ARIZONA &
NEW MEXICO

MACMILLAN • USA

Macmillan Travel
A Simon & Schuster Macmillan Company
15 Columbus Circle
New York, NY 10023

MACMILLAN is a registered trademark of Macmillan, Inc.

Manufactured in the United States of America

10 9 8 7 6 5 4 3 2 1

ISSN: 1079-3569
ISBN: 0-02-860144-0

SPECIAL SALES
Bulk purchases (10+ copies) of Frommer's travel guides are available to corporations at special discounts. The Special Sales Department can produce custom editions to be used as premiums and/or for sales promotion to suit individual needs. Existing editions can be produced with custom cover imprints such as corporate logos. For more information write to Special Sales, Simon & Schuster, 1230 Avenue of the Americas, New York, NY 10020

CONTENTS

INTRODUCTION

America on Wheels introduces a brand-new lodgings rating system—one that factors in the latest trends in travel preferences, technologies, and amenities and is based on thorough inspections by experienced travel professionals. We rate establishments from 1 to 5 flags, plus a unique rating we call Ultra, a special award reserved for only a handful of outstanding properties in each category. Our restaurant selections represent the ethnic diversity of today's dining scene and are categorized with symbols according to their special features, ambience, and services available. In addition, the series provides in-depth sightseeing information, including driving tours and best-of-the-state highlights.

STATE INTRODUCTIONS

Our coverage of each state in the *America on Wheels* series begins with background information that will help familiarize you with your destination. Included is a summary of the state's history and an overview of its geography, followed by practical tips that we hope you will find useful in planning your trip—what kind of weather to expect, what to pack, sources of information within the state, driving rules and regulations, and other essentials.

The "Best of the State" section provides you with a rundown of the top sights and attractions and the most popular festivals and special events around the state. It also includes infomation on spectator sports and an "A to Z" list of recreational activities available to you.

DRIVING TOURS

The scenic driving tours guide you along some of the most popular sightseeing routes. Every tour is keyed to a map and includes mileage information and precise directions, refreshment stops, and, for longer tours, recommended places to stay.

THE LISTINGS

The cities are organized alphabetically within each state. Below each city name, you'll find a map page number and map location. These refer to the color maps at the back of the book.

Types of Lodgings

Here's how we define the lodging categories used in *America on Wheels*.

Motel

A motel usually has 1 to 3 floors, and many of the guest rooms have doors facing the parking lot or outdoor corridors. A motel may only have a small, serviceable lobby and usually offers only limited services; the nearest restaurant may be down the street. A motel is most likely to be located alongside a highway or in a resort area.

Hotel

A hotel usually has 3 or more floors with elevators. It may or may not have parking, but if it does, entry to the guest rooms is likely to be through the lobby rather than directly from the parking lot. A range of lodgings is available (such as standard rooms, deluxe rooms, and suites), and a range of services is available (such as bellhops, room service, and a concierge). Many hotels have a restaurant or coffee shop open for breakfast, lunch, and dinner; they may have a cocktail lounge/bar. Recreational facilities may be available (such as a swimming pool, fitness center, and tennis courts).

Resort

A resort usually has more extensive facilities and recreational activities than a hotel, and offers 3 meals a day. The atmosphere is generally more informal than at comparable hotels.

Lodge

A lodge is essentially a small hotel in a rural, remote, or mountainous location. The atmosphere, service, and furniture may be more casual than you'd find in a regular hotel, and there may not be televisions or telephones in every guest room. The facilities usually include a coffee shop or restaurant, bar or cocktail lounge, game room, and indoor or outdoor swimming pool or hot tub. In ski areas, the lounge usually has a fireplace and facilities for storing ski gear.

Inn

An inn is a small-scale hotel or lodge, usually in an older building that may or may not have been designed for lodgings, and it is often located in interesting surroundings. An inn should have a warm, welcoming atmosphere, with a more homelike quality to its furnishings and facilities. The guest rooms may be individually decorated in a style appropriate to the inn's age and location, and the rooms may or may not have telephones, televisions, or private bathrooms. An inn usually has a lounge or sitting room for guests (with parlor games and perhaps a television) and a small dining room that may or may not be open to the public. Breakfast, however, is almost always served.

How the Lodgings Are Rated

Every hotel, motel, resort, inn, and lodge rated in this series has been subjected to a thorough hands-on inspection by our team of accomplished travel professionals. We ask the kinds of questions that readers would ask if they could inspect the rooms in advance for themselves (How good is the soundproofing? How firm is the bed? What condition are the room furnishings in?). Then all of the inspection reports are reviewed by regional editors who are experts on their territories. The top-rated properties are then rechecked by a special consultant who has been reviewing and critiquing luxury hotels around the world for almost 25 years. *Establishments are not charged to be included in our series.*

Our ratings are based on *average* guest rooms—not lavish suites or concierge floors—so they're not artificially high. Therefore, in some cases a hotel rated 4 flags may indeed have individual rooms or suites that might fall into the 5-flag category; conversely, a 4-flag

hotel may have a few rooms in its lowest price range that might otherwise warrant 3 flags.

The detailed ratings vary by category of lodgings—for example, the criteria imposed on a hotel are more rigorous than those for a motel—and some features that are considered essential in, for example, a 4-flag city hotel are relaxed for a resort that offers alternative attractions, sporting facilities, and/or beautiful and spacious grounds. Likewise, amenities such as telephones and televisions—essential in hotels and motels—are not required in inns, often the destination for lovers of peace and quiet. Instead, the criteria take into account such features as individually decorated rooms and complimentary afternoon tea.

There are, of course, several basic attributes that apply to all lodgings across the board: the cleanliness and maintenance of the building as a whole; the housekeeping in individual rooms; safety, both indoors and out; the quality and practicality of the furnishings; the quality and availability of the amenities; the caliber of the facilities; the extent and/or condition of the grounds; the ambience and cleanliness in the dining rooms; and the caliber and professionalism of the service in relation to the rates and types of lodging. Since the *America on Wheels* rating system is highly rigorous, just because a property has garnered only 1 flag does not mean it is inadequate or substandard.

WHAT THE INDIVIDUAL RATINGS MEAN

1 Flag

These properties have surpassed the minimum requirements of cleanliness, safety, convenience, and amenities; the staff may be limited, but guests can generally expect a friendly, hospitable greeting. They will have basic amenities, such as air conditioning or heating where appropriate, telephones, and televisions. The bathrooms may have only showers rather than tubs, and just 1 towel for each guest, but showers and towels must be clean. The 1-flag properties are by no means places to avoid, since they can represent exceptional value.

2 Flags

In addition to having all of the basic attributes of 1-flag lodgings, these properties will have some extra amenities, such as bellhops to help with the luggage, ice buckets in each room, and better quality furnishings. Some extra services may include availability of cribs and irons, and wake-up service.

3 Flags

These properties have all the basics noted above but also offer a more generous complement of amenities, such as firmer beds, larger desks, more drawer space, extra blankets and pillows, cable or satellite TV, alarm clock/radios, room service (although hours may be limited), and dry cleaning and/or laundry services.

4 Flags

This is the realm of luxury, with refinements in amenities, furnishings, and service—such as larger rooms, more dependable soundproofing, 2 telephones per room, in-room movies, in-room safes, thick towels, hair dryers, twice-daily maid service, turndown service, concierge service, and 24-hour room service.

5 Flags

These properties have everything the 4-flag properties have, plus a more personal level of service and more sumptuous amenities, among them bathrobes, superior linens, and blackout drapes for lightproofing. Facilities normally include a business center and fitness center. Generally speaking, guests pay handsomely to stay in these properties.

Ultra

This crème-de-la-crème rating is reserved for those rare hotels and resorts, possibly also motels and inns, that are truly outstanding in every or almost every department—places with a "Grand Hotel" presence, an almost flawless level of service, and a standard of dining equal to that of the finest restaurants.

Unrated

In the few cases where an inspector was not able to make a detailed inspection, the property is listed as "Unrated." Also, in some cases where a property was in the process of changing owners or managers, or if the property was undergoing the kind of major renovations that made formal evaluation impossible, then, again, the inspectors have listed it as "Unrated."

Types of Dining

Restaurant

A restaurant serves complete meals.

Refreshment Stop

A refreshment stop serves drinks and/or snacks only (such as an ice cream parlor, bakery, or coffee bar).

How the Restaurants Were Evaluated

All of the restaurants reviewed in this series have been through the kind of thorough inspection described for accommodations, above. Our inspectors have evaluated everything from freshness of ingredients to noise level and spacing of tables.

Unique to the *America on Wheels* series are the easy-to-read symbols that identify for you a restaurant's special features, ambience, and services. With them you can determine at a glance whether a place is a local favorite, offers exceptional value, or is "worth a splurge."

How to Read the Listings

LODGINGS

Introductory Information

The rating is followed by the establishment's name, address, neighborhood (if located in a major city), telephone numbers, and fax number (if there is one). When appropriate, you'll also find the location of the establishment, highway information with exit number, and/or more specific directions. In the resort listings, the number of acres is indicated. Also included are our inspectors' comments, which provide some description and discuss any outstanding features or special information about the establishment. If the lodging is not rated, it will be noted at the end of this section.

Rooms

The number and type of accommodations available is followed by the information on check-in/check-out times. If there is anything worth noting about rooms, whether the size or decor or furnishings, inspectors' comments will follow.

Amenities

The amenities available in the majority of the guest rooms are indicated by symbols and then a list. Because travelers usually expect air conditioning, telephones, and televisions in their guest rooms, we specifically note when those amenities are not available. If the accommodations have minibars, terraces, fireplaces, or Jacuzzis, we indicate that here.

Services

The services available are indicated by symbols and then a list. There may be a fee for some of the services. "Babysitting available" means the establishment can put you in touch with local babysitters and/or agencies. An establishment that accepts pets may nevertheless place restrictions on the types or size of pets allowed.

Facilities

The facilities available are indicated by symbols followed by a list; all are on the premises, except for cross-country and downhill skiing, which are within 10 miles. The lifeguard listed refers to a beach lifeguard, not a pool lifeguard. Our "Accessible for People With Disabilities" symbol appears where establishments claim to have guest rooms with such accessibility.

Rates

If the establishment's rates vary throughout the year, then the rates given are for the high season. The rates listed are EP (no meals included), unless otherwise noted. We'll tell you if there is a charge for an extra person to stay in a room; if children stay free, and if so, up to what age; if there are minimum stay requirements; if the rates are ever higher for special events or holidays; if AP (3 meals) or MAP (breakfast and dinner) rates are also available; and/or if special packages are available. The parking rates (if the establishment has parking) are followed by the credit card information.

Always confirm the rates when you are making your reservations, and ask about taxes and other charges, which are not included in our rates.

RESTAURANTS

Introductory Information

If a restaurant is a local favorite, an exceptional value, or "worth a splurge," this will be noted by a special symbol at the beginning of the listing. Then the establishment's name, address, neighborhood (if located in a major city), and telephone number are listed. Next comes the location of the establishment, highway information with exit number, and/or more specific directions, as appropriate. The types of cuisine are followed by our inspectors' comments on everything from decor to menu highlights.

The "FYI" Heading

After the reservations policy, we tell you if there is live entertainment, a children's menu, a dress code, and a no-smoking policy for the entire restaurant. If the restaurant does not offer a full bar, we tell you what the liquor policy is.

Hours of Operation

Under the "Open" heading, "HS" indicates that the hours listed are for the high season only; otherwise, the hours listed are year-round. It's a good idea to call ahead to confirm the hours of operation, especially in the off-season.

Prices

Prices given are for the dinner main courses (unless otherwise noted). If a prix-fixe dinner is offered during all of the dinner hours, that price is listed here, too. This section ends with credit card information, followed by any appropriate symbol(s).

Accessibility for People With Disabilities

The accessibility symbol appears in listings where the restaurant has a level entrance or an access ramp, a doorway at least 36 inches wide, and restrooms that are on the same floor as the dining room, with doorways at least 32 inches wide and properly outfitted stalls.

ATTRACTIONS

Introductory Information

The name, street address, neighborhood (if located in a major city), and telephone number are followed by a brief rundown of the attraction's high points and key attributes—so you can quickly determine if it's worth a full day of exploration or just a brief detour.

Hours of Operation & Admission

Service information includes hours of operation and the cost of admission. The cost is indicated by 1 to 4 dollar signs ($, $$, $$$, or $$$$) or by "Free," if no fee is charged. It's a good idea to call ahead to confirm the hours.

DISABLED TRAVELER INFORMATION

The Americans with Disabilities Act (ADA) of 1990 required that all public facilities and commercial establishments be made accessible to disabled persons by January 26, 1992. Any property opened after January 26, 1993, must be built in accordance with the ADA Accessible Guidelines. Note, however, that not all establishments have completed their renovations to conform with the law; be sure to call ahead to determine if your specific needs can be met.

TAXES

State and city taxes vary widely and are not included in the prices in this book. Always ask about the taxes when you are making your reservations. State sales tax is given under "Essentials" in the introduction to each state.

A DISCLAIMER

Readers are advised that prices fluctuate in the course of time and travel information changes under the impact of the varied and volatile factors that affect the travel industry. The publisher cannot be held responsible for the experiences of readers while traveling. Readers are invited to send ideas, comments, and suggestions for future editions to: *America on Wheels,* Macmillan Travel, 15 Columbus Circle, New York, NY 10023.

ABBREVIATIONS

A/C	air conditioning
AP	American Plan (rates include breakfast, lunch, and dinner)
avail	available
BB	Bed-and-Breakfast Plan (rates include full breakfast)
bldg	building
CC	credit cards
CI	check-in time
CO	check-out time
CP	Continental Plan (rates include continental breakfast)
ctges	cottages
ctr	center
D	double
effic	efficiencies
evnts	events
HS	high season
info	information
int'l	international
ltd	limited
maj	major
MAP	Modified American Plan (rates include breakfast and dinner)
Mem Day	Memorial Day
mi	miles
min	minimum
MM	mile marker
PF	prix fixe (a fixed-price meal)
pking	parking
refrig	refrigerator
rms	rooms
rsts	restaurants
S	single
satel	satellite
spec	special
stes	suites
svce	service
tel	telephone
univ	university
w/	with
wknds	weekends

The following toll-free telephone numbers were accurate at press time; *America on Wheels* cannot be held responsible for any number that has changed. The "TDD" numbers are answered by a telecommunications service for the deaf and hard-of-hearing. Be sure to dial "1" before each number.

Lodgings

Best Western International, Inc
(800) 528-1234 Continental USA and Canada
(800) 528-2222 TDD

Budgetel Inns
(800) 4-BUDGET Continental USA and Canada

Budget Host
(800) BUD-HOST Continental USA

Clarion Hotels
(800) CLARION Continental USA and Canada
(800) 228-3323 TDD

Comfort Inns
(800) 228-5150 Continental USA and Canada
(800) 228-3323 TDD

Courtyard by Marriott
(800) 321-2211 Continental USA and Canada
(800) 228-7014 TDD

Days Inn
(800) 325-2525 Continental USA and Canada
(800) 325-3297 TDD

Doubletree Hotels
(800) 222-TREE Continental USA

Drury Inn
(800) 325-8300 Continental USA and Canada
(800) 325-0583 TDD

Econo Lodges
(800) 446-6900 Continental USA and Canada
(800) 228-3323 TDD

Embassy Suites
(800) 362-2779 Continental USA and Canada

Exel Inns of America
(800) 356-8013 Continental USA and Canada

Fairfield Inn by Marriott
(800) 228-2800 Continental USA and Canada
(800) 228-7014 TDD

Fairmont Hotels
(800) 527-4727 Continental USA

Forte Hotels
(800) 225-5843 Continental USA and Canada

Four Seasons Hotels
(800) 332-3442 Continental USA
(800) 268-6282 Canada

Friendship Inns
(800) 453-4511 Continental USA
(800) 228-3323 TDD

Guest Quarters Suites
(800) 424-2900 Continental USA

Hampton Inn
(800) HAMPTON Continental USA and Canada

Hilton Hotels Corporation
(800) HILTONS Continental USA and Canada
(800) 368-1133 TDD

Holiday Inn
(800) HOLIDAY Continental USA and Canada
(800) 238-5544 TDD

Howard Johnson
(800) 654-2000 Continental USA and Canada
(800) 654-8442 TDD

Hyatt Hotels and Resorts
(800) 228-9000 Continental USA and Canada
(800) 228-9548 TDD

Inns of America
(800) 826-0778 Continental USA and Canada

Intercontinental Hotels
(800) 327-0200 Continental USA and Canada

ITT Sheraton
(800) 325-3535 Continental USA and Canada
(800) 325-1717 TDD

La Quinta Motor Inns, Inc
(800) 531-5900 Continental USA and Canada
(800) 426-3101 TDD

Loews Hotels
(800) 223-0888 Continental USA and Canada

Marriott Hotels
(800) 228-9290 Continental USA and Canada
(800) 228-7014 TDD

Master Hosts Inns
(800) 251-1962 Continental USA and Canada

Meridien
(800) 543-4300 Continental USA and Canada

Omni Hotels
(800) 843-6664 Continental USA and Canada

Park Inns International
(800) 437-PARK Continental USA and Canada

Quality Inns
(800) 228-5151 Continental USA and Canada
(800) 228-3323 TDD

Radisson Hotels International
(800) 333-3333 Continental USA and Canada

Ramada
(800) 2-RAMADA Continental USA and Canada
(800) 228-3232 TDD

Red Carpet Inns
(800) 251-1962 Continental USA and Canada

Red Lion Hotels and Inns
(800) 547-8010 Continental USA and Canada

Red Roof Inns
(800) 843-7663 Continental USA and Canada
(800) 843-9999

Residence Inn by Marriott
(800) 331-3131 Continental USA and Canada
(800) 228-7014 TDD

Resinter
(800) 221-4542 Continental USA and Canada

Ritz-Carlton
(800) 241-3333 Continental USA and Canada

Rodeway Inns
(800) 228-2000 Continental USA and Canada
(800) 228-3323 TDD

Scottish Inns
(800) 251-1962 Continental USA and Canada

Shilo Inns
(800) 222-2244 Continental USA and Canada

Signature Inns
(800) 822-5252 Continental USA and Canada

Stouffer Renaissance Hotels International
(800) HOTELS-1 Continental USA and Canada
(800) 833-4747 TDD

Super 8 Motels
(800) 800-8000 Continental USA and Canada
(800) 533-6634 TDD

Susse Chalet Motor Lodges & Inns
(800) 258-1980 Continental USA and Canada

Travelodge
(800) 255-3050 Continental USA and Canada

Vagabond Hotels Inc.
(800) 522-1555 Continental USA and Canada

Westin Hotels and Resorts
(800) 228-3000 Continental USA and Canada
(800) 254-5440 TDD

Wyndham Hotels and Resorts
(800) 822-4200 Continental USA and Canada

Car Rental Agencies

Advantage Rent-A-Car
(800) 777-5500 Continental USA and Canada

Airways Rent A Car
(800) 952-9200 Continental USA

Alamo Rent A Car
(800) 327-9633 Continental USA and Canada

Allstate Car Rental
(800) 634-6186 Continental USA and Canada

Avis
(800) 331-1212 Continental USA and Canada

Budget Rent A Car
(800) 527-0700 Continental USA and Canada

Dollar Rent A Car
(800) 800-4000 Continental USA and Canada

Enterprise Rent-A-Car
(800) 325-8007 Continental USA and Canada

Hertz
(800) 654-3131 Continental USA

National Car Rental
(800) CAR-RENT Continental USA and Canada

Payless Car Rental
(800) PAYLESS Continental USA and Canada

Rent-A-Wreck
(800) 535-1391 Continental USA

Sears Rent A Car
(800) 527-0770 Continental USA and Canada

Thrifty Rent-A-Car
(800) 367-2277 Continental USA

U-Save Auto Rental of America
(800) 272-USAV Continental USA and Canada

Value Rent-A-Car
(800) 327-2501 Continental USA and Canada

Airlines

American Airlines
(800) 433-7300 Continental USA and Canada

Canadian Airlines International
(800) 426-7000 Continental USA
(800) 665-1177 Canada

Continental Airlines
(800) 525-0280 Continental USA
(800) 421-2456 Canada

Delta Air Lines
(800) 221-1212 Continental USA

Northwest Airlines
(800) 225-2525 Continental USA and Canada

Southwest Airlines
(800) 435-9792 Continental USA and Canada

Trans World Airlines
(800) 221-2000 Continental USA

United Airlines
(800) 241-6522 Continental USA and Canada

USAir
(800) 428-4322 Continental USA and Canada

Train

Amtrak
(800) USA-RAIL Continental USA

Bus

Greyhound
(800) 231-2222 Continental USA

THE TOP-RATED LODGINGS

5 Flags

The Boulders, Carefree, AZ

Loews Ventana Canyon Resort, Tucson, AZ

The Phoenician, Scottsdale, AZ

4 Flags

Arizona Biltmore, Phoenix, AZ

Arizona Inn, Tucson, AZ

The Bishop's Lodge, Santa Fe, NM

Enchantment Resort, Sedona, AZ

Hyatt Regency, Scottsdale, AZ

Inn of the Anasazi, Santa Fe, NM

Inn on the Alameda, Santa Fe, NM

John Gardiner's Tennis Ranch, Scottsdale, AZ

Las Cruces Hilton Inn, Las Cruces, NM

L'Auberge de Sedona, Sedona, AZ

Rancho Encantado, Santa Fe, NM

The Ritz-Carlton, Phoenix, AZ

Scottsdale Princess, Scottsdale, AZ

The Westin La Paloma, Tucson, AZ

Westward Look Resort, Tucson, AZ

The Wigwam, Litchfield Park, AZ

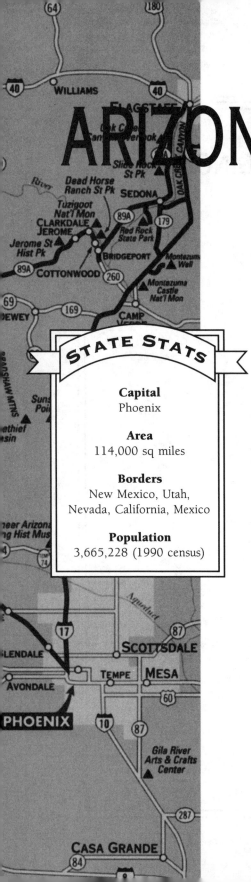

ARIZONA

A LAND OF EXTREMES

Arizona is a land of extremes. "And today in Phoenix, the mercury topped 120°F for the fifth day in a row" is the sort of weather report that conjures up visions of a vast, baking desert and makes people sweat a thousand miles away. What many non-Arizonans don't realize is that when it's topping 100° in Phoenix, it can be snowing on the rim of the Grand Canyon, and when Phoenix is warm enough for sunbathing in January, skiers are sliding down the slopes outside Flagstaff.

Arizona's elevation ranges from near sea level at Yuma to 12,760 feet on Humphreys Peak, producing a variety of landscapes that includes not only the familiar Sonoran Desert, which is home to the massive saguaro cactus, but also the ponderosa pine forests of the Mogollon Rim and the alpine meadows of the San Francisco Peaks. Nowhere are these contrasts more evident than in the Grand Canyon, which appears suddenly, full-blown and vertiginous, from the forests of the Kaibab Plateau.

Man has had a hand in creating Arizona's extremes. Except for where it flows through the Grand Canyon, most of the Colorado River has been dammed, creating huge mirage-like reservoirs in the desert or, at Lake Powell, an otherworldly landscape in which arches of red sandstone are reflected in quiet waters hundreds of feet deep. And in the cities, where high-tech and service industries foster an increasingly cosmopolitan atmosphere, glass-and-steel skyscrapers rise into the desert sky and Mercedes compete with BMWs for parking spaces at upscale shopping malls. However, away from the cities, the old Arizona of cattle ranches, copper mines, and cactus survives. In this "real" Arizona, pickup trucks are the vehicle of choice, Indians still shop at trading posts, and people still make a living riding the range and digging for gold.

At guest ranches all over the state, the Wild West comes alive as wranglers turn city slickers into cowpunchers for whom a night out means a chuck-wagon dinner under the stars and a cowboy singalong. But at the resort hotels of Phoenix, Scottsdale, Tucson, and Sedona, manicured golf courses, health spas, elaborate swimming pools, and gourmet restaurants have created a new image for the state, one that is almost diametrically opposed to the rough-and-rugged life of the cowboy. In this new land of good living, 2-pound steaks are replaced by smoked-duck tamales with mango-chilpotle sauce, and a night out might mean Pavarotti or the latest Broadway play.

The New West and the Old West ride side by side in the western art that is so prevalent in Arizona. This art captures on canvas and in bronze the none-too-glamorous real life of Arizona's cowboys. It also reflects the state's Indian heritage, although the works of the Indian craftspeople themselves are even more reflective of these cultures. Navajo rugs and sand paintings, Hopi kachinas and pottery, and Zuni silver-and-turquoise jewelry are quintessential Arizona, the crafts of people who were living on this land long before the first Spanish explorers marched north from Mexico in search of riches.

Ever since the Anasazi built their pueblos high on cliff walls, Arizonans have been coping with this region's extremes. The advent of air conditioning may have tempered the climatic excesses somewhat, allowing people to live year-round in the desert, but Arizona is still a place where the extremes are what give the state its unique character.

A BRIEF HISTORY

CLIFF DWELLINGS TO MISSION CHURCHES

Mammoth bones found in southeastern Arizona indicate that Paleo-Indians roamed this region more than 10,000 years ago. However, it was not until around the year AD 200 that the area's inhabitants began to leave permanent records of their presence. Early Indians lived in pit houses (houses partially dug into the ground), but by 700, they had begun building multistory pueblos (villages). The best preserved and most fascinating of these are the cliff dwellings of the Anasazi, who lived in the canyons of northeastern Arizona. Other tribes of the period were Sinagua, Mogollon, Hohokam, and Salado. Between 1250 and 1450, all of these early tribes abandoned their villages and disappeared; instead of an archeological forwarding address, they left behind one of the great mysteries of the Southwest.

In 1539, Marcos de Niza led the first European expedition into the area. He came in search of the fabled Seven Cities of Cíbola, and his claims to have seen them prompted Francisco Vásquez de Coronado to march northward from New Spain (Mexico). Rather than the riches he sought, Coronado found only primitive villages of stone and mud, but members of his expedition did make the first recorded sightings of both the Grand Canyon and the Hopi pueblos. Oraibi, the oldest of the latter, had by then been occupied for more than 400 years, and it is today one of the oldest continuously inhabited communities in the country.

More than 100 years went by before the Spanish again displayed an interest in this rugged region. In 1670 Franciscan friars founded missions among the Hopi, but the Pueblo Revolt of 1680 eliminated the Spanish presence. In 1691 Father Eusebio Francisco Kino, a Jesuit, visited the Pima Indian village of Tumacacori, south of present-day Tucson, but it was not until 1751 that a permanent mission and presidio (military post) were established at Tumacacori and nearby Tubac. These became the first permanent European settlements in Arizona.

In 1776, the presidio was moved to Tucson and in 1821, when Mexico won its independence from Spain, Tucson and the rest of Arizona became a part of Mexico. In 1848, in the wake of the Mexican-American War, most of northern Mexico was ceded to the United States, but because the Mexican-American border was then drawn just north of Tucson, it was not until the United States bought southern Arizona from Mexico as part of the Gadsden Purchase of 1853 that all of Arizona passed into US hands.

TERRITORIAL TIMES   During the early years of the Civil War, Arizona sided with the Confederacy, partly

---

·§ *Fun Facts* §·

• *Spaniards were in Arizona 25 years before Spain established its colony at St Augustine, Florida, and 70 years before the English founded Jamestown.*

• *Arizona has more mountainous regions than Switzerland and more forested land than Minnesota.*

• *Strange as it seems, Arizona claims more boats per capita than any other state! (That's because of the abundance of lakes created to store water in the desert.)*

• *The city of Yuma enjoys the most days of sunshine—311 of them a year—of any spot in the United States.*

because of US resistance to giving the region territorial status. However, Union troops quickly reclaimed it, and Arizona was made a territory in 1863.

Because the Spanish had mistreated Arizona's Indian inhabitants, the Spanish occupation had not been peaceful, and when the United States acquired the territory, the new Americans found themselves facing Indian hostilities. In 1864, Colonel Kit Carson led a force against the Navajo, who had migrated into the region in the 1400s, and by destroying their winter food supply was able to bring about a Navajo surrender.

It was the Apache, living in the mountains of eastern Arizona, who put up the greatest resistance to white settlement, however. Led by Cochise and Geronimo, they attacked settlers, forts, and towns, forcing the United States to conduct a protracted war against them that did not end until Geronimo surrendered to US troops in 1886.

In the meantime, as the California gold rush got under way, miners making their way westward stopped in Arizona and eventually struck silver and gold throughout the state. It was on this mineral wealth that the territory's early fortunes were made, and mining towns such as Tombstone and Bisbee became the biggest, wildest boomtowns between New Orleans and San Francisco.

In 1867, the first white farmers to settle in Arizona began reusing the ancient system of canals that the Hohokam had dug centuries earlier. About this same time, cattle ranching was introduced in southeastern and northwestern Arizona. Life in the territory was changing, and when the railroads came in the 1880s, it began to change drastically. Previously, Spanish culture had dominated the region, but the railroads forged closer links with the east, and Arizona towns began to reflect the new influence.

THE DESERT BLOSSOMS   Just as the United States had resisted giving Arizona territorial status, so too did it resist giving the territory statehood. However, in 1911, with the construction of the Roosevelt Dam on the Salt River, eastern attitudes began to change. The reservoir behind this dam provided central Arizona with water for irrigation, and cotton fields and orange groves soon sprouted in the desert. On February 14, 1912, Arizona was granted statehood, the last of the 48 contiguous states to enter the Union.

Throughout the early part of the 20th century,

copper mining dominated the Arizona economy, and with the onset of World War II, the state's mines gained greater importance. Fortunately, by the time many mines across the state shut down after the war, the economy had begun to diversify, with large-scale agriculture and cattle ranching gaining importance, and then manufacturing ultimately overtaking agriculture as the state's primary revenue earner. In the early 1980s, Arizona experienced rapid economic growth, with aerospace engineering, electronics, and other high-tech industries in the forefront.

However, it is tourism that has brought the state its greatest recognition. As early as the 1920s, cold-weary northerners had begun spending their winters in the Arizona desert. Guest ranches offered visitors a chance to relive the Wild West, and soon the word spread about the great Arizona vacations to be had. Guest ranches eventually gave way to more sophisticated resorts, and today Phoenix and Scottsdale together boast the nation's greatest resort concentration.

Although the economic boom of the early 1980s soon went bust (its demise aggravated by cutbacks in military spending that hurt the region's aerospace firms), the state is now recovering from the recession and Phoenix and Tucson are once again booming, their growth fueled in part by corporate confidence in the opportunities being created by the North American Free Trade Agreement (NAFTA).

Phoenix and Tucson today face many of the same problems that other cities around the nation are facing —smog, congestion, urban sprawl, gang violence, and water shortages. But urban planners are beginning to confront these problems, and urban renewal projects have begun luring people back into the Tucson and Phoenix downtown areas. As long as the water supply holds out, Arizona should have a sunny future.

A Closer Look
Geography

Although most people associate Arizona with the desert, the state encompasses far more than just cactus and mesquite. There are snow-capped mountain peaks, rolling grasslands, oak-shaded canyons, huge lakes busy with boats, and dense forests of tall pines. There are, in fact, more mountains in Arizona than in Switzerland and more forests than in Minnesota.

Northern Arizona, sometimes referred to as Canyon Country, encompasses arid, windswept plains as well as dense forests of ponderosa pine. It is dominated by the Colorado River's Grand Canyon, which carves its way through the Colorado Plateau for 277 twisted miles. The Grand Canyon is the state's top tourist attraction and the inspiration for its nickname—the Grand Canyon State. Flagstaff, a college and former railroad town, is the region's largest city. North of Flagstaff stand the San Francisco Peaks, the state's highest mountains. The Arizona Snowbowl ski area keeps people flocking up this way even during the dead of winter, when this is the coldest part of the state. South of Flagstaff is Oak Creek Canyon, a popular summer recreation area that offers a cool respite from the heat of the central Arizona desert. At its mouth lies Sedona, a retirement and arts community dominated by eroded red sandstone rock formations.

Northeastern Arizona, known as the Four Corners region because of the four states (Arizona, New Mexico, Utah, and Colorado) that meet at a single point, is a high, windswept plain punctuated by mesas and buttes. This is the land of the Navajo and Hopi Indians and it is here that some of the state's most breathtaking landscapes are to be found. Sculpted by wind and water, the region's layers of colorful sandstone have been eroded into strange shapes.

Eastern Arizona, endowed with high mountains and snow-capped peaks, is where Phoenicians flee in the summer to beat the desert heat. The region's cool forests are dotted with lakes and laced with streams, which makes fishing and other outdoor activities particularly popular. However, the most prominent feature of eastern Arizona is the Mogollon Rim, a 1,000-foot-high escarpment that stretches for 200 miles. The Mogollon Rim was made famous years ago by the author Zane Grey, who for many years lived near the town of Payson. Much of this eastern region is today Apache reservation land.

The saguaro cactus is the quintessential symbol of Arizona's **Sonoran Desert,** and it is in the central region of the state that these cacti begin to dominate the landscape. The desert extends from north of Phoenix southward into Mexico and westward into California, and, surprisingly, it was in the midst of this harsh environment that early settlers chose to establish both Phoenix and Tucson, which today are the state's two largest cities.

Though there is no ocean, Arizona claims a **"West**

DRIVING DISTANCES:

Phoenix

116 miles NW of Tucson
125 miles SW of Sedona
141 miles SW of Flagstaff
180 miles NW of Nogales
226 miles S of the Grand Canyon
290 miles SE of Las Vegas, NV

Tucson

64 miles N of Nogales
70 miles NW of Tombstone
116 miles SE of Phoenix
129 miles SE of Ajo
156 miles SW of Lordsburg, NM
237 miles SE of Yuma

Flagstaff

63 miles NW of Winslow
84 miles SE of Grand Canyon Village
136 miles SW of Page
141 miles NE of Phoenix
204 miles SW of Canyon de Chelly
248 miles SE of Las Vegas, NV

Coast" along its border with California and Nevada. Lakes Havasu, Mohave, and Mead, the 3 long reservoirs that stretch along this border, were created by the damming of the Colorado River and offer vacationing Arizonans year-round water-sports activities. This region also happens to be the hottest part of the state, with Yuma and Bullhead City frequently registering the nation's highest summer temperatures.

Southern Arizona encompasses part of the Sonoran Desert and includes some of the state's most rugged and remote areas. It is here that the organ pipe cactus, which is similar to the saguaro, reaches the northern limits of its range. In the southeast corner, high plains are home to large cattle ranches. Rising above these plains are numerous small mountain ranges that were once Apache strongholds.

Climate

Sure it's hot, but, as they like to say, "it's a dry heat." Arizona often claims the hottest spots in the nation during the summer, but because of the desert's low humidity, 100°F isn't nearly as uncomfortable here as it would be in other locales. Hot is also relative in Arizona. Tucson brags that it is usually 10° cooler than Phoenix, and Bullhead City is always considerably hotter than Phoenix. However, from October to May temperatures are generally moderate in Phoenix, Tucson, and the rest of the desert, with mid-winter lows rarely dipping below freezing and highs in the 60°s. Winter or summer, the desert basks in the sun. Phoenix and Tucson each get more than 300 days of sunshine each year.

Arizona's many mountain ranges give the state its climatic diversity—as you climb into the mountains, the temperature drops, even in Arizona. Snow keeps the North Rim of the Grand Canyon closed from November through April each year and provides good skiing at the Sunrise and Arizona Snowbowl ski areas.

Any time of year and anywhere in the state, it's a good idea to wear a good sunscreen if you plan to spend much time outdoors. The desert sun is strong, even in winter. At higher elevations, the sunlight is even stronger and skin burns much faster.

What to Pack

The heat, the landscape, and western heritage dictate what to wear in Arizona. Though people here generally dress casually throughout the year, in the warmer months, dressing for the heat is paramount. Bring plenty of cool clothes, preferably cotton. Also be sure to bring a bathing suit. If you have them, don't forget your cowboy boots and jeans. In the winter a jacket or wool sweater is fine for the desert, but if you are heading up into the mountains, bring a heavy coat and plenty of warm clothes. A few restaurants in Phoenix and Tucson require jackets for men, and if you plan on attending the symphony or some other cultural event, you'll want to have some formal attire.

Tourist Information

Contact the Arizona Office of Tourism, 1100 W Washington St, Phoenix, AZ 85007 (tel 602/542-TOUR or toll free 800/842-8257), at least a month before you plan to visit and they'll send you a package of information on the state. Nearly every Arizona town of any size also has a visitors bureau or chamber of commerce that can provide specific local or regional information. You'll find a list of these chambers of commerce and visitors bureaus in *Arizona Traveler,* a magazine available from the Arizona Office of Tourism. The Phoenix and Valley of the Sun Convention and Visitors Bureau, One Arizona Center, 400 E Van Buren St, Phoenix, AZ 85004-2290 (tel 602/254-6500), and the Metropolitan Tucson Convention and Visitors Bureau, 130 S Scott Ave, Tucson, AZ 85701 (tel 602/624-1817 or toll free 800/638-8350), are also good sources of information.

Driving Rules & Regulations

The use of seat belts is required of drivers and front-seat passengers. Children 4 years old or younger or who weigh 40 pounds or less must be in a child's car seat. Unless posted otherwise, a right turn is permitted on

AVERAGE MONTHLY HIGH/LOW TEMPERATURES (°F)			
	Phoenix	**Tucson**	**Flagstaff**
Jan	65/39	64/38	42/15
Feb	68/43	67/40	45/17
Mar	75/47	72/44	49/20
Apr	83/53	80/50	57/26
May	92/62	89/56	67/33
June	102/71	99/67	78/41
July	105/80	99/74	82/50
Aug	102/78	96/72	79/49
Sept	98/71	94/67	74/41
Oct	88/59	84/57	64/31
Nov	74/47	72/45	51/26
Dec	66/40	65/39	44/16

red after you've come to a complete stop. General speed limits are 25 to 35 mph in towns and cities, 15 mph in school zones, and 55 mph on highways, except rural interstates, where the speed limit is 65 mph.

Renting a Car

Because they are major resort destinations, Phoenix and Tucson offer some of the lowest car rental rates in the country. Outside of these two cities, rates tend to be a bit higher. To get the best prices, make your reservation as far in advance as possible, because the fewer cars a company has available, the more it charges. Also call several companies, as rates vary considerably from one company to the next, and you might run across a special promotional rate in effect for the time of your visit. If you're a member of an organization such as AAA or AARP, you may be able to get a discount, and some credit card companies also offer discount rates to cardholders. Also, be sure to find out if your credit card or personal automobile insurance extends coverage to rental cars. Using existing insurance saves a bundle.

Major rental companies with offices in Arizona include:

- **Alamo** (tel toll free 800/327-9633)
- **Avis** (tel 800/331-1212)
- **Budget** (tel 800/527-0700)
- **Dollar** (tel 800/800-4000)
- **Hertz** (tel 800/654-3131)
- **National** (tel 800/227-7368)
- **Thrifty** (tel 800/367-2277)

Essentials

Area Code: The area code for all of Arizona is **602;** however, on July 23, 1995, it will change to **520** for that part of the state *outside* the Phoenix metropolitan area. The area code for the Phoenix area will remain 602. (Unfortunately, because the announcement of this changeover occurred as this book went to press, telephone numbers provided do not reflect this change.)

Emergencies: For the police, an ambulance, or the fire department, dial **911.**

Liquor Laws: To purchase or consume alcoholic beverages, you must be 21 years old and have proper identification.

Taxes: Arizona's state sales tax is 5%; local sales taxes sometimes apply as well. Hotel taxes range from 6.5 to 8.5%. There is also a car-rental tax of 8.7 to 8.8%.

Time Zone: Arizona is in the Mountain time zone and does not switch to daylight saving time in summer, with the exception of the Navajo and Hopi reservations.

BEST OF THE STATE
What to See

GRAND CANYON NATIONAL PARK   A mile deep, 18 miles across at its widest, and 277 miles long, the Grand Canyon is one of the world's greatest natural wonders. More than 2 billion years of geologic time have been exposed by the weathering action of the Colorado River as it slices through the scrubland and forests of northern Arizona. However you choose to experience the Grand Canyon—from overlooks on the North and South rims; on a mule ride down into it; by hiking its trails; by helicopter or small plane; from a raft bouncing over the Colorado's many rapids—it will undoubtedly leave you awestruck. Keep in mind that the Grand Canyon is one of the most popular national parks in the United States, and a summertime visit requires some advance planning. If you want to stay at one of the Grand Canyon lodges, be sure to make your reservation 6 to 12 months in advance. The park's campgrounds also fill up nightly in summer.

OTHER NATURAL WONDERS   Arizona abounds in national monuments, state parks, and other preserves dedicated to natural wonders. The northeast part of the state, which is taken up almost entirely by the Navajo and Hopi reservations, offers the greatest concentration. Between Flagstaff and Winslow is **Meteor Crater,** a mile-wide, 570-foot-deep crater formed when a meteorite struck the earth 49,000 years ago. At **Petrified Forest National Park,** near Holbrook, you can see the country's greatest array of petrified wood. This park also protects the rainbow-hued hills of the **Painted Desert.** North of the Petrified Forest is **Canyon de Chelly National Monument,** a deep, narrow canyon with sandstone walls. Within the canyon are numerous cliff dwellings, as well as farms that are still worked by

Navajo families. Northwest of here is **Monument Valley Navajo Tribal Park,** one of the most photographed spots in the entire Southwest. Its famous buttes have served as backdrops for countless films and television commercials. Nearby, within Glen Canyon National Recreation Area, stands **Rainbow Bridge,** a 290-foot-high arch that spans 275 feet.

East and west of Tucson are units of **Saguaro National Monument,** which preserves vast stands of huge saguaro cacti. About 120 miles west of Tucson is **Organ Pipe National Monument,** a preserve for a similar, large cactus that resembles a pipe organ. **Chiracahua National Monument,** 100 miles east of Tucson, is a fascinating landscape of naturally sculpted rock formations.

MANMADE WONDERS Biosphere II, a sort of giant terrarium for people rising out of the desert north of Tucson, has become one of Arizona's most impressive manmade wonders. Another surprising structure is **London Bridge,** which now spans the waters of Lake Havasu in western Arizona. Some distance up the Colorado from Lake Havasu is the **Hoover Dam,** the tallest concrete dam in the western hemisphere. Equally impressive is the **Glen Canyon Dam** in Page. This latter dam creates Lake Powell, which stretches for more than 180 miles.

Mission San Xavier del Bac, known as "The White Dove of the Desert" and located south of Tucson, is a beautiful mission church built by the Spanish in the 18th century. In the 20th century, the desert inspired architect Frank Lloyd Wright to build his **Taliesin West** school on the outskirts of Phoenix. Italian architect Paolo Soleri, after studying at Taliesin West, went out into the desert 60 miles north of Phoenix and began building the futuristic cast-concrete city of **Arcosanti,** which is still under construction.

RUINS Arizona has an abundance of ancient Indian ruins. By far the most impressive, though rather difficult-to-visit, ruins are the Anasazi cliff dwellings of Betatakin and Keet Seel in **Navajo National Monument.** Other Anasazi cliff dwellings can be seen at Canyon de Chelly National Monument. Near Flagstaff, there are the Sinagua Indian pueblo ruins at **Wupatki National Monument** and cliff dwellings at **Walnut Canyon National Monument.** South of Flagstaff, you'll find **Montezuma's Castle National Monument,** which preserves a Sinagua cliff dwelling. Not far

from this monument is **Tuzigoot National Monument,** a hilltop pueblo ruin near the town of Clarkdale.

THE WILD WEST Arizona can lay claim to some of the wildest western history. Southeast of Tucson is **Tombstone**—"the town too tough to die." However, if you're looking for something familiar from the movie *Tombstone,* you'll have to pay a visit to **Old Tucson Studios,** a western theme park that has served as a set for hundreds of film and television productions, including *Tombstone,* since 1939. One other setting that will be familiar to fans of Hollywood westerns is **Monument Valley,** on the Navajo Indian Reservation in northern Arizona. The valley and its stunningly picturesque sandstone buttes have served as a backdrop for countless films, television shows, commercials, and print ads. Throughout the state there are also dozens of genuine ghost towns, and while some are little more than foundations, others, such as Bisbee, Tombstone, Oatman, and Goldfield, have become regular tourist attractions and acquired a few too many residents to be proper ghost towns.

For a look at what pioneer life in Arizona was really like, stop in at the **Pioneer Arizona Living History Museum** north of Phoenix to see costumed interpreters practicing 19th-century crafts and skills. At the **Sharlot Hall Museum** in Prescott, you'll also find historic buildings and exhibits on pioneer life. At **Yuma Crossing Quartermaster Depot Historic Site,** a reconstructed military outpost brings the history of this important site to life, and at the **Fort Huachuca Museum,** a 19th-century military fort, you can learn the history of the fort and the buffalo soldiers, a troop of African-American soldiers that were once stationed here.

MUSEUMS Among the not-to-be-missed museums in Arizona are several that focus on Native American culture and history. These include the **Heard Museum** in Phoenix, the **Museum of Northern Arizona** in Flagstaff, and the **Amerind Foundation** in Texas Canyon, 60 miles east of Tucson. The smaller **Smoki Museum** in Prescott also features exhibits of Native American artifacts. To learn more about the state's cowboy history, visit the **Desert Caballeros Western Museum** in Wickenburg, and for a look at cowboy art, visit Prescott's **Phippen Museum of Western Art.** For an introduction to general statewide history, visit the **Arizona Historical Society Tucson Museum.**

The **Phoenix Art Museum** is strong on contemporary art, but it also has a display of miniature period rooms as well as an impressive collection of Spanish colonial furniture and religious art. The **Tucson Art Museum** also focuses on contemporary art. At the **Arizona State University Art Museum,** changing exhibits feature works by contemporary artists.

PARKS & ZOOS   The **Arizona-Sonora Desert Museum** is a combination zoo and botanical garden that focuses on life in the Sonoran Desert and has some of the finest wildlife displays in the country. To see animals from other parts of the world, go to the **Phoenix Zoo.** If you're interested in the plants of the desert, visit the **Desert Botanical Garden** in Phoenix, **Tucson Botanical Gardens,** or the **Boyce Thompson Southwestern Arboretum,** east of Phoenix.

FAMILY FAVORITES   Many of the attractions listed above will appeal to children of various ages. Particularly popular are **Old Tucson Studios** in Tucson, the real town of **Tombstone** southeast of Tucson, the **Arizona-Sonora Desert Museum,** and the **Phoenix Zoo.**
    Wild West experiences that kids will probably enjoy are rodeos, horseback rides, and chuck-wagon cookouts. Around Phoenix and Tucson, you'll also find restaurants that are built to resemble old western towns and often offer cowboy shootouts, country music bands, hay rides, and other activities. Both Phoenix and Tucson have several miniature-golf courses that include other activities with kid appeal. Museums that children will enjoy include the **Tucson Children's Museum,** Phoenix's **Arizona Museum of Science and Technology,** and the **Mesa Southwest Museum** in Mesa. You'll also find planetariums in Tucson and Flagstaff. Most guest (dude) ranches specialize in family vacations and many of the state's big resorts have special children's programs during holidays and the summer months.

ART COMMUNITIES   The Arizona desert has attracted artists for years, and many of them have congregated in towns that were once nearly deserted. Among these artists' communities are **Bisbee,** a former copper-mining town (90 miles southeast of Tucson); **Tubac,** site of the first Spanish settlement in Arizona (60 miles south of Tucson); and **Jerome,** a former mining town high on a mountainside above Cottonwood (25 miles southwest of Sedona). Art galleries in

Scottsdale and Sedona attract collectors from around the world.

Events/Festivals

Phoenix & Central Arizona
- **Fiesta Bowl Football Classic,** Tempe. New Year's Day. Call 602/350-0900 for information.
- **Phoenix Open Golf Tournament,** Phoenix. Mid- to late January. Call 602/870-0163.
- **Heard Museum Guild Indian Fair,** Phoenix. Indian crafts sale. First weekend of March. Call 602/252-8840.
- **Scottsdale Arts Festival,** Scottsdale. Second weekend of March. Call 602/994-ARTS.
- **Phoenix Jaycee's Rodeo of Rodeo's,** Phoenix. Mid-March. Call 602/252-6771.
- **Arizona State Fair,** Phoenix. Mid- to late October. Call 602/252-6771.
- **George Phippen Memorial Day Western Art Show and Sale,** Prescott. Memorial Day weekend. Call 602/778-1385.
- **Prescott Frontier Days,** Prescott. Oldest rodeo in the United States. First week of July. Call 602/445-3103.
- **Annual Cowboy Artists of America Exhibition,** Phoenix. Late October to late November. Call 602/257-1880.

Tucson & Southern Arizona
- **Northern Telecom Open Golf Tournament,** Tucson. Mid-January. Call toll free 800/882-7660 for information.
- **Cinco de Mayo,** Tucson. Celebration of Mexican victory over the French. Parade, music, dancing. May 5. Call 602/623-8344.
- **Wyatt Earp Days,** Tombstone. Gunfight reenactments and Wild West entertainment. Memorial Day weekend. Call 602/457-2211.
- **Helldorado Days,** Tombstone. 1880s fashion show, tribal dances, street entertainment. Late October. Call 602/457-2211.

Flagstaff & Northern Arizona
- **Flagstaff Winterfest,** Flagstaff. Arts and crafts festival, sports events. Early to mid-February. Call 602/556-9900 for information.

- **Annual Festival of Native American Arts,** Flagstaff. Early July to early August. Call 602/779-6921.
- **Navajo Nation Fair,** Window Rock. Rodeo, dances, parade. Early September. Call 602/871-6659.
- **Grand Canyon Chamber Music Festival,** Grand Canyon Village. September. Call 602/638-9215.
- **Jazz on the Rocks,** Sedona. Late September. Call 602/282-1985.

Spectator Sports

BASEBALL   Because of the mild spring climate in Arizona's desert areas, the state is the site of **spring training** camps for numerous pro baseball teams. In the Phoenix area, you can catch games by the Oakland A's, the San Francisco Giants, the California Angels, the Chicago Cubs, the Milwaukee Brewers, the San Diego Padres, the Seattle Mariners, and the Colorado Rockies (who have their spring training camp in Tucson). During the summer, the AAA Pacific Coast League's **Phoenix Firebirds** (tel 602/275-0500) play at Scottsdale Stadium and the **Tucson Toros** (tel 602/325-2621) play at Hi Corbett Field.

BASKETBALL   The NBA's **Phoenix Suns** (tel 602/379-7867) play at the America West Arena in Phoenix. You can also see college basketball at **Arizona State University** in Tempe (tel 602/965-6592) and the **University of Arizona** in Tucson (tel 602/621-4163).

FOOTBALL   The **Arizona Cardinals** (tel 602/379-0101) play at Arizona State University's Sun Devil Stadium in Tempe, the same stadium where **Arizona State University** plays Pac-10 Conference football (tel 602/965-6592). More Pac-10 Conference college football action takes place in Tucson at the University of Arizona (tel 602/621-4163).

GREYHOUND RACING   You can watch the greyhounds run at the **Phoenix Greyhound Park** (tel 602/273-7181) in Phoenix and the **Tucson Greyhound Park** (tel 602/884-7576) in Tucson.

HORSE RACING   The only permanent racetrack in Arizona is **Turf Paradise** (tel 602/942-1101) in Phoenix. However, country fairs in Arizona often have horse races.

Activities A to Z

BALLOONING   The climate and wind conditions in the Arizona desert are ideal for hot-air ballooning, and more than a dozen companies offer trips. Companies to contact include A Aerozona Adventure (tel 602/991-4260 or toll free 800/421-3056) in Phoenix, Balloon America (tel 602/299-7744) in Tucson, and Northern Lights Balloon Expeditions (tel 602/282-2274) in Sedona.

BIRD WATCHING   Arizona is nationally renowned for its bird watching, particularly in the mountains and in the riparian (riverside) areas of the southern part of the state. Some top bird watching spots are Madera Canyon (south of Tucson), Ramsey Canyon (south of Sierra Vista), the San Pedro Riparian National Conservation Area (east of Tombstone), Patagonia Creek (between Nogales and Sierra Vista), and the South Fork of Cave Creek Canyon (in the Chiracahua Mountains near Portal).

BOATING   Thanks to the many lakes created to store water in the desert, Arizona has more boats per capita than any other state! Houseboating on Lakes Powell, Mead, Mohave, and Havasu are popular summer vacation activities, and motorboating and waterskiing are popular on bodies of water throughout the state. On Saguaro and Canyon lakes east of Phoenix there are paddlewheeler excursions.

CAMPING   With more than a dozen national monuments and parks and numerous state parks, Arizona offers a wealth of campgrounds. Most are either in the mountains, where Arizona families go to escape the summer heat, or on lakes, which are popular both for fishing and powerboating. The *Arizona Campground Directory,* a free map and guide to the state's public campgrounds, is available from the **Arizona Office of Tourism,** 1100 W Washington St, Phoenix, AZ 85007 (tel 602/542-TOUR or toll free 800/842-8257).

FISHING   Arizona has great lake fishing for bass, perch, brown and rainbow trout, and northern pike, and some good trout fishing on rivers and streams in the White Mountains region. For more information, contact the **Arizona Game and Fish Department,** 2222 W Greenway Rd, Phoenix, AZ 85023 (tel 602/942-3000).

GOLF   The Phoenix area alone has more than 100 golf courses. The state's mild winters mean golfers can keep swinging all through the months when snow, ice, and freezing weather make golfing impossible in more northern latitudes. For more information, contact the **Arizona Golf Association** (tel 602/944-3035), or request a copy of *The Phoenix & Valley of the Sun Golf Guide* or *The Tucson & Southern Arizona Golf Guide* from one of the visitors bureaus mentioned above.

GUIDED OUTDOOR ADVENTURES Among the most popular guided adventures in Arizona are the 1- to 3-day mule rides down into the Grand Canyon; for more information, contact **Grand Canyon National Park Lodges** (tel 602/638-2401). Also very popular are **desert jeep tours** in the Phoenix and Sedona areas; for more information, contact Desert/Mountain Jeep Tours (tel 602/860-1777) in Scottsdale or Pink Jeep Tours (tel 602/282-5000 or toll free 800/8-SEDONA) in Sedona. To lend a hand at an archaeological dig, contact the White Mountain Archaeological Center (tel 602/333-5857) or Casa Malpais Archaeological Project (tel 602/333-5375), both located near Springerville on the edge of the White Mountains.

HORSEBACK RIDING Arizona is cowboy country, and while there are still those who ride horses for a living, horseback riding for pleasure is one of the state's favorite activities. You'll find riding stables all over the state, and overnight horseback rides, wagon train rides, and cattle drives are all available. For more information, contact Don Donnelly Stables (tel 602/982-7822 or toll free 800/346-4403), Desert/Mountain Jeep Tours (tel 602/860-1777), or Double D Ranch and Wagon Train Company (tel 602/636-0418).

SNOW SKIING Despite its image as a vast desert, Arizona does have several downhill ski areas, as well as cross-country ski trails. **Arizona Snowbowl** (tel 602/779-1951) outside of Flagstaff has the most reliable snowfall. **Sunrise** (tel 602/735-7669) on the White Mountain Apache Reservation near the town of McNary also offers good skiing. On Mount Lemmon just outside Tucson, you'll find the **Mount Lemmon Ski Valley** (tel 602/576-1321), the most southerly ski area in the United States.

TENNIS In winter, tennis is nearly as popular in Arizona as golf. You'll find tennis courts at resorts and hotels—even some budget hotels—in Phoenix, Tucson, and elsewhere. There are also numerous public tennis courts in Phoenix and Tucson.

TRAIN EXCURSIONS Fans of rail travel won't want to miss the chance to travel by steam train from Williams to the Grand Canyon on the **Grand Canyon Railway** (tel toll free 800/843-8724). The Verde River Canyon Excursion Train (tel 602/639-0010) makes runs up a roadless canyon near Sedona.

WHITE-WATER RAFTING Rafting through the Grand Canyon on the **Colorado River** is one of the world's premiere white-water trips. These trips range in length from 3 days to 2 weeks and can be done in wooden dories, huge rubber rafts with outboard motors, or in smaller rafts powered only by oars. Companies offering Grand Canyon raft trips include Arizona Raft Adventures (tel 602/526-8246 or toll free 800/786-RAFT), Grand Canyon Expeditions (tel 801/644-2691 or toll free 800/544-2691), and Western River Expeditions (tel 801/942-6669 or toll free 800/453-7450). Less demanding and less expensive white-water rafting takes place in the White Mountains northeast of Phoenix; contact Salt River Rafting (tel 602/577-1824 or toll free 800/242-6335) for more information.

For a more relaxing experience, there are half-day float trips from Glen Canyon Dam to Lee's Ferry. For more information, contact Wilderness River Adventures (tel 602/645-3279). Tubing (in inner tubes) down the Salt River east of Phoenix is another favorite summer activity; contact Salt River Recreation (tel 602/984-3305) for information.

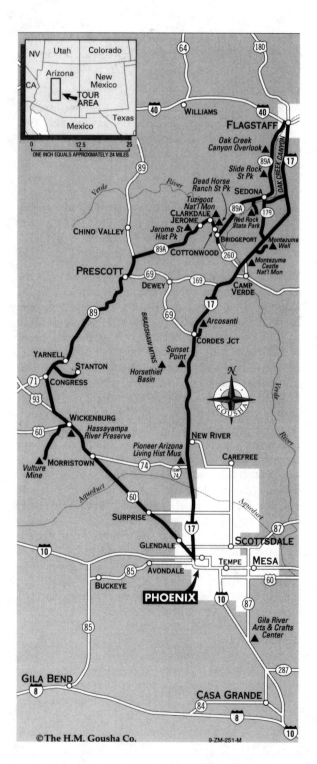

©The H.M. Gousha Co.   9-ZM-251-M

SCENIC DRIVING TOUR #1

PHOENIX, PRESCOTT & SEDONA

Start: Phoenix
Finish: Pioneer Arizona Living History Museum
Distance: 362 miles
Time: 3–5 days
Highlights: Rock formations, Victorian buildings, old mining towns, Native American ruins

From Phoenix's fine art museums to Sedona's red rocks, this tour of central Arizona's top attractions wanders through historic mining towns and the state's most sophisticated, modern communities, as well as past some of the most spectacular scenery in America. Mileages listed are from stop to stop only and do not include travel within a stop or side trips, which may easily add another hundred miles. Some mountain driving is included, and although most roads are paved and well-maintained, motorists should allow extra time. The section of Ariz 89A north of Sedona, through spectacular Oak Creek Canyon, is not recommended for large trailers.

For additional information on accommodations, restaurants, and attractions in the region covered by the tour, look under specific cities in the listings portion of this book.

1. **Phoenix.** When you hear people talking about the "New West," they're talking about Phoenix (elevation 1,132 feet), the 8th-largest US city. Although this metropolis is known for its fancy resorts, 117 golf courses, fine shopping, and urban sophistication, it has not forgotten its past. The area's first known inhabitants, the Hohokam, arrived about AD 300 and vanished in the 15th century, before Spanish conquistadors arrived in the mid-16th century. The present city of Phoenix began in the 1860s as a small settlement on the Salt River banks, named by an early settler who correctly predicted that a great city would grow from the ancient ruins, as the mythical phoenix rose from its own ashes.

   Phoenix and its surrounding cities—known collectively as the Valley of the Sun—attract both visitors and transplants with over 300 days of sunshine a year, mild temperatures, a robust economy, and an easy-going outdoor lifestyle. Although summers are hot, consistently topping 100 degrees, Phoenicians, as they like to call themselves, remind us that afternoon humidity averages a very low 17 percent, making the city far more comfortable than a number of other, cooler areas in the state. Although the Valley of the Sun actually includes 22 incorporated cities covering over 9,000 square miles, you're most likely to visit Phoenix, Scottsdale, Mesa, and Tempe.

The Phoenix area has numerous fine lodging possibilities, and is particularly known for its luxurious resorts, such as **John Gardiner's Tennis Ranch, Safari Resort,** and **Scottsdale Hilton Resort & Villas,** all in Scottsdale. Besides resorts, you have a good variety of hotel choices, including **Fairfield Inn, Hampton Inn,** and **La Quinta Inn.**

A good way to start your trip is by visiting some of the excellent museums in the area, where you may learn something about its past, people, and cultures. **Pueblo Grande Museum and Cultural Park,** 4619 E Washington St, Phoenix (tel 602/495-0900), contains ruins of an ancient Hohokam village. A "must stop" for anyone interested in Native American cultures is the **Heard Museum,** 22 E Monte Vista Rd, Phoenix (tel 602/252-8848), with extensive exhibits on Southwest tribes. Local artists and craftsworkers provide daily demonstrations here.

The **Arizona State Capitol Museum,** 1700 W Washington St, Phoenix (tel 602/542-4675), which served as the territorial capitol from 1900 to 1912, has been restored to the way it looked in 1912, the year Arizona became a state; it contains historical exhibits. Although many of Phoenix's early buildings have disappeared, more than a half-dozen turn-of-the-century structures have been saved in the 3-square-block area called **Heritage Square,** 115 N 6th St, at Monroe St, Phoenix (tel 602/262-5029), including **Rosson House,** which is open for tours; a 1912 school house that contains the **Arizona Doll and Toy Museum;** and an 1899 bungalow.

Arizona's largest western theme park, **Rawhide 1880s Western Town,** 23023 N Scottsdale Rd, Scottsdale (tel 602/563-1880), is a replica Old West town, complete wi[th] and burro rides, a museum,

Art lovers will enjoy the **Ph...um,** 1625 N Central Ave, Phoeni... 1222), with works from the Renais... present; and the **Arizona State Unive... Museum,** Nelson Fine Arts Center, 10th ... Mill Ave, Tempe (tel 602/965-ARTS), showca... the work of contemporary American artists. An ar... museum just for kids is **Arizona Museum for Youth,** 35 N Robson St, Mesa (tel 602/644-2468), with interactive exhibits.

The **Desert Botanical Garden,** 1201 N Galvin Pkwy, in Papago Park, Phoenix (tel 602/941-1225), has more than 20,000 desert plants from around the world. Next door, also in Papago Park, you'll find more than 1,300 animals at **Phoenix Zoo,** 455 N Galvin Pkwy, Phoenix (tel 602/273-1341), along with a tropical rain forest and a children's zoo.

Architecture mavens should head for Scottsdale. **Cosanti,** 6433 Doubletree Ranch Rd, Scottsdale (tel 602/948-6145), a unique complex of cast-concrete structures, houses foundries where Paolo Soleri windbells are made and sold; there is also a model of Soleri's futuristic solar-powered city Arcosanti, under construction north

---

REFRESHMENT STOP

The popular **Christopher's,** 2398 E Camelback Rd in Phoenix's Biltmore area, may be the Valley of the Sun's most elegant restaurant, serving contemporary French cuisine; **Bistro,** next door in Suite 220, and with the same owner/chef, is equally admired. For unusual Mexican dishes, try **Los Olivos,** 7328 Second St, a landmark Scottsdale dining spot. The **Hungry Hunter** chain of restaurants at 3102 E Camelback Rd, Phoenix; 4455 S Rural Rd, Tempe; 10825 N Scottsdale Rd, Scottsdale; and other locations offers good medium-priced American meals.

h gun fights, stagecoach
and shops.

oenix Art Muse-
(tel 602/257-
ance to the
sity Art
t and
es

Cactus Rd,
itect Frank
o.

askets, you
m Phoenix
fts Center
The center
an villages,
y, arts, and
The restau-
food.

northwest

out of the city on US 60 (Grana Ave), and follow the railroad for 58 miles to:

2. **Wickenburg.** Founded in 1863 by Prussian immigrant Henry Wickenburg, who discovered what would become Arizona's richest gold and silver mine, this town is a good place to relive the Old West. As you enter Wickenburg on US 60, turn right (north) onto Tegner St, and then left (west) on Yavapai St, which takes you to Frontier St and the Chamber of Commerce, located in the old Santa Fe Depot; here you can pick up a historic walking tour map. On **Frontier Street,** you'll see false front buildings dating to the turn of the century. **Desert Caballeros Western Museum,** 21 N Frontier St (tel 602/684-2272), displays a 1900 street scene, rooms from a Victorian home, minerals, and Native American artifacts. Don't miss the **Jail Tree,** near the corner of Wickenburg Way and Tegner St, where outlaws were once chained because no one wanted to take time out from mining to build a real jail.

About 12 miles south of town on Vulture Mine Rd, you'll find Wickenburg's original reason for existence, **Vulture Mine** (tel 602/377-0803), where you can take a self-guided, above-ground tour and explore some of the remaining 1884 buildings of Vulture City. About 3 miles south of Wickenburg on US 60 is the **Hassayampa River Preserve** (tel 602/684-2772), with self-guided nature walks along the Hassayampa River, Palm Lake, and through cottonwood-willow forests.

From Wickenburg, continue northwest on US 93 for 6 miles to Ariz 89, which branches off to the north along the railroad tracks for 10 miles to

Congress, and continue north about 2 miles on Ariz 89 to a rough dirt road heading east onto the plain. Follow that about 7 miles to:

3. **Stanton.** Established in 1863 after gold nuggets reportedly the size of potatoes were discovered, Stanton (originally called Antelope Station) had 3,500 residents by 1868, but both its population and gold prospects had dwindled by the early 1900s. Today the town is owned by the **Lost Dutchman Mining Association** (tel 602/427-9908), which hosts "recreational" miners. Drop-in visitors are also welcome, and they can visit the 1870s Stanton Hotel, opera house, saloon, and other original buildings.

From Stanton, drive back to Ariz 89 and turn north. You'll soon climb Yarnell Hill, which presents a breathtaking valley view to the south. Follow Ariz 89 north from the Stanton turn-off for 43 miles to:

4. **Prescott.** Another Arizona town (elevation 5,347 feet) born during the 1860s gold rush, Prescott was twice the capital of the Arizona Territory—from 1864 to 1867 and from 1877 to 1889. Today this pleasant small city is notable for its historic sites, museums, and arts and crafts. It also makes a good overnight stop. Among the local lodging choices are the historic 1927 **Hassayampa Inn;** the homey **Prescott Pines Inn;** and the economical **Super 8 Motel.**

Upon your arrival, stop at the Chamber of Commerce, 117 W Goodwin St (tel 602/445-2000) for the **Historic Downtown Walking Tour Guide,** which describes close to 3 dozen historic buildings. Near the Chamber of Commerce, you can see

---

🍺

REFRESHMENT STOP

For a trip back to the 1950s, head for **Kendall's Famous Burgers and Ice Cream,** 113 S Cortez St, or for a more formal dinner in an 1892 building, try the beef, ribs, or pasta at **Murphy's,** 201 N Cortez.

the 1864 Governor's Mansion, built of logs, and a number of other historic edifices and exhibits at **Sharlot Hall Museum,** 415 W Gurley St (tel 602/445-3122). The **Smoki Museum,** 100 N Arizona St (tel 602/445-1230) contains baskets, rugs, pottery, and other artifacts from a variety of Native American tribes, as well as a collection of western art.

Leaving Prescott, take Ariz 89 north for 5 miles, passing through the beautiful, wild-looking red, pink, and gray rock formations of **Granite Dells.** Then branch off to the northeast on Ariz 89A for 25 miles to:

5. **Jerome.** Once upon a time the town of Jerome had 15,000 residents and was labeled "the wickedest town in the West" by a New York newspaper. But when the copper mines closed in 1950 after operating more than 70 years, the town was practically deserted until it was rediscovered in the 1960s by artists who were attracted by the Verde Valley's magnificent scenery. Much of the old town has been restored, and in addition to exploring its art galleries and crafts shops, you can delve into its past. **Gold King Mine, Museum and Ghost Town,** 1 mile west of Main St on Perkinsville Rd (tel 602/634-5477), has exhibits on Jerome's early mining days. **Jerome State Historic Park,** off Ariz 89A (tel 602/634-5381), features a 1916 mansion built for mine owner James "Rawhide Jimmy" Douglas that reveals how rich miners lived during that time. The park has a spectacular view of the town and Verde Valley.

From Jerome, continue north on Ariz 89A about 4 miles, then leave Ariz 89A and follow 11th St into:

6. **Clarkdale.** During copper-mining days Clarkdale was home to the smelter for copper mined at Jerome; when the mines closed, Clarkdale almost shut down, but it was revived by the establishment of a cement company in the 1950s. **Tuzigoot National Monument** (tel 602/634-5564), about 2 miles east of Clarkdale (turn east on Main St and follow the signs), contains remnants of a Sinaguan Indian village built of mud and rock between 1125 and 1400. For a good view of the beautiful Verde Valley, take a ride on the **Arizona Central Rail-**

road, 300 N Broadway (tel 602/639-0010), which passes areas inaccessible by car.

From Clarkdale, go east on Broadway about 2 miles into Cottonwood, where it becomes Main St; turn north onto 10th St and follow it to:

7. **Dead Horse Ranch State Park** (tel 602/634-5283). No dead horses here, this state park is best known for bird watching, but it also has opportunities for canoeing, stream and pond fishing, horseback riding, picnicking, camping, and leisurely walks along the Verde River.

Leaving the park, drive east about 2 miles on Main St through Cottonwood, then follow Ariz 89A north 20 miles to:

8. **Sedona.** Surrounded by huge red rocks and rugged terrain, and blessed by a mild climate, Sedona (elevation 4,400 feet) has become a haven for artists and other free spirits; more recently, it has attracted increasing numbers of retirees. The town boasts numerous art galleries, shops, and restaurants, and serves as a base for explorations into the back country on foot, horseback, or 4-wheel drive vehicle. Sedona has a number of fine resorts and hotels, including **Best Western Arroyo Roble Hotel, Enchantment Resort, Quality Inn King's Ransom,** and **Sedona Motel.** However, local lodging is likely to fill up quickly, especially during the summer, and reservations are strongly recommended. An alternative is to drive on to Flagstaff (see stop #11 below), about 28 miles north, where there are many more lodging choices. Also, although the scenery in Flagstaff is not as pretty as in Sedona, the prices are lower.

Scenery is one of the main reasons to visit Sedona. For a spectacular view, visit **Schnebly Hill Overlook.** To get there, head south from Sedona on Ariz 179, crossing a bridge over Oak Creek, and turn east onto Schnebly Hill Rd, which you follow 12 miles to the top of the Mogollon Rim. It takes 40 to 60 minutes to drive this latter dirt road, but the view is well worth it. For another scenic perspective, drive south on Ariz 89A about 4 miles from downtown Sedona, turn east onto Upper Red Rock Loop Rd, and follow it about 2 miles to the turnoff for **Red Rock Crossing.** About 1 mile down this dirt road you'll find a parking and picnic area, from where you can view Cathedral Rock and the gigantic red box canyon that surrounds you. This area is beautiful, tree-shaded, and serene when not too crowded, with several paths to explore, a few old buildings, and a number of huge fallen trees. Back on the Red Rock Loop Rd, which soon becomes a narrow and rough dirt thoroughfare, drive about 2 miles to return to paving and the entrance to **Red Rock State Park** (tel 602/282-6907), with hiking and horseback trails available during the day. From the park, follow Lower Red Rock Loop Rd about 3 miles back to Ariz 89A and turn north, and go 5 miles back to Sedona. Just south of Sedona, high above Ariz 179, you'll see the **Chapel of the Holy Cross** (tel 602/282-4069), a modern Roman Catholic chapel built from the canyon's red rock.

Back in town, the **Sedona Arts Center,** at Ariz 89A and Art Barn Rd (tel 602/282-3809), has exhibits of works by local and regional artists, as well as theater and music performance. Sedona's more than 40 local art galleries provides art lovers with hours of browsing.

From Sedona, drive 7 miles farther north on Ariz 89A to:

9. **Slide Rock State Park** (tel 602/282-3034). Especially popular on hot summer days, this park is named for its 30-foot water slide worn into rocks in Oak Creek. Swimmers often wear old cut-off blue jeans instead of bathing suits to protect themselves (and their suits) from the rough rocks.

After cooling off at the park, continue north on Ariz 89A for another 8 miles to:

10. **Oak Creek Canyon Overlook.** This stretch of highway through the inspirational red rocks and pine forests of Oak Creek Canyon is considered one of the most scenic in America, and the overlook provides an awesome view down the valley.

Now, continue north on Ariz 89A for another 13 miles to:

11. **Flagstaff.** Located at the junction of 2 interstate highways and within easy reach of **Grand Canyon National Park,** Flagstaff is an ideal overnight stop, with numerous lodging and dining choices. But even here, reservations are recommended.

From Flagstaff, you can head south down I-17 for 47 miles to exit 293 and then north 4 miles to Montezuma Well (see directions to #12, below), or drive back to Sedona, 28 miles south on Ariz 89A, for a different perspective on beautiful **Oak Creek Canyon.** Along the way you'll pass US Forest Service camp and picnic grounds, parking for hiking trails, and Slide Rock State Park, before finding yourself back in Sedona.

From Sedona, go south past more magnificent red rock formations on Ariz 179 for 15 miles to I-17 (exit 298), and then head south on the interstate for 5 miles to exit 293, and 4 miles north on an unmarked road, following signs to:

12. **Montezuma Well.** Actually a limestone sink formed by the collapse of an ancient underground cavern, Montezuma Well was home to first the Hohokam and then the Sinagua, who built irrigation ditches for growing corn, beans, squash, and cotton. You can see remnants of the ditches, an AD 1100 Hohokam pit house, and a variety of structures used by the Sinaguan between 1125 and 1400. Montezuma Well is managed as part of Montezuma Castle National Monument (see below).

Now go back to I-17 and drive 4 miles south to exit 289 for:

13. **Montezuma Castle National Monument** (tel 602/567-3322). Here you'll find a 5-story 20-room cliff dwelling believed to have been constructed by the Sinagua some 800 years ago, plus the ruins of a larger, 6-story pueblo built against the base of a cliff.

From here, head south 5 miles on Montezuma Castle Hwy, following signs into:

14. **Camp Verde.** East of I-17 exit 287, this area was established as a cavalry outpost in 1865 to protect settlers along the Verde River from raids by the Apache and Yavapai. **Fort Verde State Historic Park,** in the center of Camp Verde (tel 602/567-3275), includes 5 of the fort's original buildings, with exhibits depicting life in a late 19th-century fort.

Now, go west through town to I-17, head south about 23 miles to Cordes Junction (exit 262A), and go northeast about 3 miles on a dirt road, following signs to:

15. **Arcosanti** (tel 602/632-7135). This city of the future, designed by Paolo Soleri, remains under construction by Soleri's students. When it is eventually completed, it will be an ecologically friendly, 25-story-tall city of some 5,000 residents, with solar energy for both heating and cooling. At present, Arcosanti has a visitor's center, guest rooms, and a bakery, and guided tours.

Leaving Arcosanti, return to I-17 and continue south about 10 miles to:

16. **Sunset Point.** An interstate rest stop (between exits 256 and 248), Sunset Point sits on a promontory with a stunning view, taking in a ghost town site, an old stagecoach trail, Horsethief Basin, and the Bradshaw Mountains. It has photo displays and maps, as well as the usual rest stop facilities.

Now go south on I-17 about 26 more miles to Pioneer Rd (exit 225) and:

17. **Pioneer Arizona Living History Museum** (tel 602/993-0212). Costumed pioneers demonstrate life in Arizona's early days at this living history museum, with close to 2 dozen original and reconstructed buildings, including a stagecoach station, a Victorian mansion, a miner's cabin, a church, several farm houses, and carpenter's, blacksmith's, and wagon maker's shops. Melodramas and other performances are presented in the opera house, and each fall, there is a reenactment of Civil War events.

From the museum it's about 12 miles south on I-17 back to Phoenix.

SCENIC DRIVING TOUR #2

TUCSON, SONORA DESERT & THE WILD WEST

Start: Tucson
Finish: Saguaro National Monument
Distance: 386 miles
Time: 3–4 days
Highlights: Old West and mining towns, rock formations, historic sites, early Spanish missions

This tour visits old Arizona, stopping at the Wild West town of Tombstone, the Spanish colonial Tumacacori mission, and the Arizona State Museum, with exhibits dealing with the area's first inhabitants, the Hohokam people. The route also takes in some of Arizona's most beautiful natural wonders, at Saguaro National Monument, Colossal Cave, and Chiricahua National Monument, as well as the desert life at the Arizona-Sonora Desert Museum. If possible, allow 3 days after leaving Tucson. Mileages listed are from stop to stop only, and do not include driving within a park or area or any side trips.

For additional information on accommodations, restaurants, and attractions in the region covered by the tour, look under specific cities in the listings portion of this book.

1. **Tucson** (elevation 2,389 feet). If there is one city that epitomizes the American Southwest, it's Tucson. This appealing destination offers lovely year-round weather (though it gets quite hot in summer), impressive mountain and desert scenery, a rich Native American and Hispanic heritage, remnants of the Old West, a varied and exciting arts community, and numerous recreational opportunities.

The Tuscon area was farmed by the Hohokam in the 1st century, and later became the home of Pima and Tohono O'odham tribes (formerly known as Papago). Europeans first discovered the region in 1687 with a visit by Spanish missionary Father Eusebio Francisco Kino. The city itself was founded in 1775 by Irishman Hugh O'Connor, who explored the region for Spain. Tuscon was under the Mexican flag from 1821, the year Mexico gained independence from Spain, until

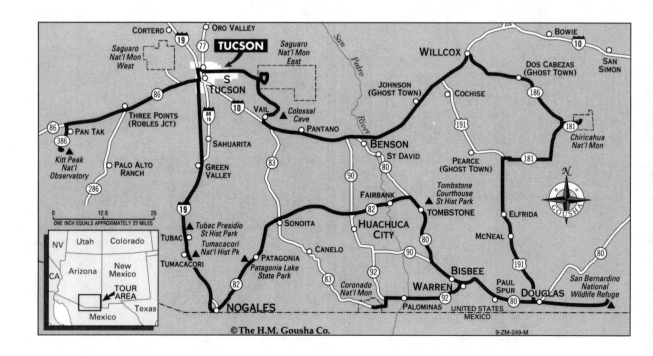

©The H.M. Gousha Co.

1846, when it was taken over by US troops during the Mexican War. The 1854 Gadsden Purchase joined southern Arizona, including Tucson, with the rest of the Arizona Territory.

Tucson has a broad selection of lodging choices, with posh resorts, comfortable hotels and motels, and historic inns. The luxurious **Loew's Ventana Canyon Resort** pampers its guests unmercifully; a more economical resort is **The Lodge on the Desert.** The historic **Arizona Inn** combines Old World charm with all the modern conveniences. Other attractive lodgings include **Hampton Inn, Econo Lodge,** and **Embassy Suites.**

Start your visit to southern Arizona by visiting one or more of Tucson's fine historical museums. At the **Arizona State Museum,** on the University of Arizona campus at University Blvd and Park Ave (tel 602/621-6302), you learn about the state's first inhabitants, the Hohokam, and about tribes that lived here later, including the Pima, Tohono O'odham, Hopi, Navajo, and Apache. The **Arizona Historical Society Tucson Museum,** 949 E Second St (tel 602/628-5774), explores the state's fascinating past from Spanish colonial days to the Wild West period to the modern age.

At the University of Arizona, be sure to visit **Flandrau Science Center & Planetarium,** at Cherry Ave and University Blvd (tel 602/621-STAR), where you can see a variety of programs and laser light shows. On clear nights, which most are, you can peruse the heavens through the planetarium's 16-inch telescope. Before leaving downtown, stop by the **University of Arizona Museum of Art,** at Park Ave and Speedway Blvd, with its excellent collection of European paintings dating back to the Renaissance and more recent American works. Nearby, also on the university campus, the **John P. Schaefer Center for Creative Photography,** just east of the Museum of Art, has one of the best and largest collections of works by the world's finest photographers.

For Western art, visit the **Tucson Museum of Art,** 140 N Main Ave (tel 602/624-2333), which also features pre-Columbian art of Mexico and South and Central America. Also downtown, you'll find **Tucson Botanical Gardens,** 2150 N Alvernon Way (tel 602/326-9255); **Tucson Children's Museum,** 200 S Sixth Ave (tel 602/884-7511); and **Reid Park Zoo,** 1100 S Randolph Way (tel 602/791-4022).

History and airplane buffs will enjoy the **Pima Air & Space Museum,** 6000 E Valencia Rd, south of Davis Monthan Air Force Base (tel 602/574-9658), which houses more than 180 aircraft, spanning over 90 years of aviation history.

Mission San Xavier del Bac, 1950 W San Xavier Rd, 9 miles south of Tucson via I-19 to the Valencia Rd exit (tel 602/294-2624), is perhaps the finest existing example of mission architecture in the United States; it incorporates Moorish, Byzantine, and Mexican Renaissance styles.

About a dozen miles west of the city, via Speedway Blvd, **Old Tucson Studios,** 201 S Kinney Rd (tel 602/883-0100), was created for the filming of the 1939 classic western *Arizona;* since then, the location has been used for more than 300 films (including *The Outlaw Josey Wales, Gunfight at the O.K. Corral,* and *Rio Bravo*) and for television shows and commercials. Old Tucson Studios is also a theme park, with gun fights, a steam railroad train, stagecoach rides, and behind-the-scenes tours and demonstrations of the making of western movies.

Two of Tucson's top attractions lie on the city's west side. Despite its name, the **Arizona-Sonora Desert Museum,** 2021 N Kinney Rd (tel 602/883-2702), is actually one of the finest zoos and botanical gardens in the country, with more than 200 species of animals and 1,200 species of plants indigenous to the Sonora Desert. Among animals you may see are mountain lions, black bears, otters, javelinas, birds, fish, scorpions, and tarantulas. There are also displays on prehistoric desert life, volcanos, and erosion. **Saguaro National Monument** (tel 602/883-6399), just north of the museum, is the home of the giant saguaro cactus, a symbol of the American West that can tower 50 feet above the desert, weigh more than 8 tons, and drink some 200 gallons of water a year. The monument has 2 sections; one west and one east of Tucson. In the western section, called the Tucson Mountain District, an information center just inside the monument's boundary has brochures and exhibits describing the life cycle of the saguaro. You also have access to a 6-mile loop drive and hiking trails. See below for information on the eastern section.

About 35 miles west of Tucson, off Ariz 86, is **Kitt Peak National Observatory** (tel 602/322-3350). Take Ajo Way, Ariz 86, west for 35 miles, turn south onto Ariz 386 and drive 11½ miles up a narrow and winding but well-maintained road to the conservatory. This part of the drive takes about 20 minutes, and there are stops at regular intervals for you to appreciate the view. This road is not recommended for those with a fear of heights or who suffer from high-altitude sickness. Perched atop 6,882-foot Kitt Peak, this observatory has close to two dozen telescopes, including the world's largest solar telescope and another telescope that contains a 30,000-pound quartz mirror. The site has a **Visitor Center and Museum** and **Visitor Galleries** for up-close views of the big telescopes, as well as tours.

♨

REFRESHMENT STOP

If Tucson's Hispanic influences make you hungry for Mexican food, try **La Parilla Suiza,** in the center of Tucson at 5602 E Speedway Blvd, which specializes in Mexico City–style cuisine. **Pronto,** 2955 E Speedway, serves Italian specialties and has a gourmet bakery. And **Bobby McGee's Conglomeration,** with several restaurants in the Tucson area, one of which is at 6464 E Tanque Verde Rd, offers traditional American food in an Old West setting.

From Tucson, go about 60 miles south on I-19 to the next stop at:

2. **Tubac,** exit 34. Considered the oldest European settlement in Arizona, Tubac today is a laid-back community of artists, who own galleries and shops, and retirees. But life was really more active in the 1750s when the Spanish government established a fort here to protect settlers from raids by hostile Native Americans. Remnants of the fort and days past may be seen at **Tubac Presidio State Historic Park,** Presidio Dr (tel 602/398-2252), a 10-acre area with an underground display showing portions of the original structure. The park also has a visitor center with exhibits tracing Tubac's sometimes-violent history and an 1885 schoolhouse. Modern Tubac is evident at the **Tubac Center of the Arts,** Plaza Rd (tel 602/398-2371), where you'll discover works by local artists, traveling exhibits, and theater and music performances.

From Tubac, return to I-19 and go south 3 miles to exit 29 for:

3. **Tumacacori National Historical Park** (tel 602/398-2341). The mission at Tumacacori, located just under 1 mile from I-19, was founded in 1691 by Father Eusebio Francisco Kino to convert the Pima Indians to Christianity. After a revolt in 1751 that left 2 priests and more than 100 settlers dead, the Spanish established a fort in nearby Tubac, and moved the mission across the Santa Cruz River. The handsome adobe ruins of this second Tumacacori mission church, a cemetery, and a mortuary chapel are what you see on a self-guided walking tour. The park also has a museum containing displays on mission life, and a garden with plants of the mission period. Nearby, within the boundaries of the park, you can see ruins of 2 other missions.

From Tumacacori, return to I-19 and go south for 18 miles to exit 1 and:

4. **Nogales.** Actually there are 2 Nogaleses—one in Arizona and a much larger one across the border in Mexico. Although definitely not Mexico at its best, this border town allows you a convenient opportunity to visit Mexico for some quick shopping and sightseeing. Most visitors park their cars on the Arizona side and walk across the border. If you do want to take your car into Mexico, you need to buy Mexican motor vehicle insurance before leaving the United States. You don't need a passport or tourist card to visit the Mexican Nogales, and you can bring back up to $400 worth of merchandise duty free, including 1 liter of liquor. The city has a variety of markets and shops

where you can find leather goods, baskets, pottery, clothing, and other items, often at very attractive prices, although some visitors feel uncomfortable with the large number of beggars on the streets and the merchants' persistent efforts to lure shoppers into stores.

Back on the Arizona side is the **Pimeria Alta Historical Society Museum,** 136 N Grand Ave (tel 602/287-5402), which has exhibits on the history of this section of southern Arizona and northern Mexico. 2 miles east of Nogales on Ariz 82 is **Arizona Vineyard Winery** (tel 602/287-7972), where you can take a tour and try free samples of wine, including an interesting Rattlesnake Red.

From Nogales, take Ariz 82 northeast 12 miles to **Patagonia Lake State Park** (tel 602/287-6965), with plenty of recreational opportunities, including a 250-acre lake, boating, fishing, hiking, and camping.

Back on Ariz 82, continue northeast for 56 miles, then turn south onto Ariz 80 and go 4 miles until you reach:

5. **Tombstone.** This town may be the most famous community of the Old West, thanks to numerous books and movies that have glorified its wild and wicked days, and particularly the famous "Gunfight at the OK Corral," during which Wyatt Earp and his brothers fought it out with the outlaw Clanton family. The town got its name from prospector Ed Schieffelin, who was warned that before he found any silver he'd find his own tombstone. When he made his first strike, Schieffelin gave the town its present name, probably to mock any doubters.

There's less shooting in Tombstone now, except for staged gunfights Sunday afternoons, but the place continues to live up to its nickname as "the town too tough to die" with a thriving tourist business. Historic Allen St has been beautifully restored, and you're likely to find film crews at work here. Half real and half make-believe, Tombstone is fun, especially if you don't take it too seriously.

At the **OK Corral,** on Allen St between 3rd and 4th Sts (tel 602/457-3456), you'll see where the famous 1881 gunfight took place. Next to the OK Corral's main entrance is **Historama** (tel 602/457-3456), with a program on Tombstone's past. **Boot Hill Graveyard,** off Ariz 80 on the north side of town (tel 602/457-9344), has a number of telling tombstones reflecting the town's genuinely violent history. Considered the West's wildest whorehouse and saloon, the **Bird Cage Theatre,** at 6th and Allen Sts (tel 602/457-3421), remains much like it was in 1881, when prostitutes were perched in cages hung from the ceiling. In contrast to the noisy shoot-em-up atmosphere in most of Tombstone in the 1880s, a sophisticated Victorian courthouse was built in 1882 at a cost of $50,000. Today it is the **Tombstone Courthouse State Historic Park,** 219 E Toughnut St (tel 602/457-3311), containing displays on the town's history. Another sign that Tombstone was home to more than gunslingers and ladies-of-the-night is **St Paul's Episcopal Church,** a handsome adobe structure built in 1882, at the corner of 3rd and Safford Sts.

🍵

REFRESHMENT STOP

For a variety of food choices in a historic building, stop at **The Nellie Cashman Restaurant,** 117 S 5th St.

Leaving Tombstone, take US 80 south 24 miles to the next stop:

6. **Bisbee** (elevation 5,490 feet). One of the region's best remaining examples of a turn-of-the-century town, Bisbee is another of the western boom towns that almost disappeared when the minerals —in this case copper—finally ran out. In 1919, Bisbee reportedly was the largest city between New Orleans and San Francisco, a wild place with 25,000 residents and close to 50 saloons and bordellos. Today, with a bit over 6,000 people, Bisbee is a fascinating mix of retired miners, artists, and transplanted city dwellers looking for a better life. Built on the exceedingly steep sides of

Tombstone Canyon, the houses seem almost to grow out of one another.

At the **Bisbee Chamber of Commerce,** Naco Rd (tel 602/432-5421), you'll find several brochures describing walking tours among the historic buildings. **Queen Mine,** 118 Arizona St (tel 602/432-2071), closed in 1975, but it offers underground tours as well as tours of the nearby **Lavender Pit** open mine. For a look at the history of mining and Bisbee, stop at the **Bisbee Mining and Historical Museum,** 5 Copper Queen Plaza (tel 602/432-7071). The **Mulheim Heritage House Museum,** 207 Youngblood Hill (tel 602/432-7071), has been restored to its early 20th-century elegance, with period furnishings. Situated on a hill overlooking Old Bisbee, the museum site offers magnificent panoramic views of the surrounding countryside. For an interesting side trip from Bisbee, visit **Coronado National Memorial,** 30 miles west on Ariz 92 and Montezuma Canyon Rd (tel 602/366-5515), which commemorates the first major European exploration of the Southwest, when Francisco Vásquez de Coronado of Spain arrived in 1540.

If it's late in the day, you may want to consider spending the night here. In historic Old Bisbee, the **Bisbee Grand Hotel** and the **Copper Queen Hotel** offer a trip back to the turn of the century, while **High Desert Inn** has modern facilities in a historic building.

From Bisbee, follow Ariz 80 east for 23 miles to get to:

7. **Douglas.** Founded in 1901, Douglas (elevation 3,990 feet) began as the roundup site for the surrounding ranches. Today, with its convenient location on the US-Mexico border, Douglas's main industry is international commerce, with 15 manufacturing plants, and another 26 across the Mexican border in Agua Prieta. While in Douglas, stop at the historic **Gadsden Hotel,** 1046 G Ave. Built in 1907, this "last of the grand hotels" has a beautiful marble lobby, vaulted stained-glass skylights, and a Tiffany stained-glass window.

From Douglas, take Ariz 80 west for 2 miles, head north on US 191 for 37 miles, turn east onto Ariz 181, and drive 22 miles to:

8. **Chiricahua National Monument** (tel 602/824-3560). Called "Land of the Standing-up Rocks" by the Chiricahua Apache for whom it is named, this monument is a wonderland of exotic and extraordinary rock sculptures, created by volcanic activity followed by millions of years of wind and water erosion. The park is a fantasy world of delicate spires, gigantic balanced rocks, massive columns, and intriguing rock grottos. A **visitor center** offers a slide show, exhibits, maps, and books. You can take a 16-mile scenic drive, and walk more than 20 miles of hiking trails past unusual rock formations such as Duck on a Rock. Also on the monument grounds is the turn-of-the-century **Faraway Ranch and Stafford Cabin,** with tours daily.

From Chiricahua National Monument, follow Ariz 186 northwest 32 miles to:

9. **Willcox,** at I-10 exit 340. Once called the "Cattle Capital of America," Willcox is still a major cattle shipping area, with the state's largest livestock auction. Lodging possibilities here include the modern, comfortable, and clean **Best Western Plaza Inn** and **Econo Lodge,** both just off the interstate highway.

Fans of older-style country western music will want to stop at the **Rex Allen Arizona Cowboy Museum,** 155 N Railroad Ave (tel 602/384-4583), dedicated to hometown boy Allen, a popular country western singer and actor in the 1940s and 1950s. The **Cochise Visitor Center and Museum of the Southwest,** at I-10 exit 340, 1500 N Circle I Rd (tel 602/384-2272), contains exhibits on southeastern Arizona's Wild West days, cattle ranching, and geology.

From Willcox, take I-10 west 61 miles to exit 279 and:

10. **Vail.** The **RW Webb Winery** (tel 602/762-5777), on the frontage road, offers informal guided tours and wine tasting. Founded in 1980, this operation is said to be the first bonded winery in the state since Prohibition.

Next, follow the steep and winding Colossal Cave Rd on its roller coaster way north about 5 miles to:

11. **Colossal Cave** (tel 602/647-7275). Among the world's largest dry limestone caves, Colossal Cave

was a favorite hideout for bandits in Arizona's Wild West days. The cave has a constant temperature of 72 degrees. There are lighted passageways among the numerous stalagmites and stalactites, and guided ½-mile tours are offered.

As you exit the cave property, the road becomes Old Spanish Trail, which you follow west 5 miles to the east section of:

12. **Saguaro National Monument** (tel 602/296-8576). Here you'll find an aging forest of giant saguaro cacti at the base of the Rincon Mountains. Stop first at the **visitor center** for hiking and driving guides, and to look at exhibits on saguaro and other desert life. You'll also learn about a fire that occurred on Mother's Day, 1994, destroying a number of giant saguaros. The monument area has an 8-mile **Cactus Forest Drive** winding through the saguaro forest, and close to 130 miles of hiking trails, including a short **Desert Ecology Trail** that shows the vital role of water in the desert.

From the monument, continue along Old Spanish Trail west about 12 miles to Broadway, which you follow about 8 miles into downtown Tucson.

SCENIC DRIVING TOUR #3

GRAND CANYON & NAVAJO AND HOPI COUNTRY

Start: Flagstaff
Finish: Meteor Crater Natural Landmark
Distance: 535 miles
Time: 2–5 days
Highlights: Grand Canyon, Native American trading
                 posts, Painted Desert

This northeast Arizona tour includes some of the state's most stunning scenery as well as opportunities to see and buy beautiful Native American jewelry, rugs, baskets, and pottery. Early morning and late evening are best for viewing the canyons and Painted Desert. It's wise not to travel after dark in the remote reaches of the Hopi and Navajo reservations, where you might encounter sheep on the road. Highways in this tour are good, all-weather roads, but there can be great distances between services of any kind.

When traveling through the reservations keep in mind that these are considered sovereign nations, with their own laws. Also remember that although the Hopi and Navajo generally welcome visitors, these areas are made up of their homes and villages; you are asked to respect their privacy by only going inside buildings where you are obviously invited and by obeying all signs. Often, photography is prohibited, and even where it is permitted you're expected to ask for permission before photographing any individuals. Religious ceremonies are fascinating to watch, but keep in mind that these are serious services and behave accordingly.

For additional information on accommodations, restaurants, and attractions in the region covered by the tour, look under specific cities in the listings portion of this book.

1. **Flagstaff.** Located at the base of the San Francisco Peaks, Flagstaff looks up at Mount Humphreys, the highest point in Arizona at an elevation of 12,633 feet. The combination of its 7,000-foot elevation and clear, dry air gives Flagstaff a mild climate year-round, with an average of 288 days of sunshine each year. You'll find recreational, cultural, and historical activities in and around the city, with opportunities for both downhill and cross-country skiing; and hiking, camping, hunting, and fishing in the Coconino National Forest, which surrounds Flagstaff and has the largest stand of ponderosa pine in the nation.

A good place to begin your tour of northern Arizona, and possibly use as a home base, Flagstaff has a variety of lodgings from which to choose, from basic to fancy. The historic **Monte Vista Hotel,** built in 1929, is located downtown. For a quiet, rustic retreat just outside the city try **Arizona Mountain Inn.** The **Best Western Woodlands Plaza Inn** is considered to be among Flagstaff's finest, and the attractive **Econo Lodge West,** in southwest Flagstaff, is a comfortable and economical choice.

Downtown Flagstaff has several historical buildings; you can obtain a map for a self-guided walking tour at the visitors center at the corner of Route 66 and Beaver St (tel 602/774-9541 or toll free 800/842-7293). Highlights include the 1888 **McMillan Building,** now housing an art gallery; the 1889 **Weatherford Hotel,** now a youth hostel and nightclub; and the 1929 **Monte Vista Hotel,** with several specialty shops. The **Riordan State Historic Park,** 1300 Riordan Ranch St, has guided tours of the 2-story mansion, built in 1904 for 2 Riordan brothers and their families.

Lowell Observatory, 1400 W Mars Rd (tel 602/774-2096), about a mile from downtown Flagstaff on the top of Mars Hill, is one of the oldest astronomical observatories in the Southwest, founded in 1894. Early observations at this site supported the expanding universe theory, and it was here in 1930 that the 9th planet, Pluto, was discovered. The observatory welcomes visitors with daytime guided tours and nighttime astronomical programs.

Northern Arizona University (tel 602/523-9011), off Old Route 66 via Riordan Rd in downtown Flagstaff, first opened in 1899 as a school for teacher preparation. The oldest of its several entries on the National Register of Historic Places is **Old Main,** built in 1894 and today housing a museum and art galleries. The university also has

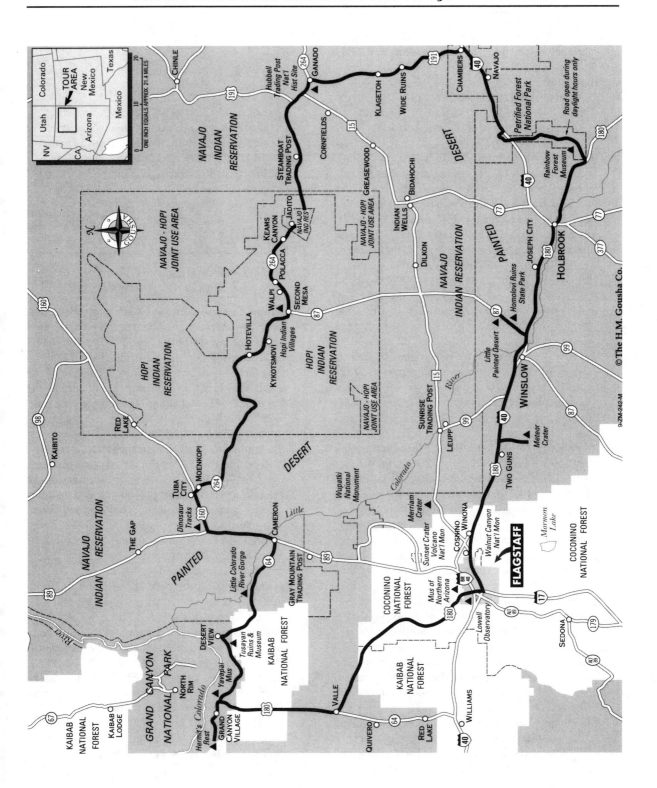

the **Richard E. Beasley Art Museum and Gallery** (tel 602/523-3471) with exhibits of contemporary art.

Just northwest of downtown on US 180 (N Fort Valley Rd), you'll find 3 museums. Created in 1928, the **Museum of Northern Arizona,** N Fort Valley Rd (tel 602/774-5211), explores the cultural and natural history of the Colorado Plateau, a geographic area encompassing northern Arizona and the Four Corners region. It also exhibits work by Native American artists. **Pioneer Museum,** 2340 N Fort Valley Rd (tel 602/774-6272), opened in 1963. Here you can see Flagstaff's first fire engine, a sheepherder's wagon, and pioneer tools and artifacts. Also notable are photographs of the Grand Canyon taken between 1902 and 1906 by Emery Kolb. **Coconino Center for the Arts,** N Fort Valley Rd (tel 602/779-6921), is a regional art center with changing exhibits every 5 to 6 weeks, plus musical performances and workshops.

Head southwest about 4 miles from Flagstaff on Woody Mountain Rd to the **Arboretum at Flagstaff** (tel 602/774-1441), the highest US botanical garden conducting horticultural research; it is located on 200 acres of ponderosa pine forest land.

Walnut Canyon National Monument, Walnut Canyon Rd (tel 602/526-3367), is on the east side of Flagstaff, about 10 minutes from downtown. Take Exit 204 off I-40. The 3-mile drive to the monument takes you through a beautiful ponderosa forest to the **visitor center.** Sometime before 1400, Sinagua Indians built over 300 rooms in the recesses of the high desert canyon walls. A steep foot trail takes you to 25 of the cliff dwelling ruins.

Sunset Crater Volcano and Wupatki National Monuments are on a loop road that takes off from US 89 about 13 miles north of Flagstaff. The Sunset Crater visitors center is 2 miles down the road, and there are numerous vistas and walking trails in the area. The visitors center for Wupatki is 22 miles north on the road; it features displays on the Indian ruins that comprise this monument, which were inhabited in the 12th and 13th centuries. Another 14 miles brings you back to US 89, and it's about 39 miles back to Flagstaff.

Once you've seen the sights of the Flagstaff area, head north on US 180 for 81 miles to:

2. **Grand Canyon National Park.** Considered the most popular natural attraction in the United States, the awe-inspiring Grand Canyon is some 2 billion years old. It is about 1 mile deep, 277 miles long, and 11 to 12 miles across. Elevation at the South Rim is 7,000 feet, and 8,200 feet at the North Rim. But the Grand Canyon's appeal consists of much more than numbers. Its quiet magnificence attains an almost spiritual beauty. It's not unusual to be standing at an overlook crowded with people and hear nothing but the sound of the wind. Sculpted by the Colorado River as it slices through layers of rock, the canyon is a maze of colorful and majestic towers, valleys, walls, and pinnacles.

Because of the Grand Canyon's popularity, it is advisable to make reservations for lodging, camping, and especially mule rides as far in advance as possible. Call the park operator (tel 602/638-2631) to be connected with the proper offices.

Once you're at the South Rim, stop first at the **visitor center** in Grand Canyon Village for helpful brochures and information on the free shuttle that operates during summer months. Then head out to see the canyon, either from the various overlooks, or by foot or mule into the canyon. On the 8-mile 1-way **West Rim Drive** (only by shuttle and tour bus in summer), you get a fine canyon view and see a historic log and stone building at **Hermit's Rest,** named for an 1890s prospector. Then, the 25-mile **East Rim Drive** takes you out the park's east gate.

Just east of Grand Canyon Village at **Yavapai Point,** you experience a different view; the **Yavapai Museum** has exhibits on the canyon's geological history. From here, continue east, stopping at the various overlooks. At **Tusayan Ruins,** you find the ruins of an ancient Anasazi village and a small museum. At **Desert View,** at the east end of East Rim Dr, climb to the top of the **Watchtower,** the highest point along the South Rim, for a spectacular view of the canyon, the Painted Desert to the east, and San Francisco Mountains to the south.

From Desert View, drive east on Ariz 64 for 15 miles to:

3. **Little Colorado River Gorge,** an awesome vista looking down into the Little Colorado River Canyon. Here you're also likely to find local Native Americans selling their crafts.

From the overlook, continue east on Ariz 64 another 17 miles, then go north 1 mile on US 89 until you reach:

4. **Cameron,** and the historic **Cameron Trading Post** (tel 602/679-2231 or toll free 800/338-7385). This genuine trading post, established in 1890, has a huge selection of rugs, pottery, textiles, beadwork, jewelry, and other Native American crafts, including museum-quality late 19th- and early 20th-century Navajo rugs. Still actively used by local Native Americans, the trading post also contains a general store with packaged foods and household goods.

From Cameron, continue 15 miles north on US 89 through the Painted Desert to US 160, turn east and travel about 6 miles to an unpaved road heading north toward Moenave. Follow this dirt road about ¼ mile to find:

5. **Dinosaur Tracks.** Left in the mud flats over 200 million years ago, these dinosaur tracks and part of a dinosaur skeleton may be seen within about 200 feet of the unpaved road.

From the tracks, return to US 160, go east about 5 miles to Ariz 264, and continue east on Ariz 264, through the Painted Desert and red rock country for about 60 miles to:

6. **Second Mesa,** home of the Hopi Native Americans, who trace their ancestry to the ancient Anasazi. Visit the **Hopi Cultural Center** (tel 602/734-2401), with a fine museum telling the story of the Hopis through historic photos and artifacts. This is also a good place to find out what other parts of the reservation are open to visitors. Usually you can take a tour of **Walpi,** on First Mesa, about 10 miles east of Second Mesa, with its cliff homes. Most other Hopi villages are usually open to the public; the exception is Old Oraibi, a spiritual center, which is closed to all outsiders.

You'll find arts and crafts vendors at the cultural center, as well as next door at the **Hopi Arts and Crafts Silvercraft Cooperative Guild** (tel 602/734-2463), which offers excellent quality pottery, textiles, baskets, silver jewelry, paintings, and Kachina dolls. If you would like to spend the night, you'll find comfortable rooms at the **Hopi Cultural Center Restaurant and Motel.**

After exploring Hopi country, continue east on Ariz 264 for 70 miles (from Second Mesa) to Ganado and:

7. **Hubbell Trading Post National Historic Site** (tel 602/755-3475). John Lorenzo Hubbell, who founded this trading post in 1878, was the foremost Navajo trader of the time, respected by both Navajos and whites. The site includes the original trading post, which still sells food, fabric, and household goods. You can look at Navajo rugs, silver and turquoise jewelry, baskets, and other crafts. A **visitor center and museum** covers the trading post's history, and you can watch Navajo weavers and jewelers at work.

From Ganado, head south on US 191 for 44 miles to I-40 at Chambers (exit 333), and take the I-40 west 22 miles to exit 311 for:

8. **Petrified Forest National Park** (tel 602/524-6228), which consists of 6 forests worth of petrified wood and some of the most colorful parts of the Painted Desert. Stop at the **Painted Desert Visitor Center** for orientation before driving 27 miles through the park, with some 2 dozen scenic overlooks and short walks. The **Painted Desert,** a pastel wonderland of colors and shapes, dominates the park's northern part, where you entered;

most of the petrified logs are in the southern part. The area is particularly colorful at sunrise and sunset, and even better if you can catch it immediately after a rain shower has washed the dust away.

Heading south through the park you'll find the **Puerco Indian Ruins** and petroglyphs at **Newspaper Rock.** Other stops include **Jasper Forest Overlook,** where you'll see petrified roots as well as trunks, and **Agate House,** a partially restored pueblo. The **Giant Logs** self-guided trail passes by some of the park's largest petrified logs, and nearby, at the park's southern edge, you'll find **Rainbow Forest Museum,** with exhibits on the area's geological and human history, plus displays of petrified wood.

From the park's southern entrance, follow US 180 west for 21 miles into Holbrook, rejoining I-40 at exit 285. Then continue west on I-40 for 28 miles to exit 257 and head north on Ariz 87 for 2 miles to:

9. **Homolovi Ruins State Park** (tel 602/289-4106), which includes ruins supposedly occupied between 1250 and 1600 by ancestors of today's Hopi tribe. (Homolovi is a Hopi word that means "place of the mounds.") Several hiking trails wind among pueblo ruins and petroglyphs, and another trail leads to **Sunset Cemetery,** all that remains of an 1870s Mormon settlement.

From the ruins, drive northeast 13 miles on Ariz 87 to:

10. **Little Painted Desert.** This small country park is a wonderful place to have a picnic supper while watching the everchanging colors of the Painted Desert.

Return 15 miles to I-40 and drive 2 miles west to exit 253 for:

11. **Winslow.** A good place to spend the night, you'll find clean, attractive accommodations at **Best Western Town House Lodge.** Before leaving town, take time to stop at **Old Trails Museum,** 212 Kinsley Ave (tel 602/289-5861), in a 1916 bank building. The museum focuses on northeast Arizona history.

From Winslow, continue west on I-40 for 20 miles to exit 233, and then 6 miles south on Meteor Crater Rd to:

12. **Meteor Crater Natural Landmark** (tel 602/289-2362). A giant rock smashed into the earth here 49,000 years ago at more than 30,000 miles per hour. The meteor destroyed all plant and animal life within 100 miles, leaving this crater 570 feet deep and over 4,000 feet across; it has been used by US astronauts to train for moon walks. The **Museum of Astrogeology** has exhibits on the crater's creation, and there's also an **Astronaut Hall of Fame.**

Return 6 miles back to I-40, and continue west for 34 miles to return to Flagstaff.

ALPINE

Map page M-2, C4

Lodge 🏨

≣≣ **Tal-Wi-Wi Lodge**, 40 County Rd 2220, PO Box 169, Alpine, AZ 85920; tel 602/339-4319. 3 mi N of Alpine. County Rd 2220 exit off US 191. A lovely mountain setting, terrific for getting away from it all. **Rooms:** 20 rms and stes. CI 2pm/CO 11am. Basic but comfortable rooms. **Amenities:** 🛁 No A/C or TV. All units w/terraces, some w/fireplaces, some w/Jacuzzis. **Services:** 🛠 🖇 **Facilities:** 🚲 📶 ⛵ 🎣 🎿 ♿ 1 rst, 1 bar, lawn games, spa. **Rates:** HS May–Sept $49 S; $57 D; from $55 ste. Children under 14 stay free. Lower rates off-season. Spec packages avail. Pking: Outdoor, free. Ltd CC.

BISBEE

Map page M-2, E4

Hotels 🏨

≣≣ **The Bisbee Grand Hotel**, 61 Main St, PO Box 825, Bisbee, AZ 85603; tel 602/432-5900 or toll free 800/421-1909. A charming, historic Old West hotel in the center of Old Bisbee. No smoking throughout. **Rooms:** 11 rms and stes. CI 1pm/CO 11am. Beautifully furnished turn-of-the-century rooms. The Victorian and Oriental suites are especially distinctive. **Amenities:** A/C. No phone or TV. **Services:** Twice-daily maid svce. **Facilities:** 🍺 1 bar (w/entertainment). **Rates:** $50–$75 S or D; from $95 ste. Pking: Outdoor, free. Maj CC. Special packages for Murder Mystery Weekends.

≣≣ **Copper Queen Hotel**, 11 Howell Ave, Bisbee, AZ 85603; tel 602/432-2216 or toll free 800/247-5829 in AZ; fax 602/432-4298. 24 mi S of Tombstone. Old Bisbee exit off US 80. This charming, historic hotel, built in 1902, offers a trip to Bisbee's glorious past. **Rooms:** 43 rms. CI 2pm/CO 11am. Nonsmoking rms avail. Comfortable, restored rooms are furnished with turn-of-the-century antiques. **Amenities:** 🛁 A/C, cable TV. **Services:** 🚐 🛠 🖇 Twice-daily maid svce. **Facilities:** 🍴 🏊 💻 1 rst, 1 bar (w/entertainment), whirlpool. **Rates:** $65–$95 S or D. Extra person $5. Children under 10 stay free. Higher rates for spec evnts/hols. Spec packages avail. Pking: Outdoor, free. Maj CC.

Inn

≣≣ **Bisbee Inn**, 45 OK St, PO Box 1855, Bisbee, AZ 85603; tel 602/432-5131. A comfortable inn located in a historic building.

Rooms: 18 rms and stes (17 w/shared bath). CI 3pm/CO 11am. No smoking. Rooms are furnished with antiques. Only the suite has a private bath; other rooms share 7 toilets and 5 showers. **Amenities:** 🛁 A/C. **Services:** 🖇 🖇 Twice-daily maid svce. **Facilities:** 📶 Washer/dryer, guest lounge w/TV. **Rates (CP):** $29–$45 S or D w/shared bath, $65 S or D w/private bath; from $65 ste. Extra person $6. Children under 1 stay free. Pking: Outdoor, free. Ltd CC.

Restaurant 🍴

Cafe Roka, 35 Main St, Bisbee (Old Bisbee); tel 602/432-5153. 24 mi S of Tombstone. **Italian.** An attractive, modern restaurant, with photographs on the walls. The somewhat limited menu includes sea scallops and angel hair pasta, and breast of chicken baked in phyllo. The chef trained at the Biltmore Hotel in Phoenix. **FYI:** Reservations recommended. Guitar. No smoking. **Open:** Tues–Sat 5–9pm. Closed some hols. **Prices:** Main courses $8.50–$15.50. Ltd CC. ♥ ♿

Attractions 🏛

Bisbee Mining and Historical Museum, 5 Copper Queen Plaza; tel 602/432-7071. Housed in the 1897 Copper Queen Consolidated Mining Company office building, this small museum features several rooms of old mining equipment. In the mine tunnel room visitors learn how underground mines were blasted and "mucked" out. There's also an exhibit of minerals that are found in the ground beneath Bisbee. Other diplays pertain to the history of the town itself. **Open:** Daily 10am–4pm. Closed some hols. $

Queen Mine Tours, 478 N Dart Rd; tel 602/432-2071. Copper built Bisbee, and between 1880 and 1975 the mines here produced $6.1 billion worth of metals. Though the mines are no longer productive, tours still take visitors into the tunnels. Go deep underground by train into the Queen Mine or travel by van to the Lavendar Pit to view a surface mine. Tours are conducted Mon–Fri at 9am, 10:30am, noon, 2pm, and 3:30pm. $$$

Muheim Heritage House, 207 Youngblood Hill; tel 602/432-7071. Built in 1908 by local merchant Joseph Muheim, this restored home houses a small museum. Inside there is period furniture and old wine-making equipment used in the several saloons in town that Muheim owned. **Open:** Thurs–Mon 10am–5pm. $

BULLHEAD CITY

Map page M-2, B1

Hotel

Days Inn, 2200 Karis Dr, Bullhead City, AZ 86442; tel 602/758-1711 or toll free 800/DAYS INN; fax 602/758-7937. Karis Dr exit off Ariz 95. This attractive, basic hotel is centrally located in Bullhead City, just across the river from Laughlin, Nevada, casinos. **Rooms:** 70 rms and stes. CI 3pm/CO 11am. Nonsmoking rms avail. **Amenities:** A/C, cable TV w/movies, refrig. **Services:** **Facilities:** Whirlpool, washer/dryer. **Rates:** HS May–Sept $40–$60 S or D; from $70 ste. Extra person $6. Children under 11 stay free. Lower rates off-season. Pking: Outdoor, free. Maj CC. Senior discounts available.

Motel

Best Western Grand Vista Hotel, 1817 Arcadia Plaza, Bullhead City, AZ 86442; tel 602/763-3300 or toll free 800/547-4464; fax 602/763-4447. Arcadia exit off Ariz 95. This motel is set high on a hill and offers a view of the Colorado River. **Rooms:** 80 rms. CI noon/CO noon. Nonsmoking rms avail. Some rooms have river views. **Amenities:** A/C, cable TV. All 1st-floor rooms have refrigerators. **Services:** **Facilities:** Whirlpool. **Rates:** HS Apr–Sept $39–$55 S or D. Children under 18 stay free. Lower rates off-season. Higher rates for spec evnts/hols. Pking: Outdoor, free. Maj CC. Rates are higher on weekends. Weekly rates are available.

Resort

Lake Mohave Resort, Katherine Landing, Bullhead City, AZ 86430-4016; tel 602/754-3245 or toll free 800/752-9669. 3 mi N of Ariz 68 at Lake Mead Nat'l Rec Area. A complete resort for the boating enthusiast, with houseboats, ski boats, patio boats, fishing boats, plus facilities for personal watercraft. **Rooms:** 52 rms. CI 2pm/CO 11am. Some rooms have fully equipped kitchenettes. **Amenities:** A/C, satel TV, refrig. Some units w/terraces. Some rooms have ceiling fans. **Services:** **Facilities:** 1 rst, 1 bar, 1 beach (lake shore). There are a picnic area available for guests and an RV park on the property. **Rates:** HS Mar–Nov $60 S; $69–$83 D. Extra person $6. Children under 5 stay free. Lower rates off-season. Pking: Outdoor, free. Ltd CC.

CAMP VERDE

Map page M-2, C3

Attractions

Fort Verde State Historic Park, 3 miles east of I-17; tel 602/567-3275. 35 miles SE of Sedona. Established in 1871, this was the 3rd military post in the Verde Valley and was occupied until 1891, by which time tensions with the Native American population had subsided and made the fort unnecessary. Today the state park, which covers 10 acres, preserves 3 officers' quarters, an administration building, and some ruins. The buildings that have been fully restored house exhibits on the fort's history. **Open:** Daily 8am–4:30pm. Closed Dec 25. $

Montezuma Castle National Monument, exit 289 off I-17; tel 602/567-3322. This Sinagua cliff dwelling, perhaps the best preserved of all the cliff dwellings in Arizona, consists of 2 stone pueblos built in the early 12th century. Located a few miles north of Monetzuma Castle is **Montezuma Well**, another prehistoric Indian site. Occupied by both the Hohokam and Sinagua at different times in the past, this desert oasis measures 368 feet across and 65 feet deep. **Open:** Daily 8am–5pm. $

CAREFREE

Map page M-2, C2

Resort

The Boulders, 34631 N Tom Darlington Dr, PO Box 2090, Carefree, AZ 85377; tel 602/488-9009 or toll free 800/553-1717; fax 602/488-4118. 270 acres. One of America's most dramatically sited and masterfully conceived resorts. It is situated in the shadow of massive mounds of 12-million-year-old boulders, part of a 1,300-acre gated community located 2,500 feet up in the Sonora Desert. Navajo artifacts and art complement the regional styling of the beamed and vaulted public rooms. **Rooms:** 159 rms; 20 ctges/villas. CI 4pm/CO noon. Express checkout avail. Nonsmoking rms avail. Grouped in clusters of pueblo-style, 2-story casitas. Unique interiors skillfully combine southwestern architecture and earth-tone colors with modern amenities. **Amenities:** A/C, cable TV, refrig, in-rm safe, shoe polisher, bathrobes. All units w/minibars, all w/terraces, all w/fireplaces. Wet bars and wood-burning fireplaces in each room; patios and terraces with loungers, tables, and chairs; roomy walk-in closets with stacks of drawers; carafes of iced water with slices of lemon for tennis players. **Services:** VP Twice-daily maid svce, car-rental desk, masseur, children's program, babysitting. Staff, primed for an urbane and pampered clientele, outnumber guests 2 to 1. **Facilities:** 🔥 🚴 ▶36 🏖 ⚓6 🏓 🎱 ♿ 6 rsts (*see also* "Restaurants" below), 2 bars (1 w/entertainment), lifeguard, lawn games, spa, sauna, steam rm, whirlpool, day-care ctr. Two golf courses shared with 250 members of Boulders Club (one course for guests and one for members, rotating daily); dramatic pool beneath the boulders, second lap pool near the tennis courts; 3 jogging/hiking trails; enlarged fitness center and new spa. Resort-supervised dining at the small, whimsical El Pedregal Festival Marketplace next door. **Rates:** HS Jan 14–May 14/Dec 23–Jan 1 $400 S; $425 D. Extra person $25. Children under 12 stay free. Lower rates off-season. MAP rates avail. Spec packages avail. Pking: Outdoor, free. Maj CC. Highest rates in the region. All rooms and rates identical except for views: fairways and coyotes or arroyos and jackrabbits. A service charge of $15 per night is added to each room for tips to staff other than waiters and bartenders.

Restaurants 🍴

Latilla Room, in The Boulders, 34631 Tom Darlington Dr, Carefree; tel 602/488-9009. 1 mi S of Carefree. **New American.** This dramatic dining room has tremendous views of huge, weather-beaten boulders. There are thick adobe-like walls and wood-beam ceilings, and the mauve chairs and carpet are the color of the mountains just after sunset. Unusual offerings include appetizers like griddle Dungeness crab cakes with sun-dried tomato sauce, and entrees such as fresh pasta with lobster, andouille sausage, tomato, and sweet corn sauce. **FYI:** Reservations recommended. Jacket required. **Open:** HS Sept–May breakfast daily 7–10:30am; dinner daily 6–9:30pm; brunch Sun 11:30am–2pm. Reduced hours off-season. **Prices:** Main courses $19.50–$28. Maj CC. ♥ 🏔 VP ♿

🌸 **The Palo Verde**, in The Boulders, 34631 N Tom Darlington Dr, Carefree; tel 602/488-9009. 20 mi N of Scottsdale. Carefree Hwy exit off I-17; go east on Carefree to Scottsdale Rd then left to the resort. **Southwestern.** The creative southwestern cuisine is worth a detour on the drive north to the Grand Canyon. Adobe-style architecture, with latilla and viga wood ceilings, open-tiled kitchen, booths, and banquettes; glass doors open to the circular terrace. Specialties are fire-roasted eggplant and anasazi beans, served with nopal cactus salsa, basil, and queso fresca; pecan-crusted rack of lamb with quinoa and goat cheese; basted veal chop with pumpkinseed cream; and breast of ranch chicken with grilled apple mashed potatoes. **FYI:** Reservations recommended. Dress code. **Open:** Lunch daily 11:30am–2:30pm; dinner daily 6–9:30pm. Closed Jul 5–Sept 2. **Prices:** Main courses $19.50–$28. Maj CC. ♥ ⚓ VP ♿

CASA GRANDE

Map page M-2, D3

Hotel 🏨

🏨 **Sunland Inn**, 7190 S Sunland Gin Rd, Casa Grande, AZ 85222; tel 602/836-5000. Sunland Gin Rd exit off I-10. Mid-sized hotel offering basic accommodations. **Rooms:** 100 rms. CI open/CO 11am. Nonsmoking rms avail. **Amenities:** 🛁 A/C, satel TV. **Facilities:** 🔥 ♿ 1 rst, 1 bar, washer/dryer. **Rates:** HS Jan–Mar $20 S; $26–$32 D. Extra person $6. Children under 18 stay free. Lower rates off-season. Spec packages avail. Pking: Outdoor, free. Maj CC.

Resort

🏨🏨🏨 **Francisco Grande Resort & Golf Club**, 26000 Gila Bend Hwy, Casa Grande, AZ 85222; tel 602/836-6444 or toll free 800/237-4238; fax 602/836-6444. 5 mi W of Casa Grande, exit 185 off I-10. Take Ariz 387 S to Ariz 84 W. This hotel/golf resort outside the small town of Casa Grande was originally built to house the San Francisco Giants baseball team during spring training. The resort claims to have the longest golf course in Arizona. **Rooms:** 112 rms and stes. CI 3pm/CO noon. Nonsmoking rms avail. Rooms range from basic motel style to more luxurious tower rooms and executive suites, with large bathtubs and hide-a-beds. **Amenities:** 🛁 ⚓ A/C, satel TV. Some units w/terraces. Tower rooms and suites have coffeemakers. **Services:** ✕ 🚐 🛄 🔧 **Facilities:** 🔥 ▶18 🎱 🏓 🎱 ♿ 1 rst, 1 bar (w/entertainment), lawn games, spa. **Rates:** $56–$106 S or D; from $126 ste. Extra person $15. Children under 18 stay free. Spec packages avail. Pking: Outdoor, free. Maj CC.

CHANDLER

Map page M-2, D3

Hotel 🏨

🏨🏨🏨 **Wyndham Garden Hotel**, 7475 W Chandler Blvd, Chandler, AZ 85226; tel 602/961-4444 or toll free 800/822-4200 in the US, 800/631-4200 in Canada; fax 602/940-0269. Chandler Blvd exit off I-10. Open, partially sunken lobby is nicely furnished and has a fireplace. **Rooms:** 159 rms and stes. CI 3pm/CO noon. Express checkout avail. Nonsmoking rms avail. Simply furnished and comfortable. **Amenities:** 🛁 ⚓ 📺 🍴 A/C, satel TV w/movies, stereo/tape player. **Services:** ✕ 🚐 🛄 🔧 **Facilities:** 🔥 🏓 🎱 ♿ 1 rst, 1 bar, spa, whirlpool, washer/dryer. **Rates:** HS Jan–May $109 S; $119 D; from $119 ste. Extra person $10. Children under 10 stay free. Lower rates off-season. Spec packages avail. Pking: Outdoor, free. Maj CC.

Resort

≣≣≣ Sheraton San Marcos Resort, 1 San Marcos Place, Chandler, AZ 85224; tel 602/963-6655 or toll free 800/325-3535; fax 602/899-5441. Chandler Blvd exit off I-10. 123 acres. The original part of this historic hotel was built in 1912 and for years it was a playground for Hollywood celebrities. The property is well landscaped, with a trellis-shaded walkway and attractive pools. 250 rooms were added in 1986. **Rooms:** 295 rms and stes. CI 3pm/CO noon. Nonsmoking rms avail. Very comfortable. **Amenities:** 🛅 🅰 🔳 A/C, cable TV w/movies. All units w/terraces, some w/Jacuzzis. **Services:** 🍽 🖛 🛆 🛋 ⬳ Babysitting. **Facilities:** 🔂 ▶18 🏌 ➁ 🏊 800 🖳 ⅊ 3 rsts, 2 bars (1 w/entertainment), lawn games, whirlpool, beauty salon. **Rates:** HS Jan 15–May 15 $195–$225 S or D; from $450 ste. Extra person $10. Children under 18 stay free. Lower rates off-season. Spec packages avail. Pking: Outdoor, free. Maj CC.

Restaurant 🍴

⑤ ★ Guedo's Taco Shop, 71 E Chandler Blvd, Chandler; tel 602/899-7841. Exit Chandler Blvd off I-10. At corner of Arizona Blvd. **Mexican.** Everything is served à la carte at this informal eatery decorated with photos of sports figures and Mexican revolutionaries. Choice of a variety of tacos, burritos, and quesadillas. Also at: 108 W Broadway Rd, Mesa (602/461-3660). **FYI:** Reservations not accepted. Beer and wine only. **Open:** Tues–Sat 11am–9pm. Closed some hols. **Prices:** Main courses $1.45–$3. No CC. 🅿 ⅊

CHINLE

Map page M-2, A4

Motels 🛏

≣≣ Canyon de Chelly Motel, Rte 7, PO Box 295, Chinle, AZ 86503; tel 602/674-5875 or toll free 800/327-0354. Rte 7 exit off Ariz 191. One of only 3 hotels in Chinle, the gateway to Canyon de Chelly National Monument. **Rooms:** 102 rms. CI 2pm/CO 11am. Nonsmoking rms avail. All rooms have either 2 queen beds or 1 king. **Amenities:** 🛅 🅰 🔳 A/C, cable TV. **Services:** ⅊ **Facilities:** 🔂 1 rst. **Rates:** HS May 10–Oct $92 S; $96 D. Extra person $4. Children under 12 stay free. Lower rates off-season. Pking: Outdoor, free. Maj CC.

≣≣ Holiday Inn Canyon de Chelly, Garcia Trading Post BIA Rte 7, PO Box 1889, Chinle, AZ 86503; tel 602/674-5000 or toll free 800/23-HOTEL; fax 602/674-8264. 2½ mi E of US 191. Opened in 1992, this is a pleasant addition to the accommodation choices in Chinle. **Rooms:** 108 rms. CI 3pm/CO noon. Nonsmoking rms avail. **Amenities:** 🛅 🅰 A/C, cable TV. Some units w/terraces. **Services:** ✕ ⅊ ⬳ **Facilities:** 🔂 🅰 123 ⅊ 1 rst (see also "Restaurants" below). Hiking and off-road vehicle tours of Canyon de Chelly are available. There are American Indian dance performances nightly. **Rates:** HS Apr–Sept $89–$109 S or D. Extra person $10. Children under 18 stay free. Lower rates off-season. Spec packages avail. Pking: Outdoor, free. Maj CC.

≣≣ Thunderbird Lodge, Rte 7, PO Box 548, Chinle, AZ 86503; tel 602/674-5841. 3½ mi E of Ariz 191. This motel is actually within the boundaries of Canyon de Chelly National Monument at the mouth of the canyon. The gift shop is located in the original Indian trading post. The entire motel is nonsmoking. **Rooms:** 72 rms and stes. CI 2pm/CO 11am. **Amenities:** 🛅 🅰 A/C, cable TV. **Services:** 🚐 ⅊ **Facilities:** 🅰 🏌 50 ⅊ 1 rst. Jeep tours of Canyon de Chelly are run by the lodge, and full- and half-day tours of the Anasazi ruins are available; hiking tours are also available. **Rates:** HS Apr 1–Nov 15 $80 S; $84 D; from $145 ste. Extra person $4. Children under 2 stay free. Lower rates off-season. Spec packages avail. Pking: Outdoor, free. Maj CC.

Restaurant 🍴

Garcia's Trading Post Restaurant, in Holiday Inn Canyon de Chelly, BIA Rte 7, Chinle; tel 602/674-5000. **American/Southwestern.** In addition to lamb chops, fish, steaks, and fajitas, there are such traditional dishes as Navajo fry bread and Navajo stew, a hardy mixture of lamb and vegetables in a tomato broth. **FYI:** Reservations not accepted. Children's menu. No liquor license. **Open:** Daily 6:30am–10pm. **Prices:** Main courses $7.95–$16.95. Maj CC. ⅊

Attraction 🏛

Canyon de Chelly National Monument, US 191; tel 602/674-5500. The park consists of 2 major canyons—**Canyon de Chelly** and **Canyon del Muerto**—as well as several smaller canyons. Together they extend for more than 100 miles through the rugged, slick-rock landscape of northeastern Arizona, draining the seasonal runoff from the snow melt of the Chuska Mountains. These streams have for centuries carved the canyons as they bring water for farming the fertile soils of the canyon bottoms. The smooth vertical sandstone walls of rich reds and yellows sharply contrast with the deep greens of corn, pasture, and cottonwood on the canyon floor.

A different view of the canyons is provided by the **North and South Rim drives**. Each drive is around 20 miles in each direction, and with stops it can easily take 3 hours to visit each rim.

The first stop on the **North Rim** is the Ledge Ruin Overlook, occupied by the Anasazi between 1050 and 1275. Nearby are Dekaa Kiva Viewpoint and Antelope House Overlook, which takes its name from the paintings of antelopes on a nearby cliff wall. Across the wash is the Tomb of the Weaver, where the well-preserved body of an old man wrapped in a blanket of golden eagle feathers was discovered in the 1920s. Visible from the overlook is Navajo Fortress, a red sandstone butte that the Navajo once used as a refuge from attackers. Continue on to Mummy Cave Overlook, named for 2 mummies found in burial urns, and then to Massacre Cave Overlook, the site of a mass slaying of Navajo by the Spanish military in 1805.

The **South Rim** drive begins at Tségi Overlook with a view of Chinle Wash. The second stop is Junction Overlook, where the view includes the junction of Canyon del Muerto and Canyon de Chelly. Next is White House Overlook, which provides the only opportunity for descending into Canyon de Chelly without a guide or ranger. The trail descends 600 feet to the canyon floor, crosses Chinle Wash, and then approaches the White House ruins (named after a long white wall in the upper ruin) and the best-known Anasazi cliff dwelling in the canyon. The ruins are located on both the canyon floor and 50 feet up the cliff wall in a small cave. (Note: Visitors cannot enter the ruins.) The 2½-mile round-trip hike takes about 2 hours; visitors should be sure to bring water for the trek.

Farther on is Sliding House Overlook, where Navajo ruins built on a narrow shelf appear to be sliding into the canyon. The drive finishes with stops at Wild Cherry Overlook, Face Rock Overlook, Spider Rock Overlook, and Speaking Rock, all providing glimpses of the ever-deepening canyon.

The visitor center, open daily 8am–6pm, is an essential first stop at Canyon de Chelly. Access to the canyons is restricted, and visitors must be accompanied by either a park ranger or an authorized guide; the only exception is on the White House Ruins trail. Free.

CHLORIDE

Map page M-2, B1

Attraction 💼

Chloride Historic District, US 93; tel 602/565-3872. Located about 20 miles northwest of Kingman, the town was founded in 1862 when silver was discovered in the nearby Cerbat Mountains. By the 1920s there were 75 mines and 2,000 people, but when the mine shut down in 1944 the town lost most of its population. Much of the downtown area has been preserved as a historic district and includes the oldest continuously operating post office in Arizona, the old jail, and the Jim Fritz Museum. Melodramas are performed at the Silverbelle Playhouse on the 1st and 3rd Saturday of each month.

CLARKDALE

Map page M-2, C2

Attractions 💼

Tuzigoot National Monument, US 89A; tel 602/634-5564. Perched atop a hill overlooking the Verde River, this Sinagua ruin was inhabited between 1100 and 1400. Built of stones and mud, the village had 77 ground-floor rooms and may have housed as many as 200 people. Inside the visitor center is a small museum displaying many of the artifacts unearthed at Tuzigoot. Interpretive trail. **Open:** Daily 8am–5pm. Closed Dec 25. $

Arizona Central Railroad, 300 N Broadway; tel 602/639-0010. Once used to transport copper from the mining town of Jerome to the territorial capital of Prescott, the railroad today operates excursions from Clarkdale to Perkinsville. The route through the Verde River Canyon traverses unspoiled desert, inaccessible by car, that is part of Prescott National Forest. The railroad operates both sightseeing trips and barbecue dinner excursions; call ahead for departure times. $$$$

COOLIDGE

Map page M-2, D3

Attraction 💼

Casa Grande Ruins National Monument, 1100 Ruins Dr; tel 602/723-3172. An earth-walled ruin that was built 650 years ago by the Hohokam peoples. An amazing example of ancient architecture in the Southwest, it is built of shaped earth rather than adobe bricks. Casa Grande ruin had a 4-foot-deep foundation and was 3 stories high. The large ruin is surrounded by many smaller buildings, which were probably homes, and indicate that Casa Grande was not used as living quarters. **Open:** Daily 7am–6pm. $

DOUGLAS

Map page M-2, E4

Hotel 🛄

≣≣ **The Gadsden Hotel**, 1046 G Ave, Douglas, AZ 85607; tel 602/364-4481; fax 602/364-4005. This "last of the grand hotels," as the Gadsden calls itself, has a lovely art deco lobby with stained glass windows depicting western scenes; marble stairs leading to the mezzanine; art deco chandeliers; and stained glass skylights. It's listed on the National Register of Historic Places. **Rooms:** 150 rms. CI 1pm/CO 11am. Nonsmoking rms avail. Rooms are steeped in historic charm. **Amenities:** 🛅 A/C, cable TV. 1 unit w/terrace. **Services:** ✗ 🚐 🖼 ⏰ Twice-daily maid svce. **Facilities:** 🔟 2 rsts, 2 bars, beauty salon. **Rates:** $29–$85 S or D. Extra person $5. Children under 18 stay free. Spec packages avail. Pking: Outdoor, free. Maj CC.

Attraction 🏛

Cochise Stronghold, Coronado National Forest; tel 602/826-3593. By the mid-1880s only Cochise and Geronimo and their Chiracahua Apaches were still fighting the US Army. Cochise used this rugged section of the Dragoon Mountains as his hideout and managed to elude capture for years because the granite boulders and pine forests made it impossible for the army to track him. Cochise was buried at an unknown spot somewhere within the area. Hiking trails, campground, picnic area. **Open:** Daily 24 hours. Free.

DRAGOON

Map page M-2, E4 (SW of Willcox)

Attraction 🏛

Amerind Foundation Museum, exit 318 off I-10; tel 602/586-3666. Established in 1937 and dedicated to the study, preservation, and interpretation of prehistoric and historic Native American cultures. To that end the foundation has compiled the nation's finest private collection of Native American archeological artifacts and contemporary items. The museum comprises 2 buildings, one containing the anthropology museum and the other the art gallery. Located 64 miles east of Tucson in the heart of Texas Canyon between Benson and Willcox. There is no museum sign on the highway. **Open:** Daily 10am–4pm. Closed some hols. $

ELGIN

Map page M-2, E4 (NW of Sierra Vista)

Attraction 🏛

Sonoita Vineyards Winery, Elgin exit off Ariz 83; tel 602/455-5893. Produces a large variety of wines sold exclusively in Arizona. The success of the grape-growing here is the result of a "terra rossa"–type soil, most commonly found in France's Burgundy region. Tours include explanations of the wine-making process and tastings. **Open:** Daily 10am–4pm. Closed some hols. Free.

FLAGSTAFF

Map page M-2, B3

Hotels 🛄

≣≣≣ **AmeriSuites**, 2455 S Beulah Blvd, Flagstaff, AZ 86001; tel 602/774-8042 or toll free 800/833-1516; fax 602/774-5524. Exit 195-B off I-40. Opened in 1993, this is an attractive offering in Flagstaff's mid- to upper-range accommodations. **Rooms:** 118 stes. CI 3pm/CO noon. Nonsmoking rms avail. **Amenities:** 🛅 🅰 🖭 A/C, satel TV w/movies, refrig, VCR. Kitchenettes in the suites are equipped with microwaves, as well as coffee and tea. **Services:** 🗝 🖼 ⏰ Babysitting. Unlimited free local phone calls. **Facilities:** 🏋 🏊 🔟 🖥 👥 Whirlpool, washer/dryer. **Rates (CP):** HS May–Oct from $63 ste. Extra person $6–$10. Children under 18 stay free. Lower rates off-season. Spec packages avail. Pking: Outdoor, free. Maj CC.

≣≣≣ **Best Western Woodlands Plaza Hotel**, 1175 W US 66, Flagstaff, AZ 86001; tel 602/773-8888 or toll free 800/528-1234. Exit 195B off I-40. 1½ mi N to US 66, ¼ mi W. One of Flagstaff's better hotels. **Rooms:** 183 rms and stes. CI 2pm/CO noon. Nonsmoking rms avail. **Amenities:** 🛅 🅰 A/C, cable TV w/movies. Some units w/minibars, 1 w/Jacuzzi. Toiletry kits are available. **Services:** ✗ 🗝 🚐 🖼 ⏰ Babysitting. **Facilities:** 🏋 🏊 🍽 🔟 🖥 👥 2 rsts (*see also* "Restaurants" below), 1 bar, spa, sauna, steam rm, washer/dryer. There are 2 whirlpools. **Rates:** HS May–Oct $99–$109 S or D; from $109 ste. Extra person $10. Children under 12 stay free. Lower rates off-season. Spec packages avail. Pking: Outdoor, free. Maj CC.

≣≣≣ **Little America Hotel**, I-40 E at Butler Ave, PO Box 3900, Flagstaff, AZ 86003; tel 602/779-2741 or toll free 800/352-4386; fax 602/779-7983. Exit 198 off I-40. A pleasant, older hotel set on 400 acres. Easy freeway access. **Rooms:** 248

rms and stes. CI 4pm/CO 1pm. Express checkout avail. Non-smoking rms avail. **Amenities:** ☎ ⚫ A/C, cable TV w/movies, refrig. All units w/terraces, some w/fireplaces. Most rooms have refrigerators. **Services:** ✗ ▤ 🚗 △ ↵ Car-rental desk, babysitting. **Facilities:** 🗑 🗑 ⚡ 🗑 ⓐ □ ⚫ 1 rst, 1 bar (w/entertainment), lawn games, washer/dryer. **Rates:** HS May 11–Oct 15 $99 S or D; from $109 ste. Extra person $10. Children under 12 stay free. Lower rates off-season. Spec packages avail. Pking: Outdoor, free. Maj CC.

▤▤ Monte Vista Hotel, 100N San Francisco St, Flagstaff, AZ 86001; tel 602/779-6971 or toll free 800/545-3068. This downtown hotel, built in 1929, has character and is listed on the National Register of Historic Places. **Rooms:** 45 rms and stes. CI 2pm/CO 11am. Each room is named for a famous actor or actress who supposedly stayed in that room. Most rooms have private baths. **Amenities:** ☎ Cable TV. No A/C. **Services:** ↵ **Facilities:** ⚡ 🗑 □ 1 rst, 1 bar (w/entertainment), beauty salon, washer/dryer. **Rates:** HS May–Oct $46–$60 S or D; from $75 ste. Children under 18 stay free. Lower rates off-season. Pking: Outdoor, free. Maj CC.

▤▤▤ Quality Suites, 706 S Milton Rd, Flagstaff, AZ 86001; tel 602/774-4333 or toll free 800/228-5151. Exit 195B off I-40. An all-suites hotel for those wanting more space or staying several days. The lobby is luxurious and features a handsome stone fireplace. Close to Northern Arizona University. **Rooms:** 102 stes. CI 2pm/CO noon. Nonsmoking rms avail. All units have comfortable sitting rooms. **Amenities:** ☎ ⚫ A/C, cable TV w/movies, refrig, VCR, stereo/tape player. All suites have 2 TVs and a microwave. **Services:** △ ↵ Babysitting. Complimentary afternoon cocktails are served. **Facilities:** 🗑 ⚡ 🗑 🗑 □ ⚫ Whirlpool. There is a library in the lounge. **Rates (BB):** HS Mid-June–mid-Sept from $100 ste. Extra person $10. Children under 3 stay free. Lower rates off-season. Higher rates for spec evnts/hols. Spec packages avail. Pking: Outdoor, free. Maj CC.

Motels

▤▤ Econo Lodge West, 2355 S Beulah Blvd, Flagstaff, AZ 86001; tel 602/774-2225 or toll free 800/424-4777; fax 602/774-2225 ext 250. Exit 195B off I-40. Turn left at first traffic light. An attractive motel in southwest Flagstaff, close to Sedona (21 miles) and other mountain and scenic areas. It's a good alternative to more expensive lodging in Sedona and other nearby resort communities. **Rooms:** 85 rms and stes. CI 3pm/CO 11am. Nonsmoking rms avail. Pleasant, light-colored rooms with wood furnishings. **Amenities:** ☎ A/C, cable TV w/movies. **Services:** ↵ Complimentary coffee and donuts available mornings in the lobby. **Facilities:** 🗑 ⚫ Whirlpool, washer/dryer.

Rates: HS May–Sept $79 S; $89 D; from $99 ste. Extra person $10. Children under 12 stay free. Lower rates off-season. Higher rates for spec evnts/hols. Pking: Outdoor, free. Maj CC.

▤▤ Evergreen Inn, 1008 E Santa Fe Ave, Flagstaff, AZ 86001; tel 602/779-7356 or toll free 800/524-9999. Exit 198 off I-40. Pleasant, moderately priced establishment. **Rooms:** 132 rms and stes. CI 2pm/CO 11am. Nonsmoking rms avail. Rooms are simply decorated with a southwestern flavor. Some have kitchenettes. **Amenities:** ☎ A/C, cable TV w/movies. **Services:** ↵ ⟨⟩ **Facilities:** 🗑 ⚡ 🗑 🗑 🗑 Washer/dryer. **Rates (CP):** HS June 15–Sept $50 S; $59–$75 D; from $85 ste. Extra person $10. Children under 17 stay free. Lower rates off-season. Spec packages avail. Pking: Outdoor, free. Maj CC.

▤ Motel Dubeau, 19 W Phoenix Ave, Flagstaff, AZ 86001; tel 602/774-6731 or toll free 800/332-1944; fax 602/774-1371. An unusual cross between a motel and hostel that caters to younger, international travelers. **Rooms:** 26 rms. CI 12:30pm/CO 11am. Nonsmoking rms avail. Six campsites also available on the premises. **Amenities:** No A/C, phone, or TV. Community room has cable TV and a piano. **Services:** 🚗 Breakfast, and coffee and tea all day long, are included in the room rate. **Facilities:** 🚲 ⚡ 🗑 Free indoor-outdoor cooking facilities. **Rates (CP):** $12 S; $24–$25 D. Pking: Outdoor, free. No CC. Campsites are $6 per person.

▤▤ Super 8 Flagstaff, 3725 Kasper Ave, Flagstaff, AZ 86004; tel 602/526-0818 or toll free 800/800-8000. Exit 201 off I-40. A pleasant motel with easy freeway access. **Rooms:** 86 rms. CI 3pm/CO 11am. Nonsmoking rms avail. **Amenities:** ☎ A/C, cable TV w/movies. **Services:** ↵ ⟨⟩ **Facilities:** ⚡ 🗑 ⚫ **Rates:** HS May–Sept $47–$52 S; $57 D. Extra person $5. Children under 12 stay free. Lower rates off-season. Pking: Outdoor, free. Maj CC.

Resort

▤▤ Arizona Mountain Inn, 685 Lake Mary Rd, Flagstaff, AZ 86001; tel 602/774-8959. Lake Mary Rd exit off I-17. 13 acres. This is a rustic, quiet retreat on the outskirts of Flagstaff. Peace and quiet is the main attraction here, although it's close to town and nearby activities. **Rooms:** 3 rms; 15 ctges/villas. CI noon/CO 11am. Nonsmoking rms avail. Cabins are self-catering, and include fully furnished kitchenettes. **Amenities:** ▤ Refrig. No A/C, phone, or TV. Some units w/terraces, all w/fireplaces, 1 w/Jacuzzi. Cabins come with barbecues and some firewood. **Services:** 🚗 ↵ ⟨⟩ **Facilities:** 🗑 ⚡ 🗑 🗑 Lawn games, playground, washer/dryer. There's ping pong, horseshoes, and basketball, and hiking opportunities abound in the surrounding national forest. **Rates:** $70–$110 S or D; from $65 ctge/villa.

Children under 3 stay free. Min stay wknds. Pking: Outdoor, free. Ltd CC. Cabin rates are based on the number of people occupying a cabin.

Restaurants 🍴

Beaver Street Brewery and Whistle Stop Cafe, 11 S Beaver St, Flagstaff (South Flagstaff); tel 602/779-0079. **American/ Pizza.** Cafe popular with the college crowd and known locally for its wood-fired pizzas. Sandwiches and burgers are offered as well. The on-site brewery produces 5 hand-crafted beers. **FYI:** Reservations not accepted. **Open:** Daily 11:30am–midnight. Closed some hols. **Prices:** Main courses $5.25–$8.50. Maj CC. 🍺&

Black Bart's, 2760 E Butler Ave, Flagstaff; tel 602/779-3142. Exit 198 off I-40. **Steak.** A large steakhouse, where local college students wait on tables and provide the musical entertainment. Decor is fittingly western, with cowhides and bull horns adorning the walls. Besides steak, there's also shrimp, swordfish, and salmon. **FYI:** Reservations not accepted. Piano/sing along/singer. Children's menu. No smoking. **Open:** Sun–Thurs 5–9pm, Fri–Sat 5–10pm. Closed some hols. **Prices:** Main courses $12–$20. Maj CC. 👥🍺&

Brix Grill and Wine Bar, 801 S Milton Rd, Flagstaff; tel 602/779-5117. Exit 195B off I-40. **Southwestern.** Opened in 1993. Casual, comfortable feel. Grilled seafood and meats are served; the grilled yellow fin tuna with couscous is especially popular. **FYI:** Reservations recommended. Jazz. Children's menu. Beer and wine only. No smoking. **Open:** HS May–Sept lunch Mon–Sat 11am–3pm; dinner daily 5–10pm. Reduced hours off-season. Closed some hols. **Prices:** Main courses $10.95–$19.95. Maj CC. ♥✉&

★ **Cafe Express**, 16 N San Francisco St, Flagstaff (Downtown); tel 602/774-0541. **Health/Spa.** This comfortable, coffee house/ bakery is particularly popular with students from nearby Northern Arizona University. It has wood floors and large original paintings. Offerings include vegetable dishes, pastas, various coffee drinks, and lots of muffins, cookies, and cakes. **FYI:** Reservations not accepted. Beer and wine only. No smoking. **Open:** Sun–Thurs 7am–10pm, Fri–Sat 7am–11pm. Closed some hols. **Prices:** Main courses $4.50–$8.50. Ltd CC. 🍺&

Cottage Place Restaurant, 126 W Cottage Ave, Flagstaff (South Flagstaff); tel 602/774-8431. **Continental.** Located in a small house, with an elegant and intimate atmosphere. The glassed-in front porch is filled with plants; original art by local artists adorns the walls. House specialties include veal regina (scallops of veal loin sautéed with sun-dried tomatoes and mushrooms), chateaubriand, and rack of lamb Provençale. Many dishes are prepared tableside, and over 130 wines are offered. **FYI:** Reservations recommended. Beer and wine only. No smoking. **Open:** Tues–Sun 5–9:30pm. Closed some hols. **Prices:** Main courses $13–$19. Maj CC. ♥&

★ **El Charro**, 409 S San Francisco St, Flagstaff (Downtown); tel 602/779-0552. **American/Mexican.** A popular Mexican diner. Beer advertisements hang on the walls, and a mural of a rural Mexican scene separates the dining rooms. Traditional Mexican fare—tostadas, enchiladas, chile rellenos—as well as American dinners. **FYI:** Reservations accepted. Guitar. Children's menu. No smoking. **Open:** Mon–Thurs 11am–8:30pm, Fri–Sat 11am–10pm. Closed some hols. **Prices:** Main courses $4.25–$9.50. Ltd CC. 🍺&

Kelly's Christmas Tree Restaurant, in Continental Plaza Shopping Center, 5200 E Cortland Blvd, Flagstaff (East Flagstaff); tel 602/526-0776. Exit 201 off I-40. **Continental.** For those who enjoy the holiday spirit all year round, this might be the perfect place. Christmas decorations are everywhere. There are several separate dining rooms, and a pleasant lounge with a fireplace. House specialties include chicken and dumplings, barbecued baby-back ribs, sautéed chicken livers, curried chicken, and fettuccine alfredo primavera. **FYI:** Reservations recommended. Children's menu. No smoking. **Open:** Lunch Mon–Sat 11:30am–3pm; dinner Mon–Sat 5–10pm, Sun 4–10pm. Closed some hols. **Prices:** Main courses $7.95–$19.95. Ltd CC. ♥✉&

Sakura Restaurant, in Best Western Woodlands Plaza Hotel, 1175 W Hwy 66, Flagstaff; tel 602/773-9118. Exit 195B off I-40. **Japanese.** A dimly lit restaurant decorated with Japanese lanterns and sake baskets. Teppan cooking (in which meats and fish are grilled right at the table) is the specialty. Extensive menu. **FYI:** Reservations recommended. Children's menu. Dress code. No smoking. **Open:** Lunch Mon–Sat 11:30am–2pm; dinner daily 5–10pm; brunch Sun 10am–2pm. **Prices:** Main courses $11.95–$18.95. Maj CC. ♥&

Woodlands Cafe, in Best Western Woodlands Plaza Hotel, 1175 W US 66, Flagstaff; tel 602/773-9118. Exit 195B off I-40. **Southwestern.** A southwestern cafe, decorated with antler chandeliers and Native American pottery. One side of the dining room is an atrium. The ample menu includes seafood, chicken, lamb, duck, steaks, pasta, and a number of burgers. Specialties include trout Arizona and vegetable fettuccine. **FYI:** Reservations recommended. Children's menu. Dress code. No smoking. **Open:** Daily 6am–10pm. **Prices:** Main courses $10–$17. Maj CC. ♥&

Attractions

Lowell Observatory, 1400 W Mars Hill Rd; tel 602/774-2096. Located atop Mars Hill, this is one of the oldest observatories in the Southwest. Founded in 1894 by Percival Lowell, the observatory has played important roles in contemporary astronomy. Among the work carried out here was Lowell's study of the planet Mars and his calculations that led him to predict the existence of the planet Pluto. Call ahead for evening viewing hours. **Open:** Daily 10am–5pm. Closed some hols. $

Museum of Northern Arizona, 3000 N Fort Valley Rd; tel 602/774-5211. State-of-the-art exhibits about the archeology, ethnology, geology, biology, and fine arts of the region. One exhibit is "Native Peoples of the Colorado Plateau," an exploration of both the archeology and cultural anthropology of the region from 15,000 BC to the present. A video theater provides continuous showings of documentaries on regional history and Native American crafts. **Open:** Daily 9am–5pm. Closed some hols. $$

The Arboretum at Flagstaff, Woody Mountain Rd; tel 602/774-1441. Covering 200 acres, it focuses on plants of the high desert, coniferous forests, and alpine tundra, all of which are environments found in the vicinity of Flagstaff. **Open:** Mon–Sat 10am–3pm, Sun noon–3pm. $

Coconino Center for the Arts, 2300 N Fort Valley Rd; tel 602/779-6921. The center houses both a performance hall and a gallery space. The gallery exhibits contemporary and traditional arts and crafts from around northern Arizona. Performances include music and dance, including Native American dances. Gift shop. **Open:** Tues–Sun 9am–5pm. Closed some hols. Free.

Arizona Historical Society Pioneer Museum, 2340 N Fort Valley Rd; tel 602/774-6272. A historical collection from northern Arizona's pioneer days. The main museum building is a large stone structure that was built in 1908 as a hospital for the indigent. In an old barn behind the main building is a large art gallery featuring works by local artists. **Open:** Mon–Sat 9am–5pm. Closed some hols. Free.

Wupatki National Monument, US 89; tel 602/556-7040. 36 mi N of Flagstaff. The largest of the prehistoric pueblos in the area is Wupatki ruin in the southeastern part of the monument. Here the Sinagua people built a sprawling 3-story pueblo containing nearly 100 rooms. The visitor center in this location has exhibits on the Sinagua and Anasazi who once inhabited the region.

The most unusual feature of Wupatki is a natural phenomenon—a blowhole—that may have been the reason for building the pueblo on this site. A network of small underground tunnels and chambers acts as a giant barometer, blowing air when the underground air is under greater pressure than the outside air. On hot days, cool air rushes out of the blowhole. **Open:** Daily 8am–6pm. $$

Walnut Canyon National Monument, Walnut Canyon Rd; tel 602/526-3367. The remains of hundreds of 13th-century Sinagua cliff dwellings can be seen in this dry, wooded canyon 7 miles east of Flagstaff. The undercut layers of limestone in the 400-foot-deep canyon proved ideal for building dwellings well protected both from the elements and from enemies. A self-guided trail leads from the visitor center on the canyon rim down 185 feet to a section of the canyon wall where 25 cliff dwellings can be entered. **Open:** Daily 8am–5pm. Closed some hols. $$

Sunset Crater National Monument, US 89; tel 602/556-7042. 15 mi N of Flagstaff. Taking its name from the sunset colors of the cinders near its summit, this volcanic crater, which began forming in 1064, stands 1,000 feet tall. Over a period of 100 years the volcano erupted repeatedly, creating the red-and-yellow cinder cone seen today and eventually covering an area of 800 square miles with ash, lava, and cinders. A mile-long interpretative trail passes through a desolate landscape of lava flows, cinders, and ash as it skirts the base. Visitor center, small campground. **Open:** Daily sunrise–sunset. $$

Riordan Mansion State Park, 1300 Riordan Ranch St; tel 602/779-4395. Built in 1904 for local lumber merchants Michael and Timothy Riordan, this 13,000-square-foot mansion is actually 2 houses connected by a large central hall. The Riordans played important roles in the early history of Flagstaff: They built the first Roman Catholic church, the first library, the power company, and the phone company. **Open:** May–Sept, daily 8am–5pm; Oct–Apr, daily 12:30–5pm. Closed Dec 25. $

Fairfield Snowball, Ariz 180 and Snowbowl Rd; tel 602/779-1951. Located on the slopes of Mount Agassiz, this popular ski site has 4 chair lifts, 32 runs, and 2,300 vertical feet of slopes. In the summer the ski lift carries hikers, bikers, and any other visitors who want to enjoy the views. **Open:** Daily 9am–4pm. $$$$

FREDONIA

Map page M-2, A2

Lodge 🛏

≣≣ **Kaibab Lodge**, Ariz 67, PO Box 30, HC64, Fredonia, AZ 86022; tel 602/638-2389. 18 mi N of the North Rim of Grand Canyon National Park. This rustic lodge, open in both summer and winter when the North Rim is generally closed, is popular with hunters because of easy access to the Kaibab National Forest. The lodge is inaccessible by car after the snows fall, however, so transportation is by special "snow vans." **Rooms:** 24 ctges/villas. CI 3pm/CO 10am. All bathrooms have showers only. **Amenities:** No A/C, phone, or TV. Some units w/terraces. The common room has a fireplace, piano, and cable TV. At an altitude of 8,700 feet, air conditioning will not be missed. **Services:** 🛎️ **Facilities:** 🚴 🏊 📷 🎿 🔫 1 rst, 1 bar, games rm, whirlpool. There's a store and a gas station with diesel fuel on the premises. The restaurant serves only breakfast and dinner, although bag lunches are available. **Rates:** HS May–Oct from $60 ctge/villa. Extra person $10. Lower rates off-season. Spec packages avail. Pking: Outdoor, free. Ltd CC. Cross-country ski packages are available.

GANADO

Map page M-2, B4

Attraction 🖼️

Hubbell Trading Post National Historic Site, Ariz 264; tel 602/755-3475. The oldest continuously operating trading post on the Navajo Reservation. The trading post includes a small museum where visitors can watch Navajo weavers in the slow process of creating rugs. In the trading post visitors may encounter individuals trading jewelry or rugs for goods or cash. The rug room is filled with a variety of traditional and contemporary Navajo rugs for sale. There are also baskets, kachinas, and several cases of jewelry by Navajo, Hopi, and Zuni craftspeople in another room. In the general store there are basic foodstuffs and bolts of cloth used by Navajo women for sewing traditional clothing. **Open:** Apr–Oct, daily 8am–6pm; Nov–Mar, daily 8am–5pm. Free.

GILA BEND

Map page M-2, D2

Motel 🛏️

🔳🔳 **Best Western Space Age Lodge**, 401 E Pima St, PO Box C, Gila Bend, AZ 85337; tel 602/683-2273 or toll free 800/528-1234. Single-story modern motel in downtown Gila Bend. **Rooms:** 41 rms. CI noon/CO noon. Nonsmoking rms avail. **Amenities:** 🛁 A/C, cable TV w/movies. Some rooms have refrigerators. **Services:** 🛎️ 🍽️ **Facilities:** 🗄️ 🏋️ 1 rst, 1 bar, whirlpool, washer/dryer. 24-hour restaurant. **Rates:** HS Jan–May $56 S; $60 D. Extra person $4. Children under 17 stay free. Lower rates off-season. Pking: Outdoor, free. Maj CC.

GLENDALE

Map page M-2, D2

Restaurant 🍴

★ **Portofino Ristorante**, in Gateway Village Shopping Center, 6020 W Bell Rd, Glendale; tel 602/938-1902. At 59th Ave. **Italian.** Pleasant shopping center restaurant, with a fountain in the center of the dining room. A sibling restaurant, Portofino West, is in the Crossroads Towne Center, 12851 W Bell Rd, Surprise (602/583-1931). **FYI:** Reservations recommended. **Open:** Lunch Mon–Fri 11:30am–2:30pm; dinner Mon–Thurs 5–10pm, Fri–Sat 5–10:30pm, Sun 4pm. Closed some hols. **Prices:** Main courses $7.50–$15.50. Maj CC. 🟢 🔵

Attraction 🖼️

Waterworld Safari, 4243 West Pinnacle Peak Rd; tel 602/581-1947. A water park featuring a wave pool, 9 water slides, and a special children's area. **Open:** June–Sept, Mon–Fri 10am–9pm, Sun 11am–7pm. $$$$

GLOBE

Map page M-2, D3

Attractions 🖼️

Besh-Ba-Gowah Archaeological Park, 150 N Pine St; tel 602/425-0320. An excavation of this city park resulted in the discovery of the remains of a Salado pueblo. Built and occupied from about 1225 to 1400, this site once housed over 400 people in 300 rooms. Today visitors can view the ruins on an interpretive trail. A museum displays artifacts, models, and photographs relating to the site. Across from the dig is a park area with picnic facilities. **Open:** Daily 8am–5pm. Free.

Tonto National Monument, Ariz 88; tel 602/467-2241. 30 mi NW of Globe on US 88. The southernmost cliff dwellings in Arizona, built between 1100 and 1400 by the Salado peoples. The 3 cliff dwellings here are some of the only remaining pueblos of the Salado, who disappeared around 1400. They are built into the caves above the Salt River where they were protected from the elements and were thus well preserved. The largest ruin, Upper Ruin, has 40 rooms and is 3 stories high in some places. The only time the public may visit Upper Ruin is on Saturday at 9:30am. It's a 3-mile round-trip hike and reservations are required. **Open:** Daily 8am–5pm. Closed Dec 25. $

GRAND CANYON

Map page M-2, B2

Hotels 🔑

≣≣≣ **El Tovar Hotel**, South Rim, PO Box 699, Grand Canyon, AZ 86023; tel 602/638-2401; fax 602/638-9247. A historic 1905 hotel perched on the South Rim of the Grand Canyon. **Rooms:** 74 rms and stes. CI 4pm/CO 11am. Nonsmoking rms avail. Standard rooms are comfortable but small. **Amenities:** 🕿 Cable TV. No A/C. Some units w/terraces. **Services:** ✗ 🔑 🚗 ⌇ Babysitting. **Facilities:** 🏊 ᠔ 1 rst (see also "Restaurants" below), 1 bar. The restaurant has a wonderful view. **Rates:** HS May–Sept $114–$169 S or D; from $185 ste. Extra person $7–$9. Children under 16 stay free. Lower rates off-season. Spec packages avail. Pking: Outdoor, free. Maj CC.

≣≣≣ **Grand Canyon Squire Inn**, Ariz 64, PO Box 130, Grand Canyon, AZ 86023; tel 602/638-2681 or toll free 800/622-6966; fax 602/638-0162. On the South Rim of Grand Canyon National Park. A modern hotel just outside the entrance to Grand Canyon National Park, in the village of Tusayan. **Rooms:** 250 rms and stes. CI 3pm/CO noon. Nonsmoking rms avail. **Amenities:** 🕿 ᠔ A/C, satel TV, stereo/tape player. Some units w/Jacuzzis. **Services:** 🔑 🚗 ⌇ **Facilities:** 🕳 ᠔ 🎾 🛶 🏊 ᠔ 2 rsts, 2 bars, games rm, spa, whirlpool, washer/dryer. Bowling alley on premises. **Rates:** HS Mar 15–Oct 22 $100–$125 S or D; from $150 ste. Extra person $8. Children under 12 stay free. Lower rates off-season. Higher rates for spec evnts/hols. Spec packages avail. Pking: Outdoor, free. Maj CC.

≣≣ **Quality Inn Grand Canyon**, Ariz 64, PO Box 520, Grand Canyon, AZ 86023; tel 602/638-2673 or toll free 800/221-2222; fax 602/638-9537. An attractive hotel 1 mile south of the entrance to Grand Canyon National Park, in Tusayan. **Rooms:** 176 rms. CI 3pm/CO 11am. Nonsmoking rms avail. **Amenities:** 🕿 🚰 A/C, cable TV, refrig. Some units w/minibars, some w/terraces. **Services:** 🚗 ⌇ **Facilities:** 🕳 🏊 ᠔ 1 rst, 1 bar. There's an indoor Jacuzzi and an outdoor hot tub. **Rates:** HS Mar 25–Oct $125 S or D. Extra person $10. Children under 5 stay free. Lower rates off-season. Higher rates for spec evnts/hols. Pking: Outdoor, free. Maj CC.

Motel

≣≣ **Thunderbird & Kachina Lodges**, South Rim, PO Box 699, Grand Canyon, AZ 86023; tel 602/638-2401. On the South Rim of Grand Canyon National Park. Pleasant, basic lodging. Registration for Thunderbird is at the Bright Angel Lodge, for Kachina at El Tovar Hotel. **Rooms:** 104 rms. CI 4pm/CO 11am.

Nonsmoking rms avail. There are 48 rooms in Kachina, and 55 in Thunderbird. Some rooms face the canyon. **Amenities:** 🕿 Cable TV. No A/C. **Services:** 🔑 ⌇ **Facilities:** 🏊 ᠔ **Rates:** HS Apr–Oct $96–$106 S or D. Extra person $9. Children under 16 stay free. Lower rates off-season. Spec packages avail. Pking: Outdoor, free. Maj CC.

Lodges

≣≣ **Bright Angel Lodge and Cabins**, W Rim Dr, PO Box 699, Grand Canyon, AZ 86023; tel 602/638-2631. A rustic lodge on the South Rim of Grand Canyon National Park. **Rooms:** 34 rms; 55 ctges/villas. CI 4pm/CO 11am. Nonsmoking rms avail. There are a variety of accommodations, from motel-type rooms to historic cabins. Some have magnificent canyon views. **Amenities:** 🕿 Cable TV. No A/C. Some units w/minibars, some w/terraces, some w/fireplaces. There's no air conditioning, but it's rarely needed at the 7,000-foot elevation. **Services:** 🚗 ⌇ **Facilities:** 2 rsts (see also "Restaurants" below), 1 bar (w/entertainment), beauty salon. **Rates:** $56 S or D; from $64 ctge/villa. Extra person $9. Children under 15 stay free. Pking: Outdoor, free. Maj CC.

≣≣ **Moqui Lodge**, Ariz 64, PO Box 369, Grand Canyon, AZ 86023; tel 602/638-2424 or toll free 800/538-6267. On the South Rim of Grand Canyon National Park. Rustic lodge. **Rooms:** 136 rms. CI 4pm/CO 11am. Nonsmoking rms avail. **Amenities:** 🕿 Cable TV. No A/C. **Services:** 🔑 🚗 ⌇ **Facilities:** ᠔ 🎾 🏊 ᠔ 1 rst, 1 bar, beauty salon. There's a picnic and barbecue area, and a gas station on the premises. Wagon rides are available. **Rates:** HS Mar–Oct $82 S or D. Extra person $9. Children under 16 stay free. Lower rates off-season. Pking: Outdoor, free. Maj CC.

Restaurants 🍴

Arizona Steakhouse, in the Bright Angel Lodge, South Rim, Grand Canyon; tel 602/638-2631 ext 6296. **American.** A simple steakhouse that features breathtaking views. The barbecue sampler lets you try pork ribs, beef ribs, and a chicken leg and thigh. **FYI:** Reservations not accepted. Children's menu. No smoking. **Open:** Daily 5–10pm. Closed Jan–Feb. **Prices:** Main courses $9.30–$17.90. Maj CC. 🏔 ᠔

Babbitt's Delicatessen, in Babbitt's General Store, South Rim, Grand Canyon; tel 602/638-2262. **Fast food.** Basic deli, located inside a grocery store. A good choice for a snack or light lunch. **FYI:** Reservations not accepted. No liquor license. No smoking. **Open:** Daily 8am–6pm. Closed some hols. **Prices:** Lunch main courses $3–$6. No CC. 🍽 ᠔

Canyon Cafe, in the Yavapai Lodge, South Rim, Grand Canyon; tel 602/638-2631. **American.** No-frills cafeteria dining, with traditional American fare. **FYI:** Reservations not accepted. Children's menu. No liquor license. No smoking. **Open:** Daily 6am–10pm. **Prices:** Main courses $6–$10. Maj CC. 🈳 &

El Tovar Dining Room, in El Tovar Hotel, South Rim, Grand Canyon; tel 602/638-2631 ext 6432. **Southwestern.** Elegant dining in a historic setting. The lovely lodge-style dining room was built with Oregon pine and boasts a stone fireplace and high-beamed ceilings. Southwestern sauces and spices add punch to traditional dishes: Prickly-pear jalapeño honey is combined with roast duckling; smoked tomato pinenut sauce with chicken breast; and tomatillo salsa and chile-lime aioli with grilled salmon. During high season, lighter fare is served on the mezzanine between 2pm and 8pm. The private dining room, which seats 2 to 8 persons, is available with 48-hour advance reservation. **FYI:** Reservations recommended. Singer. Children's menu. No smoking. **Open:** Breakfast daily 6:30–11am; lunch daily 11:30am–2pm; dinner daily 5–10pm. **Prices:** Main courses $14.25–$25.25. Maj CC. 🏔 &

Grand Canyon Lodge Dining Room, in Grand Canyon Lodge, North Rim, Grand Canyon; tel 602/638-2611 ext 160. **American.** The magnificent, lodge-style dining room provides spectacular views of the canyon. Open-beamed ceiling, chandeliers, and wall sconces. Seafood, beef, and vegetarian dishes; a specialty is the mountain red trout. **FYI:** Reservations recommended. Children's menu. No smoking. **Open:** Breakfast daily 6:30–10am; lunch daily 11:30am–2:30pm; dinner daily 5–10pm. Closed end of Oct–mid-May depending on snowfall. **Prices:** Main courses $8.20–$16.20. Maj CC. 🏔 &

Hermits Snack Bar, in Hermits Curio Shop, W Rim Dr, Grand Canyon; tel 602/638-2351. On the South Rim. **Fast food.** Simple snack bar, serving items like hot dogs, chicken nuggets, chips, cookies, and soft drinks. **FYI:** Reservations not accepted. No liquor license. No smoking. **Open:** HS May 27–Sept 30 daily 8am–8pm. Reduced hours off-season. **Prices:** Lunch main courses $1–$2.99. No CC.

Maswik Cafeteria, in the Maswik Lodge, South Rim, Grand Canyon; tel 602/638-2631. **American/Mexican.** Basic cafeteria. Sandwiches, traditional hot American dishes, some Mexican plates. **FYI:** Reservations not accepted. Children's menu. No liquor license. No smoking. **Open:** Daily 6am–10pm. **Prices:** Main courses $4–$8. Maj CC. 🈳 &

Attractions

GRAND CANYON NATIONAL PARK

About the Park. Geologists believe that it has taken between 3 and 6 million years for the Colorado River to carve the Grand Canyon a mile deep and up to 18 miles wide. Banded layers of sandstone, limestone, shale, and schist give the canyon its color, and the interplays of shadows and light from dawn to dusk create an ever-changing palette of hues and textures.

The park is divided into 3 sections: the North Rim, the South Rim, and the inner canyon. Grand Canyon Village and Desert View in the South Rim are open year-round with full facilities, including lodging, dining, and entertainment. The North Rim is open May to October and has lodging, food, camping facilities, and a service center.

To view the Grand Canyon from the rim there are several scenic drives, including the 8-mile West Rim Drive from Grand Canyon Village to Hermits Rest, and the 25-mile East Rim Drive from Grand Canyon Village to Desert View. Popular ways to see the inner canyon are rafting down the Colorado River, taking a mule ride, flying over in a helicopter or small airplane, and hiking and backpacking. All trips into the inner canyon are physically exerting, but up close visitors can see fossils, old mines, petroglyphs, wildflowers, and extensive wildlife. Details about the canyon and inner canyon trips are available in *The Guide*, a free newspaper available by calling the park visitor center. The Grand Canyon is located 80 miles northeast of Flagstaff and 60 miles north of Williams; take US 180 directly to the South Rim, or US 89 to Ariz 64, which leads to the east entrance of the park. $$$

Grand Canyon Visitor Center, Village Loop Dr; tel 602/638-7888. In addition to providing answers to questions about the Grand Canyon, the center also contains exhibits on its natural history and exploration. Throughout the day slide and video programs are shown. **Open:** Mar–Nov, daily 8am–7pm; Dec–Feb, daily 8am–5pm. Free.

Grand Canyon IMAX Theatre, South Rim; tel 602/638-2203. Located at the south entrance to the park. A huge 7-story screen completely fills the field of vision with incredibly realistic, high-definition film images. Every hour there is a 34-minute film about the canyon. **Open:** Mar–Nov, daily 8:30am–8:30pm; Dec–Feb, daily 10:30am–6:30pm. $$$

Over the Edge Theatres, Community Building, Village Loop Dr; tel 602/638-2224. This audiovisual program introduces the visitor to the geology and history of the canyon. The narration is given from the point of view of Capt. John Hance, one of the canyon's first guides. **Open:** Daily 9am–9pm. $$

Yavapai Museum, Village Loop Dr; tel 602/638-7890. Located less than a mile east of the visitor center, with exhibits on the geologic history of the Grand Canyon. A panorama of the canyon is visible through the museum's large windows. **Open:** Mar–Nov, daily 8am–7pm; Dec–Feb, daily 9am–5pm. Free.

Tusayan Museum, East Rim Dr; tel 602/638-2305. Dedicated to the Hopi tribe and ancient Anasazi people who inhabited this region 800 years ago. Inside the small museum are artfully displayed exhibits on various aspects of Anasazi life. Outside is a short self-guided trail through actual Anasazi ruins. **Open:** Daily 9am–5pm. Closed some hols. Free.

The Watchtower, Desert View, East Rim Dr; tel 602/638-2736. Architect Mary Jane Colter, who is responsible for much of the Grand Canyon's historic architecture, designed this to resemble the prehistoric towers that dot the southwestern landscape. Built as an observation post and rest stop for tourists, the watchtower incorporates Native American design and traditional art. **Open:** Mar–Nov, daily 8am–8pm; Dec–Feb, daily 9am–5pm. $

Kolb and Lookout Studios, South Rim; tel 602/638-2631, ext 6087. Due to their location precariously close to the rim of the canyon, both of these buildings are listed on the National Register of Historic Places. **Kolb Studio** was built by the brothers Ellsworth and Emory Kolb, who used it as a photography studio beginning in 1904. Today it serves as a bookstore. **Lookout Studio,** built in 1914, was designed with native limestone and an uneven roofline to allow the studio to blend in with the canyon walls. Originally built by the Fred Harvey Company to compete with the Kolb brothers, it now houses a souvenir store and 2 lookout points. **Open:** Daily 9am–6pm. Free.

GREER

Map page M-2, C4

Lodge 🛏

≣≣ **Greer Lodge**, Ariz 373, PO Box 66, Greer, AZ 85927; tel 602/735-7216. 45 mi E of Show Low. Ariz 373 exit off Ariz 260. A large log lodge set in a beautiful mountain setting, with 3 ponds and the Little Colorado River running directly behind the property. **Rooms:** 9 rms; 7 ctges/villas. CI 2pm/CO 11am. Besides the rooms in the main lodge, there are also cabins. **Amenities:** No A/C, phone, or TV. All units w/terraces, all w/fireplaces. **Services:** ⌂ Twice-daily maid svce. Breakfast included with lodge rooms, but not cabins. Hay rides and fly-fishing school in summer; sleigh rides and ice skating in winter.

Facilities: 🍴 🏊 🛶 📺 🎱 1 rst, 1 bar, lawn games. **Rates:** $90 S; $120 D; from $95 ctge/villa. Extra person $20. Children under 1 stay free. Min stay wknds. Pking: Outdoor, free. Ltd CC.

HEREFORD

Map page M-2, E4 (SE of Sierra Vista)

Attractions 📷

Ramsey Canyon Preserve, 27 Ramsey Canyon Rd; tel 602/378-2785. Internationally known wildlife preserve home to 14 species of hummingbirds—more than can be found anywhere else in the United States. Covering 280 acres, it is situated in a wooded gorge in the Huachuca Mountains. A short nature trail leads through the canyon. Because there are only a few parking spaces, a parking reservation is required on weekends and is suggested during the week. August is the best time to see hummingbirds. **Open:** Daily 8am–5pm. $$

Coronado National Memorial, 4101 E Montezuma Canyon Rd; tel 602/458-9333. A visitor center tells the story of Francisco Vásquez de Coronado's fruitless quest for riches in the San Pedro River valley. The 5,000-acre memorial features a bird observation area where visitors might see some of the more than 140 species of birds that make their home here. **Open:** Daily 8am–5pm. Free.

HOLBROOK

Map page M-2, B4

Motels 🏨

≣≣ **Comfort Inn**, 2602 Navajo Blvd, Holbrook, AZ 86025; tel 602/524-6131 or toll free 800/228-5150; fax 602/524-2281. Exit 289 off I-40. A good, basic motel. **Rooms:** 83 rms. CI noon/CO 11am. Simple, clean rooms. **Amenities:** 🔒 🛁 A/C, cable TV w/movies, stereo/tape player. **Services:** ✕ 🚐 ⌂ 🐕 **Facilities:** 🎱 🖥 ⌂ Whirlpool, washer/dryer. **Rates (CP):** HS June–Sept $48 S or D. Extra person $5. Children under 18 stay free. Lower rates off-season. Spec packages avail. Pking: Outdoor, free. Maj CC.

≣ **Days Inn**, 2601 Navajo Blvd, Holbrook, AZ 86025; tel 602/524-6949 or toll free 800/325-2525; fax 602/524-6665. Exit 289 off I-40. One of the newest motels in the area. **Rooms:** 54 rms and stes. CI 11am/CO 11am. Express checkout avail. Nonsmoking rms avail. Rooms are simple but have some nice touches, especially the king suites, which have in-room whirlpool baths. **Amenities:** 🔒 A/C, cable TV w/movies, voice mail. Some units w/Jacuzzis. **Services:** 🖨 🍴 Twice-daily maid svce. **Facilities:** 🏊 ♿ Spa, whirlpool, washer/dryer. **Rates (CP):** HS June–Aug $38–$48 S; $56–$58 D; from $65 ste. Extra person $6. Children under 12 stay free. Lower rates off-season. Higher rates for spec evnts/hols. Pking: Outdoor, free. Maj CC. A good deal for singles.

📧 **Wigwam Motel**, 811 W Hopi Dr, PO Box 788, Holbrook, AZ 86025; tel 602/524-3048. Exit 285 off I-40. Built in 1950, this motel is a must-see. Each room is designed as an Indian wigwam or teepee. **Rooms:** 15 rms. CI 2pm/CO noon. 1950s furnishings. **Amenities:** A/C, TV. No phone. 1 unit w/Jacuzzi. **Services:** 🍴 🍴 Twice-daily maid svce. **Rates:** HS May–Sept $30 S; $35 D. Lower rates off-season. Pking: Outdoor, free. Ltd CC. A bargain.

Attraction 🏛

Petrified Forest National Park (Painted Desert), I-40 or US 180; tel 602/524-6228. The petrified wood found here began its journey 225 million years ago as giant prehistoric trees. When the trees fell they were washed downstream and became preserved from decay by a layer of volcanic ash, silt, and mud. Silica later formed from the ash and filled the cells of the wood, eventually recrystallizing it into stone.

The Painted Desert is named for the vivid colors of the soil and stone that cover the barren expanses of eroded hills; these colors were created by minerals dissolved in the sandstone and clay soils that were deposited during different geologic periods.

The park's visitors centers both have maps and books about the region and both give out the free permits necessary to backpack and camp in the park. The **Painted Desert Visitor Center** is at the north end of the park and the **Rainbow Forest Museum** is at the south end. They are connected by a 27-mile scenic road with more than 20 overlooks. The petrified logs are concentrated in the southern part of the park, while the northern section overlooks the Painted Desert. At the north end, the Painted Desert Oasis provides a full-service cafeteria. **Open:** Daily 8am–5pm. $$

HOPI RESERVATION

Completely surrounded by the Navajo Reservation in the 4 Corners region of the state, the Hopi Reservation is a grouping of mesas that are home to the Hopi pueblos. This remote region of Arizona, with its flat-topped mesas and rugged, barren landscape, is the center of the universe for the Hopi people. The handful of villages here are ancient, independent communities that have today been brought together under the guidance of the Hopi Tribal Council. This land has been inhabited by the Hopi and their ancestors for nearly 1,000 years, and many aspects of the ancient pueblo culture remain intact. Photographing, sketching, and recording are all prohibited in the villages and at ceremonies, and kivas (ceremonial rooms) and ruins are off limits to visitors.

The reservation is divided into 3 mesas known simply as First, Second, and Third Mesa, which are numbered from east to west. Villages on First Mesa include Polacca, Walpi, Sichomovi, and Hano. Second Mesa is today the center of tourism in Hopiland, and the location of the **Hopi Cultural Center**. Second Mesa villages include Sungopavi, Mishongnovi, and Shipaulovi. **Oraibi**, which the Hopi claim is the oldest continuously occupied town in the United States, is located on Third Mesa, along with Hotevilla, Kykotsmovi, and Bacavi.

The Hopi have developed the most complex religious ceremonies of any of the southwestern tribes. **Masked kachina dances**, for which the Hopi are most famous, are held from January to July, while the **snake dances**, particularly popular with non-Hopis, are held from August through December. For more information about ceremonies or the reservation call the Hopi Tribal Council at 602/734-2441.

JEROME

Map page M-2, C2 (NE of Prescott)

Attraction 🏛

Jerome State Historic Park, US 89A; tel 602/634-5381. Located in the former mining town of Jerome, a national historic landmark, the park contains the partially restored 1916 mansion of mine owner "Rawhide Jimmy" Douglas. The mansion's library has been restored as a period room, while other rooms contain exhibits on copper mining and the town's history, displays of colorful ores, and tools that were once used to extract the ore from the mountain. **Open:** Daily 8am–5pm. Closed Dec 25. $

KAYENTA

Map page M-2, A4

Hotel 🏨

📧📧 **Holiday Inn–Kayenta**, Junction of US 160 and US 163, PO Box 307, Kayenta, AZ 86033; tel 602/697-3221 or toll free 800/343-1122. In a convenient location for visiting the Navajo National Monument and Monument Valley. **Rooms:** 164 rms and stes. CI 3pm/CO noon. Nonsmoking rms avail. **Amenities:**

🛏 A/C, cable TV w/movies. **Services:** ✗ 🚐 ♫ **Facilities:** ⛱ 🅿 ♿ 1 rst. **Rates:** HS June–Sept $109–$112 S or D; from $112 ste. Extra person $10. Children under 17 stay free. Lower rates off-season. Pking: Outdoor, free. Maj CC.

Motels

▤ Anasazi Inn at Tsegi Canyon, US 60, PO Box 1543, Kayenta, AZ 86033; tel 602/697-3793. 10 mi W of downtown Kayenta. In a remote location, with great views of Tsegi Canyon in all directions. **Rooms:** 56 rms. CI 2pm/CO 11am. Nonsmoking rms avail. Some rooms have kitchenettes. **Amenities:** A/C, satel TV. No phone. **Services:** ♫ **Facilities:** 1 rst. Arts and crafts center on premises. **Rates:** HS May–Oct $65 S or D. Extra person $6. Children under 12 stay free. Lower rates off-season. Pking: Outdoor, free. Maj CC.

▤▤ Wetherill Inn Motel, US 163, PO Box 175, Kayenta, AZ 86033; tel 602/697-3231. US 163 exit off US 160. A pleasant, basic motel, close to the Navajo National Monument and Monument Valley. **Rooms:** 54 rms. CI 2pm/CO 11am. Nonsmoking rms avail. **Amenities:** 🛏 🛁 A/C, cable TV. **Services:** ♫ **Facilities:** ♿ **Rates:** HS Apr 15–Oct 15 $72 S; $78 D. Extra person $6. Children under 12 stay free. Lower rates off-season. Pking: Outdoor, free. Maj CC.

KINGMAN

Map page M-2, B1

Hotel 🛎

▤▤ Quality Inn–Kingman, 1400 E Andy Devine Ave, Kingman, AZ 86401; tel 602/753-4747 or toll free 800/4-CHOICE. Exit 48 or 53 off I-40. 2 mi E of exit 48 / 2 mi W of exit 53 on Business Loop 40. Located on historic Route 66. The lobby is decorated with 1950s memorabilia, and the hotel sells Route 66 souvenirs. **Rooms:** 98 rms and stes. CI noon/CO noon. Nonsmoking rms avail. Room 165 is the Wild Bill Hickok room. Actor Guy Madison, who played Hickok in the 1950s TV series, once stayed in this room; his photo is on the door. **Amenities:** 🛏 🛁 📺 A/C, cable TV w/movies. 1 unit w/minibar. **Services:** 🚐 🛅 ♫ **Facilities:** ⛱ 🎿 📶 💻 ♿ Sauna, whirlpool, beauty salon, washer/dryer. **Rates (CP):** HS May–Sept $49–$59 S; $54–$64 D; from $70 ste. Extra person $5. Children under 18 stay free. Lower rates off-season. Higher rates for spec evnts/hols. Pking: Outdoor, free. Maj CC.

Motels

▤▤ Holiday Inn–Kingman, 3100 E Andy Devine Ave, Kingman, AZ 86401; tel 602/753-6262 or toll free 800/HOLIDAYS; fax 602/753-7137. Exit 53 off I-40. A basic motel close to major highways. **Rooms:** 120 rms. CI 1pm/CO noon. Express checkout avail. Nonsmoking rms avail. **Amenities:** 🛏 🛁 A/C, cable TV. **Services:** ✗ 🚐 🛅 ♫ 🔔 **Facilities:** ⛱ 📶 ♿ 1 rst, 1 bar (w/entertainment), washer/dryer. **Rates:** HS Feb–Sept $49–$84 S or D. Extra person $5. Children under 19 stay free. Lower rates off-season. Higher rates for spec evnts/hols. Pking: Outdoor, free. Maj CC. Senior discounts available.

▤▤ Super 8 Motel, 3401 E Andy Devine Ave, Kingman, AZ 86401; tel 602/757-4808 or toll free 800/800-8000. Exit 53 off I-40. A clean, basic motel with good interstate access. **Rooms:** 61 rms and stes. CI 2pm/CO 11am. Nonsmoking rms avail. **Amenities:** 🛏 A/C, cable TV w/movies. Some rooms have waterbeds. **Services:** ♫ 🔔 Free local calls. **Facilities:** 📶 ♿ Large-vehicle parking available. **Rates (CP):** HS Apr–Sept $30 S; $38 D; from $43 ste. Extra person $6. Children under 12 stay free. Lower rates off-season. Pking: Outdoor, free. Maj CC.

Restaurants 🍴

House of Chan, 960 W Beale St, Kingman; tel 602/753-3232. **American/Chinese.** A landmark Kingman restaurant serving up Chinese and traditional American food. Cantonese dishes include moo goo gai pan, which is sliced chicken, mushrooms, water chestnuts, bamboo shoots, and peas; and hot and spicy kung pao chicken. Seafood, beef, and chicken offerings fill out the American side of the menu. Chinese beer and wines and Japanese sake are available. **FYI:** Reservations accepted. Children's menu. **Open:** Mon–Fri 11am–10pm, Sat noon–10pm. **Prices:** Main courses $4.95–$25.95. Maj CC. 💳 ♿

JR's, 1410 E Andy Devine Ave, Kingman; tel 602/753-1066. Beale St exit off I-40. **American.** Family restaurant with pleasant coffeeshop atmosphere. A variety of breakfast items are served: corned beef hash and eggs, 10 kinds of omelettes, pork chop and eggs, french toast, pancakes, and waffles. The lunch and dinner menu includes cold sandwiches, burgers, steak, prime rib, hot roast beef or turkey sandwiches, plus a number of salads. **FYI:** Reservations accepted. Children's menu. **Open:** Daily 7am–10pm. Closed Dec 25. **Prices:** Main courses $2.95–$6.95. Maj CC. 💳 ♿

Attractions 📷

Hoover Dam, US 93; tel 702/293-8367. Constructed between 1931 and 1935, this National Historic Landmark was the first major dam on the Colorado River. It is unique for several reasons. By providing the huge amounts of electricity and water needed by Arizona and California, it helped set the stage for the phenomenal growth the region has experienced this century. At 726 feet from bedrock to roadway, it is the highest concrete dam in the western hemisphere. 110-mile-long Lake Mead, which was created by damming the Colorado River, is the largest human-made reservoir in the United States. Guided tours begin at the Nevada side of the dam. **Open:** June–Aug, daily 9am– 7pm; Sept–May, daily 9am–4pm. Closed Dec 25. $

Bonelli House, 430 E Spring St; tel 602/753-3195. Two-story, territorial-style mansion built in 1915. It is constructed of locally quarried tufa stone to make it fire-resistant. Rooms are decorated in period style with many of the original furnishings. **Open:** Thurs–Mon 1–5pm. Closed some hols. Free.

Mohave Museum of History and Arts, 400 W Beale St; tel 602/753-3195. Exhibits representing the history of Kingman fill this small museum. Dioramas and murals depict the history of the region, while an outdoor display contains wagons, railroad cars, and other large vehicles and machines that helped shape Kingman. **Open:** Mon–Fri 10am–5pm, Sat–Sun 1–5pm. Closed some hols. $

Hualapai Mountain Park, Hualapai Mountain Rd; tel 602/ 757-0915. Located 7,000 feet up in the Hualapai Mountains, this park was developed in 1930 by the Civilian Conservation Corps as a pine-shaded escape from the desert. A popular spot for picnicking, hiking, and camping. **Open:** Daily 24 hours. Free.

Oatman, Old US 66; tel 602/768-7400. Located 30 miles southwest of Kingman. Founded in 1906 when gold was discovered nearby, the town was home to 12,000 people in its heyday. In 1942, the US government closed down many of Arizona's gold-mining operations and Oatman's population plummeted. Today, the 250 inhabitants live amid the once-abandoned old buildings that have been preserved as a ghost town.

One of the biggest attractions of Oatman is its population of almost-wild **burros.** These animals, which roam the streets begging for handouts, are descendants of burros used by gold miners. The historic look of the town has also attracted filmmakers for years; among the movies filmed here was *How the West Was Won*. On weekends there are staged shootouts in the streets and dancing to western music in the evening. **Open:** Daily 10am–5pm. Free.

LAKE HAVASU CITY

Map page M-2, C1

Hotel 🏨

≡≡≡ **Holiday Inn Lake Havasu City**, 245 London Bridge Rd, Lake Havasu City, AZ 86403; tel 602/855-4071 or toll free 800/HOLIDAY; fax 602/855-2379. Exit 9 off I-40. A pleasant hotel set back from the lake, with lower rates than comparable area hotels. **Rooms:** 162 rms and stes. CI 3pm/CO noon. Express checkout avail. Nonsmoking rms avail. Rooms are spacious and comfortable. **Amenities:** 🛏 🖐 A/C, satel TV w/movies, refrig. Some units w/minibars, some w/terraces. **Services:** ✕ 🚐 🖐 🎶 ✍ Free transportation to Laughlin, Nevada, casinos. **Facilities:** 🔧 200 💻 🖐 1 rst, 1 bar (w/entertainment), 1 beach (lake shore), games rm, whirlpool, beauty salon, washer/dryer. Discounts on greens fees are available for nearby PGA championship golf courses. **Rates:** HS Mar–Oct $53–$78 S or D; from $105 ste. Extra person $8. Children under 18 stay free. Min stay spec evnts. Lower rates off-season. Higher rates for spec evnts/hols. Spec packages avail. Pking: Outdoor, free. Maj CC.

Resorts

≡≡≡ **London Bridge Resort**, 1477 Queens Bay, Lake Havasu City, AZ 86403; tel 602/855-0888 or toll free 800/ 624-7939; fax 602/855-9209. Swanson Ave exit off Ariz 95. 110 acres. Large "theme park" hotel on the shores of Lake Havasu. Everything pertains to British royalty; a replica of the royal family's gold coronation coach is displayed in the lobby. **Rooms:** 183 rms and stes. CI 3pm/CO 11am. Nonsmoking rms avail. A variety of accommodations are available, from deluxe rooms to 2-bedroom suites. **Amenities:** 🛏 🖐 A/C, cable TV w/movies. Some units w/minibars, some w/terraces, some w/Jacuzzis. **Services:** ✕ 🗝 🚐 🖐 🎶 ✍ Babysitting. Complimentary shuttle to Laughlin, Nevada, casinos. **Facilities:** 🔧 🛝 🖐 ▶9 🖐 🔧 🖐 500 💻 🖐 3 rsts, 3 bars (2 w/entertainment), 1 beach (lake shore), lawn games, whirlpool, beauty salon, washer/dryer. There are 62 boat slips available at the hotel. **Rates (BB):** HS Apr–Oct $59–$159 S or D; from $99 ste. Extra person $5. Children under 18 stay free. Lower rates off-season. Higher rates for spec evnts/hols. Spec packages avail. Pking: Outdoor, free. Maj CC. Rates are increased on weekends.

≡≡ **Nautical Inn Resort & Conference Center**, 1000 McCulloch Blvd, Lake Havasu City, AZ 86403; tel 602/855-2141 or toll free 800/892-2141. Mesquite or Swanson exit off Ariz 95. 127 acres. Popular with boaters. **Rooms:** 124 rms and stes. CI 4pm/CO 11am. Nonsmoking rms avail. Some rooms have kitchenettes. **Amenities:** 🔒 📺 A/C, cable TV. 1 unit w/minibar, all w/terraces. Some rooms have coffeemakers. **Services:** ✗ ⌷ 🔔 Babysitting. **Facilities:** 🎣 ⛳ 📁 ▶18 🏊 ⛷ 🐎 ♿ 2 rsts (*see also* "Restaurants" below), 2 bars (w/entertainment), 3 beaches (lake shore), lawn games, whirlpool, washer/dryer. Barbecues are available. Parasailing is offered. **Rates:** HS Mar 15–Oct $90–$149 S or D; from $150 ste. Children under 18 stay free. Min stay wknds. Lower rates off-season. Higher rates for spec evnts/hols. Spec packages avail. Pking: Outdoor, free. Maj CC.

Restaurants 🍽

Captain's Table, in Nautical Inn Resort & Conference Center, 1000 McCulloch Blvd, Lake Havasu City; tel 602/855-2141 ext 410. Mesquite or Swanson Ave exit off Ariz 95. **Seafood.** Lakefront restaurant offering diners pretty views. Seafood is prepared grilled, blackened, charbroiled, baked, or Provençale. Chicken and beef are served as well. **FYI:** Reservations recommended. Singer. Children's menu. **Open:** HS May–Sept Sun–Thurs 7am–10pm, Fri–Sat 7am–11pm. Reduced hours off-season. **Prices:** Main courses $7.95–$48. Maj CC. 🏞 💟 ♿

Shugrue's, 1425 McCulloch Blvd, Lake Havasu City; tel 602/453-1400. **Seafood/Steak.** Attractive, comfortable restaurant that features a solarium dining room providing exceptional views of London Bridge. Primarily seafood and steak, but some Cajun dishes as well. House specialties include pan-fried southwestern catfish and broiled lemon-garlic shrimp. **FYI:** Reservations accepted. Children's menu. **Open:** Lunch Mon–Sat 11am–3pm, Sun 10am–3pm; dinner Sun–Thurs 5–10pm, Fri–Sat 5–11pm. Closed Dec 25. **Prices:** Main courses $6.95–$29.95. Maj CC. 🏞 ♿

Attractions 💼

London Bridge, 1550 London Bridge Rd; tel 602/855-4115. In the mid-1960s the British government decided to sell London Bridge, which was sinking into the Thames River, to Robert McCulloch, founder of Lake Havasu City. Reconstruction of the bridge began in 1968 and the grand reopening was held in 1971. When originally rebuilt, the bridge was located on a desert peninsula jutting into Lake Havasu, connecting desert to more desert. Since then a mile-long channel was dredged through the base of the peninsula, creating an island offshore from Lake Havasu City. Today the bridge is the 2nd largest attraction in Arizona. Visitors can also explore the more than 50 British-style shops that comprise the **English Village** located near the bridge. **Open:** Daily 24 hours. Free.

LAKE POWELL
Map page M-2, A3

Attractions 💼

Glen Canyon Dam, US 89; tel 602/645-2481. Built across a section of Glen Canyon that's less than ⅓ mile wide, the dam impounds the waters of the Colorado River to form Lake Powell. Built to provide water for the desert communities of the Southwest and West, the dam also provides hydroelectric power. Self-guided tours of the dam take 30–45 minutes. **Open:** Nov–Mar daily 8am–5pm; Mar–Nov, daily 7am–7pm. Free.

John Wesley Powell Memorial Museum, 6 N Lake Powell Blvd; tel 602/645-9496. Lake Powell is named after John Wesley Powell, the one-armed Civil War hero who led the first expedition through the Grand Canyon in 1869. This small museum documents the Powell expedition with photographs, etchings, and artifacts. In addition, there are Native American artifacts ranging from Anasazi pottery to contemporary Navajo and Hopi crafts. Gift shop, information center. **Open:** Mon–Sat 8am–6pm, Sun 10am–6pm. Closed some hols. Free.

LAKESIDE
Map page M-2, C4 (S of ShowLow)

Motel 🛏

≣≣≣ **Lakeside Inn**, 1637 Ariz 260, PO Box 1130-D, Lakeside, AZ 85935; tel 602/368-6600 or toll free 800/843-4792; fax 602/368-6600. 9 mi SE of Show Low. An attractive, comfortable motel. **Rooms:** 55 rms and stes. CI 3pm/CO 11am. Nonsmoking rms avail. **Amenities:** 🔒 ♨ A/C, cable TV w/movies. Some units w/minibars, some w/fireplaces. VCRs are available at the office. **Services:** 🔔 Twice-daily maid svce, babysitting. **Facilities:** 🚲 🎿 📁 🐎 🎱30 ♿ Games rm, spa, whirlpool. **Rates (CP):** HS Nov–Mar/July–Aug $55–$114 S or D; from $114 ste. Extra person $8. Children under 12 stay free. Min stay HS. Lower rates off-season. Higher rates for spec evnts/hols. Spec packages avail. Pking: Outdoor, free. Maj CC.

Lodge

≣≣ **Lake of the Woods**, 2244 W White Mt Blvd (Ariz 260), PO Box 777, Lakeside, AZ 85929; tel 602/368-5353. 7 mi SE of Show Low. A pleasant get-away-from-it-all, cabin-in-the-woods kind of resort, situated on a pretty lake. **Rooms:** 26 ctges/villas. CI 2pm/CO 11am. Old-fashioned-style cabins, with lots of stone and wood. **Amenities:** Cable TV, refrig. No A/C or phone. Some units w/terraces, all w/fireplaces, some w/Jacuzzis. **Services:** ⊋ ⊲⊳ Babysitting. **Facilities:** ⚠ 🔲 🛦 🖾 ⛲ 🎣 ⛳ ⚁ Games rm, lawn games, spa, playground, washer/dryer. **Rates:** HS June–Aug from $69 ctge/villa. Extra person $5. Children under 1 stay free. Min stay spec evnts. Lower rates off-season. Higher rates for spec evnts/hols. Spec packages avail. Pking: Outdoor, free. Ltd CC.

Resort

▤▤ **The Place Resort**, 3179 White Mt Rd (Ariz 260), PO Box 2675, Lakeside, AZ 85929; tel 602/368-6777. 5½ acres. A quiet retreat, perfect for relaxing and enjoying the lovely surroundings, or as use as a base camp for fishing, hunting, skiing, or golfing. **Rooms:** 20 ctges/villas. CI 1pm/CO 11am. Simple cabins with stone fireplaces and complete kitchens. **Amenities:** Cable TV, refrig. No A/C or phone. 1 unit w/minibar, all w/terraces, all w/fireplaces. **Services:** ⊋ ⊲⊳ Twice-daily maid svce, children's program, babysitting. **Facilities:** 🔲 🛦 🖾 ⚁ Lawn games, playground. Groceries can be purchased nearby. **Rates:** HS Nov 15–Mar 15/June 1–Sept 15 from $82 ctge/villa. Extra person $6. Min stay HS. Lower rates off-season. Spec packages avail. Pking: Outdoor, free. Maj CC.

LITCHFIELD PARK

Map page M-2, D2 (W of Glendale)

Resort 🎞

▤▤▤▤ **The Wigwam**, 300 E Indian School Rd, Litchfield Park, AZ 85340; tel 602/935-3811 or toll free 800/327-0396; fax 602/935-3737. 17 mi W of Phoenix. Litchfield Rd exit off I-10. Turn right after you exit and right again at 2nd traffic light. 75 acres. Dating from the 1920s, this 75-acre resort retains much of its original casita-style ambience, though it is now less a desert hideaway than a suburban playground. Ideal for meetings in winter and congenial for families in summer, it's also perfect for golfers year-round. **Rooms:** 331 rms and stes; 2 ctges/villas. CI 4pm/CO 1pm. Express checkout avail. Nonsmoking rms avail. Recent $44-million renovation restored original 1-story casitas and added new 2-story wings grouped around a 2nd swimming pool complex. Original rooms (a tad smaller, less expensive) have more southwestern flavor but their patios offer little shade and less privacy (the best bets are the casitas facing the first fairway). **Amenities:** 🔒 ⛾ 🍽 A/C, cable TV, refrig, in-rm safe, shoe polisher, bathrobes. All units w/minibars, all w/terraces, some w/fireplaces, some w/Jacuzzis. **Services:** 🍽 🖙 VP 🚐 🖾 ⊋ ⊲⊳ Twice-daily maid svce, car-rental desk, social

director, masseur, children's program, babysitting. Welcoming, responsive staff. **Facilities:** 🔋 🚴 🏌54 🛦 🖾 🏊 ⛲ 🎣 ⚡ 🖳 ⚁ 4 rsts (see also "Restaurants" below), 4 bars (1 w/entertainment), lifeguard, games rm, lawn games, spa, sauna, steam rm, whirlpool, beauty salon, day-care ctr, playground. Golfers can use caddies rather than carts; golf facilities are shared with club members, but guests get "first priority." Tennis courts include 500-seat stadium court. Trap and skeet shooting; day camp for kids. Live entertainment and dancing most evenings. **Rates:** HS Jan 9–Apr 30 $250–$280 S; $270–$300 D; from $355 ste; from $1,000 ctge/villa. Children under 18 stay free. Lower rates off-season. AP and MAP rates avail. Spec packages avail. Pking: Outdoor, free. Maj CC. Given the resort's not-too-convenient location, the MAP rate of $48 extra per person (with choice of 3 restaurants, gratuities included) is worth considering.

Restaurant 🍴

⑤ **Arizona Kitchen**, in The Wigwam, 300 E Indian School Rd, Litchfield Park; tel 602/935-3811. 17 mi W of Phoenix. From I-10, take Litchfield Rd exit, then go right to 2nd traffic light then right again. **Southwestern/Native American.** A cozy, informal setting for sampling innovative dishes. The inviting room is marked by timber-beamed ceilings, adobe walls, and sturdy wooden furniture—all dominated by a big, open kitchen with lots of tiles and copperware. The menu includes blue corn piki rolls (with shredded capon and jalapeño spinach); rattlesnake fritters; and chilequiles pizza (with spiced chicken and tortillas); and roasted pheasant (with chipotle-pomegranate honey). **FYI:** Reservations accepted. Guitar. Children's menu. **Open:** Breakfast Mon–Fri 7–11am, Sat–Sun 8am–noon; lunch Mon–Fri noon–2:30pm; dinner daily 6–10:30pm. **Prices:** Main courses $11.50–$26.75. Maj CC. 🖫 VP ⚁

Attraction 💼

Wildlife World Zoo, 16501 W Northern Ave; tel 602/935-9453. Features a large collection of animals housed in their natural surroundings on 45 acres, including over 350 species and 1,400 individual animals such as dromedary camels, llamas, kangaroos, jaguars, and tigers. A unique attraction is the lory parrot feeding, in which visitors feed apples to the birds as they ride a tram through the enclosure. **Open:** Daily 9am–5pm. $$$

MARBLE CANYON

Map page M-2, A3

Motel 🛏

≣ **Cliff Dwellers Lodge**, US 89A, PO Box 30, HC67, Marble Canyon, AZ 86036; tel 602/355-2228 or toll free 800/433-2543. 9 mi W of Navajo Bridge. A serene escape in the remote high mesas of northern Arizona, with beautiful views of the Vermillion Cliffs. **Rooms:** 21 rms. CI 2pm/CO 11am. **Amenities:** A/C. No phone or TV. Some units w/terraces. **Services:** 🚐 🛎 River rafting is available nearby. **Facilities:** ⚠ 🍽 ♿ 1 rst, 1 bar. Gas station, general store, and restaurant on premises. Landing strips for small planes nearby. **Rates:** HS May–Oct $57–$67 S or D. Extra person $4. Lower rates off-season. Pking: Outdoor, free. Ltd CC.

Lodge

≣≣ **Marble Canyon Lodge**, US 89A, Marble Canyon, AZ 86036; tel 602/355-2225 or toll free 800/726-1789. 5 mi S of Lee's Ferry. An attractive lodge close to the Colorado River, particularly popular with rafters and fishermen. **Rooms:** 50 rms and effic. CI 2pm/CO 11am. **Amenities:** 🛁 🖥 A/C, satel TV. **Services:** 🛎 🐾 Airstrip directly across the highway from the lodge for fly-ins. **Facilities:** ⚠ 🍽 🅿 ♿ 1 rst, 1 bar, lawn games, washer/dryer. Several buildings have small sitting rooms with libraries. Gas station, store, and post office on site. Rafting. **Rates:** HS Apr–Sept $45 S; $55 D; from $125 effic. Extra person $5. Children under 14 stay free. Lower rates off-season. Pking: Outdoor, free. Ltd CC.

MAYER

Map page M-2, C2

Attraction 📷

Arcosanti, I-17 at Cordes Junction; tel 602/632-7135. Paolo Soleri, an Italian architect who came to Arizona to study with Frank Lloyd Wright, has a dream of merging architecture and ecology. He calls this merger *arcology*, and Arcosanti is the realization of his ideas. An experiment in urban living, the energy-efficient town blends with the desert and preserves as much of the surrounding landscape as possible. Visitors cannot tour the grounds unescorted; there are hourly tours. **Open:** Daily 9am–5pm. Closed some hols. $$

MCNARY

Map page M-2, C4

Attraction 📷

Sunrise, Ariz 273; tel 602/735-7669. The only ski area in the White Mountains, an area known for its ponderosa pine forests, lakes, and mountains. The resort is located on the Apache Reservation and is operated by the Apache people. Lots of winter sun, 11 lifts, and more than 60 trails make this a very popular winter spot for Arizonans. During the summer there is hiking and fishing. **Open:** Nov–Apr, daily 9am–4:30pm. $$$$

MESA

Map page M-2, D3

Hotels 🛏

≣≣≣ **Courtyard by Marriott**, 1221 S Westwood Ave, Mesa, AZ 85210; tel 602/461-3000 or toll free 800/321-2210; fax 602/461-0179. Alma School Rd exit off US 60; take Southern Ave east to Westwood Ave. A pleasant establishment especially good for stays of several days. **Rooms:** 149 rms and stes. CI 3pm/CO 1pm. Express checkout avail. Nonsmoking rms avail. **Amenities:** 🛁 🍴 🖥 A/C, cable TV w/movies. All units w/terraces. Standard kings have sofa beds. All rooms have a special hot water faucet for tea or coffee making. **Services:** 🔺 🛎 Babysitting. **Facilities:** 🏋 🍳 🅿 ♿ 1 rst, 1 bar, games rm, whirlpool, washer/dryer. Restaurant serves breakfast only. **Rates (CP):** HS Jan–Apr $99–$109 S or D; from $114 ste. Children under 18 stay free. Lower rates off-season. Pking: Outdoor, free. Maj CC.

≣≣ **Hampton Inn**, 1563 S Gilbert Rd, Mesa, AZ 85204; tel 602/926-3600 or toll free 800/HAMPTON; fax 602/926-4892. Gilbert Rd exit off US 60. A good choice for families. **Rooms:** 116 rms. CI 3pm/CO noon. Nonsmoking rms avail. **Amenities:** 🛁 🍴 🍽 A/C, cable TV w/movies, shoe polisher. All units w/minibars. King rooms have 2 phones, and some have sofa sleepers. **Services:** 🔺 🛎 🐾 **Facilities:** 🏋 🅿 💻 ♿ Whirlpool, washer/dryer. **Rates (CP):** HS Jan 1–Apr 15 $67–$92 S or D. Extra person $5. Children under 18 stay free. Lower rates off-season. Higher rates for spec evnts/hols. Pking: Outdoor, free. Maj CC.

≣≣≣ **Holiday Inn**, 1600 S Country Club Dr, Mesa, AZ 85210; tel 602/964-7000 or toll free 800/HOLIDAY. Country Club Dr exit off US 60. Pleasant lobby, with lots of plants.

Rooms: 245 rms and stes. CI 3pm/CO noon. Express checkout avail. Nonsmoking rms avail. Rooms are comfortable, with excellent views of the Superstition Mountains from the upper floors. **Amenities:** 🛏 🕭 A/C, cable TV w/movies. Some units w/terraces. **Services:** ✕ 🖃 🗐 🍽 Car-rental desk, children's program. **Facilities:** 🛦 🗟 🕭 1 rst, 3 bars (1 w/entertainment), sauna, steam rm, whirlpool, washer/dryer. Attractive indoor-outdoor pool with lots of trees. **Rates:** HS Jan–Apr $109–$129 S or D; from $139 ste. Extra person $10. Children under 18 stay free. Lower rates off-season. Spec packages avail. Pking: Outdoor, free. Maj CC. Reasonable rates considering the quality and location.

≣≣ Lexington Hotel Suites, 1410 S Country Club Dr, Mesa, AZ 85210; tel 602/964-2897 or toll free 800/53-SUITE. Country Club Dr exit off US 60. All-suites hotel popular with golfers, good for short or long stays. Attractively furnished lobby. **Rooms:** 121 stes. CI 4pm/CO noon. Nonsmoking rms avail. **Amenities:** 🛏 🕭 🗐 A/C, cable TV w/movies, refrig. Studios and 1- and 2-bedroom suites have refrigerators, ovens, and cooking utensils. **Services:** 🛒 🖃 🗐 Children's program, babysitting. **Facilities:** 🛦 🗟 🖵 🕭 Whirlpool, washer/dryer. **Rates (CP):** HS Jan 1–mid-Apr from $49 ste. Extra person $5. Children under 16 stay free. Lower rates off-season. Spec packages avail. Pking: Outdoor, free. Maj CC. Extended-stay rates for studios.

≣≣≣ Mesa Pavilion Hilton, 1011 W Holmes Ave, Mesa, AZ 85210; tel 602/833-5555 or toll free 800/544-5866; fax 602/649-1886. Alma School Rd exit off US 60. Attractive 8-story atrium lobby, palm-filled with circular bar in center. **Rooms:** 263 rms and stes. Exec-level rms avail. CI 3pm/CO noon. Express checkout avail. Nonsmoking rms avail. Some rooms for the disabled have roll-in showers. **Amenities:** 🛏 🕭 A/C, cable TV w/movies, refrig. Some units w/minibars, all w/terraces, some w/Jacuzzis. **Services:** ✕ 🖘 🖃 🗐 Car-rental desk, masseur, babysitting. **Facilities:** 🛦 🗟 🗟 🖵 🕭 1 rst, 2 bars (1 w/entertainment), spa, whirlpool, beauty salon. **Rates:** HS Jan 16–Apr 16 $105–$160 S; $115–$170 D; from $140 ste. Extra person $10. Children under 18 stay free. Lower rates off-season. Spec packages avail. Pking: Outdoor, free. Maj CC.

≣ Rodeway Inn, 5750 E Main St, Mesa, AZ 85205; tel 602/985-3600 or toll free 800/888-3561; fax 602/832-1230. Exit Higley Rd off US 60. A no-frills suburban hotel. **Rooms:** 116 rms and stes. CI 1pm/CO 11am. Nonsmoking rms avail. Basic, comfortable rooms. **Amenities:** 🛏 A/C, cable TV. All units w/terraces. **Services:** 🖃 🗐 **Facilities:** 🛦 🗟 🖵 1 rst, 1 bar, whirlpool, washer/dryer. **Rates (CP):** HS Jan–Apr $99 S or D; from $119 ste. Extra person $5. Children under 5 stay free. Lower rates off-season. Higher rates for spec evnts/hols. Spec packages avail. Pking: Outdoor, free. Maj CC.

≣≣≣ Sheraton Mesa Hotel, 200 N Centennial Way, Mesa, AZ 85201; tel 602/898-8300; fax 602/964-9279. A large hotel in a quiet part of Mesa, featuring attractive landscaping and fountains. **Rooms:** 269 rms and stes. Exec-level rms avail. CI 3pm/CO noon. Express checkout avail. Nonsmoking rms avail. **Amenities:** 🛏 🕭 🗐 🍽 A/C, cable TV w/movies, refrig, stereo/tape player, in-rm safe. All units w/minibars. **Services:** ✕ 🖘 🖃 🗐 🍽 Babysitting. Secretarial services available. **Facilities:** 🛦 🗟 🗟 🕭 2 rsts, 1 bar (w/entertainment), spa, whirlpool. New ballroom under construction at time of inspection. **Rates:** HS Jan 1–Apr 15 $119–$139 S or D; from $175 ste. Extra person $10. Children under 18 stay free. Lower rates off-season. Spec packages avail. Pking: Outdoor, free. Maj CC.

Motel

≣≣ Days Inn, 333 W Juanita Ave, Mesa, AZ 85210; tel 602/844-8900 or toll free 800/325-2525. Country Club Dr exit off US 60. Pleasant southwestern-style lobby with plants. **Rooms:** 128 rms and stes. CI 2pm/CO noon. Express checkout avail. Nonsmoking rms avail. **Amenities:** 🛏 🕭 A/C, satel TV w/movies, refrig. **Services:** 🖃 🗐 🍽 **Facilities:** 🛦 🗟 🕭 Spa, sauna, whirlpool, washer/dryer. **Rates (CP):** HS Feb–Mar $74–$79 S or D; from $95 ste. Extra person $5. Children under 18 stay free. Lower rates off-season. Spec packages avail. Pking: Outdoor, free. Maj CC.

Resorts

≣≣≣ Arizona Golf Resort & Conference Center, 425 S Power Rd, Mesa, AZ 85206; tel 602/832-3202 or toll free 800/528-8282; fax 602/981-0151. Power Rd exit off US 60. 150 acres. A large complex set amid an 18-hole golf course. **Rooms:** 160 rms and stes. CI 4pm/CO noon. Nonsmoking rms avail. **Amenities:** 🛏 🕭 🗐 🍽 A/C, cable TV w/movies, refrig, in-rm safe. Some units w/terraces. **Services:** ✕ 🖃 🗐 🍽 **Facilities:** 🛦 🏌 ▶18 🎾 🏐2 🏊 🗟 🗟 🕭 1 rst, 1 bar, lawn games, spa, whirlpool. **Rates:** HS Jan–May $129–$150 S or D; from $169 ste. Extra person $15. Children under 12 stay free. Lower rates off-season. Higher rates for spec evnts/hols. Spec packages avail. Pking: Outdoor, free. Maj CC.

≣≣≣ Saguaro Lake Ranch Resort, 13020 Bush Hwy, Mesa, AZ 85205; tel 602/984-2194; fax 602/380-1490. 20 mi N of Mesa. Bush Hwy exit off Ariz 87. 20 acres. An older but very comfortable resort on the Salt River, a half-mile from Saguaro Lake. Built in 1927, this ranch has been a resort for over 60 years. **Rooms:** 24 rms. CI 11am/CO 2pm. Nonsmoking rms avail. Some rooms sleep as many as 8; all have a homey feel with southwestern prints on the walls, and many have Monterey furniture from the 1940s. **Amenities:** 🕭 A/C, refrig. No phone or

TV. **Services:** 🛎 Babysitting. **Facilities:** 🏠 🖪 ⛵ 🏌️ 1 rst, 1 bar, games rm, lawn games, day-care ctr, playground, washer/dryer. Also basketball, volleyball, and horseshoes. Nearby activities include hiking, rafting, bird watching, waterskiing, and horseback riding. **Rates (AP):** HS Dec 15–May 31 $110 S; $190 D. Extra person $50. Children under 6 stay free. Lower rates off-season. Higher rates for spec evnts/hols. AP and MAP rates avail. Pking: Outdoor, free. Maj CC. There are 5 B&B-style rooms in the lodge that offer the full American plan. $100 double, $85 single. Rates do not include fees for rafting or horseback riding.

Restaurants 🍴

Jade Empress, in K-mart Mall, 1840 W Broadway Rd, Mesa; tel 602/833-3577. Exit Dobson Rd off US 60. **Chinese.** Low light, lots of plants, and Chinese prints. Specialties include Cantonese barbecue, subgum chop suey, and Szechuan chicken. **FYI:** Reservations recommended. Children's menu. **Open:** Mon–Sat 11am–10pm, Sun 11:30am–9pm. Closed some hols. **Prices:** Main courses $4.50–$15. Maj CC. 🎰 🚗 💟 ♿

The Landmark, 809 W Main St, Mesa; tel 602/962-4652. At Extension Rd. **American.** Housed in a 1908 building that was formerly a Mormon church. The decor is early Americana, the cuisine is midwestern homestyle cooking. Large soup and salad bar. **FYI:** Reservations not accepted. Children's menu. No smoking. **Open:** Lunch Mon–Fri 11:30am–2pm; dinner Mon–Sat 4–9pm, Sun noon–7pm. Closed some hols. **Prices:** Main courses $11–$15. Maj CC. 🍺 ♿

Raffaele's, in Dobbs Plaza Shopping Center, 2909 S Dobson Rd, Mesa; tel 602/838-0090. **Italian.** A bright dining room, with soft colors and trompe l'oeil murals. Specialties include fettuccine Smirnoff—fettuccine topped with shallots, fresh tomatoes, basil, and vodka. Also at: 2999 N 44th St, Phoenix (602/952-0063). **FYI:** Reservations recommended. Dress code. **Open:** Lunch Mon–Fri 11:30am–3pm; dinner Sun–Thurs 5–10pm, Fri–Sat 5–11pm. Closed some hols. **Prices:** Main courses $8.95–$19.95. Maj CC. 💟 🚗 ♿

Zur Kate, in Main St Plaza Shopping Center, 4815 E Main St, Mesa; tel 602/830-4244. Between Higley and Greenfield Rds. **German.** Decorated in the style of a German inn, with steins, antlers, and German banners on the walls. Wide variety of German specialties, including homemade bratwurst. Call for holiday and summer hours. **FYI:** Reservations not accepted. **Open:** HS Sept–May Mon–Thurs 11am–8pm, Fri–Sat 11am–close. Reduced hours off-season. Closed some hols. **Prices:** Main courses $5.50–$9.25. Ltd CC. 🚗 ♿

Attractions 💼

Champlin Fighter Museum, 4636 Fighter Aces Dr; tel 602/830-4540. Aeronautical museum dedicated exclusively to fighter planes and the men who flew them. Restored aircraft from World Wars I and II, the Korean War, and the Vietnam War are on display, with a strong emphasis on the wood-and-fabric biplanes and triplanes of World War I. Also memorabilia of famous flying fighter aces. **Open:** Daily 10am–5pm. Closed some hols. $$$

Arizona Temple, 525 E Main; tel 602/964-7164. A Mormon Church completed in 1927 from a plan based on classical Greek architecture. Visitor center, flower gardens, reflecting pool, guided tours. **Open:** Daily 9am–9pm. Free.

Navajo Reservation

Map Page M-2, A3 to A4

Roughly the size of West Virginia, the Navajo Reservation covers 25,000 square miles of northeastern Arizona, as well as parts of New Mexico, Colorado, and Utah. It is the largest Native American reservation in the United States and is home to nearly 200,000 Navajo. Though there are now modern towns with supermarkets, shopping malls, and hotels on the reservation, most Navajo still follow a pastoral life-style as herders. Flocks of sheep and goats, as well as herds of cattle and horses, have free range of the reservation and often graze beside the highways. Visitors should drive with care, especially at night.

A familiar sight on the reservation are the small hexagonal buildings with rounded roofs called **hogans,** the traditional homes of the Navajo. They are usually made of wood and earth. Hogans are on display at the Canyon de Chelly and Navajo National Monument visitor centers.

The Navajo are well known for their woven rugs, silverwork, and sandpaintings. The historic **Hubbell Trading Post** (see "Attractions" under Ganado) has an excellent selection of rugs and jewelry, and the **Cameron Trading Post,** at the crossroads of Cameron where Ariz 64 branches off US 89 to Grand Canyon Village, specializes in museum-quality crafts including Navajo textiles from between 1860 and 1940.

The biggest event open to the public on the reservation is the **Navajo Nation Fair,** held in Window Rock every September featuring traditional dances, a rodeo, pow wow, parade, Miss Navajo Pageant, and arts and crafts exhibits and sales. For more information about the fair and the reservation contact the Navajoland Tourism Office at 602/871-6659.

NOGALES
Map page M-2, E3

Motels 🛏

≣≣ **Best Western Time Motel**, 921 N Grand Ave, Nogales, AZ 85621; tel 602/287-4627 or toll free 800/528-1234; fax 602/287-6949. Attractive, recently renovated motel a little over a mile from the Mexican border. **Rooms:** 43 rms. CI 10am/CO noon. Nonsmoking rms avail. Rooms are small but adequate, with relatively new furnishings. **Amenities:** 📞 A/C, cable TV. Some units w/terraces. **Services:** 🛆 ⊋ ⊲ **Facilities:** 🛗 ⬜ Whirlpool. **Rates (CP):** HS Oct 15–Apr 30 $40–$46 S or D. Extra person $3. Children under 12 stay free. Lower rates off-season. Spec packages avail. Pking: Outdoor, free. Maj CC.

≣≣ **Super 8 Motel**, 547 W Mariposa Rd, Nogales, AZ 85621; tel 602/281-2242 or toll free 800/800-8000; fax 602/281-2242 ext 400. Exit 4 off I-19. Close to shopping, this is a good choice for vacationers. **Rooms:** 117 rms and stes. CI 1pm/CO noon. Nonsmoking rms avail. **Amenities:** 📞 ⊘ A/C, cable TV w/movies. Some units w/terraces. Some rooms have refrigerators. **Services:** ✗ 🛆 ⊋ ⊲ **Facilities:** 🛗 🔟 ⬜ ⚿ 1 rst, 1 bar, whirlpool, washer/dryer. **Rates:** HS Dec–May $42–$45 S; $48 D; from $69 ste. Extra person $2. Children under 15 stay free. Lower rates off-season. Pking: Outdoor, free. Maj CC.

Restaurant 🍴

Mr C's Supper Club, 282 W View Point Dr, Nogales; tel 602/281-9000. Exit 4 off I-19. **Seafood/Steak.** Modern-looking restaurant considered by many locals to be Nogales's finest. With fresh fish prepared a variety of ways, and steak. **FYI:** Reservations recommended. Band. Children's menu. **Open:** Daily 11:30am–midnight. Closed some hols. **Prices:** Main courses $10–$25. Ltd CC. ♥ ☑ ⚿

Attractions 💼

Pimeria Alta Historical Society, 131 N Grand Ave; tel 602/287-4621. Near the border-crossing in downtown Nogales. Maintains a small museum, library, and archives on this region from southern Arizona to northern Mexico. **Open:** Tues–Sat 10am–5pm. Closed some hols. Free.

Arizona Vineyard Winery, 1830 Patagonia Hwy; tel 602/287-7972. 19th-century-style winery produces 50,000 gallons a year of white burgundy, blanc de blanc, chablis, rosé, tino tinto, haute sauterne, mountain Rhine, and worker's red. The wine,

produced in wood barrels, can be sampled in rooms filled with movie props that the owner rents out for the frequent filmings in the area. **Open:** Daily 10am–5pm. Closed Dec 25. Free.

OAK CREEK CANYON
Map page M-2, B3

Attraction 💼

Slide Rock State Park, Ariz 179; tel 602/282-3034. Located 7 miles north of Sedona on the site of an old homestead, this park preserves a natural water slide. A popular location for swimming and fishing. **Open:** Daily sunrise–sunset. $

ORACLE
Map page M-2, D3 (NE of Tucson)

Attraction 💼

Biosphere 2, Ariz 77, MM 96.5; tel 602/825-6400. On September 26, 1991, 4 men and 4 women were sealed inside a large and elaborate greenhouse to begin the first 2-year stint of what will be a 100-year experiment to attain a better understanding of the human role in the future of the planet. More than 4,000 species of plants and animals are part of the experiment, which includes a rain forest, desert, savannah, marsh, and even a tiny "ocean" complete with waves and tides. Facilities open to visitors include the orientation center, Biofair, test module, research and development center, and Biospherian Theater. Visitors cannot enter Biosphere 2. Arrive before 2pm to have time to see all exhibits. Cafe and snackbar. **Open:** Daily 9am–5pm. Closed Dec 25. $$$$

ORGAN PIPE CACTUS NATIONAL MONUMENT
Map page M-2, E2

Located 70 miles south of Gila Bend on Ariz 5. A preserve for the rare organ pipe cactus and the plants and animals of the Sonoran Desert. The massive cactus forms many trunks, some 20 feet tall, that resemble organ pipes. It grows on south-facing slopes where it can absorb the most sun, and blooms in May, June, and July, showing its lavender and white flowers only at night.

Two scenic loop roads allow visitors to drive through the monument. The 21-mile **Ajo Mountain Drive** winds along the foothills of the Ajo Mountains, the highest range in the area. Desert landscapes and large groups of organ pipe cactus are among the highlights of this 2-hour tour. The 53-mile **Puerto Blanco Drive** circles the colorful Puerto Blanco Mountains and passes **Quitobaquito Spring,** upon which Native Americans and pioneers once relied for the only source of water for miles around; the trip takes half a day. For more information contact the park information office, open daily 8am–5pm, at 602/387-6849.

PAGE

Map page M-2, A3

Hotel 🛏

Inn at Lake Powell, 716 Rim View Dr, PO Box C, Page, AZ 86040; tel 602/645-2466 or toll free 800/826-2718. Rim View Dr exit off Lake Powell Blvd, ¾ mi E of US 89. Situated on a hilltop overlooking Lake Powell and Glen Canyon Dam. **Rooms:** 103 rms and stes. CI 3pm/CO noon. Nonsmoking rms avail. Half the rooms have views. **Amenities:** A/C, cable TV w/movies. **Services:** **Facilities:** 1 rst, 1 bar, whirlpool. Parking for RVs is available. **Rates:** HS May–Sept $69–$92 S or D; from $125 ste. Extra person $10. Children under 18 stay free. Lower rates off-season. Pking: Outdoor, free. Maj CC.

Motels

Best Western Weston Inn, 201 N Lake Powell Blvd, Page, AZ 86040; tel 602/645-2451 or toll free 800/637-9183. Page exit off US 89A. Located on a hill overlooking spectacular Glen Canyon Dam and Lake Powell. **Rooms:** 90 rms. CI 2pm/CO 11am. Nonsmoking rms avail. Some rooms have views of the lake. **Amenities:** A/C, cable TV w/movies. Some units w/terraces. **Services:** **Facilities:** Washer/dryer. A golf course is 2 miles away, Lake Powell is 6 miles away, and shopping centers are within 2 blocks. **Rates (CP):** HS Apr–Oct $63 S; $76–$81 D. Extra person $5. Children under 12 stay free. Lower rates off-season. Pking: Outdoor, free. Maj CC.

Lake Powell Motel, US 89, PO Box 1597, Page, AZ 86040; tel 602/645-2477 or toll free 800/528-6154; fax 602/331-5258. 4 mi N of Glen Canyon Dam. Great views of Lake Powell from this motel set high on a hill away from Page and the marinas. **Rooms:** 25 rms. CI 3pm/CO 11am. Nonsmoking rms avail. All rooms have sliding glass doors giving access to lawn furniture out front. **Amenities:** A/C, cable TV. **Services:**

Rates: HS Apr–Oct $66 S or D. Extra person $6. Children under 18 stay free. Lower rates off-season. Pking: Outdoor, free. Maj CC.

Lodge

Wahweap Lodge, Lakeshore Dr, PO Box 1597, Page, AZ 86040; tel 602/645-2433 or toll free 800/528-6154. Lake Shore Dr exit off US 89. 4 mi N of Glen Canyon Dam. This large lodge is located at a marina on the shores of Lake Powell. **Rooms:** 375 rms and stes. CI 3pm/CO 11am. Express checkout avail. Nonsmoking rms avail. **Amenities:** A/C, cable TV w/movies. Some units w/terraces. **Services:** **Facilities:** 2 rsts (see also "Restaurants" below), 1 bar, whirlpool. Full boating facilities are available. **Rates:** HS Apr–Oct $83–$100 S or D; from $165 ste. Extra person $9. Children under 18 stay free. Lower rates off-season. Spec packages avail. Pking: Outdoor, free. Maj CC.

Restaurants 🍴

M Bar H Cafe, in Bar H Mercantile Center, 819 N Navajo Dr, Page; tel 602/645-1420. **American.** A simple cafe done in a western motif, with deer heads and mounted ducks on the walls. That famous western specialty, chicken-fried steak with mashed potatoes, gets top billing here. Homemade pies. **FYI:** Reservations accepted. Beer and wine only. **Open:** HS Apr–Oct daily 5am–11pm. Reduced hours off-season. Closed Dec 25. **Prices:** Main courses $7.65–$11.95. Ltd CC.

Rainbow Room, in the Wahweap Lodge, Lakeshore Dr, Page; tel 602/645-2433 ext 1017. 5 mi N of Page. Lake Shore Dr exit off US 89. **Southwestern.** Sweeping, panoramic views of Lake Powell are visible through the curved glass wall of the dining room. Varied seafood and beef dishes offered. **FYI:** Reservations not accepted. Guitar. Children's menu. No smoking. **Open:** HS May 15–Oct 15 breakfast daily 6–11am; lunch daily 11am–3pm; dinner daily 5–10pm. Reduced hours off-season. **Prices:** Main courses $10–$25. Maj CC.

Attractions 💼

Glen Canyon National Recreation Area, US 89; tel 602/645-2471. One of the nation's most popular national recreation areas. Lake Powell, a manmade lake, is the main attraction, set amid the slick-rock canyons of northern Arizona and southern Utah. It is more than 500 feet deep in some places and bounded by more than 2,000 miles of shoreline. Few roads penetrate the recreation area, so the only way to appreciate this rugged region is by boat; bring your own or rent one here. Houseboats, waterskiing, jet skiing, fishing, and camping. For more information write: PO Box 1507, Page, AZ 86040. **Open:** Daily 24 hours. Free.

Rainbow Bridge National Monument, Glen Canyon National Recreation Area, off US 89; tel 602/645-2471. The world's largest natural bridge, this sandstone arch stands 290 feet high and spans 275 feet, a product of the powerful erosion that has sculpted the entire region. Located 50 miles from Glen Canyon Dam; accessible only by boat or on foot. **Open:** Daily 24 hours. Free.

PARKER

Map page M-2, C1

Resort 🏨

≣≣ **Havasu Springs Resort**, Rte 2, PO Box 624, Parker, AZ 85344; tel 602/667-3361. 16 mi S of Lake Havasu City. There's a small motel in this resort at the south end of Lake Havasu, augmented by an RV park and houseboat rentals. **Rooms:** 44 rms and stes. CI 2pm/CO 11am. Some rooms have kitchenettes and half have lake views. **Amenities:** 🛁 A/C, satel TV w/movies. **Services:** 🐕 **Facilities:** 🛗 ⛰ 🗑 ▶₉ 🛥 🛶 ₂₅₀ 1 rst, 2 bars, 1 beach (lake shore), games rm, washer/dryer. Full marina services are available. Barbecues and picnic tables are close by. **Rates:** HS Apr–Oct $70–$80 S or D; from $90 ste. Extra person $5. Children under 3 stay free. Lower rates off-season. Pking: Outdoor, free. Ltd CC.

Attraction 💼

Colorado River Indian Tribes Museum and Library, 2nd Ave and Mohave Rd; tel 602/669-9211. Permanent and changing exhibits explain the history of the 4 tribes of the Colorado River area—the Mohave, the Chemehuevi, the Navajo, and the Hopi. Also on display are works by local artists, and Native American baskets and pottery. **Open:** Mon–Fri 8am–5pm, Sat 10am–3pm. Closed some hols. Free.

PATAGONIA

Map page M-2, E3

Motel 🏨

≣≣ **Stage Stop Motel**, 303 McKeown Ave, PO Box 777, Patagonia, AZ 85624; tel 602/394-2211. 18 mi N of Nogales. A comfortable motel, the only lodging available in Patagonia, a quiet town with several art galleries. The nearby Patagonia-Sonoita Creek Preserve, run by the Arizona chapter of the Nature Conservancy, is great for birdwatching. **Rooms:** 43 rms, stes, and effic. CI 2pm/CO noon. Express checkout avail. Rooms have sliding glass doors. **Amenities:** 🛁 A/C, cable TV, voice mail. Some units w/terraces. **Services:** ✗ VP 🐕 🐕 **Facilities:** 🛗 ₅₀ 1 rst, 1 bar, washer/dryer. **Rates:** $40–$50 S or D; from $80 ste; from $60 effic. Extra person $10. Children under 5 stay free. Spec packages avail. Pking: Outdoor, free. Maj CC.

Attraction 💼

Patagonia-Sonoita Creek Preserve, along Ariz 82; tel 602/394-2400. A nature preserve owned by the Nature Conservancy that protects a mile and a half of Sonoita Creek riparian (riverside) habitat. More than 250 species of birds have been spotted on the preserve, making it a popular spot for bird watchers. Among the rare birds that may be seen here are 22 species of flycatchers, kingbirds, and phoebes, and the Montezuma quail. Free.

PAYSON

Map page M-2, C3

Motels 🏨

≣≣ **Best Western Paysonglo Lodge**, 1005 S Beeline Hwy, Payson, AZ 85541; tel 602/474-2382 or toll free 800/772-9766, 800/872-9766 in AZ; fax 602/474-1937. 1 mi S of intersection with Ariz 260. Pleasant motel catering to senior citizens; strictly enforced quiet hours. **Rooms:** 39 rms. CI 3pm/CO noon. Nonsmoking rms avail. **Amenities:** 🛁 🐕 A/C, cable TV, refrig. Some units w/fireplaces. **Services:** 🐕 **Facilities:** 🛗 ⚲ Whirlpool, washer/dryer. **Rates (CP):** HS Apr–Oct $58–$108 S; $68–$108 D. Children under 18 stay free. Min stay spec evnts. Lower rates off-season. Higher rates for spec evnts/hols. Pking: Outdoor, free. Maj CC. Senior discount.

≣≣≣ **Majestic Mountain Inn**, 602 E Ariz 260, Payson, AZ 85541; tel 602/474-0185 or toll free 800/408-2442. Ariz 260 exit off Ariz 87. Opened in late 1993. One of the nicest in Payson. **Rooms:** 37 rms. CI 1pm/CO 11am. Nonsmoking rms avail. **Amenities:** 🛁 🐕 📺 A/C, cable TV w/movies, refrig, stereo/tape player. Some units w/terraces, some w/fireplaces, some w/Jacuzzis. Coffee cups and glasses are furnished in all rooms, and luxury rooms have VCR and hot tubs. **Services:** 🚐 🐕 🐕 **Facilities:** ⚲ **Rates:** HS May–Sept $52–$130 S or D. Extra person $6. Min stay spec evnts. Lower rates off-season. Higher rates for spec evnts/hols. Pking: Outdoor, free. Maj CC.

≣≣ **Payson Pueblo Inn**, 809 E Ariz 260, Payson, AZ 85541; tel 602/474-5241 or toll free 800/888-9828. 1 mi E of intersection of Ariz 87 and Ariz 260. A modern pueblo-style motel, which is being expanded to include 6 suites with fireplaces and hot tubs. **Rooms:** 39 rms and stes. CI noon/CO 11am. Nonsmoking rms avail. Three of the suites have skylights over the hot tubs. **Amenities:** 📞 🐕 A/C, cable TV w/movies, refrig. Some units w/fireplaces, some w/Jacuzzis. Suites have coffeemakers, wet bars, and microwave ovens. **Services:** 🛎 Free local calls. **Facilities:** 🖥 🔥 **Rates:** HS May–Sept $39–$54 S; $44–$54 D; from $75 ste. Extra person $5. Children under 3 stay free. Min stay wknds. Lower rates off-season. Higher rates for spec evnts/hols. Pking: Outdoor, free. Maj CC.

Resort

≣≣≣ **Kohl's Ranch Resort**, E Ariz 260, Payson, AZ 85541; tel 602/478-4211 or toll free 800/331-5645 in AZ. 17 mi E of Payson. 12 acres. A lovely mountain resort on the banks of a stream. **Rooms:** 41 rms; 8 ctges/villas. CI 4pm/CO 11am. Nonsmoking rms avail. There are rooms in the main lodge, and 1- and 2-bedroom cabins, which sleep 4 to 6 adults. All cabins have full kitchens and a deck overlooking the stream. **Amenities:** 📞 A/C, cable TV. Some units w/terraces, some w/fireplaces. All cabins have fireplaces. **Services:** ✕ 🛎 🏌 **Facilities:** 🏌🚣🔥🎿🏊 🔟 1 rst, 2 bars (1 w/entertainment), games rm, sauna. **Rates:** HS Mid-May–mid-Oct $65–$95 S; $75–$105 D; from $140 ctge/villa. Extra person $5. Children under 12 stay free. Min stay spec evnts. Lower rates off-season. Spec packages avail. Pking: Outdoor, free. Maj CC. Specialized corporate retreats are offered.

Restaurants 🍴

Heritage House Garden Tea Room, 202 W Main St, Payson; tel 602/474-5501. **American.** Sandwich shop located inside a crafts and gift store. Wooden tables and chairs, lots of plants, and an old jukebox in the center of the room. Serving soups, salads, sandwiches, and desserts. **FYI:** Reservations accepted. No liquor license. **Open:** HS May–Oct Mon–Sat 11am–3pm. Reduced hours off-season. Closed some hols. **Prices:** Lunch main courses $4.50–$5.25. Ltd CC. 👥 🔥

The Oaks Restaurant, 302 W Main St, Payson; tel 602/474-1929. **American.** A cozy, comfortable restaurant with an early American look: wainscoted walls, patterned curtains, hurricane lamps, and a brick fireplace. The basic American menu includes prime rib, broiled salmon filets, lamb chops, roast cornish game hens, and a fresh vegetable platter. **FYI:** Reservations recommended. Children's menu. **Open:** HS May–Oct lunch Tues–Sun 11am–2pm; dinner Sun–Thurs 5–8pm, Fri–Sat

5–9pm; brunch Sun 11am–2pm. Reduced hours off-season. Closed Dec 25. **Prices:** Main courses $10.25–$14.95. Maj CC. 📷 🔥

Attraction 🏛

Tonto Natural Bridge State Park, Ariz 87; tel 602/476-4202. Located 15 miles north of Payson. The largest natural travertine bridge in the world. Discovered in 1877 by gold prospector David Gowan, who was being chased by Apaches, the bridge is 183 feet high and 150 feet across. There is also a restored historic lodge built in 1927 by Gowan's nephew. **Open:** Apr–Oct, daily 8am–6pm, Nov–Mar, daily 9am–5pm. Closed Dec 25. $

PEACH SPRINGS
Map page M-2, B2

Motel 🛏

≣≣ **Grand Canyon Caverns Inn and Campground**, Ariz 66, PO Box 180, Peach Springs, AZ 86434; tel 602/422-3223. 20 mi W of Seligman. A rustic motel on old Route 66, halfway between Kingman and Seligman. The limestone Grand Canyon Caverns, located on the property, are the largest dry caverns in the United States. **Rooms:** 48 rms. CI 4pm/CO 11am. Nonsmoking rms avail. Quaint rooms are partially pine-panelled and contain decorative rock collections under glass. **Amenities:** 📞 A/C, satel TV. Some rooms have rollout beds. **Services:** 🚗 🏌 Guided tours of the caverns are available for a fee. **Facilities:** 🔟 🔥 1 rst, games rm, playground, washer/dryer. Picnic tables, barbecues, and a landing strip for small planes are on the premises; a gift shop and cafeteria are at the caverns. **Rates:** HS Feb–Nov $34 S; $40 D. Extra person $3. Lower rates off-season. Spec packages avail. Pking: Outdoor, free. Ltd CC. American Plan available at certain times of the year.

PHOENIX
Map page M-2, C2

See also **Carefree, Chandler, Glendale, Mesa, Scottsdale, Tempe**

TOURIST INFORMATION
Phoenix and Valley of the Sun Convention and Visitors Bureau 505 N 2nd St, on the northwest corner of Adams and 2nd Sts (tel 602/254-6500). Open Mon–Fri 8am–5pm.

The **Information Hotline** (tel 602/252-5588) has recorded information about Phoenix 24 hours a day.

Also see "Tourist Information" on page 18.

PUBLIC TRANSPORTATION

Downtown Area Shuttle (DASH) Operates Mon–Fri 6:30am–6pm. Runs every 5–10 minutes and makes regular stops. Attractions along route include state capitol, visitors information center, Museum of Science and Technology, Heritage Square, and Arizona Center. Fare 25¢. For information call 602/253-5000.

Hotels

≡≡≡ Courtyard by Marriott, 9631 N Black Canyon Fwy, Phoenix, AZ 85021 (Metrocenter); tel 602/944-7373 or toll free 800/321-2211; fax 602/944-0079. This is a good choice for corporate travelers, close to many Phoenix high-tech companies and just off I-17. **Rooms:** 146 rms and stes. CI 3pm/CO 1pm. Express checkout avail. Nonsmoking rms avail. **Amenities:** A/C, cable TV w/movies. Some units w/terraces. Suites have refrigerators. **Services:** Babysitting. **Facilities:** 1 rst, 1 bar, whirlpool, washer/dryer. **Rates:** HS Jan–Apr $98–$108 S or D; from $108 ste. Extra person $10. Children under 18 stay free. Lower rates off-season. Pking: Outdoor, free. Maj CC.

≡≡≡ The Crescent Hotel, 2620 W Dunlap Ave, Phoenix, AZ 85021 (Metrocenter); tel 602/943-8200 or toll free 800/423-4126; fax 602/371-2856. Dunlap exit off I-17. A luxurious hotel, with particularly attractive public areas. There's a lovely fountain in the lobby, and outside dining under a tent. **Rooms:** 342 rms and stes. CI 3pm/CO noon. Express checkout avail. Nonsmoking rms avail. Rooms are large and well furnished. **Amenities:** A/C, satel TV, refrig, in-rm safe, bathrobes. All units w/minibars, all w/terraces, some w/Jacuzzis. **Services:** Social director, masseur, babysitting. **Facilities:** 1 rst, 2 bars (1 w/entertainment), lawn games, racquetball, squash, spa, sauna, steam rm, whirlpool. Excellent recreational facilities. **Rates:** HS Oct–Apr $119–$135 S; $119–$175 D; from $190 ste. Extra person $15. Children under 18 stay free. Lower rates off-season. Higher rates for spec evnts/hols. Spec packages avail. Pking: Outdoor, free. Maj CC. A good value considering features and amenities.

≡≡≡ Crown Sterling Suites, 2630 E Camelback Rd, Phoenix, AZ 85016 (Biltmore); tel 602/955-3992 or toll free 800/433-4600. Good location in Phoenix's upscale shopping center,

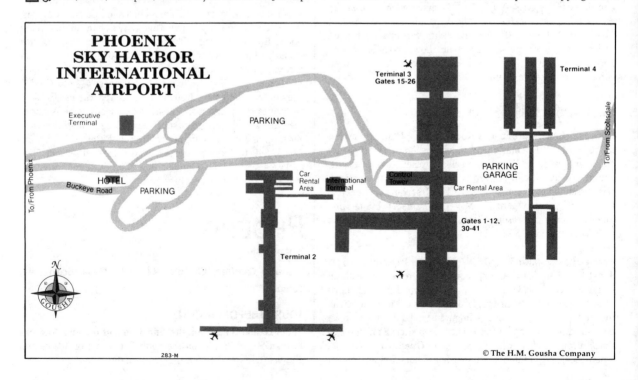

PHOENIX SKY HARBOR INTERNATIONAL AIRPORT

283-M

© The H.M. Gousha Company

Biltmore Fashion Park. Perfect for those who wish to shop in the Park's clothing stores and bookstores or dine in one of the numerous fine restaurants. The 5-story atrium lobby has huge fish ponds with large fish, and a piano bar. **Rooms:** 232 stes. CI 3pm/CO noon. Express checkout avail. Nonsmoking rms avail. Rooms are attractively furnished and very comfortable. **Amenities:** 🛁 👓 📺 A/C, satel TV w/movies, refrig. All units w/minibars, some w/terraces. **Services:** ✕ 🍴 🖼 🛏 🚶 Masseur, children's program, babysitting. Complimentary full breakfast and cocktails. **Facilities:** 🏊 320 🖥 👤 1 rst, 1 bar (w/entertainment), whirlpool. 70 stores and 10 restaurants in Biltmore Fashion Park. **Rates (BB):** HS Jan 3–May 26 from $195 ste. Extra person $10. Children under 12 stay free. Lower rates off-season. Spec packages avail. Pking: Outdoor, free. Maj CC.

▤▤ Fairfield Inn, 1241 N 53rd Ave, Phoenix, AZ 85043; tel 602/269-1919 or toll free 800/228-2800; fax 602/269-1919. 51st Ave exit off I-10. Conveniently located, with easy freeway access. **Rooms:** 126 rms. CI 3pm/CO noon. Nonsmoking rms avail. All rooms have coded key-cards for security. **Amenities:** 🛁 👓 A/C, cable TV w/movies. **Services:** 🖼 🚶 **Facilities:** 🏊 12 👤 **Rates (CP):** HS Jan–mid-Apr $60 S or D. Extra person $3–$6. Children under 18 stay free. Lower rates off-season. Pking: Outdoor, free. Maj CC.

▤▤ Fountain Suites, 2577 W Greenway Rd, Phoenix, AZ 85023 (Metrocenter); tel 602/375-1777 or toll free 800/338-1338; fax 602/375-1777 ext 5555. Greenway Rd off I-17. Spectacular landscaping. Large, airy lobby with lots of light. **Rooms:** 314 stes. CI 3pm/CO noon. Express checkout avail. Nonsmoking rms avail. The spacious, well-appointed rooms are a comfortable place to spend several days. **Amenities:** 🛁 🍴 A/C, cable TV w/movies, refrig, voice mail. All units w/minibars, some w/Jacuzzis. **Services:** ✕ 🚗 🖼 🚶 🛎 Car-rental desk, masseur, children's program. **Facilities:** 🏊 🎾 🚴 300 🖥 👤 1 rst, 3 bars (1 w/entertainment), lawn games, racquetball, sauna, whirlpool, washer/dryer. Close to golf courses and horse racing. There's a very pleasant lounging area around the pool. **Rates:** HS Jan–Apr from $75 ste. Lower rates off-season. Higher rates for spec evnts/hols. Spec packages avail. Pking: Outdoor, free. Maj CC.

▤▤ Hampton Inn Airport, 4234 S 48th St, Phoenix, AZ 85040; tel 602/428-8688 or toll free 800/HAMPTON; fax 602/431-8339. Exit 48th St off I-10. Easy airport access, good for business travelers. **Rooms:** 128 rms and stes. CI 3pm/CO noon. Nonsmoking rms avail. All rooms have video players. **Amenities:** 🛁 👓 A/C, satel TV, VCR. **Services:** ✕ 🚗 🖼 🚶 🛎 Free local calls and newspapers. **Facilities:** 🏊 🚴 50 🖥 👤 1 rst, 1 bar, spa, whirlpool, washer/dryer. **Rates (CP):** HS Dec–

Apr $79–$89 S or D; from $109 ste. Extra person $10. Children under 18 stay free. Lower rates off-season. Pking: Outdoor, free. Maj CC.

▤▤▤ Holiday Inn, 1500 N 51st Ave, Phoenix, AZ 85043; tel 602/484-9009 or toll free 800/HOLIDAY; fax 602/484-9009 ext 505. 51st Ave exit off I-10. Conveniently located. Attractive atrium in the lobby. **Rooms:** 144 rms and stes. CI 2pm/CO noon. Express checkout avail. Nonsmoking rms avail. **Amenities:** 🛁 👓 🍴 A/C, satel TV w/movies. Some units w/minibars, some w/Jacuzzis. **Services:** ✕ 🖼 🚶 🛎 **Facilities:** 🏊 🚴 250 🖥 👤 1 rst, 1 bar, sauna, whirlpool. **Rates:** HS Jan–Apr $139 S; $149 D; from $150 ste. Extra person $10. Children under 18 stay free. Lower rates off-season. Spec packages avail. Pking: Outdoor, free. Maj CC. Group rates are available.

▤▤▤ Holiday Inn Crowne Plaza, 111 N Central Ave, Phoenix, AZ 85004 (Downtown); tel 602/257-1525 or toll free 800/HOLIDAY; fax 602/253-9755. In the heart of downtown Phoenix, popular with convention attendees and corporate travelers. **Rooms:** 532 rms and stes. Exec-level rms avail. CI 4pm/CO noon. Nonsmoking rms avail. **Amenities:** 🛁 👓 A/C, satel TV w/movies. Some units w/minibars, some w/terraces. **Services:** ✕ 🍴 VP 🚗 🖼 🚶 🛎 Car-rental desk. **Facilities:** 🏊 🚴 1.5K 🖥 👤 3 rsts, 2 bars, spa, sauna, beauty salon. Conveniently located for sports facilities. **Rates:** HS Nov–May $129 S or D; from $149 ste. Extra person $10. Children under 12 stay free. Lower rates off-season. Spec packages avail. Pking: Indoor, $6. Maj CC.

▤▤▤ Hotel Westcourt, 10220 N Metro Pkwy E, Phoenix, AZ 85021 (Metrocenter); tel 602/997-5900 or toll free 800/858-1033. Peoria Ave exit off I-17. Convenient to the freeway and Metrocenter shopping center, with 200 stores, 37 restaurants, and 17 theaters. **Rooms:** 300 rms and stes. Exec-level rms avail. CI 3pm/CO noon. Express checkout avail. Nonsmoking rms avail. **Amenities:** 🛁 👓 📺 🍴 A/C, satel TV w/movies, refrig, voice mail. Some units w/terraces. **Services:** ✕ 🍴 🚗 🖼 🚶 Car-rental desk, babysitting. **Facilities:** 🏊 🎾 🚴 500 🖥 👤 1 rst, 1 bar, spa, sauna, whirlpool. Golf nearby. **Rates:** HS Jan–Apr $125 S; $135 D; from $250 ste. Extra person $10. Children under 12 stay free. Lower rates off-season. Spec packages avail. Pking: Outdoor, free. Maj CC.

▤▤▤ Hyatt Regency Phoenix at Civic Plaza, 122 N 2nd St, Phoenix, AZ 85004 (Downtown); tel 602/252-1234 or toll free 800/223-1234; fax 602/254-9472. Popular with convention and business travelers, this Hyatt Regency claims to be the largest hotel in Arizona. **Rooms:** 712 rms and stes. Exec-level rms avail. CI 3pm/CO noon. Express checkout avail. Nonsmoking rms avail. **Amenities:** 🛁 👓 📺 🍴 A/C, satel TV w/movies, voice mail. Some units w/minibars, some w/terraces. **Services:**

X ⌨ VP 🚗 🛄 ⟲ Car-rental desk, babysitting. **Facilities:** ⛱
♨ 1.5K 💻 ♿ 2 rsts, 2 bars, spa, whirlpool, beauty salon. The Compass Rose is a rooftop, revolving restaurant. The hotel is close to golf, tennis, and horseback riding. **Rates:** HS Jan–Apr $175 S; $200 D; from $350 ste. Extra person $25. Children under 18 stay free. Lower rates off-season. Spec packages avail. Pking: Indoor, $6. Maj CC.

≡≡≡ **InnSuites Phoenix Best Western**, 1615 E Northern Ave, Phoenix, AZ 85020; tel 602/997-6285 or toll free 800/752-2204; fax 602/943-1407. ¾ mi N of Glendale Ave. A lovely property nestled in Phoenix's Squaw Peak Mountain Preserve resort area. **Rooms:** 123 rms and stes. CI 2pm/CO noon. Express checkout avail. Nonsmoking rms avail. There are standard rooms, studio suites, and 2-room suites available. **Amenities:** 🛁 🅰 🖥 🍴 A/C, satel TV w/movies, refrig. Some units w/Jacuzzis. All units have microwaves, free juices, and in-room coffee, tea, and microwave popcorn. King rooms have sofa sleepers. **Services:** ⌨ 🚗 🛄 ⟲ 🍽 There's a complimentary deluxe continental breakfast, complimentary cocktails daily from 5pm to 6:30pm, and complimentary newspapers. Local calls are free, as is fax service within the United States. 24-hour front desk. **Facilities:** ⛱ ♨ 100 ♿ Whirlpool, playground, washer/dryer. There's a barbecue on site. **Rates (CP):** HS Jan 1–Apr 16 $75–$89 S or D; from $95 ste. Children under 18 stay free. Lower rates off-season. Spec packages avail. Pking: Outdoor, free. Maj CC.

≡≡≡ **Lexington Hotel and City Square Sports Club**, 100 W Clarendon Ave, Phoenix, AZ 85013; tel 602/279-9811 or toll free 800/272-2439; fax 602/631-9358. Exit 7th St off I-10. This midtown property is within walking distance of museums and other attractions. **Rooms:** 180 rms. CI 3pm/CO 11am. Nonsmoking rms avail. **Amenities:** 🛁 🅰 A/C, cable TV, refrig. Some units w/minibars, some w/terraces. **Services:** X VP 🚗 🛄 ⟲ 🍽 Masseur. **Facilities:** ⛱ ♨ 300 1 rst, 1 bar, racquetball, spa, sauna, steam rm, whirlpool, beauty salon. Use of adjacent health club included in rates. **Rates:** HS Mid-Jan–Apr $109 S or D. Extra person $7. Children under 18 stay free. Lower rates off-season. Pking: Indoor, free. Maj CC.

≡≡≡ **Marriott Residence Inn**, 8242 N Black Canyon Fwy, Phoenix, AZ 85051 (Metrocenter); tel 602/864-1900 or toll free 800/331-3131. Dunlap Ave exit off I-17. Good freeway access. Popular for extended stays. **Rooms:** 128 stes. CI 3pm/CO noon. Nonsmoking rms avail. All suites have full-sized kitchens with appliances. **Amenities:** 🛁 🅰 A/C, cable TV w/movies, refrig. Some units w/terraces, some w/fireplaces. VCR rentals available. **Services:** 🛄 ⟲ 🍽 Hospitality hour (Monday–Thursday) with soft drinks, beer, wine, and snacks. **Facilities:** ⛱🅰🎾 ♨ 20 💻 ♿ Lawn games, spa, whirlpool, washer/dryer. Basketball and

tennis available on a "sports court." **Rates (CP):** HS Jan–Apr from $159 ste. Children under 18 stay free. Lower rates off-season. Higher rates for spec evnts/hols. Pking: Outdoor, free. Maj CC.

≡≡≡ **Phoenix Hilton Suites**, 10 E Thomas Rd, Phoenix, AZ 85012; tel 602/222-1111 or toll free 800/445-8667; fax 602/265-4811. Exit 7th St N off I-10. An all-suite hotel, especially attractive to business travelers. **Rooms:** 226 stes. Exec-level rms avail. CI 3pm/CO noon. Express checkout avail. Nonsmoking rms avail. All rooms have sofabeds and dining tables. Seven rooms are being converted for the sight/hearing impaired. **Amenities:** 🛁 🅰 🖥 A/C, cable TV w/movies, refrig, VCR, voice mail. Some units w/terraces. All units have microwave ovens. **Services:** X ⌨ 🚗 🛄 ⟲ Children's program, babysitting. Free photocopier, personal computer, and fax services within the United States. Complimentary beverage hour nightly and full breakfast. **Facilities:** ⛱ ♨ 100 💻 ♿ 1 rst, 1 bar, spa, sauna, whirlpool, washer/dryer. **Rates (BB):** HS Jan–May from $174 ste. Extra person $15. Children under 18 stay free. Lower rates off-season. Spec packages avail. Pking: Indoor, free. Maj CC. Children stay free with parents.

≡≡ **Premier Inn**, 10402 Black Canyon Fwy, Phoenix, AZ 85051 (Metrocenter); tel 602/943-2371 or toll free 800/786-6835; fax 602/943-5847. Peoria exit off I-17. A good choice for those who like to shop, located in one of the Southwest's largest malls. Also close to almost 40 restaurants and several golf courses. **Rooms:** 253 rms and stes. CI 3pm/CO noon. Nonsmoking rms avail. Rooms are clean, comfortable, and spacious. **Amenities:** 🛁 A/C, satel TV. Some units w/terraces. Special business traveler rooms have extra-large work areas, refrigerators, and coffeemakers. **Services:** ⟲ 🍽 **Facilities:** ⛱ 🎿 ♨ 25 Whirlpool, washer/dryer. **Rates:** HS Mid-Jan–mid-Apr $54–$67 S or D; from $100 ste. Lower rates off-season. Pking: Outdoor, free. Maj CC.

≡≡ **Quality Inn South Mountain**, 5121 E LaPuente Ave, Phoenix, AZ 85044; tel 602/893-3900 or toll free 800/562-3332; fax 602/496-0815. Elliot Rd exit off I-10. Comfortable and quiet, with good freeway access. Close to the airport, Tempe, and Mesa. **Rooms:** 193 rms and stes. CI 3pm/CO noon. Nonsmoking rms avail. **Amenities:** 🛁 🅰 A/C, cable TV w/movies. Some units w/minibars. Microwaves and refrigerators are available. **Services:** X 🛄 ⟲ 🍽 **Facilities:** ⛱ 175 ♿ 1 rst, 1 bar, whirlpool, washer/dryer. There are 5 golf courses within 5 miles. **Rates:** HS Dec–Apr $89 S; $99 D; from $119 ste. Extra person $5. Children under 16 stay free. Lower rates off-season. Pking: Outdoor, free. Maj CC. Discounts available for seniors and tours.

▇▇▇ **Radisson Hotel–Midtown**, 401 W Clarendon Ave, Phoenix, AZ 85013; tel 602/234-2464 or toll free 800/527-3467. This is an older midtown hotel with a small but attractive lobby. **Rooms:** 106 rms and stes. CI 3pm/CO noon. Nonsmoking rms avail. **Amenities:** 🕾 👁 A/C, cable TV. All 37 suites have 2 telephones, 2 TVs, and a stocked minibar. **Services:** ✗ 🚗 🖼 🗘 **Facilities:** 🖪 73 1 rst, 1 bar, whirlpool. **Rates (CP):** HS Mid-Jan–Apr $110 S or D; from $125 ste. Extra person $10. Children under 17 stay free. Lower rates off-season. Spec packages avail. Pking: Outdoor, free. Maj CC.

▇▇ **Ramada Hotel Downtown**, 401 N First St, Phoenix, AZ 85004; tel 602/258-3411 or toll free 800/272-6232; fax 602/258-3171. Downtown hotel with good access to the convention center, Symphony Hall, and America West Arena. **Rooms:** 160 rms and stes. CI 3pm/CO noon. Nonsmoking rms avail. Some rooms have a view of the pool. **Amenities:** 🕾 A/C, cable TV. Some units w/terraces. **Services:** ✗ 🖼 🗘 **Facilities:** 🖪 300 👍 1 rst, 1 bar (w/entertainment). **Rates:** HS Jan 15–Apr 15 $79–$105 S or D. Extra person $10. Children under 18 stay free. Lower rates off-season. Higher rates for spec evnts/hols. Spec packages avail. Pking: Outdoor, free. Maj CC.

▇▇▇▇ **The Ritz-Carlton Phoenix**, 2401 E Camelback Rd, Phoenix, AZ 85016 (Biltmore Fashion Park); tel 602/468-0700 or toll free 800/241-3333; fax 602/468-9883. From I-17 take Camelback exit and go east to Biltmore Fashion Park. In a city of resort hotels, this is 11 floors of no-nonsense, businesslike luxury, with only a pool, fitness center, and 1 tennis court. Close to major new commercial center. **Rooms:** 281 rms and stes. Exec-level rms avail. CI 3pm/CO noon. Express checkout avail. Nonsmoking rms avail. All the usual Ritz-Carlton refinements, including Italian marble bathrooms; but even in a climate where temperatures climb over 100°F, many guests might prefer windows that can be opened. **Amenities:** 🕾 👁 🍽 A/C, cable TV w/movies, refrig, in-rm safe, bathrobes. All units w/minibars, 1 w/Jacuzzi. Small 9-hanger closets, dataports, and 3 phones indicate that most guests are executives on overnight stays. Rosenthal china for room service. **Services:** 🍽 🗝 VP 🚗 🖼 🗘 🖐 Twice-daily maid svce, masseur, babysitting. Smart, efficient, obliging staff. **Facilities:** 🖪 🚲 🏊 🎾 700 🖳 👍 3 rsts (*see also* "Restaurants" below), 2 bars (1 w/entertainment), lifeguard, sauna. 2nd-floor sports roof with attractive pool, and poolside service; sun deck cooled by misting system. Complimentary transportation to nearby golf courses. Dancing with dinner in elegant Grill Room. **Rates:** HS Sept 5–May 27 $70–$195 S or D; from $250 ste. Children under 18 stay free. Lower rates off-season. Spec packages avail. Pking: Indoor, $9.50. Maj CC. A bargain compared with the nearby resorts, and summer rates give everyone a chance to sample Ritz-Carlton swank for just $95 double.

Motels

▇▇ **Hampton Inn**, 8101 N Black Canyon Hwy, Phoenix, AZ 85021; tel 602/864-6233 or toll free 800/HAMPTON; fax 602/995-7503. Northern Ave exit off I-17. A step above the average basic motel, this is a good choice for family vacationers. **Rooms:** 149 rms. CI 3pm/CO noon. Nonsmoking rms avail. Rooms are pleasant, comfortable, and quiet. **Amenities:** 🕾 👁 🍽 A/C, cable TV. **Services:** 🖼 🗘 🖐 **Facilities:** 🖪 10 🖳 👍 Whirlpool. **Rates (CP):** HS Jan 9–Apr 17 $69–$79 S or D. Children under 18 stay free. Lower rates off-season. Higher rates for spec evnts/hols. Pking: Outdoor, free. Maj CC.

▇▇ **La Quinta Inn**, 2510 W Greenway Rd, Phoenix, AZ 85023 (Metrocenter); tel 602/993-0800 or toll free 800/531-5900; fax 602/789-9172. Greenway Rd exit off I-17. A good, basic motel for those who want to be on the north side of Phoenix. **Rooms:** 147 rms and stes. CI 3pm/CO noon. Nonsmoking rms avail. Comfortable rooms are attractively furnished. **Amenities:** 🕾 👁 🍽 A/C, satel TV, refrig. **Services:** ✗ 🖐 **Facilities:** 🖪 🍽 250 🖳 👍 1 rst, 1 bar, sauna, whirlpool. Golf pro on premises. **Rates:** HS Feb 15–May 1 $72–$80 S or D; from $85 ste. Extra person $10. Children under 18 stay free. Lower rates off-season. Higher rates for spec evnts/hols. Spec packages avail. Pking: Outdoor, free. Maj CC.

▇▇ **Travelodge Metrocenter**, 8617 N Black Canyon Fwy, Phoenix, AZ 85021 (Metrocenter); tel 602/995-9500 or toll free 800/255-3050; fax 602/995-0150. Northern Ave exit off I-17. Close to the freeway and Metrocenter Mall. **Rooms:** 180 rms. CI 3pm/CO noon. Nonsmoking rms avail. **Amenities:** 🕾 A/C, satel TV w/movies. **Services:** 🚗 🖼 🗘 🖐 Free shuttle to the Metrocenter Mall. **Facilities:** 🖪 👍 Whirlpool, washer/dryer. **Rates (CP):** HS Jan–May $56 S; $61 D. Extra person $7. Children under 17 stay free. Lower rates off-season. Pking: Outdoor, free. Maj CC.

Resorts

▇▇▇▇ **Arizona Biltmore**, 24th St and Missouri Ave, Phoenix, AZ 85016; tel 602/955-6600 or toll free 800/950-0086; fax 602/381-7646. Camelback Rd exit off I-17. E on Camelback to 24th St then left to Missouri Ave. 39 acres. A major renovation (to the tune of $33 million) has enhanced the 65-year-old resort's one-of-a-kind architecture and appointments, inspired by Frank Lloyd Wright. But yet another change in management and the addition of still more homes and conference rooms on the Biltmore estate means this rating is conditional. **Rooms:** 500 rms and stes. CI 3pm/CO noon. Express checkout avail. Nonsmoking rms avail. Deployed in 4-story wings around main low-rise building, newly renovated to re-create the 1920s character of the resort's debut. Art deco styling gives them a special charm. Many patios face other patios (corner rooms on the 4th floor have extra-large terraces with more privacy). **Amenities:** 🕾 ⚷ 🍽 A/C, cable TV w/movies, voice mail, shoe polisher. All units w/minibars, some w/terraces. Bathrobes and 2-line phones provided on request. Energy-saving sensors adjust heat and air conditioning. **Services:** ✕ 📠 VP 🚗 🖨 ⤴ ⟳ Twice-daily maid svce, car-rental desk, social director, masseur, children's program, babysitting. Turndown service on request. Regular shuttle to Biltmore Fashion Park. **Facilities:** 🏌 🚴 ▶₃₆ 🎾 🏐 🎳 12K 💻 🔥 3 rsts (*see also* "Restaurants" below), 2 bars (1 w/entertainment), lifeguard, games rm, lawn games, spa, sauna, steam rm, whirlpool, beauty salon, day-care ctr. The original Catalina pool has been relegated to the status of adjunct to a new $4 million, 5-pool complex with waterslide, swim-up bar, and poolside cabanas with TV and phones. Athletic Club, tennis, and golf shared with 5,000 local members. **Rates:** HS Sept 11–June 5 $280–$320 S or D; from $650 ste. Children under 18 stay free. Lower rates off-season. AP and MAP rates avail. Spec packages avail. Pking: Outdoor, free. Maj CC. Cabanas cost an additional $30 to $150 a day. Incidental services fee of $4 added daily to include admission to health and fitness center and cover unlimited local phone calls and long-distance access.

≡≡≡ Hermosa Inn, 5532 N Palo Cristi Rd, Phoenix, AZ 85253 (Paradise Valley); tel 602/955-8614 or toll free 800/254-8870; fax 602/955-8299. 6 acres. A unique resort, built in 1930 as the home of cowboy artist Lon Megargee. The lodge was rebuilt in 1994 after a fire. **Rooms:** 35 rms and stes; 4 ctges/villas. CI 3pm/CO noon. There are a variety of individually decorated accommodations, from suites to casitas and villas, and many with kitchenettes or full kitchens. **Amenities:** 🕾 A/C, cable TV, refrig. All units w/terraces, some w/fireplaces, some w/Jacuzzis. **Services:** ✕ 📠 🖨 ⤴ **Facilities:** 🏌 🍴₃ 🍽 1 rst, 1 bar, spa, whirlpool, washer/dryer. There's a barbecue on the grounds. **Rates:** HS Jan 14–Apr 17 $95–$125 S or D; from $185 ste; from $245 ctge/villa. Lower rates off-season. Pking: Outdoor, free. Maj CC. Weekly and monthly rates are available.

≡≡≡ The Pointe Hilton at Squaw Peak, 7677 N 16th St, Phoenix, AZ 85020; tel 602/997-2626 or toll free 800/876-4683; fax 602/943-4633. 300 acres. Another of Phoenix's plush Hilton resorts. **Rooms:** 497 stes; 76 ctges/villas. CI 4pm/CO noon. Express checkout avail. Nonsmoking rms avail. Rooms are comfortable and well appointed. **Amenities:** 🕾 ⚷ 🖭 A/C, cable TV w/movies, refrig, voice mail. All units w/minibars, all w/terraces, 1 w/fireplace. **Services:** ✕ 📠 VP 🚗 🖨 ⤴ Car-rental desk, social director, masseur, children's program, babysitting. **Facilities:** 🏌 🚴 ⛳ 🎾 🏐₄ 🏐 🎳 1K 💻 🔥 4 rsts, 7 bars (4 w/entertainment), games rm, lawn games, racquetball, sauna, steam rm, whirlpool, beauty salon, day-care ctr, play-ground, washer/dryer. There's a flowing canal called Lazy River whose current carries guests on air mattresses. **Rates:** HS Jan–Apr from $199 ste; from $245 ctge/villa. Children under 12 stay free. Lower rates off-season. Higher rates for spec evnts/hols. MAP rates avail. Spec packages avail. Pking: Outdoor, free. Maj CC.

≡≡≡ The Pointe Hilton at Tapatio Cliffs, 11111 N 7th St, Phoenix, AZ 85020 (North Phoenix); tel 602/866-7500 or toll free 800/876-4683; fax 602/993-0276. 2 miles north of Dunlap Ave. 650 acres. A large, plush resort on the side of Phoenix's North Mountain. Caters to both leisure and business travelers. **Rooms:** 584 stes. CI 4pm/CO noon. Express checkout avail. Nonsmoking rms avail. Rooms are comfortable and attractively furnished. **Amenities:** 🕾 ⚷ 🖭 A/C, cable TV w/movies. All units w/minibars, all w/terraces, some w/fireplaces, some w/Jacuzzis. **Services:** ✕ 📠 VP 🚗 🖨 ⤴ Car-rental desk, social director, masseur, children's program, babysitting. Complimentary cocktails. **Facilities:** 🏌 🚴 ▶₁₈ ⛳ 🎾 🏐 🎳 1K 💻 🔥 3 rsts, 4 bars (2 w/entertainment), spa, sauna, steam rm, whirlpool, beauty salon, day-care ctr, washer/dryer. **Rates (CP):** HS Jan–May $209–$225 S or D. Extra person $10. Children under 18 stay free. Lower rates off-season. AP rates avail. Spec packages avail. Pking: Outdoor, free. Maj CC.

≡≡≡ The Pointe Hilton Resort on South Mountain, 7777 S Pointe Pkwy, Phoenix, AZ 85044; tel 602/438-9000 or toll free 800/572-7222; fax 602/431-6528. Baseline Rd exit off I-10. 886 acres. A large, luxurious resort, popular for conventions. **Rooms:** 638 stes. CI 4pm/CO noon. Nonsmoking rms avail. **Amenities:** 🕾 ⚷ 🖭 A/C, cable TV w/movies, refrig, stereo/tape player, voice mail. All units w/minibars, all w/terraces, some w/fireplaces. **Services:** ✕ 📠 🚗 🖨 ⤴ Car-rental desk, social director, masseur, children's program, babysitting. Complimentary cocktails are served daily from 4:30 to 6pm. Daily mall shuttle and 24-hour transportation around the resort. **Facilities:** 🏌 🚴 ▶₁₈ ⛳ 🎾 🏐 🎳 2.5K 💻 🔥 4 rsts (*see also* "Restaurants" below), 4 bars (2 w/entertainment), games rm, lawn games, racquetball, spa, sauna, steam rm, whirlpool, beauty salon, day-care ctr, washer/dryer. On-premise sports bar. **Rates:** HS Jan–mid-May from $200 ste. Extra person $10. Children under 18 stay free. Lower rates off-season. Spec packages avail. Pking: Outdoor, free. Maj CC.

Restaurants 🍴

Bistro, in the Biltmore Financial Center, 2398 E Camelback Rd, Suite 220, Phoenix (Biltmore); tel 602/957-3214. **New American.** One of the most popular restaurants in Phoenix, this is a less formal version of Christopher's next door (see listing), with the same owner/chef. As the name suggests, it is a bistro-style eatery, with tile floors and a marble bar. Innovative dinner specialties include braised lamb shank with lentils and wheatberries, and shallot steak with red wine sauce and pommes frites. Seafood dishes include John Dory, ahi tuna, scallops, and grilled halibut. **FYI:** Reservations recommended. **Open:** Mon–Sat 11am–10:30pm. Closed some hols. **Prices:** Main courses $15.95–$22.95. Maj CC. 🆅🅿 ♿

Christopher's, in the Biltmore Financial Center, 2398 E Camelback Rd, Suite 180, Phoenix (Biltmore); tel 602/957-3214. **French.** Considered by many to be Phoenix's premier dining experience, Christopher's has a small, elegant dining room with original country scenes and still-lifes on cream walls above wood-panelled wainscoting. A special appetizer is the house smoked salmon with ahi tuna and caviar. Dinner specialties include salad of foie gras with yams, smoked squab with tarragon and quinoa, and sautéed lamb with fried basil and curried potatoes. There's also a selection of tantalizing desserts. **FYI:** Reservations recommended. Jacket required. No smoking. **Open:** Wed–Sun 6–10pm. Closed some hols. **Prices:** Main courses $29; PF dinner $70. Maj CC. ♥ 🆅🅿 ♿

Christo's, 6327 N 7th St, Phoenix (Midtown); tel 602/264-1784. **Continental/Italian.** A bright, modern restaurant with a sophisticated atmosphere. Art deco–style prints adorn the walls. Northern Italian cooking is the order of the day, with such specialties as scampi Christo's and shrimp Florentine. **FYI:** Reservations recommended. **Open:** Lunch Mon–Fri 11:30am–2:30pm; dinner Mon–Thurs 5:30–10pm, Fri–Sat 5:30–10:30pm. Closed some hols. **Prices:** Main courses $16–$25. Maj CC. ♿

Ed Debevic's, 2102 E Highland Ave, Phoenix; tel 602/956-2760. **American.** A trendy, 1950s-style diner. Sandwiches, hamburgers, and hot dogs are the main fare, but plates such as Ed's Mom's meatloaf, macaroni and cheese, and homemade pot roast are also offered. **FYI:** Reservations not accepted. Children's menu. **Open:** Sun–Thurs 11am–10pm, Fri–Sat 11am–11pm. Closed some hols. **Prices:** Main courses $3.75–$6.75. Maj CC. 👫 ♿

The Fish Market, 1720 E Camelback Rd, Phoenix (E Phoenix); tel 602/277-FISH. **Pizza/Seafood.** A large seafood restaurant in a fashionable part of Phoenix, it's actually two restaurants in one: the simple downstairs restaurant with a sushi bar, and the fancier Top of the Market upstairs. A retail fish market also operates downstairs and provides the place with a "working" feel. Selections include mesquite-charbroiled fish, plus blackened, grilled, and fried fish. There are also pasta and seafood dishes. **FYI:** Reservations recommended. Children's menu. **Open:** Sun–Thurs 11am–9:30pm, Fri–Sat 11am–10pm. Closed some hols. **Prices:** Main courses $6.85–$31.75. Maj CC. ♥ ♿

Garcia's, 4420 E Camelback Rd, Phoenix (Arcadia); tel 602/952-8031. **Mexican.** This large eatery offers basic Mexican fare: enchiladas, burritos, and chile rellenos, plus Olivia's Sampler, with mini tacos, flautas, chimichangas, and refried beans. Also at: 5509 N 7th St, Phoenix (602/274-1176); 3301 W Peoria Ave, Phoenix (602/886-1850); 1940 E University Dr, Mesa (602/844-0023); 17037 North 59th Ave, Glendale (602/843-3296); 2394 North Alma School Rd, Chandler (602/963-0067). **FYI:** Reservations recommended. Children's menu. **Open:** Sun–Thurs 11am–10pm, Fri–Sat 11am–11pm. Closed some hols. **Prices:** Main courses $4.95–$8.25. Maj CC. 👫 ♿

Gourmet House of Hong Kong, 1438 E McDowell Rd, Phoenix (Midtown); tel 602/253-4859. **Chinese.** Basic Chinese food in a no-frills, diner atmosphere. Large variety of Canton/Hong Kong–style Chinese food. House specialties include orange-flavored duck, and scallops with ginger and onion. **FYI:** Reservations accepted. No liquor license. **Open:** Sun–Thurs 11am–10pm, Fri–Sat 11am–11pm. Closed some hols. **Prices:** Main courses $4.50–$11. Ltd CC. ♿

Greekfest, in Greekfest Center, 1940 E Camelback Rd, Phoenix (Midtown); tel 602/265-2990. At 20th St. **Greek.** Archways, white-washed walls, Greek plates and artwork, and wood-beam ceiling give the feel of the Greek island of Chios, childhood home of owner-chef Tony Makridis. The menu is educational and enlightening, with detailed descriptions. Hot and cold appetizers and salads, mezethes, casseroles, souvlaki. **FYI:** Reservations recommended. **Open:** Lunch Mon–Sat 11am–2:30pm; dinner Mon–Thurs 5–10pm, Fri–Sat 5–11pm, Sun 5–9pm. Closed some hols. **Prices:** Main courses $12.95–$18. Maj CC. ♥ ♿

The Grill, in the Ritz-Carlton Phoenix, 2401 E Camelback Rd, Phoenix (Biltmore); tel 602/468-0700. **American.** Fine dining in an English gentleman's club setting. Marble fireplace in the lounge, marble bar, soft chandelier lighting, dark paneling. Entrees include roast Colorado lamb (carved tableside), roast prime rib, veal chop, range chicken, Dover sole, Norwegian salmon, and yellowtail snapper. **FYI:** Reservations recommended. Piano. Children's menu. Jacket required. **Open:** HS Sept–May Mon–Fri 11:30am–10:30pm, Sat–Sun 5–10:30pm. Reduced hours off-season. **Prices:** Main courses $18–$28. Maj CC. ♥ 🆅🅿 ♿

Havana Cafe, 4225 E Camelback Rd, Phoenix (E Phoenix); tel 602/952-1991. At 44th St. **Cuban/Spanish.** A modern cafe, popular with the Latino community and all lovers of Caribbean and Spanish food. Specialties include masas de puerco fritas, containing pork seasoned with a lime-cumin marinade and fried to a golden brown; pollo chilendron, boneless chicken sautéed with pork, onions, pimientos, herbs, white wine and artichoke hearts; and zarzuela de mariscos, a medley of seafood in a spicy fresh tomato sauce. **FYI:** Reservations not accepted. Dress code. **Open:** Mon–Sat 11:30am–10pm, Sun 4–9:30pm. Closed some hols. **Prices:** Main courses $7.50–$14.95. Maj CC. 🍴 🚫

Houston's, in the Camelback Esplanade, 2425 E Camelback Rd, Phoenix (Biltmore); tel 602/957-9700. **New American.** Very comfortable restaurant with a southwestern look. The bar is popular with singles. Tables have lamps, and the leather booths have sconce lighting. Offering unusual pizzas, burgers, salads, fish, chicken, beef, and ribs. **FYI:** Reservations not accepted. No smoking. **Open:** Mon–Thurs 11am–11pm, Fri–Sat 11am–midnight, Sun 11am–10pm. Closed some hols. **Prices:** Main courses $6.25–$14.95. Maj CC. 🚫

Hungry Hunter, in Safeway Plaza Shopping Center, 3102 E Camelback Rd, Phoenix (Biltmore); tel 602/957-7180. **Seafood/ Steak.** Popular, medium-priced chain restaurant serving traditional seafood and meat dishes. Also at: 10237 N Metro Pkwy, Phoenix (602/371-0240); 2511 W Indian School Rd, Phoenix (602/266-2471); 4455 S Rural Rd, Tempe (602/838-8388); 10825 N Scottsdale Rd, Scottsdale (602/998-8777). **FYI:** Reservations recommended. Children's menu. **Open:** Lunch Mon–Fri 11am–2:30pm; dinner Mon–Thurs 5–9:30pm, Fri 5–10pm, Sat 4:30–10pm, Sun 4:30–9pm. Closed some hols. **Prices:** Main courses $14.95–$17.95. Maj CC. 🚫 🚫 🚫

Indian Delhi Palace, 5050 E McDowell Rd, Phoenix (Midtown); tel 602/244-8181. **Indian.** Simple, busy Indian restaurant in a commercial area of Phoenix. Chef's specialties include murg makhani, tandoori chicken cooked in butter in tomato gravy; vegetable korma, mixed vegetables and nuts cooked in cream and delicately spiced; and lamb boti kebab masala, boneless tandoori lamb in tomatoes and buttered gravy. Also at: 2626 N 75th Ave, Phoenix (602/849-6533); Fiesta Mall, 1261 W Southern Ave, Mesa (602/890-0440). **FYI:** Reservations recommended. **Open:** Lunch Mon–Fri 11:30am–2:30pm, Sat–Sun 11:30am–4:30pm; dinner daily 5–10pm. **Prices:** Main courses $6–$13. Maj CC. 🚫

Los Dos Molinos, 8646 S Central Ave, Phoenix (South Phoenix); tel 602/243-9113. 1 mi S of Baseline Rd. **Mexican.** Small, busy dining room with tiled floor, Mexican artifacts, posters, chile wreaths, murals, old license plates, and piñatas. Chef Victoria Chavez's specialties include chimichangas, enchiladas, chile rellenos, and pork ribs marinated in red chile. Also at: 260 S Alma School Rd, Mesa (602/835-5356). **FYI:** Reservations not accepted. **Open:** Daily 11am–9pm. Closed some hols; July. **Prices:** Main courses $5.25–$8.75. Ltd CC. 🚫

Matador Restaurant, 125 E Adams St, Phoenix (Downtown); tel 602/254-7563. **American/Greek/Mexican.** A spacious downtown Mexican, with a dining room lit by large street lamps and bullfight prints decorating the walls. In addition to standard Mexican fare, the menu offers steaks and Greek dishes. The green corn tamales are especially popular. **FYI:** Reservations accepted. Band. Children's menu. **Open:** Daily 7am–11pm. Closed some hols. **Prices:** Main courses $4.95–$16.95. Maj CC. 🚫 🚫

Mrs White's Golden Rule Cafe, 808 E Jefferson St, Phoenix (Downtown); tel 602/262-9256. At S 8th St. **Soul/Southern.** A southern soul food diner. Chicken-fried steak, catfish, pork chops, and barbecue head the entrees. Okra gumbo is also served up. Desserts include peach cobbler, and apple, sweet potato, and pecan pies. **FYI:** Reservations not accepted. Children's menu. No liquor license. No smoking. **Open:** Mon–Fri 11am–7:30pm. Closed some hols. **Prices:** Main courses $5.95–$10. No CC. 🚫

⭐ **The Olive Garden**, 10223 N Metro Pkwy E, Phoenix (Metro-Center); tel 602/943-4573. Peoria exit off I-17. **Italian.** A busy Italian offering basic fare, including a variety of pastas and meat and seafood dishes. **FYI:** Reservations accepted. Children's menu. Beer and wine only. **Open:** Daily 11am–10pm. Closed some hols. **Prices:** Main courses $7–$14. Maj CC. 🚫 🚫

🍴 **Orangerie**, in Arizona Biltmore Hotel, 24th St and Missouri, Phoenix; tel 602/955-6600. Camelback exit off I-17; continue east on Camelback to 24th then turn left to Missouri. **New American.** Fine dining in a setting of unique ambience. Intriguing art deco walls and spectacular chandeliers; contemporary southwestern art; an entire wall of conservatory-style windows. Knowledgeable wait staff in white tuxedos. The refined cuisine, served on Royal Doulton china, features seared scallops and roasted eggplant ravioli; butter-browned baby turbot with quinoa and braised fennel; cherry wood–smoked roast loin of venison with truffle-herb spaetzle; and warm apple tart with marionberry ice cream. 8,000-bottle wine cellar. **FYI:** Reservations recommended. Jacket required. No smoking. **Open:** HS Sept–June breakfast Mon–Fri 7–11am; lunch Mon–Fri 11am–2:30pm; dinner Mon–Sat 6–10pm; brunch Sun 10am–2:30pm. Reduced hours off-season. **Prices:** Main courses $21.25–$29. Maj CC. 🚫 🚫 🚫

Oscar Taylor, in Biltmore Fashion Park, 2420 E Camelback Rd, Phoenix (Biltmore); tel 602/956-5705. **American/Barbecue.** Situated in an upscale shopping center. Walls are brick and natural stone; one dining room has glass walls. Menu includes stuffed pork chops, buffalo pot roast, and farmhouse-style roast chicken. **FYI:** Reservations recommended. Children's menu. No smoking. **Open:** HS Dec–Mar daily 11am–10pm. Reduced hours off-season. Closed Dec 25. **Prices:** Main courses $15.95–$23.95. Maj CC. 🚫 🚫 🚫

Remington's, in The Scottsdale Plaza Resort, 7200 N Scottsdale Rd, Phoenix (Paradise Valley); tel 602/948-5000. **Regional American.** Low light and plants contribute to the ambience of this lovely restaurant. Specialties include Santa Fe roast pork and scallops Nantucket. **FYI:** Reservations recommended. Jazz/piano. **Open:** Lunch Mon–Fri 11am–2:30pm; dinner daily 5–10pm. **Prices:** Main courses $14.95–$22.95. Maj CC. ♥ 🔲 💌 🆅🅿 ⛤

⑤ **The Restaurant at the Ritz-Carlton**, in the Ritz-Carlton Phoenix, 2401 E Camelback Rd, Phoenix (Camelback Esplanade); tel 602/468-0700. Camelback exit off I-17; go east on Camelback to Biltmore Fashion Park and the Camelback Esplanade. **American/Continental.** Mansion decor, with original paintings and well-spaced tables. Popular for lunch with executives from the neighboring offices and with shoppers from Biltmore Fashion Park across the street, it is one of the classiest settings in America for a $7.50 sandwich or $8.50 plate of pasta. For dinner, the Grill Room offers a more expensive menu and live music. Specialties offered: tortilla soup with mini smoked chicken tamale; seared chicken breast with asparagus and cream cheese baked in phyllo; southwestern caesar salad with tortilla-crusted chicken strips; caramelized papaya tart with Midori sabayon. **FYI:** Reservations recommended. Piano. Children's menu. Dress code. **Open:** Breakfast daily 6:30–11:30am; lunch Mon–Sat 11:30am–2:30pm; brunch Sun 11am–2:30pm. **Prices:** Lunch main courses $7.50–$15. Maj CC. 👥 🆅🅿 ⛤

Richardson's, 1582 E Bethany Home Rd, Phoenix; tel 602/265-5886. At 16th St. **Southwestern.** A busy southwestern-style bar and grill. New Mexico decor features chile ristras and wreaths, Indian wall blankets, and adobe booths surrounding a horseshoe-shaped bar. Among the specialties are grilled pork chop stuffed with chorizo with cilantro chutney sauce, and Chimayo chicken stuffed with spinach, sun-dried tomatoes, poblano chile and asiago cheese. Daily specials and desserts. **FYI:** Reservations not accepted. **Open:** Daily 11am–midnight. Closed Dec 25. **Prices:** Main courses $7.95–$17.95. Maj CC. ♥ ⛤

Roxsand, 2594 E Camelback Rd, Phoenix (Biltmore); tel 602/381-0444. **Eclectic.** The modernistic, high-tech look features a two-tiered dining room, track lighting, hanging lamps, and a huge metal pineapple suspended from the ceiling. The "fusion" cuisine (a blending of foods from different cultures) includes grilled New York steak with "Texas chain saw" chili sauce, polenta cake and grilled vegetables; and air-dried duck with Szechuan black bean sauce, "'evil jungle prince" sauce, plum sauce, and moo shu pancakes. **FYI:** Reservations recommended. **Open:** Lunch Mon–Fri 11am–4pm, Sat–Sun noon–4pm; dinner Mon–Thurs 5–10pm, Fri–Sat 5–10:30pm, Sun 5–9:30pm. Closed some hols. **Prices:** Main courses $9–$24. Maj CC. ♥ 🆅🅿 ⛤

Rustler's Rooste, in the Pointe Hilton Resort on South Mountain, 7777 S Pointe Pkwy, Phoenix; tel 602/231-9111. Baseline Rd exit off I-10. **Southwestern/Steak.** A fun-filled raucous steakhouse: buffalo heads on the walls, sawdust on the floor, and a longhorn steer in a pen outside the entrance. There's a slide from the upstairs bar to the downstairs dining room for patrons' use. Beef is the chief offering, but the menu also includes mesquite-grilled catfish, marinated broiled swordfish, halibut steaks, barbecued or mesquite-grilled chicken, and even a vegetarian plate. Appetizers include deep-fried rattlesnake. A light menu is served until 11pm in the lounge. Also at: 4868 E Cactus Rd, Scottsdale (602/494-4327). **FYI:** Reservations recommended. Band. Children's menu. **Open:** HS Dec–Apr daily 5–11pm. Reduced hours off-season. **Prices:** Main courses $8.95–$19.95. Maj CC. ■ 🆅🅿 ⛤

★ **The Rusty Pelican**, 9801 N Black Canyon Hwy, Phoenix (Metro Center); tel 602/944-9646. Exit Dunlap off I-17. **Seafood.** Fresh fish dominates the menu, with many charbroiled specialties. **FYI:** Reservations recommended. Sing along. Children's menu. **Open:** Daily 11am–10pm. **Prices:** Main courses $10.95–$18.95. Maj CC. ■ 💌 ⛤

Sam's Cafe, in Biltmore Fashion Park, 2566 E Camelback Rd, Suite 201, Phoenix; tel 602/954-7100. **Southwestern.** Located in a popular Phoenix mall. Decorated in southwestern style with open beams and stucco walls. Selection of salads, pastas, and sandwiches, plus southwestern fare including tamales, quesadillas, burritos, and tacos. Entrees may include chile-rubbed tuna and blue corn–fried catfish. Also at: 455 N 3rd, Phoenix (602/252-3545). **FYI:** Reservations recommended. Children's menu. **Open:** Sun–Thurs 11am–10pm, Fri–Sat 11am–midnight. Closed some hols. **Prices:** Main courses $9.95–$15.95. Maj CC. 🔲 🆅🅿 ⛤

Shogun, in Abco Shopping Center, 12615 N Tatum Blvd, Phoenix; tel 602/953-3264. At Cactus Rd. **Japanese.** A small, simple establishment with Japanese prints on the walls and wooden-shaded lamps hanging over the booths. Traditional Japanese fare, along with interesting appetizers such as ika panko, deep-fried, breaded squid strips. House specialties include tempura Alaskan codfish, chicken, and shrimp, all with tempura vegetables. Sushi bar. **FYI:** Reservations accepted. Beer and wine only. No smoking. **Open:** Lunch Mon–Fri 11am–2:30pm; dinner Mon–Sat 5–10pm, Sun 5–9pm. Closed some hols. **Prices:** Main courses $6.75–$20.50. Maj CC. ⛤

Sing High Chop Suey House, 27 W Madison, Phoenix (Downtown); tel 602/253-7848. **Chinese.** Specializes in Cantonese dishes. **FYI:** Reservations accepted. Children's menu. No liquor license. **Open:** Mon–Thurs 11am–9pm, Fri–Sat noon–11pm, Sun noon–9pm. Closed some hols. **Prices:** Main courses $5.95–$10. Maj CC.

Steamer's Genuine Seafood, in Biltmore Fashion Park, 2576 E Camelback Rd, Phoenix (Biltmore); tel 602/956-3631. **Seafood.** A popular place for seafood. Extensive selection, including live Maine lobster. Smoking is allowed only in the bar. **FYI:** Reservations recommended. Children's menu. **Open:** Mon–Thurs 11am–10pm, Fri 11am–11pm, Sat noon–11pm, Sun 5–10pm. Closed some hols. **Prices:** Main courses $13.95–$22.95. Maj CC.

Vincent Guerithault on Camelback, 3930 E Camelback Rd, Phoenix; tel 602/224-0225. **Southwestern.** Decorated in French country style, with open beams, fresh and dried flower arrangements, arched windows, and still life studies on the walls. The large selection of appetizers includes spinach salad with wild boar bacon, and duck tamale with Anaheim green chile. Entrees are prepared with a southwestern touch. **FYI:** Reservations recommended. **Open:** Lunch Mon–Fri 11:30am–2:30pm; dinner Sun–Fri 6–10:30pm, Sat 5:30–10:30pm. Closed some hols. **Prices:** Main courses $20–$22. Maj CC.

Attractions

MUSEUMS

Heard Museum, 22 E Monte Vista Rd; tel 602/252-8848. One of the finest museums in the country that deals exclusively with Native American cultures. "Native Peoples of the Southwest" is an extensive exhibit that explores the culture of each of the major tribes of the region. "Our Voices, Our Land" is an audiovisual presentation in which contemporary Native Americans express their thoughts on their heritage. "Old Ways, New Ways" is an interactive exhibit where visitors can join a drumming group on a video, duplicate a Northwest tribal design, or design a Navajo rug. On weekends there are performances by singers and dancers. The biggest event of the year is the **Annual Guild Indian Fair and Market**, which is held on the first weekend in March. Guided tours daily. **Open:** Mon–Sat 10am–5pm, Sun noon–5pm. Closed some hols. $$

Phoenix Art Museum, 1625 N Central Ave; tel 602/257-1222. The largest art museum in the Southwest, with a collection that spans the major artistic movements from the Renaissance to the present. The modern and contemporary art includes works by Diego Rivera, Frida Kahlo, Pablo Picasso, Karel Appel, Willem de Kooning, Henri Rousseau, Georgia O'Keeffe, and Auguste Rodin.

The Thorne Miniature Collection is one of the museum's most popular exhibits and consists of tiny, exquisitely detailed rooms on a scale of 1 inch to 1 foot. **Open:** Tues and Thurs–Sat 10am–5pm, Wed 10am–9pm, Sun noon–5pm. Closed some hols. $$

Arizona Museum of Science and Technology, 147 E Adams St; tel 602/256-9427. Aimed primarily at children, the hands-on museum has more than 100 interactive exhibits. Visitors can walk inside a giant camera obscura or conduct electricity with their own bodies. Frequent physics and chemistry demonstrations; small collection of reptiles. **Open:** Mon–Sat 9am–5pm, Sun noon–5pm. Closed some hols. $$

Gila River Arts and Crafts Center, exit 175 off I-10; tel 602/963-3981. Located on the Gila River Indian Reservation, the center provides visitors with an opportunity to learn more about the history and culture of the tribes that inhabit this region of the Arizona desert. In Heritage Park, there are replicas of villages of 5 different tribes, the Tohono O'oodham, Pima, Maricopa, Apache, and Hohokam. Inside the museum there are historical photos, artifacts, and an excellent collection of Pima baskets. Other exhibits tell the story of the Gila River Basin. **Open:** Daily 8am–5pm. Free.

Pueblo Grande Museum and Cultural Park, 4619 E Washington St; tel 602/495-0900. The ruins of an ancient Hohokam tribal village, one of several villages located along the Salt River between 300 and 1400. Sometime around 1450, this and other villages were mysteriously abandoned. Small museum. **Open:** Mon–Sat 9am–4:45pm, Sun 1–4:45pm. Closed some hols. $

Hall of Flame Firefighting Museum, 6101 E Van Buren St; tel 602/ASK-FIRE. The world's largest firefighting museum. There are more than 100 vintage fire trucks on display, including an 1855 hand-pumper from Philadelphia. **Open:** Mon–Sat 9am–5pm, Sun noon–4pm. Closed some hols. $$

HISTORIC BUILDINGS & HOMES

Heritage Square, 115 N Sixth St; tel 602/262-5029. A collection of some of the few remaining houses in Phoenix that date to the last century and the original Phoenix townsite. All the buildings are listed on the National Register and most display Victorian architectural styles popular just before the turn of the century. Among the buildings located here are the ornate **Rosson House,** which is open for tours; the **Silva House,** a neoclassical-revival-style home that now houses historical exhibits on water and electricity use in the Valley of the Sun; the **Carriage House**; and the **Bouvier-Teter House.** Also located here is the **Arizona Doll and Toy Museum**. Inside is a reproduction of a 1912 schoolroom in which all the children are antique dolls. Closed Aug. **Open:** Wed–Sat 10am–4pm, Sun noon–4pm. $$

Pioneer Arizona Living History Museum, Pioneer Rd exit off I-17; tel 602/993-0212. A living-history museum with 28 original and reconstructed buildings from the 1890s. Costumed guides practice traditional pioneer occupations and create 19th-century crafts. The old Opera House hosts live melodramas every weekend. Each year in October there are Civil War battle reenactments and a gathering of modern mountain men. **Open:** Oct–June; call ahead for hours. $$$

Arizona State Capitol Museum, 1700 W Washington St; tel 602/542-4675. The former state capitol, but has recently been restored to its original 1912 appearance. Among the rooms on view are the Senate and House chambers, as well as the governor's office and historical exhbits. **Open:** Mon–Fri 8am–5pm. Closed some hols. Free.

Arizona Biltmore, 24th St and Missouri; tel toll free 800/950-0086. A landmark for 65 years, the resort's design was inspired by architect Frank Lloyd Wright, who collaborated with Albert Chase McArthur. One of the architectural points to look for is the detailed, patterned concrete blocks used in the building's structure. These were the first incidence of pre-cast concrete blocks in the history of architecture and are now known as Biltmore Blocks. All of the furnishings in the dining area are Wright-designed, as are several of the sculptures in the entrance and one of the stained-glass windows. Also see listing under "Resorts." Free.

Mystery Castle, S Mountain Rd; tel 602/268-1581. A giant sand castle located on the edge of South Mountain Park, it was built over a period of 18 years by a single man for his daughter. The castle, which is on the National Historic Registry, contains 18 rooms, 13 fireplaces, and a small chapel where wedding ceremonies are often performed. **Open:** Tues–Sun 11am–4pm. $

PARKS & GARDENS

Desert Botanical Garden, 1201 N Galvin Pkwy; tel 602/941-1225. Devoted exclusively to cacti and the more than 10,000 desert plants from all over the world that make their home here. The Plants and People of the Sonoran Desert trail explains the science of ethnobotany through interactive displays that demonstrate how the inhabitants of the Sonoran Desert once utilized wild and cultivated plants. **Open:** Oct–Apr, daily 8am–8pm; May–Sept, daily 7am–10pm. Closed Dec 25. $$

Phoenix Zoo, 5810 E Van Buren St; tel 602/273-7771. Home to more than 1,200 animals, known for its 4-acre African Veldt exhibit and its baboon colony. The southwestern animal exhibits are also of particular interest. In addition, there is an 11-acre children's zoo with baby animals and a petting area. **Open:** Daily 7am–4pm. Closed some hols. $$$

Salt River Recreation Area, Bush Hwy; tel 602/984-3305. Located 20 miles northeast of Phoenix in Tonto National Forest. Visitors can take an inner tube trip down the river—a tame and relaxing ride and one of the best ways to see the desert. **Open:** Apr–Sept, daily 9am–4pm. $$$

ENTERTAINMENT VENUES

Desert Sky Pavilion, N 83rd Ave; tel 602/254-7200. An 18,500-seat amphitheater. Hosts a wide variety of entertainment from Broadway musicals to rock concerts. **Open:** Box office, Mon–Fri 8am–5pm. $$$$

Herberger Theater Center, 222 E Monroe St; tel 602/252-TIXS. From the outside this theater resembles a colonial church. Inside, its 2 Broadway-style theaters host more than 600 performances each year by Arizona companies and traveling shows. **Open:** Box office, Mon–Fri 10am–6pm, Sat noon–6pm. $$$$

America West Arena, 201 E Jefferson; tel 602/379-7800. Home of the NBA's Phoenix Suns, this stadium also hosts a wide range of programs throughout the year featuring everything from rodeos to rock music. **Open:** Box office, Mon–Fri 8:30am–5pm, Sat 10am–4pm.

PINETOP

Map page M-2, C4 (NW of McNary)

Motels 🛏

≣≣ **Best Western Inn of Pinetop**, 404 White Mt Blvd (Ariz 260), PO Box 1006, Pinetop, AZ 85935; tel 602/367-6667 or toll free 800/525-1234; fax 602/367-6672. 10 mi S of Show Low. A comfortable, modern motel. **Rooms:** 41 rms. CI 2pm/CO 11am. Nonsmoking rms avail. **Amenities:** 🛏 A/C, cable TV. 1 unit w/terrace. **Services:** 🛎 🐾 Twice-daily maid svce. **Facilities:** 🏋 📺 👍 Spa. **Rates:** HS Dec–Mar/June–Sept 15 $59–$79 S; $64–$89 D. Extra person $5. Children under 12 stay free. Min stay HS. Lower rates off-season. Pking: Outdoor, free. Maj CC.

≣≣ **Econo Lodge**, 458 White Mt Blvd (Ariz 260), PO Box 1226, Pinetop, AZ 85935; tel 602/367-3636 or toll free 800/544-4444; fax 602/367-1543. 9 mi S of Show Low. A clean, comfortable motel centrally located to lakes, horseback riding, hiking, and other outdoor activities. **Rooms:** 44 rms. CI open/ CO 11am. Nonsmoking rms avail. **Amenities:** ☎ 🕭 A/C, cable TV w/movies, refrig. **Services:** 🖴 🖐 Twice-daily maid svce. Laptop computer jacks are available in the office. **Facilities:** 🏌 🏊 🖳 🕭 Spa. **Rates (CP):** HS Oct–Apr $59–$89 S or D. Extra person $5. Children under 18 stay free. Lower rates off-season. Spec packages avail. Pking: Outdoor, free. Maj CC.

Resort

🎜🎜 **Whispering Pines Resort**, 237 Ariz 260, PO Box 1043, Pinetop, AZ 85935; tel 602/367-4386. 8 mi SE of Show Low. 12½ acres. A quiet mountain retreat. **Rooms:** 4 rms; 29 ctges/ villas. CI 1pm/CO 10am. A variety of cabins are offered. **Amenities:** 🖳 Cable TV, refrig. No A/C or phone. All units w/terraces, some w/fireplaces. **Services:** 🚐 🖐 **Facilities:** ⚠ 🔄 🏊 🏌 🏊 🕭 Lawn games, spa, playground, washer/dryer. **Rates:** $30–$40 S; $59–$84 D; from $59 ctge/villa. Extra person $6. Children under 3 stay free. Min stay spec evnts. Spec packages avail. Pking: Outdoor, free. Ltd CC.

PRESCOTT

Map page M-2, C2

Hotels 🖭

🎜🎜🎜 **Hassayampa Inn**, 122 E Gurley St, Prescott, AZ 86301 (Downtown); tel 602/778-9434; fax 602/778-9434. Built in 1927, this historic hotel is on the National Register of Historic Places. The lobby is done in art deco/pueblo style, with a huge painted mural above the fireplace, a tile floor, 2 pianos, and leather chairs. **Rooms:** 67 rms and stes. CI 3pm/CO noon. Nonsmoking rms avail. Each room is distinctly decorated, with original watercolors of local scenes, and period furnishings. **Amenities:** ☎ 🕭 A/C, cable TV. 1 unit w/terrace, 1 w/Jacuzzi. Suites have hair dryers. **Services:** ✗ 🖾 🖴 **Facilities:** 🔢 🖳 🕭 1 rst (see also "Restaurants" below), 1 bar. Superbly decorated dining room. **Rates (BB):** HS Apr–Oct $89–$109 S or D; from $135 ste. Extra person $10. Children under 6 stay free. Lower rates off-season. Higher rates for spec evnts/hols. Spec packages avail. Pking: Outdoor, free. Maj CC.

🎜🎜 **Hotel St Michael**, 205 W Gurley St, Prescott, AZ 86301; tel 602/776-1999 or toll free 800/678-3757; fax 602/776-7318. A historic downtown hotel located on Prescott's famous "Whiskey Row." **Rooms:** 72 rms and stes. CI 2pm/CO 11am. **Amenities:** ☎ A/C, cable TV. **Services:** 🚐 🖴 Babysitting. **Facilities:** 1 rst. The Caffe St Michael in the hotel offers specialty coffee drinks. **Rates (CP):** $32–$62 S or D; from $62

ste. Extra person $8. Children under 12 stay free. Higher rates for spec evnts/hols. Spec packages avail. Pking: Outdoor, free. Maj CC.

🎜🎜🎜 **Sheraton Resort and Conference Center**, 1500 Ariz 69, Prescott, AZ 86301; tel 602/776-1666 or toll free 800/ 967-4637. Located high on a hill above Prescott, this hotel has a commanding view, especially of the jagged San Francisco Peaks to the north. **Rooms:** 160 rms and stes. CI 3pm/CO noon. Nonsmoking rms avail. **Amenities:** ☎ 🖭 A/C, satel TV, refrig. 1 unit w/minibar, all w/terraces, 1 w/fireplace, 1 w/Jacuzzi. **Services:** ✗ 🚐 🖾 🖴 🖐 Masseur, babysitting. **Facilities:** 🔄 🕭 ⛳ 🔢 🖳 🕭 1 rst, 2 bars (1 w/entertainment), racquetball, spa, sauna, whirlpool, beauty salon. There's a slot machine casino on the premises. The swimming pool has retractable doors to become an indoor pool during inclement weather. **Rates:** HS Apr–Sept $140 S or D; from $160 ste. Extra person $10. Children under 17 stay free. Lower rates off-season. Spec packages avail. Pking: Outdoor, free. Maj CC.

Motel

🎜🎜 **Super 8 Motel**, 1105 E Sheldon St, Prescott, AZ 86303; tel 602/776-1282 or toll free 800/800-8000; fax 602/778-6736. Sheldon St exit off Ariz 89. This is a good, economical motel for vacationers or business travelers on a budget. Close to local colleges and the Veterans Administration hospital. **Rooms:** 70 rms. CI 3pm/CO 11am. Nonsmoking rms avail. **Amenities:** ☎ A/C, cable TV. **Services:** 🖴 Fax and copy services are available, and there's a 24-hour front desk. Free local calls. **Facilities:** 🔄 🕭 **Rates (CP):** HS Apr–Sept $46–$50 S; $52–$60 D. Children under 12 stay free. Lower rates off-season. Spec packages avail. Pking: Outdoor, free. Maj CC.

Inns

🎜🎜 **Prescott Country Inn**, 503 S Montezuma St (US 89), Prescott, AZ 86303; tel 602/445-7991. With comfortable cottages, a good choice for a romantic getaway. **Rooms:** 12 ctges/ villas. CI 3pm/CO 11am. Each room is unique. **Amenities:** ☎ 🕭 Cable TV, refrig. No A/C. Some units w/terraces, some w/fireplaces. **Services:** 🕭 🚐 🖴 Twice-daily maid svce. Complimentary cookies provided. **Rates (CP):** HS May–Sept from $89 ctge/ villa. Extra person $15. Children under 6 stay free. Min stay spec evnts. Lower rates off-season. Spec packages avail. Pking: Outdoor, free. Ltd CC.

🎜🎜 **Prescott Pines Inn**, 901 White Spar Rd (US 89), Prescott, AZ 86303; tel 602/445-7270 or toll free 800/541-5374; fax 602/ 778-3665. A good choice for those who enjoy the atmosphere of a small bed-and-breakfast but prefer a bit more privacy. The main guest house dates from 1902. **Rooms:** 13 rms and stes. CI 3pm/CO noon. No smoking. The comfortable rooms are individually decorated. **Amenities:** 🔒 ⚐ 🔟 A/C, cable TV, refrig. All units w/terraces, some w/fireplaces. **Services:** ☎ 🚙 ⟲ A full-service breakfast is available at $5 per person, if reserved by 7pm the previous evening. **Facilities:** Guest lounge. **Rates (BB):** $55–$95 S or D; from $69 ste. Extra person $20. Higher rates for spec evnts/hols. Pking: Outdoor, free. Ltd CC. Rates are $4 to $10 higher Friday and Saturday nights than week nights.

Restaurants 🍴

★ **El Charro**, 120 N Montezuma, Prescott; tel 602/445-7130. **American/Mexican.** Popular and affordable downtown Mexican eatery, with local artists' work for sale. **FYI:** Reservations accepted. Beer and wine only. No smoking. **Open:** Sun–Thurs 11am–8pm, Fri–Sat 11am–8:30pm. Closed some hols. **Prices:** Main courses $2.75–$8.25. Ltd CC. 🈳 &

★ **Kendall's Famous Burgers and Ice Cream**, 113 S Cortez St, Prescott; tel 602/778-3658. **Burgers/Ice cream.** A 1950s and '60s–style hamburger and ice cream joint, complete with pictures of Elvis, James Dean, and Corvettes. Flame-broiled burgers, fresh-cut fries, beer-batter onion rings, and old-fashioned ice cream sundaes fit the mood. **FYI:** Reservations not accepted. No liquor license. **Open:** Mon–Sat 11am–8pm, Sun 11am–6pm. Closed Dec 25. **Prices:** Main courses $3.09–$4.65. No CC. 🈳 &

★ **Murphy's**, 201 N Cortez, Prescott; tel 602/445-4044. **American/Seafood.** The building housing this large restaurant dates from 1892 and is listed on the National Register of Historic Places. Animal head trophies and historic photos are on the walls; a collection of antiques sits above the bar, which has the original tin ceiling. The menu includes ribs, meat, and pastas. With 60 bottled beers and 3 specialty beers on tap. **FYI:** Reservations accepted. Children's menu. **Open:** HS June–Aug lunch daily 11am–3pm; dinner daily 4:30–11pm. Reduced hours off-season. Closed Dec 25. **Prices:** Main courses $10.95–$16.95. Maj CC. ▮

The Peacock Room, in the Hassayampa Inn, 122 E Gurley St, Prescott; tel 602/778-9434. **Continental.** Comfortable booths with art deco lamps, chandeliers, and soft music all contribute to the relaxed atmosphere. Specialties include shrimp scampi and chicken Venezia. **FYI:** Reservations recommended. Children's menu. Dress code. No smoking. **Open:** Breakfast Mon–Fri 7–11am, Sat–Sun 7–11:30am; lunch Mon–Fri 11am–2pm, Sat–Sun noon–2pm; dinner Sun–Thurs 5–9pm, Fri–Sat 5–9:30pm. **Prices:** Main courses $9.95–$19.95. Maj CC. ● ▮ ▼

Attractions 🖼

Sharlot Hall Museum, 415 W Gurley St; tel 602/445-3122. A complex of historic buildings and gardens started by territorial historian Sharlot Hall. Restored buildings include the Old Governor's Mansion, built in 1864; the 1875 John C Frémont House; the William Bashford House, an example of Victorian architecture; and the Sharlot Hall Building, a museum. In addition, the grounds include a schoolhouse, a gazebo, a ranch house, and an old windmill. **Open:** Mon 10am–5pm, Sun 1–5pm. Closed some hols. Free.

The Smoki Museum, 126 N Arizona St; tel 602/445-1230. Houses a large collection of American Indian artifacts as well as a collection of western art. Annual ceremonial dances held in August at Yavapai County Fairgrounds. **Open:** May–Sept, Mon, Tues, Thurs–Sat 10am–4pm; Sun 1–4pm. Closed Oct–May. $

Prescott's Phippen Museum of Western Art, 4701 US 89 N; tel 602/778-1385. Exhibits works by both established western artists and newcomers. Throughout the year there are several one-person shows, as well as group exhibitions. The museum gift shop represents more than 100 Arizona artists. **Open:** Mon, Wed–Sat 10am–4pm, Sun 1–4pm. $

Prescott National Forest, 344 S Cortez St; tel 602/445-1762. Pine forest containing hiking trails, several artificial lakes, and campgrounds. The Forest Service Office, located at the entrance, has maps and information about the area. Free.

RIO RICO

Map page M-2, E3 (N of Nogales)

Resort 🛏

Rio Rico Resort and Country Club, 1069 Camino Caralampi, Rio Rico, AZ 85648; tel 602/281-1901 or toll free 800/288-4746; fax 602/281-7132. 10 mi N of Nogales, exit 17 off I-19. 23 acres. A major remodeling is under way. When completed, this is expected to be a beautiful resort. Unrated. **Rooms:** 180 rms and stes. CI 4pm/CO noon. Express checkout avail. Nonsmoking rms avail. Extremely well-appointed, very comfortable rooms. **Amenities:** 🔒 ⚐ A/C, cable TV w/movies. All units w/terraces. **Services:** ✕ ☎ VP 🚙 ⬧ ⟲ **Facilities:** 🎿 ▶18 ♣ 🏌 ⛳ 600 ⬜ & 1 rst, 1 bar (w/entertainment), spa, sauna, whirlpool, beauty salon. **Rates:** HS Jan–Apr/Oct–Dec $115–$125 S or D; from $150 ste. Extra person $10. Children under 12 stay free. Lower rates off-season. Higher rates for spec evnts/hols. Spec packages avail. Pking: Outdoor, free. Maj CC.

SAFFORD

Map page M-2, D4

Motel ⬛

≣≣ Best Western Desert Inn, 1391 Thatcher Blvd, Safford, AZ 85546; tel 602/428-0521 or toll free 800/528-1234; fax 602/428-7653. A pleasant, attractive motel. **Rooms:** 70 rms and stes. CI 1pm/CO noon. Nonsmoking rms avail. **Amenities:** ⬛ ⬛ A/C, cable TV, refrig. **Services:** ✗ 🚗 ⬛ ⬐ ⬙ **Facilities:** 🔥 ⬛ 1 rst, 1 bar, washer/dryer. **Rates:** $46–$48 S; $50–$54 D; from $65 ste. Extra person $4. Children under 12 stay free. Pking: Outdoor, free. Maj CC.

Attraction ⬛

Roper Lake State Park, I-10; tel 602/428-6760. Located in the foothills of Mt Graham, the 240-acre park features natural hot springs that are accessible in a continually flowing hot tub area. A man-made lake offers fishing and swimming; motor boats are not allowed on the lake. Camping, hiking, nature trails. **Open:** Daily 6am–10pm. $

SCOTTSDALE

Map page M-2, D2

Hotels ⬛

Courtyard by Marriott, 13444 E Shea Blvd, Scottsdale, AZ 85259; tel 602/860-4000 or toll free 800/321-2211; fax 602/860-4308. Close to Mayo Clinic. Unrated. **Rooms:** 124 rms and stes. CI 3pm/CO 1pm. Express checkout avail. Nonsmoking rms avail. **Amenities:** ⬛ ⬛ A/C, cable TV w/movies. Some units w/minibars, some w/terraces. **Services:** ✗ 🔑 ⬛ ⬐ Twice-daily maid svce, babysitting. **Facilities:** 🔥 ⬛ ⬛ ⬛ 1 rst, 1 bar, whirlpool, washer/dryer. **Rates:** HS Jan 1–Apr 23 $104 S; $114 D; from $125 ste. Extra person $10. Children under 5 stay free. Lower rates off-season. Higher rates for spec evnts/hols. Pking: Outdoor, free. Maj CC.

≣≣≣ Embassy Suites Resort Scottsdale, 5001 N Scottsdale Rd, Scottsdale, AZ 85250; tel 602/949-1414 or toll free 800/528-1456; fax 602/949-1414 ext 525. An attractive all-suites hotel, with fountains outside the lobby. **Rooms:** 310 stes. CI 3pm/CO noon. Express checkout avail. Nonsmoking rms avail. Rooms are spacious, particularly nice for those with children and for business travelers who need extra space. Handicapped-accessible room does not have roll-in shower, but bathroom floor

has a drain for showering outside the tub. **Amenities:** ⬛ ⬛ A/C, satel TV w/movies. All units w/minibars, some w/Jacuzzis. **Services:** ✗ 🔑 🚗 ⬛ ⬐ ⬙ Car-rental desk, babysitting. Complimentary cocktails. **Facilities:** 🔥 ⬛ ⬛ ⬛ ⬛ 1 rst, 1 bar, games rm, spa, whirlpool, washer/dryer. **Rates (BB):** HS Jan–Apr from $145 ste. Extra person $10. Children under 12 stay free. Lower rates off-season. Spec packages avail. Pking: Outdoor, free. Maj CC.

≣≣ Fairfield Inn, 13440 N Scottsdale Rd, Scottsdale, AZ 85254; tel 602/483-0042 or toll free 800/228-2800. 8 mi N of downtown. A step above the basic hotel/motel, recommended for both business travelers and vacationers. **Rooms:** 133 rms. CI 3pm/CO noon. Express checkout avail. Nonsmoking rms avail. Rooms are simple but very pleasant. **Amenities:** ⬛ A/C, cable TV. **Services:** ⬛ ⬐ Free morning coffee and tea, and free local phone calls. Fax service available. **Facilities:** 🔥 ⬛ ⬛ Whirlpool. **Rates:** HS Jan–Apr $85–$95 S or D. Children under 18 stay free. Lower rates off-season. Higher rates for spec evnts/hols. Spec packages avail. Pking: Outdoor, free. Maj CC. A particularly good value in off-season.

≣≣≣ Holiday Inn Hotel and Conference Center, 7353 E Indian School Rd, Scottsdale, AZ 85251; tel 602/994-9203 or toll free 800/695-6995; fax 602/941-2567. At Civic Center Plaza Dr. Centrally located Scottsdale hotel with its own conference center. **Rooms:** 206 rms and stes. CI 3pm/CO noon. Express checkout avail. Nonsmoking rms avail. All ground-floor rooms have patios. **Amenities:** ⬛ ⬛ ⬛ ⬛ A/C, cable TV w/movies, voice mail. Some units w/minibars, some w/terraces. **Services:** ✗ 🚗 ⬛ ⬐ ⬙ Babysitting. **Facilities:** 🔥 ⬛ ⬛ ⬛ ⬛ ⬛ 1 rst (see also "Restaurants" below), 1 bar (w/entertainment), spa, whirlpool. **Rates:** HS Jan–Apr $140–$160 S; $150–$170 D; from $175 ste. Extra person $10. Children under 19 stay free. Lower rates off-season. Spec packages avail. Pking: Outdoor, free. Maj CC.

≣≣≣ Howard Johnson, 5101 N Scottsdale Rd, Scottsdale, AZ 85250; tel 602/945-4392 or toll free 800/446-4656. A handsome hotel, good for both business and pleasure travelers. Close to airports and shopping in old Scottsdale. **Rooms:** 216 rms and stes. CI 3pm/CO 1pm. Express checkout avail. Nonsmoking rms avail. Pleasant, comfortable rooms. **Amenities:** ⬛ ⬛ A/C, satel TV. **Services:** ✗ 🚗 ⬛ ⬐ ⬙ Car-rental desk. **Facilities:** 🔥 ⬛ ⬛ 1 rst, 1 bar, washer/dryer. **Rates:** HS Jan 15–Apr 15 $95–$118 S or D; from $153 ste. Extra person $10. Children under 18 stay free. Lower rates off-season. Spec packages avail. Pking: Outdoor, free. Maj CC. A good value.

≣≣≣ Scottsdale Manor Suites, 4807 N Woodmere Fairway Dr, Scottsdale, AZ 85251; tel 602/994-5282 or toll free 800/523-5282. Ideal for longer, self-catering visits. **Rooms:** 72 stes.

CI 3pm/CO 10am. All units have fully equipped kitchens, 2 bedrooms and 2 baths. Very spacious. **Amenities:** ⛶ ⛁ ⛶ A/C, cable TV, refrig, stereo/tape player. Some units w/terraces. Linens, towels, vacuum cleaners, ironing boards, and irons are provided. **Services:** ⊐ Daily maid service is available at an extra charge. Free local calls. **Facilities:** ⛶ ⛰ ⛶2 ⛶ Lawn games, whirlpool, washer/dryer. Putting green and 25 barbecues on premises. **Rates:** HS Jan 15–Apr 15 from $200 ste. Children under 18 stay free. Min stay. Lower rates off-season. Spec packages avail. Pking: Outdoor, free. No CC. There's a 2-night minimum stay. Each unit can house up to 4 persons for the base rate, and weekly and monthly rates are available.

≡≡≡ **Sunburst Hotel & Conference Center**, 4925 N Scottsdale Rd, Scottsdale, AZ 85251 (Downtown); tel 602/945-7666 or toll free 800/528-7867; fax 602/946-4056. Centrally located hotel, close to shopping and sports facilities. **Rooms:** 209 rms and stes. CI 3pm/CO noon. Express checkout avail. Nonsmoking rms avail. **Amenities:** ⛶ ⛶ A/C, cable TV w/movies, refrig. All units w/terraces. Some rooms have coffeemakers. **Services:** ✕ ⛶ ⛶ ⊐ Babysitting. **Facilities:** ⛶ ⛶ ⛶ ⛶ ⛶ 1 rst, 2 bars, whirlpool. **Rates:** HS Jan 2–Apr $125–$150 S; $140–$165 D; from $200 ste. Extra person $15. Children under 18 stay free. Lower rates off-season. Spec packages avail. Pking: Outdoor, free. Maj CC.

Motels

≡≡≡ **Best Western Papago Inn and Resort**, 7017 E McDowell Rd, Scottsdale, AZ 85257; tel 602/947-7335 or toll free 800/528-1234; fax 602/994-0692. This pleasant, modern motel adjoins Papago Plaza Shopping Center and is close to Desert Botanical Gardens. **Rooms:** 56 rms and stes. CI 2pm/CO noon. Express checkout avail. Nonsmoking rms avail. **Amenities:** ⛶ ⛁ ⛶ ⛶ A/C, cable TV, refrig. 1 unit w/fireplace. Telephone adapts for machines for the hearing impaired. **Services:** ✕ ⛟ ⛶ ⊐ Complimentary wine for guests. **Facilities:** ⛶ ⛟ ⛶ ⛶ 1 rst, 1 bar, spa, sauna, washer/dryer. There's a bird aviary by the pool, and a large outdoor chess game. A small meeting room is free for guest use. **Rates:** HS Jan–Apr $88–$110 S or D; from $175 ste. Extra person $6. Children under 12 stay free. Lower rates off-season. Spec packages avail. Pking: Outdoor, free. Maj CC.

≡≡ **Rodeway Inn**, 7110 E Indian School Rd, Scottsdale, AZ 85251; tel 602/946-3456 or toll free 800/424-4777; fax 602/946-4248. Basic, centrally located lodging. **Rooms:** 64 rms and stes. CI 3pm/CO noon. Nonsmoking rms avail. Rooms are simply but comfortably furnished. **Amenities:** ⛶ ⛁ A/C, cable TV. 1 unit w/Jacuzzi. **Services:** ⊐ **Facilities:** ⛶ Whirlpool. **Rates (CP):** HS Jan 14–Apr 17 $78–$117 S; $86–$125 D; from

$125 ste. Extra person $8. Children under 17 stay free. Lower rates off-season. Higher rates for spec evnts/hols. Pking: Outdoor, free. Maj CC.

≡≡≡ **Scottsdale Pima Motel**, 7330 N Pima Rd, Scottsdale, AZ 85258; tel 602/948-3800 or toll free 800/344-0262; fax 602/443-3374. This motel offers a wide range of accommodations and is good for long stays. Popular with golfers and business travelers. **Rooms:** 93 rms and stes. CI 3pm/CO noon. Nonsmoking rms avail. All suites have kitchens. **Amenities:** ⛶ ⛁ ⛶ A/C, cable TV w/movies, refrig. Some units w/minibars, some w/terraces. **Services:** ⛶ ⊐ ⛶ Complimentary 24-hour coffee bar. Free shuttle service within a 5-mile radius. **Facilities:** ⛶ ⛟ ⛶ ⛶ 1 rst, 1 bar, games rm, spa, sauna, steam rm, whirlpool, washer/dryer. Game room with pool table. **Rates (CP):** HS Apr 17–May 21/Sept 9–Dec 29 $59 S; $69 D; from $89 ste. Extra person $10. Children under 16 stay free. Lower rates off-season. Spec packages avail. Pking: Outdoor, free. Maj CC. Weekly and monthly rates available.

≡≡ **Scottsdale's 5th Avenue Inn**, 6935 5th Ave, Scottsdale, AZ 85251 (Downtown); tel 602/994-9461 or toll free 800/528-7396; fax 602/947-1695. In a good location in the very hub of Scottsdale. More than 250 shops and galleries are within walking distance. **Rooms:** 92 rms. CI 2pm/CO noon. Nonsmoking rms avail. **Amenities:** ⛶ ⛁ A/C, satel TV. **Services:** ⛶ ⊐ Babysitting. **Facilities:** ⛶ ⛶ ⛶ 1 rst, washer/dryer. **Rates (CP):** HS Jan 15–Apr $71 S; $82–$87 D. Extra person $8. Children under 16 stay free. Lower rates off-season. Pking: Outdoor, free. Maj CC. Good value for the location.

Resorts

≡≡≡ **Holiday Inn Sunspree Resort**, 7601 E Indian Bend Rd, Scottsdale, AZ 85250; tel 602/991-2400 or toll free 800/991-2400. 23 acres. A good, basic resort; was undergoing renovation. Caters to golfers and tennis players. **Rooms:** 200 rms and stes. CI 3pm/CO noon. Nonsmoking rms avail. Well-appointed, comfortable rooms. **Amenities:** ⛶ ⛁ ⛶ A/C, cable TV, refrig. Some units w/minibars. **Services:** ✕ ⛶ ⛟ ⛶ ⊐ Car-rental desk, children's program, babysitting. **Facilities:** ⛶ ⛟ ⛶18 ⛶ ⛟ ⛶ ⛶ 1 rst, 1 bar, lawn games, whirlpool, washer/dryer. **Rates (CP):** HS Jan–Apr $110 S or D; from $175 ste. Extra person $10. Children under 20 stay free. Lower rates off-season. Spec packages avail. Pking: Outdoor, free. Maj CC.

≡≡≡≡ **Hyatt Regency Scottsdale**, 7500 E Doubletree Ranch Rd, Scottsdale, AZ 85258 (Gainey Ranch); tel 602/991-3388 or toll free 800/233-1234; fax 602/483-5550. 5 mi N of downtown Scottsdale. From I-17 take Greenway Pkwy 15 miles east to Scottsdale Rd. 27 acres. Splendidly landscaped grounds covering 27 acres of a 560-acre spread known as the Gainey Ranch, with lagoons and fountains, tall stands of date palms, and stunning architecture incorporating textured concrete blocks à la Frank Lloyd Wright. **Rooms:** 493 rms and stes; 7 ctges/villas. Exec-level rms avail. CI 4pm/CO noon. Express checkout avail. Nonsmoking rms avail. Attractive decor with southwestern colors and artworks. Fireplaces and patios in casitas, larger-than-average rooms in Regency Club wing. **Amenities:** 🛅 ⚱ 🍴 A/C, cable TV w/movies, refrig, in-rm safe. All units w/minibars, all w/terraces, some w/fireplaces. Bathrobes in season only, on request at other times. **Services:** 🍽 🗝 VP 🚐 🖼 🛏 Car-rental desk, social director, masseur, children's program, babysitting. Turndown service in season only, on request other times. Free shuttle to nearby shopping malls. Young, cordial staff. **Facilities:** 🏊 🚲 🏌 27 🎾 🌊 4 🏐 🥎 1.5K 💻 ♿ 4 rsts, 3 bars (1 w/entertainment), lifeguard, spa, sauna, steam rm, whirlpool, beauty salon, day-care ctr, playground. 2.5-acre water playground with sandy beach; 10 pools (including one for adults only); 3-story waterslide; 25-foot-wide Jacuzzi (open until midnight); 14-foot waterfalls that are floodlit at night; and poolside bars. Boat rides on lagoons. Gainey Ranch golf courses shared with neighboring homeowners. Complimentary bicycles. Free spa features Mollen Clinic for health evaluations and exercise counseling. One restaurant has singing servers; the other overlooks a Japanese koi pond. **Rates:** HS Jan 1–Jun 12 $285–$375 S or D; from $450 ste; from $1,000 ctge/villa. Children under 18 stay free. Min stay HS. Lower rates off-season. Spec packages avail. Pking: Outdoor, free. Maj CC. $40 premium for pool, fairway, or mountain views. Summer rates are less than half winter rates and are a bargain.

≣≣≣≣**John Gardiner's Tennis Ranch**, 5700 E McDonald Dr, Scottsdale, AZ 85253 (Paradise Valley); tel 602/948-2100 or toll free 800/245-2051; fax 602/483-7314. McDonald Dr exit off Scottsdale Rd. 53 acres. A superb facility designed for the tennis enthusiast who wants to improve his or her game in a luxury setting. **Rooms:** 82 rms and stes. CI 3pm/CO 1pm. Express checkout avail. Nonsmoking rms avail. All rooms have views of Camelback Mountain. **Amenities:** 🛅 ⚱ 🖼 A/C, cable TV, refrig, voice mail, bathrobes. Some units w/minibars, all w/terraces, some w/fireplaces. Most rooms have VCRs and stereos. **Services:** ✕ 🗝 🚐 🖼 🛏 🕊 Twice-daily maid svce, car-rental desk, social director, masseur, children's program, babysitting. Complimentary orange juice, newspapers, and soft drinks daily. Tennis pros on hand. **Facilities:** 🏊 🎾 🌊 24 🥎 100 💻 ♿ 1 rst, 1 bar (w/entertainment), spa, whirlpool, washer/dryer. Pro shop. **Rates:** HS Dec–Apr $225 S or D; from $335 ste. Extra person $15. Children under 18 stay free. Lower rates off-season. AP and MAP rates avail. Spec packages avail. Pking: Outdoor, free. Maj CC. There are several tennis packages to choose from. Also, 5 homes are available to rent.

≣≣≣**Marriott's Camelback Inn Resort, Golf Club & Spa**, 5402 E Lincoln Dr, Scottsdale, AZ 85253 (Paradise Valley); tel 602/948-1700 or toll free 800/242-2635; fax 602/951-8469. Glendale Ave exit off I-17; continue east until Glendale becomes Lincoln. One of the original desert resorts and still a landmark, with its pueblo-style architecture. Spread over 125 natural desert acres. Highly popular with people who organize business meetings, but individual vacationers may feel crowded out. Attractive, adobe-style lobby and lounge. **Rooms:** 423 rms and stes. CI 4pm/CO noon. Express checkout avail. Nonsmoking rms avail. Attractive, southwestern-style oak furniture, with seating areas in each 550-square-foot room, but balconies and patios often look out on walkways or other patios. Cramped bathrooms. **Amenities:** 🛅 ⚱ 🍴 A/C, cable TV w/movies, refrig, voice mail, in-rm safe, shoe polisher, bathrobes. All units w/minibars, all w/terraces, some w/fireplaces, some w/Jacuzzis. In-room video services for messages and accounts review; some suites with private pools. **Services:** ✕ 🗝 VP 🚐 🖼 🛏 🕊 Twice-daily maid svce, car-rental desk, social director, masseur, children's program, babysitting. Bellmen double as doormen and car valets; turndown service may be fastest on record, but in their rush housekeepers sometimes leave behind out-of-date activities list. **Facilities:** 🏊 🚲 🏌 36 🎾 🌊 5 🏐 🥎 2.2K 💻 ♿ 5 rsts (see also "Restaurants" below), 4 bars (1 w/entertainment), lifeguard, games rm, lawn games, spa, sauna, steam rm, whirlpool, beauty salon, day-care ctr, playground, washer/dryer. Striking circular swimming pool with tiered flower gardens, and handsome, 25,000-square-foot spa and wellness center (membership fee $22 per day) offering Adobe Clay Purification Treatments; the 2 championship courses are among the best bargains for golfers (but they are located several miles away at the Camelback Country Club Estates). Also Hopalong College for kids (seasonal), including cookouts and "camelhunts." **Rates:** HS Jan 1–May 21 $275–$340 S or D; from $360 ste. Children under 18 stay free. Lower rates off-season. AP and MAP rates avail. Spec packages avail. Pking: Outdoor, free. Maj CC.

≣≣≣≣≣**The Phoenician**, 6000 E Camelback Rd, Scottsdale, AZ 85251; tel 602/941-8200 or toll free 800/888-8234; fax 602/947-4311. Camelback Rd exit off I-17. 130 acres. Grand and affluent, filled with antiques and artworks and surrounded by estate-like gardens and ponds wedged between lush fairways and a hillside of cacti and ocotillos. But the extravagantly elegant lobby can be overwhelmed by business groups—60% of the clientele—and many rooms are a long hike from both the lobby and restaurants. **Rooms:** 580 rms and stes; 15 ctges/villas. CI 4pm/CO noon. Express checkout avail. Nonsmoking rms avail. Some have stunning views of the grounds and city lights, others have less-than-stunning views of other rooms and balconies. For some guests, the choicest (not the priciest) lodgings face the hillside at the rear; golfers and tennis players prefer the convenience of the casitas in a cluster of villas below the spectacular water playground. All rooms are distinguished by spaciousness (600 square feet and up) and refined appointments, down to brass doorknobs and hinges. Bathrooms, swathed in marble, are the size of most hotel rooms. **Amenities:** 📱 🛁 🍴 A/C, cable TV w/movies, refrig, in-rm safe, shoe polisher, bathrobes. All units w/minibars, all w/terraces, some w/fireplaces. Balconies/patios large enough for proper tables, chairs and loungers; double walk-in closets; Nintendo and other playthings for kids; 2-line speakerphones; TV message service and account reports. **Services:** 🍽 🔑 📹 🚐 🛄 ↵ Twice-daily maid svce, car-rental desk, social director, masseur, children's program, baby-sitting. Young and eager, if not always polished, staffers outnumber the guest rooms 2 to 1. **Facilities:** ⛳ 🚲 ▶18 🎿 🏊 🎾 📺 🖥 ♿ 6 rsts (*see also* "Restaurants" below), 4 bars (2 w/entertainment), lifeguard, lawn games, spa, sauna, steam rm, whirlpool, beauty salon, day-care ctr, playground. Most resorts measure their pool areas in feet; here it's in acres, with 5 pools, 100-foot slides, lagoons, sundecks, and swim-up bars. Immaculate health spa and Center for Wellbeing with Meditation Atrium; first-rate tennis complex with automated practice court and pros who chill towels for perspiring players; golf course reserved exclusively for hotel guests, with an additional 9 holes of golf promised for 1995. Delightful restaurants. **Rates:** HS Sept 15–July 1 $290–$425 S or D; from $850 ste. Extra person $50. Children under 12 stay free. Lower rates off-season. Spec packages avail. Pking: Indoor/outdoor, free. Maj CC. Rates slightly higher than nearby Camelback and Princess resorts, but there's more to offer here than either.

≋≋≋ **Radisson Resort**, 7171 N Scottsdale Rd, Scottsdale, AZ 85253; tel 602/991-3800 or toll free 800/333-3333; fax 602/948-1381. 76 acres. A very attractive resort in the center of Scottsdale. **Rooms:** 116 rms and stes; 202 ctges/villas. CI 4pm/CO noon. Express checkout avail. Nonsmoking rms avail. Rooms are plush and finely decorated. **Amenities:** 📱 🛁 📹 🍴 A/C, cable TV, refrig, voice mail, bathrobes. All units w/minibars, all w/terraces, some w/fireplaces, 1 w/Jacuzzi. **Services:** 🍽 🔑 🛄 ↵ 🚐 Twice-daily maid svce, car-rental desk, social director, masseur, children's program, babysitting. **Facilities:** ⛳ 🚲 ▶36 🎿 🏊 🎾 1.5K ♿ 2 rsts, 3 bars (2 w/entertainment), board surfing, games rm, lawn games, spa, sauna, steam rm, whirlpool, beauty salon, playground, washer/dryer. **Rates:** HS Jan–Apr $100–$215 S or D; from $150 ste; from $100 ctge/villa. Extra person $10. Children under 18 stay free. Min stay spec evnts. Lower rates off-season. Spec packages avail. Pking: Outdoor, free. Maj CC.

≋≋≋ **Red Lion's La Posada Resort**, 4949 E Lincoln Dr, Scottsdale, AZ 85253; tel 602/952-0420 or toll free 800/547-8010; fax 602/852-0151. 30 acres. The hotel has an

attractive arched adobe entrance and well-kept flower gardens. **Rooms:** 264 rms and stes. CI 4pm/CO noon. Express checkout avail. Nonsmoking rms avail. Rooms are large and well furnished. An increasing number of handicapped-accessible rooms are planned for 1995. **Amenities:** 📱 🛁 📹 A/C, satel TV w/movies. All units w/minibars, all w/terraces, some w/Jacuzzis. **Services:** ✕ 🔑 🛄 ↵ 🚐 Car-rental desk, masseur, children's program, babysitting. Signs are posted showing handicap accessible routes. **Facilities:** ⛳ 🚲 🎿 🎾 600 🖥 ♿ 3 rsts, 1 bar (w/entertainment), lawn games, racquetball, sauna, whirlpool, beauty salon. The main pool is divided by "Flintstone"-like man-made rocks, with cave and swim-through tunnel and waterfall. **Rates:** HS Jan 1–May 15 $209–$239 S or D; from $520 ste. Extra person $15. Children under 18 stay free. Min stay wknds. Lower rates off-season. Spec packages avail. Pking: Outdoor, free. Maj CC.

≋≋≋ **Regal McCormick Ranch**, 7401 N Scottsdale Rd, Scottsdale, AZ 85253; tel 602/948-5050 or toll free 800/243-1332. 70 acres. Beautiful but unpretentious resort. Lobby is decorated in southwestern decor. **Rooms:** 125 rms and stes; 51 ctges/villas. CI 3pm/CO noon. Nonsmoking rms avail. Rooms are especially well appointed. **Amenities:** 📱 🛁 A/C, cable TV w/movies. All units w/minibars, all w/terraces, some w/fireplaces. Villas have full kitchens. **Services:** ✕ 🔑 🛄 ↵ Masseur, children's program, babysitting. **Facilities:** ⛳ 🚲 ⛵ 🚣 ▶18 🎿 🏊 ⛵ 200 ♿ 2 rsts, 1 bar (w/entertainment), lawn games, whirlpool, day-care ctr. Attractive lake. Additional golf courses nearby. **Rates:** HS Jan–Apr $165–$230 S; $175–$240 D; from $295 ste; from $320 ctge/villa. Extra person $10. Children under 18 stay free. Min stay HS. Lower rates off-season. Spec packages avail. Pking: Outdoor, free. Maj CC.

≋≋≋ **Resort Suites of Scottsdale**, 7677 E Princess Blvd, Scottsdale, AZ 85255; tel 602/585-1234 or toll free 800/541-5203. 12 acres. Ideal for the golfer and those who want the conveniences and comforts of home while on vacation. **Rooms:** 287 stes. CI 3pm/CO 10am. Express checkout avail. Nonsmoking rms avail. Condominium-style suites have full kitchens and walk-in closets, and a pool view. **Amenities:** 📱 🛁 📹 A/C, cable TV w/movies, refrig. All units w/terraces. The 2- and 4-bedroom suites have their own washers and dryers. **Services:** ✕ 🔑 🚐 🛄 ↵ Babysitting. Helicopter transport to area golf courses is available. **Facilities:** ⛳ 🚲 ▶36 🎿 🎾 100 🖥 ♿ 1 rst, 1 bar (w/entertainment), games rm, spa, whirlpool, washer/dryer. The resort can arrange golf at any of 35 area courses. **Rates:** HS Jan–Apr from $185 ste. Children under 18 stay free. Lower rates off-season. Spec packages avail. Pking: Outdoor, free. Maj CC. Several golf packages are available.

≡≡≡ **Safari Resort**, 4611 N Scottsdale Rd, Scottsdale, AZ 85251; tel 602/945-0721 or toll free 800/845-4356; fax 602/946-4703. 12 acres. A landmark Scottsdale resort—the city's first—at the hub of downtown activities. **Rooms:** 188 rms and stes. CI 3pm/CO noon. Nonsmoking rms avail. Some units have kitchenettes. **Amenities:** 📺 🅰 A/C, cable TV w/movies, refrig. Some units w/terraces. Most rooms have refrigerators. **Services:** ✕ 🔑 🖼 🛏 🐕 The lounge has complimentary appetizers during happy hour. **Facilities:** 🏌 🅿 💻 🚹 2 rsts, 1 bar (w/entertainment), lawn games, spa, whirlpool, beauty salon, playground, washer/dryer. The resort has a golf putting and pitching green, and is close to major shopping and dining districts. **Rates (CP):** HS Jan–mid Apr $92–$104 S; $102–$114 D; from $130 ste. Extra person $10. Children under 18 stay free. Lower rates off-season. Spec packages avail. Pking: Outdoor, free. Maj CC.

≡≡≡ **Scottsdale Conference Resort**, 7700 E McCormick Pkwy, Scottsdale, AZ 85258; tel 602/991-9000 or toll free 800/528-0293. 50 acres. This plush resort books mainly groups and corporate meetings. **Rooms:** 308 rms and stes; 12 ctges/villas. CI 3pm/CO 1pm. Nonsmoking rms avail. **Amenities:** 📺 🅰 🍴 A/C, cable TV, refrig, bathrobes. All units w/minibars, some w/terraces, some w/fireplaces, 1 w/Jacuzzi. **Services:** ✕ 🔑 VP 🚌 🖼 🐕 Twice-daily maid svce, car-rental desk, masseur. **Facilities:** 🏌 ⛳ ⛵36 🎾 🏊 🛳 ⛹ 💻 🚹 1 rst, 1 bar, games rm, lawn games, spa, sauna, steam rm, whirlpool, beauty salon. **Rates (AP):** HS Jan–Mar $340 S; $245–$490 D; from $515 ste; from $300 ctge/villa. Children under 18 stay free. Lower rates off-season. Spec packages avail. Pking: Indoor/outdoor, free. Maj CC.

≡≡≡ **Scottsdale Hilton Resort and Villas**, 6333 N Scottsdale Rd, Scottsdale, AZ 85250; tel 602/948-7750 or toll free 800/528-3119; fax 602/948-2232. 20 acres. Lavish property, with a high-ceilinged lobby, southwestern-style carpets, and recorded background music. **Rooms:** 187 rms, stes, and effic; 45 ctges/villas. CI 4pm/CO 1pm. Nonsmoking rms avail. Rooms are unusually spacious. **Amenities:** 📺 🅰 A/C, cable TV w/movies. Some units w/terraces, some w/fireplaces, some w/Jacuzzis. **Services:** ✕ 🔑 VP 🖼 🐕 🐾 Car-rental desk, social director, masseur, children's program. **Facilities:** 🏌 🍴 🛳 🍴 💻 🚹 1 rst, 1 bar (w/entertainment), spa, sauna, steam rm, whirlpool, beauty salon. Golf courses nearby, and numerous recreational opportunities on site. **Rates (CP):** HS Jan–May $140–$175 S or D; from $195 ste; from $300 effic; from $310 ctge/villa. Extra person $10. Children under 10 stay free. Min stay spec evnts. Lower rates off-season. Spec packages avail. Pking: Outdoor, free. Maj CC. An especially good value during the summer off-season.

≡≡≡ **Scottsdale Plaza Resort**, 7200 N Scottsdale Rd, Scottsdale, AZ 85253; tel 602/948-5000 or toll free 800/832-2025; fax 602/951-5151. 40 acres. A plush property in the center of the resort area. **Rooms:** 404 rms and stes. CI 3pm/CO noon. Express checkout avail. Nonsmoking rms avail. Rooms are attractively and comfortably furnished. **Amenities:** 📺 🅰 A/C, cable TV, refrig, in-rm safe, bathrobes. All units w/minibars, some w/terraces, some w/fireplaces. **Services:** ✕ 🔑 🚌 🖼 🐕 Car-rental desk, masseur, babysitting. **Facilities:** 🏌 ⛳ 🍴3 🎾 🛳 🍴 💻 🚹 3 rsts, 3 bars (1 w/entertainment), lawn games, racquetball, spa, sauna, steam rm, whirlpool, beauty salon. **Rates:** HS Jan–Apr $210–$225 D; from $300 ste. Extra person $15. Children under 18 stay free. Lower rates off-season. Higher rates for spec evnts/hols. Spec packages avail. Pking: Outdoor, free. Maj CC.

≡≡≡≡ **Scottsdale Princess**, 7575 E Princess Dr, Scottsdale, AZ 85255 (North Scottsdale); tel 602/585-4848 or toll free 800/344-4758; fax 602/585-0086. Bell Rd exit off I-17; continue east on Bell to Scottsdale Rd. 450 acres. Big and sprawling, with echoes of colonial Spain in its terra-cotta columns and red-tiled roofs, fountains and flagstone walkways, terraced lawns and gardens; but the sense of desert is eroded by surrounding subdivisions. **Rooms:** 600 rms and stes; 125 ctges/villas. CI 4pm/CO noon. Express checkout avail. Nonsmoking rms avail. Asymmetric configuration makes 525-square-foot rooms more interesting than usual cookie cutters; comfortable and efficient. Oval tubs, separate toilets. Marginal views. **Amenities:** 📺 🅰 🍴 A/C, cable TV w/movies, refrig, in-rm safe, shoe polisher, bathrobes. All units w/minibars, all w/terraces, some w/fireplaces, 1 w/Jacuzzi. In-room video services (telephone messages, accounts review, room service orders); speakerphones with dataport, call-waiting, and 2 extensions; swimsuit bags in closets; wood-burning fireplaces in casitas. **Services:** 🍽 🔑 VP 🖼 🐕 Twice-daily maid svce, car-rental desk, masseur, children's program, babysitting. Genial, generally competent staff. **Facilities:** 🏌 ⛳ ⛵36 🎾 🍴3 🎾 🛳 🍴 💻 🚹 5 rsts (see also "Restaurants" below), 6 bars (1 w/entertainment), lifeguard, games rm, lawn games, racquetball, squash, spa, sauna, steam rm, whirlpool, beauty salon. Golf courses, a short drive away, are operated by TPC (one of them is home of the Phoenix Open), owned by the city, and open to all, but Princess guests get priority tee times. 10-station fitness course; 10,000 square feet of workout space. Kids' Club activities include sand painting and Native American bead art. **Rates:** HS Jan 1–May 21 $260–$350 S or D; from $480 ste. Extra person $30. Children under 12 stay free. Lower rates off-season. MAP rates avail. Spec packages avail. Pking: Outdoor, free. Maj CC. A good value, given the wide range of activities and moderately priced dining options.

Stouffer Cottonwoods Resort, 6160 N Scottsdale Rd, Scottsdale, AZ 85253; tel 602/991-1414 or toll free 800/HOTELS-1; fax 602/951-3350. Near Lincoln Dr. 25 acres. This southwestern-style resort lies adjacent to the upscale Borgata of Scottsdale shopping center. **Rooms:** 170 rms and stes. CI 3pm/CO noon. Express checkout avail. Nonsmoking rms avail. **Amenities:** A/C, cable TV w/movies, refrig, in-rm safe. All units w/minibars, all w/terraces, some w/fireplaces, some w/Jacuzzis. **Services:** VP Social director, masseur, babysitting. There's an on-site tennis pro. **Facilities:** 2 250 1 rst, 1 bar, lawn games, whirlpool. Both swimming pools are open 24 hours. Putting green, tennis shop. **Rates (CP):** HS Jan–May $205 S or D; from $235 ste. Extra person $10. Children under 18 stay free. Min stay spec evnts. Lower rates off-season. Spec packages avail. Pking: Outdoor, free. Maj CC.

Wyndham Paradise Valley Resort, 5401 N Scottsdale Rd, Scottsdale, AZ 85250 (Downtown); tel 602/947-5400 or toll free 800/WYNDHAM in the US, 800/631-4200 in Canada; fax 602/481-0209. 22 acres. Beautiful and luxurious, with a large, open lobby with glass enclosed aviary, palms, and skylights. **Rooms:** 387 rms and stes. CI 3pm/CO noon. Express checkout avail. Nonsmoking rms avail. There are wood-beamed ceilings in the spacious rooms, which have individual climate controls. **Amenities:** A/C, cable TV w/movies, refrig, bathrobes. All units w/minibars, all w/terraces. **Services:** X VP Car-rental desk, masseur, children's program, babysitting. Trolley transportation available to nearby shops. **Facilities:** 2K 2 rsts, 1 bar (w/entertainment), lawn games, racquetball, spa, sauna, steam rm, whirlpool, beauty salon. Waterfalls flow into the large swimming pools; poolside bar for beverages and snacks. Championship golf available at nearby courses. **Rates:** HS Jan–Apr $195–$275 S or D; from $295 ste. Extra person $20. Children under 18 stay free. Lower rates off-season. Spec packages avail. Pking: Outdoor, free. Maj CC.

Restaurants

Baby Kay's Cajun Kitchen, 7216 E Shoeman Lane, Scottsdale; tel 602/990-9080. **Cajun.** A small Cajun diner and bar with funky New Orleans decor. The menu includes a spicy gumbo, catfish filets in sherry or crawfish sauce, barbecue shrimp, and red beans and rice. A specialty is chicken and sausage jambalaya. Also at: 2119 E Camelback Rd, Phoenix (602/955-6011). **FYI:** Reservations not accepted. Jazz. **Open:** Mon–Thurs 5–10pm, Fri–Sat 5–11pm. Closed some hols. **Prices:** Main courses $6.95–$13.95. Maj CC.

Bola's Grill, in the Holiday Inn Hotel and Conference Center, 7353 E Indian School Rd, Scottsdale (Old Town); tel 602/994-9203. **New American.** A southwestern grill in the Scottsdale Civic Center Mall in Old Town Scottsdale. The dining area is in a semi-circle around the exposed kitchen. Specialties include grilled lamb chops, baby-back ribs, lemon oregano chicken, southwestern duck, and medallions of beef. **FYI:** Reservations recommended. Band. Children's menu. **Open:** Lunch Mon–Sat 11am–2pm; dinner Sun–Thurs 5–9pm, Fri–Sat 5–10pm; brunch Sun 11am–2pm. **Prices:** Main courses $6.95–$15.95. Maj CC.

Cantina del Pedregal, in El Pedregal Marketplace, 34505 N Scottsdale Rd, Scottsdale; tel 602/488-0715. 1 mi S of Carefree. **Mexican.** This comfortable Mexican restaurant in the hills north of Phoenix offers patio dining and splendid views. Attractively decorated in folk art style, with "rock art" painted on the stucco walls. The Sonoran cuisine is highlighted by the Mexican Gulf shrimp with smoked red chile sauce. Also offered are hot pork tamales; chicken, beef, and shrimp fajitas; chiles rellenos; and chicken with mole sauce. The margaritas are very popular. **FYI:** Reservations recommended. Children's menu. **Open:** HS Sept–July daily 11:30am–10pm. Reduced hours off-season. Closed some hols. **Prices:** Main courses $8.75–$13.95. Maj CC.

★ **The Chaparral**, in Marriott's Camelback Inn Resort, Golf Club & Spa, 5402 E Lincoln Dr, Scottsdale (Paradise Valley); tel 602/948-1700. Glendale Ave exit off I-17; continue east until Glendale becomes Lincoln. **Continental/French.** Formal but not stuffy restaurant, with a well-informed staff and attentive, gracious service. Circular adobe rooms with Native American motifs, soft lighting, and picture windows for views of Camelback Mountain. Grilled eggplant with mascarpone cheese, pesto, and roasted tomato vinaigrette; veal medallions with crabmeat, lobster, and shrimp; grilled jumbo shrimp with corn fritters and melon salsa. **FYI:** Reservations recommended. Combo. Jacket required. **Open:** Daily 6–10pm. **Prices:** Main courses $21–$28. Maj CC. VP

Chart House, 7255 E McCormick Pkwy, Scottsdale (McCormick Ranch); tel 602/951-2550. 1/10 mi E of Scottsdale Road. **Seafood/Steak.** The large dining room, which seats 220, has a nautical theme; outdoor action photos cover the walls. Mostly steak and seafood. Slow-roasted prime rib is a house specialty. **FYI:** Reservations recommended. Children's menu. **Open:** Mon–Thurs 5–10pm, Fri–Sun 5–11pm. **Prices:** Main courses $14–$35. Maj CC. VP

Don and Charlie's, 7501 E Camelback Rd, Scottsdale; tel 602/990-0900. At Scottsdale Rd. **American.** One word—sports—sums up the decor of this central Scottsdale eatery. With an emphasis on baseball, the restaurant is decorated with sports memorabilia, from photos to signed baseballs and footballs. The menu offers ribs, steaks, barbecue, prime rib, fish, and seafood pasta. **FYI:** Reservations recommended. Children's menu. **Open:** Mon–Thurs 5–10pm, Fri–Sat 5–10pm, Sun 4:30–9pm. Closed Thanksgiving. **Prices:** Main courses $7.95–$23.95. Maj CC.

Eddie Chan's, in Mountain View Plaza, 9699 N Hayden Rd, Scottsdale (McCormick Ranch); tel 602/998-8188. **Chinese.** A pleasant, intimate, quiet spot in a Scottsdale shopping center. The walls and floor are dark green, and attractive carved wooden partitions separate dining areas. A large selection of Hunan and Cantonese specialties are featured. **FYI:** Reservations accepted. **Open:** Mon–Fri 11am–10pm, Sat noon–10pm, Sun 4:30–10pm. Closed some hols. **Prices:** Main courses $4.25–$21. Maj CC.

8700, in the Citadel, 8700 E Pinnacle Peak Rd, Scottsdale (Pinnacle Peak); tel 602/994-8700. At Pima Rd. **Continental.** This lovely restaurant is handsomely decorated with original paintings and sculpture, antiques, dried-flower arrangements, a travertine floor, and fireplace. Selections are continental with a Southwest flavor: roast rack of black buck antelope in jerk and juniper marinade; charbroiled veal chop with ancho chile-honey glaze; sautéed scallops with salmon and sole poached in cabbage. Variety of desserts prepared daily. **FYI:** Reservations recommended. **Open:** Daily 6–10pm. Closed Dec 25. **Prices:** Main courses $18.95–$29.50; PF dinner $35. Maj CC.

El Chorro Lodge, 5550 E Lincoln Dr, Scottsdale (Paradise Valley); tel 602/948-5170. **American/Continental.** Built in 1934 as a girls school, the building was converted to a lodge and restaurant in 1937. Today, the original schoolroom is the main bar. Decor is western, with numerous prints and sculptures. The fare is traditional—steaks, lamb chops, baby back ribs, and some seafood. **FYI:** Reservations recommended. Children's menu. **Open:** Breakfast Sat 9am–3pm; lunch daily 11am–3pm; dinner daily 5:30–11pm; brunch Sun 9am–3pm. **Prices:** Main courses $14.95–$22.95. Maj CC.

Golden Swan, in the Hyatt Regency Scottsdale, 7500 E Doubletree Ranch Rd, Scottsdale; tel 602/991-3388 ext 79. **Regional American.** The indoor dining area, decorated with etched glasswork, opens onto a patio and overlooks a duck pond. Traditional American dishes are prepared with an international flair. **FYI:** Reservations recommended. Dress code. **Open:** Dinner daily 6–10pm; brunch Sun 10am–2pm. **Prices:** Main courses $18–$31. Maj CC.

The Grill, in the Scottsdale Princess, 7575 E Princess Dr, Scottsdale; tel 602/585-4848. **American.** A relaxed, casual golf course restaurant, offering great views of the course and nearby mountains. The ceiling is open-beamed, and caricatures of local personalities decorate the walls; there are TVs at the bar. The menu includes a variety of salads and sandwiches, plus full dinners including charbroiled meats and grilled fish. **FYI:** Reservations accepted. Children's menu. Dress code. **Open:** Daily 6am–10pm. **Prices:** Main courses $13.95–$18.95. Maj CC.

Jean-Claude's Petit Cafe, 7340 E Shoeman Lane, Scottsdale; tel 602/947-5288. **French.** Tucked away on a side street, this small French cafe has a faithful following. Hors d'oeuvres range from pâté to escargots in garlic butter to fresh seafood in a puff pastry. Entrees include duck cooked in a raspberry vinegar or green peppercorn sauce, and grilled salmon with tarragon. The dessert soufflés are popular. **FYI:** Reservations recommended. **Open:** Lunch Mon–Fri 11:30am–2:30pm; dinner Mon–Sat 6–10pm. Closed some hols. **Prices:** Main courses $12.95–$17.95. Maj CC.

Jewel of the Crown, in Financial Center 2, 4141 N Scottsdale Rd Ste 110, Scottsdale; tel 602/840-2412. At Indian School Rd. **Indian.** Delightful East Indian restaurant hidden away in the back of a business complex. Carved wooden elephants, urns, and screens. Tapestries adorn the walls. The tandoori and curry specialties feature chicken, shrimp, and fish. East Indian desserts served. **FYI:** Reservations recommended. **Open:** Lunch daily 11:30am–2pm; dinner daily 5–10pm. **Prices:** Main courses $8.95–$14.95. Maj CC.

La Hacienda, in the Scottsdale Princess, 7575 E Princess Dr, Scottsdale; tel 602/271-9000. **Mexican.** As the name might suggest, this is a Mexican hacienda–style restaurant, with thick stucco walls, 2 fireplaces, a stone floor in the lounge, and chile ristras throughout. The exotic Mexican menu includes cochinillo asado—suckling pig marinated in bitter orange, black pepper, and tamarind, carved at your table. Seafood entrees include swordfish steamed in banana leaves, and wood-grilled ahi tuna. Strolling mariachi musicians perform nightly. **FYI:** Reservations recommended. Guitar. Children's menu. **Open:** HS Jan–June Sun–Thurs 6–10pm, Fri–Sat 6–11pm. Reduced hours off-season. **Prices:** Main courses $14.95–$21. Maj CC.

★ **L'Ecole**, in the Scottsdale Culinary Institute, 8100 E Camelback Rd, Scottsdale; tel 602/990-7639. **International.** This locally popular restaurant is a training ground for students at the Scottsdale Culinary Institute. The menu includes veal, chicken, and fish dishes, some of which are prepared tableside. All meals include appetizer, salad, dessert, tea or coffee. **FYI:** Reservations recommended. Dress code. No smoking. **Open:** Lunch Mon–Fri

11:30am–3pm; dinner Mon–Fri 6:30–10pm. Closed some hols. **Prices:** Main courses $15–$19; PF dinner $13–$20. Ltd CC. ♥ ♿

★ **Los Olivos**, 7328 2nd St, Scottsdale (Downtown); tel 602/946-2256. **American/Mexican.** This Scottsdale landmark opened in 1945 and is well-known for its wonderful margaritas and live Latin music. Chef Juanita Recalde has been preparing unusual Mexican cuisine here for 30 years. There are 2 large dining rooms and a dance floor. **FYI:** Reservations recommended. Guitar. Children's menu. **Open:** Sun–Thurs 11am–10pm, Fri–Sat 11am–11pm. Closed some hols. **Prices:** Main courses $6–$13. Maj CC. ♿

Malee's on Main Street, 7131 E Main St, Scottsdale (Old Town); tel 602/947-6042. **Thai.** Intimate restaurant with a small bar and lounge, soft sconce lighting, and muted watercolor paintings. A second dining room has a fireplace. The gourmet Thai dishes are rated for spiciness. **FYI:** Reservations recommended. **Open:** Lunch Mon–Fri 11:30am–2:30pm, Sat noon–2:30pm; dinner Mon–Thurs 5–9:30pm, Fri–Sat 5–10pm, Sun 5–9pm. Closed some hols. **Prices:** Main courses $8.50–$15.95. Maj CC. ♥ ♿

Mancuso's Restaurant, in the Borgata, 6166 N Scottsdale Rd, Scottsdale; tel 602/948-9988. **French/Italian.** Set in an elegant château with chandeliers. The menu features about a dozen different pastas, plus veal saltimbocca, veal sweetbreads, and numerous beef, chicken, and seafood selections. **FYI:** Reservations recommended. Piano. Dress code. **Open:** Daily 5–10pm. Closed some hols. **Prices:** Main courses $12.95–$25.95. Maj CC. ♥ VP ♿

★ **Marché Gourmet**, 4121 N Marshall Way, Scottsdale (Old Town); tel 602/994-4568. **French.** Small, intimate French bistro. The main dining room has vine-covered windows. Specialties include cassoulet toulousain, Spanish paella, and merquez—spicy lamb sausages with fries. **FYI:** Reservations recommended. No smoking. **Open:** Breakfast daily 7:30–11am; lunch daily 11am–2pm; dinner Mon–Sat 5:30–9pm. Closed some hols. **Prices:** Main courses $10–$20. Maj CC. ♥ ♿

Maria's When in Naples, in Scottsdale Promenade Shopping Center, 7000 E Shea Blvd, Scottsdale; tel 602/991-6887. **Italian.** Authentic Italian food, with pastas made fresh on the premises, in the heart of Scottsdale. Murals and hanging garlic highlight the Italian peasant decor. **FYI:** Reservations recommended. Dress code. **Open:** Lunch Mon–Fri 11:30am–2:30pm; dinner daily 5–10pm. Closed some hols. **Prices:** Main courses $9.95–$18.95. Maj CC. ♥ VP

The Market at the Citadel, in The Inn at the Citadel, 8700 E Pinnacle Peak Rd, Scottsdale (North Scottsdale); tel 602/585-0635. **Southwestern.** A combination deli-restaurant, with a market-like dining room decorated with baskets, chile wreaths, and glassware. Wide variety of soups and salads, plus roast chicken, ribs, and meat loaf. Also fajitas, enchiladas, and seafood. **FYI:** Reservations recommended. Children's menu. **Open:** Daily 7am–10pm. **Prices:** Main courses $7.25–$17.95. Maj CC. ♿

♣ **Marquesa**, in the Scottsdale Princess, 7575 E Princess Dr, Scottsdale; tel 602/585-4848. Bell Rd continue east on Bell to Scottsdale Road. **Mediterranean/Spanish.** Catalan cuisine prepared and served in elegant surroundings. Stylish Estancia decor; tapas bar and patio with fireplace for outdoor dining. Among dishes offered are crabmeat and fontina cheese in baked sweet red peppers with garlic aioli; and veal tenderloin and breast of duckling with polenta and asparagus. Marquesa is also noted for its Sunday "marketplace" brunch—a buffet of some 4 dozen dishes, not including paellas and desserts. **FYI:** Reservations recommended. Jacket required. **Open:** Dinner Sun–Thurs 6–10pm, Fri–Sat 6–11pm; brunch Sun 10:30am–2:30pm. Closed July–Aug. **Prices:** Main courses $17–$26. Maj CC. ♥ 🏊 🖼 VP ♿

♣ **Mary Elaine's**, in The Phoenician, 6000 E Camelback Rd, Scottsdale; tel 602/941-8200. Camelback exit off I-17; continue east on Camelback Rd to 44th Street. **New American/Continental.** Opulent setting of softly lit gold-leaf accents, 18th-century paintings, and wall-to-wall window looking out to the lights of Scottsdale. The custom-designed Mikasa china, Schott-Zwiessel crystal, and waiters dressed in formal attire enhance the air of elegance. Entrees include garlic-and-herb-crusted rack of Colorado lamb; grain of herbed cannelloni; and roasted sea scallops with curry-coconut sauce and mango chutney. Award-winning wine list, knowledgeable sommelier. The terrace is an ideal spot for after-dinner cognac. **FYI:** Reservations recommended. Jacket required. **Open:** Tues–Sun 6–10pm. **Prices:** Main courses $26–$29; PF dinner $65–$70. Maj CC. ♥ VP ♿

Palm Court, in the Scottsdale Conference Resort, 7700 E McCormick Pkwy, Scottsdale (McCormick Ranch); tel 602/991-3400. **Continental.** Elegant dining among palm trees and flowers; a glass-fronted wine cabinet is the centerpiece. The continental menu emphasizes seafood but also includes roast tenderloin, rack of lamb, duckling, and veal. **FYI:** Reservations recommended. Piano. Jacket required. **Open:** Breakfast daily 7–10am; lunch daily 11am–2pm; dinner daily 5–10pm; brunch Sun 10:30am–2pm. **Prices:** Main courses $21–$28; PF dinner $45. Maj CC. ♥ VP ♿

Pepin Restaurante Español, in Scottsdale Civic Center Mall, 7363 Scottsdale Mall, Scottsdale; tel 602/990-9026. **Spanish.** Spanish atmosphere abounds: white stuccoed arches, bota wine flasks, and flamenco dancing and guitar music. The chef prepares dishes from the Spanish coastal province of Galicia, his homeland. **FYI:** Reservations accepted. Guitar. **Open:** HS Sept–May lunch Mon–Sat 11:30am–3pm; dinner daily 5–11pm. Reduced hours off-season. Closed some hols. **Prices:** Main courses $9.95–$19.95; PF dinner $14.95. Maj CC. ● ✉ &

The Piñon Grill, in the Regal McCormick Ranch, 7401 N Scottsdale Rd, Scottsdale; tel 602/948-5050. **Southwestern.** Offering innovative seafood selections, as well as beef and chicken. A dessert specialty is the chocolate taco. **FYI:** Reservations recommended. Children's menu. Dress code. **Open:** Breakfast daily 6–11am; lunch daily 11am–2pm; dinner daily 5–10:30pm. **Prices:** Main courses $14.95–$24.95. Maj CC. ▲ ✉ &

Reay's Cafe, in Reay's Ranch Market, 9689 N Hayden Rd, Scottsdale (North Scottsdale); tel 602/596-9496. **Health/Spa.** Bright and cheery cafe located in a health food supermarket. There's patio dining under a large covered awning; a misting system keeps patrons cool. Limited entrees, mostly grilled fish and chicken. **FYI:** Reservations accepted. Beer and wine only. No smoking. **Open:** Sun–Thurs 7am–9pm, Fri–Sat 7am–10pm. Closed some hols. **Prices:** Main courses $11–$14. Ltd CC. ▲ &

Sfuzzi, in Fashion Sq Shopping Center, 4720 N Scottsdale Rd, Scottsdale; tel 602/946-9777. **Italian.** High-ceilinged bistro serving imaginative pastas and pizzas. **FYI:** Reservations recommended. Children's menu. **Open:** Mon–Sat 11am–10pm, Sun 10:30am–10pm. **Prices:** Main courses $9.50–$21. Maj CC. ● ✉

Va Bene Trattoria, in Mountain View Plaza, 9619 N Hayden Rd, Scottsdale (North Scottsdale); tel 602/922-3576. **Italian.** Small, intimate cafe specializing in Northern Italian cuisine. Specialties include nodino di vitello alla Valdostana, a veal chop sautéed with sage and baked with ham and cheese, and tris, or triple pasta. **FYI:** Reservations recommended. **Open:** Lunch Tues–Fri 11am–2pm; dinner Tues–Sun 5–10pm. Closed some hols. **Prices:** Main courses $15–$22. Maj CC. ● &

Voltaire, 8340 E MacDonald Dr, Scottsdale; tel 602/948-1005. **Continental.** Red leather chairs, red carpet, and a mirrored wall give Voltaire a sophisticated, continental atmosphere. Some tables have their own chandeliers. Specialties include duckling in orange sauce, and calf sweetbreads sautéed in lemon butter with capers. **FYI:** Reservations recommended. Jacket required.

Open: HS Oct–May Tues–Sat 5:30–10pm. Reduced hours off-season. Closed some hols; June–Sept. **Prices:** Main courses $16–$20.50. Ltd CC. &

⑤ **Windows on the Green**, in The Phoenician, 6000 E Camelback Rd, Scottsdale; tel 602/941-8200. Camelback exit off I-17; continue east on Camelback to 44th Street. **Southwestern.** Golf course clubhouses don't come more stylish than this 120-seater, with its custom-designed china and original art. The airy, sunny room overlooks the fairways, and there is a striking collection of southwestern glass and pottery. The bar has a big-screen TV for major sporting events. The imaginative, refreshing cuisine ranges from lobster and roasted corn chili, to chile and sugar-cured black buck antelope. **FYI:** Reservations recommended. Guitar. Children's menu. **Open:** Lunch Mon–Sat 11am–3pm; dinner Sun 6–10pm, Tues–Thurs 6–10pm, Fri–Sat 6–11; brunch Sun 10am–3pm. **Prices:** Main courses $17–$26. Maj CC. ▲ ▣ &

Yamakasa, in Mercado Del Rancho Shopping Center, 9301 E Shea Blvd, Scottsdale; tel 602/860-5605. **Japanese.** Simply decorated Japanese serving a broad range of traditional dishes. **FYI:** Reservations recommended. Beer and wine only. **Open:** Lunch Mon–Fri noon–2pm; dinner Mon–Fri 5:30–10pm, Sat 5:30–10pm, Sun 5:30–9pm. Closed some hols. **Prices:** Main courses $7.50–$23.50. Maj CC. &

Attractions 🛍

Taliesin West, Frank Lloyd Wright Blvd and Cactus Rd; tel 602/860-2700. The headquarters of the Frank Lloyd Wright Foundation and School of Architecture. Tours offer background on Wright and an introduction to his theories of architecture. Wright believed in using local materials in his designs, which is evident here in the campus buildings. **Open:** Oct–May, daily 10am–4pm; June–Sept, daily 8–11am. Closed some hols. $$$

Cosanti, 6433 Doubletree Ranch Rd; tel 602/948-6145. This complex of cast-concrete structures served as a prototype and learning project for architect Paolo Soleri's much larger Arcosanti project, located north of Phoenix (see listing under "Mayer"). Soleri designs brass wind bells, which are cast here and sold all over Arizona to finance his architecture projects. **Open:** Daily 9am–5pm. Closed some hols. $

Fleischer Museum, 17207 N Perimeter Dr; tel 602/585-3108. This is the only museum in the United States devoted exclusively to the California school of American impressionism. **Open:** Daily 10am–4pm. Closed some hols. Free.

Scottsdale Center for the Arts, 7380 N Second St; tel 602/994-2301. Anchoring the Scottsdale Mall sculpture park at the heart of downtown Scottsdale, this cultural center hosts both visual-art exhibitions and performing-arts productions. The center includes 3 art galleries with rotating exhibits, an indoor theater, and an outdoor amphitheater. **Open:** Call for schedule. $$$$

Kerr Cultural Center, 6110 N Scottsdale Rd; tel 602/965-KERR. An adobe building that provides an intimate setting for an eclectic and diversified season. Offerings include everything from cowboy bands to classical jazz. **Open:** Box office, Mon–Fri 10am–5pm, Sat noon–5pm. $$$

Rawhide, 23023 N Scottsdale Rd; tel 602/502-1880. A replica of an 1880s western town featuring a main street with 20 traditional craft shops, stagecoach rides, and a western stunt show every hour. New to the town is a Native American Village, built and staffed by Native Americans representing the 7 local tribes of the area. Special events include rodeos and country music performances. **Open:** June–Sept, daily 5–10pm; Oct–May, daily 11am–10pm. Closed Dec 25. $

SECOND MESA

Map page M-2, B3

Motel 🛏

≣ **Hopi Cultural Center Restaurant and Motel**, Ariz 264, PO Box 67, Second Mesa, AZ 86043; tel 602/734-2401. 22 mi W of Keams Canyon. In this very remote area accommodations are limited, so reservations are imperative in the summer. Although the exterior of the building has an "institutional" look, the motel rooms are very pleasant. **Rooms:** 33 rms. CI 3pm/CO 11am. All rooms are nonsmoking. **Amenities:** 🛁 A/C, cable TV. **Services:** ⌂〰 **Facilities:** [50] 1 rst. **Rates:** HS May–Sept $55 S; $60 D. Extra person $5–10. Children under 12 stay free. Lower rates off-season. Pking: Outdoor, free. Maj CC. There is a $5 key deposit.

Attraction 🎫

Hopi Cultural Center, AZ 264; tel 602/734-6650. The tourism headquarters for the area. A museum has educational displays about Hopi culture and history. Signs indicate when villages are open to visitors. **Open:** Mon–Fri 8am–5pm. $

SEDONA

Map page M-2, B3

Hotel 🛏

≣≣ **Bell Rock Inn**, 6246 Ariz 179, Sedona, AZ 86351; tel 602/282-4161. 8 mi W of I-17. A southwestern-style hotel in scenic Oak Creek, just south of Sedona. **Rooms:** 47 rms. CI 3pm/CO 11am. Nonsmoking rms avail. Rooms are finished in rough wood and beamed ceilings and decorated with southwestern art. **Amenities:** 🛁 A/C, cable TV. **Services:** ⌂〰 Complimentary champagne provided. **Facilities:** 🛢 ⚫2 [80] 🚶 1 rst, 1 bar (w/entertainment), whirlpool. **Rates:** HS Apr–Nov $59–$65 S; $79–$115 D. Extra person $9. Lower rates off-season. Higher rates for spec evnts/hols. Spec packages avail. Pking: Outdoor, free. Maj CC.

Motels

≣≣ **Best Western Arroyo Roble Hotel**, 400 N US 89A, PO Box NN, Sedona, AZ 86339; tel 602/282-4001 or toll free 800/528-1234; fax 602/282-4001 ext 550. A striking 5-story motel set above Oak Creek. **Rooms:** 53 rms; 7 ctges/villas. CI 2pm/CO 11am. Nonsmoking rms avail. Some rooms have views of the canyon's spectacular red rock formations. **Amenities:** 🛁 🖥 A/C, cable TV. All units w/terraces, some w/fireplaces, some w/Jacuzzis. **Services:** ⌂〰 **Facilities:** 🛢 ⚫ 🚩 🚶 Games rm, racquetball, spa, sauna, steam rm, whirlpool, washer/dryer. Close to golf, hiking trails, and horseback riding, and within walking distance of numerous restaurants. **Rates:** HS Feb 15–Nov 30 $105–$120 S; $115–$130 D; from $250 ctge/villa. Extra person $10. Children under 12 stay free. Lower rates off-season. Pking: Outdoor, free. Maj CC.

≣≣≣ **Quality Inn King's Ransom**, 771 Ariz 179, PO Box 180, Sedona, AZ 86339; tel 602/282-7151 or toll free 800/221-2222. A conveniently located motel, with peaceful and attractive rose gardens. **Rooms:** 65 rms. CI 3pm/CO 11am. Nonsmoking rms avail. Rooms have good lighting and southwestern furnishings. **Amenities:** 🛁 A/C, cable TV. Some units w/terraces. **Services:** 🔑〰 🍽 Babysitting. **Facilities:** 🛢 🚶 1 rst (see also "Restaurants" below), 1 bar, whirlpool. **Rates:** HS Feb 15–Nov 30 $68–$78 S; $78–$95 D. Extra person $10. Children under 18 stay free. Lower rates off-season. Higher rates for spec evnts/hols. Pking: Outdoor, free. Maj CC.

≣ **Sedona Motel**, 218 Ariz 179, PO Box 1450, Sedona, AZ 86339 (Downtown); tel 602/282-7187. Economical lodging right in the heart of Sedona. **Rooms:** 16 rms and stes. CI 3pm/CO 10am. Nonsmoking rms avail. Many rooms offer spectacular views. **Amenities:** 🛅 A/C, cable TV. **Services:** ♫ **Rates:** HS Mar–Nov $69–$79 S or D; from $89 ste. Extra person $6. Lower rates off-season. Pking: Indoor, free. Maj CC.

Inn

≣≣≣ **Canyon Villa Bed and Breakfast Inn**, 125 Canyon Circle Dr, Sedona, AZ 86351 (Oak Creek); tel 602/284-1226 or toll free 800/453-1166; fax 602/284-2114. 6 mi S of Sedona. Bell Rock Blvd exit off Ariz 179. A lovely inn, with marvelous furnishings and original art in the common areas. The inn adjoins national forest lands and has unobstructed views of Sedona's famous red rocks. Unsuitable for children under 10. **Rooms:** 11 rms. CI 3pm/CO 11am. No smoking. Each room is decorated in its own unique motif, some with handmade quilts and rocking chairs. **Amenities:** 🛅 ⚬ 🍴 A/C, cable TV, bathrobes. All units w/terraces, some w/fireplaces, some w/Jacuzzis. **Services:** 🗝 Afternoon tea served. **Facilities:** 🔂 Guest lounge w/TV. The outdoor swimming pool is delightful. **Rates (BB):** HS Feb–Oct $95–$155 S or D. Extra person $25. Min stay wknds and spec evnts. Lower rates off-season. Pking: Outdoor, free. Ltd CC.

Resorts

≣≣≣ **Enchantment Resort**, 525 Boynton Canyon Rd, Sedona, AZ 86336; tel 602/282-2900 or toll free 800/522-2282; fax 602/282-9249. 3 mi W of Sedona. Dry Creek Rd exit off US 89A. 70 acres. A secluded pueblo-style resort offering among the most spectacular views in Sedona. **Rooms:** 162 ctges/villas. CI 4pm/CO noon. Express checkout avail. Nonsmoking rms avail. Rooms are attractively decorated in southwestern style. **Amenities:** 🛅 ⚬ 🖵 A/C, satel TV w/movies, refrig. Some units w/minibars, all w/terraces, some w/fireplaces. All casita studios have gas barbecues. **Services:** ✗ 🗝 🚗 🖄 ♫ Social director, masseur, children's program, babysitting. Guests receive complimentary orange juice and faxed versions of the *New York Times* each morning. **Facilities:** 🔂 ⚲₆ ▶₆ 🖾 ⚲ 12 🍴 🏊 140 🖵 ⚐ 1 rst (*see also* "Restaurants" below), 1 bar (w/entertainment), lawn games, spa, sauna, steam rm, whirlpool, day-care ctr, playground, washer/dryer. Hiking and other activities nearby. **Rates:** HS Mar 17–July 5/Sept–Nov from $145 ctge/villa. Extra person $20. Children under 12 stay free. Min stay wknds. Lower rates off-season. Higher rates for spec evnts/hols. AP and MAP rates avail. Spec packages avail. Pking: Outdoor, free. Maj CC.

≣≣≣≣ **L'Auberge de Sedona**, 301 L'Auberge Lane, PO Box B, Sedona, AZ 86336; tel 602/282-7131 or toll free 800/272-6777; fax 602/282-2885. Ariz 179 exit off Ariz 89A. 6 acres. A resort with a diverse selection of accommodations. This is actually two resorts in one, with the Orchards at L'Auberge atop a hill above L'Auberge. The two are connected by a walkway and cable car. L'Auberge has rooms in the lodge and cottages; the Orchard has rooms only. Scenery along Oak Creek, which runs beside the cottages, is lovely. No smoking throughout. **Rooms:** 68 rms and stes; 31 ctges/villas. CI 3pm/CO 11am. Express checkout avail. All rooms and cottages have canopy beds and are individually decorated. **Amenities:** 🛅 ⚬ 🖵 A/C, cable TV, refrig, in-rm safe, bathrobes. Some units w/minibars, all w/terraces, some w/fireplaces, some w/Jacuzzis. Cottages have no TV. **Services:** ✗ 🗝 🚗 🖄 ♫ Twice-daily maid svce, social director, masseur, babysitting. **Facilities:** 🔂 200 🖵 ⚐ 2 rsts (*see also* "Restaurants" below), 1 bar, whirlpool, day-care ctr. **Rates:** HS Mar–Oct $160–$180 S or D; from $225 ctge/villa. Extra person $20. Lower rates off-season. Spec packages avail. Pking: Outdoor, free. Maj CC.

≣≣≣ **Los Abrigados**, 160 Portal Lane, Sedona, AZ 86336; tel 602/282-1777 or toll free 800/521-3131; fax 602/282-2614. Behind the Tlaquepaque Shopping Center. 22 acres. This Spanish revival–style resort, with red-tile roofs and brick and stucco walls, is reminiscent of Old Mexico. **Rooms:** 172 stes. CI 4pm/CO noon. Express checkout avail. Nonsmoking rms avail. **Amenities:** 🛅 ⚬ 🖵 🍴 A/C, cable TV w/movies, refrig. All units w/minibars, all w/terraces, some w/fireplaces, some w/Jacuzzis. **Services:** ✗ 🗝 🚗 🖄 ♫ Social director, masseur, children's program, babysitting. **Facilities:** 🔂 🖾 ⚲3 🍴 275 ⚐ 2 rsts (*see also* "Restaurants" below), 1 bar (w/entertainment), lawn games, spa, sauna, steam rm, whirlpool, beauty salon, day-care ctr, playground, washer/dryer. **Rates:** HS Feb–Dec from $210 ste. Extra person $20. Children under 16 stay free. Min stay spec evnts. Lower rates off-season. Spec packages avail. Pking: Outdoor, free. Maj CC.

≣≣≣ **Poco Diablo Resort**, 1752 S Ariz 179, PO Box 1709, Sedona, AZ 86336; tel 602/282-7333 or toll free 800/542-4253; fax 602/282-2090. 22 acres. Full-featured golf and tennis resort. **Rooms:** 109 rms and stes. CI 3pm/CO noon. Express checkout avail. Nonsmoking rms avail. Rooms are decorated with contemporary southwestern art and furnishings, and some offer splendid views of the surrounding canyon walls. **Amenities:** 🛅 ⚬ 🖵 A/C, cable TV, refrig. All units w/minibars, some w/terraces, some w/fireplaces, some w/Jacuzzis. **Services:** ✗ 🗝 🚗 🖄 ♫ Masseur, babysitting. **Facilities:** 🔂 ▶₉ 🖾 ⚲2 🍴 300 🖵 ⚐ 1 rst, 1 bar (w/entertainment), lawn games, racquetball, whirlpool. **Rates:** HS Mid-Mar–Nov 30 $95–$155 S or D; from $160 ste. Extra person $15. Children under 16 stay free. Min stay HS. Lower rates off-season. Spec packages avail. Pking: Outdoor, free. Maj CC.

Restaurants 🍴

The Canyon Rose, in Los Abrigados, 160 Portal Lane, Sedona; tel 602/282-7073. **Southwestern.** Attractive restaurant with modern southwestern decor. An etched glass wall separates the dining room from the lounge. Specialties include a sea scallop and lobster tamale and mesquite-broiled quail. **FYI:** Reservations recommended. Piano. Children's menu. Dress code. **Open:** Breakfast daily 7–11am; lunch Sat 11am–2pm; dinner daily 5–10pm. **Prices:** Main courses $15–$23. Maj CC. ♥ 🖤 ⅙

El Rincon del Tlaquepaque, in Tlaquepaque Shopping Center, Ariz 179, Sedona; tel 602/282-4648. **Mexican.** Adobe-like interior; traditional Mexican food, with some Navajo dishes. **FYI:** Reservations recommended. Children's menu. **Open:** HS Mar–Oct Tues–Sat 11am–9pm, Sun noon–5pm. Reduced hours off-season. Closed some hols; Feb. **Prices:** Main courses $7.50–$12.95. Ltd CC. 🍷 🖼 ⅙

★ **La Mediterranée de Sedona**, in the Quality Inn Kings Ransom, 771 Ariz 179, Sedona; tel 602/282-7006. **Mediterranean/Middle Eastern.** Modern southwestern look, with a 10-foot-square window facing the red rocks to the north. There are 2 balconies for outdoor dining. Extensive menu contains many Mediterranean specialties as well as vegetarian dishes. **FYI:** Reservations recommended. **Open:** Daily 7am–10pm. **Prices:** Main courses $9.25–$18.50. Maj CC. 🏞 ⅙

L'Auberge, in L'Auberge de Sedona, 301 L'Auberge Lane, Sedona; tel 602/282-2885. L'Auberge Lane exit off AZ 89. **French.** Offers a total dining experience for the connoisseur of French cuisine. The dining room, done in French country style, overlooks a shaded creek. **FYI:** Reservations recommended. Jacket required. No smoking. **Open:** Breakfast daily 7–11am; lunch daily noon–3pm; dinner daily 6–10pm. **Prices:** Main courses $28–$36; PF dinner $49. Maj CC. ♥ ⅙

René at Tlaquepaque, in Tlaquepaque Shopping Center, Ariz 179, Sedona; tel 602/282-9225. **French.** Decorated with paintings by local artists and flowers and enhanced with soft light. Selection of relatively simple French dishes. Rack of lamb is a specialty. **FYI:** Reservations recommended. Piano. Children's menu. Dress code. **Open:** Lunch daily 11:30am–2:30pm; dinner Sun–Thur 5:30–9pm, Fri–Sat 5:30–9:30pm. Closed some hols. **Prices:** Main courses $16.95–$25.50. Maj CC. ♥ ⅙

★ **Sedona Swiss Restaurant & Cafe**, 350 Jordan Rd, Sedona; tel 602/282-7959. Jordan Rd exit off US 89A. **French/Swiss.** An authentic Swiss restaurant, offering patio dining. The Swiss owners fell in love with Sedona while vacationing here and never left. Most popular are the veal dishes, such as veal eminc Zurichois, which is veal sautéed in a cognac-mushroom sauce.

Also on the menu are chicken, seafood, beef, and lamb. The pastries and chocolates are locally famous. **FYI:** Reservations recommended. Children's menu. No smoking. **Open:** Mon–Sat 7:30am–9:30pm. **Prices:** Main courses $9.95–$23.95. Ltd CC. ⅙

★ **Shugrue's Restaurant, Bakery & Bar**, 2250 W US 89A, Sedona; tel 602/282-2943. **New American.** A large, roomy restaurant, with 3 dining rooms, book-lined walls, and wood beams. One room holds a large fish tank. The prime rib is especially popular. Diners can create their own combinations, such as prime rib with shrimp scampi. **FYI:** Reservations recommended. Guitar/piano. Children's menu. Dress code. **Open:** Breakfast Tues–Sun 8–11:30am; lunch daily 11:30am–3pm; dinner Mon–Fri 5–9pm, Sat–Sun 5–10pm; brunch Sun 8am–3pm. Closed Dec 25. **Prices:** Main courses $12–$18. Maj CC. 🏞 🖤 ⅙

Yavapai Room, in the Enchantment Resort, 525 Boynton Canyon Rd, Sedona; tel 602/282-2900. 3 mi W of Sedona; exit Dry Creek Rd off AZ 89. **Southwestern.** Two walls of the dining room are glass, giving diners terrific views of Sedona's famous red rock formations. The menu offers innovative variations of standard dishes, like pasta Anasazi and Enchantment beef Wellington. **FYI:** Reservations recommended. Piano. Children's menu. Dress code. **Open:** Breakfast daily 7–11am; lunch daily 11:30am–2:30pm; dinner daily 6–10pm; brunch Sun 11:30am–2:30pm. **Prices:** Main courses $14–$26. Maj CC. 🏞 ⅙

Attraction 💼

Sedona Arts Center, Art Barn Road exit off US 89A; tel 602/282-3809. Serves as both a gallery for artworks by local and regional artists and a theater for plays and music performances. Fine Arts and Crafts Exhibition in April.

SIERRA VISTA

Map page M-2, E4

Motel 🛏

≣ ≣ ≣ **Ramada Inn**, 2047 S Ariz 92, Sierra Vista, AZ 85635; tel 602/459-5900 or toll free 800/825-4656; fax 602/458-1347. 2 miles south of junction Ariz 90/92. A motel in the center of Sierra Vista. **Rooms:** 149 rms and stes. CI 4pm/CO 11am. Nonsmoking rms avail. Rooms are basic and comfortable. Refrigerators available upon request. **Amenities:** 📺 🅰 🖥 A/C, cable TV. 1 unit w/Jacuzzi. **Services:** ✕ 🚗 🖼 🔜 🍽 Twice-daily maid svce, babysitting. **Facilities:** 🎣 🔟 🖵 ⅙ 1 rst, 1 bar (w/entertainment), whirlpool. **Rates (BB):** HS Feb–Oct $48–

$86 S or D; from $95 ste. Extra person $8. Children under 12 stay free. Lower rates off-season. Spec packages avail. Pking: Outdoor, free. Maj CC.

Attractions

Fort Huachuca, junction of Ariz 90 and Ariz 92; tel 602/533-7536. This army base was established in 1877 and the buildings of the old post have been declared a National Historic Landmark. The Fort Huachuca Museum is dedicated to the many forts that dotted the Southwest in the latter part of the 19th century. Also on the base is one of Sierra Vista's most famous attractions, the **B Troop, 4th Regiment, US Cavalry Memorial**. This troop of about 30 members dress in the blue-and-gold uniforms of the 1880s cavalry and perform on horseback. Call 602/533-2714 for appearance schedule. **Open:** Mon–Fri 9am–4pm, Sat, Sun 1–4pm. Free.

San Pedro Riparian National Conservation Area, Ariz 90; tel 602/458-3559. A rare example of a natural riparian (riverside) habitat. Fossil findings indicate that people were living along this river 11,000 years ago. At that time the area was not a desert but a swamp, and the San Pedro River is all that remains of this ancient wetland. The conservation area is home to more than 300 species of birds, 80 species of mammals, 14 species of fish, and 40 species of amphibians and reptiles. The headquarters building has handouts and maps of the area. The San Pedro House, a 1930s ranch, operates as a visitor center and bookstore. **Open:** Daily sunrise to sunset. Free.

SPRINGERVILLE

Map page M-2, C4

Attraction

Apache-Sitgreaves National Forests, Ariz 260; tel 602/333-4301. Over 800 miles of hiking trails are located on 2 million acres in these 2 connecting national forests. The many lakes provide excellent fishing opportunities, but the high elevation may make the water too cold for most swimmers. There are 2 visitor centers located at Mogollan Rim and Big Lake. **Open:** Daily 24 hours. Free.

SUPERIOR

Map page M-2, D3

Attraction

Boyce Thompson Southwestern Arboretum, 37615 US 60; tel 602/689-2811. Built in the 1920s as an educational facility to promote the gardening of drought-tolerant plants, the arboretum's visitor center building is now on the National Register of Historic Places. Because of the presence of both a creek and a small lake, the arboretum has displays on the more water-demanding plants of the desert. Though the cactus gardens are impressive, it's the 2 boojum trees from Baja California that visitors find most fascinating. Spring, when the desert wildflowers are in bloom, is the best time to visit. **Open:** Daily 8am–5pm. Closed Dec 25. $$

TEMPE

Map page M-2, D2

Hotels

Embassy Suites, 4400 S Rural Rd, Tempe, AZ 85282; tel 602/897-7444 or toll free 800/EMBASSY; fax 602/897-6112. Rural Rd exit off US 60. A good-quality, mid-range, all-suites hotel. **Rooms:** 224 stes. CI 3pm/CO 1pm. Express checkout avail. Nonsmoking rms avail. **Amenities:** A/C, satel TV w/movies, refrig, voice mail. Some units w/terraces. **Services:** Guest service information is in both English and Spanish. There is a 2-hour complimentary cocktail hour nightly. **Facilities:** 1 rst, 1 bar, games rm, spa, sauna, whirlpool, washer/dryer. **Rates (BB):** HS Jan–Apr from $149 ste. Extra person $10. Children under 12 stay free. Lower rates off-season. Higher rates for spec evnts/hols. Spec packages avail. Pking: Outdoor, free. Maj CC.

Fiesta Inn, 2100 S Priest Dr, Tempe, AZ 85282; tel 602/967-1441 or toll free 800/528-6481; fax 602/967-0224. Broadway exit off I-10. Frank Lloyd Wright–inspired, partially sunken lobby. Beautiful landscaping. **Rooms:** 270 rms and stes. CI 1pm/CO 1pm. Nonsmoking rms avail. The 100 mini-suites have a pool view. **Amenities:** A/C, cable TV w/movies, refrig, stereo/tape player. **Services:** Babysitting. Free local calls. **Facilities:** 1 rst, 1 bar, spa, sauna, whirlpool. Guests have free use of bicycles, and there's a golf practice range. **Rates:** HS Jan 1–May

14 $128–$138 S or D; from $135 ste. Extra person $8. Children under 16 stay free. Lower rates off-season. Higher rates for spec evnts/hols. Spec packages avail. Pking: Outdoor, free. Maj CC.

≡≡ La Quinta Inn, 911 S 48th St, Tempe, AZ 85281; tel 602/967-4465 or toll free 800/531-5900; fax 602/921-9172. An attractive hotel with a pleasant lobby. **Rooms:** 129 rms and stes. CI 2pm/CO noon. Nonsmoking rms avail. Rooms are comfortable and nicely furnished. **Amenities:** 🔒 👤 A/C, satel TV. **Services:** 🚐 🖥 🛎 🛎 **Facilities:** 🏊 🏐 🔥 Washer/dryer. Putting green in courtyard. **Rates (CP):** HS Jan–Apr $75–$82 S or D; from $87 ste. Extra person $10. Children under 18 stay free. Lower rates off-season. Higher rates for spec evnts/hols. Pking: Outdoor, free. Maj CC.

≡≡≡ Radisson Tempe Mission Palms Hotel, 60 E 5th St, Tempe, AZ 85281 (Old Town); tel 602/894-1400 or toll free 800/333-3333. An attractive hotel close to Arizona State University and Old Town Tempe. **Rooms:** 303 rms and stes. CI 3pm/CO 10am. Nonsmoking rms avail. **Amenities:** 🔒 👤 🖥 🎵 A/C, cable TV w/movies. Some units w/terraces, some w/Jacuzzis. **Services:** ✕ 📠 🚐 🖥 🛎 Car-rental desk, babysitting. **Facilities:** 🏊 🏐 🔥 🛄 💻 🔥 1 rst, 1 bar, spa, sauna, steam rm, whirlpool. **Rates:** HS Jan–May 27 $139 S; $169 D; from $325 ste. Extra person $10. Children under 12 stay free. Lower rates off-season. Higher rates for spec evnts/hols. Spec packages avail. Pking: Outdoor, free. Maj CC.

Motels

≡≡ Comfort Inn, 5300 S Priest St, Tempe, AZ 85283; tel 602/820-7500 or toll free 800/228-5150. Baseline Rd exit off I-10. A good, comfortable motel. **Rooms:** 160 rms. CI noon/CO noon. Nonsmoking rms avail. Rooms are simple and comfortable. **Amenities:** 🔒 A/C, satel TV w/movies. **Services:** 🚐 🖥 🛎 🛎 **Facilities:** 🏊 🔥 💻 🔥 Whirlpool. **Rates (CP):** HS Jan–Apr $69–$89 S or D. Extra person $10. Children under 18 stay free. Lower rates off-season. Higher rates for spec evnts/hols. Spec packages avail. Pking: Outdoor, free. Maj CC. Reasonable rates for the area.

≡ Days Inn, 1221 E Apache Blvd, Tempe, AZ 85281; tel 602/968-7793 or toll free 800/325-2525; fax 602/966-4450. Basic motel close to cultural activities at Gammage Center and to Arizona State University. **Rooms:** 100 rms. CI noon/CO 11am. Nonsmoking rms avail. **Amenities:** 🔒 👤 A/C, cable TV w/movies. **Services:** 🖥 🛎 Free local calls. **Facilities:** 🏊 🔥 🔥 Whirlpool, washer/dryer. **Rates (CP):** HS Jan–May 30 $41 S; $45–$55 D. Extra person $5. Children under 12 stay free. Lower rates off-season. Spec packages avail. Pking: Outdoor, free. Maj CC.

≡≡ Econo Lodge, 2101 E Apache Blvd, Tempe, AZ 85281; tel 602/966-5832 or toll free 800/424-4777. A basic motel 8 miles from Phoenix's Sky Harbor International Airport. **Rooms:** 39 rms. CI 11am/CO 11am. Nonsmoking rms avail. **Amenities:** 🔒 A/C, cable TV w/movies. **Services:** 🛎 🛎 Free local calls. **Facilities:** 🏊 🔥 Washer/dryer. **Rates (CP):** HS Jan–Apr $32–$85 S or D. Extra person $5. Children under 18 stay free. Lower rates off-season. Pking: Outdoor, free. Maj CC.

Resort

≡≡≡ The Buttes, 2000 Westcourt Way, Tempe, AZ 85282; tel 602/225-9006 or toll free 800/843-1986; fax 602/438-8622. 25 acres. This hilltop resort has commanding views of the area. There is a waterfall and fish pond in the lobby, and a desert garden behind the check-in desk. **Rooms:** 370 rms and stes. Exec-level rms avail. CI 4pm/CO noon. Express checkout avail. Nonsmoking rms avail. Rooms are large, with shuttered, double French doors. **Amenities:** 🔒 👤 🖥 🎵 A/C, cable TV w/movies, refrig. All units w/minibars, some w/terraces, 1 w/fireplace. **Services:** 🍴 📠 🅥🅟 🚐 🖥 🛎 🛎 Car-rental desk, masseur, babysitting. **Facilities:** 🏊 🎾 🏐 🛄 🔥 💻 🔥 3 rsts (see also "Restaurants" below), 3 bars (1 w/entertainment), lawn games, spa, whirlpool. 4 whirlpools. **Rates:** HS Jan 1–May 26 $200–$225 S or D; from $475 ste. Extra person $10. Children under 18 stay free. Lower rates off-season. Spec packages avail. Pking: Outdoor, free. Maj CC.

Restaurants 🍴

House of Tricks, 114 E 7 St, Tempe (Old Town); tel 602/968-1114. **New American.** Located in a house with hardwood and tiled floors and a stone fireplace. The regularly changing menu offers innovative variations on American and international dishes. Gourmet food shop due to open adjacent to the restaurant. **FYI:** Reservations recommended. Beer and wine only. **Open:** Lunch Mon–Fri 11am–4pm; dinner Tues–Fri 4–9pm, Sat 5–9pm. Closed some hols; first 2 weeks of July.. **Prices:** Main courses $10.25–$12.50. Maj CC. ♥ 🔥

Monti's La Casa Vieja, 3 W 1st St, Tempe (Old Town); tel 602/967-7594. **American/Barbecue.** A historic restaurant in the oldest building in Tempe, with beam and stone walls, animal heads and western paintings on the walls, and a fountain in one of its 13 dining rooms. Barbecued baby-back ribs, steak, deep-fried fish and seafood, and spaghetti and meatballs are among the offerings. **FYI:** Reservations recommended. **Open:** Sun–Thurs 11am–11pm, Fri–Sat 11am–midnight. Closed some hols. **Prices:** Main courses $5.75–$19. Maj CC. 🍴 🔥

The Paradise Bar and Grill, 401 S Mill Ave, Tempe (Old Town); tel 602/829-0606. At 4th St. **American.** Original brick walls, lots of wood, and photos of old Tempe dominate this pub-type restaurant, located in an 1899 building that is listed on the National Register of Historic Places. Pastas, chicken, catch of the day, steak. **FYI:** Reservations not accepted. Children's menu. **Open:** Sun–Thurs 11am–10pm, Fri–Sat 11am–11pm. Closed some hols. **Prices:** Main courses $9.95–$14.95. Maj CC. 🍴 &

Top of the Rock, in The Buttes, 2000 Westcourt Way, Tempe; tel 602/225-9000. **Southwestern.** Located in a modern, high-beamed circular building that affords diners stunning views of the valley. Creative southwestern cuisine; specialties include pesto-crusted rack of lamb. **FYI:** Reservations recommended. Children's menu. Dress code. **Open:** Dinner Sun–Thurs 5–11pm, Fri–Sat 5pm–midnight; brunch Sun 10am–2pm. **Prices:** Main courses $14.95–$23.95; PF dinner $19.95. Maj CC. ▲ VP

Attractions 🖼

Arizona State University Art Museum, at the Nelson Fine Arts Center, 10th St and Mill Ave; tel 602/965-ARTS. Inside are galleries for crafts, prints, contemporary art, American artists, a temporary exhibition gallery, and 2 outdoor sculpture courts. The museum's collection by American artists includes works by Georgia O'Keeffe, Edward Hopper, and Frederic Remington. **The Matthews Center**, at the corner of Cady and Taylor malls, is affiliated with the museum. It contains Latin American art, American ceramics, and South Pacific and African art. **Open:** Tues 10am–9pm, Wed–Sat 10am–5pm. Closed some hols. Free.

Grady Gammage Memorial Auditorium, Mill Ave and Apache Blvd; tel 602/965-3434. Designed by architect Frank Lloyd Wright, this venue is both graceful and massive. The auditorium, which is on the Arizona State University campus, hosts a wide variety of music and theater performances throughout the year. **Open:** Box office, Mon–Fri 10am–6pm, Sat 10am–4pm. $$$$

Sun Devil Stadium, 6th St and Stadium Dr; tel 602/965-3434. Home of Arizona State University's Sun Devils football team, and the location of the Fiesta Bowl Football Classic. The stadium also hosts pro football's Arizona Cardinals. **Open:** Box office, Mon–Fri 10am–6pm, Sat 10am–4pm. $$$$

Big Surf, 1500 N McClintock; tel 602/947-SURF. A water park with 10 waterslides, 2 children's areas, and a wave pool. Also on the premises are volleyball courts, an arcade, and a picnic area. **Open:** June–Sept, Mon–Sat 10am–6pm, Sun 11am–7pm. $$$$

TOMBSTONE
Map page M-2, E4

Motel 🏨

🏨🏨 **Best Western Look-Out Lodge**, US 80 W, PO Box 787, Tombstone, AZ 85638; tel 602/457-2223 or toll free 800/652-6772; fax 602/457-3870. 24 mi N of Bisbee. Popular with vacationers; offers splendid views of the mountains. **Rooms:** 40 rms. CI 2pm/CO 11am. Nonsmoking rms avail. Rooms were renovated in 1993; they feature king- or queen-size beds and large bathrooms decorated with pretty tile. **Amenities:** 🛋 A/C, cable TV. Some units w/terraces. **Services:** 🛎 🗝 **Facilities:** 🖥 💻 **Rates (CP):** HS Dec 26–May 31 $50–$55 S; $55–$70 D. Extra person $5. Children under 12 stay free. Lower rates off-season. Higher rates for spec evnts/hols. Pking: Outdoor, free. Maj CC.

Restaurant 🍴

The Nellie Cashman Restaurant, 117 S 5th and Toughnut, Tombstone; tel 602/457-2212. 24 mi N of Bisbee. **American.** Located in a historic part of Tombstone and named for a legendary pioneer woman philanthropist. Basic diner food, with several types of hamburgers plus hot sandwiches, salads, steaks, chicken, and fish. **FYI:** Reservations accepted. No liquor license. **Open:** Daily 7am–9pm. **Prices:** Main courses $5.75–$15.25. Ltd CC. 🍴

Attraction 🖼

Tombstone Historic District, US 80; tel 602/457-2211. Known as "the town too tough to die" and declared a National Historic Landmark in 1962, downtown Tombstone has come to epitomize the image of the Wild West for most people. The star attraction is the **OK Corral**, site of the gun battle between the Earps and the Clantons that has taken on mythic proportions. Each Sunday at 2pm there is a live reenactment of the famous shootout. Next door is Historama, a 30-minute audiovisual presentation on the history of Tombstone narrated by Vincent Price. Included in the price of a Tombstone pass is a 4-page epitaph of the testimonies after the gun battle. This document is available at the Office of the Tombstone Epitaph, the oldest newspaper in Arizona, begun in 1880.

Other Tombstone attractions include the **Rose Tree Inn Museum,** home of the world's largest rose bush, measuring over 8,000 square feet; the Crystal Palace, a restored 1879 saloon;

and the Bird Cage Theater, named for the velvet-draped cages hanging from the ceiling that were used by prostitutes to ply their trade.

On the outskirts of town is the **Boot Hill Graveyard**. The cemetery is the final resting place of several members of the OK Corral shootout, as well as other notorious gunslingers. **Open:** Daily 9am–5pm. Closed Dec 25. $$

TONALEA

Map page M-2, A3 (SW of Kayenta)

Attraction

Navajo National Monument, Ariz 564; tel 602/672-2366. Located 30 miles west of Kayenta and 60 miles northeast of Tuba City, it encompasses Tsegi Canyon and 3 of the best-preserved Anasazi cliff dwellings in the region: Betatakin, Keet Seel, and the Inscription House. Fragile Inscription House has been closed to the public since 1968. **Betatakin**, which means "ledge house" in Navajo, is the only one of the 3 ruins that can be easily seen. The round-trip, ranger-led hike to Betatakin from the visitor center, conducted May–October, takes about 5 hours and involves descending more than 700 feet to the floor of Tsegi Canyon. **Keet Seel**, which means "broken pieces of pottery" in Navajo, was occupied beginning as early as 950 and continuing until 1300. The 16-mile round-trip hike to Keet Seel is strenuous and requires an overnight stay at a primitive campground. The visitor center at the entrance to the monument has informative displays on the Anasazi culture, including numerous artifacts from Tsegi Canyon. **Open:** National monument, daily 24 hours; visitor center, daily 8am–5pm. Free.

TUBAC

Map page M-2, E3 (N of Nogales)

Resort

≣≣≣ **Tubac Golf Resort**, 1 Otero Rd, PO Box 1297, Tubac, AZ 85646; tel 602/398-2211 or toll free 800/848-7893. Exit 34 off I-19. 400 acres. A golf resort on a restored historic ranch, with splendid views of the Santa Rita Mountains. **Rooms:** 32 stes. CI 3pm/CO noon. Comfortable rooms have unusual brick interiors. **Amenities:** 🛏 📺 A/C, cable TV. Some units w/fireplaces. **Services:** ⇄ 🐕 Babysitting. **Facilities:** 🏨 ▶18 🏊1 🏌50 🖥 ⚷ 1 rst, 1 bar (w/entertainment), whirlpool, washer/dryer. **Rates:** HS Jan–Apr $105–$142 S or D. Extra person $15. Children under 12 stay free. Lower rates off-season. Spec packages avail. Pking: Outdoor, free. Ltd CC.

Attractions

Tubac Center of the Arts, 9 Plaza Rd; tel 602/398-2371. The center of cultural activities for the active arts community in Tubac. Showcases rotating exhibits of artwork by members of the Santa Cruz Valley Art Association and also stages traveling exhibits, juried shows, an annual craft show, and theater and music performances. **Open:** Oct–May, Tues–Sat 10am–4:30pm, Sun 1–4:30pm. Closed some hols. Free.

Tubac Presidio State Historic Park, Presidio Dr; tel 602/398-2252. The park museum houses exhibits that explore the European background and Native American history of Tubac and Southern Arizona. On display is the 1859 press from Arizona's first newspaper. Park grounds feature an adobe schoolhouse built in 1885, and an archeological exhibit featuring a Spanish captain's house. **Open:** Daily 8am–5pm. Closed Dec 25. $

TUCSON

Map page M-2, D3

TOURIST INFORMATION

Metropolitan Tucson Convention and Visitors Bureau 130 S Scott Ave (tel 602/624-1817). Open Mon–Fri 8am–5pm, Sat–Sun 9am–4pm.

PUBLIC TRANSPORTATION

Sun Tran Buses Operate 5:30am–10pm over much of the Tucson metropolitan area. Fares 75¢ adults, 50¢ students, 30¢ seniors, children under 6 free. For information call 602/792-9222.

Sun Tran Trolley Operates Mon–Sat in downtown Tucson. Stops include University of Arizona, Downtown Arts District, Visitors Bureau, Convention Center, and Museum of Art. Fare 75¢. For information call 602/792-9222.

Hotels

≣≣≣≣ **Arizona Inn**, 2200 E Elm St, Tucson, AZ 85719 (Midtown); tel 602/325-1541 or toll free 800/933-1093; fax 602/881-5830. Old-world charm combines with modern elegance in this historic Tucson hotel. Grounds are superbly manicured, with luxurious gardens and flowers. The bar, restaurant, and study in the main lodge are beautifully decorated. **Rooms:** 83 rms and stes. CI 3pm/CO noon. Each room is individually furnished with antiques and period furniture. **Amenities:** 🛏 ⚷ A/C, cable TV, stereo/tape player. Some units w/terraces, some w/fireplaces. **Services:** ✗ ☎ 🆅🅿 🛄 ⇄

Babysitting. Complimentary afternoon tea is served November–April. **Facilities:** 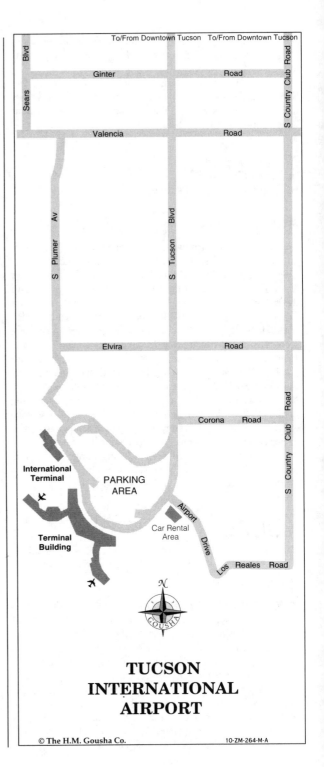 2 rsts (*see also* "Restaurants" below), 2 bars (1 w/entertainment), lawn games. The 14-acre property includes a croquet court. The book-filled study with overstuffed chairs allows for comfortable reading. **Rates:** HS Jan 2–May 26 $134–$162 S; $144–$172 D; from $175 ste. Extra person $15. Children under 10 stay free. Lower rates off-season. AP and MAP rates avail. Spec packages avail. Pking: Outdoor, free. Maj CC.

Aztec Inn, 102 N Alvernon Way, Tucson, AZ 85711 (Central Tucson); tel 602/795-0330 or toll free 800/227-6086; fax 602/326-2111. Exit 258 off I-10. This centrally located, older hotel was being sold at this writing; renovation is expected. **Rooms:** 157 rms, stes, and effic. CI 11am/CO 1pm. Express checkout avail. Nonsmoking rms avail. Rooms are attractive and comfortable. **Amenities:** A/C, cable TV, refrig. Some units w/terraces. **Services:** ✗ **Facilities:** 1 rst, 1 bar, washer/dryer. **Rates (CP):** HS Feb–Apr $70 S or D; from $80 ste; from $90 effic. Extra person $10. Children under 12 stay free. Lower rates off-season. Spec packages avail. Pking: Outdoor, free. Maj CC. $10 charge for third and fourth person in a room.

Best Western–A Royal Sun Inn and Suites, 1015 N Stone Ave, Tucson, AZ 85705; tel 602/622-8871 or toll free 800/545-8858; fax 602/623-2267. Attractive downtown hotel. **Rooms:** 80 rms and stes. CI 2pm/CO noon. Nonsmoking rms avail. **Amenities:** A/C, satel TV w/movies, refrig, VCR, stereo/tape player. Some units w/minibars, some w/terraces. **Services:** ✗ **Facilities:** 1 rst, 1 bar, spa, sauna, whirlpool. **Rates:** HS Jan–Apr $89 S; $99 D; from $120 ste. Extra person $10. Lower rates off-season. Pking: Outdoor, free. Maj CC.

Best Western Inn Suites Hotel, 6201 N Oracle Rd, Tucson, AZ 85704; tel 602/297-8111 or toll free 800/554-4535; fax 602/297-2935. Popular with both business and leisure travelers. **Rooms:** 159 rms and stes. CI 2pm/CO noon. Express checkout avail. Nonsmoking rms avail. There are 2 types of suites: studio inn suites, with living rooms; and executive suites, with both living rooms and kitchenettes. **Amenities:** A/C, cable TV w/movies. Some units w/minibars, some w/terraces, some w/Jacuzzis. **Services:** Babysitting. **Facilities:** 1 rst, whirlpool, washer/dryer. **Rates (BB):** HS Jan 15–Apr 15 $99 S or D; from $125 ste. Extra person $10. Children under 16 stay free. Lower rates off-season. Higher rates for spec evnts/hols. Spec packages avail. Pking: Outdoor, free. Maj CC.

TUCSON INTERNATIONAL AIRPORT

© The H.M. Gousha Co.   10-ZM-264-M-A

≣≣≣ **Clarion Hotel Tucson Airport**, 6801 S Tucson Blvd, Tucson, AZ 85706; tel 602/746-3932 or toll free 800/526-0550; fax 602/889-9934. Valencia Rd exit off I-19 proceed 4 miles east to Tucson Blvd. Better-than-average hotel close to the airport. **Rooms:** 191 rms and stes. CI 3pm/CO noon. Nonsmoking rms avail. Very attractively appointed with southwestern decor. **Amenities:** 🛍 🖑 ⌕ A/C, cable TV w/movies. Some units w/terraces. **Services:** ✗ 🚐 🗚 ⌂ ⌘ Masseur, babysitting. In addition to full breakfast, guests receive complimentary cocktails and late-night snacks. 24-hour airport shuttle. **Facilities:** 🔔 ⌂ 🏊 🖑 🌣 1 rst, 1 bar, whirlpool, washer/dryer. **Rates (BB):** HS Jan–May $85–$105 S; $95–$115 D; from $125 ste. Extra person $10. Children under 18 stay free. Lower rates off-season. Spec packages avail. Pking: Outdoor, free. Maj CC.

≣≣ **Country Suites by Carlson**, 7411 N Oracle Rd, Tucson, AZ 85704; tel 602/575-9255 or toll free 800/456-4000; fax 602/575-8671. A fine, basic hotel, good for both business travelers and vacationers. **Rooms:** 156 stes. CI 3pm/CO noon. Nonsmoking rms avail. Rooms are attractively and comfortably furnished. **Amenities:** 🛍 🖑 🖥 A/C, satel TV, refrig. **Services:** ⌘ 🚐 🗚 ⌂ ⌘ **Facilities:** 🔔 🏊 🖥 🌣 Whirlpool, washer/dryer. Putting green. **Rates (CP):** HS Jan–Apr from $75 ste. Extra person $6. Children under 12 stay free. Lower rates off-season. Pking: Outdoor, free. Maj CC. Long-term rates for 6 or more nights.

≣≣≣ **Courtyard by Marriott**, 2505 E Executive Dr, Tucson, AZ 85706; tel 602/573-0000 or toll free 800/321-2211; fax 602/573-0470. Conveniently located a half-mile from Tucson International Airport. **Rooms:** 149 rms and stes. CI 3pm/CO noon. Express checkout avail. Nonsmoking rms avail. Half the rooms look out at the pool. Two thirds of the hotel is nonsmoking. **Amenities:** 🛍 🖑 A/C, satel TV w/movies, stereo/tape player, voice mail. Some units w/terraces. All suites have wet bars and refrigerators, as well as 2 telephones and 2 televisions. Most first- and second-floor king rooms have sofabeds. **Services:** ✗ 🚐 🗚 ⌂ Babysitting. **Facilities:** 🔔 🚑 🖥 🌣 1 rst, 1 bar, whirlpool, washer/dryer. **Rates:** HS Jan–mid-May $109 S; $119 D; from $129 ste. Extra person $10. Children under 15 stay free. Lower rates off-season. Pking: Outdoor, free. Maj CC.

≣≣≣ **The Doubletree Hotel Tucson**, 445 S Alvernon Way, Tucson, AZ 85711 (Midtown); tel 602/881-4200 or toll free 800/222-8733. A centrally located and well-appointed hotel. **Rooms:** 295 rms and stes; 3 ctges/villas. Exec-level rms avail. CI 3pm/CO 1pm. Express checkout avail. Nonsmoking rms avail. **Amenities:** 🛍 🖑 🖥 🖑 A/C, cable TV w/movies, refrig, bathrobes. Some units w/minibars, some w/terraces. Rooms in the tower have minibars and coffeemakers. King rooms in the tower also have sofas. Bathrobes and hair dryers provided on the executive level. **Services:** ✗ ⌘ 🆅🅿 🚐 🗚 ⌂ ⌘ Masseur,

babysitting. Complimentary box of specialty chocolate chip cookies presented to guests on arrival. **Facilities:** 🔔 🍷🖥 🚑 🔑 🌣 2 rsts, 2 bars (1 w/entertainment), spa, whirlpool, beauty salon. **Rates:** HS Jan–Apr 15 $120–$140 S; $135–$155 D; from $250 ste. Extra person $15. Children under 18 stay free. Lower rates off-season. Spec packages avail. Pking: Outdoor, free. Maj CC.

≣≣≣ **Embassy Suites Hotel**, 7051 S Tucson Blvd, Tucson, AZ 85706; tel 602/573-0700 or toll free 800/573-0700; fax 602/741-9645. All-suites hotel right next door to the airport; it's especially popular with corporate travelers. **Rooms:** 204 stes. CI 1pm/CO 1pm. Express checkout avail. Six suites have adjoining conference suites, and all suites have kitchenettes. Half the rooms are nonsmoking. **Amenities:** 🛍 🖑 🖥 🖑 A/C, cable TV w/movies, refrig, stereo/tape player, voice mail. Some units w/terraces. There are 2 televisions in every suite. **Services:** ✗ 🚐 🗚 ⌂ ⌘ Car-rental desk, babysitting. Complimentary cocktails are served daily from 5:30 to 7:30pm. **Facilities:** 🔔 🍷🖥 🚑 🖥 🌣 1 rst, 1 bar, whirlpool, washer/dryer. **Rates (BB):** HS Jan–May from $129 ste. Extra person $10. Children under 12 stay free. Lower rates off-season. Spec packages avail. Pking: Outdoor, free. Maj CC. Special weekend rates available.

≣≣ **Hampton Inn**, 6971 S Tucson Blvd, Tucson, AZ 85706; tel 602/889-5789 or toll free 800/HAMPTON; fax 602/889-4002. Located next to Tucson International Airport. **Rooms:** 125 rms and stes. CI 1pm/CO noon. Nonsmoking rms avail. Half the rooms are nonsmoking. **Amenities:** 🛍 🖑 A/C, satel TV w/movies, stereo/tape player. Some units w/terraces. **Services:** 🚐 🗚 ⌂ ⌘ Free local calls. The hotel has a "100% satisfaction guaranteed" program. **Facilities:** 🔔 🚑 🌣 Whirlpool, washer/dryer. **Rates (CP):** HS Jan–mid-May $75 S; $79 D; from $85 ste. Children under 18 stay free. Lower rates off-season. Higher rates for spec evnts/hols. Pking: Outdoor, free. Maj CC.

≣≣≣ **Holiday Inn**, 181 W Broadway, Tucson, AZ 85701 (Downtown); tel 602/624-8711 or toll free 800/HOLIDAY; fax 602/623-8121. Exit W Congress St off I-10. A downtown hotel close to the convention center and oriented to the business traveler. **Rooms:** 309 rms and stes. CI 3pm/CO noon. Express checkout avail. Nonsmoking rms avail. Rooms are comfortable and attractive. **Amenities:** 🛍 🖑 🖥 A/C, cable TV. **Services:** ✗ 🚐 🗚 ⌂ ⌘ Car-rental desk. **Facilities:** 🔔 🚑 🌣 1 rst, 1 bar (w/entertainment), games rm. Ample meeting space, and the exhibition area has space for 50 booths. **Rates (BB):** HS Jan–Apr $115 S or D; from $150 ste. Extra person $10. Children under 18 stay free. Lower rates off-season. Higher rates for spec evnts/hols. Spec packages avail. Pking: Indoor, free. Maj CC.

≣≣≣ Hotel Park Tucson and Conference Center, 5151 E Grant Rd, Tucson, AZ 85712 (Midtown); tel 602/323-6262 or toll free 800/257-7275; fax 602/325-2989. Midtown hotel suitable for both business and vacation travelers. **Rooms:** 216 rms and stes. CI 3pm/CO 1pm. Express checkout avail. Nonsmoking rms avail. Many rooms have mountain views. **Amenities:** 🛏 ⚥ 📻 A/C, satel TV, refrig, stereo/tape player, voice mail. Some units w/terraces. Suites have wet bars, 2 televisions, and 2 telephones. **Services:** ✕ 🖂 🚗 🖼 🛎 Babysitting. **Facilities:** 🛗 🍴 325 🖥 ⛇ 2 rsts (see also "Restaurants" below), 2 bars (1 w/entertainment), spa, whirlpool, washer/dryer. 4,300-square-foot ballroom, executive board room, and smaller meeting rooms. **Rates (BB):** HS Jan 18–May 27 $115 S; $125 D; from $125 ste. Extra person $15. Children under 12 stay free. Min stay spec evnts. Lower rates off-season. Higher rates for spec evnts/hols. Spec packages avail. Pking: Outdoor, free. Maj CC.

≣≣ Howard Johnson Lodge, 750 W Starr Pass Blvd, Tucson, AZ 85713; tel 602/624-4455; fax 602/624-4455. 22nd St exit off I-10. Recently renovated. **Rooms:** 99 rms and stes. CI 3pm/CO noon. Nonsmoking rms avail. Some rooms have a pool view. **Amenities:** 🛏 A/C, satel TV w/movies. All units w/terraces. **Services:** 🚗 🛎 **Facilities:** 🛗 🍴 50 ⛇ Sauna, whirlpool. **Rates (CP):** HS Jan–Apr $85 S; $95 D; from $130 ste. Extra person $10. Children under 12 stay free. Lower rates off-season. Higher rates for spec evnts/hols. Pking: Outdoor, free. Maj CC.

≣≣≣ Marriott Residence Inn, 6555 E Speedway Blvd, Tucson, AZ 85710 (Midtown); tel 602/721-0991 or toll free 800/331-3131. An attractive, comfortable hotel. Ideal for longer stays. **Rooms:** 128 stes. CI 3pm/CO noon. Nonsmoking rms avail. **Amenities:** 🛏 ⚥ 📻 A/C, satel TV w/movies, refrig, stereo/tape player. Some units w/terraces, some w/fireplaces. All units have VCRs. **Services:** 🖂 🚗 🖼 🛎 Babysitting. Complimentary afternoon snacks. **Facilities:** 🛗 50 Lawn games, whirlpool, washer/dryer. Outdoor game court for volleyball, basketball, and paddle ball. **Rates (CP):** HS Jan–Apr from $135 ste. Extra person $10. Children under 13 stay free. Lower rates off-season. Spec packages avail. Pking: Outdoor, free. Maj CC.

≣≣≣ Park Inn International, 2803 E Valencia Rd, Tucson, AZ 85706; tel 602/294-2500 or toll free 800/864-2145; fax 602/741-0851. Valencia Rd exit off I-19. This hotel close to the airport is good for business travelers. Management stresses personal service. **Rooms:** 95 rms and stes. CI noon/CO noon. Nonsmoking rms avail. Rooms have simple southwestern decor and good lighting. **Amenities:** 🛏 📻 A/C, cable TV w/movies. Some units w/terraces. **Services:** ✕ 🚗 🖼 🛎 Fax and photocopy services available. **Facilities:** 🛗 100 🖥 ⛇ 1 rst, 1 bar,

whirlpool. **Rates:** HS Dec–Mar $85 S; $90 D; from $120 ste. Extra person $5. Children under 16 stay free. Lower rates off-season. Pking: Outdoor, free. Maj CC.

≣≣≣ Plaza Hotel and Conference Center, 1900 E Speedway Blvd, Tucson, AZ 85719; tel 602/327-7341 or toll free 800/843-8052, 800/654-3010 in AZ; fax 602/327-0276. Exit 257 off I-10. Centrally located high-rise hotel close to the University of Arizona and University Medical Center. **Rooms:** 150 rms. CI 3pm/CO noon. Nonsmoking rms avail. All rooms have mountain views. **Amenities:** 🛏 ⚥ A/C, cable TV. Some rooms have refrigerators. **Services:** ✕ 🚗 🖼 🛎 🖧 Complimentary newspapers, cocktails, and snacks. **Facilities:** 🛗 500 🖥 ⛇ 1 rst, 1 bar, whirlpool. **Rates:** HS Feb–Mar $58–$83 S or D. Extra person $8. Children under 16 stay free. Lower rates off-season. Higher rates for spec evnts/hols. Spec packages avail. Pking: Indoor/outdoor, free. Maj CC.

≣≣≣ Radisson Suite Hotel Tucson, 6555 E Speedway Blvd, Tucson, AZ 85710 (Central Tucson); tel 602/721-7100 or toll free 800/333-3333. Exit Speedway Blvd off I-10. An all-suites hotel, good for long-term visitors and business travelers who need extra working space. **Rooms:** 304 stes. CI 3pm/CO noon. Express checkout avail. Nonsmoking rms avail. Second- to fifth-floor suites have balconies. Many rooms have mountain views. **Amenities:** 🛏 ⚥ 📻 A/C, satel TV w/movies, refrig. Some units w/terraces, some w/fireplaces, some w/Jacuzzis. Many standard suites have microwaves. **Services:** ✕ 🖂 🚗 🖼 🛎 🖧 Twice-daily maid svce, car-rental desk. Complimentary cocktails. **Facilities:** 🛗 🍴 500 ⛇ 1 rst, 2 bars, spa, whirlpool, washer/dryer. **Rates (BB):** HS Oct–May from $115 ste. Extra person $10. Children under 17 stay free. Lower rates off-season. Higher rates for spec evnts/hols. Spec packages avail. Pking: Outdoor, free. Maj CC.

≣≣≣ Ramada Downtown, 475 N Granada Rd, Tucson, AZ 85701; tel 602/622-3000 or toll free 800/228-2828; fax 602/623-8922. Exit St Mary's Rd off I-10. 12 acres. Downtown hotel with good freeway access. **Rooms:** 297 rms and stes. CI 3pm/CO noon. Express checkout avail. Nonsmoking rms avail. Rooms are simply and comfortably furnished. **Amenities:** 🛏 ⚥ 📻 A/C, satel TV w/movies, voice mail. Some units w/terraces. **Services:** ✕ 🖂 🚗 🖼 🛎 🖧 Lifeguards at pool in summer. **Facilities:** 🛗 600 ⛇ 1 rst, 1 bar (w/entertainment), lifeguard, lawn games, washer/dryer. **Rates (BB):** HS Jan–Apr $99 S or D; from $135 ste. Extra person $10. Children under 18 stay free. Min stay spec evnts. Lower rates off-season. Spec packages avail. Pking: Outdoor, free. Maj CC. Summer rates available.

≣≣ Rodeway Inn, 1365 W Grant Rd, Tucson, AZ 85745; tel 602/622-7791 or toll free 800/228-2000; fax 602/629-0201. Exit Grant Rd off I-10. An attractive, basic motel located close to downtown, with good freeway access. **Rooms:** 146 rms and stes. CI 3pm/CO noon. Express checkout avail. Nonsmoking rms avail. **Amenities:** 🔒 🌡 A/C, satel TV w/movies. **Services:** ✗ 🚐 🖨 🍴 🍽 **Facilities:** 🚴 🚷 🚳 1 rst, 1 bar, whirlpool, washer/dryer. **Rates (CP):** HS Mid-Jan–Apr $50–$80 S or D; from $125 ste. Extra person $6. Children under 18 stay free. Lower rates off-season. Higher rates for spec evnts/hols. Spec packages avail. Pking: Outdoor, free. Maj CC.

🏨🏨 **Tanque Verde Inn**, 7007 E Tanque Verde, Tucson, AZ 85715 (Eastside); tel 602/298-2300 or toll free 800/882-8484. Very pleasant, medium-priced hotel featuring attractive court-yards and gardens. **Rooms:** 90 rms, stes, and effic. CI 3pm/CO 11am. Nonsmoking rms avail. 60 rooms have kitchenettes. **Amenities:** 🔒🌡🖨 🍴 A/C, cable TV w/movies, refrig. **Services:** 🖨 🍴 🍽 Poolside happy hour from 5:30 to 7:30pm daily. **Facilities:** 🚴 🚷 Whirlpool, washer/dryer. **Rates (CP):** HS Feb–Mar $80–$125 S or D; from $130 ste; from $95 effic. Extra person $8. Children under 18 stay free. Lower rates off-season. Spec packages avail. Pking: Outdoor, free. Maj CC. Weekly and monthly rates available.

🏨🏨🏨 **Tucson East Hilton**, 7600 E Broadway, Tucson, AZ 85710 (Eastside); tel 602/721-5600 or toll free 800/648-7177; fax 602/721-5696. Kolb Rd exit off I-10. A large eastside hotel popular with business travelers. The 7-story atrium lobby boasts a fountain. **Rooms:** 232 rms and stes. Exec-level rms avail. CI 3pm/CO noon. Express checkout avail. Nonsmoking rms avail. **Amenities:** 🔒🌡🖨 A/C, cable TV w/movies, voice mail. 1 unit w/minibar, some w/terraces. **Services:** ✗ 🚐 🖨 🍴 Babysitting. **Facilities:** 🚴 🏋 🖨 🚳 🚷 1 rst, 1 bar (w/entertainment), whirlpool. **Rates:** HS Feb–Apr $95–$175 S; $108–$188 D; from $170 ste. Extra person $13. Children under 18 stay free. Lower rates off-season. Spec packages avail. Pking: Outdoor, free. Maj CC. Corporate rates are available.

🏨🏨🏨 **Viscount Suite Hotel**, 4855 E Broadway, Tucson, AZ 85711; tel 602/745-6500 or toll free 800/527-9666; fax 602/790-5144. Located in the heart of the business district, 4 miles from downtown. A fountain graces the lobby. **Rooms:** 215 stes. Exec-level rms avail. CI 3pm/CO noon. Nonsmoking rms avail. **Amenities:** 🔒🌡🖨 🍴 A/C, satel TV w/movies. Suites have 2 telephones and 2 TVs. **Services:** ✗ 🖙 🚐 🖨 🍴 A complimentary cocktail reception runs from 5 to 7pm daily. The director of guest services can arrange tours and other activities. **Facilities:** 🚴 🏋 🚳 🚷 3 rsts, 1 bar, sauna, whirlpool. There's a popular sports bar on premises. **Rates (BB):** HS Jan–Apr from $135 ste. Extra person $10. Children under 12 stay free. Lower rates off-season. Spec packages avail. Pking: Outdoor, free. Maj CC.

Motels

🏨 **Discovery Inn**, 1010 S Freeway, Tucson, AZ 85745; tel 602/622-5871 or toll free 800/622-5871; fax 602/620-0097. 22nd St exit off I-10. A pleasant, modern motel just off the interstate. **Rooms:** 148 rms and stes. CI open/CO 11am. Nonsmoking rms avail. Comfortable, although not all are well soundproofed. **Amenities:** 🔒 A/C, cable TV w/movies. **Services:** 🖨 🍴 **Facilities:** 🚴 🚳 🚷 1 rst, 1 bar, washer/dryer. **Rates:** HS Jan–Apr $65–$70 S or D; from $70 ste. Children under 18 stay free. Lower rates off-season. Spec packages avail. Pking: Outdoor, free. Maj CC. All rooms are $35 in the off-season.

🏨🏨 **Econo Lodge**, 3020 S 6th Ave, Tucson, AZ 85713; tel 602/623-5881 or toll free 800/623-5881. Basic, clean, comfortable accommodations. **Rooms:** 88 rms. CI 11am/CO 11am. Nonsmoking rms avail. **Amenities:** 🔒 A/C, satel TV. **Services:** 🍴 **Facilities:** 🚴 🚷 Washer/dryer. **Rates:** HS Jan–Apr $39 S; $49 D. Extra person $5. Children under 15 stay free. Lower rates off-season. Spec packages avail. Pking: Outdoor, free. Maj CC.

🏨 **Motel 6**, 755 E Benson Hwy, Tucson, AZ 85706; tel 602/622-4614. Exit 262 off I-10. A clean, well-kept, no-frills motel on the east side of Tucson, with attractive cactus gardens on the property. **Rooms:** 120 rms. CI noon/CO noon. Nonsmoking rms avail. Simple, comfortable rooms. **Amenities:** 🔒 A/C, cable TV. **Services:** 🍴 🍽 **Facilities:** 🚴 🚷 **Rates:** $26 S; $32 D. Extra person $3. Children under 18 stay free. Pking: Outdoor, free. Maj CC.

🏨 **Palm Court Inn**, 4425 E 22nd St, Tucson, AZ 85711 (Midtown); tel 602/745-1777 or toll free 800/288-1650. Popular with long-term visitors. **Rooms:** 40 rms and effic. CI 2pm/CO 11am. Nonsmoking rms avail. All rooms have full kitchenettes. **Amenities:** 🔒 A/C, cable TV, refrig. Some units w/terraces. **Facilities:** 🚴 Whirlpool, washer/dryer. **Rates:** HS Oct–Apr $60 S or D; from $120 effic. Lower rates off-season. Pking: Outdoor, free. Ltd CC. Weekly rates are available.

🏨🏨🏨 **Smuggler's Inn**, 6350 E Speedway Blvd, Tucson, AZ 85710 (Central Tucson); tel 602/296-3292 or toll free 800/525-8852; fax 602/722-3713. A nice mid-priced hotel with a lagoon. **Rooms:** 150 rms and stes. CI 3pm/CO 1pm. Nonsmoking rms avail. All rooms have easy chairs and views of the lake, pool, or garden. **Amenities:** 🔒🌡 A/C, cable TV w/movies. All units w/terraces. **Services:** ✗ 🚐 🖨 🍴 Complimentary cocktail and snacks daily. **Facilities:** 🚴 🏊 🚳 🚷 1 rst, 1 bar (w/entertainment), whirlpool, washer/dryer. A putting green adjoins the lagoon. **Rates:** HS Jan–May $89 S; $99 D; from $119 ste. Children under 16 stay free. Lower rates off-season. Spec packages avail. Pking: Outdoor, free. Maj CC.

Resorts

≣≣≣ **Best Western Ghost Ranch Lodge**, 801 W Miracle Mile, Tucson, AZ 85705; tel 602/791-7565 or toll free 800/456-7565; fax 602/791-3898. Exit Miracle Mile off I-10. 8 acres. This unusual resort, which dates from 1941, is steeped in history. The "Ghost Ranch" name was inspired by the original owner's friendship with New Mexico artist Georgia O'Keeffe. The lobby has a saltillo-tiled floor and Mexican furniture, and there are lovely cactus gardens. **Rooms:** 68 rms; 13 ctges/villas. CI 2pm/CO noon. Nonsmoking rms avail. Cottages have private patios. **Amenities:** 🛅 🐬 🖃 A/C, satel TV w/movies, refrig. Some units w/terraces. Cottages have fold-out sofas, microwaves, and cooking stoves. **Services:** 🚗 🖳 🖐 🐬 Babysitting. Airport transportation free with 5-day stay. **Facilities:** 🖪 🖐 🖭 🖭 👌 1 rst, 1 bar, lawn games, whirlpool, washer/dryer. Outdoor, awning-covered dining. **Rates (CP):** HS Jan–Apr $68–$92 S; $74–$98 D; from $84 ctge/villa. Extra person $6. Children under 12 stay free. Lower rates off-season. Spec packages avail. Pking: Outdoor, free. Maj CC.

≣≣≣ **Lazy K Bar Ranch**, 8401 N Scenic Dr, Tucson, AZ 85743; tel 602/744-3050 or toll free 800/321-7018; fax 602/744-7628. 160 acres. Although surrounded by wide-open spaces, this lovely ranch is only 17 miles from Tucson. **Rooms:** 23 rms and stes. CI 1pm/CO noon. **Amenities:** 🐬 A/C. No phone or TV. Some units w/terraces, some w/fireplaces, 1 w/Jacuzzi. Deluxe king rooms have hide-a-beds; suites have fireplaces. Videos are available in the TV room. **Services:** 🚗 🖐 Babysitting. **Facilities:** 🖪 ൽ 🚣 🖭 🖭 1 rst, 1 bar, games rm, lawn games, whirlpool, playground, washer/dryer. There's a pleasant library with a card table and piano. **Rates (AP):** HS Feb–Apr/Dec 18–Jan 1 $145–$165 S; $230–$290 D; from $165 ste. Extra person $25–80. Min stay. Lower rates off-season. Higher rates for spec evnts/hols. Pking: Outdoor, free. Maj CC. Minimum 3-night stay; rates include daily horseback riding (except Sunday). The charge for a third person in the room varies according to age.

≣≣≣ **The Lodge on the Desert**, 306 N Alvernon Way, PO Box 42500, Tucson, AZ 85733 (Central Tucson); tel 602/325-3366 or toll free 800/456-5634; fax 602/327-5834. 5 acres. A quiet, centrally located old-style adobe resort dating from the 1930s. It feels and looks like a Mexican hacienda, and has lovely grounds. The original home is now a central lodge for the resort. **Rooms:** 40 rms and stes. CI 2pm/CO noon. Four types of rooms: Standard, Deluxe, Luxury, and Elegant. All rooms are decorated differently with furniture from the 1940s and '50s. Some rooms have separate tubs and showers. **Amenities:** 🛅 A/C, TV. Some units w/terraces, some w/fireplaces. Some rooms have hide-a-beds; most have refrigerators and kiva fireplaces. **Services:** ✗ 🖂 🖳 🖐 🐬 Free airport transportation available for those staying at least 7 days during high season. **Facilities:** 🖪 🖭 👌 1 rst (*see also* "Restaurants" below), 1 bar, games rm, lawn games. The lodge has a good library with easy chairs. There's outdoor dining by the fountain. Recreational sports include ping pong, croquet, horseshoes, and darts. **Rates (CP):** HS Nov–May $80–$100 S; $90–$112 D; from $109 ste. Extra person $10. Children under 2 stay free. Lower rates off-season. AP and MAP rates avail. Pking: Outdoor, free. Maj CC.

≣≣≣≣≣ **Loews Ventana Canyon Resort**, 7000 N Resort Dr, Tucson, AZ 85715 (Ventana Canyon); tel 602/299-2020 or toll free 800/234-5117; fax 602/299-6832. 20 mi NE of downtown Tucson. From I-10, take Ina Rd or Orange Grove Rd exits to Skyline Dr and turn left at Craycroft Rd. 93 acres. Located 3,000 feet up in the foothills of the Catalina Mountains, between desert slopes and Tom Fazio–designed fairways. Imposing, award-winning architecture fits 398 rooms into 4 stories of earth-toned wings with hints of Native American cliff dwellings and pueblos. Grand lobby/lounge echoes art deco of Arizona Biltmore in Phoenix, with artwork and sculpture and a wall of windows overlooking 1.5-acre tiered lake. **Rooms:** 398 rms and stes. CI 3pm/CO noon. Express checkout avail. Nonsmoking rms avail. All with roomy balconies—from some, guests can almost reach to touch the cactus and squawbrush, others have expansive views of the city below. Oversized bathtubs, southwestern art, attractive furniture of burnished pine. **Amenities:** 🛅 🐬 🖳 A/C, cable TV w/movies, refrig, shoe polisher, bathrobes. All units w/minibars, all w/terraces, some w/fireplaces, some w/Jacuzzis. In-room video for messages and accounts review; 2-line phones; dataports due in 1995. **Services:** 🍽 ☛ 🖵 🚗 🖳 🖐 Twice-daily maid svce, car-rental desk, masseur, children's program, babysitting. Young, alert staff; regular room service menu augmented by candlelight dinners catered by swank Ventana Room and served course by course. **Facilities:** 🖪 ൽ ▶18 🖭 🖳 🖭 🖭 🖭 👌 4 rsts (*see also* "Restaurants" below), 2 bars (w/entertainment), lifeguard, games rm, lawn games, spa, sauna, steam rm, whirlpool, beauty salon, playground. Beautiful freeform pool with heated whirlpool and waterfall-chilled plunge pool, surrounded by wispy palo verde and African sumac trees (open until 10pm); brand-new children's playground; pathways to natural 80-foot-high waterfall. **Rates:** HS Jan 10–May 31 $265–$305 S; $285–$325 D; from $425 ste. Extra person $10. Children under 18 stay free. Min stay spec evnts. Lower rates off-season. AP and MAP rates avail. Spec packages avail. Pking: Outdoor, free. Maj CC. Room rates, in 3 categories, vary by floor and view. Although two thirds of guests are there for meetings, the resort has many romantic features; the special Celebration Packages are a good deal.

≣≣≣ **Sheraton El Conquistador Resort and Country Club**, 10000 N Oracle Rd, Tucson, AZ 85737; tel 602/544-5000 or toll free 800/325-7832; fax 602/544-1228. Exit Ina Rd off

I-10. 300 acres. Set at the base of Catalina State Park and National Park property, this resort has excellent views. **Rooms:** 434 rms and stes. CI 4pm/CO noon. Express checkout avail. Nonsmoking rms avail. Standard double rooms have queen beds; standard king rooms have king bed, couch, and coffee table. **Amenities:** 🛏 ⓐ 🎿 ☎ A/C, cable TV w/movies, voice mail, in-rm safe. All units w/minibars, all w/terraces, some w/fireplaces, some w/Jacuzzis. **Services:** ⏧ 🖙 ⛱ ↵ ⏧ Twice-daily maid svce, car-rental desk, social director, masseur, children's program, babysitting. Complimentary morning newspapers. **Facilities:** ⛳ 🚲 ⏃45 ⛵ 🎾 🏂 🎣 ⛹31 🍸 📶1.2k 🖥 ♿ 6 rsts, 4 bars (2 w/entertainment), lawn games, racquetball, spa, sauna, whirlpool, beauty salon, day-care ctr. Hiking and bicycling opportunities available on the adjacent lands. **Rates:** HS Jan–May $250–$260 S or D; from $280 ste. Extra person $15. Children under 18 stay free. Lower rates off-season. Spec packages avail. Pking: Outdoor, free. Maj CC.

≋≋≋ **Tanque Verde Ranch**, 14301 E Speedway Blvd, PO Box 66, Tucson, AZ 85748; tel 602/296-6275 or toll free 800/234-DUDE; fax 602/721-9426. 20 mi E of Tucson. 640 acres. Dude ranch in the Catalina foothills, popular with both European and American visitors. **Rooms:** 67 rms and stes. CI 2pm/CO noon. **Amenities:** 🛏 A/C, refrig. Some units w/terraces, some w/fireplaces. Rooms do not have TVs, although they are available; there's also one in the lodge. **Services:** 🖙 🚐 ⛱ ↵ Social director, masseur, children's program, babysitting. Free airport transportation with stays of 4 nights or more. **Facilities:** ⛳ 🏊 🎣 ⛹4 🎣 🍸 📶200 ♿ 1 rst, 1 bar, games rm, lawn games, spa, sauna, whirlpool, day-care ctr, playground, washer/dryer. The ranch has a fishing lake and offers bird watching and banding, and nature hikes. More than 130 horses available to ride. **Rates (AP):** HS Dec 16–Apr 30 $230–$270 S; $260–$320 D; from $260 ste. Lower rates off-season. AP rates avail. Pking: Outdoor, free. Maj CC. Rates include riding, tennis, sports, and all ranch activities. Add $65 to $75 (to double rate) for a third person in room.

≋≋≋ **Tucson National Golf and Conference Center**, 2727 W Club Dr, Tucson, AZ 85741; tel 602/297-2271 or toll free 800/528-4856; fax 602/297-7544. 650 acres. Beautiful golf resort in a magnificent setting. Home of the PGA Northern Telecom Open. **Rooms:** 142 rms and stes; 25 ctges/villas. CI 3pm/CO noon. Nonsmoking rms avail. Minisuites have sofas and throw pillows on the beds. Some rooms have makeup tables. **Amenities:** 🛏 ⓐ 🎿 ☎ A/C, cable TV w/movies, refrig, bathrobes. All units w/minibars, all w/terraces, some w/fireplaces. Each room has irons and ironing boards; minisuites have minibars. **Services:** ✗ 🖙 VP ⛱ ↵ Twice-daily maid svce, masseur, children's program, babysitting. **Facilities:** ⛳ 🚲 ⏃27 🎾 🏂 🎣 🍸 🍸 📶1k 🖥 ♿ 3 rsts, 5 bars, games rm, lawn

games, spa, sauna, steam rm, whirlpool, beauty salon, playground, washer/dryer. **Rates:** HS Jan–May $265 S or D; from $275 ste; from $350 ctge/villa. Extra person $10. Children under 18 stay free. Lower rates off-season. MAP rates avail. Spec packages avail. Pking: Outdoor, free. Maj CC.

≋≋≋ **Ventana Canyon Golf and Racquet Club**, 6200 N Clubhouse Lane, Tucson, AZ 85715 (Sabino Canyon); tel 602/577-1400 or toll free 800/828-5701; fax 602/299-0256. 1,100 acres. This small, intimate resort is good for corporate outings and retreats. **Rooms:** 49 stes. CI 3pm/CO noon. Nonsmoking rms avail. Rooms have picture-postcard scenic views. All suites have kitchens. **Amenities:** 🛏 ⓐ 🎿 ☎ A/C, cable TV, refrig, bathrobes. All units w/terraces. **Services:** ✗ 🖙 VP ⛱ ↵ Masseur, babysitting. **Facilities:** ⛳ 🚲 ⏃36 🎾 🍸 🍸 📶70 🖥 ♿ 2 rsts, 1 bar, lawn games, spa, sauna, steam rm, whirlpool, beauty salon, day-care ctr. **Rates:** HS Jan 15–Apr 30 $280–$384 S or D; from $300 ste. Extra person $38. Children under 17 stay free. Lower rates off-season. Higher rates for spec evnts/hols. Spec packages avail. Pking: Outdoor, free. Maj CC.

≋≋≋≋ **The Westin La Paloma**, 3800 E Sunrise Dr, Tucson, AZ 85718 (La Paloma); tel 602/742-6000 or toll free 800/876-3683. A large, nicely appointed hotel at the base of the mountains. The expansive lobby's 50-foot arched windows frame stunning mountain views. **Rooms:** 487 rms and stes. CI 4pm/CO noon. Express checkout avail. Nonsmoking rms avail. All rooms have double sinks in the bathrooms. **Amenities:** 🛏 ⓐ 🎿 ☎ A/C, cable TV w/movies, refrig, voice mail, in-rm safe, bathrobes. All units w/minibars, all w/terraces, some w/fireplaces, some w/Jacuzzis. Resort suites have whirlpools and barbecues on their patios. **Services:** ✗ 🖙 VP 🚐 ⛱ ↵ Car-rental desk, masseur, children's program, babysitting. **Facilities:** ⛳ 🚲 ⏃27 🎾 🏂 🎣 ⛹2 🍸 🍸 📶18k 🖥 ♿ 5 rsts, 2 bars, lawn games, racquetball, spa, sauna, steam rm, whirlpool, beauty salon, day-care ctr, playground. The hotel has 3 whirlpools, a lap pool, and a swim-up bar. **Rates:** HS Jan–May 27 $205–$315 S or D; from $425 ste. Extra person $20. Children under 18 stay free. Lower rates off-season. Spec packages avail. Pking: Indoor/outdoor, free. Maj CC.

≋≋≋≋ **Westward Look Resort**, 245 E Inn Rd, Tucson, AZ 85704; tel 602/297-1151 or toll free 800/722-2500; fax 602/297-9023. Exit Ina Rd off I-10. 80 acres. A lovely resort in the foothills of the Catalina Mountains. Large lobby with tile floor and fireplace. **Rooms:** 244 rms and stes. CI 3pm/CO noon. Nonsmoking rms avail. **Amenities:** 🛏 ⓐ 🎿 A/C, cable TV w/movies, refrig, voice mail. All units w/minibars, all w/terraces. **Services:** ✗ 🖙 ⛱ ↵ ⏧ Masseur, babysitting. Tennis lessons are available. **Facilities:** ⛳ 🎾 🍸3 🍸 🍸 📶300 ♿ 2 rsts (*see also* "Restaurants" below), 1 bar (w/entertainment), lawn games, spa, whirlpool. There's a pro shop on the premises. Also, facilities for volleyball, basketball, and baseball. **Rates:** HS Jan 16–Apr 15 $130–$260 S or D; from $260 ste. Extra person $10. Children under 16 stay free. Lower rates off-season. AP rates avail. Spec packages avail. Pking: Outdoor, free. Maj CC.

≡≡≡ **White Stallion Ranch**, 9251 W Twin Peaks Rd, Tucson, AZ 85743; tel 602/297-0252 or toll free 800/782-5546; fax 602/744-2786. 17 mi N of downtown Tucson, exit Ina Rd off I-10. 3,000 acres. This sprawling guest ranch has beautiful mountain views, and a lobby that's homey and comfortable, with a fireplace. **Rooms:** 29 rms and stes. CI 2pm/CO 11am. Most rooms have western-style furniture. Rooms range in size from small (in the main lodge) to spacious suites. **Amenities:** A/C. No phone or TV. All units w/terraces, some w/fireplaces, some w/Jacuzzis. **Services:** 🚗 🍴 Babysitting. **Facilities:** 🛁 ⛵ 🎿 🎱 🏊 1 rst, 1 bar, games rm, lawn games, whirlpool, playground, washer/dryer. The main lodge has a TV. There's a children's petting zoo, and about 80 horses for riding (no riding on Sunday). Free airport pickup for stays of 4 days or more. **Rates (AP):** HS Dec 18–Apr 29 $134 S; $218–$242 D; from $129 ste. Extra person $79. Children under 2 stay free. Min stay HS. Lower rates off-season. AP rates avail. Spec packages avail. Pking: Outdoor, free. No CC.

Restaurants 🍽️

Anthony's in the Catalinas, 6440 N Campbell Ave, Tucson (Catalina Foothills); tel 602/299-1771. **Continental.** An elegant restaurant with terrific views of the Catalina mountains and Tucson. The main dining room has a large fireplace, huge ceiling beams, and tapestries depicting scenes from the Middle Ages. Specialties include duck à l'orange with Grand Marnier sauce, and pork calvados stuffed with apples, mushrooms, and spinach. **FYI:** Reservations recommended. Piano. **Open:** Lunch Mon–Sat 11:30am–2:30pm; dinner daily 5:30–10pm. Closed some hols. **Prices:** Main courses $13.95–$25.95. Maj CC. ♥ 🏔️ VP ⴕ

Arizona Inn, in the Arizona Inn, 2200 E Elm St, Tucson (Midtown); tel 602/325-1541. **Regional American/Continental.** Well-regarded restaurant located in a hotel steeped in tradition, with high, open-beamed ceilings, Indian blankets on the walls, a kiva fireplace, furniture from the 1920s, and soft lighting. A popular entree is chicken and shrimp in tequila with grilled red onion and prickly pear sauce. The menu also includes a daily pasta, venison, wild boar, duck, veal, chicken, and a number of grilled beef choices. **FYI:** Reservations recommended. Guitar. Children's menu. Dress code. **Open:** HS Sept–May breakfast daily 6:15–10:30am; lunch daily 11:30am–2pm; dinner daily 5–10pm. Reduced hours off-season. **Prices:** Main courses $14–$21. Maj CC. ♥ 🏺 ⴕ

Bobby McGee's Conglomeration, 6464 E Tanque Verde Rd, Tucson (Eastside); tel 602/886-5551. **American.** Features an Old West look, with fringed stained-glass lamp shades, wood paneling, comfortable booths, and lots of memorabilia. Servers are dressed as Old West characters, from "school marms" to cowpunchers. The menu offers just about everything—chicken, steak, prime rib, seafood, pasta, and vegetarian dishes. **FYI:** Reservations recommended. Children's menu. Dress code. **Open:** Mon–Thurs 5–10pm, Fri–Sat 5–11pm, Sun 4–10pm. Closed Dec 25. **Prices:** Main courses $6.25–$15.95. Maj CC. 👫 💟 ⴕ

Boccata, in River Center, 5605 E River Rd, Tucson; tel 602/577-9309. **Continental.** Large second-floor restaurant offering dining on the balcony. Decorated in dark colors, with prints by artist Miguel Martinez and large flower arrangements. A variety of pastas are served as well as pork, beef, and fresh fish. **FYI:** Reservations recommended. Children's menu. **Open:** Sun–Thurs 5:30–9pm, Fri–Sat 5–10pm. Closed some hols. **Prices:** Main courses $9.50–$21. Maj CC. 🏔️ ⴕ

Cafe Magritte, 254 E Congress, Tucson (Downtown); tel 602/884-8004. At 6th Ave. **Eclectic.** Arty downtown cafe decorated with original artwork (available for purchase). A bar and lounge connect to the dining room, and there are sidewalk tables. High-carbohydrate foods are the specialty—numerous pasta, vegetable, and bean dishes. **FYI:** Reservations accepted. Cabaret/jazz. Beer and wine only. **Open:** Tues–Thurs 11am–11pm, Fri–Sat 11am–midnight. Closed some hols. **Prices:** Main courses $5.25–$9.75. Ltd CC. 🍰 ⴕ

Cafe Terra Cotta, in St. Philip's Plaza, 4310 N Campbell, Tucson; tel 602/577-8100. **Southwestern.** A bright, modern-looking restaurant with a contemporary Southwest flair. Southwestern specialties, with lots of chiles and herbs, plus pizza and pastas. **FYI:** Reservations recommended. Children's menu. **Open:** Sun–Thurs 11am–9:30pm, Fri–Sat 11am–10:30pm. Closed some hols. **Prices:** Main courses $14–$19. Maj CC. 🍰 ⴕ

Capriccio, 4825 N 1st Ave, Tucson; tel 602/887-2333. At River Rd. **Italian.** Elegant Italian dining, perfect for special occasions, with romantic candlelight and creamy walls with black tile borders, decorated with brass plates and artwork. Wide-ranging menu. A specialty is bacciolini d'agnello, sautéed lamb with spinach served with demi-glace garlic-caper sauce. **FYI:** Reservations recommended. Dress code. **Open:** Mon–Sat 5:30–9:30pm. Closed some hols. **Prices:** Main courses $13.95–$19.95. Maj CC. ♥ ⴕ

Carlos Murphy's, 419 W Congress, Tucson (Downtown); tel 602/628-1956. Exit West Congress off I-10. **Mexican.** Spacious restaurant housed in an old train station; a large model airplane hangs from the ceiling. Traditional Mexican fare, plus barbecued ribs, chicken, burgers, and salads. **FYI:** Reservations accepted. Children's menu. **Open:** Sun–Thurs 11am–10pm, Fri–Sat 11am–11pm. Closed some hols. **Prices:** Main courses $6.95–$12.95. Maj CC. 🎭 ♿

Casa Molina, 6225 E Speedway Blvd, Tucson (Midtown); tel 602/886-5468. **Mexican.** A landmark Tucson restaurant, with a large statue of a bull standing guard outside. There are several dining rooms; an unusual one is the Redondo, or round, room, which has all-brick walls with beam spokes extending outward from a brick "hub." Variety of typical Mexican dishes. Also at: 1138 N Belvedere, Tucson (602/325-9957). **FYI:** Reservations recommended. Children's menu. **Open:** Daily 11am–10pm. Closed some hols. **Prices:** Main courses $4.65–$14.75. Maj CC. 🎭♿

Daniel's Restaurant and Trattoria, in St Phillips Plaza, 4340 N Campbell Ave, Suite 107, Tucson; tel 602/742-3200. **Italian.** Dark, plush, and elegant, with gold frond palm trees, etched glass partitions, mirrors, and vases of flowers. Food is prepared light with only "very natural, fresh ingredients." Entrees include grilled fish, seafood, and lamb. **FYI:** Reservations recommended. Dress code. **Open:** Daily 5–10pm. Closed some hols. **Prices:** Main courses $12.50–$26.50. Maj CC. 🆅🅿 ♿

Da Vinci, 3535 E Fort Lowell Rd, Tucson (Ft Lowell); tel 602/881-0947. **Italian.** A little slice of Italy in Tucson. Filled with statues and columns, plants, and murals. The menu includes a variety of Italian specialties and pizzas; desserts are all homemade. **FYI:** Reservations not accepted. Children's menu. **Open:** Mon–Sat 3:30–10pm. Closed some hols. **Prices:** Main courses $9.95–$15.95. Maj CC. ♥ ♿

The Dining Room, in The Lodge on the Desert, 306 N Alvernon Way, Tucson (Midtown); tel 602/325-3366. **American.** Features a Mexican hacienda look, emphasized by the fascinating collection of Mexican ceramic folk art, tin chandeliers, and tiled entryways. The menu includes simple, hearty, traditional fare, like charbroiled steaks and scallops with sharp sauce, plus 3 different nightly dinner specials. **FYI:** Reservations recommended. Dress code. **Open:** Breakfast Mon–Fri 7–9:30am, Sat–Sun 7:30am–9:30pm; lunch daily noon–1:30pm; dinner daily 6–8:30pm; brunch Sun 11am–2pm. **Prices:** Main courses $7–$21. Maj CC. ♥ ♨ ♿

El Adobe, 40 W Broadway, Tucson (Downtown); tel 602/791-7458. **Mexican.** Located in the historic 1850s Charles O Brown house in downtown Tucson. The menu includes a large selection of Mexican dishes, as well as "heart healthy" items. **FYI:** Reservations recommended. Children's menu. **Open:** HS Summer May–Sept Mon–Thurs 11am–9pm, Fri–Sat 11am–10pm. Reduced hours off-season. Closed some hols. **Prices:** Main courses $7.95–$10.95. Maj CC. ♨

El Charro Cafe, 311 N Cart Ave, Tucson; tel 602/622-1922. **Mexican.** A popular cafe located in a historic district. An extensive collection of old Mexican prints graces the walls. The dining patio has a fountain, and the bar is delightfully decorated with colorful folk art. Entrees range from seafood enchiladas to country-style spareribs to traditional Mexican combination plates. Spanish, Mexican, and Brazilian wines are served. **FYI:** Reservations recommended. Children's menu. **Open:** Sun–Thurs 11am–9pm, Fri–Sat 11am–10pm. Closed some hols. **Prices:** Main courses $6–$15. Maj CC. ♨ ♿

The Gold Room, in Westward Look Resort, 245 E Ina Rd, Tucson (North Tucson); tel 602/297-1151 ext 413. **Continental.** A large, spacious restaurant with exposed beams and lots of windows providing splendid views of Tucson. Beef, veal, and seafood are the main offerings. **FYI:** Reservations recommended. Piano. Children's menu. **Open:** Breakfast daily 8–11am; lunch daily 11am–2pm; dinner daily 5:30–10pm; brunch Sun 11am–2pm. **Prices:** Main courses $18–$25. Maj CC. ♥ 🆅🅿 ♿

Janos, 150 N Main St, Tucson (El Presidio District); tel 602/884-9426. **Southwestern.** Considered among Tucson's best restaurants and located in one of the city's oldest homes. There are 4 dining rooms, including a porch at the rear of the house and several smaller rooms with fireplaces. Award-winning chef Janos Wilder makes generous use of cilantro, tomatillo salsa, and chile sauces in his southwestern dishes. The menu includes fish, meats, game, and vegetarian plates. **FYI:** Reservations recommended. **Open:** HS Oct–May Mon–Sat 5:30–9:30pm. Reduced hours off-season. Closed some hols. **Prices:** Main courses $19–$30. Maj CC. ♥ ◗ ♿

Japanese Kitchen, 8424 E Old Spanish Trail, Tucson; tel 602/886-4131. **Japanese.** Japanese prints, paper lanterns, and indoor and outdoor fish ponds set the tone at this Japanese eatery, noted for its teppan cooking (in which meat is sliced and grilled on table-top stoves). Featuring a sushi bar, teriyaki seafood and meat dishes, and combination plates, including steak and sushi and steak and sashimi. **FYI:** Reservations recommended. Children's menu. **Open:** Lunch Mon–Fri 11:30am–2pm; dinner Sun–Thurs 5–9:30pm, Fri–Sat 5–10:30pm. Closed some hols. **Prices:** Main courses $9.95–$18.50. Maj CC. ♥♿

Jerome's, 6958 E Tanque Verde Rd, Tucson; tel 602/721-0311. At Sabino Canyon Rd. **Cajun.** Two dining rooms: one with wood paneling and low light, the other with a fireplace. The menu offers a variety of grilled seafood and meat dishes. **FYI:** Reservations accepted. Children's menu. **Open:** Daily 5–10pm. **Prices:** Main courses $10–$15. Maj CC. ♥ ✉ &

Keaton's, in Foothills Mall, 7401 N La Cholla, Tucson; tel 602/297-1999. Ina Rd exit off I-10. **Seafood.** Shopping mall restaurant with a large lounge and sports bar–like atmosphere. Mesquite-grilled ribs and seafood; lots of soups, salads, sandwiches, and pastas. With some 70 different beers and 35 brands of tequila to choose from. **FYI:** Reservations recommended. Children's menu. **Open:** Daily 11:30am–10pm. Closed some hols. **Prices:** Main courses $9.95–$16.95. Maj CC. ▦ &

La Parrilla Suiza, 5602 E Speedway Blvd, Tucson (Midtown); tel 602/747-4838. **Mexican.** A festive, bustling Mexican restaurant with a low ceiling, brick interior, and attractive tile-inlaid tables. Chile Christmas lights decorate the bar. Dishes feature traditional charro beans and homemade corn tortillas. Many items are charcoal-grilled. Also at: 2720 N Oracle, Tucson (602/624-4311). **FYI:** Reservations recommended. **Open:** Mon–Thurs 11am–10pm, Fri–Sat 11am–11pm, Sun 11am–10pm. Closed some hols. **Prices:** Main courses $4.35–$9.75. Maj CC. &

★ **La Placita Cafe**, in Plaza Palomino Shopping Center, 2950 N Swan Rd, Tucson; tel 602/881-1150. Swan Rd at Ft Lowell. **Mexican.** Located in a small, upscale shopping plaza. Offers patio dining under awnings. The interior dining area is adorned with Mexican folk art and Oaxacan black pottery, as well as a fireplace. The Oaxaca-born chef offers unusual and sometimes exotic Mexican fare. Dinners include escalopas callos de hacha (sautéed deep sea scallops), chiles rellenos de cangrejo (fresh green chiles stuffed with crab), and planta de hueva berenjena (fried eggplant filet). There are also steaks and carne seca (marinated dried beef). **FYI:** Reservations recommended. **Open:** Lunch Mon–Sat 11:30am–2:30pm; dinner daily 5–9pm. Closed Dec 25. **Prices:** Main courses $5.95–$14.95. Maj CC. &

Le Rendez-Vous, 3844 E Ft Lowell Rd, Tucson; tel 602/323-7373. **French.** A popular French bistro with plenty of atmosphere. There is an enclosed patio with a red canvas roof and tile floor throughout. French music plays in the background. The menu is small but select; the house specialty is duck à l'orange. **FYI:** Reservations recommended. **Open:** Lunch Tues–Fri 11:30am–2pm; dinner Tues–Sun 6–10pm. Closed some hols. **Prices:** Main courses $13.95–$23.95. Maj CC. ♥ &

Lotus Garden, 5975 E Speedway Blvd, Tucson (Central Tucson); tel 602/298-3351. **Chinese.** Decorated in subtle tones, this popular Chinese features an array of dishes, ranging from chop suey to house specialties like ying yang, whole shrimp and slices of beef in tomato and hot chile sauce. Chinese and

Japanese wines are available. **FYI:** Reservations recommended. **Open:** Sun–Thurs 11:30am–11pm, Fri–Sat 11:30am–midnight. Closed some hols. **Prices:** Main courses $7.75–$29; PF dinner $8.50–$20. Maj CC. ♥ &

Penelope's, 3071 N Swan Rd, Tucson (Central Tucson); tel 602/325-5080. **French.** Housed in an old adobe building in a residential area, with a stained-glass window/mural, ceiling fans, and original art. Entrees change regularly, but typical choices might be filet mignon with peppercorns, salmon with fruit relish, or rack of lamb. **FYI:** Reservations recommended. Beer and wine only. **Open:** Lunch Tues–Fri 11:30am–2pm; dinner Tues–Sun 5:30pm–close. Closed some hols. **Prices:** PF dinner $25–$28.50. Maj CC. ♥ &

Pinnacle Peak, in Trail Dust Town, 6541 E Tanque Verde Rd, Tucson; tel 602/296-0911. **American/Barbecue/Steak.** This western-style steakhouse is famous for cutting off neckties—wearer beware—and hanging the ends from the ceiling. Besides a large selection of steaks, they offer chicken, trout, and salmon specialties. **FYI:** Reservations accepted. Children's menu. **Open:** Daily 5–10pm. Closed some hols. **Prices:** Main courses $3.95–$12.95. Maj CC. ▮ ▦ &

Presidio Grill, in Rancho Shopping Center, 3352 E Speedway Blvd, Tucson; tel 602/327-4667. **Southwestern.** A popular, modern grill in central Tucson, with a colonnade entrance and soft black leather booths. Pastas, salads, pizzas, meat, fish. **FYI:** Reservations recommended. Children's menu. **Open:** Mon–Thurs 11am–10pm, Fri–Sat 11am–midnight, Sun 8am–10pm. Closed some hols. **Prices:** Main courses $14–$21. Maj CC. ♥ &

Pronto, 2955 E Speedway, Tucson (Midtown); tel 602/326-9707. **Italian/Southwestern.** A bright, happy place with birthday cake and coffee cup designs—and the command "Mangia!" (eat!)—on the walls. There are soups, salads, regular and grilled sandwiches, burgers, pasta, pizzas, and several vegetarian dishes. Everything is made from scratch. The gourmet bakery produces innovative desserts. **FYI:** Reservations not accepted. Children's menu. Beer and wine only. **Open:** Mon–Thurs 7:30am–9pm, Fri–Sat 7:30am–11pm. Closed some hols. **Prices:** Main courses $4–$6. Ltd CC. &

The Rancher's Club of Arizona, in Hotel Park Tucson and Conference Center, 5151 E Grant Rd, Tucson (Midtown); tel 602/321-7621. **Southwestern.** Everything is western here, from the cowhide and leather chairs to the western paintings and photos to the cow horn chandelier and staring animal trophy heads. Steaks are grilled on a variety of aromatic woods. Seafood is also available. **FYI:** Reservations recommended. Harp. Dress code. **Open:** Lunch Mon–Fri 11:30am–2pm; dinner Mon–Sat 5:30–10pm. **Prices:** Main courses $19–$64. Maj CC. ▮ ✉ &

Scordato's, 4405 W Speedway Blvd, Tucson; tel 602/792-3055. 6 mi W of Tucson. **Italian.** A Tucson landmark since 1971, Scordato's represents the epitome of fine dining. Decor is elegant, with a lovely glass wine storage unit in the entryway and soft chandelier lighting. The menu is extensive; veal is a house specialty. **FYI:** Reservations recommended. Children's menu. **Open:** Tues–Sat 5–10pm, Sun 4–10pm. Closed some hols; July 1–15. **Prices:** Main courses $15.95–$22.95. Maj CC. ⚕ �👦

Solarium, 6444 E Tanque Verde Rd, Tucson (Eastside); tel 602/886-8186. **Eclectic.** Designed by a group of artists, the restaurant has a bi-level dining room with lots of windows and plants, stone floors with inlaid tiles, and sculptured metal doors. The menu ranges from meat to fowl to pasta to seafood. Items are rated according to a "good for the heart" scale. **FYI:** Reservations recommended. Guitar. **Open:** Lunch Mon–Fri 11:30am–2:30pm; dinner Sun–Thurs 5–10pm, Fri–Sat 5–11pm. Closed some hols. **Prices:** Main courses $6.95–$16.25. Maj CC. 🔲 �👦

The Tack Room, 2800 N Sabino Rd, Tucson; tel 602/722-2800. **Southwestern.** Set in the main house of an old Spanish-style resort. Original art hangs between picture windows framing mountain views. Southwestern-style dishes; special summer grill menu. **FYI:** Reservations recommended. Children's menu. **Open:** Daily 6pm–close. Closed some hols. **Prices:** Main courses $24.50–$32; PF dinner $45. Maj CC. ⚕ 🔼 VP �👦

⚕ **The Ventana Room**, in Loews Ventana Canyon Resort, 7000 N Resort Dr, Tucson (Ventana Canyon); tel 602/299-2020 ext 5195. From I-10, take Ina Rd or Orange Grove Rd exits, then go east to Skyline Dr to Craycroft Rd. **French/Southwestern.** The ventanas (or windows) in question are filled with wall-to-wall, floor-to-ceiling panoramas of the flickering lights of Tucson below. The split-level room gives most diners a view, but in a short while the professional and courteous service and outstanding cuisine are of more interest than Tucson. Even the coffee service is special. Sample dishes include seared venison carpaccio; fillet of Hawaiian onaga, oven-braised with pappardelle of leeks; pepper-crusted veal chop with madeira truffle sauce; plum sorbet. **FYI:** Reservations recommended. Harp. Jacket required. **Open:** Daily 6–10:30pm. **Prices:** Main courses $18–$26. Maj CC. ⚕ VP �👦

Attractions

MUSEUMS

Arizona State Museum, University of Arizona, University Blvd and Park Ave; tel 602/621-6302. Founded in 1892. Extensive collection of artifacts from prehistoric and contemporary Native American cultures of the Southwest. Featured is a mock-up of a cave with displays of artifacts from ancient cave-dwelling cultures. A large exhibit covers the Hohokam, an ancient farming culture that mysteriously disappeared around 1450. **Open:** Mon–Sat 9am–5pm, Sun 2–5pm. Closed some hols. Free.

University of Arizona Museum of Art, Park Ave and Speedway Blvd; tel 602/621-7567. The museum is home to both an extensive permanent collection, featuring European works from the Renaissance to the 17th century and a large group of 20th-century painting and sculpture, as well as 2 halls with changing exhibits. The star attraction is the *Retable of Ciudad Rodrigo*, which consists of 26 paintings from 15th-century Spain. **Open:** Sept 2–May 14, Mon–Fri 9am–5pm, Sun noon–4pm; May 15–Sept 1, Mon–Fri 10am–3:30pm, Sun noon–4pm. Free.

Tucson Museum of Art and Historic Block, 140 N Main Ave; tel 602/624-2333. The museum boasts a large collection of western and pre-Columbian art, most notably realistic and romantic portrayals of life in the Old West. Free guided tours of the restored homes that make up the historic block are conducted October–May, Wednesday at 11am and Thursday at 2pm. **Open:** Tues–Sat 10am–4pm, Sun noon–4pm. Closed some hols. $

Arizona Historical Society Tucson Museum, 949 E Second St; tel 602/628-5774. As Arizona's oldest historical museum, this repository of all things Arizonan is a treasure trove for the history buff. A full-scale reproduction of an underground mine tunnel is on display that includes an assayer's office, miner's tent, blacksmith shop, and a stamp mill. Transportation through the years is another interesting exhibit, with silver-studded saddles of Spanish ranchers, steam locomotives, and "horseless carriages." **Open:** Mon–Sat 10am–4pm, Sun noon–4pm. Closed some hols. Free.

Frémont House Museum, 151 S Granada Ave; tel 602/622-0956. Built in 1858 as a small adobe house, the structure was enlarged after 1866 and is a classic example of Sonoran Mexican adobe architecture. The house has been fully restored and is decorated with period antiques. **Open:** Wed–Sat 10am–4pm. Closed some hols. Free.

Center for Creative Photography, 1030 N Olive Rd; tel 602/621-7968. Conceived by Ansel Adams, the research facility holds more than 500,000 negatives, 200,000 study prints, and 40,000 master prints by the world's greatest photographers, making it one of the best and largest collections in the world. Photography exhibits are mounted year-round; prints may be examined in a special room. It is suggested that visitors make an appointment and decide in advance whose works they would like to see. **Open:** Mon–Fri 10am–5pm, Sun noon–5pm. Free.

Flandrau Science Center and Planetarium, Cherry and University Aves; tel 602/621-STAR. On the campus of the University of Arizona. Exhibits include a mineral museum and displays on the sun, moon, planets, asteroids, meteorites, and the exploration of space. Evening shows in the planetarium range from astronomy programs by guest lecturers to laser shows set to music. **Open:** Mon–Fri 8am–5pm, Sat–Sun 1–5pm; evening hours, Tues 7–9pm, Wed–Thurs 7–10pm, Fri–Sat 7pm–12:30am. Closed some hols. $$

Pima Air and Space Museum, 6000 E Valencia Rd; tel 602/574-9658. On display are more than 180 aircraft covering the evolution of American aviation. The collection includes replicas of the Wright Brothers' 1903 Wright Flyer and the X-15, the world's fastest aircraft. The museum also operates the Titan Missile Museum in nearby Grass Valley. This is the only intercontinental ballistic missile (ICBM) complex in the world open to the public. **Open:** Daily 9am–5pm. Closed Dec 25. $$

Tucson Children's Museum, 200 S Sixth Ave; tel 602/792-9985. Hands-on children's museum. Touchable displays include a health and wellness exhibit called "Mind Your Own Business," and a firehouse where visitors learn about fire safety. **Open:** Hours vary, call ahead. $

Old Tucson Studios, 201 S Kinney Rd; tel 602/883-6457. A movie set used for more than 50 years to film western movies and television shows such as *Gunfight at the O K Corral* and *Little House on the Prairie*. There are shootout enactments on Main Street, rodeos, stagecoach rides, and an old steam train. **Open:** Daily 9am–8pm. Closed some hols. $$$$

MONUMENTS & LANDMARKS

El Tiradito, S Granada Ave at W Cushing St. Dedicated to a sinner who had been buried on unconsecrated ground at this spot, the now-crumbling shrine has long played an important role in local folklore and the life of Roman Catholic Tucsonans. Listed on the National Register of Historic Places. Free.

Mission San Xavier del Bac, 1950 W San Xavier Rd; tel 602/294-2624. Called the "White Dove of the Desert," the mission is considered to be the finest example of mission architecture in the United States. Masses are held Monday through Saturday at 8:30am and on Sunday at 8am, 9:30am, 11am, and 12:30 pm. **Open:** Daily 8am–5:30pm. Free.

Saguaro National Monument, 3693 S Old Spanish Trail; tel 602/883-6366 (west) or 602/296-8576 (east). The saguaro cactus has been called the monarch of the desert; it is the largest cactus native to the United States and can attain a height of 50 feet and a weight of more than 8 tons. Many species of bird live in holes in the cactus trunk. Coyotes, foxes, squirrels, and javelinas all eat the fruit and seeds. Since 1933 the 2 sections of Saguaro National Monument have protected the saguaro and all the other inhabitants of this section of the Sonoran Desert. Both sections of the park have loop roads, nature trails, hiking trails, and picnic grounds. **Open:** Daily 8am–5pm. $$

Sabino Canyon, 5900 N Sabino Canyon Rd; tel 602/749-8700. Located in the Santa Catalina Mountains of Coronado National Forest, this desert oasis has attracted people and animals for thousands of years. Along the length of the canyon are waterfalls and pools where vistiors can swim. Moonlight horseback rides are held 3 times each month April–December; call for reservations (602/749-2861). Narrated scenic tram ride through lower canyon. **Open:** Daily 24 hours. Free.

Kitt Peak National Observatory, Ariz 86; tel 602/325-9200. Located atop 6,882-foot Kitt Peak in the Quinlan Mountains, 40 miles southwest of Tucson, this is the largest of the astronomical observatories in Arizona. The world's largest solar telescope and 4 other major telescopes are located here. Guided tours are offered daily. People with medical problems are advised that the tour includes a great deal of walking, high altitudes, and steep mountain paths. **Open:** Daily 10am–4pm. Closed some hols. Free.

ZOOS & GARDENS

Arizona-Sonora Desert Museum, 2021 N Kinney Rd; tel 602/883-1380. Actually a zoo, and one of the best in the country. The Sonoran Desert encompasses much of central and southern Arizona as well as parts of northern Mexico. The region contains not only arid lands but also forested mountains, springs, rivers, and streams. The full spectrum of desert life is represented at the zoo, including black bears, mountain lions, beavers, tarantulas, fish, scorpions, prairie dogs, and javelinas. In addition, there is a simulated cave with exhibits on prehistoric desert life and more than 400 species of native plants, including the giant saguaro cactus. **Open:** Mar–Sept, daily 7:30am–6pm; Oct–Feb, daily 8:30am–5pm. $$$

Reid Park Zoo, Country Club Rd and 22nd St; tel 602/791-4022. The zoo is a breeding center for several endangered species. Among the animals in the zoo's programs are giant anteaters, white rhinoceroses, tigers, ruffed lemurs, and zebras. **Open:** Daily 9am–4pm. Closed Dec 25. $

Hi Corbett Field, Randolph Way; tel 602/325-2621. This baseball field is located in the Reid Park complex. The **Colorado Rockies** pitch spring training camp here in March, and the **Tucson Toros**, the Houston Astros AAA team in the Pacific Coast League, play during the summer. **Open:** Feb–Sept $$

Tucson Botanical Gardens, 2150 N Alvernon Way; tel 602/326-9255. A 5-acre oasis of greenery in downtown Tucson dedicated to demonstrating the variety of plants that can be grown in southern Arizona. **Open:** Daily 8:30am–4:30pm. Closed some hols. $

PERFORMING ARTS

Tucson Convention Center Music Hall, bounded by Church Ave, Broadway Blvd, Cushing St, and Granada Ave; tel 602/791-4101 or 791-4266. Large performing arts and convention complex. The Tucson Symphony Orchestra, the oldest continuously performing symphony in the Southwest, performs here October–May; concerts feature classics, pops, and chamber music. Also part of the complex is the the Arizona Opera Company, which stages 4 annual productions. **Open:** Box office, Mon–Sat 10am–6pm. $$$$

Temple of Music and Art, 330 S Scott Ave; tel 602/884-8210 or 622-2823. Completely renovated in 1991, this landmark 1927 theater is the center of Tucsons's arts district. The temple's main venue is the 605-seat Hosclaw Theatre, which serves as a home for the Arizona Theatre Company. ATC presents 6 productions a year, from comedies and dramas to Broadway-style musicals. Other venues at the Temple include the 90-seat Cabaret Theatre and an art gallery. Tours available; restaurant. **Open:** Box office, Mon–Fri 10am–6pm, Sat 10am–5pm, Sun 10am–2pm. $$$$

TUMACACORI

Map page M-2, E3

Attraction 🖼

Tumacacori National Monument, Frontage Rd; tel 602/398-2341. Mission founded by Jesuit missionary and explorer Fr Eusebio Francisco Kino in 1691 to convert the Pima Indians. Much of the old brick-and-stucco mission church still stands, and Spanish architectural influence can easily be seen. On weekends, Native American and Mexican craftspeople give demonstrations of Native arts. The Tumacacori Fiesta is held in early December. Small museum. **Open:** Daily 8am–5pm. Closed some hols. $

WICKENBURG

Map page M-2, C2

Motel 🛏

≣≣ **Best Western Rancho Grande**, 293 E Wickenburg Way, PO Box 1328, Wickenburg, AZ 85358; tel 602/684-5445 or toll free 800/854-7235; fax 602/684-7380. 53 mi NW of Phoenix. A Spanish-style, tile-roofed motel in the center of Wickenburg. **Rooms:** 80 rms and stes. CI noon/CO noon. Nonsmoking rms avail. Rooms are attractively furnished, with an Old West feel. **Amenities:** 🛁 🕭 📺 A/C, cable TV, refrig. Some units w/terraces. **Services:** ✕ 🚗 ▣ 🛎 🐾 Babysitting. **Facilities:** 🛗 🎖 ₺ 1 rst, 1 bar, whirlpool. Two public golf courses are nearby. **Rates:** HS Dec–May $54–$70 S; $56–$79 D; from $65 ste. Extra person $3. Lower rates off-season. Pking: Outdoor, free. Maj CC.

Resorts

≣≣ **Flying E Ranch**, 2801 W Wickenburg Way, PO Box EEE, Wickenburg, AZ 85358; tel 602/684-2173; fax 602/684-5304. 2 mi N of Wickenburg. 20,000 acres. This working ranch has accepted guests since the 1940s. There's plenty of room for horseback riding, but the cattle are not for guest use. **Rooms:** 17 rms, stes, and effic. CI open/CO noon. **Amenities:** A/C, cable TV. No phone. All units w/minibars, some w/terraces, 1 w/Jacuzzi. **Services:** 🛎 **Facilities:** 🛗 🎖 🌊 🎱 1 rst, games rm, lawn games, sauna, whirlpool. Comfortable guest lounge with piano. Also, shuffleboard court and giant outdoor chess game. Livery stable for guests' horses. **Rates (AP):** HS Nov–Apr $110–$140 S; $175–$220 D; from $175 ste; from $175 effic. Min stay. Lower rates off-season. Pking: Outdoor, free. No CC.

≣≣ **Kay El Bar Guest Ranch**, Rincon Rd, PO Box 2480, Wickenburg, AZ 85358; tel 602/684-7593. 60 mi N of Phoenix, exit Rincon Rd off US 89/93. 60 acres. The Kay El Bar has been a guest ranch since 1926, and a cattle ranch from about the turn of the century. It may not be fancy, but it has lots of charm, with buildings listed on the National Register of Historic Places. **Rooms:** 10 rms; 2 ctges/villas. CI 4pm/CO noon. Nonsmoking rms avail. **Amenities:** A/C. No phone or TV. 1 unit w/fireplace. **Services:** 🚗 🛎 **Facilities:** 🛗 🎖 1 rst, 1 bar, lawn games. One horseback ride per day is included in rates. **Rates (AP):** $115–$215 S or D; from $230 ctge/villa. Extra person $70. Children under 2 stay free. Min stay. Pking: Outdoor, free. Ltd CC.

≣≣≣ **Rancho de los Caballeros**, 1551 S Vulture Mine Rd, PO Box 1148, Wickenburg, AZ 85390; tel 602/684-5484; fax 602/684-2267. 3 mi N of Wickenburg. Vulture Mine Rd exit off US 60. 120,000 acres. This large, quiet, desert resort features a comfortable lobby with leather chairs, a billiard table, a piano, and a fireplace. Hummingbird feeders are placed throughout the property. **Rooms:** 73 rms and stes. CI 4pm/CO 1pm. Nonsmoking rms avail. Some rooms have great views of the Bradshaw Mountains. **Amenities:** 🛏 ⚲ A/C, refrig. Some units w/minibars, all w/terraces, some w/fireplaces. **Services:** 🚐 ⛱ ⤴ Twice-daily maid svce, social director, masseur, children's program, babysitting. **Facilities:** 🎣 ▶₁₈ ⛳ ⚑ ⛵₄ 150 ⌨ ♿ 1 rst, 1 bar (w/entertainment), games rm, lawn games, day-care ctr, playground. **Rates (AP):** HS Oct 15–May 15 $145–$185 S; $264–$332 D; from $265 ste. Extra person $65. Lower rates off-season. Spec packages avail. Pking: Outdoor, free. No CC.

≡≡≡ **Wickenburg Inn**, US 89, PO Box P, Wickenburg, AZ 85358; tel 602/684-7811 or toll free 800/942-5362; fax 602/684-2981. 8 mi N of Wickenburg. 4,700 acres. A deluxe riding and tennis resort. **Rooms:** 6 rms and stes; 41 ctges/villas. CI 3pm/CO noon. Range of accommodations, from rooms in the lodge to 3 sizes of casitas, each with its own personality. Some casitas have spiral staircases to the roof. **Amenities:** 🛏 A/C. Some units w/minibars, some w/terraces, some w/fireplaces. **Services:** 🚐 ⤴ Social director, masseur, children's program, babysitting. **Facilities:** 🎣 ⛳ ⛵₁₁ 100 1 rst, 1 bar, lawn games, spa, whirlpool, playground, washer/dryer. There are nature and wildlife studies and an arts and crafts center. There are about 85 horses, with plenty of space to ride. Golf is nearby. **Rates (AP):** HS Jan–May $175–$260 S; $265–$300 D; from $230 ste; from $260 ctge/villa. Extra person $50. Children under 5 stay free. Min stay spec evnts. Lower rates off-season. Higher rates for spec evnts/hols. Pking: Outdoor, free. Maj CC.

Attractions 🧳

Vulture Mine, Vulture Mine Rd; tel 602/377-0803. Wickenburg was founded as a mining town in 1863 when Henry Wickenburg struck gold. Today visitors can see the old mine where he struck his claim as well as the ghost town of Vulture City. Most of the buildings were built in 1884, including the assay office which was constructed with more than $600,000 worth of gold and silver ore. Visitors can also pan for gold. **Open:** Sept–Apr, Thurs–Mon 9am–5pm. $$

Hassayampa River Preserve, US 60; tel 602/684-2772. The riparian (riverside) habitat supports trees and plants that require more water than is usually available in the desert. This lush growth provides food and shelter for hundreds of species of birds, mammals, and reptiles. Nature trails lead along the river beneath cottonwoods and willows and past the spring-fed Palm Lake. Naturalist-guided walks; reservations are required. **Open:** Sept–May, Wed–Sun 8am–5pm; May–Sept, Wed–Sun 6am–noon. $$

Desert Caballeros Western Museum, 21 N Frontier St; tel 602/684-2272. Displays western art depicting life on the range in the days of "cowboys and Indians." Exhibits on the history of central Arizona include a branding and barbed-wire exhibit covering the ranching history of the area, and a re-created street from 1900. **Open:** Mon–Sat 10am–4pm, Sun 1–4pm. Closed some hols. $$

WILLCOX

Map page M-2, D4

Motels 🏨

≡≡≡ **Best Western Plaza Inn**, 1100 W Rex Allen Dr, Willcox, AZ 85643; tel 602/348-3556 or toll free 800/262-2645; fax 602/384-2679. Exit 340 off I-10. A pleasant, better-than-average motel, good for both vacationers and business travelers. **Rooms:** 92 rms and stes. CI open/CO noon. Nonsmoking rms avail. The attractive, comfortable rooms were renovated in 1993. **Amenities:** 🛏 ⚲ ▦ A/C, cable TV w/movies, refrig. Some units w/minibars, some w/Jacuzzis. **Services:** ✕ 🚐 ⤴ ⥁ **Facilities:** 🎣 150 ⌨ ♿ 1 rst, 1 bar (w/entertainment), spa, whirlpool, beauty salon, washer/dryer. **Rates (BB):** $50–$80 S or D. Extra person $5. Children under 12 stay free. Spec packages avail. Pking: Outdoor, free. Maj CC.

≡≡ **Econo Lodge**, 724 N Bisbee Ave, Willcox, AZ 85643; tel 602/384-4222 or toll free 800/424-4777; fax 602/384-3785. Exit 340 off I-10. Basic motel with easy access to area attractions. **Rooms:** 72 rms and stes. CI 11am/CO 11am. Nonsmoking rms avail. **Amenities:** 🛏 A/C, satel TV w/movies, refrig. Video players and movies are available to rent. **Services:** 🚐 ⤴ ⥁ Twice-daily maid svce. **Facilities:** 🎣 15 ⌨ ♿ Washer/dryer. **Rates:** $40–$65 S; $46–$75 D; from $75 ste. Extra person $5. Children under 18 stay free. Higher rates for spec evnts/hols. Spec packages avail. Maj CC.

Attractions 🧳

Chiricahua National Monument, Ariz 186; tel 602/824-3560. These gravity-defying rock formations sculpted by nature—called "the land of the standing-up rocks" by the Apaches and the "wonderland of rocks" by pioneers—are the equal of any of Arizona's many amazing rocky landmarks. Formed about 25 million years ago by a massive volcanic eruption, these rhyolite badlands were once the stronghold of renegade Apaches. Many species of birds, mammals, and plants now live in the mountains, taking advantage of a climate usually found farther to the south in Mexico. Campground, picnic area, visitor center. **Open:** Visitor center, daily 8am–5pm. $$

Fort Bowie National Historic Site, Ariz 186; tel 602/847-2500. Fort Bowie was established in 1862 near the mile-high Apache Pass to protect the slow-moving Butterfield Stage, which carried mail, passengers, and freight, as it traversed this difficult region through the heart of Apache territory. It was from Fort Bowie that federal troops battled Geronimo until the Apache chief finally surrendered in 1886. Today there's little left of the fort but some crumbling adobe walls. It's a 1.5-mile hike to the ruins. **Open:** Ranger station, daily 8am–5pm; grounds, daily sunrise to sunset. Free.

Museum of the Southwest, 1500 N Circle I Rd; tel 602/384-2272. Exhibits on the geology of southeastern Arizona, the Apaches, settlement by pioneers, and cattle ranching. It also includes a cowboy hall of fame and an information center where visitors can find out more about Willcox and the surrounding region. **Open:** Mon–Sat 9am–5pm, Sun 1–5pm. Free.

Rex Allen Museum, Rail Road Ave; tel 602/384-4583. Rex Allen was a singing cowboy, famous for the song "Streets of Laredo" and the television program *Frontier Doctor*. The museum houses memorabilia from the entertainer's career. A life-size bronze statue is in the park across from the museum; Allen's horse, Koko, is buried beneath his statue. **Open:** Daily 10am–4pm. $

WILLIAMS
Map page M-2, B2

Hotel 🛏

Ramada Inn at the Mountain Side, 642 E Bill Williams Ave, Williams, AZ 86046; tel 602/635-4431 or toll free 800/462-9381; fax 602/635-2292. Exit 161 off I-40. A large hotel set amidst 27 acres of pine forest at the eastern edge of Williams. **Rooms:** 96 rms and stes. CI 2pm/CO noon. Nonsmoking rms avail. **Amenities:** A/C, cable TV. **Services:** X Facilities: 2 rsts, 1 bar, whirlpool. Both restaurants have live entertainment. Winter sports close by. **Rates:** HS Apr–Oct $115–$125 S or D; from $125 ste. Extra person $10. Children under 18 stay free. Lower rates off-season. Spec packages avail. Pking: Outdoor, free. Maj CC.

Motels

Canyon Country Inn, 442 W Bill Williams Ave, Williams, AZ 86046; tel 602/635-2349 or toll free 800/643-1020; fax 602/635-9898. A comfortable motel located in an older home. **Rooms:** 13 rms and stes. CI 2pm/CO 11am. Nonsmoking rms avail. **Amenities:** A/C, cable TV. **Services:** **Rates (CP):** HS May–Aug $75–$95 S or D; from $95 ste. Extra person $10. Children under 10 stay free. Lower rates off-season. Spec packages avail. Pking: Outdoor, free. Ltd CC. Packages are available that include the steam train ride from Williams to Grand Canyon National Park.

Comfort Inn, 911 W Bill Williams Ave, Williams, AZ 86046; tel 602/635-4045 or toll free 800/221-2222; fax 602/635-9060. Exit 161 off I-40. An attractive, basic motel located in Williams's historic district, with convenient access to Grand Canyon National Park and other area attractions. **Rooms:** 77 rms and stes. CI noon/CO 11am. Nonsmoking rms avail. Rooms are simply but comfortably furnished. **Amenities:** A/C, cable TV. Some units w/minibars. **Services:** **Facilities:** Games rm, whirlpool, washer/dryer. **Rates (CP):** HS Apr 16–Oct 15 $82 S; $98–$118 D; from $140 ste. Extra person $10. Children under 12 stay free. Lower rates off-season. Spec packages avail. Pking: Outdoor, free. Maj CC.

Holiday Inn Express, 831 W Bill Williams Ave, Williams, AZ 86046; tel 602/635-9000 or toll free 800/HOLIDAY. Exit 161 off I-40. Built in 1992, this attractive hotel is a good addition to the range of accommodations in Williams. It has a large lobby with a fireplace. **Rooms:** 52 rms and stes. CI 2pm/CO 11am. Nonsmoking rms avail. **Amenities:** A/C, cable TV. **Services:** **Facilities:** Whirlpool, washer/dryer. **Rates (CP):** HS Apr–Oct $95 S or D; from $125 ste. Extra person $5. Children under 18 stay free. Lower rates off-season. Pking: Outdoor, free. Maj CC.

Norris Motel, 1001 W Bill Williams Ave, Williams, AZ 86046; tel 602/635-2202 or toll free 800/341-8000; fax 602/635-9202. Exit 161 off I-40. Simple, comfortable motel; a good choice within this price range. Note that the newer wing has larger rooms, indoor corridors, and sprinklers. **Rooms:** 33 rms and stes. CI noon/CO 11am. Nonsmoking rms avail. Rooms are attractively furnished. **Amenities:** A/C, cable TV w/movies, refrig. **Services:** Complimentary bus service is provided to the historic downtown area and the Grand Canyon Railway Depot. **Facilities:** Whirlpool. There's a hot tub in a gazebo. **Rates:** HS May 18–Sept 7 $58 S; $62–$70 D; from $95 ste. Extra person $5. Children under 3 stay free. Lower rates off-season. Pking: Outdoor, free. Maj CC.

≣≣ **Quality Inn Mountain Ranch**, Rte 1, PO Box 35, Williams, AZ 86046; tel 602/635-2693 or toll free 800/221-2222. 5 mi E of Williams, exit 171 off I-40. Set on 26 acres, this pleasant, clean motel offers a variety of outdoor activities for the vacationer. **Rooms:** 73 rms. CI 2pm/CO 11am. Nonsmoking rms avail. **Amenities:** 🛜 📺 A/C, cable TV. **Services:** 🍽 **Facilities:** 🏊 🏋 ⛵ 🎿 🏃 🎣 ♨2 📶 1 rst, games rm, lawn games, whirlpool. **Rates:** HS Apr–Oct $96 S or D. Extra person $6. Children under 6 stay free. Lower rates off-season. Pking: Outdoor, free. Maj CC.

≣≣ **Travelodge**, 430 E Bill Williams Ave, Williams, AZ 86046; tel 602/635-2651 or toll free 800/578-7878; fax 602/635-2651. Exit 163 off I-40. A basic motel with easy access to I-40. **Rooms:** 41 rms and stes. CI 1pm/CO 11am. Nonsmoking rms avail. **Amenities:** 🛜 📺 A/C, cable TV w/movies. **Services:** 🍽 🍷 **Facilities:** 🏊 ♿ Whirlpool. Swimming pool was scheduled for renovation at time of this property's inspection. **Rates:** HS May 15–Sept 15 $74–$89 S; $79–$89 D; from $149 ste. Extra person $6. Children under 17 stay free. Lower rates off-season. Higher rates for spec evnts/hols. Pking: Outdoor, free. Maj CC.

WINDOW ROCK

Map page M-2, B4

Hotel 💼

≣≣ **Navajo Nation Inn**, 48 W Ariz 264, PO Drawer 2340, Window Rock, AZ 86515; tel 602/871-4108 or toll free 800/662-6189; fax 602/871-5466. Intersection of Ariz 264 and Rte 12. An attractive hotel, located in the capitol of the Navajo Nation, the largest reservation in the United States. Close to many historical attractions, including Hubbell Trading Post, a National Historic Site. **Rooms:** 56 rms and stes. CI 2pm/CO 11am. Nonsmoking rms avail. **Amenities:** 🛜 A/C, cable TV w/movies. **Services:** 🍷 **Facilities:** 📶 🖥 ♿ 1 rst. **Rates:** HS May–Sept $55–$60 S or D; from $70 ste. Extra person $5. Children under 12 stay free. Lower rates off-season. Higher rates for spec evnts/hols. Spec packages avail. Pking: Outdoor, free. Maj CC.

Attractions 💼

Window Rock, Ariz 264; tel 602/871-6647. Named for a huge natural opening in a sandstone cliff wall on the Navajo Reservation, this has long been an important site to the Navajo. At one time there was a spring at the base of the rock, and water from it was used by medicine men performing the Tohee Ceremony, a water ceremony intended to bring rain. Another legend says that evil monsters were banished from the world through Window Rock during the time of creation. **Open:** Daily 24 hours. Free.

Navajo Nation Zoological and Botanical Park; tel 602/871-6573. The only Native American–operated zoo in the country. On view are animals and plants that are part of the Navajo culture. Among the animals featured here are those considered to be "guardian animals" such as elk, deer, coyotes, black bears, and golden eagles. All animals on display have either been found injured, abandoned, or have been donated by other zoos. **Open:** Daily 8am–5pm. Closed some hols. Free.

St Michael's Mission Museum, 24 Mission Rd; tel 602/871-4171. Exhibits explore the impact of the Franciscan Friars on the Navajo people, and life in Arizona in the late 1800s. The museum is housed in the original mission built in 1898. Inside are pottery, artifacts, and the first typewriter for the Navajo language. The new church is located nearby and is open year-round. **Open:** June–Sept, daily 9am–5pm. Free.

WINSLOW

Map page M-2, B3

Motel 💼

≣≣ **Best Western Town House Lodge**, 1914 W 3rd St, Winslow, AZ 86047; tel 602/289-4611 or toll free 800/528-1234. Exit 252 off I-40. This is an attractive, older motel, with no surprises. **Rooms:** 68 rms and stes. CI 1pm/CO 11am. Nonsmoking rms avail. Rooms are simple, uncluttered, comfortable, and clean. **Amenities:** 🛜 A/C, cable TV. **Services:** 🍽 🍷 **Facilities:** 🏊 📶 1 rst, 1 bar, playground, washer/dryer. **Rates:** HS May–Sept $44–$48 S; $48–$52 D; from $80 ste. Extra person $6. Children under 12 stay free. Lower rates off-season. Pking: Outdoor, free. Maj CC.

Attraction 💼

Meteor Crater, exit 233 off I-40; tel 602/526-5259. 49,000 years ago a meteor estimated to be 100 feet in diameter slammed into the ground here at 45,000 miles per hour. It formed what is today the best-preserved crater in the world, measuring 570 feet deep and nearly a mile across. The resemblance of the crater landscape to the surface of the moon prompted NASA to use this as a training site for Apollo program astronauts. Part of the small museum at this site has a section dedicated to the exploration of space; the rest is devoted to exhibits on astrogeology, including a meteorite weighing nearly three quarters of a ton. **Open:** Daily 6am–6pm. $$$

YUMA
Map page M-2, D1

Hotels ⌷

▤▤▤ **Best Western Chilton Inn and Conference Center**, 300 E 32nd St, Yuma, AZ 85364; tel 602/344-1050 or toll free 800/528-1234. A centrally located hotel close to Yuma International Airport. **Rooms:** 119 rms. CI 3pm/CO noon. Nonsmoking rms avail. **Amenities:** ☎ ⌕ A/C, cable TV. **Services:** ⚟ 🚐 ⚟ ⚟ Free local phone calls. **Facilities:** 🛱 🖃 300 ⅙ 1 rst, 1 bar, whirlpool, washer/dryer. The restaurant is open 24 hours. **Rates (CP):** HS Sept–Apr $79 S; $84–$89 D. Extra person $5. Children under 18 stay free. Lower rates off-season. Spec packages avail. Pking: Outdoor, free. Maj CC. Weekly rates are available.

▤▤ **Best Western Coronado Motor Hotel**, 233 4th Ave, Yuma, AZ 85364; tel 602/783-4453 or toll free 800/528-1234. 4th Ave exit off I-8. An attractive, better-than-average hotel within walking distance of Yuma's major historic and cultural attractions. **Rooms:** 49 rms and stes. CI 1pm/CO 11am. Nonsmoking rms avail. Large family suites are available. Some rooms have kitchenettes. **Amenities:** ☎ ⌕ ⚟ A/C, cable TV w/movies, refrig, VCR. Some units w/terraces, some w/Jacuzzis. All rooms have microwaves. **Services:** ⚟ ⚟ **Facilities:** 🛱 99 ⅙ 1 rst, 1 bar, whirlpool, washer/dryer. A free video library is available for guest use. **Rates (CP):** HS Jan–Mar $56–$70 S; $61–$80 D; from $55 ste. Extra person $5. Children under 12 stay free. Lower rates off-season. Pking: Outdoor, free. Maj CC.

▤▤▤ **Best Western InnSuites Hotel Yuma**, 1450 S Castle Dome Ave, Yuma, AZ 85365; tel 602/783-8341 or toll free 800/922-2034; fax 602/783-1349. US 95 exit off I-8. Popular with both business travelers and vacationers, this upscale hotel has easy freeway access, and is good for extended stays. **Rooms:** 166 stes. CI 2pm/CO noon. Nonsmoking rms avail. A variety of suite sizes are available, from the smaller Studio to the more luxurious Executive or Presidential Suites. **Amenities:** ☎ ⌕ 🖃 ⚟ A/C, cable TV w/movies, refrig. Some units w/minibars. **Services:** ⚟ ⚟ ⚟ Free local phone calls. Also, complimentary cocktails and morning newspapers are offered. **Facilities:** 🛱 ⚟ 🖃 200 ⅙ 1 rst, spa, whirlpool, playground, washer/dryer. **Rates (CP):** HS Jan 15–Apr 10 from $74 ste. Children under 18 stay free. Lower rates off-season. Spec packages avail. Pking: Outdoor, free. Maj CC.

▤▤ **Park Inn International**, 2600 S Fourth Ave, Yuma, AZ 85365; tel 602/726-4830 or toll free 800/437-PARK. I-8 Business Loop exit off I-8. All-suites hotel popular for multi-night stays. It's conveniently located within 3 miles of downtown and I-8, 2 miles of the airport, and a half-mile from shopping malls. **Rooms:** 164 stes. CI noon/CO 2pm. Nonsmoking rms avail. Every suite is decorated with southwestern art. Many have sofabeds. **Amenities:** ☎ ⌕ 🖃 ⚟ A/C, cable TV w/movies, refrig. Some units w/minibars, some w/Jacuzzis. All suites have a microwave oven and 2 TVs. **Services:** ⚟ ⚟ Complimentary cocktails are served from 5 to 7pm nightly. **Facilities:** 🛱 150 ⅙ Whirlpool, washer/dryer. **Rates (CP):** HS Sept–Apr from $53 ste. Extra person $10. Children under 16 stay free. Lower rates off-season. Spec packages avail. Pking: Outdoor, free. Maj CC.

Motels

▤▤ **Yuma Cabana**, 2151 4th Ave, Yuma, AZ 85364; tel 602/783-8311 or toll free 800/874-0811. I-8 Business Loop exit off I-8. Attractive, renovated motel, centrally located. **Rooms:** 66 rms and stes. CI 3pm/CO noon. Nonsmoking rms avail. Kitchenettes are available. **Amenities:** ☎ 🖃 A/C, satel TV. **Services:** ⚟ **Facilities:** 🛱 ⅙ **Rates:** HS Sept–May $25–$62 S or D; from $38 ste. Extra person $3. Children under 3 stay free. Lower rates off-season. Pking: Outdoor, free. Maj CC. Senior discounts are available.

▤▤ **Yuma 4th Ave Travelodge**, 2050 4th Ave, Yuma, AZ 85364; tel 602/782-3831 or toll free 800/255-3050; fax 602/783-4616. I-8 Business Loop exit off I-8. Comfortable, standard motel on Yuma's "motel row." **Rooms:** 48 rms. CI noon/CO 11am. Nonsmoking rms avail. **Amenities:** ☎ 🖃 A/C, cable TV w/movies, refrig. **Services:** ⚟ There are free local phone calls and complimentary morning newspapers. Fax and photocopying services are available. **Facilities:** 🛱 ⅙ Washer/dryer. **Rates (CP):** HS Jan–Mar $42 S; $62–$72 D. Extra person $4. Children under 17 stay free. Lower rates off-season. Pking: Outdoor, free. Maj CC. There are off-season rate discounts.

Restaurants ⍾

Garden Cafe and Coffee House, 221 Main St, Yuma; tel 602/783-1491. **Health/Spa.** This could be the coolest spot in what is often the hottest location in the United States. All seating is outdoors in the garden (which includes an aviary); a misting water system cools patrons. The menu includes homemade quiche and sweet basil chicken salad, plus sandwiches, soups, and salads. A new coffeehouse section offers espresso, cappuccino, and specialty drinks. **FYI:** Reservations recommended. No liquor license. No smoking. **Open:** Tues–Fri 9am–2:30pm, Sat–Sun 8am–2:30pm. Closed some hols; June–Aug. **Prices:** Lunch main courses $4.50–$7.25. Maj CC. ♥ ⬛

★ **Lutes Casino**, 221 Main St, Yuma; tel 602/782-2192. **American.** Built in 1901 as a general store with a hotel upstairs, Lute's became a pool hall in the 1920s and is now billed as the oldest continually operating pool hall in the state. Old photos, movie star posters, signs, and other memorabilia seem to be everywhere. Noted for its hamburgers and something called a "special," a cross between a hamburger and a hot dog. **FYI:** Reservations not accepted. **Open:** Mon–Thurs 9am–7pm, Fri 9am–8pm, Sat 9am–7pm, Sun 9am–6pm. Closed some hols. **Prices:** Main courses $2.75–$3.50. No CC. 🍖 📷 ⑆

Yuma Landing, 195 4th Ave, Yuma; tel 602/782-7427. **American.** The first plane to land in Arizona touched down near this site in 1911. Seafood, steaks, pasta. **FYI:** Reservations accepted. Children's menu. **Open:** Daily 5am–9pm. **Prices:** Main courses $2.95–$17.95. Maj CC. 📷 ⑆

Attractions 📷

Arizona Historical Society Century House Museum and Gardens, 240 S Madison St; tel 602/782-1841. Once the home of a prosperous Yuma merchant, today the old house is surrounded by palm trees and lush gardens. Inside the museum are historic photographs and artifacts from Arizona's territorial period. **Open:** Tues–Sat 10am–4pm. Closed Dec 25. Free.

Yuma Territorial Prison State Historic Park, Prison Hill Rd; tel 602/783-4771. Yuma is one of the hottest places in the world, so it comes as no surprise that in 1876 the Arizona Territory chose this bleak spot for a prison. The prison museum has some interesting displays, including photos of many of the 3,069 prisoners who were incarcerated at Yuma over the years. **Open:** Daily 8am–5pm. Closed Dec 25. $

Quartermaster Depot State Historic Park, 100 N 4th Ave; tel 602/329-0471. Yuma was a busy river port during the mid-19th century and a depot for military supplies shipped from California. Today, the large wooden buildings that comprised the port hold exhibits that tell the story of the people who lived and worked at Yuma Crossing. Costumed guides answer questions about the depot and its role in Arizona history. **Open:** Daily 10am–5pm. Closed Dec 25. $

NEW MEXICO

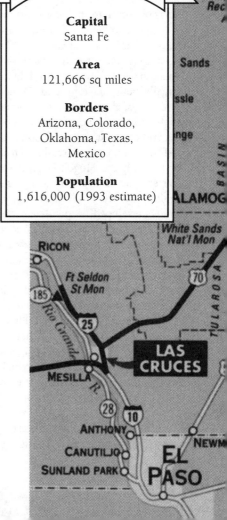

LAND OF ENCHANTMENT

Prickly pear cactus and tall evergreens, sun-baked desert and deep powder snow. New Mexico is a land of contrasts and contradictions. Its 3 dominant cultures—Native American, Hispanic, and Anglo—are unique but intertwined, each retaining its individual identity while influencing the other in a sometimes uneasy alliance. In many ways, a trip to New Mexico is an excursion to a foreign country, a exotic land of enchantment and excitement, yet no passport is needed.

When many people think of New Mexico they see American Indians, wrapped in blankets in their centuries-old adobe pueblos. And certainly many visitors come to experience the state's thriving Native American culture. But others are also curious to follow the trail of legendary gunslinger Billy the Kid or explore crumbling ghost towns where sagebrush and cactus have taken over once-busy streets. Railroad romantics can tour the depots from turn-of-the-century mining days that dot the state and climb aboard a historic steam train for a memorable trip into the past.

Besides being a treasure trove of Old West history, New Mexico is also a vibrant art center. There are hundreds of galleries, studios, and museums to explore. From ancient Indian petroglyphs to the most modern mediums, art lovers cannot only see and buy, but can join classes, tour studios, and watch many of today's artists at work.

Museums explore the cultural and historic, including beautiful Indian pottery and blankets, artifacts from the state's Spanish colonial days, Civil War and Old West memorabilia, and feats of science and engineering like the first atom bomb and the space shuttle.

A land of spectacular scenic beauty, New Mexico encompasses the towering Rocky Mountains, pristine desert sands, and vast underground caverns. Hunting, fishing, and camping are extremely popular, and hikers revel in the state's unspoiled wilderness. Winter snows turn New Mexico into a skiers' paradise, with deep powder and plenty of sunshine. In addition to world-class downhill ski resorts, there are plenty of opportunities for cross-country skiing and snowmobiling.

In short, there are many reasons to visit New Mexico and a great variety of activities that are bound to satisfy almost every taste. Take time to explore the state's hidden treasures as well as its major attractions. See its mountains and deserts. Taste its foods. Meet its people. A New Mexico vacation really is like a trip to a distant land—without having to leave the country.

STATE STATS

Capital
Santa Fe

Area
121,666 sq miles

Borders
Arizona, Colorado, Oklahoma, Texas, Mexico

Population
1,616,000 (1993 estimate)

A Brief History

PREHISTORIC PEOPLES Somewhere between 20,000 and 25,000 years ago, Paleo-Indians roamed into the area we now know as New Mexico, following the mastodon, bison, and early forms of the camel and horse that provided the necessities of their nomadic life. The earliest evidence of their passage—a projectile point found in the Clovis area of southeast New Mexico—is about 12,000 years old.

As the glaciers receded and the climate became drier, man became more dependent on plants, and sometime in the first few centuries AD corn was introduced from Mexico. The people in the western two-thirds of New Mexico settled in villages, often located along river drainages, while those in the eastern third remained primarily nomadic. Those who settled in the northwestern corner of New Mexico are known as Anasazi; those in the southwestern part as Mogollon.

The Mogollon lived in pit houses, dug partially into the ground, and carried on a lively trade with the peoples to the south, in present-day Mexico. The Anasazi were more urbanized, living in complex houses usually built above ground. Discovering the increased strength of cluster-type construction, the Anasazi eventually created elaborate stone buildings of several stories and often hundreds of rooms, as well as ceremonial below-ground structures known as kivas. During this time, both the Mogollon and Anasazi began making pottery and baskets. The size of settlements increased, regional styles in architecture, ceramics, and other crafts developed, dependence on agriculture intensified, and trade networks expanded.

The Anasazi territory included nearly 40,000 square miles of the Four Corners area—northwestern New Mexico and adjacent corners of Colorado, Utah, and Arizona. In this area, archaeologists have located ruins of over 10,000 structures created between AD 400 and 1300, some half of them built between AD 950 and 1100. One of the largest is Chaco Canyon, an extremely complex and highly developed settlement in northwestern New Mexico, from which a great network of roads radiated to outlying settlements, the only known prehistoric planned transportation system north of Mexico.

Around AD 1200, the Anasazi left the Four Corners area, inexplicably abandoning their villages. Modern scientists hypothesize that although specific reasons may vary from area to area, the move probably was triggered by subtle changes in climate. The Mogollon also began moving northwards at this time, settling in smaller villages along rivers and often building with adobe.

CONQUISTADORS & COLONIZERS When Spanish conquistadors arrived in the 1500s, they called the people they found "Pueblo" Indians, because their buildings resembled Spanish villages, or pueblos. What they had hoped to find, however, was an area as rich in gold and silver as Aztec Mexico. Francisco Vásquez de Coronado, who set out from Mexico in 1540, and the leaders of later expeditions were among those who were sorely disappointed. Then in 1598, Don Juan de

---

✎ *Fun Facts* ✎

• *The design of the state flag combines the ancient sun symbol of the Zuni Indians native to the state with the colors of the flag of Spain, which ruled the region for more than 250 years.*

• *In 1950, the town of Hot Springs, NM, became Truth or Consequences when it won a contest run by the legendary radio program of the same name. It was seeking an American town that was willing to change its name in honor of the show's 10-year anniversary.*

• *Taos is home to more artists per capita than Paris.*

• *The Acoma Pueblo is the oldest continually inhabited city in the United States: It can trace its occupation back to AD 1150. It's also famed as the "Sky City," because of its location 7,000 feet above sea level.*

• *It was in the town of Lincoln that Billy the Kid was to be hanged for cattle rustling and other crimes in 1878. The shackled and manacled Kid, however, managed to escape the hangman's noose at the final moment of truth. After a 3-year manhunt, Sheriff Pat Garrett gunned down the outlaw at Fort Sumner in eastern New Mexico.*

Oñate was appointed the Spanish governor of New Mexico and directed to colonize it.

With some 200 settlers, including soldiers, families, and priests, and 7,000 head of livestock in tow, Oñate established the first Spanish colony on the east bank of the Rio Grande near its confluence with the Rio Chama, close to Española, at present-day San Juan Pueblo.

He was succeeded by Pedro de Peralta, who, in 1610, when the King of Spain made New Mexico a royal colony, became the first royal governor of the province. Peralta promptly made Santa Fe the provincial capital. Thus, Santa Fe is not only the oldest capital in the nation, it also predates the English settlement at Plymouth, Massachusetts by a decade.

European settlements appeared all along the Rio Grande and its tributaries, from Taos to Socorro. Life was not altogether peaceful, however, with both civil and religious conflicts between settlers and Indians. In 1680, in an unprecedented demonstration of unity, the Pueblos revolted against Spanish oppression and forced conversion to Christianity and drove the hated Spanish conquerors south to El Paso. But only 13 years later, Captain General Diego de Vargas peacefully recaptured the province for Spain. To encourage increased settlement, he and his successors issued land grants for agriculture and grazing to Spanish colonists, and the communities that sprang up served as outposts against Indian attacks. Even so, life in New Mexico was defined by almost continuous warfare with marauding Indians, and an increasingly defensive posture.

THE FRONTIER PERIOD BEGINS In 1821, Spain's influence came to an end with the Mexican revolution, and under Mexican control New Mexico was encouraged to trade with its American neighbors. That same year, the Santa Fe Trail opened, linking Santa Fe with St Louis, an event that changed forever the course of New Mexican history. So many traders and settlers came over the Trail that the ruts from their wagon wheels are still visible in the northeastern part of the state. Santa Fe soon became a bustling hub of trade, through which caravans made their way onward to northern Mexico along the *Camino Real* (Royal Highway) and to California via the Old Spanish Trail.

Soon, not only traders were marching west. In 1841 the new Republic of Texas invaded New Mexico in an effort to control the trade route through the state. The Texans were defeated, but Mexico's inability to protect the province from attack led inevitably to its absorption by the United States.

In 1846, Brigadier General Stephen Watts Kearny led the US Army of the West from Fort Leavenworth, Kansas in a peaceful takeover of New Mexico. They walked into Santa Fe unopposed, just as Vargas had done 150 years earlier, and although they suffered a setback 4 months later when a group of New Mexicans rebelled, fearing their land rights would be invalidated by a new government, the revolt was quickly suppressed, and New Mexico was effectively claimed for the United States. The Treaty of Guadalupe Hidalgo officially ended the Mexican War in 1848 and made almost all of New Mexico, Arizona, and California part of the United States. The remainder came in 1853, when the Gadsden Purchase set the present-day Mexican-American boundary.

By this time gold had been discovered in the dusty mountains above San Francisco, and hundreds of thousands of people left their homes in the East and headed for the gold fields. Many of those who were unable to complete the journey settled in New Mexico, however, and in a mere 10 years between the 1850 and 1860 censuses, New Mexico's population increased over 30 percent.

With the advent of the Civil War, the South looked to the West for Colorado and California gold, and for military supplies from centers such as Fort Union, near Las Vegas, New Mexico. In July 1861, a Confederate army from Texas invaded New Mexico, and by early 1862 had captured both Albuquerque and Santa Fe. For 2 weeks, the Confederate flag flew over the territory's capitol. But in March 1862, hundreds of Union and Confederate troops fought the Battle of Glorieta, just east of Santa Fe. Afterwards, it was apparent that the Confederates had won, except that the Union troops had destroyed their supplies, forcing them to retreat to Texas and ending any further threat.

In the last decades of the 19th century, the Indians were confined to reservations around the territory, and there were dramatic changes in the way title to land was held. Theoretically protected by the Treaty of Guadalupe Hidalgo, Hispanic landowners found their land grants going to newcomers through crafty legal maneuvers. The Atchison, Topeka and Santa Fe Railroad arrived in 1880, and within 10 years, railroads had reached into every corner of the territory, bringing new residents and new ideas. The Santa Fe Trail closed, new towns sprang up along the rails, and the territory contributed to the folklore of the Wild West with William (Billy the Kid) Bonney, Clay Allison, and other notorious outlaws among its more infamous residents.

A CLOUD IN THE DESERT SKY   On January 6, 1912, New Mexico became the 47th state in the Union. Farming and ranching flourished alongside a rapidly expanding mining industry in the early part of the century, and after Taos and Santa Fe gained national recognition as art colonies in the 1920s, tourism also became an important industry. The artists were drawn by such qualities as the purity of the New Mexico light and the serenity of the desert, and it is ironic that at least the latter characteristic also led to the selection of Los Alamos, a small town in the mountains northwest of Santa Fe, as the secret location of the top secret Manhattan Project, which developed the atom bomb. After 2 years of work, a team of scientists drove to the Trinity Test Site, and in the early hours of July 16, 1945, exploded their handiwork, ushering in the atomic age. New Mexico remains in the forefront of scientific research and development. White Sands Missile Range is an important site for the study of astrophysics; Albuquerque derives much economic support from aerospace research and defense contracts; the Air Force Special Weapons Center is located at Kirtland Air Force Base; and Los Alamos National Laboratory continues to work in nuclear research.

But even as the state moves toward the next century, shifting from a reliance on oil, gas, and minerals to high technology and manufacturing, it remains rooted in its past. The computer whiz may be telecommuting to some big city corporation, but Chimayo weavers still work at the looms their ancestors built a hundred years ago, and Pueblo potters quietly release the beauty hidden in a lump of clay.

A CLOSER LOOK

Geography

As America's 5th-largest state and the meeting ground for the Great Plains, the southern Rockies, and the Colorado Plateau, New Mexico offers a wide variety of terrain. Elevations range from 2,800 to over 13,000 feet and include 6 of the 7 life zones found in the

DRIVING DISTANCES:

Albuquerque
59 miles SW of Santa Fe
129 miles SW of Taos
138 miles E of Gallup
173 miles W of Tucumcari
182 miles SE of Farmington
223 miles N of Las Cruces
224 miles SW of Raton
275 miles NW of Tucson, AZ
449 miles SW of Denver, CO

Las Cruces
47 miles NW of El Paso, TX
208 miles W of Carlsbad
223 miles S of Albuquerque
275 miles E of Tucson, AZ
282 miles SW of Santa Fe
352 miles SW of Taos
405 miles SE of Farmington
413 miles SW of Raton

Santa Fe
59 miles NE of Albuquerque
70 miles SW of Taos
165 miles SW of Raton
199 miles SE of Farmington
268 miles NW of Carlsbad
282 miles NE of Las Cruces

Taos
70 miles NE of Santa Fe
95 miles SW of Raton
129 miles NE of Albuquerque
214 miles E of Farmington
338 miles NW of Carlsbad
352 miles NE of Las Cruces

United States: Arctic-Alpine, Hudsonian, Canadian, Transition, Upper Sonoran, and Lower Sonoran. (The one you won't find is Tropical.)

Northeastern New Mexico encompasses the 6 counties of the Great Plains. There's ranching in this sparsely populated, wide-open country, with the railroad running north to south through the center and along the southern boundary. It's a fairly dry region, averaging about 14 to 18 inches of rain per year; the wettest season is summer.

North Central New Mexico includes the Sangre de Cristo Mountains of the southern Rockies and the northern valley of the Rio Grande and Rio Chama. Elevations are the highest in the state, and winters tend to be long, with much of the annual precipitation in the form of snow. Tourism supports the region, which contains some of New Mexico's most picturesque Indian pueblos, most of the state's ski areas, and the 2 major art centers of **Taos** and **Santa Fe.**

The mesas of **Northwestern New Mexico** were home to the great Anasazi civilization of the first few centuries AD and are now part of the reservation of America's largest Native American tribe, the Navajo. The San Juan River flows through the northern part; much of the remainder is arid and stark. **Farmington,** the largest city in the area, has a mild climate that encouraged farming and ranching for many years, before the discovery of oil, coal, and gas.

Albuquerque dominates **Central New Mexico.** The Sandia Mountains border the eastern edge of the state's largest city (an estimated 398,492 people in 1992), and the Rio Grande wends its way south through the western part. Summer daytime temperatures can exceed 100°F, and winters are mild and sunny. The University of New Mexico is located here, and technology, including aerospace and defense research, is a major economic factor, along with light manufacturing and tourism.

Southwestern New Mexico has the San Mateo and Mogollon Mountains and the Black Range soaring above the desert, where temperatures also soar, often to over 100° during June, July, and August. Rainfall is low. The state's second largest city, **Las Cruces,** with 66,466 people (1992 estimate), is located here. The railroad was a major contributor to the growth of the area in the early part of the century. Mining remains important, since copper and gold are still coming out of the hills near Silver City. Ranching and farming are also key industries.

The landscape of **Southeastern New Mexico** is dominated by oil rigs and cattle ranches. **Roswell** is the area's largest city. Tourism is an important part of the economy; **Carlsbad Caverns National Park** receives almost 700,000 visitors per year. The climate is warm and dry, with little snow except in the Sacramento and Guadalupe Mountains in the west. Precipitation averages 8 to 14 inches yearly.

Climate

Elevation and terrain have a tremendous influence on weather, and New Mexico, with mountains, deserts, canyons, and plains, experiences weather that is dramatic, exciting, and capricious. You may not like what it's doing, but it will never bore you. Be prepared for extreme changes in temperature at any time of year, and watch for summer afternoon thunderstorms that can leave you drenched and shivering in minutes. In

AVERAGE MONTHLY HIGH/LOW TEMPERATURES (°F)			
	Albuquerque	**Las Cruces**	**Santa Fe**
Jan	47/22	57/26	40/19
Feb	53/26	63/29	44/22
Mar	61/32	69/35	51/28
Apr	71/40	77/42	60/35
May	80/49	85/49	69/43
June	91/58	94/59	79/52
July	93/65	94/65	82/57
Aug	89/63	92/63	80/56
Sept	83/55	87/56	74/49
Oct	72/43	78/44	63/38
Nov	57/31	66/32	50/27
Dec	48/23	57/26	41/20

winter, mountain temperatures can drop well below zero.

Health & Safety

Cities range in altitude from 3,030 feet at Jal in the southeast corner to 8,750 feet at Red River in the northern mountains. Santa Fe, Cloudcroft, and several other popular destinations are at 7,000 feet and above. These elevations can be taxing to lowlanders, so take things slow, especially at first, and drink plenty of water. Those with heart or respiratory problems should consult their doctors before planning a trip to the state's higher reaches. Because the sun's rays are more direct in New Mexico's thinner, clearer air, sunburn can be a real problem. Be sure to bring good-quality sun block, a hat, and sunglasses that protect against ultraviolet rays.

Always carry plenty of extra water in the desert, and be on the lookout for rattlesnakes and other poisonous creatures. If you're heading into the wilderness, let someone know where you're going and when you expect to return, and then stick to your schedule.

What to Pack

The bywords are comfortable and casual. Even the state's most elegant restaurants are more informal than those in New York or Chicago, and you'll be welcome almost everywhere wearing casual clothes.

You'll want comfortable walking shoes, a light jacket, preferably water resistant, and a sweater. Warm clothing is needed in mountain areas even in summer, as evenings cool down very quickly once the sun dips below the horizon. Layers are the best way to dress, since it tends to be cool at both ends of the day and temperatures can be delightfully warm when the sun is out, even in the middle of winter. Sunglasses, hats, and sunscreen are essential at any time of year.

Tourist Information

For a copy of the *New Mexico Vacation Guide* and information on attractions statewide, contact the New Mexico Department of Tourism, PO Box 2003, Santa Fe, NM 87503-2003 (tel 505/827-7400 or toll free 800/545-2040). When in Santa Fe, visit the Welcome Center in the historic Lamy Building at 491 Old Santa Fe Trail. There are also welcome centers distributing brochures and maps at both the Texas and Arizona ends of I-40 and I-10. Topographical maps are available from the US Geological Survey Distribution Section, Federal Center, Building 41, Denver, CO 80225 (tel 303/234-3832), and state and county maps are available from the New Mexico State Highway and Transportation Department, 1120 Cerrillos Rd, Santa Fe, NM 87501 (tel 505/827-5250).

For road conditions and closure information, call the state's Highway Hotline (tel toll free 800/432-4269).

Driving Rules & Regulations

The speed limit on interstate highways is 65 mph outside city limits, 55 mph within city limits. The statewide speed limit elsewhere is 55 mph outside city limits, unless otherwise posted. Seat belts are mandatory for all front-seat occupants in passenger cars and pickup trucks with a gross weight of 10,000 pounds or less, and approved child restraints or safety belts are required for all children under the age of 11. Motorcyclists under 18 must wear helmets. Charges of driving while intoxicated (DWI) are determined by minimum blood alcohol levels of 0.02% for those under age 21, and 0.08% for those 21 and over. Drivers convicted of a first offense can face up to 90 days in jail and a $500 fine, plus 90 days to 1-year license revocation.

Indian reservations are considered sovereign nations, and each enforces its own laws. For instance, many prohibit the transportation of alcoholic beverages and may require motorcyclists to wear helmets.

Renting a Car

Most major car rental agencies have outlets in Albuquerque, and some are also represented in Santa Fe, Las Cruces, and other cities. Among companies serving Albuquerque and Albuquerque International Airport are:

- **Advantage** (tel toll free 800/777-5500)
- **Agency** (tel 800/321-1972)
- **Alamo** (tel 800/327-9633)
- **Avis** (tel 800/331-1212)
- **Budget** (tel 800/527-0700)
- **Dollar** (tel 800/800-4000)
- **Enterprise** (tel 800/325-8007)

- **Hertz** (tel 800/654-3131)
- **National** (tel 800/227-7368)
- **Payless** (tel 800/729-5377)
- **Rent-A-Wreck** (tel 800/247-9556)
- **Thrifty** (tel 800/367-2277)
- **Wheelchair Getaways of New Mexico** (wheelchair-accessible vans) (tel 800/367-2277)

Essentials

Area Code: The area code for all of New Mexico is 505.

Emergencies: Call 911.

Liquor Laws: The minimum legal age to drink any alcoholic beverage in New Mexico is 21. Liquor can be sold by the glass Monday through Saturday from 7am to 2am, and Sunday noon to midnight. Package liquor can be sold Monday through Saturday from 7am to midnight, and not at all on Sunday. Some counties are entirely dry on Sunday, and most Indian reservations are not only dry but forbid possession of alcoholic beverages.

Smoking: The New Mexico Clean Indoor Air Act requires designated smoking and nonsmoking areas in all public (government-owned) buildings. At press time there was no statewide smoking policy for restaurants, but many counties and cities had passed their own ordinances. For instance, in Albuquerque, most restaurants are required to have nonsmoking areas.

Taxes: New Mexico has a gross receipts tax, administered as a sales tax, of 5% on goods and services. Additional county and city taxes bring the combined tax to about 6% in most communities. Most cities and counties also add a tax of 2 to 5% to lodging bills. For instance, the combined sales and lodgers tax in Albuquerque was about 10.8% in 1994. State and local taxes do not apply on Indian reservations.

Time Zone: New Mexico is in the Mountain time zone and observes daylight saving time from April through October.

BEST OF THE STATE
What to See & Do

Luring visitors for hundreds and perhaps thousands of years, New Mexico has scenic beauty and historical attractions, as well as a cultural mix—American Indian, Hispanic, and Anglo—that flavors not only the cuisine, but also the activities, art and architecture, language, and customs. The best plan of attack may be to pick and choose, like at one of those all-you-can-eat buffets. Here's the menu.

ART Attracted by clear mountain light and picturesque Indian and Hispanic villages, Anglo artists from the eastern United States "discovered" New Mexico about the beginning of the 20th century. Their work can be seen in the museums and galleries of **Taos, Santa Fe,** and **Albuquerque.** Check local newspapers for gallery openings, where you can talk with artists one-on-one about their work, often while sipping a glass of wine and nibbling cheese and crackers. Many communities also have annual or semi-annual arts festivals, such as the **Taos Arts Festival** each fall, with exhibits, tours of artists' studios, and arts-and-crafts markets. While there has been a long-time appreciation of Native American and Hispanic crafts, such as world-famous pottery made at **San Ildefonso Pueblo** and carved wooden *santos* (saints) by Hispanic artists, there is a growing awareness that there are also a number of Native American and Hispanic painters and sculptors. Check out the galleries in Albuquerque's **Old Town.**

HISTORIC SITES & BUILDINGS From prehistoric Indian pit houses to the **Kit Carson Home and Museum** in Taos to the spot where the world's first atomic bomb was assembled, New Mexico is covered with wonderful historic sites and buildings. Among them, you'll find the huge home of the ancient Anasazi Indians at **Chaco Culture National Historic Park,** ruins of an important military post at **Fort Union National Monument,** and the **Mission of San Miguel** in Santa Fe, one of the oldest surviving churches in the United States.

Guided tours of the ghost towns of **Shakespeare** and **Steins,** near Lordsburg, let you see the real thing, and in Chama the **Cumbres and Toltec Scenic Railroad** offers rides on a historic narrow-gauge steam train.

MUSEUMS From the most elaborate temperature and humidity-controlled buildings housing priceless works of art to funky small-town collections from grandma's attic, you'll find plenty to look at in New Mexico. Albuquerque, Santa Fe, and Taos have sophisticated museums housing extensive collections of American Indian and Spanish Colonial art and artifacts, like Taos's **Millicent Rogers Museum,** the **Albuquerque Museum,** and the **Museum of Indian Arts and Culture** in Santa Fe. But almost every small town has some sort of museum, and they're often fascinating, like the **Santa Fe Trail Museum** in Springer, with the only electric chair ever used in New Mexico.

NATURAL WONDERS Simply put, New Mexico is a beautiful state. You'll find pristine lakes among tall pines near **Red River,** waves of gleaming gypsum at **White Sands National Monument,** and a spectacular fairyland of sculpture at the state's most popular national park, **Carlsbad Caverns.** The **Wild Rivers National Recreation Area,** near the state's northern border, offers spectacular views of the Rio Grande, and you'll find 400-foot tall rock formations at **Cimarron Canyon State Park.**

While most of us find it easy to appreciate the green, lush beauty of the mountains or an intricately carved rock formation, sometimes it's harder to appreciate the splendor of the desert. Take time to gaze across the vast expanses of seemingly nothing to distant peaks, and look for the red, purple, and yellow blooms of cactus, and the gnarled, weathered trunks of the sturdy piñon pine. Just watch where you step—there may be a rattler out there.

WILDLIFE The state's abundant wildlife ranges from elk, antelope, and deer that watch you drive by along US 64 near **Cimarron,** to the rare whooping crane at **Bosque del Apache National Wildlife Refuge.** You can see exotic and endangered fish at the **National Fish Hatchery** in Dexter and get up close to numerous desert dwellers at **Living Desert State Park** in Carlsbad.

FAMILY FAVORITES New Mexico doesn't offer much in the way of pre-fab family fun—there are no major theme parks. But most children are fascinated by the vestiges of the real Old West in New Mexico, where you can count the bullet holes in the ceiling of the **St James Hotel** in Cimarron, or walk the same streets as outlaw Billy the Kid at **Lincoln State Monument.** And don't forget outer space, the new frontier, at Alamogordo's **Space Center** or the **UFO museums** in Roswell; and those state-of-the-art computers and science exhibits at Los Alamos's **Bradbury Science Museum.** Albuquerque has several attractions geared for families, including **Albuquerque Children's Museum,** with hands-on activities. Finally, head for a campsite along a pure mountain stream in one of the state's national forests.

CUISINE It isn't really Mexican, it isn't Tex-Mex, and it certainly isn't traditional American. New Mexicans have developed their own style of cooking. Travel the state from end-to-end and you'll find some subtle differences, but in general, New Mexicans like lots of green or red chile peppers, onion, garlic, cumin, and both Monterey jack and cheddar cheeses. The beans of choice are pinto, but don't expect any if you order a bowl of chile. In a true New Mexico restaurant a bowl of chile means chile stew—made from whole chile peppers, possibly with a bit of meat—and it's guaranteed to open your sinuses.

Events/Festivals

Santa Fe, Taos & Northern New Mexico

- **New Year's Celebration,** Taos, Santo Domingo, San Felipe, Cochiti, Santa Ana, and Picuris pueblos. Turtle, matachines, and other traditional dances. January 1. Call 505/843-7270 for information.
- **Red River Winterfest,** Red River. Ski, sled dog, and snowmobile races, ice sculpture, country music, and dancing. Last weekend in January. Call toll free 800/348-6444.
- **Taos Spring Arts Celebration,** Taos. Studio tours, gallery exhibits, poetry readings, and music. 2nd and 3rd weeks in May. Call toll free 800/732-8267.
- **Rails 'n' Trails Days,** Las Vegas. Old-time Atchison, Topeka, and Santa Fe Railroad exhibits, working-ranch tours, and a western dance. Late May. Call 505/425-8631 or toll free 800/832-5947.
- **Spring Festival,** El Rancho de las Golondrinas, south of Santa Fe. Costumed villagers, Spanish colonial crafts, and festive Spanish music. Early June. Call 505/471-2261 or toll free 800/777-CITY.

- **Summer Chamber Music Festival,** Taos. Concerts and seminars. Mid-June through early July. Call 505/776-2388.
- **Santa Fe Opera,** Santa Fe. Internationally acclaimed operatic productions with distinguished guest artists. Early July to late August. Call toll free 800/982-3851 for schedule and information.
- **Nambe Waterfall Ceremonial,** Nambe Pueblo. Dance teams present all-afternoon buffalo, Comanche, corn, deer, and eagle dances. July 4. Call 505/455-2036.
- **Fiesta de Santiago y Santa Ana,** Taos. Live music, parades, a fiesta queen, food, and dancing. Late July. Call 505/758-4568.
- **Spanish Market,** Santa Fe. Top Hispanic artisans display and sell traditional Spanish colonial arts and crafts. Last weekend in July. Call 505/983-4038 or toll free 800/777-CITY.
- **Fort Union Founder's Day,** Las Vegas. Living history groups recall military and pioneer life of the 1850s to 1870s. Last weekend in July. Call 505/425-8025 or toll free 800/832-5947.
- **Inter-Tribal Indian Ceremonial,** Gallup. A nationwide gathering of tribes at Red Rock State Park for 4 days of parades, dances, arts-and-crafts demonstrations, fairs, and rodeo competition. Mid-August. Call toll free 800/242-4282.
- **Indian Market,** Santa Fe. High-quality arts-and-crafts show, with competition for best Native American artisans. 2nd weekend before Labor Day. Call 505/983-5220 or toll free 800/777-CITY.
- **La Fiesta de Santa Fe,** Santa Fe. Colorful celebration commemorating the reconquest of New Mexico by Don Diego de Vargas in 1692; Spanish music, dancing, and food vendors. 1st or 2nd week after Labor Day. Call 505/984-6760 or toll free 800/777-CITY.
- **Fall Arts Festival,** Taos. Tours of artists' homes and special exhibits of Taos art. Last 2 weeks of September and 1st week of October. Call 505/758-3873 or toll free 800/732-8267.
- **San Geronimo Feast Day,** Taos Pueblo. Afternoon buffalo, Comanche, and corn dances; ceremonial foot races; and an arts-and-crafts fair. September 30. Call 505/758-9593 or toll free 800/732-8267.

- **Harvest Festival,** El Rancho de las Golondrinas, south of Santa Fe. A traditional Spanish colonial fiesta. 1st weekend in October. Call 505/471-2261 or toll free 800/777-CITY.
- **Annual Shiprock/Navajo Nation Fair,** Shiprock. A rodeo, carnival, mud bog, 10-kilometer run, country-western dancing, various Indian dances, a powwow, agricultural and arts-and-crafts exhibits, and the traditional 9-day chant called the Night Way or "Yeibichai." October. Call 602/871-6436.
- **Taos Mountain Balloon Rally,** Taos. Hot-air balloon rides, mass ascensions at dawn, an arts-and-crafts fair. Last weekend in October. Call toll free 800/732-8267.

Albuquerque

- **Albuquerque Gem and Mineral Show,** Albuquerque. Geologists, mineralogists, and amateur rock hounds build competitive displays, demonstrate gold panning and mining techniques, and identify ore samples. Mid-March. Call 505/334-6174 for information.
- **San Felipe Fiesta,** Albuquerque. Three days of food and entertainment in Old Town in honor of Albuquerque's patron saint. Early June. Call 505/243-4628.
- **Aztec Dances,** Albuquerque. Dancers soar from the top of an 80-foot pole to the ground in a traditional Aztec ceremony. July. Call 505/843-7270.
- **New Mexico State Fair,** Albuquerque. A 17-day extravaganza with horse racing, a top rodeo event, living Indian and Spanish villages, nightly country-western concerts, livestock show, games, and rides. September. Call 505/265-1791 or toll free 800/284-2282.
- **Kodak Albuquerque International Balloon Fiesta,** Albuquerque. More than 650 hot-air balloons in mass ascensions at daybreak; evening balloon "glows." Early October. Call 505/821-1000 or toll free 800/284-2282.
- **Old Town Luminaria Tours,** Albuquerque. "Luminarias," candles in sand-weighted paper bags, decorate walls, walkways, and roof lines to light the way for the Santo Niño (Christ Child). Christmas Eve. Call 505/243-3696 or toll free 800/284-2282.

Southern New Mexico

- **Rock-Hound Roundup,** Deming. More than 500 hobbyists from 45 states attend this nationally famous informal tailgate-style convention. Includes a mineral-sample auction and guided field trips for semi-precious agate, jasper, and pink onyx. 2nd week in March. Call 505/546-2674 for information.

- **Trinity Site Tour,** Alamogordo. Open to the public only 2 days each year, this is where the world's first atomic bomb was detonated on July 16, 1945. 1st Saturday in April and October. Call 505/678-1134.

- **Wild Wild West Pro Rodeo,** Silver City. More than 300 contestants from surrounding states compete. May. Call 505/538-3229.

- **Pioneer Days Celebration and Balloon Fiesta,** Clovis. One of the top national rodeos, plus hot air balloon rally, parades, and western music. Early June. Call 505/763-3435.

- **Old Fort Days,** Fort Sumner. Reenactments of the death of outlaw Billy the Kid, Old West bank robberies, trials, and hangings. Early to mid-June. Call 505/355-7705.

- **National Standard-Class Glider and Soaring Championships,** Hobbs. Features the top pilots of high-performance sailplanes. Early July. Call 505/397-3202 or toll free 800/658-6291.

- **Frontier Days,** Silver City. Historic celebration with parades, a cowboy breakfast and barbecue, hot air balloon rally, art show, ice cream social, and junior rodeo. Early July. Call 505/538-3785 or toll free 800/548-9378.

- **Great American Duck Race,** Deming. Watch 500 ducks compete for $10,000 in prizes; with duck parade and duck dance. Last weekend in August. Call 505/546-2674.

- **Carlsbad Caverns Bat Flight Breakfast,** Carlsbad. Breakfast followed by an eerie, hour-long spectacle as some 500,000 Mexican freetail bats return at dawn to roost. Mid-August. Call 505/785-2232.

- **Hatch Chile Festival,** Hatch. Traditional and contemporary red and green chile dishes, chile ristras, and bushel baskets and sacks of chiles from the autumn harvest. September. Call 505/267-3071.

- **The Whole Enchilada Fiesta,** Las Cruces. The world's largest enchilada, Spanish music concerts, dances, and parades. Early October. Call toll free 800/FIESTAS.

Spectator Sports

AUTO RACING　The season generally runs from late spring through early fall and concentrates on sprint cars, stocks and hobby stocks, and IMCA modifieds. In Albuquerque, check with **Duke City Raceway** (tel 505/873-7223); race fans in Las Cruces, head for **The Speedway,** at Southern New Mexico State Fairgrounds (tel 505/524-7913). In the Farmington area there's **Aztec Speedway,** south of the community of Aztec on Legion Rd (tel 505/334-6629). Drag race fans should check the schedule at **Albuquerque National Dragway** (tel 505/299-9478).

BASEBALL　Albuquerque Dukes, the Triple-A farm team of the Los Angeles Dodgers, play at Albuquerque Sports Stadium (tel 505/243-1791) from mid-April through early September.

BASKETBALL & FOOTBALL　The action is at the **University of New Mexico** in Albuquerque (tel 505/277-2116) and **New Mexico State University** in Las Cruces (tel 505/646-1420 or 505/646-NMSU for recorded information).

HORSE RACING　Some of the country's best quarter horses and thoroughbreds run at New Mexico's four tracks. The **Downs at Albuquerque** (tel 505/262-1188), in the State Fairgrounds, offers nearly $2 million in purses from January to mid-June and during the state fair in September. Racing takes place at the **Downs at Santa Fe,** just south of Santa Fe off I-25 (tel 505/471-3311), from late June through Labor Day. **Ruidoso Downs** (tel 505/378-4431), considered the quarter horse capital of the world, has races from mid-May through Labor Day, when the All American Futurity takes place. Located on New Mexico's southern border, just 5 miles from El Paso, Texas, **Sunland Park** (tel 505/589-1131) has the state's longest season—from early October to early May.

RODEO　Many New Mexico communities have rodeo grounds and host regional events. Among major rodeos on the professional circuit are the **All-American Pro Rodeo** (tel toll free 800/235-FAIR), at the New Mexico State Fair in Albuquerque each September, and the **Clovis Rodeo** (tel 505/763-3435) in June during the Pioneer Days Celebration.

Activities A to Z

BALLOONING   Major hot-air balloon rallies take place in both Albuquerque and Taos each October, and companies throughout the state offer balloon rides. Among firms advertising that they are fully insured and certified by the FAA are Braden's Balloons Aloft (tel 505/281-2714) and Naturally High Balloon Company (tel 505/843-6888), both in Albuquerque.

BICYCLING   Popular throughout the state, although many roads in rural areas are narrow, with no shoulders or bike paths. Urban biking is best in Albuquerque, where information and bike maps are available from the **Albuquerque Cultural and Recreational Services Dept** (tel 505/768-3550). For information on mountain biking trails in New Mexico's national forests, contact the **USDA Forest Service Office** (tel 505/842-3292). For bike rentals try Recreational Equipment Inc (tel 505/247-1191) or Rio Mountainsport (tel 505/766-9970), both in Albuquerque. Northeast Cyclery (tel 505/299-1210), also in Albuquerque, repairs all brands of bicycles.

BOATING   For information on lake boating, contact **New Mexico State Parks,** PO Box 1147, Santa Fe, NM 87504-1147 (tel 505/827-7465 or toll free 800/451-2541). Those interested in white-water rafting or kayaking on the Rio Grande or Rio Chama should contact the **Bureau of Land Management,** NM State Office, PO Box 27115, Santa Fe, NM 87502-0115 (tel 505/438-7400).

CAMPING & HIKING   With 5 national forests, dozens of state and national parks, and vast tracts of other public land, there is no excuse to stay indoors. Information on state parks can be obtained from **New Mexico State Parks,** PO Box 1147, Santa Fe, NM 87504-1147 (tel 505/827-7465 or toll free 800/451-2541). National

forest and wilderness maps are available from the USDA Forest Service Office, 517 Gold Ave SW, Albuquerque, NM 87102 (tel 505/842-3292). Topographical maps can be obtained from the US Geological Survey Distribution Section, Federal Center, Building 41, Denver, CO 80225 (tel 303/234-3832). A variety of maps is also available from the Bureau of Land Management, NM State Office, PO Box 27115, Santa Fe, NM 87502-0115 (tel 505/438-7400); and a geologic highway map and rock-hound guide is available from the New Mexico Bureau of Mines and Mineral Resources, Campus Station, Socorro, NM 87801 (tel 505/835-5410).

FISHING & HUNTING   Opportunities for fishing and hunting are particularly numerous in the northern mountains. Licenses, information, and equipment can be obtained at sporting goods stores throughout the state. You can also contact the **New Mexico Department of Game and Fish,** PO Box 25112, Santa Fe, NM 87503 (tel 505/827-7911). The department maintains a 24-hour hotline (tel toll free 800/ASK-FISH), with information on the best places to fish, fishing conditions, licenses, and regulations. Those interested in guided trips can contact the **New Mexico Council of Outfitters and Guides,** 160 Washington St SE, No. 175, Albuquerque, NM 87108 (tel 505/243-4461), for a brochure and state outfitters' directory.

GOLF   Generally mild weather and more than 60 golf courses cater to golfers. Check with the **Sun Country Golf Association** (tel 505/897-0864) concerning private clubs throughout the state. For information on municipal courses in Albuquerque, contact the **Albuquerque Parks Division** (tel 505/888-8115).

SKIING   New Mexico's mountains and an abundance of snow offer some of the best skiing in the country at the state's 9 downhill and 2 cross-country ski areas. For information, contact **Ski New Mexico,** PO Box 1104, Santa Fe, NM 87504 (tel 505/982-5300); and for recorded daily snow conditions call the **Sno-Phone** (tel 505/984-0606).

SCENIC DRIVING TOUR #1

SANTA FE, TAOS & BEYOND

Start: Santa Fe
Finish: Pecos National Historic Park
Distance: 496 miles
Time: 2–4 days
Highlights: Art galleries, museums, Native American pueblos, historic steam railroad, Spanish colonial churches, wildlife

A longtime favorite of ranchers, artists, writers, fortune hunters, and more than a few outlaws, north-central New Mexico claims some of the state's most impressive mountain scenery, a rich and exciting history, and a wide range of attractions. This tour visits the Santa Fe and Taos art centers, several Native American pueblos, an old fort, more than a dozen museums, several pristine lakes, and plenty of scenic beauty. Keep in mind that mountain driving can be slow. Mileage totals are from stop to stop only, and in-town and side trip travel may add several hundred miles. Those driving in winter should check on road conditions on US 64 between Chama and Taos before leaving Santa Fe by contacting the New Mexico Highway Department (tel toll free 800/432-4269). Snow storms often close a mountain section of this road for a day or more.

For additional information on accommodations, restaurants, and attractions in the region covered by the tour, look under specific cities in the listings portion of this book.

1. **Santa Fe.** This "City Different" combines Old World charm with modern urban sophistication. Steeped in history, the city has a busy and prosperous artists colony, excellent museums, an abundance of musical and theatrical events, and some of the state's most popular shops and restaurants.

   Originally inhabited by ancestors of present-day Pueblo Indians, Santa Fe (elevation 7,000 feet) was established in 1610 as Spain's New Mexico provincial capital. In the late 1600s, it was the site of a bloody Native American revolt and later reconquest. In the mid-19th century US troops invaded and secured the city without firing a shot.

   If you seek lodging, the downtown **Eldorado Hotel** (Santa Fe's largest) and **Hilton of Santa Fe** are close to Santa Fe Plaza and very convenient. The more economical **El Rey Inn** on Cerrillos Rd, southwest of downtown, is a favorite of New Mexicans visiting their capital city.

   Several of the city's main attractions are within easy walking distance of the **Plaza,** which makes it a good place to begin your sightseeing. On the plaza's north side, the **Palace of the Governors** (tel 505/827-6483), believed to be the oldest public US building, has a long "portal," or covered porch, where local Native Americans display and sell their jewelry, pottery, baskets, and other arts and crafts. Inside, there's a regional history museum, with exhibits on regional developments over the past 400 years. Across Lincoln St from the Palace of the Governors, off the northwest corner of the Plaza, the **Museum of Fine Arts** (tel 505/827-4455) showcases New Mexico's 20th-century artists. Just east of the Plaza, the **Institute of American Indian Arts Museum,** 108 Cathedral Pl (tel 505/988-6281), has a Native American arts collection representing numerous US tribes. **St Francis Cathedral,** at Cathedral Place and San Francisco St (tel 505/982-5619), was constructed in the late 19th century to emulate the great cathedrals of Europe. The **Loretto Chapel,** 211 Old Santa Fe Trail, at Water St (tel 505/984-7971), by the same architects that built St Francis Cathedral, is famous for its "miraculous" spiral staircase, which appears to hang without visible support.

   Southwest of the Plaza area, **Santuario de Guadalupe,** 100 Guadalupe St (tel 505/988-2027), is reputedly the oldest existing US shrine to Mexico's patron saint, Our Lady of Guadalupe. Built in the late 1700s and extensively remodeled a century later, it is not used as a church today, but serves as a center for performing arts events and art exhibits. Southeast of the Plaza, the **Mission of San Miguel** (tel 505/983-3974) was built in the early 1600s on the site of a 12th-century pueblo. Inside the mission church is a bell considered to have been made in Spain in the 1350s.

   The **State Capitol,** commonly called the Roundhouse, on Old Santa Fe Trail at Paseo de Peralta (tel 505/986-4589), offers tours that include a visit to the art gallery in the governor's office, with works by New Mexican artists.

   Three museums are located on Camino Lejo,

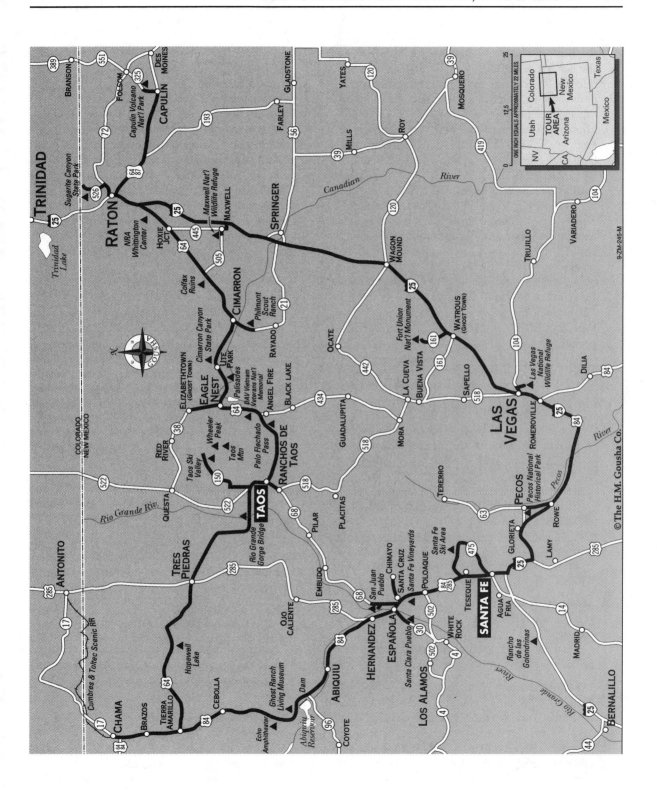

south of downtown. **Wheelwright Museum of the American Indian,** 704 Camino Lejo (tel 505/982-4636), contains both historic and contemporary Native American arts and crafts, with an especially impressive collection of Navajo art. The **Museum of International Folk Art,** 706 Camino Lejo (tel 505/827-6350), has folk art from more than 100 countries, including 1 wing devoted to the Spanish colonial period. At the **Museum of Indian Arts and Culture,** 710 Camino Lejo (tel 505/827-6344), exhibits focus on the Apache, Navajo, and Pueblo cultures. Art lovers may also explore the more than 75 galleries, studios, and antique shops along **Canyon Road,** just a few blocks southeast of the Plaza.

About 15 miles south of Santa Fe Plaza via I-25, **El Rancho de las Golondrinas** (tel 505/471-2261) is a living history museum of restored buildings devoted to New Mexico's Spanish colonial period.

Ⓤ☕

REFRESHMENT STOP

For a quick bite in downtown Santa Fe, stop at **The Burrito Co,** 111 Washington Ave. You'll find extremely elegant dining at **The Compound,** 653 Canyon Rd, which serves fine American cuisine, and a taste of old Santa Fe at **El Farol,** 808 Canyon Rd, a Mexican restaurant.

From Santa Fe, drive 20 miles north on US 84/285 to:

2. **Santa Fe Vineyards** (tel 505/753-8100), where you can take an informal winery tour and sample the local wines.

From the winery, continue north on US 84/285 for about 4 miles to:

3. **Española.** Settled by Spanish colonists in 1598, Española (elevation 5,590 feet) owes its modern-day importance as a trading center to the railroad, and specifically the narrow gauge "chili line," so-named because of the drying strings of red chiles hanging on the flat-roofed adobe homes along its route. The line ran from Antonito, Colo-

rado, to Santa Fe from the 1880s to 1941, and a section of the line survives today as a scenic railroad based in Chama.

You can learn about the area's history and see work by local artists at **Bond House Museum,** 710 Bond St (tel 505/753-2377), a Victorian-style adobe home. **Santa Clara Pueblo** (tel 505/753-7326) is located about 2 miles south of Española via Los Alamos Ave (NM 30). Known for its distinctive, highly polished black pottery, the pueblo administers the **Puye Cliff Dwellings,** the impressive ruins of an ancient village where some 1,500 people once lived. To see artists at work, stop at **San Juan Pueblo,** 4 miles north of Española on NM 68 and then another mile west on NM 74 (tel 505/852-4400). At San Juan, arts and crafts from different northern New Mexico pueblos are for sale, and artists are often seen working, at **Oke-Oweenge Crafts Cooperative** (tel 505/852-2372). The tiny community of **Chimayo,** 10 miles east of Española on NM 76, is a worthwhile side trip where you can see traditional Rio Grande weaving at **Ortega's Weaving Shop** (tel 505/351-4215), or visit the beautiful **Santuario de Chimayo,** which contains dirt that believers say has miraculous healing powers.

From Española continue west for about 6 miles to the village of:

4. **Hernandez,** stopping along the road to try to find the exact spot where photographer Ansel Adams took his famous photo, *Moonrise, Hernandez, New Mexico,* in 1941.

Now, continue 16 miles west on US 84 to:

5. **Abiquiu.** Site of an ancient Native American pueblo, Abiquiu was settled by Spanish colonists in the mid-1700s, but became famous as the home of 20th-century artist Georgia O'Keeffe. Although the home is not open to the public, visitors can explore the village plaza and gaze at the sandstone bluffs and mesas that helped inspire the artist.

From Abiquiu, continue west on US 84 for 7 miles to:

6. **Abiquiu Dam and Lake.** (tel 505/685-4371). This large lake is a favorite of northern New Mexicans for boating, water skiing, fishing, swimming, camping, and picnicking.

Now continue 5 more miles west on US 84 to:

7. **Ghost Ranch Living Museum** (tel 505/685-4312). Operated by the US Forest Service and a private foundation, Ghost Ranch is a home for northern New Mexico wildlife creatures that have been severely injured or orphaned, or for other reasons are not able to survive in the wild. Residents include a bear, owls, eagles, skunks, foxes, and other animals.

From Ghost Ranch, head another 6 miles west on US 84 to:

8. **Echo Amphitheater.** This US Forest Service campground (tel 505/684-2486), at 6,600 feet elevation, is a pleasant stop to stretch your legs and spend some time exploring the high desert, with its red rock walls.

Now, continue west and north on US 84 for 40 miles to:

9. **Chama.** This isolated mountain village, at 7,860 feet elevation, is a delightful overnight stop, or home base for fishing, hiking, hunting, snowmobiling, or cross-country skiing jaunts. Most lodging here is a bit rustic, but you'll find all the modern conveniences. Especially recommended are **Chama Trails Inn** and **Elk Horn Lodge and Cafe.**

The number-one attraction is the **Cumbres and Toltec Scenic Railroad** (tel 505/756-2151),

---

☕ REFRESHMENT STOP

For homemade Mexican food and American burgers and sandwiches, stop at **Viva Vera's,** on Main St, 2/10 mile north of the "Y." You'll find an Old West atmosphere and good beef at **High Country Restaurant,** on Main St, 1/10 mile north of the "Y."

---

a narrow-gauge steam train line that runs from Chama into southern Colorado each summer and fall, passing through some of the region's most beautiful scenery.

From Chama, retrace your route 13 miles south on US 84, turn east onto US 64, and go 30 miles through spectacular mountain scenery to:

10. **Hopewell Lake.** This US Forest Service campground (tel 505/758-6200) has a popular fishing lake and is a good place to stretch your legs and perhaps have a picnic lunch.

From the lake, continue 35 miles east, through the tiny community of Tres Piedras (Spanish for "three rocks") to:

11. **Rio Grande Gorge Bridge.** Spanning the Rio Grande, this impressive bridge has fantastic views 650 feet down into the gorge, and both up and down the river.

From the bridge, continue east 15 miles on US 64 to:

12. **Taos** (elevation 6,965 ft). Already home to Native Americans for hundreds of years, Europeans arrived in 1615 with the establishment of Fernando de Taos village by Spanish colonists. Next came French-Canadian trappers, mountain men, artists, writers, and entrepreneurs. The end result is the Taos of today, a mixture of old and new, with some 100 art galleries, quaint adobe homes, historic haciendas, the ancient Taos Pueblo, and a world-class ski resort.

You have plenty of lodging choices. **Holiday Inn Don Fernando de Taos** and **Kachina Lodge** offer fine, modern rooms with a southwestern touch; the older but well-kept **El Monte Lodge** is cozy and economical; and **The Historic Taos Inn** is within easy walking distance of the main sights.

From most parts of town you can see **Taos Mountain,** most prominent as you look north down Paseo del Pueblo Norte; it has been painted and photographed countless times, and numerous variations on the landmark may be seen in local art galleries. Legend has it that this is a magic mountain, with its own mind. If the mountain likes you, you must return. But if you displease it, the mountain banishes you for life.

Most visits to Taos begin at **Taos Plaza,** with an abundance of art galleries, shops, and restaurants. Benches in the Plaza's center provide a shady break from sightseeing and provide good people-watching opportunities. Walking off the southwest corner of the plaza, watch for Ledoux St, where you'll find the **Blumenschein Home and Museum,** at #222 (tel 505/758-0330), with antique furnishings and paintings by Ernest

Blumenschein, one of the East Coast artists who founded the Taos Society of Artists in 1915. The **Harwood Foundation Museum of Taos Art,** 238 Ledoux St (tel 505/758-9826), has changing displays of local artists' works.

Walking east of Taos Plaza about ½ block takes you to another era of Taos's heritage, the Old West, at **Kit Carson Home and Museum,** 113 Kit Carson Rd (tel 505/758-4741). The famous scout made Taos his headquarters for much of his life. His home, which he presented to his Mexican bride, Josefa Jaramillo, as a wedding present, has exhibits on Carson's career and New Mexico's mountain-man period. **Bent House Museum,** at 117 Bent St (tel 505/758-2376), just north of Taos Plaza, was the home of the first governor of the American territory of New Mexico, and the site where he was killed during the Taos Pueblo Rebellion of 1847.

Several blocks north of Taos Plaza at 227 Paseo del Pueblo Norte is the **Fechin Institute** (tel 505/758-1710). Nicolai Fechin was a Russian-born artist who painted in Taos and rebuilt an old adobe home, adding unique Russian-style carvings. His former house is open to the public during the summer and fall. Nearby, **Kit Carson Park** (tel 505/758-4160) contains a cemetery with the graves of Carson and his family and other prominent Taos citizens.

Taos's most popular attraction is **Taos Pueblo** (tel 505/758-9593), located 2 miles north of Taos Plaza via Paseo del Pueblo Norte and the pueblo access road. Home to Taos Indians since long before Columbus arrived in the so-called New World, this site is considered New Mexico's most beautiful pueblo. Visitors can watch Native American ceremonial dances, shop for handmade jewelry, pottery, and drums, and eat the traditional fried bread. The pueblo often closes to the public for about a month in late winter, so check before making the trip at this time.

Among Taos's best historic homes is the **Martinez Hacienda,** located 2 miles west of Taos Plaza on NM 240 (tel 505/758-1000). The fort-like building, with 21 rooms around 2 courtyards, contains Spanish colonial furniture and artifacts of the early 19th century, a working blacksmith

shop, and exhibits on Spanish culture and Taos history.

Millicent Rogers Museum, 4 miles north of Taos Plaza via Paseo del Pueblo Norte/US 64 and Millicent Rogers Rd (tel 505/758-2462), has an excellent selection of Hispanic and Native American art and artifacts, including the best collection you'll see anywhere of San Ildefonso Pueblo pottery by famed artist Maria Martinez.

South of Taos about 4 miles on Paseo del Pueblo Sur/NM 68, in the community of Ranchos de Taos, is the much-photographed adobe **San Francisco de Asis Church** (tel 505/758-2754), which offers a glimpse into the religious past and present of northern New Mexico. The church houses a mystery painting of Christ; it contains a scientifically unexplained image of a cross that appears when viewed in total darkness.

Of course, if you're a skier, it will be hard to resist a day on the slopes at **Taos Ski Valley,** about 16 miles northeast of Taos via US 64 and NM 150 (tel 505/776-2291).

⊡

REFRESHMENT STOP

On Taos Plaza, a convenient stop for lunch is **The Garden Restaurant,** 127 N Plaza. Nearby, **Doc Martin's** at the Historic Taos Inn, 125 Paseo del Pueblo Norte, provides more formal dining, and the busy, somewhat noisy **Michael's Kitchen,** 305 Paseo del Pueblo Norte, is a local favorite, especially for breakfast.

From Taos, head east on US 64 for 22 miles, crossing 9,101-foot Palo Flechado Pass, to:

13. **DAV Vietnam Veterans National Memorial** (tel 505/377-6900). Built by Dr. Victor Westphall in memory of his son David, a US marine who died in the Vietnam War, this stunning structure has a visitor center and chapel, honoring all US soldiers who gave their lives in that war.

From the memorial, continue east on US 64, but look southwest to **Wheeler Peak,** New

Mexico's highest mountain at 13,161 feet. From the DAV Memorial, it's 9 miles to:

14. **Eagle Nest.** Sitting at the junction of NM 38 and US 64, Eagle Nest is a favorite recreation spot, with boat and bank fishing at **Eagle Nest Lake** in warm weather, and ice fishing in winter. The lake is also popular for windsurfing.

From Eagle Nest, continue east on US 64 for about 8 miles into Cimarron Canyon and the:

15. **Palisades.** These spectacular cliffs with their striking rock formations were cut by the Cimarron River through igneous rock known as a sill, composed of the rock monzonite, left here some 40 million years ago when this section of the Rocky Mountains was uplifted. Popular with rock climbers, the cliffs are 800 feet high in some areas. **Cimarron Canyon State Park** is part of the 33,000-acre **Colin Neblett Wildlife Area.** Especially during early mornings and late evenings, watch for elk, mule deer, wild turkey, and maybe even a black bear as you drive carefully through the canyon.

From the Palisades it's about 16 miles east on US 64 to:

16. **Cimarron** (elevation 6,427 feet). This historic Old West town grew up in the mid-1800s as a Santa Fe Trail stop. It was the scene of the bloody Colfax County War over ownership of the gigantic Maxwell land grant, which covered much of north-central New Mexico. **St James Hotel,** opened as a saloon in 1873, counts 26 men killed within its thick adobe walls, and infamous gunman Clay Allison is said to have danced on the bar. The hotel, a National Historic Landmark, has been restored and offers tours. It's also a good place to eat or spend a night, with historic rooms decorated with antiques, and modern rooms in a motel annex. Visitors to Cimarron should also browse through the **Old Mill Museum,** on NM 21 south of US 64, a 4-story building built as a grist mill in 1864 that now displays historic photos and memorabilia from Cimarron's past.

Philmont Scout Ranch, 4 miles southwest of Cimarron on NM 21 (tel 505/376-2281), hosts thousands of scouts from around the world each summer, and has 3 museums. **Kit Carson Museum,** furnished in 1850s style, includes part of a ranch house built by the famous scout; **Villa Philmonte** was once the lavish home of Oklahoma oil man Waite Phillips; and **Philmont Museum and Seton Memorial Library** houses the library, art, and natural history collections of Boy Scouts of America founder Ernest Thompson Seton. While driving to Philmont from Cimarron watch for bison, raised by the scout ranch, and deer and pronghorn antelope.

From Cimarron, follow US 64 east for 12 more miles to:

17. **Colfax Ruins.** Sitting along the northwest side of the road, these ruins and some abandoned railroad coaches are all that's left of an early 20th-century town.

From the ruins, continue east for about 20 miles to:

18. **NRA Whittington Center,** operated by the National Rifle Association, provides instruction in pistol, rifle, and shotgun shooting, as well as firearms safety.

From here, continue east on US 64 for about 4 miles to I-25 (exit 446), and take I-25 north about 3 miles to:

19. **Raton** (elevation 6,640 feet). First just a water hole on the Santa Fe Trail, the town was founded in 1879 as a railroad, mining, and ranching center. Start a self-guided walking tour of the city's historic district, described in a brochure available at the **Raton Museum,** 216 1st St (tel 505/445-8979). Housed in a 1906 brewery warehouse, the museum has a variety of memorabilia and displays depicting Raton's early days. Nearby, you'll see the 1903 **Santa Fe Railroad Depot,** the 1896 **Palace Hotel,** and the 1929 **Swastika Hotel,** which became the Yucca Hotel during World War II when the swastika symbol was adopted by the German Nazi Party. Also, don't miss the **Shuler Theater,** 131 N 2nd St (tel 505/445-5528), built in 1915 in European rococo style and recently restored to its former elegance.

Sugarite Canyon State Park, about 8 miles east of Raton via NM 72 and 2 miles north on US

526 (tel 505/445-5607), has hiking trails, picnicking, camping, and fishing in lakes stocked with trout. Watch for wild turkeys, mule deer, and beaver, as well as migratory waterfowl in the fall.

Capulin Volcano National Monument, 30 miles east of Raton via US 64/87 and north 3 miles on NM 325 (tel 505/278-2201), allows you to walk inside a volcano that erupted only a short 10,000 years ago.

For comfortable lodging in Raton, your best bets are the **Best Western Sands Motel** or **Harmony Manor Motel.**

☕ REFRESHMENT STOP

Renowned for its margaritas, **Pappa's Sweet Shop Restaurant,** 1201 S 2nd St, also specializes in steak and prime rib. Locals recommend the Mexican food at **El Matador,** 1012 S 2nd St.

From Raton, go south for 24 miles on I-25 to exit 426 at Maxwell, go west off the interstate into Maxwell, and follow NM 445 north less than a mile and then NM 505 west about 2 miles to:

20. **Maxwell National Wildlife Refuge** (tel 505/375-2331). Fall is the best time to visit this refuge with 3 lakes, when you're likely to sight ducks, Canadian geese, bald eagles, and possibly American white pelicans and sandhill cranes. There's also a black-tailed prairie dog town, and you may see deer and antelope. Stop at the visitors center for a map.

From the refuge, return to I-25 and continue south about 13 miles to:

21. **Springer** (exits 414 and 412). Settled in 1879, Springer was the Colfax County seat from 1882 to 1897. The old courthouse, on Maxwell St, today houses the **Santa Fe Trail Museum** (tel 505/483-2341), with memorabilia and historic photographs, as well as the state's only electric chair, used in Santa Fe from 1933 to 1956, when 7 convicted murderers were executed.

From Springer, continue south 48 miles on I-25 to exit 366, then travel 8 miles north on NM 161 to:

22. **Fort Union National Monument** (tel 505/425-8025). Opened in 1851 to protect Santa Fe Trail travelers from Native American attacks, the fort was expanded 10 years later to repel Confederate attacks during the Civil War. There's a self-guided walking trail among the fort's ruins.

From the fort, return 8 miles to I-25, and continue south 22 miles to:

23. **Las Vegas.** Founded in 1835 as a land grant from the Mexican government, Las Vegas has been a Santa Fe Trail stop, a military outpost, a railroad depot, a commerce center, and a Wild West town. You can view ornate Victorian buildings dating from the town's days of ranching prosperity in the late 1800s, as well as pre-Victorian Spanish Colonial adobes. Begin your visit at the **Rough Riders Museum,** 729 Grand Ave (tel 505/425-8726), with exhibits on Teddy Roosevelt's Rough Riders and area history. Next door at the **Las Vegas/San Miguel County Chamber of Commerce,** 727 Grand Ave (tel 505/425-8631 or toll free 800/832-5947), you can obtain a visitors' guide with a walking tour of the historic plaza and Bridge Street areas, with stops at late 18th- and early 19th-century buildings, including the handsome 1881 **Plaza Hotel,** 230 Old Town Plaza (tel 505/425-3591), beautifully restored in the 1980s. **Las Vegas National Wildlife Refuge,** 6 miles southeast of town via NM 104 and NM 281 (tel 505/425-3581), has opportunities to sight a variety of birds, including geese, bald eagles, and sandhill cranes. There's an overlook and a nature trail.

From Las Vegas, continue south on I-25 for 40 miles to exit 307, then take NM 63 north for 5 miles to:

24. **Pecos National Historical Park** (tel 505/757-6414). This park has a 1¼-mile self-guided trail through 13th-century pueblo ruins, a Spanish mission, and a visitors center with exhibits and brochures.

From the park, return 5 miles to I-25, and continue south for 26 miles back to Santa Fe.

SCENIC DRIVING TOUR #2

ALBUQUERQUE & THE GREAT NORTHWEST

Start: Albuquerque
Finish: Coronado State Monument, Bernalillo
Distance: 611 miles
Time: 2–5 days
Highlights: Native American ruins, pueblos, lava flows, museums

When travelers plan a vacation to New Mexico, their itinerary usually covers Santa Fe and Taos, while it overlooks Albuquerque; yet Albuquerque is also an enjoyable city to visit with a good choice of attractions. It's also a fine place to begin your trip before exploring the rest of the state. This tour takes you from Albuquerque to the northwest corner of the state, a sparsely populated, somewhat primitive area, with great distances between services and some of the state's worst roads. However, the tour also takes in Chaco Canyon,

the biggest ancient Native American ruin in the Southwest, as well as other cultural, historic, and scenic sites worth visiting. Be advised before setting out that there is no way to get to Chaco Canyon without driving on 20–25 miles of dirt road; rain or snow can make the road impassable.

For additional information on accommodations, restaurants, and attractions in the region covered by the tour, look under specific cities in the listings portion of this book.

1. **Albuquerque** (elevation 5,000 feet). New Mexico's largest city is a pleasant blend of cultures—Native American, Spanish, and Anglo. Ancient Native Americans lived in the Sandia Mountains near here some 10,000 years ago, followed by the Anasazi tribe around AD 1100. Next came Spanish conquistadors in the mid-16th century. The railroad brought Anglo-Americans to the region in the 1880s, and the automobile and Route 66 brought even more transplants in the 1930s. Visitors to

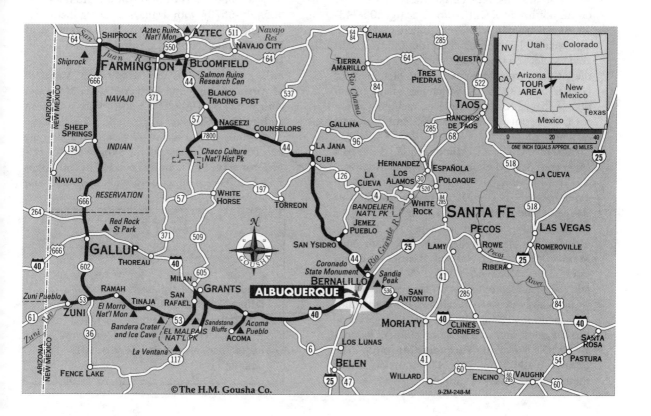

©The H.M. Gousha Co.

Albuquerque today find it a comfortable city—just a big Western town, really–with excellent museums, a pleasant climate, and even its own baseball team.

You'll probably want to spend a few days here, perhaps to allow your body to adapt to the elevation. The city has plenty of lodging choices, including most of the usual chain hotels and motels. In Old Town, you may enjoy the luxurious **Sheraton Old Town** or the historic charm of **Casas de Sueños.** Close to Old Town, off I-40, **Travelers Inn** is an economical choice. For an airport motel, you'll find **Best Western Airport Inn** surprisingly homey and quiet.

Start your Albuquerque visit in **Old Town,** bounded by Rio Grande Blvd on the west and Central Ave on the south. Browse through some of the area's more than 100 art galleries and specialty shops, where you'll find art for practically any taste, and exquisite pottery, jewelry, weavings, and baskets created by New Mexico's Native American artisans. **San Felipe de Neri Church,** on the north side of Old Town Plaza (tel 505/243-4628), has been in almost continuous use since it was built in 1706. A brochure describing a self-guided Old Town walking tour is available from the **Albuquerque Museum,** 2000 Mountain Rd NW (tel 505/243-7255), which has a huge collection of Spanish colonial artifacts, including armor used by Spanish conquistadors, and historical exhibits.

Also in Old Town is **Albuquerque Children's Museum,** 800 Rio Grande NW (tel 505/842-5525), with interactive exhibits and activities for children age 2–12. **American International Rattlesnake Museum,** 202 San Felipe St NW (tel 505/242-6569), displays just what you'd expect, including an albino rattler. The excellent **New Mexico Museum of Natural History and Science,** 1801 Mountain Rd (tel 505/841-8837), takes a participatory hands-on look at the natural world that's fun and educational for both adults and children; exhibits include an "active" volcano, dinosaurs, and an Ice Age cave. About ½ block west of Old Town, the **Turquoise Museum,** 2107 Central Ave NW (tel 505/247-8650), deals with the mining and uses of turquoise.

Heading away from Old Town, but still on Albuquerque's west side, the 600-acre **Rio Grande Zoo,** 903 10th St SW (tel 505/843-7413), has more than 1,300 animals from around the world. **Rio Grande Nature Center State Park,** 2901 Candelaria Rd NW (tel 505/344-7240), contains a 3-acre pond and marsh, and 2 miles of nature trails along the Rio Grande. Among New Mexico's newest parks, established in 1990, is **Petroglyph National Monument,** 4735 Unser Blvd NW (tel 505/839-4429). Still in development, the park has more than 15,000 prehistoric Native American petroglyphs in lava flows along Albuquerque's West Mesa. Guided tours are offered in summer. The **Indian Pueblo Cultural Center,** 2401 12th St NW, 1 block north of I-40 (tel 505/843-7270), has exhibits on New Mexico's 19 pueblos; Native American dance and craft demonstrations are held on weekends.

In southeast Albuquerque, on Kirtland Air Force Base at the corner of Wyoming Blvd and K St, you'll find the **National Atomic Museum** (tel 505/845-6670), with displays detailing the development of nuclear energy. The **University of New Mexico,** north of Central Ave and east of University Blvd (tel 505/277-0111), has 5 museums, including the acclaimed **Maxwell Museum of Anthropology** and **University Art Museum,** with works by 19th- and 20th-century American and European artists.

If you want a great view of Albuquerque, particularly at sunset, take the **Sandia Peak Aerial Tramway,** 10 Tramway Loop NE (tel 505/856-7325), 2.7 miles up to the summit of 10,378-foot

---

REFRESHMENT STOP

For the best malt in town, or a burger, sandwich, or blue-plate special, stop at **66 Diner,** 1405 Central Ave NE, west of the University of New Mexico. In Old Town, you can have a genuine New Mexico dining experience at **Maria Teresa,** 618 Rio Grande Blvd NW.

Sandia Peak. Those looking for a similar view at a different location might opt for the road to **Sandia Crest.** It's about a 1-hour drive from downtown Albuquerque, taking I-40 east to NM 14, which you follow north to NM 536; the latter road takes you to the crest.

Albuquerque visitors may also want to take in an **Albuquerque Dukes** baseball game, 1601 Stadium Blvd SE (tel 505/243-1791), or tackle the slopes at **Sandia Peak Ski Area,** 20 miles northeast of the city (tel 505/242-9052).

Next head west 52 miles on I-40 to exit 108, the Acoma/Sky City turnoff, then 13 miles southwest to:

2. **Acoma Pueblo.** Perched on a high rock mesa, "Sky City," as it is called, is believed to be the oldest continuously occupied US city. Begin your tour at the **Visitor Center** (tel 505/252-1139 or toll free 800/747-0181), with a museum, a cafe, and shops, at the base of the mesa; then board the pueblo's tour bus for a ride to the top. You'll see a large mission church, built in 1629, containing numerous Spanish colonial artifacts; flat-roofed adobe homes; and members of the Acoma tribe selling fry-bread and distinctive white pottery with brown and black designs.

From Acoma, return 13 miles to I-40 and continue west for 19 miles to NM 117 (exit 89), then turn south and go 14 miles to:

3. **El Malpais National Monument** (tel 505/285-5406). El Malpais (which means "the badlands" in Spanish) is a seemingly endless lava-filled valley, produced by more than 3 million years of volcanic eruptions. **Sandstone Bluffs Overlook,** about 10 miles south of I-40, provides fine views of the lava flows, and several miles further south you can see **La Ventana,** one of the state's largest natural arches.

This is the eastern section of El Malpais; you'll see the west side later. Now return 14 miles north on NM 117 back to I-40 (exit 89), and go west 4 miles to exit 85 and:

4. **Grants.** Although Grants began some 100 years ago as a railroad and ranching center, it was not until 1950, with the discovery of uranium, that the

---

> ☕
>
> **REFRESHMENT STOP**
>
> You can get breakfast all day at **Grants Station Restaurant,** 200 W Santa Fe Ave, which displays railroad memorabilia, including a caboose. The menu has a variety of American and Mexican standard dishes.

---

town really boomed. Although there is little mining done here today, Grants keeps its short-lived mining tradition alive at **New Mexico Mining Museum,** 100 N Iron St at Santa Fe Ave (tel 505/287-4802 or toll free 800/748-2142), the only uranium mine museum in the world; it offers the experience of a simulated uranium mine, with authentic machinery and equipment.

From Grants, at I-40 exit 81, take NM 53 south and west, through the lava flows on the west side of **El Malpais National Monument,** about 25 miles to the next stop:

5. **Bandera Crater and Ice Cave** (tel 505/783-4303), where you can see a gigantic volcanic crater and its lava flows, and the ice cave, which is actually a lava tube that maintains a perpetual mass of ice year-round.

Now continue west on NM 53 for about 16 miles to:

6. **El Morro National Monument** (tel 505/783-4226). This fascinating national monument has something for everyone—spectacular scenery, Anasazi pueblo ruins, several self-guiding trails, and the famous **Inscription Rock,** where conquistadors, pioneers, and other travelers have left messages dating back to 1605. Much earlier Anasazi petroglyphs may be seen along the cliffs, including carvings of geometric designs and animals.

From the monument, drive west on NM 53 about 34 miles to:

7. **Zuni Pueblo** (tel 505/782-4481). Famous for its inlaid silver and turquoise jewelry, Zuni is among New Mexico's largest inhabited pueblos. Stop at

Zuni Arts and Crafts (tel 505/782-5532), a tribal-owned arts and crafts market, and explore the exhibits at the **Zuni Museum Project** to learn about Zuni culture. **Our Lady of Guadalupe Mission** is decorated with murals by Zuni artist Alex Seowtewa.

From Zuni, return 10 miles east on NM 53 to the intersection with NM 602, and go north about 30 miles to:

8. **Gallup.** Traditionally a commerce center for Navajo, Zuni, and other tribes, Gallup has dozens of trading posts, galleries, and shops that specialize in Native American arts and crafts. Just east of town, **Red Rock State Park** (tel 505/722-3829) contains several archeological sites of the Anasazi, an 1888 trading post building, and a museum with exhibits on both prehistoric and modern Native Americans in the area and displays of Native American arts and crafts.

Also in Gallup, look for historic buildings along a remaining section of old US Route 66, here designated 66 Ave. Among these gems is **El Rancho Hotel & Motel,** built in 1937 and New Mexico and Arizona headquarters for film companies from the 1930s through the 1960s. El Rancho makes a fun stop for the night; for a more modern motel, try the economical **Blue Spruce Lodge** or 1 of the 3 **Best Westerns** in town.

From Gallup, take US 666 north through the Navajo Reservation 86 miles to:

9. **Ship Rock.** This prominent rock formation (1,700 feet tall), which you can see off to the west from several view points, is called "Rock with Wings" by the Navajos; others find it resembles a tall sailing ship. The rock is sacred to the Navajos and climbing it is prohibited.

From Ship Rock, continue about 7 miles to its namesake town of Shiprock, and take US 64 east for 29 miles to:

10. **Farmington** (elevation 5,395 feet). By far the biggest city in northwest New Mexico, this is a good home base for trips into the Navajo Reservation, Mesa Verde National Park in southeast Colorado, and Chaco Culture National Historical Park. Lodging choices here include **Holiday Inn of Farmington** and the **Anasazi Inn,** and the nostalgic 1950s-style **Enchantment Lodge** in nearby Aztec.

Aztec Ruins National Monument, about 15 miles northeast of Farmington and just past the town of Aztec on US 550 (tel 505/334-6174), includes the ruins of a 500-room pueblo, apparently abandoned by the Anasazi 7 centuries ago. The monument contains the only reconstructed Anasazi great kiva (religious chamber) in existence. The visitors center has exhibits of baskets and pottery discovered in the ruins. Back in Farmington, visit the **Farmington Museum,** 302 N Orchard St (tel 505/599-1174), with exhibits on the area's history, including a replica of a 1930s trading post.

⛾

REFRESHMENT STOP

You'll find good Mexican food at **Señor Pepper's Restaurant,** Four Corners Regional Airport; and for those who enjoy a classic pub atmosphere there's **Clancy's Pub,** 2703 E 20th St.

From Farmington, go east 11 miles on US 64 until you reach:

11. **Salmon Ruin Research Center** (tel 505/632-2013). This large pueblo, built in the late 11th century, contains a rare elevated kiva, as well as a more traditional kiva. The center also has a museum displaying artifacts from the site, and **Heritage Park,** with reconstructed buildings representing different periods of the area's history.

From Salmon Ruin, continue east on US 64 for 2 miles to Bloomfield, take NM 44 south about 44 miles to Nageezi, go southwest on San Juan County Rd 7800 for 11 miles, then south on NM 57 for 15 miles to:

12. **Chaco Culture National Historical Park** (tel 505/988-6727). This was once the New York City of the ancient Anasazi, when all roads led to Chaco. Occupied from about AD 900 to 1200, this historical park (elevation 6,300 feet), includes ruins of more than a dozen large Anasazi villages

and hundreds of smaller sites. At its height in the 12th century, the oldest and largest village, Pueblo Bonito, towered 4 stories with some 600 rooms and 40 kivas. Although many parts of Chaco may be seen from roadways, some of the best views involve at least short hikes. A visitors center has exhibits and shows films on area history and cultures. *Warning:* In rainy or snowy weather the road from Nageezi into Chaco Culture National Historical Park may be impassable. Check with the park office before setting out.

From Chaco, return the 26 miles to Nageezi, turn east onto NM 44 and go 91 miles to San Ysidro, turn north onto NM 4 and drive 4 miles to:

13. **Jemez Pueblo.** Stop at the **Walatowa Visitor Center** (tel 505/834-7235) for information on this pueblo, known for its dances, pottery, and sculpture. In the **Red Rock Scenic Area,** you'll find roadside stands with traditional foods and arts and crafts. No photography is permitted.

From the Pueblo, return 4 miles to San Ysidro and continue southeast on NM 44 for about 23 miles to:

14. **Coronado State Monument** (tel 505/867-5351). This state monument preserves the ruins of a 15th-century Anasazi pueblo called Kuaua, with hundreds of excavated rooms and a reconstructed kiva ceremonial chamber. Anasazi murals with drawings of people and animals are also on display.

Continue on NM 44 about 2 miles into Bernalillo, then go south on I-25 for 12 miles to return to Albuquerque.

ACOMA PUEBLO

Map page M-3, B2

The spectacular "Sky City," a walled adobe village perched high atop a sheer rock mesa 357 feet above the valley floor, Acoma Pueblo is said to have been inhabited since at least the 11th century. This makes it the longest continuously occupied community in the United States. Tour buses board at the visitor center at the base of the mesa and then climb through a rock garden of 50-foot sandstone monoliths to the mesa's summit. Transparent mica stone windows are prevalent among the 300-odd adobe structures.

Also located on the mesa is the mission church of **San Estevan del Rey.** Built in 1639, it contains numerous masterpieces of Spanish colonial art. The annual San Estevan del Rey feast day is held September 2, when the pueblo's patron saint is honored with a midmorning mass, a procession, an afternoon corn dance, and an arts-and-crafts fair. To reach Acoma from Grants, drive east 15 miles on I-40 to McCartys, then south 13 miles on paved tribal roads to the visitor center. For more information about Sky City contact Acoma Pueblo at 505/252-1139, or toll free at 800/747-0181.

ALAMOGORDO

Map page M-3, D3

Motel 🏨

🏨🏨 **Days Inn Alamogordo**, 907 S White Sands Blvd, Alamogordo, NM 88310; tel 505/437-5090 or toll free 800/325-2525; fax 505/434-5667. A pleasant, standard motel, offering basic services and amenities. **Rooms:** 40 rms. CI 2pm/CO 11am. Nonsmoking rms avail. **Amenities:** 🕾 A/C, cable TV w/movies. **Services:** 🖐 🕹 **Facilities:** 🔧 ♿ Washer/dryer. **Rates (CP):** $38–$45 S; $45–$52 D. Extra person $5. Children under 13 stay free. Pking: Outdoor, free. Maj CC.

Restaurants 🍴

Furgi's Pub, 817 Scenic Dr, Alamogordo; tel 505/437-9564. **Seafood/Steak.** A friendly, dimly lit place, with ceiling fans and record albums and movie and car posters on the walls. Offers steaks and fresh seafood, including mako shark steak, as well as pasta, salads, and Mexican dishes. The bar is open until 2am. **FYI:** Reservations accepted. Band/country music/rock. Children's menu. **Open:** Mon–Sat 11am–10pm. Closed Dec 25. **Prices:** Main courses $7.95–$21.95. Ltd CC.

Ramona's, 2913 N White Sands Blvd, Alamogordo; tel 505/437-7616. **American/Mexican.** Cheerful, open dining room. Specializes in Mexican food, but also serves steak, chicken, trout, hamburgers, and sandwiches. Favorites are the special Mexican plate and the chimichangas. Locally grown chile peppers are used. **FYI:** Reservations accepted. Children's menu. Beer and wine only. **Open:** Daily 6am–10pm. Closed some hols. **Prices:** Main courses $4.75–$9.50. Maj CC. 🎬

Attractions 💼

White Sands National Monument, US 70/82; tel 505/479-6124. The park preserves the best part of the world's largest gypsum dune field, an area of 275 miles of pure white gypsum sand that reaches out over the floor of the Tularosa Basin in wavelike dunes. The 16-mile Dunes Drive loops through the "heart of sands" from the visitor center. Visitors can leave their cars at established parking areas to explore the area on foot. **Open:** Visitors center, daily 8am–4:30pm; dunes, daily 7am–sunset. $

Space Center, Scenic Dr and Indian Wells Rd; tel 505/437-2840. This is in 2 parts—the **International Space Hall of Fame** and the **Clyde W Tombaugh Space Theater**. The Space Hall of Fame occupies the Golden Cube, a 5-story building with walls of golden glass. Exhibits recall the accomplishments of the first astronauts and cosmonauts. Also on display are a spacecraft and a lunar exploration model, a space-station plan, a hands-on cutaway of a crew module called Space Station 2001, and explanations of life in space aboard Skylab and Salyut. On adjacent grounds is the Sonic Wind sled, which tested human endurance to speeds exceeding 600 mph in preparation for future space flights. At the Tombaugh Theater, OMNIMAX and Spitz 512 Planetarium Systems create earthly and cosmic experiences on a 2,700-square-foot screen. Twenty special-effects projectors can show 2,354 stars, the Milky Way, all the visible planets, and the sun and moon. Call ahead for show times. **Open:** Daily 9am–5pm. Closed Dec 25. $

Alameda Park Zoo, 1021 N White Sands Blvd; tel 505/439-4290. Established in 1898, it is the oldest zoo in the Southwest. Its collection includes hundreds of mammals and birds from around the world. **Open:** Daily 9am–5pm. Closed some hols. $

Tularosa Basin Historical Society Museum, 1301 N White Sands Blvd; tel 505/437-6120. Artifacts and photographs recall regional history. **Open:** Mon–Sat 10am–4pm, Sun 1–4pm. Closed some hols. Free.

Oliver Lee Memorial State Park, 409 Dog Canyon Rd; tel 505/437-8284. Nestled at the mouth of Dog Canyon in a stunning break in the steep escarpment of the Sacramento Mountains, this site has drawn human visitors for thousands of years. Dog Canyon was one of the last strongholds of the Mescalero Apache, and was the site of battles between them and the US Cavalry in the 19th century. Today springs and seeps support a variety of rare and endangered plant species, as well as a rich wildlife. Hiking trails into the foothills are well marked; the park also offers picnic and camping grounds. **Open:** Daily 7am–sunset; visitor center 9am–4pm. Closed some hols. $

ALBUQUERQUE

Map page M-3, B2

TOURIST INFORMATION

Albuquerque Convention and Visitors Bureau Main office at 121 Tijeras NE, 1st floor (tel 505/243-3696 or toll free 800/284-2282). Open Mon–Fri 8am–5pm. Additional information center at Albuquerque International Airport, bottom of escalator, lower level; open daily 9:30am–8pm. Also, on Romero St in Old Town; open Mon–Sat 10am–5pm, Sun 11am–5pm.

PUBLIC TRANSPORTATION

Sun Tran of Albuquerque Buses Operate 6am–6pm, depending on route. Fares 75¢ adults, 25¢ children 5–18, children under 5 free. For information call 505/843-9200.

Hotels

Albuquerque Hilton, 1901 University Blvd NE, Albuquerque, NM 87102; tel 505/884-2500 or toll free 800/821-1901; fax 505/889-9118. Menaul Blvd exit off I-25. A lovely, well-kept, and surprisingly quiet hotel just a block off I-25, with a gracious, comfortable atmosphere. **Rooms:** 264 rms and stes. CI 3pm/CO noon. Express checkout avail. Nonsmoking rms avail. Rooms have southwestern decor and New Mexican art. Top-floor rooms have cathedral ceilings. **Amenities:** A/C, cable TV w/movies, voice mail, shoe polisher. All units w/terraces. Refrigerators are available; some rooms have bathroom telephones. **Services:** Car-rental desk, babysitting. **Facilities:** 2 rsts (see also "Restaurants" below), 1 bar (w/entertainment), sauna, steam rm, whirlpool. **Rates:** $95–$125 S; $105–$130 D; from $350 ste. Extra person $10. Children under 18 stay free. Spec packages avail. Pking: Outdoor, free. Maj CC.

Albuquerque Marriott Hotel, 2101 Louisiana Blvd NE, Albuquerque, NM 87110; tel 505/581-6800 or toll free 800/334-2086; fax 505/881-1780. This is a luxurious, full-service high-rise hotel close to Albuquerque's 2 major shopping centers and uptown businesses. **Rooms:** 410 rms and stes. CI 3pm/CO noon. Express checkout avail. Nonsmoking rms avail. **Amenities:** A/C, cable TV w/movies, refrig, voice mail. Some units w/minibars. **Services:** Babysitting. **Facilities:** 2 rsts (see also "Restaurants" below), 1 bar, spa, sauna, whirlpool, washer/dryer. **Rates:** $125 S; $140 D; from $250 ste. Extra person $10. Higher rates for spec evnts/hols. Spec packages avail. Pking: Outdoor, free. Maj CC.

Best Western Fred Harvey, 2910 Yale Blvd SE, Albuquerque, NM 87106; tel 505/843-7000 or toll free 800/227-1117; fax 505/843-6307. Exit 222A (Gibson Ave) off I-25. In a good location for business travelers, right near the airport. **Rooms:** 266 rms and stes. CI 2pm/CO 1pm. Nonsmoking rms avail. **Amenities:** A/C, cable TV w/movies. All units w/terraces. **Services:** Babysitting. **Facilities:** 2 rsts, 1 bar, spa, sauna, washer/dryer. **Rates:** $90 S; $100 D; from $150 ste. Extra person $10. Children under 12 stay free. Pking: Outdoor, free. Maj CC.

Best Western Winrock Inn, 18 Winrock Center NE, Albuquerque, NM 87110; tel 505/883-5252 or toll free 800/866-5252; fax 505/889-3206. Louisiana Blvd exit off I-40. A conveniently located, urban motel adjacent to a major shopping center and close to I-40. **Rooms:** 173 rms and stes. CI 3pm/CO noon. Nonsmoking rms avail. **Amenities:** A/C, cable TV w/movies. Some units w/terraces. Suites have refrigerators. **Services:** Car-rental desk. Rates include 2 evening cocktails per adult and soft drinks for children. **Facilities:** Washer/dryer. **Rates (BB):** $62 S; $72 D; from $85 ste. Extra person $7. Children under 12 stay free. Higher rates for spec evnts/hols. Spec packages avail. Pking: Outdoor, free. Maj CC.

Holiday Inn Midtown, 2020 Menaul Blvd NE, Albuquerque, NM 87007; tel 505/884-2511 or toll free 800/HOL-IDAY; fax 505/881-4806. An attractive motel conveniently located near both I-25 and I-40. **Rooms:** 363 rms. CI 2pm/CO noon. Nonsmoking rms avail. There are king leisure rooms designed for business travelers. **Amenities:** A/C, cable TV w/movies. Some units w/terraces, some w/Jacuzzis. **Services:** Car-rental desk, babysitting. **Facilities:** 1 rst, 1 bar (w/entertainment), games rm, spa, sauna, whirlpool, washer/dryer. Exercise facilities include a full Nautilus gym. **Rates:** HS Mar–Oct $89 S; $99 D. Extra person $10. Children under 18 stay free. Lower rates off-season. Higher rates for spec evnts/hols. Pking: Outdoor, free. Maj CC.

Holiday Inn Pyramid, 5151 San Francisco Rd NE, Albuquerque, NM 87109; tel 505/821-3333 or toll free 800/HOL-IDAY; fax 505/828-0230. Exit 232 off I-25. A luxurious hotel on the north side of Albuquerque, especially suitable for business travelers and conventioneers. **Rooms:** 311 rms and stes. CI 3pm/CO noon. Express checkout avail. Nonsmoking rms avail. Rooms are well-appointed and very comfortable. **Amenities:** 🔳 🅰 🔲 A/C, cable TV w/movies, refrig, shoe polisher. Some units w/terraces. **Services:** ✗ 🔑 🚗 🖨 ⬅ ⬉ Car-rental desk, children's program, babysitting. **Facilities:** 🏊 🍴 🔲 ⬇ 2 rsts, 2 bars (1 w/entertainment), spa, sauna, steam rm, whirlpool, washer/dryer. **Rates:** $100–$130 S; $110–$140 D; from $115 ste. Extra person $10. Children under 17 stay free. Higher rates for spec evnts/hols. Spec packages avail. Pking: Outdoor, free. Maj CC.

≋≋≋ **Howard Johnson Plaza Hotel**, 6000 Pan American Fwy NE, Albuquerque, NM 87109; tel 505/821-9451 or toll free 800/544-9881; fax 505/858-0239. Handsome hotel in the

northeast part of Albuquerque, close to I-25 access to Santa Fe and northern New Mexico. **Rooms:** 150 rms and stes. CI 3pm/CO noon. Nonsmoking rms avail. **Amenities:** 🔳 🅰 🔲 🍽 A/C, cable TV w/movies, refrig, in-rm safe. Some units w/minibars, some w/terraces. **Services:** ✗ 🚗 🖨 ⬅ ⬉ Babysitting. **Facilities:** 🏊 🍴 🔲 ⬇ 1 rst, 1 bar, spa, washer/dryer. **Rates:** $60 S; $70 D; from $65 ste. Extra person $10. Children under 12 stay free. Higher rates for spec evnts/hols. Pking: Outdoor, free. Maj CC.

≋≋≋ **Hyatt Regency**, 330 Tijeras Ave NW, Albuquerque, NM 87102; tel 505/842-1234 or toll free 800/233-1234; fax 505/766-6710. A luxurious high-rise hotel, catering to practically every need of the business or pleasure traveler. Next to the Albuquerque Convention Center. **Rooms:** 395 rms and stes. CI

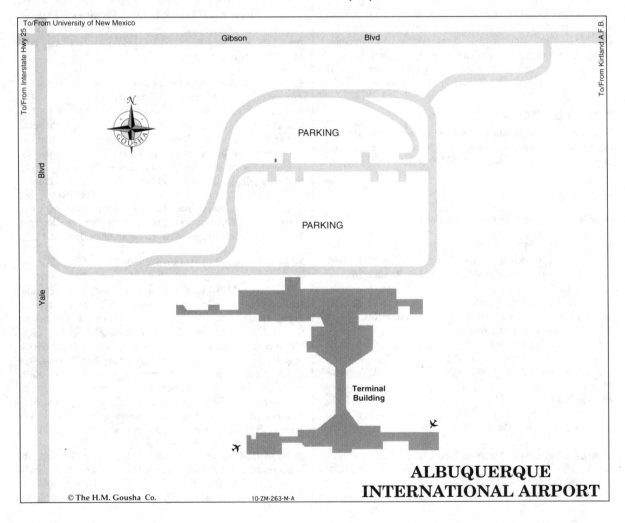

To/From University of New Mexico

To/From Interstate Hwy 25

To/From Kirtland A.F.B.

Gibson   Blvd

Blvd

Yale

PARKING

PARKING

Terminal Building

ALBUQUERQUE INTERNATIONAL AIRPORT

© The H.M. Gousha Co.   10-ZM-263-M-A

3pm/CO noon. Express checkout avail. Nonsmoking rms avail. **Amenities:** 🔒 ⚗ 🖨 🍴 A/C, cable TV w/movies, voice mail. **Services:** ✗ 🔜 VP 🚗 🗺 🛏 🍷 Car-rental desk, masseur, babysitting. **Facilities:** 🛗 🛎 1.5K 🖥 ⚽ 1 rst (see also "Restaurants" below), 2 bars (1 w/entertainment), spa, sauna, beauty salon. **Rates:** HS Aug–Oct $131 S; $151 D; from $310 ste. Extra person $10. Children under 18 stay free. Lower rates off-season. Spec packages avail. Pking: Indoor, $7. Maj CC.

🏛🏛🏛 **La Posada de Albuquerque**, 125 2nd St NW, Albuquerque, NM 87102; tel 505/242-9090 or toll free 800/777-5732; fax 505/242-8664. 1 block N of Central Ave. Charming, historic hotel, built by Conrad Hilton in 1939. **Rooms:** 114 rms and stes. CI 3pm/CO 11am. Nonsmoking rms avail. Rooms have southwestern decor, with handmade furniture and Mexican tiles. **Amenities:** 🔒 ⚗ 🍴 A/C, cable TV w/movies, refrig. **Services:** ✗ VP 🚗 🗺 🛏 Babysitting. **Facilities:** 300 ⚽ 1 rst, 2 bars (1 w/entertainment), beauty salon. Guests have access to a health club next door. **Rates:** $92 S; $102 D; from $105 ste. Extra person $10. Children under 12 stay free. Spec packages avail. Pking: Outdoor, free. Maj CC.

🏛🏛🏛 **Plaza Inn**, 900 Medical Arts Ave NE, Albuquerque, NM 87102; tel 505/243-5693 or toll free 800/237-1307; fax 505/843-6229. Located close to the University of New Mexico and the attractions and restaurants of historic Old Town. Offers similar services and amenities to larger, more expensive motels. **Rooms:** 120 rms. CI 3pm/CO noon. Express checkout avail. Nonsmoking rms avail. Pleasantly decorated rooms have large desks. **Amenities:** 🔒 ⚗ 🖨 🍴 A/C, cable TV w/movies, refrig. Some units w/terraces. **Services:** ✗ 🚗 🗺 🛏 🍷 Babysitting. **Facilities:** 🛗 🛎 50 ⚽ 1 rst, 1 bar, spa, washer/dryer. **Rates:** $70–$80 S; $80 D. Extra person $5. Children under 12 stay free. Higher rates for spec evnts/hols. Pking: Outdoor, free. Maj CC.

🏛🏛🏛 **Ramada Hotel Classic**, 6815 Menaul Blvd NE, Albuquerque, NM 87110; tel 505/881-0000 or toll free 800/252-7772; fax 505/881-3736. Exit 162 off I-40. An attractive uptown hotel, adjacent to Albuquerque's largest shopping mall and close to the city's business and financial district. A good location for both business travelers and vacationers. **Rooms:** 296 rms and stes. CI 4pm/CO noon. Nonsmoking rms avail. Rooms have a subtle southwestern decor. **Amenities:** 🔒 A/C, cable TV w/movies, refrig, voice mail. **Services:** 🍽 🚗 🗺 🛏 🍷 Social director, babysitting. There's an American Airlines ticket counter in the lobby. **Facilities:** 🛗 🛎 1K ⚽ 2 rsts, 2 bars (1 w/entertainment), spa, sauna, whirlpool, washer/dryer. Close to tennis, golf, and downhill skiing. The main ballroom has crystal chandeliers and a Wurlitzer organ. **Rates:** $89–$119 S; $99–$129 D; from $125 ste. Extra person $10. Children under 12 stay free. Spec packages avail. Pking: Outdoor, free. Maj CC.

🏛🏛🏛 **Residence Inn**, 3300 Prospect Ave NE, Albuquerque, NM 87107; tel 505/881-2661 or toll free 800/331-3131; fax 505/884-5551. Exit 160 off I-40. Centrally located, and a good choice for those staying more than a night or two. **Rooms:** 112 stes. CI 2pm/CO noon. Nonsmoking rms avail. Condominium-like units have complete kitchens. **Amenities:** 🔒 ⚗ 🖨 🍴 A/C, cable TV w/movies, refrig. Some units w/terraces, all w/fireplaces. **Services:** 🚗 🗺 🛏 🍷 Babysitting. **Facilities:** 🛗 🍷 🛎 40 ⚽ Spa, whirlpool, washer/dryer. **Rates (CP):** From $75 ste. Children under 12 stay free. Higher rates for spec evnts/hols. Spec packages avail. Pking: Outdoor, free. Maj CC.

🏛🏛🏛 **Sheraton Old Town**, 800 Rio Grande Blvd NW, Albuquerque, NM 87104 (Old Town); tel 505/843-6300 or toll free 800/237-2133; fax 505/842-9863. A luxurious hotel in historic Old Town, within walking distance of numerous restaurants, shops, and attractions. **Rooms:** 190 rms and stes. CI 3pm/CO 1pm. Nonsmoking rms avail. **Amenities:** 🔒 ⚗ 🍴 A/C, cable TV w/movies, refrig. **Services:** ✗ 🚗 🗺 🛏 Masseur, babysitting. **Facilities:** 🛗 🛎 300 ⚽ 2 rsts, 2 bars (1 w/entertainment), spa, sauna, steam rm, whirlpool, beauty salon. A downhill ski area is within 20 miles. **Rates:** $95–$140 S; $110–$140 D; from $140 ste. Extra person $10. Children under 17 stay free. Higher rates for spec evnts/hols. Spec packages avail. Pking: Outdoor, free. Maj CC.

Motels

🏛🏛🏛 **Amberly Suite Hotel**, 7620 Pan American NE, Albuquerque, NM 87109; tel 505/823-1300 or toll free 800/333-9806; fax 505/823-2896. Exit 231 off I-25. These apartment-like suites are excellent for families or business travelers who need extra room to work. **Rooms:** 170 stes. CI 3pm/CO noon. Nonsmoking rms avail. Comfortable, homey rooms. **Amenities:** 🔒 ⚗ 🖨 A/C, cable TV w/movies, refrig. **Services:** 🚗 🗺 🛏 🍷 Babysitting. **Facilities:** 🛗 🛎 100 ⚽ 1 rst, 1 bar, spa, sauna, whirlpool, washer/dryer. The fitness center is open 24 hours. **Rates:** From $94 ste. Extra person $10. Children under 12 stay free. Spec packages avail. Pking: Outdoor, free. Maj CC.

🏛 **American Inn**, 4501 Central Ave NE, Albuquerque, NM 87108 (Nob Hill); tel 505/262-1681. Good, basic lodging near the University of New Mexico campus, completely renovated in 1989. **Rooms:** 130 rms and stes. CI open/CO 11am. Nonsmoking rms avail. **Amenities:** 🔒 A/C, cable TV w/movies. Some units w/terraces. **Services:** 🛏 Babysitting. **Facilities:** 🛗 30 **Rates:** $23 S; $27–$33 D; from $35 ste. Extra person $10. Children under 12 stay free. Higher rates for spec evnts/hols. Pking: Outdoor, free. Maj CC.

≣≣ Best Western Airport Inn, 2400 Yale Blvd SE, Albuquerque, NM 87106; or toll free 800/528-1234; fax 505/243-0620. A Mexican hacienda–style motel, close to Albuquerque International Airport. **Rooms:** 120 rms and stes. CI 1pm/CO noon. Nonsmoking rms avail. Pleasant, comfortable rooms, decorated with silk flowers, posters, and old photos. Surprisingly quiet. **Amenities:** 🛏 ⚱ A/C, cable TV w/movies. Some units w/terraces. **Services:** 🚗 🛆 🖵 The adjacent Village Inn restaurant provides take-out and occasional room service. **Facilities:** 🚇 ᕒ Whirlpool. **Rates (CP):** HS Apr 15–Oct $59 S; $64 D; from $120 ste. Extra person $5. Children under 12 stay free. Lower rates off-season. Pking: Outdoor, free. Maj CC.

≣≣ Clubhouse Inn, 1315 Menaul Blvd NE, Albuquerque, NM 87107; tel 505/345-0010 or toll free 800/258-2466; fax 505/344-3911. Lomas Ave exit off I-25. A homey, centrally located motel. **Rooms:** 137 rms and stes. CI 2pm/CO noon. Express checkout avail. Nonsmoking rms avail. Guest rooms have plenty of work space. **Amenities:** 🛏 ⚱ 🖵 📶 A/C, cable TV w/movies, refrig. Some units w/terraces, some w/Jacuzzis. Suites have refrigerators, microwaves, and wet bars. **Services:** 🛆 🖵 Babysitting. Coffee, tea, and hot chocolate are available 24 hours. **Facilities:** 🚇 📶 ᕒ Whirlpool, washer/dryer. Besides the pool, the patio has a sun deck and barbecue grills. **Rates (BB):** $63 S; $73 D; from $79 ste. Extra person $10. Children under 11 stay free. Spec packages avail. Pking: Outdoor, free. Maj CC.

≣≣≣ Courtyard by Marriott, 1920 Yale Blvd SE, Albuquerque, NM 87106 (Albuquerque Int'l Airport); tel 505/843-6600 or toll free 800/321-2211; fax 505/843-8740. Gibson Blvd exit off I-25. Well-appointed motel, close to the airport. **Rooms:** 150 rms and stes. CI 4pm/CO 1pm. Express checkout avail. Nonsmoking rms avail. **Amenities:** 🛏 ⚱ 🖵 📶 A/C, cable TV w/movies, refrig, voice mail. There are extra-long phone cords, a large work desk, and shower massage. **Services:** ✕ 🚗 🛆 🖵 Babysitting. In-room coffee and tea service provided. **Facilities:** 🚇 📶 📶 ᕒ 1 rst, 1 bar, spa, whirlpool, washer/dryer. **Rates:** $79 S; $89 D; from $93 ste. Children under 12 stay free. Pking: Outdoor, free. Maj CC.

≣≣ Fairfield Inn, 1760 Menaul Rd NE, Albuquerque, NM 87102; tel 505/889-4000 or toll free 800/228-2800; fax 505/889-4000. Exit 227A off I-25. This new Marriott has many of the amenities and services found at full-service hotels but at more economical rates. **Rooms:** 186 rms. CI 3pm/CO noon. Express checkout avail. Nonsmoking rms avail. **Amenities:** 🛏 ⚱ A/C, cable TV w/movies. Some units w/terraces. **Services:** 🚗 🛆 🖵 Babysitting. **Facilities:** 🚇 📶 📶 🖵 ᕒ Sauna, whirlpool, washer/dryer. **Rates (CP):** $50 S; $60 D. Extra person $10. Children under 19 stay free. Higher rates for spec evnts/hols. Spec packages avail. Pking: Outdoor, free. Maj CC.

≣≣ Hampton Inn, 5101 Ellison NE, Albuquerque, NM 87109; tel 505/344-1555 or toll free 800/426-7866; fax 505/345-2216. Exit 231 off I-25. A better-than-average motel on the north side of Albuquerque, a good location for those viewing the annual balloon fiesta in October, or planning day trips to Santa Fe. **Rooms:** 125 rms. CI 2pm/CO noon. Nonsmoking rms avail. **Amenities:** 🛏 ⚱ 🖵 A/C, cable TV w/movies. **Services:** 🛆 🖵 Babysitting. **Facilities:** 🚇 📶 ᕒ Guests receive free use of a health club 1 mile away. **Rates (CP):** $54–$56 S; $59 D. Children under 18 stay free. Higher rates for spec evnts/hols. Spec packages avail. Pking: Outdoor, free. Maj CC.

≣≣ La Quinta Inn, 2116 Yale Blvd SE, Albuquerque, NM 87106; tel 505/243-5500 or toll free 800/531-5900; fax 505/247-8288. 1 mi E of I-25 Gibson/airport exit. Pleasant motel close to Albuquerque International Airport. **Rooms:** 105 rms and stes. CI 3pm/CO noon. Nonsmoking rms avail. Attractive, nicely furnished rooms. **Amenities:** 🛏 ⚱ A/C, cable TV w/movies. All units w/terraces. **Services:** 🚗 🛆 🖵 🔸 Babysitting. **Facilities:** 🚇 📶 ᕒ Washer/dryer. **Rates:** $53–$59 S; $61–$68 D; from $65 ste. Extra person $7.50. Children under 18 stay free. Pking: Outdoor, free. Maj CC.

≣≣ Le Baron Inn and Suites, 2120 Menaul Blvd NE, Albuquerque, NM 87107; tel 505/884-0250 or toll free 800/444-7378; fax 505/883-0594. Exit 160 off I-40. A well-appointed motel in the center of Albuquerque. **Rooms:** 200 rms and stes. CI 2pm/CO noon. Nonsmoking rms avail. Basic rooms are simply but nicely decorated; the suites are more plush. **Amenities:** 🛏 ⚱ A/C, cable TV w/movies, shoe polisher. Suites have refrigerators and microwave ovens. **Services:** 🚗 🛆 🖵 **Facilities:** 🚇 📶 Washer/dryer. **Rates (CP):** $52–$65 S; $62–$75 D; from $80 ste. Children under 12 stay free. Pking: Outdoor, free. Maj CC.

≣ Motel 6, 1701 University Blvd NE, Albuquerque, NM 87102; tel 505/843-9228. Exit 160 off I-40. A clean, basic motel for the budget-conscious. **Rooms:** 118 rms. CI 2pm/CO noon. Nonsmoking rms avail. Simple but quite adequate. **Amenities:** 🛏 A/C, cable TV w/movies. **Services:** 🛆 Babysitting. **Facilities:** 🚇 ᕒ **Rates:** $27 S; $33 D. Extra person $3. Children under 18 stay free. Pking: Outdoor, free. Maj CC.

≣≣ Radisson Inn, 1901 University Blvd SE, Albuquerque, NM 87106 (Albuquerque Int'l Airport); tel 505/247-0512 or toll free 800/333-3333; fax 505/843-7148. A handsome property right near the airport. **Rooms:** 148 rms and stes. CI 3pm/CO noon. Express checkout avail. Nonsmoking rms avail. Spacious rooms have queen- or king-size beds. **Amenities:** 🛏 ⚱ 🖵 📶 A/C, cable TV w/movies. **Services:** ✕ 🚗 🛆 🖵 🔸 Babysitting. **Facilities:** 🚇 📶 ᕒ 1 rst, 1 bar (w/entertainment), whirlpool.

Rates: $85 S; $95 D; from $95 ste. Extra person $10. Children under 17 stay free. Spec packages avail. Pking: Outdoor, free. Maj CC.

≣≣ **Travelers Inn**, 411 McKnight Ave NW, Albuquerque, NM 87102; tel 505/242-5228 or toll free 800/633-8300; fax 505/766-9218. Exit 159A off I-40. A well-kept motel built in 1991. Close to the shops, galleries, and attractions of historic Old Town. **Rooms:** 96 rms and stes. CI 2pm/CO 11am. Nonsmoking rms avail. The simple rooms are comfortable and furnished in wood tones, with stucco walls. **Amenities:** 🛏 A/C, cable TV w/movies. **Services:** 🚐 🛎 **Facilities:** 🔒 🏊 🛠 Whirlpool. **Rates (CP):** $41 S; $48 D; from $62 ste. Extra person $4. Children under 12 stay free. Higher rates for spec evnts/hols. Pking: Outdoor, free. Maj CC.

Inns

≣≣ **Casas de Suenos**, 310 Rio Grande Blvd SW, Albuquerque, NM 87104 (Old Town); tel 505/247-4560 or toll free 800/CHAT-W/US; fax 505/842-8493. 2 blocks S of Central Ave. A delightful getaway in historic Old Town. Lovely shaded grounds. Unsuitable for children under 13. **Rooms:** 16 ctges/villas. CI 3pm/CO 11am. No smoking. Authentic Spanish decor, with each room following an individual theme. **Amenities:** 🛏 🛁 🍴 A/C, cable TV, refrig, VCR. All units w/terraces, some w/fireplaces, some w/Jacuzzis. **Services:** ✕ 🔑 Masseur, afternoon tea served. **Facilities:** 🪑 **Rates (BB):** From $85 ctge/villa. Extra person $15. Pking: Outdoor, free. Ltd CC.

≣≣≣ **The WE Mauger Estate**, 701 Roma Ave NW, Albuquerque, NM 87102; tel 505/242-8755. A charming, historic inn. **Rooms:** 8 rms. CI 4pm/CO 11am. No smoking. Rooms are decorated with Victorian elegance. **Amenities:** 🛁 📺 🍴 A/C, refrig. No phone or TV. There are no room televisions, but the guest lounge offers a TV and about 200 recorded movies. **Services:** ✕ 🔑 🛎 Wine/sherry served. **Rates (BB):** $59–$89 S w/shared bath, $69–$109 S w/private bath. Extra person $15. Min stay spec evnts. Spec packages avail. Pking: Outdoor, free. Ltd CC.

Restaurants 🍽

Artichoke Cafe, 424 Central Ave SE, Albuquerque; tel 505/243-0200. 1½ blocks E of Broadway. **New American.** Art deco dining room with modern art on the walls. Imaginative variations on American and continental cuisine, including baked chicken stuffed with goat cheese, spinach and roasted red pepper, and New Zealand mussels with sweet Italian sausage in white wine. **FYI:** Reservations accepted. Children's menu. Beer and wine

only. No smoking. **Open:** Lunch Mon–Fri 11am–2:30pm; dinner Mon–Sat 5–10pm. Closed some hols. **Prices:** Main courses $8.95–$19.95. Maj CC. 💟 🍴 🛠

Bangkok Cafe, 5901 Central Ave NE, Albuquerque; tel 505/255-5036. 2 blocks E of San Mateo Blvd. **Thai.** Genuine Thai cuisine. Especially popular is Thai pad priew whan goong, which is Thai-style sweet-and-sour shrimp. **FYI:** Reservations not accepted. Beer and wine only. **Open:** Lunch Mon–Fri 11am–2pm; dinner Sun–Thurs 5–9pm, Fri–Sat 5–9:30pm. Closed some hols. **Prices:** Main courses $4.95–$9.25. Maj CC. 🍴 🛠

★ **Cafe Oceana**, 1414 Central Ave SE, Albuquerque; tel 505/247-2233. **Seafood.** Historic 1928 building, with tin ceilings and hardwood floors. Fresh seafood, including shrimp oceana, crab and shrimp rellenos, and a catch of the day. There's also a popular oyster bar. **FYI:** Reservations accepted. **Open:** Mon–Fri 11am–11pm, Sat 5–11pm. Closed some hols. **Prices:** Main courses $7.95–$19.95. Maj CC. 💟 🛠

★ **Catalina's Mexican Restaurant**, 400 San Felipe St NW, Albuquerque (Old Town); tel 505/842-6907. **Mexican.** Located in a historic adobe building. Traditional New Mexico–style Mexican food. **FYI:** Reservations not accepted. No liquor license. **Open:** Mon 8am–1pm, Tues–Wed 8am–4pm, Thurs–Sat 8am–8pm. Closed some hols. **Prices:** Main courses $2.95–$7.95. Maj CC. 🍴 🛒 🛠

Cervante's, 5801 Gibson Blvd SE, Albuquerque; tel 505/262-2253. At San Pedro Blvd. **Mexican.** Classic Spanish decor. New Mexico–style Mexican food, including chiles rellenos, enchiladas, burritos, and stuffed sopaipillas. Also at: 10030 Central Ave SE, Albuquerque (505/275-3266). **FYI:** Reservations accepted. **Open:** Daily 11am–10pm. Closed some hols. **Prices:** Main courses $4.95–$12.95. Maj CC. 💟 🛠

Chili's Grill and Bar, 6909 Menaul Blvd NE, Albuquerque; tel 505/883-4321. **Burgers/Southwestern.** Casual bar atmosphere. Features burgers, available with or without green chiles or guacamole, and steaks, chicken, and Mexican dishes. **FYI:** Reservations not accepted. **Open:** Mon–Thurs 11am–10:30pm, Fri–Sat 11am–11:30pm, Sun 11am–10pm. Closed Dec 25. **Prices:** Main courses $4.95–$9.95. Maj CC. 🛒 🛠

The Cooperage, 7220 Lomas Blvd NE, Albuquerque; tel 505/255-1657. 3 blocks E of NM State Fairgrounds. **Seafood/Steak.** The circular, wood-paneled dining room is decorated with reproductions of 19th-century art. There's a wide variety of beef, seafood, and chicken, plus buffalo steak. The house specialty is prime rib, and there's a popular soup and salad bar. **FYI:** Reservations recommended. Blues/combo. Children's menu. Dress code. **Open:** Lunch Mon–Fri 11am–2:30pm, Sat noon–

2:30; dinner Mon–Thurs 5–10pm, Fri–Sat 5–11pm, Sun noon–9pm. Closed Dec 25. **Prices:** Main courses $9–$19. Maj CC. ◉ ▦ ♿

The County Line Barbecue, 9600 Tramway Blvd NE, Albuquerque; tel 505/296-8822. Exit 234 off I-25. **Barbecue.** Generous portions of barbecued beef ribs, sausage, and brisket; plus chicken, smoked duck and pork, steaks, and salads. There's a spectacular view of the city, especially just after sunset as lights are coming on. **FYI:** Reservations not accepted. Children's menu. **Open:** Mon–Thurs 5–9pm, Fri–Sat 5–10pm, Sun 4–9pm. Closed some hols. **Prices:** Main courses $8.95–$13.95. Maj CC. ▲ ♿

ej's, 2201 Silver Ave SE, Albuquerque; tel 505/268-2233. 2 blocks S of Central Ave. **New American.** Classic college student hangout, serving up burgers, sandwiches, Mexican food, and salads. Entrees include sautéed snapper, stir-fried vegetables, and basil garlic pesto. **FYI:** Reservations not accepted. Band/guitar/singer. No liquor license. **Open:** Mon–Thurs 7am–11pm, Fri–Sat 7am–midnight, Sun 8am–9:30pm. Closed some hols. **Prices:** Main courses $3.50–$7.25. No CC. ♿

The Firehouse Restaurant at the Tram, 38 Tramway Rd, Albuquerque; tel 505/856-3473. **Southwestern/Steak.** Located at the base of Sandia Tramway, the Firehouse offers a spectacular view of the city and Rio Grande Valley, especially from the outdoor balcony. With fresh fish and seafood, chicken, and beef. Some entrees are grilled lime chicken, scallops with toasted piñons and white wine, and pepper steak. **FYI:** Reservations recommended. Piano. **Open:** HS June–Aug daily 11:30am–10pm. Reduced hours off-season. Closed some hols. **Prices:** Main courses $12–$17.95. Maj CC. ▲ ▲

★ Garduño's of Mexico, 5400 Academy Rd NE, Albuquerque; tel 505/821-3030. **Mexican.** Strolling musicians contribute to the noisy, festive atmosphere at this Mexican eatery, where the waitstaff dons Mexican dress and serves up large portions of chiles rellenos, chimichangas, carne adovada, and quesadillas. **FYI:** Reservations not accepted. Combo. Children's menu. **Open:** Mon–Thurs 11am–10pm, Fri–Sat 11am–10:30pm, Sun 10:30am–10pm. Closed some hols. **Prices:** Main courses $6.25–$12.95. Maj CC. ▦ ♿

❦ High Finance Restaurant and Tavern, 40 Tramway Rd NE, Albuquerque; tel 505/243-9742. Ride the train to the top of Sandia Peak. **Seafood/Steak.** Casually elegant mountain-top restaurant with a view of Albuquerque. Fresh seafood, prime rib, steaks, pasta, and chicken. Smoking is permitted only in the bar. The tram, which is necessary to get to the restaurant, is $12.50 per person without dinner reservations, $9.50 with reservations.

FYI: Reservations recommended. **Open:** Lunch daily 11am–4pm; dinner daily 5–9:30pm. Closed Thanksgiving. **Prices:** Main courses $13.95–$35. Ltd CC. ◉ ▲ ▲ ♿

★ High Noon Restaurant and Saloon, 425 San Felipe St NW, Albuquerque (Old Town); tel 505/765-1455. **Southwestern.** Housed in a building dating from 1785. With southwestern decor, historic photos. Features steak, seafood, chicken, pasta, and Mexican dishes. House specialties include rib-eye steak, mixed grill, and lamb chops. **FYI:** Reservations accepted. Guitar. **Open:** Mon–Sat 11am–10:30pm, Sun noon–9pm. Closed some hols. **Prices:** Main courses $9.95–$19.95. Maj CC. ▮ ♿

Humphrey's Cafe, in the New Mexico Museum of Natural History, 1801 Mountain Rd NW, Albuquerque (Old Town); tel 505/764-0058. **Cafeteria.** A busy lunch spot. **FYI:** Reservations not accepted. No liquor license. No smoking. **Open:** Daily 11am–3pm. Closed some hols. **Prices:** Lunch main courses $2.95–$6.95. No CC. ▦ ♿

Hunan Chinese Restaurant, 1218 San Pedro Blvd SE, Albuquerque; tel 505/266-3300. **Chinese.** Bright red and gold interior. Specializes in hot and spicy Mandarin cuisine, with a popular lunch buffet. Chinese wine is served. **FYI:** Reservations not accepted. Beer and wine only. **Open:** Daily 11am–9:30pm. Closed some hols. **Prices:** Main courses $6–$9. Maj CC. ▦ ♿

India Kitchen Restaurant, 6910 Montgomery Blvd NE, Albuquerque; tel 505/884-2333. **Indian.** A small, simple restaurant, decorated with Indian art. Both meat and vegetarian dishes are served. The menu provides spiciness ratings for individual dishes. **FYI:** Reservations accepted. Children's menu. Beer and wine only. No smoking. **Open:** Sun–Thurs 5–9pm, Fri–Sat 5–9:30pm. **Prices:** Main courses $5.95–$9.95. Maj CC. ◉ ▦ ♿

La Hacienda Restaurant, 302 San Felipe St NW, Albuquerque (Old Town); tel 505/243-3131. **Mexican.** Decorated in Mexican motif, with chile ristras and hanging plants. The New Mexico-style Mexican menu include chiles rellenos, chimichangas, enchiladas. Fajitas are a house specialty, along with several seafood dishes. More than a dozen varieties of margaritas. **FYI:** Reservations accepted. Singer. **Open:** Daily 11am–9pm. Closed some hols. **Prices:** Main courses $8.95–$16.95. Maj CC. ▮ ♿

La Placita, 208 San Felipe St NW, Albuquerque (Old Town); tel 505/247-2204. **New American/Mexican.** Located in an historic adobe home built in 1706, with hand-carved doors and decorated with regional art and furniture. Variety of Mexican specialties, plus steaks, chicken, and seafood. Wheelchair ramps are available on request. **FYI:** Reservations accepted. Children's menu. Beer and wine only. **Open:** HS June–Aug daily 11am–9:30pm. Reduced hours off-season. Closed some hols. **Prices:** Main courses $8.95–$13.95. Maj CC. ▮

♥ **Le Marmiton**, in Gourmet Plaza Shopping Center, 5415 Academy Blvd NE, Albuquerque; tel 505/821-6279. **French.** Considered Albuquerque's best French restaurant. Intimate, French provincial atmosphere, with indirect lighting. The poulet au poivre is excellent. Early bird specials Tuesday through Thursday from 5–6:30pm. **FYI:** Reservations recommended. Beer and wine only. No smoking. **Open:** Lunch Tues–Fri 11:30am–2pm; dinner Mon 6–9pm, Tues–Fri 5:30–9pm, Sun 6–9:30pm. Closed some hols. **Prices:** Main courses $15.95–$19.95. Maj CC. ♥ ♥

Maria Teresa, 618 Rio Grande Blvd NW, Albuquerque (Old Town); tel 505/242-3900. **Southwestern.** Classic elegance in an 1840s adobe home, furnished with Victorian antiques and paintings. Many entrees have a New Mexican twist, like the salmon with tequila-lime sauce. Also Mexican specialties. **FYI:** Reservations recommended. Children's menu. **Open:** Daily 11am–9pm. Closed Dec 25. **Prices:** Main courses $10–$21. Maj CC. ♥ ▮ ♿

McGrath's Restaurant, in the Hyatt Regency, 330 Tijeras Ave NW, Albuquerque; tel 505/766-6700. 1 block N of Central Ave at 3rd St. **Southwestern.** Plush but casual decor. Gourmet dishes are prepared with a southwestern twist, such as filet mignon brushed with red chile butter, and southwest chicken and chorizo confit. **FYI:** Reservations recommended. Children's menu. **Open:** Daily 6:30am–10:30pm. **Prices:** Main courses $12.50–$20. Maj CC. ♥ ▮ VP ♿

★ **Monte Vista Fire Station**, 3201 Central Ave NE, Albuquerque (Nob Hill); tel 505/255-2424. **New American.** A 1936 art deco fire station. Imaginative variations of classic American and continental dishes. The menu includes grilled sliced sirloin with forest mushroom sauce, and wild mushroom ravioli. **FYI:** Reservations recommended. **Open:** Lunch Mon–Fri 11–2:30pm; dinner Sun–Thurs 5–10:30pm, Fri–Sat 5–11pm. Closed Dec 25. **Prices:** Main courses $8.95–$16.95. Maj CC. ⚓ ♿

★ **New Chinatown**, 5001 Central Avenue NE, Albuquerque; tel 505/265-8859. 3 blocks W of San Mateo Blvd. **Chinese.** Statues of foo dogs guard the entrances. Walls are decorated with paintings of Chinese scenes and souvenirs from China; lighting is subdued and unobtrusive. Many Szechuan specialties are included on the mostly Cantonese menu. Sweet-and-sour shrimp and sweet-and-sour pork are two of the more than 40 dishes. Portions are large; there's a buffet lunch daily except Saturday.

FYI: Reservations not accepted. **Open:** Daily 11am–10pm. Closed Thanksgiving. **Prices:** Main courses $6.95–$19.95. Maj CC. ♥ ▮ ▦ ♿

♥ **Nicole's**, in the Albuquerque Marriott Hotel, 2101 Louisiana Blvd NE, Albuquerque; tel 505/881-6800. Louisiana Blvd exit off I-40. **Continental.** An intimate dining room, decorated with reproductions of 19th-century art. Creative variations on classic continental cuisine: breast of chicken with chorizo sausage, veal medallions with pink peppercorn sauce, and grilled swordfish medallions. **FYI:** Reservations recommended. Dress code. **Open:** Lunch Mon–Fri 11:30am–2:30pm; dinner daily 6–10pm. **Prices:** Main courses $19–$25. Maj CC. ♥ ♿

Pelican's, 9800 Montgomery Blvd NE, Albuquerque; tel 505/298-7678. At Eubank Blvd. **Seafood/Steak.** Decorated in maritime motif; specializing in fresh fish, seafood, prime rib, and steaks. **FYI:** Reservations recommended. Children's menu. **Open:** Sun–Thurs 5–10:30pm, Fri–Sat 5–11:30pm. Closed some hols. **Prices:** Main courses $5.95–$24.95. Maj CC. ♥ ⚓ ♿

♥ **Rancher's Club**, in the Albuquerque Hilton, 1901 University Blvd NE, Albuquerque; tel 505/884-2500. Menaul Blvd exit off I-25. **Seafood/Steak.** Considered one of Albuquerque's finest restaurants. Styled in western elegance, with polished wood and a stone fireplace. Large steaks and a wide choice of poultry and seafood are grilled over different aromatic woods on different days, producing unique flavors. **FYI:** Reservations recommended. Piano/singer. **Open:** Lunch Mon–Fri 11:30am–2pm; dinner Mon–Thurs 5:30–10pm, Fri–Sat 5:30–10:30pm, Sun 5:30–9pm; brunch Sun 10am–2pm. **Prices:** Main courses $18.95–$28. Maj CC. ♥ ▮ ▣ ♿

Rio Grande Yacht Club, in the Airport Center, 2500 Yale Blvd SE, Albuquerque; tel 505/243-6111. **Seafood/Steak.** Maritime-themed restaurant, with a tropical garden. Seafood is flown in fresh daily. Also steaks and seafood/beef combinations. **FYI:** Reservations recommended. Children's menu. **Open:** Lunch Mon–Fri 11am–2pm; dinner daily 5:30–10:30pm. Closed some hols. **Prices:** Main courses $9.95–$16.95. Maj CC. ♥ ⚓ ▣

Sadie's, 6230 4th St NW, Albuquerque; tel 505/345-5339. Exit 228 off I-25. Go 1½ miles west on Montaño Rd then north on 4th St. **American/Mexican.** A busy, no-frills restaurant specializing in burgers, steaks (some smothered in chiles), and such Mexican selections as stuffed sopaipillas, enchiladas, and carne adovada. **FYI:** Reservations not accepted. Children's menu. **Open:** Mon–Sat 11am–10pm, Sun 11am–9pm. Closed some hols. **Prices:** Main courses $5.95–$12.95. Maj CC. ▦ ♿

Scalo, in Nob Hill Center, 3500 Central Ave SE, Albuquerque; tel 505/255-8781. **Italian.** Bistro-style restaurant specializing in northern Italian cuisine, with homemade pastas as well as meat, chicken, and fish entrees. **FYI:** Reservations recommended. **Open:** Lunch Mon–Sat 11:30am–2:30pm; dinner Mon–Sat 5–11pm, Sun 5–9pm. Closed some hols. **Prices:** Main courses $9.95–$16.95. Maj CC. ♥ ♨ 🏞 ⚹

Seagull Street Fish Market, 5410 Academy Rd NE, Albuquerque; tel 505/821-0020. Exit 230 off I-25. **Seafood.** An attractive seafood restaurant offering outdoor dining beside a freshwater lagoon. Fresh mesquite-grilled fish includes Pacific snapper Vera Cruz and skewered monkfish. Beef and pasta also available. **FYI:** Reservations recommended. Island music. Children's menu. **Open:** Lunch Sun–Fri 11am–2:30pm; dinner Mon–Thurs 5–10pm, Fri–Sat 5–11pm, Sun noon–9pm. Closed Dec 25. **Prices:** Main courses $8.99–$23.95. Maj CC. ♥ ♨ 🏞 🎭 ⚹

66 Diner, 1405 Central Ave NE, Albuquerque; tel 505/247-1421. **Diner.** 1950s-style diner. Photos of Elvis and Marilyn Monroe. Burgers, sandwiches, and blue plate specials, including chicken pot pie and fried catfish. Old-fashioned malts and other fountain drinks. **FYI:** Reservations accepted. Children's menu. Beer and wine only. **Open:** Mon–Thurs 9am–11pm, Fri 9am–midnight, Sat 8am–midnight, Sun 8am–10pm. Closed some hols. **Prices:** Main courses $3.25–$6.95. Maj CC. 🎭 ⚹

Stephen's, 1311 Tijeras Ave NW, Albuquerque; tel 505/842-1773. At intersection of 14th St and Central Ave. **American.** An open, airy restaurant facing busy Central Avenue. Traditional American entrees are prepared in innovative ways. Specialties include rack of lamb, Cajun mixed grill, and pork tenderloin scaloppine. The award-winning wine cellar has some 400 selections. **FYI:** Reservations recommended. Dress code. **Open:** Lunch Mon–Fri 11am–2pm; dinner Sun–Thurs 5:30–9:30pm, Fri–Sat 5:30–10:30pm. Closed some hols. **Prices:** Main courses $16–$25. Maj CC. ♥ ⚹

Attractions 💼

HISTORIC BUILDINGS & MUSEUMS

Old Town, Central Ave and Rio Grande Blvd NW; tel 505/842-9100. A maze of cobbled courtyard walkways lead to hidden patios and gardens where many of Old Town's 150 galleries and shops are located. Adobe buildings, many refurbished in the pueblo revival style of the 1950s, ring the tree-shaded Old Town Plaza, created in 1780. Pueblo and Navajo artisans often display their wares on the sidewalks lining the plaza.

The first structure built when colonists established Albuquerque in 1706 was the **Church of San Felipe de Neri,** which faces the Plaza on its north side. The house of worship has been in almost continuous use for 285 years. The windows are 20 feet from the ground and its walls are 4 feet thick—structural details needed to make the church also serviceable as a fortress. A spiral stairway leading to the choir loft is built around the trunk of an ancient spruce.

Other notable structures include the 1877 **Our Lady of the Angels School,** 320 Romero St, the first public school in Albuquerque; **Antonio Vigil House,** 413 Romero St, an adobe-style residence with traditional viga ends sticking out over the entrance door; and **Casa Armijo,** at San Felipe St, a headquarters for both Union and Confederate troops during the Civil War. Guided walking tours are held Tuesday to Sunday during the summer.

National Atomic Museum, Wyoming Blvd and K St; tel 505/845-6670. Traces the history of nuclear-weapons development, beginning with the top-secret Manhattan Project of the 1940s. A 50-minute film, *Ten Seconds That Shook the World,* is shown 4 times daily. There are full-scale models of the "Fat Man" and "Little Boy" bombs and displays and films on peaceful applications of nuclear technology and other alternative energy sources. Outdoor exhibits include missiles and bombers. The museum is located on Kirtland Air Force Base; visitors must obtain passes at the entry gates of the base. **Open:** Daily 9am–5pm. Closed some hols. Free.

Albuquerque Museum, 2000 Mountain Rd NW; tel 505/243-7255. A permanent exhibit chronicles the city's evolution from the earliest 16th-century forays of Coronado's conquistadores to its present-day status as a center for military research and high-technology industries. An object of special note is a 17th-century *repostero*, or tapestry, once belonging to the Spanish House of Albuquerque.

A multimedia audiovisual presentation, *Albuquerque: The Crossroads,* depicts the development of the city since 1875. There's also a gallery of early and modern New Mexico art, and a photo archive. **Open:** Tues–Sun 9am–5pm. Closed some hols. Free.

University Art Museum, Cornell St; tel 505/277-4001. Located on the University of New Mexico campus in the fine arts center, this collection focuses on 19th- and 20th-century American and European artists. Exhibits of early modernist work; history of photography and prints. **Open:** Sept–May, Tues–Fri 9am–4pm, Sun 1–4pm. Closed some hols. Free.

Jonson Gallery, 1909 Las Lomas Blvd NE; tel 505/277-4967. Featured are more than 2,000 works by the late Raymond Jonson, a leading modernist painter in early 20th-century New Mexico. Located on the University of New Mexico campus. **Open:** Tues–Fri 9am–4pm. Free.

Indian Pueblo Cultural Center, 2401 12th St NW; tel 800/288-0721. Owned and operated as a nonprofit organization by the 19 pueblos of northern New Mexico, this is modeled after Pueblo Bonito, a spectacular 9th-century ruin (see under Chaco Culture National Historical Park). A permanent exhibit depicts the evolution from prehistory to the present of the various pueblos, including displays of the distinctive handcrafts of each community. Local Native American dancers perform, and artisans demonstrate their crafts on weekends. Annual craft fair is held on July 4. **Open:** Daily 9am–5:30pm. $

New Mexico Museum of Natural History, 1801 Mountain Rd NW; tel 505/841-8837. Permanent and changing exhibits on regional zoology, botany, geology, and paleontology. Innovative video displays, polarizing lenses, and black lighting enable visitors to stroll through geologic time. Visitors can walk a rocky path through the Hall of Giants, as dinosaurs fight and winged reptiles swoop overhead; step into a seemingly live volcano, complete with simulated magma flow; or share an Ice Age cave, festooned with stalagmites, with saber-toothed tigers and woolly mammoths. Hands-on exhibits in the Naturalist Center permit use of a video microscope, and viewing of an active beehive. **Open:** Daily 9am–5pm. Closed some hols. $$

Geology Museum and Meteoritic Museum, 200 Yale Blvd NE; tel 505/277-1644. Located in Northrop Hall on the University of New Mexico campus, these adjacent museums cover the gamut of recorded time from dinosaur bones to meteorites. There are 3,000 meteorite specimens in the collection, as well as minerals and fossils. **Open:** Mon–Fri 9am–5pm. Free.

Maxwell Museum of Anthropology, Redondo Dr; tel 505/277-4405. A repository of southwestern anthropological finds located on the University of New Mexico campus. Permanent galleries include "Ancestors," describing 4 million years of human evolution, and "Peoples of the Southwest," a 10,000-year summary. Regional jewelry, basketry, and textiles are on display. **Open:** Mon–Sat 9am–4pm, Sun noon–4pm. Closed some hols. Free.

Spanish History Museum, 2221 Lead St SE; tel 505/268-9981. This exclusive gallery features "From Kingdom to Statehood," an exhibit outlining Hispanics' role in New Mexico's pursuit of statehood from 1848 to 1912. **Open:** Daily 1–5pm, summer daily 10am–5pm. $

Ernie Pyle Memorial Library, 900 Girard Blvd NE; tel 505/256-2065. Memorabilia and poignant exhibits recalling the Pulitzer Prize-winning war correspondent, killed in action during World War II, are displayed in his 1939 home. **Open:** Tues, Thurs 12:30–8pm; Wed, Fri–Sat 9am–5:30pm. Free.

American International Rattlesnake Museum, 202 San Felipe St NW; tel 505/242-6569. With live specimens in landscaped habitats. Featured are both common and very rare rattlesnakes of North, Central, and South America. Over 20 species can be seen, including such oddities as albinos and patternless rattlesnakes. **Open:** Daily 10am–6:30pm. Closed some hols. $

OTHER ATTRACTIONS

Petroglyph National Monument, 6900 Unser Blvd NW; tel 505/897-8814 or 839-4429. These ancient lava flows were once hunting and gathering areas for prehistoric Native Americans, who chronicled their journeys with etched markings in the basalt. Today, 15,000 of these petroglyphs have been found in concentrated groups. Visitors may take any of the 4 levels of hiking trails to see them. **Open:** Daily 9am–6pm summer, 8am–5pm winter. $

Rio Grande Zoological Park, 903 10th St SW; tel 505/843-7413. Open-motif exhibits, including an African savanna and Amazon rain forest, are the highlights of this zoo. More than 1,200 animals of 300 species, among them endangered African hoofed animals, cats, elephants, giraffes, and native southwestern species, share the 60 acres of riverside habitat among ancient cottonwoods. **Open:** Daily 9am–5pm. Closed some hols. $$

Sandia Peak Tramway, 10 Tramway Loop NE; tel 505/298-8518. The world's longest tramway extends 2.7 miles from Albuquerque's northeastern city limits to the summit of 10,360-foot Sandia Peak. The 15-minute ride takes visitors from urban desert at its base to lush mountain foliage in the Cibola National Forest at its peak. **Open:** Daily 9am–9pm. $$$$

Sandia Peak Ski Area, 10 Tramway Loop NE; tel 505/296-9585. There are 25 trails here, 14 of which are intermediate level. The mountain has a 10,360-foot summit and a 1,700-foot vertical drop. During the summer chair lifts are operational Thursday to Sunday and mountain bikes are available for rent. **Open:** Mid-Dec–mid-Mar, daily 9am–4pm. $$$$

ENTERTAINMENT

Cliff's Amusement Park, 4800 Osuna Rd NE; tel 505/883-9063. New Mexico's largest amusement park, with 23 rides, including a roller coaster and log flume; video arcades; a recording studio; picnic grounds; and live entertainment. **Open:** Apr–early Oct; call ahead for hours. $$$$

Kimo Theatre, 419 Central Ave NW; tel 505/764-1700. This showcase of the performing arts is designed as a tribute to the region's Native American cultures. Opened in 1927, the architecture is a colorful adaptation of the adobe pueblo and its interior decor emphasizes Native American motifs. Handmade tiles adorn the lobby; wall paintings simulate Navajo sand paintings; and murals of the legendary "Seven Cities of Cíbola" stand outside the balcony seating area. The 750-seat theater is home of the New Mexico Repertory Theatre, Opera Southwest, and La Compaña de Teatro de Albuquerque. **Open:** Daily 11am–5pm.

Popejoy Hall, Cornell St; tel 505/277-3121. The area's leading venue for major musical entertainment. Seating 2,094, it is the home of the New Mexico Symphony Orchestra, the Albuquerque Civic Light Opera Association, and the New Mexico Ballet Company. **Open:** Mon–Fri 9:30am–5:30pm.

ANGEL FIRE

Map page M-3, A3   (N of Taos)

Attraction 📷

Angel Fire Ski Area, N Angel Fire Rd; tel 800/633-7463. The 30 miles of ski runs are heavily oriented toward beginning and intermediate skiers. There is a vertical drop of 2,180 feet to a base elevation of 8,500 feet. **Open:** Dec–Apr, daily 9am–4:30pm. $$$$

ARTESIA

Map page M-3, D4

Hotel 🏨

≣≣ Pecos Inn Best Western Hotel, 2209 W Main St, Artesia, NM 88210; or toll free 800/528-1234; fax 505/748-2868. ½ mi W of US 285 on US 82. Simply but attractively decorated and landscaped. **Rooms:** 81 rms and stes. CI 4pm/CO 11am. Nonsmoking rms avail. **Amenities:** 🛏 🍴 🖥 A/C, cable TV w/movies, refrig. Some units w/terraces. All regular rooms have wet bars. Hair dryers and microwave ovens are available. **Services:** ✗ 🖼 🖴 **Facilities:** 🔖 🍴 ⚑ 1 rst, 1 bar, sauna, whirlpool. **Rates:** $51–$60 S; $58–$65 D; from $65 ste. Extra person $7. Children under 12 stay free. Pking: Outdoor, free. Maj CC.

Attraction 📷

Artesia Historical Museum and Art Center, 505 W Richardson Ave; tel 505/748-2390. Housed in an old Victorian home, with exhibits of Native Americans and pioneer artifacts, as well as works by local artists. **Open:** Tues–Sat 10am–5pm. Closed some hols. Free.

AZTEC

Map page M-3, A1

Motel 🛏

≣≣ Enchantment Lodge, 1800 W Aztec Blvd, Aztec, NM 87410; tel 505/334-6143 or toll free 800/847-2194; fax 505/334-6144. Nostalgic 1950s decor, with pink neon lights, and every room door a different color. **Rooms:** 20 rms. CI noon/CO 11am. Nonsmoking rms avail. **Amenities:** 🛏 A/C, cable TV w/movies, refrig. **Services:** ✗ 🚗 🖴 Babysitting. **Facilities:** 🔖 ⚑ 🏊 Playground, washer/dryer. There are pool side umbrella tables, a grassy picnic area, and a fun, eclectic gift shop. **Rates:** HS May–Oct $28–$34 S; $38–$44 D. Extra person $5–7. Children under 1 stay free. Lower rates off-season. Spec packages avail. Pking: Outdoor, free. Ltd CC.

Attractions 📷

Aztec Ruins National Monument, US 550; tel 505/334-6174. The ruins of a 500-room pueblo, abandoned by the Anasazi 7 centuries ago and misnamed by pioneers who confused the Anasazi with the ancient Mexican Aztec people. The influence of the Chaco culture is strong at Aztec, as evidenced in the preplanned architecture, the open plaza, and the fine stone masonry in the old walls. Aztec is best know for its Great Kiva, the only completely reconstructed Anasazi kiva in existence. The circular ceremonial room is 50 feet in diameter, with a main floor sunken 8 feet below the surface. The visitor center displays some outstanding examples of Anasazi ceramics and basketry found in the ruins. **Open:** Daily 8am–5pm. Closed some hols. $

Navajo Lake State Park, NM 173; tel 505/632-2278. Three recreation sites—San Juan River, Pine River, and Sims Mesa—overlook Navajo Lake, the largest in northwestern New Mexico. Anglers can fish for trout, bass, crappie, catfish, and northern pike. Camping, hiking, boating, water sports. **Open:** Daily sunrise–sunset. $

BERNALILLO

Map page M-3, B2

Restaurant 🍴

Prairie Star, 1000 Jemez Canyon Dam Rd, Bernalillo; tel 505/867-3327. 2 mi W of Bernalillo; exit 242 off I-25. **Regional American.** A sprawling adobe home, with viga and latilla ceilings, decorated with original art. The menu features southwestern variations on standard dishes, such as trout with piñon nuts and shrimp margarita. The wine list has over 225 selections. **FYI:** Reservations recommended. Guitar. **Open:** Dinner Sun–Thurs 5–10pm, Fri–Sat 5–11pm; brunch Sun 10:30am–2:30pm. Closed some hols. **Prices:** Main courses $12–$25. Maj CC. ♥ &

Attractions 🖼

Coronado State Monument, NM 44 (PO Box 95); tel 505/867-5351. When Coronado traveled through this region in 1540 to 1541, he wintered at a village located on the ruins of the ancient Anasazi pueblo known as Kuaua. Those excavated ruins have been preserved in this state monument. Hundreds of rooms can be seen, and a kiva has been restored so that visitors may descend a ladder into the enclosed space, once the site of sacred rites. There is also a small archeological museum. **Open:** Daily 9am–5pm. Closed some hols. $

Sandia Pueblo, NM 313; tel 505/867-3317. Established about 1300, this was one of the few pueblos visited by Coronado's contingent in 1540. Remains of that village are still visible near the present church. The pueblo celebrates its St Anthony feast day on June 13 with a midmorning mass, procession, and afternoon corn dance. Photographs prohibited. **Open:** Daily sunrise to sunset. Free.

Santa Ana Pueblo, 2 Dove Rd; tel 505/867-3301. Guests are normally welcomed only on ceremonial days. Pueblo members perform the turtle and corn dances on January 1; the eagle, elk, buffalo, and deer dances on Three Kings Day, January 6; the spring corn basket dance at Easter; various dances for St Anthony's Day on June 29 and St Anne's Day on July 26; and several days of dances at Christmastime. Photographs prohibited. **Open:** Certain ceremonial days only. Free.

CAPITAN
Map page M-3, D3

Attraction 🖼

Smokey Bear Historical State Park, 118 First Street; tel 505/354-2748. Smokey Bear was found here as a cub clinging to a tree after a forest fire in the Capitan Mountains in the early 1950s. He lived a long life in the National Zoo in Washington, DC, and after his death was returned to his home for burial. Today, visitors can see his grave, walk nature paths, and view exhibits on Smokey and fire prevention in the museum (free). **Open:** Daily sunrise to sunset. $

CAPULIN
Map page M-3, A4

Attraction 🖼

Capulin Volcano National Monument, NM 325; tel 505/278-2201. A 2-mile road spirals 1,000 feet to the summit of this 8,182-foot peak. Two self-guiding trails leave from the parking area permitting visitors to explore the inactive volcano: the 1-mile Crater Rim Trail, and the 1,000-foot descent to the ancient volcanic vent. The mountain was last active about 10,000 years ago when it sent out the last of 3 lava flows. **Open:** Visitor center May–Sept, daily 7:30am–5pm; Oct–Apr, daily 8:30am–4:30pm. Closed some hols. $$

CARLSBAD
Map page M-3, D4

Hotel 🛏

▀▀▀ **Holiday Inn**, 601 S Canal St, PO Box 128, Carlsbad, NM 88220; tel 505/885-8500 or toll free 800/742-9586; fax 505/887-5999. A full-service hotel in downtown Carlsbad, in a striking New Mexico territorial-style building. **Rooms:** 100 rms. Exec-level rms avail. CI 2pm/CO 11am. Nonsmoking rms avail. **Amenities:** 🅰 ⚹ A/C, cable TV w/movies, voice mail. Some units w/Jacuzzis. Some handicapped rooms have roll-in showers. **Services:** ✕ 🚗 ⛴ ⏴ **Facilities:** 🔗 💺 🏊 & 2 rsts, 1 bar, sauna, whirlpool, playground, washer/dryer. Close to 2 18-hole golf courses. **Rates:** HS June–Aug $75–$85 S; $81–$91 D. Extra person $6. Children under 19 stay free. Lower rates off-season. Spec packages avail. Pking: Outdoor, free. Maj CC.

Motels

▀▀▀ **Best Western Motel Stevens**, 1829 S Canal St, Carlsbad, NM 88220; or toll free 800/730-2851; fax 505/887-6338. A full-service motel, newly renovated and very popular with business travelers. **Rooms:** 202 rms and stes. Exec-level rms avail. CI noon/CO noon. Nonsmoking rms avail. Most rooms have 2 queen beds, and several have kitchenettes. **Amenities:** 🅰 ⛴ A/C, cable TV w/movies. Some units w/terraces, some w/Jacuzzis. Microwave/refrigerator combination available for $5. **Services:** ✕ 🚐 ⛴ ⏴ ⛴ Babysitting. Free newspapers. **Facilities:** 🔗 💺 & 2 rsts (see also "Restaurants" below), 1 bar (w/entertainment), playground, washer/dryer.

Rates: $60–$70 S; $65–$75 D; from $65 ste. Extra person $5. Children under 13 stay free. Pking: Outdoor, free. Maj CC. Long-term rates are available.

≣≣ **Carlsbad Travelodge South**, 3817 National Parks Hwy, Carlsbad, NM 88220; tel 505/887-8888 or toll free 800/255-3050; fax 505/885-0126. Quiet accommodations at a good location on the south side of Carlsbad, 20 miles from the caverns and within 10 miles of Carlsbad's other attractions. **Rooms:** 60 rms. CI noon/CO noon. Nonsmoking rms avail. Clean, well-appointed rooms. **Amenities:** 🛁 📺 A/C, cable TV w/movies. Refrigerators and microwave ovens are available. **Services:** 🛎️ ⌁ ⌁ **Facilities:** 🛗 ⅙ Whirlpool, washer/dryer. **Rates (BB):** HS June–Aug $57 S; $65 D. Extra person $4. Children under 18 stay free. Lower rates off-season. Pking: Outdoor, free. Maj CC.

≣ **Continental Inn**, 3820 National Parks Hwy, Carlsbad, NM 88220; tel 505/887-0341; fax 505/885-0508. A pleasant, standard motel. **Rooms:** 60 rms and stes. CI 1pm/CO 11am. Nonsmoking rms avail. The honeymoon suite (room 129) has a heart-shaped tub with mirrored ceiling and shower for two. **Amenities:** 🛁 📺 A/C, cable TV w/movies. Suites have refrigerators. **Services:** ⌁ ⌁ **Facilities:** 🛗 ⅙ 24-hour restaurant within walking distance. **Rates:** HS May–Sept $33 S; $38–$43 D; from $50 ste. Extra person $5. Children under 15 stay free. Lower rates off-season. Pking: Outdoor, free. Maj CC.

≣ **Stagecoach Inn**, 1819 S Canal St, Carlsbad, NM 88220; tel 505/887-1148; fax 505/887-1148. A modest, no-frills property that's undergoing gradual refurbishment. **Rooms:** 56 rms. CI 10am/CO 11am. Nonsmoking rms avail. **Amenities:** 🛁 A/C, cable TV w/movies. **Services:** ✗ ⌁ ⌁ ⌁ **Facilities:** 🛗 ⅙ 1 rst (see also "Restaurants" below), whirlpool, playground, washer/dryer. **Rates:** HS June–Aug $30 S; $40–$54 D. Children under 18 stay free. Lower rates off-season. Higher rates for spec evnts/hols. Pking: Outdoor, free. Maj CC.

Restaurants 🍴

The Flume, in Best Western Motel Stevens, 1829 S Canal St, Carlsbad; tel 505/887-2851. **American/Mexican.** Elegant restaurant in southwest hacienda style with chandeliers and wall sconces. The menu offers a variety of seafood, beef, and chicken selections. The house specialty is teriyaki chicken breast. **FYI:** Reservations recommended. Country music/dancing. Children's menu. **Open:** Mon–Sat 6am–10pm, Sun 6am–9pm. **Prices:** Main courses $7.95–$15.95. Maj CC. 🅿️ ⅙

★ **Lucy's**, 701 S Canal, Carlsbad; tel 505/887-7714. **Mexican/Steak.** Busy cafe with partitioned areas for small family parties. Mexican dishes include burritos, enchiladas, and tacos. **FYI:**

Reservations accepted. Children's menu. **Open:** Mon–Sat 11am–10pm. Closed some hols. **Prices:** Main courses $3.75–$11.95. Maj CC. 🅿️ ⅙

★ **Stagecoach Restaurant**, in the Stagecoach Inn, 1801 S Canal St, Carlsbad; tel 505/885-2862. **Regional American.** A southwestern cafe with ceiling fans and lights with a wagon wheel design. There is seating at both booths and tables. Specializes in burgers, barbecue, and Mexican plates. A breakfast buffet is available Saturday and Sunday from 11pm to 2pm. **FYI:** Reservations not accepted. No liquor license. **Open:** Mon–Fri 5am–9pm, Sat–Sun 6am–8pm. Closed Dec 25. **Prices:** Main courses $3.95–$6.95. Ltd CC.

Attractions 💼

Carlsbad Caverns National Park, 3225 National Parks Hwy; tel 505/785-2232. One of the largest and most spectacular cave systems in the world, the caverns comprise some 75 caves that snake through the porous limestone reef of the Guadalupe Mountains. Two caves, Carlsbad Cavern and New Cave, are open to the public. At the lowest point in the trail the caverns reach 830 feet below the surface. They are filled with stalactites and stalagmites that create fantastic and grotesque formations resembling everything from waterfalls to castles. At sunset, a crowd gathers at the cavern entrance to watch a quarter-million bats take off for the night. Visitors are advised to wear flat shoes with rubber soles and heels to avoid falls on the slippery paths. **Open:** Daily 8:30am–2:30pm. Closed Dec 25. $$

Living Desert State Park, Skyline Dr; tel 505/887-5516. A 45-acre stretch of Chihuahuan Desert preserved with all its flora and fauna. There are more than 50 species of mammals, birds, and reptiles in the open-air park, and hundreds of varieties of plants. Animals arrive through a rehabilitation program that cares for sick or injured creatures. Golden eagles and great horned owls are among the birds of prey; an exhibit of nocturnal animals shows badgers, spotted skunks, kit foxes, and ringtail cats in underground burrows. Larger mammals such as deer, antelope, elk, javelina, buffalo, and bobcat also share the area. **Open:** May–Sept, daily 8am–7pm; Oct–Apr, daily 9am–4pm. Closed Dec 25. $

CHACO CULTURE NATIONAL HISTORICAL PARK

Map page M-3, B1

Chaco represents the high point of Pre-Columbian pueblo civilization. It includes more than a dozen large Anasazi ruins occupied from the early 900s to about 1200, and hundreds of smaller sites in the wide streambed of the normally dry Chaco Wash. Most of the ruins are located on the north side of the canyon, including the largest, **Pueblo Bonito,** constructed over 3 acres of land in the 11th century. It comprises 4 stories, 600 rooms, and 40 kivas and may have housed as many as 1,200 people. The Anasazi also engineered a network of 300 miles of roads, best seen from the canyon rim 100 feet above the ruins.

The visitor center houses a small museum and provides self-guided trail maps and permits for the overnight campground. Chaco is fairly isolated; Farmington is the closest city and is a 2-hour, 75-mile drive down NM 44. Nageezi Trading Post, the closest location for gas, food, and lodging, is 26 miles by way of graded dirt road. This final stretch becomes flooded and dangerous when it rains; inquire about road conditions before leaving the paved roadway. For more information contact the park at 505/988-6727, daily 8am–5pm.

CHAMA

Map page M-3, A2

Motels 🏨

🏨 **Branding Iron Motel**, W Main St, PO Box 557, Chama, NM 87520; tel 505/756-2162 or toll free 800/446-2650. A standard motel. **Rooms:** 41 rms. CI 2pm/CO 11am. Nonsmoking rms avail. **Amenities:** 🛏 A/C, cable TV. All units w/terraces. **Services:** 🛎 🛎 Babysitting. **Facilities:** 🏋 ♿ 1 rst. **Rates:** HS May 27–Oct 20 $53–$60 S; $65–$75 D. Lower rates off-season. Spec packages avail. Pking: Outdoor, free. Maj CC.

🏨🏨 **Chama Trails Inn**, W Main St, PO Box 816, Chama, NM 87520; tel 505/756-2156 or toll free 800/289-1421. At the "Y". Chile ristras adorn the white stucco facade of this handsome property. Far above the usual small-town motel. The owners are friendly and knowledgeable. **Rooms:** 16 rms. CI noon/CO 11am. Nonsmoking rms avail. Custom-made pine furnishings and hand-carved wood beams. **Amenities:** 🛏 ♨ 🖥 Cable TV, refrig. No A/C. All units w/terraces, some w/fireplaces, 1 w/Jacuzzi. **Services:** 🛎 **Facilities:** 🏋 🖼 An art gallery with local artists' work is on the premises. **Rates:** HS Late May–Oct $35 S; $41 D. Extra person $6. Lower rates off-season. Pking: Outdoor, free. Maj CC.

🏨🏨 **Elkhorn Lodge and Cafe**, US 84, Rte 1, PO Box 45, Chama, NM 87520; tel 505/756-2105 or toll free 800/532-8874; fax 505/756-2638. A charming, somewhat rustic motel, reminiscent of a mountain lodge, set beside a stream. **Rooms:** 22 rms; 11 ctges/villas. CI 2pm/CO 11am. Clean, spacious rooms, with solid wood paneling. **Amenities:** 🛏 Cable TV. No A/C. All units w/terraces. **Services:** 🚐 🛎 🛎 **Facilities:** 🏋 🏋 1 rst, lawn games, playground. Barbecue pits on the grounds. **Rates:** HS May–Oct $41 S; $57 D; from $53 ctge/villa. Extra person $6. Children under 5 stay free. Lower rates off-season. Spec packages avail. Pking: Outdoor, free. Ltd CC.

Restaurants 🍴

★ **High Country Restaurant**, Main St, Chama; tel 505/756-2384. **Seafood/Steak.** A friendly, comfortable eatery, decorated with western art and knick-knacks. Selection of steak, fish, seafood, chicken, pork, and sandwiches. **FYI:** Reservations accepted. Country music. **Open:** Daily 7am–11pm. Closed some hols. **Prices:** Main courses $7.50–$13.95. Maj CC. 🍴 🏋 🏋 ♿

Viva Vera's, Main St, Chama; tel 505/756-2557. **Regional American/Mexican.** Comfortable restaurant with Spanish touches. Basic Mexican and American food, including enchiladas, chile stew, burritos, hamburgers, and sandwiches. **FYI:** Reservations accepted. Beer and wine only. **Open:** HS May–Oct daily 7am–9:30pm. Reduced hours off-season. Closed some hols. **Prices:** Main courses $5.75–$10.50. Maj CC. 🍴 🏋 🏋 ♿

Attractions 🏛

Cumbres and Toltec Scenic Railroad, US 64; tel 505/756-2151. American's longest and highest narrow-gauge steam railroad operates on a 64-mile track between Chama and Antonito, Colorado. Built in 1880 as an extension of the Denver and Rio Grande Line to serve the mining camps of the San Juan Mountains, it is perhaps the finest surviving example of what once was a vast network of remote Rocky Mountain railways. The C&T passes through forests of pine and aspen, past striking rock formations, and through the magnificent Toltec Gorge of the Rio de los Pinos. It crests at the 10,105-foot Cumbres Pass, the highest in the United States used by passenger trains. Reservations are recommended. **Open:** June–Oct daily departure 10:30am. $$$$

Jicarilla Apache Indian Reservation, off US 64; tel 505/759-3242. About 3,200 Apache live on this 768,000-acre reservation. The tribal craftspeople are noted for their basket-weaving and both contemporary and museum-quality examples can be seen at **Jicarilla Apache Arts and Crafts Shop and Museum**. Two isolated pueblo ruins are found on the reservation: the **Cordova Canyon** ruins on Tribal Road 13 and the **Honolulu** ruin on Road 63. **Open:** Daily sunrise to sunset. Free.

CIMARRON

Map page M-3, A3

Hotel 🛏

▇▇ **St James Hotel**, Rte 1 Box 2, Cimarron, NM 87714; tel 505/376-2664; fax 505/376-2623. At 17th and Collinson Sts. This handsome historic hotel, opened in 1890, was popular with many of the legends of the Old West, including Buffalo Bill Cody, Annie Oakley, train robber Blackjack Ketchum, and gunfighter Clay Allison, who reportedly once danced on the bar. Restored to its original Victorian grandeur in 1985, the lobby and rooms are furnished with turn-of-the-century antiques. The original tin ceiling of the hotel's dining room shows off bullet holes left from its wilder days. **Rooms:** 25 rms and stes. CI 3pm/CO noon. Restored rooms in the original building are very much like they were in the 1890s, many with the original marble sinks—and no phones or TVs. Room 18 is not rented because its resident ghost, TJ Wright, does not welcome visitors. Rooms in the annex, built in the 1950s, are standard motel rooms. **Amenities:** 🐾 No A/C, phone, or TV. Annex rooms have TVs and telephones. **Services:** 🛎 Masseur. The St. James offers tours during summer months ($2 per person) and shows a 20-minute video on the history of the hotel. **Facilities:** 🍴 2 rsts (*see also* "Restaurants" below), 1 bar, games rm. Coffee shop serves 3 meals a day. Close to hiking, fishing, hunting, horseback riding, and downhill and cross-country skiing. **Rates:** $45–$85 S; $50–$85 D; from $95 ste. Extra person $5. Children under 18 stay free. Min stay spec evnts. Spec packages avail. Pking: Outdoor, free. Maj CC. Mystery Weekend packages are available; reservations are suggested at least 6 months in advance.

Restaurant 🍽

Lambert's, in St James Hotel, 17th and Collinson Sts, Cimarron; tel 505/376-2664. 1 block S of US 64 on NM 21. **Continental.** A delightful, historic dining room in the Victorian St James Hotel. It was built in 1873 by Henri Lambert, personal chef to President Lincoln and General Grant. The room is decorated with Victorian antiques, and patrons can pass time counting the numerous bullet holes in the tin ceiling. There is also a painting on display depicting one of the shootings that took place here. The menu includes steak, seafood, and continental dishes. **FYI:** Reservations recommended. Children's menu. **Open:** Dinner Mon–Sat 5pm–close, Sun noon–close. Closed Dec 25. **Prices:** Main courses $12.95–$21.95. Maj CC. ♥ 🍷

Attractions 💼

Philmont Scout Ranch, I-25; tel 505/376-2281. This 137,000-acre property was donated to the Boy Scouts of America in 1938 by Texas oilman Waite Phillips. There are 3 museums located on the property that are open to the public: The **Villa Philmonte** is a Mediterranean-style summer home built in 1927 for Phillips and is furnished with the family's European antiques. The **Philmont Museum and Seton Memorial Library** commemorates the art and taxidermy of Ernest Thompson Seton, the naturalist and author who founded the Boy Scouts of America. The **Kit Carson Museum**, located 7 miles south of Philmont headquarters in Rayado, is a period hacienda furnished in 1850s style. Tours are led by staff in historical costumes. Free.

Old Mill Museum, NM 21; tel 505/376-2913. Land baron Lucien Maxwell founded the town of Cimarron in 1848 as base of operations for his 1.7-million-acre empire. In 1857 he built the Maxwell Ranch, which he furnished opulently with heavy draperies, gold-framed paintings, and 2 grand pianos. The ranch isn't open for inspection today, but Maxwell's 1864 stone grist mill, built to supply flour to Fort Union, is. It houses an interesting collection of early photos and memorabilia of the ranch. **Open:** May–Oct, Mon–Wed and Fri–Sat 9am–5pm, Sun 1–5pm. $

Cimarron Canyon State Park, US 64; tel 505/377-6271. This designated state wildlife area lies at the foot of crenellated granite formations known as the Palisades. Covering 32,000 acres, the park is a popular spot for hunting, fishing, and hiking. **Open:** Daily sunrise to sunset. Free.

CLAYTON

Map page M-3, A4

Attraction 💼

Kiowa National Grasslands, 16 N Second St; tel 505/374-9652. This area provides food, cover, and water for a wide variety of wildlife such as antelope, quail, barbary sheep, and mule deer. Also located at Kiowa are the Canadian River and the

Canadian River Canyon. The variety of recreational options available include warm water fishing, picnicking, and camping. **Open:** Daily 8am–4:30pm. Free.

CLEVELAND

Map page M-3, B3 (E of Española)

Attraction 🖼

Cleveland Mill Historical Museum, NM 518; tel 505/387-2645. From 1901 to 1947, this 2-story adobe mill ground out 50 barrels of wheat flour a day. Today, it's been converted into a museum with exhibits on regional history and culture. **Open:** Fri–Sun 10am–5pm. $

CLOUDCROFT

Map page M-3, D3

Lodge 🏨

≣≣≣ **The Lodge at Cloudcroft**, 1 Corona Place, PO Box 497, Cloudcroft, NM 88317; or toll free 800/395-6343; fax 505/682-2715. From US 82, turn south at the USFS office. Beautiful, historic mountain lodge with 6-story tower; highly recommended for a vacation getaway. The lobby is elegantly and comfortably furnished with plush seating around a brick fireplace. **Rooms:** 63 rms and stes. CI 4pm/CO noon. Nonsmoking rms avail. Rooms are uniquely furnished in turn-of-the-century style—cozy, but not crowded. There are basic rooms, a junior suite with a small sitting room, and the more formal Governor's Suite. **Amenities:** 📺 Cable TV. No A/C. Some units w/fireplaces, 1 w/Jacuzzi. **Services:** 🛎 Masseur, babysitting. Fax and photocopying services are available. **Facilities:** 🛗 🚴 ▶9 ⚓ 🐎 300 1 rst (*see also* "Restaurants" below), 1 bar (w/entertainment), games rm, lawn games, sauna, whirlpool. The mezzanine has tables and chairs for board games. There are lots of hiking trails in the surrounding forest, and tennis at nearby public courts. The gift shop has homemade fudge. **Rates:** HS June–Aug $49–$99 S or D; from $109 ste. Children under 12 stay free. Min stay spec evnts. Lower rates off-season. Higher rates for spec evnts/hols. Spec packages avail. Pking: Outdoor, free. Maj CC.

Restaurants 🍴

Ray's Western Cafe, Burro Ave, Cloudcroft; tel 505/682-2445. **American/Mexican.** Old West–style cafe with exposed wood ceiling beams and wood and stucco walls. The cashier is behind bars like a bank teller of old. Burgers, sandwiches, and a variety of homestyle dinners, plus standard Mexican plates. Pool tables in adjoining bar. **FYI:** Reservations not accepted. Rock. Children's menu. **Open:** HS June–Aug Sun–Thurs 7am–9pm, Fri–Sat 7am–10pm. Reduced hours off-season. Closed Dec 25. **Prices:** Main courses $5.75–$15.50. Ltd CC.

♥ **Rebecca's at the Lodge**, in the Lodge at Cloudcroft, 1 Corona Place, Cloudcroft; tel 505/682-2566. **Regional American.** An elegant yet unpretentious restaurant. There are 2 dining rooms: one with a wall of windows facing west that allows diners to look out over the trees to the distant plains; the other a bit cozier with a large fireplace. A grand piano is on a slowly revolving dais centered between the two. The award-winning chef prepares innovative variations of American and continental cuisine, including sliced pork tenderloin sautéed in a creamy apple brandy sauce. The bartender proudly offers 100-year-old brandy, brought to the table in beautiful hand-painted decanters and warmed just before serving. **FYI:** Reservations recommended. Piano. Children's menu. **Open:** HS June–Sept breakfast daily 7–10:30am; lunch daily 11:30am–2:30pm; dinner daily 5:30–10pm. Reduced hours off-season. **Prices:** Main courses $12.95–$24. Maj CC. ♥ 🍷 🍽 📷 🏞

CLOVIS

Map page M-3, C4

Motels 🏨

≣≣ **Best Western La Vista Inn**, 1516 Mabry Dr (US 60/70/84), Clovis, NM 88101; tel 505/762-3808 or toll free 800/524-1234; fax 505/762-1422. A pleasant, basic motel. **Rooms:** 47 rms. CI 1pm/CO 11am. Nonsmoking rms avail. **Amenities:** 📺 A/C, cable TV. **Services:** 🚐 🛎 24-hour desk and maid service. **Facilities:** 🛗 Games rm, washer/dryer. **Rates (CP):** $30–$40 S; $36–$44 D. Extra person $4. Children under 12 stay free. Pking: Outdoor, free. Maj CC.

≣≣ **Clovis Inn**, 2912 Mabry Dr (US 60/70/84), Clovis, NM 88101; tel 505/762-5600 or toll free 800/535-3440. Pleasant accommodations. **Rooms:** 97 rms and stes. CI open/CO noon. Nonsmoking rms avail. **Amenities:** 📺 🍴 A/C, cable TV w/movies. Refrigerators and microwaves are available. **Services:** 🚐 🖨 🛎 Coffee is available in the lobby all day. **Facilities:** 🛗 135 🚻 Whirlpool, washer/dryer. Outdoor basketball court; barbecue pit and shaded picnic tables near the pool. **Rates (CP):** HS Feb–Nov $38 S; $40 D; from $45 ste. Extra person $3–6. Children under 12 stay free. Lower rates off-season. Spec packages avail. Pking: Outdoor, free. Maj CC.

Restaurant 🍴

Poor Boy's Steakhouse, 2115 N Prince, Clovis; tel 505/763-5222. **Seafood/Steak.** Early American decor, with Tiffany lamps, booths, and seating on a raised center section. Steaks, seafood, chicken dishes, and sandwiches; large salad bar. **FYI:** Reservations not accepted. Children's menu. No liquor license. **Open:** Sun–Thurs 11am–9pm, Fri–Sat 11am–10pm. Closed some hols. **Prices:** Main courses $3.99–$12.99. Maj CC. 🅿️ ♿

Attractions 📷

Hillcrest Park Zoo, 10th and Sycamore Sts; tel 505/769-7873. Located in Hillcrest Park, the 22-acre zoo displays a full range of animals from native swamp deer to zebras. **Open:** Tues–Sun 9am–5pm. Closed Dec 25. $

Lyceum Theatre, 411 Main St; tel 505/763-6085. A restored and refurbished vaudeville theater, now the city's center for performing arts. $$$$

COCHITI PUEBLO

Map page M-3, B2 (SW of Santa Fe)

Occupied continuously since the 14th century, this is the northernmost of the Keresan-speaking pueblos, stretching along the Rio Grande. Cochiti is well known for its pottery, especially the famous storyteller figures created by Helen Cordero. The San Buenaventura Feast Day is July 14, when the corn dance and rain dance are performed. Fishing and bird hunting on pueblo grounds is allowed with a permit from the pueblo governor. Water sports are available at Cochiti Lake. Photographs are prohibited. The pueblo is approximately 40 miles north of Albuquerque via US 85, then north on NM 22 and NM 16. For more information contact the Cochiti Pueblo at 505/465-2244.

DEMING

Map page M-3, D1

Motels 🏨

Best Western Mimbres Valley Inn, Frontage Rd, I-10 W, PO Box 1159, Deming, NM 88030; tel 505/546-4544 or toll free 800/528-1234. Exit 81 off I-10. Located on the west side of town. Opened in 1993. **Rooms:** 40 rms. CI 8am/CO 11am. Nonsmoking rms avail. Pleasant, pastel-colored rooms, with wood furnishings and southwestern art. **Amenities:** 🛏 A/C, cable TV. **Services:** 🕹 📞 24-hour front desk. **Facilities:** 🛗 ♿

3 miles from an 18-hole public golf course. **Rates (CP):** $42 S; $47 D. Extra person $5. Children under 13 stay free. Higher rates for spec evnts/hols. Pking: Outdoor, free. Maj CC.

Chilton Inn, 1709 E Spruce St, PO Box 790, Deming, NM 88030; tel 505/546-8813; fax 505/546-7095. Conveniently located, western-style hotel. **Rooms:** 57 rms. CI 11am/CO noon. Nonsmoking rms avail. **Amenities:** 🛏 A/C, cable TV w/movies. **Services:** 🚗 📇 🕹 📞 Babysitting. Photocopying and fax services available at the front desk. **Facilities:** 🛗 🏊 ♿ 1 rst, beauty salon. **Rates:** $36–$42 S; $40–$46 D. Extra person $5. Children under 18 stay free. Min stay spec evnts. Pking: Outdoor, free. Maj CC.

Grand Hotel, US 70/180, PO Box 309, Deming, NM 88031; tel 505/546-2631; fax 505/546-4446. Exit 81 off I-10. Located east of downtown. Attractive motel with colonial-style entrance and a large lobby. **Rooms:** 62 rms and stes. CI open/CO noon. Nonsmoking rms avail. Rooms are decorated in French provincial style and look out on the pool and lawn. **Amenities:** 🛏 A/C, cable TV w/movies. Some units w/terraces. Refrigerators available. **Services:** ✕ 🚗 📇 🕹 📞 **Facilities:** 🛗 🏊 ♿ 1 rst, 1 bar. **Rates:** $38 S; $48 D; from $65 ste. Extra person $6. Children under 12 stay free. Pking: Outdoor, free. Maj CC.

Holiday Inn, I-10 E, PO Box 1138, Deming, NM 88031; tel 505/546-2661 or toll free 800/HOLIDAY; fax 505/546-6308. Exit 85 off I-10. Built in the 1970s, this meticulously maintained motel has been completely renovated and is rated one of the top Holiday Inns in the country. **Rooms:** 89 rms, stes, and effic. CI 10am/CO noon. Nonsmoking rms avail. Rooms have a subtle southwestern decor, with comfortable chairs and southwest art. **Amenities:** 🛏 ♿ A/C, cable TV. **Services:** ✕ 🚗 📇 🕹 📞 **Facilities:** 🛗 🏊 ♿ 1 rst (*see also* "Restaurants" below), 1 bar, washer/dryer. **Rates:** $48–$50 S; $54–$56 D; from $65 ste; from $65 effic. Extra person $6. Children under 20 stay free. Higher rates for spec evnts/hols. Pking: Outdoor, free. Maj CC. The rate includes a discount on breakfast in Fat Eddie's restaurant.

Wagon Wheel Motel, 1109 W Pine, Deming, NM 88030; tel 505/546-2681. A clean, comfortable "mom and pop" motel. Much renovation recently completed and more underway. **Rooms:** 19 rms, stes, and effic. CI noon/CO 11am. Nonsmoking rms avail. Basic but homey rooms. **Amenities:** 🛏 A/C, cable TV w/movies. **Services:** ✕ 🚗 📞 **Facilities:** 🛗 ♿ Washer/dryer. Heated swimming pool open in summer only. Within walking distance of several restaurants. **Rates:** $22 S; $24–$29 D; from $31 ste; from $36 effic. Extra person $3. Children under 4 stay free. Pking: Outdoor, free. Ltd CC.

Restaurants 🍴

Cactus Cafe, 218 W Cedar St, Deming; tel 505/546-2458. Exit 82A off I-10. **Mexican/Southwestern.** Mexican cafe. The $5.75 Mexican buffet is very popular, as are the chiles rellenos and shrimp fajitas. Local wine. **FYI:** Reservations accepted. Children's menu. Beer and wine only. **Open:** Daily 7am–9pm. Closed Dec 25. **Prices:** Main courses $3.90–$9.95. Maj CC. 🏧 ⅍

Fat Eddie's at the Inn, in the Holiday Inn, PO Box 1138, Deming; tel 505/546-2661. Exit 85 off I-10. **American/Mexican.** View of hotel lawn and pool. Choice of standard American and Mexican entrees. Specialties include baby-back pork ribs and pepper steak. A soup, salad, and deli sandwich luncheon buffet is offered weekdays. **FYI:** Reservations accepted. Children's menu. **Open:** Breakfast daily 6–11am; lunch daily 11am–2pm; dinner daily 4:30–10pm. **Prices:** Main courses $3.65–$15.95. Maj CC. 🏧 ⅍

K-Bob's, 316 E Cedar St, Deming; tel 505/546-8883. Exit 82 off I-10. **Steak.** A family steak place with old guns and brands on the walls. Besides steak, K-Bob's offers catfish, trout, chicken, and sandwiches. **FYI:** Reservations accepted. Children's menu. Beer and wine only. **Open:** Daily 10:30am–10pm. Closed some hols. **Prices:** Main courses $2.99–$14.99. Maj CC. 🏧 ⅍

Attractions 📷

Deming Luna Mimbres Museum, 301 S Silver St; tel 505/546-2382. Deming was the meeting place of the second east-west railroad to connect the Pacific and Atlantic coasts, and that heritage is recalled here. Collections include pioneer-era quilts and laces, military mementos of 19th-century forts and raids, over 800 dolls, and a gem and mineral display. **Open:** Mon–Sat 9am–4pm, Sun 1:30–4pm. Closed some hols. Free.

Rockhound State Park, NM 11; tel 505/546-6182. Located at the base of the wild Florida Mountains, this arid, cactus-covered land is traversed by trails leading down into dry gullies and canyons. Visitors are encouraged to pick and take home with them as much as 15 pounds of minerals—jasper, agate, quartz crystal, and flow-banded rhyolite—from these trails. Hunting, playgrounds, camping. **Open:** Daily sunrise–sunset. Free.

Pancho Villa State Park, NM 11; tel 505/531-2711. Located 32 miles south of Deming in the tiny border town of Columbus, looking across to Mexico. The state park here marks the last foreign invasion of American soil. A temporary fort at this site was attacked in 1916 by Mexican revolutionaries led by Pancho Villa, who cut through the boundary fence at Columbus. The Mexicans retreated across the border, and an American punitive expedition, headed by Gen John J Pershing, was launched in Mexico, but Villa was never captured. Today ruins of the border fort, called Camp Furlong, can be seen at the park. Other features include a desert botanical garden, visitors center, playground, and campsites with shelters. **Open:** Daily sunrise to sunset. $

ELEPHANT BUTTE
Map page M-3, D2 (E of Truth or Consequences)

Motel 🏨

🏨 **Elephant Butte Inn**, NM 195, PO Box E, Elephant Butte, NM 87935; tel 505/744-5431. 5 mi N of Truth or Consequences, exit 83 or 79 off I-25. Popular with boaters, fishermen, and other water lovers. **Rooms:** 48 rms. CI 2pm/CO 11am. Nonsmoking rms avail. Beautiful views of the lake from the rooms at the back. **Amenities:** 🛁 A/C, TV. All units w/terraces. **Services:** ✕ 🚐 ↩ ⑬ **Facilities:** 🏊2 🛎 1 rst, 1 bar (w/entertainment), playground. Within walking distance of the public beach at Elephant Butte Lake. **Rates:** HS May–Nov $49–$62 S or D. Children under 18 stay free. Lower rates off-season. Pking: Outdoor, free. Maj CC. Higher rates on weekends.

Restaurant 🍴

Dam Site Restaurant, in Elephant Butte State Park, NM 177, Elephant Butte; tel 505/894-2073. 5 mi E of Truth or Consequences; exit 83 off I-25. **American.** Simple dining room with white walls and Mexican touches. There's a lovely view of Elephant Butte Lake on one side, and of a cactus garden on the other. Steak, seafood, chicken, and several Mexican dishes are offered. Separate patio menu. **FYI:** Reservations accepted. Jazz/singer. Children's menu. **Open:** HS Apr–Oct Sat–Sun 11am–10pm, Mon–Fri 11am–9pm. Reduced hours off-season. **Prices:** Main courses $7–$11. Maj CC. 🏧 ⅍

Attraction 📷

Elephant Butte Lake State Park, Hwy 85; tel 505/744-5421. The park contains the largest lake in New Mexico, covering 38,000 acres. Fishing, swimming, boating, sailing, waterskiing, and camping. **Open:** Daily sunrise–sunset. $

EL MORRO NATIONAL MONUMENT

Map page M-3, B1

Located on NM 53, "Inscription Rock" looms up out of the sand and sagebrush, a bluff 200 feet high holding some of the most captivating messages in North America. Between 1605 and 1906, nearly every explorer, conquistador, missionary, army officer, surveyor, and pioneer emigrant who passed the rock left a written record of their journey. Early Native Americans also left their mark in the form of petroglyph carvings. A paved walkway makes it easy to walk to the writings, and there is a stone stairway leading up to other markings.

Atop Inscription Rock via a short, steep trail are ruins of an Anasazi pueblo occupying an area 200 by 300 feet. The visitor center (505/783-4226), open daily 8am–5pm, distributes self-guided trail booklets.

ESPAÑOLA

Map page M-3, B3

Motel ▣

▤▤ **Park Inn**, 920 N Riverside Dr, Española, NM 87532; tel 505/753-7291 or toll free 800/766-7943; fax 505/753-1218. Take US 84 to NM 68. A good, basic motel. **Rooms:** 51 rms. CI 11am/CO 11am. Nonsmoking rms avail. Standard motel rooms. **Amenities:** ▨ A/C, cable TV. **Services:** ◁▷ **Facilities:** ▣ ▣ The pool is in a nice grassy area, with rose bushes about. **Rates (CP):** HS May 25–Oct 12 $48 S; $53 D. Extra person $5. Children under 16 stay free. Lower rates off-season. Pking: Outdoor, free. Maj CC.

Attractions ▣

Santa Clara Pueblo, NM 30; tel 505/753-7326. This is one of the larger pueblos in the area, with a population of about 1,600. Driving and walking tours are offered weekdays, with a week's notice, and include visits to the pueblo's historic church and artists' studios. The Puye Cliff Dwellings (see below) are on the Santa Clara reservation. **Open:** Daily sunrise–sunset. Free.

Puye Cliff Dwellings, NM 30; tel 505/753-7326. Thought to have been occupied from about 1250 to 1577 by the Santa Clara people, this site at the mouth of the Santa Clara Canyon is a national landmark. Visitors can descend the volcanic tuff via staircases and ladders from the 7,000-foot mesa top into the

740-room pueblo ruin, which includes a ceremonial chamber and community house. Petroglyphs are evident in many of the rocky cliff walls. **Open:** Summer, daily 8am–8pm; winter, daily 8am–4pm. Closed some hols. $$

FARMINGTON

Map page M-3, A1

Hotels ▣

▤▤ **Anasazi Inn**, 903 W Main St, Farmington, NM 87401; tel 505/325-4564; fax 505/326-0732. A pueblo-style hotel with friendly personnel. **Rooms:** 43 rms and stes. CI noon/CO 11am. Express checkout avail. Nonsmoking rms avail. Rooms are comfortable, with 1 king- or 2 queen-size beds and wood furnishings. **Amenities:** ▨ A/C, cable TV, refrig. **Services:** ▥ ▨ ◁▷ **Facilities:** ▣ 2 rsts, 1 bar. **Rates:** HS July–Aug $38 S or D; from $46 ste. Extra person $6. Lower rates off-season. Spec packages avail. Pking: Outdoor, free. Maj CC.

▤▤▤ **The Farmington Inn**, 700 Scott Ave, Farmington, NM 87401; tel 505/327-5221 or toll free 800/600-5221; fax 505/327-1565. Conveniently located, with a sky-lit central courtyard. **Rooms:** 194 rms. CI 1pm/CO noon. Nonsmoking rms avail. Well-appointed rooms have 1 king- or 2 queen-size beds, and 2 sinks. **Amenities:** ▨ ▨ ▣ A/C, cable TV, refrig. **Services:** ✗▥ ▨ ◁▷ Children's program. **Facilities:** ▣ ▣ ▨ 1 rst, 1 bar, games rm, sauna, steam rm, whirlpool, washer/dryer. **Rates:** HS May–Sept $59 S; $69 D. Extra person $10. Children under 12 stay free. Lower rates off-season. AP rates avail. Spec packages avail. Pking: Outdoor, free. Maj CC.

Motels ▣

▤▤▤ **Holiday Inn of Farmington**, 600 E Broadway, Farmington, NM 87401; tel 505/327-9811 or toll free 800/HOLIDAY; fax 505/325-2288. The recently renovated lobby is attractively furnished in an Aztec motif. **Rooms:** 149 rms. CI 3pm/CO noon. Nonsmoking rms avail. All king rooms have sofa beds. Some rooms open onto the pool and a grassy area with trees. **Amenities:** ▨ ▨ ▣ ▨ Cable TV w/movies. No A/C. Some units w/Jacuzzis. **Services:** ✗▥ ▨ ◁▷ Children's program. **Facilities:** ▣ ▣ ▨ 1 rst (see also "Restaurants" below), 1 bar, sauna, whirlpool. **Rates:** $58–$62 S; $64–$68 D. Extra person $6. Children under 19 stay free. Spec packages avail. Pking: Outdoor, free. Maj CC.

▤▤ **La Quinta**, 675 Scott Ave, Farmington, NM 87401; tel 505/327-4706 or toll free 800/531-5900; fax 505/325-6583. N of Broadway. Pleasant mid-size motel. **Rooms:** 106 rms. CI noon/CO noon. Express checkout avail. Nonsmoking rms avail. **Amenities:** 🔒 🛁 A/C, cable TV w/movies. **Services:** 🏊 🛒 🐕 **Facilities:** 🏋 ⚕ **Rates (CP):** HS May 27–Sept $54 S; $62 D. Extra person $8. Children under 18 stay free. Lower rates off-season. Spec packages avail. Pking: Outdoor, free. Maj CC.

📧 **Motel 6**, 1600 Bloomfield Hwy, Farmington, NM 87401; tel 505/326-4501; fax 505/326-3883. Adequate lodging for the cost-conscious. **Rooms:** 134 rms. CI 7am/CO noon. Nonsmoking rms avail. **Amenities:** 🔒 A/C, TV. **Services:** 🛒 🐕 **Facilities:** 🏋 ⚕ Washer/dryer. **Rates:** $25 S; $31 D. Extra person $6. Children under 17 stay free. Pking: Outdoor, free. Maj CC.

📧📧 **Super 8 Motel**, 1601 Bloomfield Hwy, Farmington, NM 87401; tel 505/325-1813 or toll free 800/800-8000; fax 505/325-1813. An attractive, newer motel. **Rooms:** 60 rms and stes. CI 6am/CO 11am. Nonsmoking rms avail. Clean, comfortable rooms with attractive bedspreads and art. **Amenities:** 🔒 A/C, cable TV w/movies. **Services:** 🛒 🐕 **Facilities:** ⚕ Games rm. **Rates (CP):** HS May–Sept $30 S; $37 D; from $55 ste. Extra person $4. Children under 13 stay free. Lower rates off-season. Pking: Outdoor, free. Maj CC.

Restaurants 🍴

Brass Apple, in the Holiday Inn Farmington, 600 E Broadway, Farmington; tel 505/327-9811. **Continental/Southwestern.** Modern dining room with large windows and lots of plants. Specialties include seafood chiles rellenos, pork asada, chicken dijonaise, Cajun barbecued shrimp, filet mignon, and prime rib. **FYI:** Reservations accepted. Children's menu. **Open:** Breakfast Mon–Sat 6–11am, Sun 6am–noon; lunch Mon–Sat 11am–2pm; dinner daily 3–10pm. **Prices:** Main courses $4.95–$14.50. Maj CC. 📷 ⚕

★ **Clancy's Pub**, 2703 E 20th St at Hutton Rd, Farmington; tel 505/325-8176. **Eclectic.** A classic pub, reminiscent of television's *Cheers,* with dark-green decor and an enclosed patio with lattice-work umbrella tables. There's a number of sandwiches, burgers, and southwestern dishes to choose from. Specialties include steak Clancy's, tenderloin steak with Swiss cheese, ham, and green chiles; fish and chips; and barbecued ribs. **FYI:** Reservations accepted. Blues/singer. **Open:** Mon–Sat 11am–2am, Sun noon–midnight. Closed some hols. **Prices:** Main courses $3.50–$8. Maj CC. 🍺 📷 ⚕

K B Dillon's, 101 W Broadway, Farmington; tel 505/325-0222. **Southwestern/Steak.** A comfortable, fun pub. Decorated with lots of plants and sports memorabilia. Fish, chicken, beef, and seafood. **FYI:** Reservations recommended. Blues/rock. Jacket required. **Open:** Lunch Mon–Fri 11am–2pm; dinner Mon–Sat 5–10:30pm. Closed some hols. **Prices:** Main courses $10.95–$18.95. Maj CC. ❤ ⚕

Señor Pepper's Restaurant, in Four Corners Regional Airport, Navajo St, Farmington; tel 505/327-0436. **Mexican.** Mexican fiesta-style decor. All food is prepared from fresh ingredients. Stacked and rolled enchiladas, a variety of burritos, tostadas, tacos, chiles rellenos, and combination plates. Southwestern-style steak, chicken, and seafood dishes also served. Items labeled "Life Course" contain no cheese or sour cream. **FYI:** Reservations accepted. Comedy. Children's menu. **Open:** Sun–Thurs 5am–10pm, Fri–Sat 5am–10:30pm. Closed some hols. **Prices:** Main courses $4.75–$16.95. Maj CC. 📷 ⚕

Attractions 💼

Salmon Ruin & San Juan County Archaeological Research Center, 975 US 64; tel 505/632-2013. Located 11 miles east of Farmington, this massive C-shaped pueblo overlooking the San Juan River was built in the 11th century as a Chacoan colony and is one of the most recently excavated ruins in the West. In 1990, **Heritage Park** was established on an adjoining plot of land. It comprises a series of reconstructed ancient and historic dwellings representing the area's cultures, from a paleoarchaic sand-dune site to an Anasazi pit house. Visitor center, small museum. **Open:** Daily 9am–5pm. Closed some hols. $

Angel Peak Recreation Area, NM 44; tel 505/599-8900. At the foot of the distinctive 6,800-foot pinnacle of Angel Peak is a variety of unusual, colorful geological formations and canyons to explore on foot. The Bureau of Land Management has developed 2 campgrounds and a picnic area, however there is no water and no on-site personnel. Free.

Ship Rock, US 64. This distinctive landmark is known to the Navajo as *Tes be dahi,* "Rock With Wings." Composed of igneous rock flanked by long upright walls of solidified lava, it rises 1,700 feet off the desert floor to an elevation of 7,178 feet. There are viewpoints off US 666, 6 to 7 miles south of the town of Shiprock. You can get closer by taking the tribal road to the community of Red Rock; but to get any nearer this sacred Navajo rock, you must have permission from the Navajo Tribal Council. Climbing is not permitted.

Bisti Badlands, Old NM 371; tel 505/599-8900. A federally protected area of strange rock formations, petrified logs, and prehistoric fossils. Visitors can walk among the huge turrets, buttes, spires, and pinnacles. The site is administered by the Bureau of Land Management, however there are no facilities on the premises. **Open:** Daily 24 hours. Free.

FLORA VISTA

Map page M-3, A1   (NE of Farmington)

Restaurant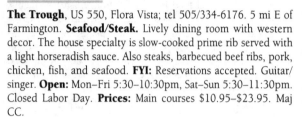

The Trough, US 550, Flora Vista; tel 505/334-6176. 5 mi E of Farmington. **Seafood/Steak.** Lively dining room with western decor. The house specialty is slow-cooked prime rib served with a light horseradish sauce. Also steaks, barbecued beef ribs, pork, chicken, fish, and seafood. **FYI:** Reservations accepted. Guitar/singer. **Open:** Mon–Fri 5:30–10:30pm, Sat–Sun 5:30–11:30pm. Closed Labor Day. **Prices:** Main courses $10.95–$23.95. Maj CC.

GALLUP

Map page M-3, B1

Hotel

El Rancho Hotel and Motel, 1000 E 66 Ave, Gallup, NM 87301; tel 505/863-9311 or toll free 800/543-6351; fax 505/722-5917. Exit 22 off I-40. This historic 1937 hotel was headquarters for numerous film crews and movie stars on location in the Southwest from the 1940s to the 1960s. There's an unmanned shoe shine stand in the lobby, and stills of movies shot in Gallup on the mezzanine level. **Rooms:** 98 rms, stes, and effic. CI 2pm/CO noon. Nonsmoking rms avail. All rooms have ceiling fans and artwork on the walls and are all named for movie stars. The Presidential Suite (Ronald Reagan stayed here when he was an actor) has a king bed, sofa, chairs, and an incredibly large bathroom with a whirlpool and bidet. The Marx Brothers Suite has 3 beds. **Amenities:** A/C, cable TV. Some units w/terraces. **Services:** 24-hour front desk. **Facilities:** 1 rst, 1 bar, washer/dryer. **Rates:** $39 S; $55 D; from $74 ste; from $39 effic. Extra person $5. Children under 10 stay free. Higher rates for spec evnts/hols. Pking: Outdoor, free. Maj CC.

Motels

Best Western Gallup Inn, 3009 W Hwy 66, Gallup, NM 87301; tel 505/772-2221 or toll free 800/528-1234; fax 505/722-7442. Exit 16 off I-40. A mid-size Best Western, noted for its large atrium courtyard containing a swimming pool and cafe. **Rooms:** 126 rms and stes. CI 1pm/CO noon. Nonsmoking rms avail. Rooms are decorated with an American Indian motif. **Amenities:** A/C, cable TV w/movies, refrig. **Services:** **Facilities:** 1 rst, 1 bar, games rm, spa, sauna, whirlpool. **Rates:** HS June–Sept $58 S; $64 D; from $64 ste. Lower rates off-season. Higher rates for spec evnts/hols. Spec packages avail. Pking: Outdoor, free. Maj CC.

Best Western Red Rock Inn, 3010 E US 66, Gallup, NM 87301; tel 505/722-7600 or toll free 800/528-1234; fax 505/722-9770. Exit 26 off I-40. Featuring a high-ceilinged lobby with comfortable furniture and Native American pictures. **Rooms:** 77 rms and stes. CI noon/CO 11am. Nonsmoking rms avail. Early American–style beds and overstuffed wing chairs; furnishings are of good quality. **Amenities:** A/C, cable TV, refrig. Some units w/terraces, some w/Jacuzzis. **Services:** **Facilities:** Spa, sauna, whirlpool, washer/dryer. **Rates:** HS May–Sept $65 S; $75 D; from $84 ste. Extra person $5. Children under 12 stay free. Lower rates off-season. Higher rates for spec evnts/hols. Spec packages avail. Pking: Outdoor, free. Maj CC.

Best Western Royal Holiday Motel, 1903 W US 66, Gallup, NM 87301; tel 505/722-4900 or toll free 800/528-1234; fax 505/722-5100. Exit 16 off I-40. A conveniently located, Spanish-style motel. **Rooms:** 50 rms. CI 3pm/CO 11am. Nonsmoking rms avail. Recently renovated and refurnished rooms are very handsome, with Early American–style beds, American Indian paintings, and deep-green carpets. **Amenities:** A/C, cable TV w/movies. **Services:** Babysitting. **Facilities:** Spa, whirlpool, playground. **Rates:** HS May 30–Sept 1 $54–$58 S; $60–$68 D. Extra person $4. Children under 12 stay free. Lower rates off-season. Spec packages avail. Pking: Outdoor, free. Maj CC.

Blue Spruce Lodge, 1119 E Hwy 66, Gallup, NM 87301; tel 505/863-5211. Exit 22 off I-40. A friendly, clean, small motel. **Rooms:** 20 rms and stes. CI noon/CO 11am. Nonsmoking rms avail. Rooms face either the highway or railroad tracks. Comfortable furnishings. There are some 2-bedroom suites. **Amenities:** A/C, cable TV w/movies. **Services:** **Facilities:** Games rm. **Rates:** $22 S; $26–$29 D; from $31 ste. Extra person $3. Children under 10 stay free. Higher rates for spec evnts/hols. Spec packages avail. Pking: Outdoor, free. Maj CC. A very good value.

El Capitan Motel, 1300 E Hwy 66, Gallup, NM 87301; tel 505/863-6828. Exit 22 off I-40. A pleasant, 1-story, adobe-style motel. **Rooms:** 42 rms and stes. CI noon/CO 11am. Nonsmoking rms avail. Southwestern decor, with prints on the walls and tile bathrooms. **Amenities:** A/C, cable TV. **Services:** **Rates:** HS May–Nov $28–$36 S; $30–$40 D; from $40 ste. Extra person $3. Children under 10 stay free. Lower rates off-season. Higher rates for spec evnts/hols. Spec packages avail. Pking: Outdoor, free. Maj CC. AARP discounts are available.

≝≝≝ **Holiday Inn**, 2915 W Hwy 66, Gallup, NM 87301; tel 505/722-2201 or toll free 800/432-2211; fax 505/722-9616. Exit 16 off I-40. A large, comfortable lobby and a patio area with welcoming green grass are hallmarks of this fine Holiday Inn. **Rooms:** 212 rms. CI noon/CO noon. Nonsmoking rms avail. Rooms are comfortable and quiet. **Amenities:** 🛅 🅰 A/C, cable TV w/movies. **Services:** ✕ 🚐 ⊠ ⌘ ⌂ Children's program, babysitting. **Facilities:** 🛗 🛍 800 ⌧ ⅙ 2 rsts, 1 bar (w/entertainment), games rm, spa, sauna, whirlpool, washer/dryer. There is a putting area in the games room, and a sun deck outside the indoor pool. Equipment for the hearing impaired is available. **Rates:** HS June–Sept $49–$87 S or D. Extra person $5. Children under 18 stay free. Min stay spec evnts. Lower rates off-season. Higher rates for spec evnts/hols. Pking: Outdoor, free. Maj CC.

Restaurants 🍴

Panz Alegra, 1201 E 66 Ave, Gallup; tel 505/722-7229. Exit 22 off I-40. **Mexican/Steak.** Brick walls and Tiffany lamps, booths and tables. Steaks, seafood, burgers, salads, and a variety of Mexican dishes, including posole, combination plates, fajitas, and burritos. **FYI:** Reservations recommended. Children's menu. Dress code. **Open:** Mon–Sat 11am–10pm. Closed some hols. **Prices:** Main courses $4–$12. Maj CC. 🖼 💟 ⅙

The Ranch Kitchen, 3001 W US 66, Gallup; tel 505/722-2537. Exit 16 off I-40. **Mexican/Southwestern.** Features 2 large, attractive dining rooms with blonde tables, white walls, corner fireplaces, low ceilings with vigas, wagon wheel chandeliers, and local art. An open-pit barbecue is outside. The menu includes New Mexican dishes, Navajo tacos, steaks, pork, and chicken; there's also a salad bar. Summer outdoor dining is offered after 5pm. A Navajo gift shop is on the premises. **FYI:** Reservations not accepted. Children's menu. Beer and wine only. **Open:** HS Apr–Oct daily 6am–10pm. Reduced hours off-season. Closed Dec 25. **Prices:** Main courses $4.95–$12.95. Maj CC. 🖼 ⅙

Attraction 🎫

Red Rock State Park, NM 566; tel 505/722-6196. Native American dancers perform nightly during the summer in the Marland Aitson Amphitheater, in a natural setting amidst red sandstone buttes. This arena is also the site of numerous annual events, including the Inter-Tribal Indian Ceremonial held in mid-August. The **Red Rock Museum** has displays on prehistoric Anasazi and modern Zuni, Hopi, and Navajo culture, as well as changing art gallery exhibits. **Open:** Park, daily sunrise–sunset; museum, Mon–Fri 8:30am–4:30pm. $

GRANTS

Map page M-3, B1

Motels 🛏

≝≝≝ **Best Western Grants Inn**, 1501 E Santa Fe Ave, Grants, NM 87020; tel 505/287-7901 or toll free 800/600-5221; fax 505/285-5751. Exit 85 off I-40. A good-looking motel. The central courtyard is graced by lush tropical plants surrounding an indoor swimming pool. **Rooms:** 126 rms. CI noon/CO noon. Nonsmoking rms avail. Rooms are quiet and spacious, with attractive artwork. Handicapped rooms have separate entrance. **Amenities:** 🛅 🅰 A/C, cable TV, refrig. **Services:** ✕ ⊠ ⌘ ⌂ **Facilities:** 500 ⅙ 1 rst, 1 bar (w/entertainment), games rm, sauna, whirlpool, washer/dryer. **Rates:** $61–$66 S; $71–$76 D. Extra person $10. Higher rates for spec evnts/hols. Spec packages avail. Pking: Outdoor, free. Maj CC.

≝≝ **Sands Motel**, 112 McArthur St, PO Box 1437, Grants, NM 87020; tel 505/287-2996 or toll free 800/424-7679. Exit 85 off I-40. A pleasant family-style motel. **Rooms:** 24 rms. CI 2pm/CO 11am. Nonsmoking rms avail. Some rooms have separate dressing areas. Handicapped-accessible room planned for 1995. **Amenities:** 🛅 🅰 A/C, cable TV w/movies, refrig. **Services:** 🚐 ⌘ ⌂ **Facilities:** Close to several restaurants; coffee shop within walking distance. **Rates:** HS May–Dec $30 S; $40–$43 D. Children under 12 stay free. Lower rates off-season. Pking: Outdoor, free. Maj CC. A very good value.

Restaurants 🍴

El Jardin Palacio's—Southwest Cuisine, 319 W Santa Fe Ave, Grants; tel 505/285-5231. Exit 81 off I-40. **Southwestern.** Mexican family-owned restaurant decorated with original oil paintings; located in a building that formerly housed the city hall, jail, and firehouse. Most selections are favorite family recipes. The menu offers Mexican combination plates, fajitas, burritos, chiles rellenos, and chimichangas. Also rainbow trout and several shrimp dishes. **FYI:** Reservations accepted. Children's menu. Beer and wine only. **Open:** Lunch Mon–Fri 11am–2:30pm; dinner Mon–Sat 5–9pm. Closed some hols. **Prices:** Main courses $2.95–$7.95. Maj CC. 🖼

Grants Station Restaurant, 200 W Santa Fe Ave, Grants; tel 505/287-2334. Exit 85 or 81 off I-40. **Regional American.** A fun place for kids and railroad buffs. Railroad memorabilia is everywhere; even the waitstaff sports railroad uniforms. A caboose outside is used as a private dining room. Steaks, fish, pork chops, chicken, shrimp, Mexican dishes, and sandwiches, plus salad bar. Breakfast is served all day. **FYI:** Reservations accepted.

Children's menu. No liquor license. **Open:** HS May–Sept daily 6am–11pm. Reduced hours off-season. Closed Dec 25. **Prices:** Main courses $2.75–$11.95. Maj CC. 🖼️ &

La Ventana, 110½ Geis St, Grants; tel 505/287-9393. Exit 81 off I-40. **Seafood/Steak.** Attractive, dimly lit restaurant with Southwest decor, and separate rooms for meetings and special events. Steaks, seafood, ribs, chicken, and a few Mexican dishes. **FYI:** Reservations recommended. Children's menu. **Open:** Mon–Sat 11am–11pm. Closed some hols. **Prices:** Main courses $3.95–$13.95. Maj CC. ♥ &

Monte Carlo Restaurant and Lounge, 721 W Santa Fe Ave, Grants; tel 505/287-9250. Exit 81 or 85 off I-40. **Mexican/ Southwestern.** A historical landmark on old Route 66, opened in 1947. Food is served in both the restaurant and lounge. Mexican decor. Both New Mexican and American dinners are offered, including a variety of beef, chicken, and shrimp entrees, plus chiles rellenos, enchiladas, fajitas, tamales, tacos, burritos, and sopaipillas. **FYI:** Reservations accepted. Guitar/singer. Children's menu. **Open:** Daily 7am–10pm. Closed Dec 25. **Prices:** Main courses $4–$13. Maj CC. 🍴 🖼️ &

Attractions 🏛️

The New Mexico Museum of Mining, 100 N Iron St; tel 505/287-4802. The world's only uranium-mining museum is structured over a re-creation of an actual underground mine, complete with original machinery and equipment. Once underground, visitors can touch and feel the mining tools, equipment, and cement walls. Retired miners often lead tours. **Open:** Summer, Mon–Sat 9am–6pm, Sun noon–6pm; winter, Mon–Sat 9am–4pm, Sun noon–4pm. Closed some hols. $

El Malpais National Monument, 620 E Santa Fe Ave; tel 505/285-5406. America's newest national monument, it is one of the outstanding examples of volcanic landscape in the United States. The area covers 115,000 acres of cinder cones, vast lava flows, hundreds of lava tubes and ice caves, sandstone cliffs, and natural bridges and arches. Anasazi ruins, ancient Indian trails, and Spanish and Anglo homesteads are located throughout.

From **Sandstone Bluffs Overlook**, many craters are visible in the lava flow. **La Ventana,** 17 miles south of I-40, is the largest natural arch in New Mexico. From NM 53 visitors have access to the **Zuni-Acoma Trail**, an ancient trade route that crosses 4 major lava flows in a 7½-mile (one-way) hike. **El Calderon**, 20 miles south of I-40, is a trailhead for exploration of a cinder cone, lava tubes, and a bat cave. **Open:** Daily 8am–4:30pm. Closed some hols. Free.

Cibola National Forest, 1800 Lobo Canyon Rd; tel 505/287-8833. Two major parcels of the forest flank I-40 on either

side of Grants. To the southeast, NM 547 leads some 20 miles into the San Mateo Mountains. The range's high point, 11,301-foot Mount Taylor, is home of the annual Mount Taylor Winter Quadrathlon in February. The route passes 2 campgrounds, Lobo Canyon and Coal Mine Canyon. Hiking and elk hunting are popular in summer, cross-country skiing in winter. **Open:** Daily 24 hours. Free.

HOBBS
Map page M-3, D4

Motels 🏨

≣≣≣ **Hobbs Motor Inn**, 501 N Marland St, Hobbs, NM 88240; tel 505/397-3251 or toll free 800/635-6635; fax 800/635-6635. A pleasant full-service motel, popular with business travelers and tour groups. **Rooms:** 76 rms and stes. CI 11am/CO 1pm. Nonsmoking rms avail. **Amenities:** 📷 A/C, cable TV w/movies. 1 unit w/minibar. Refrigerators are available. **Services:** ✕ 🍴 🖼️ 🔔 🔔 **Facilities:** �️ 🏊 2 rsts, 1 bar (w/entertainment). 15 percent discount for guests in the motel restaurants. Exercise room due to open in 1995. **Rates:** $38 S; $42–$45 D; from $65 ste. Extra person $4. Children under 15 stay free. Pking: Outdoor, free. Maj CC.

≣≣ **Zia Motel**, 619 N Marland St, Hobbs, NM 88240; tel 505/397-3591. A clean and comfortable, basic no-frills motel. Very popular with business travelers. **Rooms:** 38 rms. CI 5am/CO 11am. Nonsmoking rms avail. **Amenities:** 📷 A/C, cable TV w/movies. Some units w/terraces. **Services:** 🔔 🔔 Babysitting. Complimentary morning coffee. **Facilities:** �️ Within walking distance of 2 restaurants. **Rates:** $33 S; $36–$38 D. Extra person $3. Children under 12 stay free. Spec packages avail. Pking: Outdoor, free. Maj CC. Weekly rates are available.

Restaurant 🍽️

Cattle Baron Steak and Seafood Restaurant, 1930 N Grimes St, Hobbs; tel 505/393-2800. **Seafood/Steak.** Tastefully appointed with handsome polished wood and parquet tables. Etched-glass dividers separate booths. Three sizes of prime rib are offered. Entrees include salad bar, fresh-baked bread, and choice of baked potato, fries, rice pilaf, or steamed fresh vegetable. Happy hour weekdays 4-7pm; meals can be served in the bar. **FYI:** Reservations accepted. Children's menu. **Open:** Sun 11am–9pm, Mon–Thurs 11am–9:30pm, Fri–Sat 11am–10pm. Closed Dec 25. **Prices:** Main courses $6.95–$20.95. Maj CC. 🖼️ &

Attraction 💼

Lea County Cowboy Hall of Fame and Western Heritage Center, 5317 Lovington Hwy; tel 505/392-4510. Honors the area's ranchers and rodeo performers with displays of memorabilia and artifacts, as well as rotating exhibits by local and New Mexican artists. **Open:** Mon–Fri 10am–5pm, Sat 1–5pm. Closed some hols. Free.

JEMEZ PUEBLO

Map page M-3, B2

The 2,400 Jemez natives are the only remaining people to speak the Towa dialect of the Tanoan group. Famous for their dancing, Jemez feast days attract residents from many other pueblos. Celebration days include the Feast of Our Lady of Angels on August 12; the Feast of San Diego on November 12, when the Pecos bull dance is performed; and the Feast of Our Lady of Guadalupe on December 12, featuring the Matachines dance, based on a Spanish morality play.

There is fishing and picnicking along the Jemez River on government forest lands, and camping at the Dragonfly Recreation Area. Pueblo stores sell fishing permits, and permits for game hunting may be bought from the pueblo governor's office. The pueblo is 42 miles northwest of Albuquerque via I-25 to Bernalillo, NM 44 to San Ysidro, and NM 43 to the pueblo. Photographs prohibited. For more information contact the pueblo at 505/834-7359.

JEMEZ SPRINGS

Map page M-3, B2 (SW of Los Alamos)

Attraction 💼

Jemez State Monument, NM 4; tel 505/829-3530. All that is left of the Mission of San Jose de los Jemez, founded by Franciscan missionaries in 1621, is preserved at this site. The mission was excavated between 1921 and 1937, along with portions of a prehistoric Jemez pueblo. Artifacts found during the excavation are housed in a small museum. **Open:** May–Sept, daily 9:30am–5:30pm; Oct–Apr, daily 8:30am–4:30. Closed some hols. $

LAGUNA PUEBLO

Map page M-3, B2

The pueblo consists of a central settlement and 5 smaller villages some 32 miles east of Grants, and 45 miles west of Albuquerque. Founded after the 1680 Pueblo Revolt by refugees from the Rio Grande valley, it is the youngest of New Mexico's pueblos. Located here is the **Mission of San Jose de los Lagunas,** famous for its interior artwork. Pueblo and Navajo people from throughout the region attend the Fiesta de San Jose, held September 19, at the Laguna mission. The fair kicks off with a mass and procession, followed by a harvest dance, sports events, and a carnival. For more information contact the Laguna Pueblo at 505/552-6654.

LAMY

Map page M-3, B3 (SE of Santa Fe)

Restaurant 🍴

The Legal Tender, off US 285, Lamy; tel 505/466-8425. 15 mi SE of Santa Fe; exit 290 off I-25. **American.** Housed in a handsome old Victorian building across from the old Atchison, Topeka, and Santa Fe Railway station in Lamy, about 20 minutes south of Santa Fe. The handcarved cherrywood bar was imported from Germany in the late 1800s, when the building was a general store. The menu consists of creatively prepared vegetarian, chicken, seafood, beef, and lamb offerings. Friday and Saturday nights and Sunday lunch feature live country music; during Tuesday, Thursday, and Saturday lunch a ragtime pianist entertains. **FYI:** Reservations recommended. Country music/piano. **Open:** HS May–Oct lunch daily noon–3pm; dinner Sun–Thurs 5–8:30pm, Fri–Sat 5–9pm. Reduced hours off-season. Closed Dec 25. **Prices:** Main courses $12.50–$22.95. Ltd CC. 🍽️ 🅿️ 📷

LAS CRUCES

Map page M-3, D2

Hotel 🏨

⬛⬛⬛⬛ **Las Cruces Hilton Inn**, 705 S Telshor Blvd, Las Cruces, NM 88001; tel 505/522-4300 or toll free 800/288-1784; fax 505/522-4300. Exit 3 off I-25. Across from Mesilla Valley Mall. A luxurious downtown hotel, convenient to all Las Cruces attractions and activities, and adjacent to the city's largest shopping mall. **Rooms:** 210 rms and stes. Exec-level rms avail. CI 2pm/CO 1pm. Express checkout avail. Nonsmoking rms avail. Basic to luxurious rooms available. **Amenities:** 🛁 🖲 📺 A/C, cable TV w/movies. Some units w/terraces, some w/Jacuzzis. **Services:** ✗ 🚐 🖼 🗘 🐟 Car-rental desk, babysitting. **Facilities:** 🔂 🛥️ 🕱 🕹 1 rst, 1 bar (w/entertainment), whirlpool. Packages available that include use of the Picacho Hills private country club 18-hole golf course. **Rates:** $87 S; $97 D; from $100 ste. Extra person $10. Children under 13 stay free. Min stay spec evnts. Spec packages avail. Pking: Outdoor, free. Maj CC.

Motels

🟦🟦🟦 **Best Western Mesilla Valley Inn**, 901 Avenida de Mesilla, Las Cruces, NM 88005; tel 505/524-8603 or toll free 800/327-3314; fax 505/526-8437. Exit 140 off I-10. This modern, southwestern-style motel is close to Old Mesilla's galleries, shops, and restaurants, and to downtown Las Cruces. **Rooms:** 166 rms and effic. CI 2pm/CO 11am. Nonsmoking rms avail. **Amenities:** 🛁 🖲 A/C, cable TV w/movies. 1 unit w/terrace. Executive rooms have refrigerators and clock radios. **Services:** ✗ 🚐 🖼 🗘 🐟 Babysitting. **Facilities:** 🔂 🕱 🕹 1 rst, 1 bar (w/entertainment), games rm, whirlpool, washer/dryer. A golf course is within 3 miles. **Rates:** $48–$54 S; $52–$58 D; from $85 effic. Extra person $2. Children under 13 stay free. Pking: Outdoor, free. Maj CC. Rates include discount on restaurant meals, and children under 13 eat free.

🟦🟦 **Best Western Mission Inn**, 1765 S Main St, Las Cruces, NM 88005; tel 505/524-8591 or toll free 800/528-1234; fax 505/523-4740. An attractive Mexican mission-style building with stucco walls and a red tile roof. **Rooms:** 68 rms and stes. CI 2pm/CO noon. Nonsmoking rms avail. Rooms are adorned with Mexican tiles and western art. **Amenities:** 🛁 A/C, satel TV w/movies. **Services:** 🚐 🖼 🗘 🐟 **Facilities:** 🔂 🕱 1 rst, 1 bar, playground. The restaurant serves a daily breakfast buffet only. **Rates (BB):** $48 S; $52 D; from $74 ste. Extra person $4. Children under 12 stay free. Pking: Outdoor, free. Maj CC.

🟦🟦 **Hampton Inn**, 755 Avenida de Mesilla, Las Cruces, NM 88005; tel 505/526-8311 or toll free 800/426-7866; fax 505/527-2015. Exit 140 off I-10. Well-maintained, better-than-average motel at a convenient location on the southwest side of town, near historic Old Mesilla's shops, galleries, and restaurants. **Rooms:** 118 rms. CI 3pm/CO noon. Nonsmoking rms avail. **Amenities:** 🛁 🖲 📺 A/C, cable TV w/movies. Refrigerators and microwave ovens are available. **Services:** ✗ 🖼 🗘 🐟 Free local calls. **Facilities:** 🔂 🕱 🕹 **Rates (CP):** $48–$52 S; $53–$57 D. Children under 19 stay free. Pking: Outdoor, free. Maj CC.

Inns

🟦🟦 **Lundeen's Inn of the Arts**, 618 S Alameda Blvd, Las Cruces, NM 88005 (Downtown); tel 505/526-3327; fax 505/526-3355. 1½ acres. A historic and comfortable yet elegantly furnished inn, with wonderful artwork. **Rooms:** 18 rms and stes; 2 ctges/villas. CI 3pm/CO noon. No smoking. The rooms have no numbers, but each is named for a well-known artist and decorated in a motif recalling the artist's work. **Amenities:** 🛁 🖲 A/C, cable TV w/movies, refrig. Some units w/terraces, some w/fireplaces. Many rooms have bidets. **Services:** ✗ 🖼 🗘 🐟 Babysitting. The innkeepers often provide refreshments in the afternoon. **Facilities:** 🕱 🕹 Washer/dryer, guest lounge w/TV. The inn is close to the Wednesday and Saturday arts and crafts market on the downtown Main Street Mall. The innkeepers' Academy of the Arts program presents week-long programs on silversmithing, coil pottery, painting, and other art forms. Nearby tennis, golf, and ballroom dancing. **Rates (BB):** $53–$60 S or D; from $75 ste; from $85 ctge/villa. Extra person $10. Min stay spec evnts. Higher rates for spec evnts/hols. Spec packages avail. Pking: Outdoor, free. Ltd CC. Weekly rates are available.

🟦🟦🟦 **Meson de Mesilla**, 1803 Avenida de Mesilla, PO Box 1212, Las Cruces, NM 88046; tel 505/525-9212 or toll free 800/732-6025. Exit 140 off I-10. Head south on NM 28 toward Mesilla. A lovely adobe inn on the east side of Old Mesilla, this is a bed-and-breakfast in the European tradition. **Rooms:** 13 rms. CI 1pm/CO 11am. No smoking. Southwestern decor is uncluttered, comfortable, open and airy, with brass beds, antiques, and tile bathrooms. All rooms, except one on the ground floor, open onto an attractive second-floor veranda. **Amenities:** 🖲 📺 A/C, satel TV. No phone. All units w/terraces, some w/fireplaces. **Services:** 🚐 🗘 Full gourmet breakfast, including such items as orange yogurt pancakes or eggs Benedict. **Facilities:** 🔂 🕱 1 rst, 1 bar. **Rates (BB):** $45–$82 S or D. Extra person $10. Spec packages avail. Pking: Outdoor, free. Ltd CC.

Restaurants 🍴

Cattle Baron Steak and Seafood Restaurant, 790 S Telshor Blvd, Las Cruces; tel 505/522-7533. E of Mesilla Valley Mall. **Seafood/Steak.** Open and airy dining room with polished wood, off-white stucco walls, and lots of plants. Specializes in steak, prime rib, and fresh seafood, but grilled chicken, burgers, soups, and salads also available. **FYI:** Reservations accepted. Children's menu. **Open:** Sun–Thurs 11am–9:30pm, Fri–Sat 11am–10pm. Closed Dec 25. **Prices:** Main courses $6.95–$20.95. Maj CC. 🍽️ 🚼 🕹

♣ **Double Eagle**, 308 Calle Guadalupe, Las Cruces; tel 505/523-6700. **Continental.** An elegant restaurant in an old building, sporting a gold-leaf tin ceiling and furnished with antiques.

Especially popular are chateaubriand, filet mignon, salmon with orange-chile sauce, and lamb chops. Several entrees are prepared tableside. Homemade desserts. **FYI:** Reservations recommended. **Open:** Mon–Sat 11am–10pm, Sun 5–9pm. **Prices:** Main courses $10.95–$24.95. Maj CC. ⬤ ▮ ☚ ▣

★ **Fajitas**, 600 E Amador Ave, Las Cruces; tel 505/523-6407. **Southwestern.** Located in a historic, 100-year-old adobe home with beige walls and wood floors and ceilings, and decorated with Indian sand paintings and blankets. Serves traditional New Mexico–style Mexican food, with no chemical additives. Specialties are fajitas and enchiladas. **FYI:** Reservations accepted. **Open:** Lunch daily 11am–2pm; dinner daily 5–9pm. Closed some hols. **Prices:** Main courses $4.95–$21.95. Maj CC. ▮ ☚ ▣

La Posta, Old Mesilla Plaza, Las Cruces; tel 505/524-3524. SE corner of Old Mesilla Plaza. **Southwestern.** Housed in a historic 150-year-old adobe building with viga ceilings, rough wood, and white stucco walls. The menu features New Mexico–style Mexican food and charbroiled steaks. A house specialty is tostadas composts, which originated at the restaurant in 1939, the year it opened. It consists of a toasted corn tortilla cup filled with chile con carne and frijoles, topped with chopped lettuce, diced tomato, and grated cheese. **FYI:** Reservations recommended. Children's menu. Beer and wine only. **Open:** Sun 11am–9pm, Tues–Thurs 11am–9pm, Fri–Sat 11am–9:30pm. Closed some hols. **Prices:** Main courses $2.80–$11.95. Maj CC. ▮

Peppers, 306 Calle Guadalupe, Las Cruces; tel 505/523-4999. **Southwestern.** Located in a 150-year-old adobe, with viga and latilla ceilings, handmade Mexican-style chairs, and colorful, southwestern furnishings. Unusual southwestern fare is offered, such green chile wontons with pineapple salsa; shark fajitas; and shrimp enchiladas. **FYI:** Reservations recommended. **Open:** Mon–Sat 11am–10pm, Sun noon–9pm. **Prices:** Main courses $7.95–$13.95. Maj CC. ▮ ▣

Santa Fe Restaurant, 1410 S Solano Dr, Las Cruces; tel 505/522-0466. **Southwestern.** Wood and white-block walls, inlaid tile tables. Innovative Mexican dishes, steak, chicken, and shrimp. **FYI:** Reservations recommended. Guitar. Children's menu. Beer and wine only. No smoking. **Open:** Lunch Mon–Fri 11:30am–2pm, Sat 11:30am–4pm, Sun 11:30am–4pm; dinner Mon–Fri 5–10pm, Sat 4–10pm, Sun 4–9pm. Closed Dec 25. **Prices:** Main courses $4.95–$11.95. Maj CC. ▣

Attractions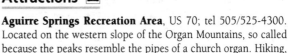

Aguirre Springs Recreation Area, US 70; tel 505/525-4300. Located on the western slope of the Organ Mountains, so called because the peaks resemble the pipes of a church organ. Hiking, camping, picnicking, horse trails. **Open:** Daily 8am–8pm. $

San Albino Church, Calle de Santiago and Calle Principal; tel 505/526-9349. Constructed in 1851, this is one of the oldest churches in the Mesilla Valley. It was named for St Albin, a medieval English bishop of North Africa. The church bells date from the early 1870s; the pews were made in Taos of Philippine mahogany. Tours, Tues–Sun 1–3pm. Free.

LAS VEGAS

Map page M-3, B3

Hotel ▣

▤▤▤ **Plaza Hotel**, 230 Old Town Plaza, Las Vegas, NM 87701; tel 505/425-3591 or toll free 800/328-1882; fax 505/425-9659. Exit 343 off I-25. A handsome, historic hotel right on Las Vegas Plaza, renovated to offer modern comforts in an 1880s setting. **Rooms:** 38 rms and stes. CI 2pm/CO 11am. Nonsmoking rms avail. Each room is uniquely decorated, with period furnishings, high ceilings, and distinctive moldings. **Amenities:** ▣ A/C, cable TV. **Services:** ✕ ⤷ ⟳ Masseur. **Facilities:** ▣ ⅃ 1 rst, 1 bar (w/entertainment). **Rates:** HS May–Nov $51–$57 S; $55–$60 D; from $80 ste. Extra person $5. Children under 12 stay free. Lower rates off-season. Higher rates for spec evnts/hols. Spec packages avail. Pking: Outdoor, free. Maj CC.

Motels

▤▤ **Comfort Inn**, 2500 N Grand Ave, Las Vegas, NM 87701; tel 505/425-1100 or toll free 800/716-1103; fax 505/454-8404. Exit 347 off I-25. A new motel on the outskirts of the city. **Rooms:** 101 rms. CI 2pm/CO 11am. Nonsmoking rms avail. **Amenities:** ▣ ▢ A/C, cable TV. **Services:** ⬤ ▣ ⤷ Babysitting. **Facilities:** ▣ ▣ ⅃ Whirlpool, washer/dryer. **Rates (CP):** $38–$53 S; $42–$59 D. Children under 18 stay free. Lower rates off-season. Pking: Outdoor, free. Maj CC.

▤▤ **Inn on the Santa Fe Trail**, 1133 Grand Ave, Las Vegas, NM 87701; tel 505/425-6791 or toll free 800/425-6791; fax 505/425-0417. Exit 345 off I-25. An attractively updated hacienda-style motel, close to the downtown plaza. **Rooms:** 42 rms and stes. CI 1pm/CO 11am. Nonsmoking rms avail. All overlook a central courtyard. The furniture was designed and hand-crafted by local artisans. **Amenities:** ▣ A/C, cable TV. Refrigerators are available in some rooms. **Services:** 🚐 🖼 🛎 🤿 Masseur, babysitting. **Facilities:** 🏋 🔲 ♿ Whirlpool, washer/dryer. **Rates (CP):** HS May 15–Oct 15 $44–$54 S; $49–$59 D; from $59 ste. Extra person $5. Children under 12 stay free. Lower rates off-season. Spec packages avail. Pking: Outdoor, free. Maj CC.

Restaurants 🍽

El Alto Supper Club, Sapello St off New Mexico Ave, Las Vegas; tel 505/454-0808. Exit 343 off I-25. **Seafood/Steak.** Situated on a hill overlooking the city, the El Alto has been run by the same family for over 50 years. It's known for its steaks, which are cut fresh daily. Some seafood and a few New Mexican combination dinners are offered as well. **FYI:** Reservations accepted. Children's menu. **Open:** HS May–Oct daily 6–9pm. Reduced hours off-season. Closed some hols. **Prices:** Main courses $9.95–$23.50. Ltd CC.

★ **El Rialto Restaurant**, 141 Bridge St, Las Vegas; tel 505/425-0037. ½ block S of the Plaza. **Mexican/Seafood/Steak.** Located in an old building with a tin ceiling; offers a good range of enchiladas, tacos, and sopaipillas, plus steak, chicken, and seafood dinners. **FYI:** Reservations accepted. Children's menu. **Open:** Mon–Sat 11am–9pm. Closed Dec 25. **Prices:** Main courses $5.29–$21.69. Maj CC. 🖼

Hillcrest Restaurant, 1106 Grand Ave, Las Vegas; tel 505/425-7211. Exit 347 off I-25. **Regional American.** Run by the same family since the 1940s, and known for its special Lenten meals. There are 2 dining areas—one a more formal dining room serving lunch and dinner, and the other a coffee shop. The homestyle cooking includes classic American fare from chicken-fried steak to hamburgers. Lunch buffet on Sunday with roast turkey and all the trimmings. **FYI:** Reservations recommended. Children's menu. **Open:** Lunch daily noon–2pm; dinner daily 5–8pm; brunch Sun 9am–3pm. Closed Dec 25. **Prices:** Main courses $5.95–$11.95. Ltd CC. 🖼

Attractions 📷

Fort Union National Monument, exit 366 off I-25; tel 505/425-8025. Although this was the largest military installation in the 19th-century Southwest, today it is in ruins. There's little to see but adobe walls and chimneys, but the very scope of the fort is impressive. The national monument visitor center has interpreted the fort's history through exhibits, booklets, and a walking trail. **Open:** Daily 8am–5pm. Closed some hols. $

Rough Riders Memorial and City Museum, Grand Ave; tel 505/425-8726. About 40 percent of Teddy Roosevelt's Spanish-American War campaigners in 1898 came from this frontier town; the museum chronicles their contribution to US history. **Open:** Mon–Sat 9am–4pm. Free.

Las Vegas National Wildlife Refuge, NM 104; tel 505/425-3581. This has 220 species of birds and animals on 8,750 acres of wetland. **Open:** Mon–Fri 8am–4:30. Closed some hols. Free.

LEMITAR

Map page M-3, C2 (N of Socorro)

Restaurant 🍽

Coyote Moon Cafe, W Frontage Rd, Lemitar; tel 505/835-2536. 7 mi N of Socorro; exit 156 off I-25. **American/Mexican.** Situated in what was originally a chile processing plant, this large restaurant adorned with chile ristras has a casual "cowboy" atmosphere. Generous portions of Mexican dishes; also beef, chicken, sandwiches, burgers, and salads. Specialties include carnitas con papas, chunks of lean beef fried with potatoes and onions; and papa llena, a baked potato stuffed with taco meat, beans, cheese, lettuce, tomato, and either chile or salsa. **FYI:** Reservations accepted. Children's menu. No liquor license. **Open:** Mon–Fri 11am–9pm, Sat–Sun 8am–8pm. Closed Dec 25. **Prices:** Main courses $2.40–$10.10. Ltd CC. 🖼 ♿

LINCOLN

Map page M-3, D3

Attraction 📷

Lincoln State Monument, Hwy 380 W; tel 505/653-4372. Lincoln is one of the last historic yet uncommercialized 19th-century towns remaining in the West. The entire town is a New Mexico State Monument and a National Historic Landmark. Billy the Kid shot his way out of the **Old Courthouse** located here, now a state museum. A hole made by a bullet from the Kid's gun still exists.

At the Lincoln County Heritage Trust's **Historical Center**, exhibits explain the role of Apaches, Hispanics, Anglo cowboys, and Buffalo Soldiers in Lincoln's history and provide details of the Lincoln County War. **Open:** Daily 9am–6pm. Closed some hols. $

LORDSBURG

Map page M-3, D1

Motels 🛏

≣≣ **Best Western American Motor Inn**, 944 E Motel Dr, Lordsburg, NM 88045; tel 505/542-3591 or toll free 800/528-1234. Exit 24 off I-10. 1 mi W on I-10 business loop. This better-than-average motel is a good choice for either business or vacation travelers. **Rooms:** 88 rms and stes. CI 11am/CO 11am. Nonsmoking rms avail. **Amenities:** 🛅 A/C, satel TV w/movies. 24-hour lobby. **Services:** ✕ 🚙 🖾 🖴 🖣 Fax service available. **Facilities:** 🖼 🏊 ⅙ 1 rst, 1 bar, playground. **Rates (BB):** $39–$49 S; $44–$49 D; from $86 ste. Extra person $5. Pking: Outdoor, free. Maj CC.

≣≣ **Best Western Western Skies Inn**, 1303 S Main St, Lordsburg, NM 88045; tel 505/542-8807 or toll free 800/528-1234; fax 505/542-8895. Exit 22 off I-10. A popular travelers' stopover, halfway between El Paso and Tucson. Reservations are highly recommended. **Rooms:** 40 rms. CI 10am/CO 11am. Nonsmoking rms avail. **Amenities:** 🛅 A/C, cable TV, refrig. **Services:** 🚙 🖴 🖣 **Facilities:** 🖼 ⅙ Lawn games. **Rates:** $44 S; $49 D. Extra person $5. Children under 13 stay free. Pking: Outdoor, free. Maj CC.

Restaurant 🍴

Kranberry's Family Restaurant, 1405 S Main St, Lordsburg; tel 505/542-9400. Exit 22 off I-10. **American/Mexican.** Large windows and southwestern art. Variety of homestyle family favorites, including burgers, sandwiches, chicken and beef entrees, and salads. Baked goods are made on the premises. **FYI:** Reservations accepted. Children's menu. No liquor license. **Open:** Daily 6am–10pm. Closed Dec 25. **Prices:** Main courses $2.69–$13.89. Maj CC. 🍴 ⅙

Attractions 💼

Shakespeare Ghost Town, I-10 exit 22; tel 542-9034. A National Historic Site, this was once the home of 3,000 miners, promoters, and dealers of various kinds. Since 1935, it's been privately owned by the Hill family, who have kept it uncommercialized with no souvenir hype or gift shop. They offer 2-hour guided tours on a limited basis, and reenactments and special events 4 times a year. Six original buildings and 2 reconstructed buildings survive in various stages of repair or disrepair. **Open:** 10am and 2pm second and fourth weekends of every month. $

Steins Railroad Ghost Town, I-10 exit 3; tel 505/542-9791. This settlement 19 miles west of Lordsburg started as a Butterfield Stage stop, then was a railroad town of about 1,000 residents from 1905 to 1945. Today there are 10 buildings with 16 rooms filled with 19th- and 20th-century artifacts and furnishings. There's also the Steins Mercantile shop and a petting zoo for kids. **Open:** Daily 9am–5pm. Closed some hols. $

LOS ALAMOS

Map page M-3, B2

Hotel 🛏

≣≣≣ **Hilltop House Hotel**, 400 Trinity, Los Alamos, NM 87544; tel 505/662-2441 or toll free 800/462-0936; fax 505/662-5913. **Rooms:** 108 rms, stes, and effic. Exec-level rms avail. CI 3pm/CO 11am. Express checkout avail. Nonsmoking rms avail. **Amenities:** 🛅 🖥 A/C, cable TV w/movies, voice mail. Some units w/terraces. **Services:** ✕ 🚙 🖾 🖴 🖣 Twice-daily maid svce, car-rental desk. **Facilities:** 🖼 🏊 🔟 ⅙ 1 rst, 1 bar, beauty salon, washer/dryer. The dining room is on the third floor and offers magnificent views of the Sangre de Cristo Mountains. **Rates (CP):** HS Mem Day–Labor Day $73 S; $83 D; from $98 ste; from $78 effic. Extra person $10. Children under 12 stay free. Lower rates off-season. Spec packages avail. Pking: Outdoor, free. Maj CC.

Attractions 💼

Bradbury Science Museum, 1309 15th St; tel 505/667-4444. Offers a glimpse into World War II's historic Manhattan Project as well as today's advanced science and technology. There are more than 35 hands-on exhibits for visitors to explore lasers and computers and view laboratory research in energy, defense, the environment, and health. **Open:** Tues–Fri 9am–5pm, Sat–Mon 1–5pm. Closed some hols. Free.

Bandelier National Monument, NM 4; tel 505/672-3861. Combines the extensive ruins of an ancient cliff-dwelling Anasazi pueblo culture with 46 square miles of canyon-and-mesa wilderness. A cottonwood-shaded 1½-mile trail along Frijoles Creek heads to the principal ruins; 60 miles of maintained trails lead to more ruins and ceremonial sites, waterfalls, and wildlife habitats. The separate Tsankawi section of the monument, reached by an ancient 2-mile trail close to White Rock, contains a large unexcavated ruin on a high mesa overlooking the Rio Grande Valley. Visitor center and museum near entrance. **Open:** Daily sunrise–sunset. Closed some hols. $$

Los Alamos Historical Museum, 1921 Juniper St; tel 505/662-6272. Recounts area history, from prehistoric cliff dwellers to the present, with exhibits ranging from Native American artifacts to school memorabilia and wartime displays. **Open:** Mon–Sat 10am–4pm, Sun 1–4pm. Closed some hols. Free.

Fuller Lodge Art Center, 2132 Central Ave; tel 505/662-9331. The massive log building that once housed the dining and recreation hall for the Los Alamos Ranch School for boys is now a National Historic Landmark known as the Fuller Lodge. Besides the art center, its current occupants include the Los Alamos Historical Museum (see above) and the Los Alamos County Chamber of Commerce, which doubles as a visitor information center. The art center has works of northern New Mexico artists and stages traveling exhibitions of regional and national importance. **Open:** Mon–Sat 10am–4pm, Sun 1–4pm. Free.

LOS LUNAS
Map page M-3, C2

Restaurant 🍽

The Luna Mansion, NM 6 and NM 85, Los Lunas; tel 505/865-7333. Exit 203 off I-25. **New American/Steak.** Located in a National Historic Landmark building dating from 1881. The menu features a variety of steaks, prime rib, game, chicken, and seafood. Specialties include lamb loin medallions with 2 sauces. **FYI:** Reservations recommended. **Open:** Dinner daily 5–10:30pm; brunch Sun 11am–2pm. Closed Dec 25. **Prices:** Main courses $9.95–$20.95. Maj CC. 🍴💟♿

MESCALERO
Map page M-3, D3

Resort 🏨

≡≡≡ **Inn of the Mountain Gods**, Carrizo Canyon Rd, PO Box 269, Mescalero, NM 88340; tel 505/257-4431 or toll free 800/545-6040; fax 505/257-6173. 3 mi SW of Ruidoso. A luxurious mountain resort operated by the Mescalero Apaches on the tribe's 460,000-acre reservation. The spectacular multi-story building has a tall copper fireplace in the center of the lobby. **Rooms:** 253 rms and stes. CI 4pm/CO noon. Nonsmoking rms avail. Beautifully decorated in a Native American motif; most have views of the pool area and Lake Mescalero. **Amenities:** 🏠 A/C, cable TV w/movies. 1 unit w/fireplace. Each has a wet bar and some have refrigerators. **Services:** ✕ 🛎 🖼 🛗 **Facilities:**

🛗 🚴 ⚠ 🔌 ▶18 🏊 🎿 🎾6 900 ♿ 3 rsts, 5 bars (2 w/entertainment), games rm, lawn games, sauna, whirlpool. Championship golf course designed by Ted Robinson. **Rates:** HS June–Sept $120 S or D; from $130 ste. Extra person $12. Children under 12 stay free. Lower rates off-season. Higher rates for spec evnts/hols. Spec packages avail. Pking: Outdoor, free. Maj CC.

Attraction 🏛

Mescalero Apache Indian Reservation, US 70; tel 505/671-4495. Immediately south and west of Ruidoso, it covers 460,000 acres and is home to about 2,800 members of the Mescalero, Chiricahua, and Lipan bands of Apache. The Mescalero Cultural Center has photos, artifacts, clothing, craftwork, and other exhibits that demonstrate the history and culture of the people.

St Joseph's Mission, just off US 70 on a hill overlooking the reservation, is a Gothic-style structure with walls 8 feet thick that was built by the Apache between the 2 World Wars. Symbols of Apache mountain gods and Roman Catholic saints appear in paintings and carvings inside. **Open:** Mon–Fri 8am–4:30pm. Free.

MESILLA
Map page M-3, E2 (SW of Las Cruces)

Restaurant 🍽

♀ **Meson de Mesilla**, 1803 Avenida de Mesilla, Mesilla; tel 505/525-2380. Exit 140 off I-10. **Continental.** Southwestern decor complimented by stained glass windows and tile floors. Entrees include duck breast, veal, lobster tail, salmon, quail, and the house specialty—chateaubriand for two—flamed in cognac and prepared tableside. **FYI:** Reservations recommended. Guitar. **Open:** Lunch Wed–Fri 11:30am–2pm; dinner Tues–Sat 5:30–9pm; brunch Sun 11am–2pm. **Prices:** Main courses $17.95–$34.95. Ltd CC. 💟 🍴 🖼 🏔

MORA
Map page M-3, B3

Attraction 🏛

Morphy Lake State Park, NM 518; tel 505/387-2328. Located 4 miles south of Mora down a dirt road. The pine forest offers primitive camping, and the lake is known for its trout fishing. **Open:** Daily sunrise to sunset. $

PINOS ALTOS
Map page M-3, D1   (N of Silver City)

Restaurant 🍽

🌶 **Buckhorn Saloon**, NM 15, Pinos Altos; tel 505/538-9911. 7 mi N of Silver City. **Seafood/Steak.** Old West atmosphere; viga ceiling, white-washed brick walls, large brick fireplaces. Steaks, seafood, chicken, and burgers. Specialties are prime rib and filet mignon. A loaf of fresh-baked bread is taken to each table. **FYI:** Reservations recommended. Guitar/jazz/piano/singer. **Open:** Mon–Sat 6–10pm. Closed some hols. **Prices:** Main courses $10.95–$26.95. Ltd CC. ♥ ▣

PORTALES
Map page M-3, C4

Attraction 🖼

Blackwater Draw Archeological Site and Museum, US 70; tel 505/562-2202. This site contains the first well-documented evidence of man in North America, dating back approximately 11,000 years. On display are artifacts uncovered at the dig, including stone tools believed to be used by the Clovis people to hunt for mammoth. **Open:** Mon–Sat 10am–5pm, Sun noon–5pm. Closed Mon Sept–May. $

RADIUM SPRINGS
Map page M-3, D2   (NW of Las Cruces)

Attraction 🖼

Fort Selden State Monument, I-25; tel 505/526-8911. Founded in 1865, the fort housed the famous African-American cavalry, the "Buffalo Soldiers," who protected settlers from marauding Apaches. Today there are only eroding ruins remaining; displays in the visitor center tell the fort's story. Adjacent to the state monument is **Leasburg Dam State Park** where visitors can picnic, camp, boat, and swim. **Open:** Daily 9am–6pm. Closed some hols. $

RATON
Map page M-3, A3

Motels 🛏

≣≣≣ **Best Western Sands Motel**, 300 Clayton Rd, Raton, NM 87740; tel 505/445-2737 or toll free 800/518-2581; fax 505/445-4053. Exit 451 off I-25. An attractive motel, with a fenced, tree-shaded area for relaxing in lawn chairs. **Rooms:** 50 rms and stes. CI open/CO 11am. Nonsmoking rms avail. Custom-made furniture and southwestern art. The family room sleeps up to 8. **Amenities:** 🕾 A/C, cable TV w/movies. All rooms in the luxury wing have refrigerators, reclining, over-stuffed lounge chairs, 25-inch TVs, coffeemakers, and clock radios. VCRs and videotapes are available for rent. **Services:** 🚐 🍸 **Facilities:** 🚣 🏊 ⟨50⟩ ⬧ 1 rst (see also "Restaurants" below), whirlpool, playground. The restaurant is open April to October only. **Rates:** HS June 16–Sept 6 $67–$78 S; $69–$80 D; from $73 ste. Extra person $3. Children under 12 stay free. Min stay spec evnts. Lower rates off-season. Pking: Outdoor, free. Maj CC.

≣≣ **Harmony Manor Motel**, 351 Clayton Rd, Raton, NM 87740; tel 505/445-2763 or toll free 800/992-0347. Exit 451 off I-25. Very clean, pleasant motel offering basic lodging. **Rooms:** 18 rms. CI 6am/CO 11am. Nonsmoking rms avail. **Amenities:** 🕾 A/C, cable TV. **Services:** 🚐 🍸 ⟨⟩ Babysitting. **Facilities:** ⬧ Playground. **Rates:** HS May 10–Sept 4 $40–$48 S; $44–$58 D. Extra person $4. Children under 18 stay free. Lower rates off-season. Pking: Outdoor, free. Maj CC.

≣ **Melody Lane Motel**, 136 Canyon Dr, Raton, NM 87740; tel 505/445-3655 or toll free 800/421-5210; fax 505/445-3641. Exit 454 off I-25. A quiet motel on the north side of downtown. **Rooms:** 26 rms. CI 1pm/CO 11am. Nonsmoking rms avail. Rooms are pleasant and well-appointed, with pine ceilings, southwestern art, and solid furnishings. **Amenities:** 🕾 A/C, cable TV w/movies. Roll-a-way beds are available. There are some in-room steam baths. **Services:** 🚐 🍸 ⟨⟩ **Facilities:** ⟨30⟩ **Rates (CP):** HS Mid-May–Labor Day $32–$49 S; $36–$55 D. Extra person $5. Lower rates off-season. Pking: Outdoor, free. Maj CC.

Restaurants 🍽

Capri Restaurant, 304 Canyon Dr, Raton; tel 505/445-9755. **American/Italian/Mexican.** A small, simple cafe. Pasta specials offered Friday and Saturday evenings cost $5.45 and include salad, garlic bread, and a glass of wine. (Reservations are recommended for those evenings, and for large parties.) At other times there's American fare, including steak sandwiches, burgers, pork chops, fish, and chicken; plus several Mexican dishes. The restaurant has a packaged liquor store. **FYI:** Reservations accepted. **Open:** HS May–Sept daily 7am–9pm. Reduced hours off-season. Closed some hols. **Prices:** Main courses $4.25–$8.95. Maj CC. 👥

★ **El Matador**, 1012 S 2nd St, Raton; tel 505/445-9575. **Southwestern.** Bright, diner-like restaurant. Recommended for its Mexican food: enchiladas, tamales, tacos, burritos, and bowls of red or green chile. Burgers, sandwiches, steak, and seafood are also available. **FYI:** Reservations accepted. Children's menu. No liquor license. **Open:** Tues–Sun 7am–8:30pm. Closed some hols. **Prices:** Main courses $3.25–$12.25. Ltd CC. 👥 &

Pappas' Sweet Shop Restaurant, 1201 S 2nd St, Raton; tel 505/445-9811. **American.** Upscale, well-established restaurant. Decorated with antiques and collectibles; furnishings include tiles and other items from the family's original 1925 candy and ice cream shop, plus old photos of the Raton area. Steak and prime rib is the specialty, and Pappas' is noted for its margaritas. Sandwiches are made on homemade breads. There's an attached gift shop, and parking for RVs and other large vehicles in back. **FYI:** Reservations recommended. Piano. Children's menu. **Open:** HS June–Sept breakfast daily 9–11am; lunch daily 11am–2pm; dinner daily 5–9pm. Reduced hours off-season. Closed some hols. **Prices:** Main courses $5.95–$22.95. Maj CC. ▮ ♥ &

Sands Restaurant, in Best Western Sands Motel, 300 Clayton Rd, Raton; tel 505/445-8041. Exit 451 off I-25. **Regional American.** Traditional American cooking in an open and spacious dining room with large picture windows. The turkey and chicken casseroles are popular. **FYI:** Reservations accepted. Children's menu. No liquor license. **Open:** Daily 6:30am–9pm. Closed Nov–Mar. **Prices:** Main courses $4.95–$13.95. Maj CC. 👥 &

Attractions 🖼

Dorsey Mansion, US 56; tel 505/375-2222. A 2-story log-and-stone home built in the 1880s by cattleman Stephen Dorsey. It features 36 rooms, hardwood floors, Italian marble fireplaces, a hand-carved cherry wood staircase, and a dining room table that seats 60. Visitation by appointment only. $

Raton Museum, 216 S First St; tel 505/455-8979. Displays a wide variety of mining, railroad, and ranching items from the early days of the town. Walking tour maps available. **Open:** Tues–Sat 10am–4pm. Free.

RED RIVER

Map page M-3, A3

Hotel 🛏

≣≣≣ **Lifts West Condominium Resort Hotel**, Main St, PO Box 318, Red River, NM 87558; tel 505/754-2778 or toll free 800/221-1859; fax 505/754-6617. The dramatic lobby is 3 stories high, with a large stone fireplace at one end and a glass elevator at the other. It's the site of classical music concerts, square dancing, and lectures, plus cozy after-ski chats around the blazing fire. **Rooms:** 86 rms and stes. CI 2pm/CO 10am. Nonsmoking rms avail. Accommodations are large and beautifully furnished, with fully equipped kitchens and dining areas. **Amenities:** 🛁 ♨ 📺 Cable TV, refrig, VCR. No A/C. Some units w/terraces, some w/fireplaces. **Services:** 🛎 Babysitting. **Facilities:** 🔥 🏋 🎿 📷 1 rst, sauna, whirlpool, washer/dryer. **Rates:** HS Nov–Mar $69–$99 S; $109–$139 D; from $179 ste. Extra person $10. Children under 12 stay free. Min stay spec evnts. Lower rates off-season. Spec packages avail. Pking: Indoor/outdoor, free. Maj CC. Rates are reasonable, considering the quality.

Motel

≣ **Ponderosa Lodge**, 200 W Main St, PO Box 528, Red River, NM 87558; tel 505/754-2988 or toll free 800/336-RSVP. A conveniently located motel in the center of town, close to all of Red River's attractions and activities. **Rooms:** 36 rms, stes, and effic. CI 1pm/CO 10am. Nonsmoking rms avail. Standard rooms with modest furnishings. **Amenities:** 🛁 📺 Cable TV, refrig. No A/C. All units w/terraces, some w/fireplaces. **Services:** 🛎 **Facilities:** 🏋 🎿 📷 Washer/dryer. **Rates:** HS Dec–Mar $81 S or D; from $99 ste; from $215 effic. Extra person $10. Children under 12 stay free. Min stay spec evnts. Lower rates off-season. Spec packages avail. Pking: Outdoor, free. Maj CC.

Lodges

≣≣ **Alpine Lodge**, Main St, PO Box 67, Red River, NM 87558; tel 505/754-2952 or toll free 800/252-2333. An attractive lodge, conveniently located, with a view of the river. A park along the river has picnic tables, grills, and benches, and a bridge connecting the property to the main ski lift. **Rooms:** 45 rms, stes, and effic; 1 ctge/villa. CI 2pm/CO 10am. Rooms are well-appointed and comfortable. Many overlook the river; others have a view of the ski slopes. **Amenities:** 🛁 📺 Satel TV w/movies, refrig. No A/C. All units w/terraces, some w/fireplaces. **Services:** 🛎 Babysitting. **Facilities:** 🔥 🏋 🎿 📷 & 1 rst, 1 bar (w/entertainment), playground, washer/dryer. **Rates:** HS July–Sept/Nov–Mar $40–$46 S; $50–$70 D; from $64 ste; from $58 effic; from $120 ctge/villa. Extra person $8. Children under 12 stay free. Min stay spec evnts. Lower rates off-season. Spec packages avail. Pking: Outdoor, free. Maj CC.

The Riverside, 210 E Main St, PO Box 249, Red River, NM 87558; tel 505/754-2252 or toll free 800/432-9999; fax 505/754-2495. Located on a full city block in the center of town. The grounds are spacious and well-kept. **Rooms:** 41 rms, stes, and effic. CI 3pm/CO 10am. Nonsmoking rms avail. Rooms are simple but large, good for families. Duplexes sleep 5. **Amenities:** Cable TV, refrig. No A/C. All units w/terraces, some w/fireplaces. **Services:** **Facilities:** Lawn games, playground. **Rates:** HS Dec–Mar/June–Sept $50–$65 S; $63–$85 D; from $89 ste; from $89 effic. Extra person $10. Lower rates off-season. Spec packages avail. Pking: Outdoor, free. Maj CC.

Restaurant

★ **Texas Red's Steakhouse and Saloon**, 111 E Main St, Red River; tel 505/754-2964. **Steak.** Down-home, Old West–style eatery. The menu is mostly steak, with some salads and chicken. There's usually a wait, but patrons can call the "waiting list hot line" at 754-2922 to check on seating availability. **FYI:** Reservations not accepted. **Open:** Daily 5–9:30pm. Closed Nov. **Prices:** Main courses $10.50–$28.50. Maj CC.

Attraction

Red River Ski Area, Pioneer Rd; tel 800/348-6444. The 27 trails on the mountain are geared toward the intermediate skier. There's a 1,500-foot vertical drop here to a base elevation of 8,750 feet. **Open:** Nov–Mar, daily 9am–4pm. $$$$

ROSWELL

Map page M-3, D3

Motels

Days Inn, 1310 N Main St, Roswell, NM 88201; tel 505/623-4021 or toll free 800/329-7466; fax 505/623-0079. 1 mi N of US 70/380 on US 285. No-frills, standard motel. **Rooms:** 62 rms. CI noon/CO 11am. Nonsmoking rms avail. **Amenities:** A/C, cable TV w/movies. **Services:** **Facilities:** 1 rst, 1 bar, whirlpool. **Rates (CP):** $36 S; $40–$44 D. Extra person $5. Children under 12 stay free. Pking: Outdoor, free. Maj CC.

Frontier Motel, 3010 N Main St, Roswell, NM 88201; tel 505/622-1400 or toll free 800/678-1401; fax 505/622-1405. 1 mi N of center of town on US 285. A well-kept "mom and pop" motel, friendly and welcoming. **Rooms:** 38 rms and stes. CI 11am/CO 11am. Nonsmoking rms avail. Simple, clean, standard motel rooms. Some smaller, less expensive rooms have showers only; larger rooms have shower/bath combinations. **Amenities:** A/C, cable TV w/movies, refrig. **Services:** **Facilities:** 1 rst. **Rates (CP):** $34–$43 S; $38–$47 D; from $50 ste. Extra person $3. Higher rates for spec evnts/hols. Pking: Outdoor, free. Maj CC.

National 9 Inn, 2001 N Main St, Roswell, NM 88201; tel 505/622-0110 or toll free 800/423-3106; fax 505/622-0110. ½ mi N of center of town on US 285. A small, no-frills motel. **Rooms:** 67 rms and effic. CI noon/CO 11am. Nonsmoking rms avail. **Amenities:** A/C, cable TV w/movies. **Services:** **Facilities:** **Rates:** $29–$33 S; $34–$40 D. Extra person $4. Children under 13 stay free. Higher rates for spec evnts/hols. Pking: Outdoor, free. Maj CC.

Sally Port Inn, 2000 N Main St, Roswell, NM 88201; tel 505/622-6430 or toll free 800/600-5221; fax 505/623-7631. ½ mi N of downtown on US 285. Attractively decorated and well maintained. **Rooms:** 124 rms. CI noon/CO noon. Nonsmoking rms avail. **Amenities:** A/C, cable TV w/movies. **Services:** Twice-daily maid svce, car-rental desk. **Facilities:** 1 rst, 1 bar, sauna, whirlpool, beauty salon, washer/dryer. There's an 18-hole golf course adjacent to the property. **Rates:** $52–$54 S; $62–$64 D. Extra person $10. Children under 18 stay free. Spec packages avail. Pking: Outdoor, free. Maj CC.

Restaurants

Keuken Dutch Restaurant, 1208 N Main St, Roswell; tel 505/624-2040. **American/Dutch.** Decorated in blue and white, with prints of Holland on the walls and Delft china (which is for sale). Choice of basic American dishes and several Dutch entrees. **FYI:** Reservations accepted. No liquor license. **Open:** Daily 5am–11pm. **Prices:** Main courses $4.99–$10.99. Maj CC.

Mario's, 200 E 2nd St, Roswell; tel 505/623-1740. 1 block E of US 285. **American/Mexican.** Southwestern steakhouse decor, with ceiling fans, painted brick walls, plants. Intimate bar. Mexican and American specialties, including steak, catfish, a number of "heart smart" dishes, and a salad bar. **FYI:** Reservations accepted. Children's menu. **Open:** Mon–Thurs 11am–9pm, Fri–Sat 11am–10pm. Closed some hols. **Prices:** Main courses $4.95–$12.95. Maj CC.

Ⓢ **Nuthin' Fancy Cafe**, 2103 N Main St, Roswell; tel 505/ 623-4098. ½ mi N of downtown Roswell on US 285. **American.** An open and airy cafe with chile ristras, neon cactus, and western prints. Seating at both booths and tables. Burgers, sandwiches, and diner-type favorites such as meatloaf, chicken-fried steak, and fried catfish. Also grilled chicken and fish, and nightly specials. **FYI:** Reservations accepted. No liquor license. **Open:** Daily 6am–9pm. Closed Dec 25. **Prices:** Main courses $3.75–$7.50. Ltd CC. 🏧 ♿

Pepper's Grill and Bar, in Sunwest Center, 500 N Main St, Roswell; tel 505/623-1700. **Mexican/Southwestern.** Delightful cartoon chile characters decorate the walls in this fun restaurant and bar. There are big, comfortable booths, as well as tables. The menu has many southwestern dinners, plus beef, chicken, and seafood entrees. Specialties include steak or chicken fajitas, mesquite-smoked baby-back ribs, and, on Friday and Saturday nights, prime rib. **FYI:** Reservations accepted. Blues/guitar. Children's menu. **Open:** Mon–Thurs 11am–9pm, Fri–Sat 11am–10pm. Closed some hols. **Prices:** Main courses $3.90– $11.95. Maj CC. 🍸 🛄 🏧 ♿

Attractions 🧰

Historical Center for Southeast New Mexico, 200 N Lea Ave; tel 505/622-8333. On the National Register of Historic Places, this 1910 mansion built by rancher J P White is a monument to turn-of-the-century style. The house is fully restored and furnished with early 20th-century antiques; there is also a gallery of changing historical exhibits. **Open:** Fri–Sun 1–4pm. Free.

Roswell Museum and Art Center, 100 W 11th St; tel 505/ 624-6744. The museum proclaims the city's role as a center for the arts and a cradle of America's space industry. The art center contains the world's finest collection of works by Peter Hurd and his wife, Henriette Wyeth, as well as representative works by Georgia O'Keeffe, Ernest Blumenschein, Joseph Sharp, and other famed members of the early 20th-century Taos and Santa Fe art colonies. The Robert Goddard Collection presents actual engines, rocket assemblies, and specialized parts developed by the rocket scientist in the 1930s, when he lived and worked in Roswell. **Open:** Mon–Sat 9am–5pm, Sun 1–5pm. Closed some hols. Free.

New Mexico Military Institute, 101 W College Blvd; tel 505/ 624-8100. Considered the "West Point of the West," the military school celebrated its centennial in 1991. The **General Douglas L McBride Military Museum** on campus houses a collection of artillery and artifacts that document New Mexico's role in America's wars. **Open:** Daily 8am–4pm. Free.

Spring River Park and Zoo, 1400 E College Blvd; tel 505/ 624-6760. The park covers 48 acres and features a miniature train, an antique carousel, a large prairie dog town, a children's fishing pond, a picnic ground, and playgrounds. The zoo contains regional animals displayed in their natural habitats as well as a children's petting zoo, and a Texas longhorn ranch. **Open:** Daily 10am–sunset. Free.

Bitter Lake National Wildlife Refuge, US 70; tel 505/ 622-6755. A great variety of waterfowl—including cormorants, herons, pelicans, sandhill cranes, and snow geese—find a winter home on these 24,000 acres of river bottomland, marsh, stands of salt cedar, and open range. **Open:** Daily sunrise–sunset. Free.

Bottomless Lakes State Park, NM 409; tel 505/624-6058. This chain of 7 lakes, surrounded by rock bluffs, is a popular recreation site for Roswell residents. Rainbow trout fishing, swimming and windsurfing, campsites. **Open:** Daily 6am–9pm. $

Ruidoso

Map page M-3, D3

Motels 🏨

≣≣≣ **Best Western Swiss Chalet Inn**, 1451 Mechem Dr, PO Box 759, Ruidoso, NM 88345; tel 505/258-3333 or toll free 800/477-9477; fax 505/258-5325. 5 mi N of Ruidoso. In an attractive white and blue chalet-style building located in a mountain setting. **Rooms:** 81 rms and stes. CI 3pm/CO noon. Nonsmoking rms avail. Rooms are modern and comfortable. **Amenities:** 🛗 A/C, cable TV w/movies. Some units w/terraces. **Services:** ✗ 🚗 ⌂ ⌂ **Facilities:** 🔥 🎿 📷 📶 1 rst, 1 bar, sauna, whirlpool, washer/dryer. Downhill skiing is 12 miles away at Ski Apache. **Rates:** HS June–Aug $62–$82 S; $69–$89 D; from $96 ste. Extra person $8. Children under 13 stay free. Min stay spec evnts. Lower rates off-season. Spec packages avail. Pking: Outdoor, free. Maj CC.

≣≣ **Dan Dee Cabins Resort**, 310 Main Rd Upper Canyon, PO Box 844, Ruidoso, NM 88345 (Upper Canyon); tel 505/ 257-2165 or toll free 800/345-4848. Go to the end of Sudderth Dr and head into Upper Canyon on Main Rd. Built in the 1930s as a retreat from the Texas heat, this property has plenty of space and privacy. **Rooms:** 12 ctges/villas. CI 4pm/CO 11am. Each cabin is unique, finished in wood with handsome stone fireplaces, and nestled among tall pine trees. All have full kitchens. **Amenities:** 📺 Cable TV w/movies, refrig. No A/C or phone. All units w/fireplaces. **Services:** ⌂ Babysitting. **Facilities:** Playground. Lots of hiking trails in the national forest just ½ mile up the creek. Good fishing nearby. **Rates:** HS June 15–Labor Day from $77 ctge/villa. Extra person $7.50. Min stay spec evnts. Lower rates off-season. Spec packages avail. Pking: Outdoor, free. Ltd CC.

≝≝≝ **Enchantment Inn**, 307 US 70 W, PO Box 4210 HS, Ruidoso, NM 88345; or toll free 800/435-0280; fax 505/378-5427. ¼ mile W of NM 48. Recently renovated. Lots of wood and glass; Mexican-tiled floor. **Rooms:** 80 rms and stes. CI 1pm/CO 11am. Nonsmoking rms avail. **Amenities:** 🛏 A/C, satel TV w/movies. Some units w/Jacuzzis. **Services:** ✗ ⌂ Babysitting. **Facilities:** 🔥 🏊 ᕼ 1 rst, 1 bar (w/entertainment), games rm, whirlpool, washer/dryer. There's a patio with barbecue grills. A major downhill ski resort is about 20 miles away. **Rates:** HS June–Aug $55–$75 S or D; from $85 ste. Extra person $10. Children under 18 stay free. Min stay spec evnts. Lower rates off-season. Spec packages avail. Pking: Outdoor, free. Maj CC.

≝≝ **Pines Motel**, 620 Sudderth Dr, Ruidoso, NM 88345; tel 505/257-4334 or toll free 800/257-4334. A handsome, meticulously maintained motel, with 6 older, completely refurbished rooms, and 4 new, more luxurious units. Owners live on premises. A very good value. **Rooms:** 10 rms. CI 2pm/CO 11am. Nonsmoking rms avail. Rooms in the new section overlook the Rio Ruidoso. **Amenities:** 🛏 🕭 📺 Cable TV w/movies, refrig. No A/C. Some units w/terraces. **Services:** 🚐 Babysitting. **Facilities:** ᕼ Lawn games. Horseshoes and a gazebo in the tree-shaded area along the river. Trout fishing in the Rio Ruidoso. **Rates:** $32–$50 S; $36–$60 D. Extra person $5. Min stay spec evnts. Spec packages avail. Pking: Outdoor, free. Maj CC.

≝≝ **Shadow Mountain Lodge**, 107 Main Rd Upper Canyon, PO Box 1427, Ruidoso, NM 88345 (Upper Canyon); tel 505/257-4886 or toll free 800/441-4331. A beautifully landscaped adult complex, with lots of trees and a nearby stream. **Rooms:** 19 stes. CI 4pm/CO 11am. Rooms are comfortable and airy, with stone fireplaces, attractive wood panelling, and kitchenettes. **Amenities:** 🛏 🕭 📺 Cable TV w/movies, refrig. No A/C. All units w/terraces, all w/fireplaces. **Facilities:** 🏊 ᕼ The lodge is located close to good fishing streams, and there are plenty of hiking trails nearby. **Rates:** HS Mem Day–Sept from $68 ste. Extra person $10. Min stay spec evnts. Lower rates off-season. Higher rates for spec evnts/hols. Spec packages avail. Pking: Outdoor, free. Maj CC.

Lodge

≝≝ **The Historic Carrizo Lodge and Condominiums**, Carrizo Canyon Rd, PO Box Drawer A, Ruidoso, NM 88345; or toll free 800/227-1224. Turn south off Sudderth Dr across from the Chamber of Commerce and go about 1 mile to Lodge. Located

on 7½ acres of lovely wooded mountain property, right alongside the road, yet it has a secluded, quiet atmosphere. **Rooms:** 84 rms and effic. CI 4pm/CO 11am. Nonsmoking rms avail. **Amenities:** 🛏 📺 A/C, cable TV, refrig. Some units w/terraces,. Condominium units have wood-burning fireplaces. **Services:** ⌂ **Facilities:** 🔥 🏊 ᕼ 1 rst, 1 bar, games rm, spa, sauna, whirlpool, washer/dryer. The Carrizo Art School operates from May through October. **Rates:** HS June–Aug $49–$79 S or D; from $79 effic. Extra person $7.50. Children under 12 stay free. Min stay spec evnts. Lower rates off-season. Spec packages avail. Pking: Outdoor, free. Maj CC.

Restaurants 🍴

★ **Cafe Rio**, 2547 Sudderth Dr, Ruidoso; tel 505/257-7746. **International/Pizza.** Decorated with red-and-white-checked tablecloths and rough wood walls, this restaurant offers a vast selection of unique foods from around the world, including pizza. The owners/chefs were trained in New York and have cooked on both the Gulf and West Coasts. The large selection of beers includes several seasonal varieties. **FYI:** Reservations not accepted. Beer and wine only. **Open:** Daily 11am–8:30pm. Closed some hols; Dec 1–21, 1 month after Easter. **Prices:** Main courses $3.95–$8.95. No CC.

Casa Blanca, 501 Mechem Dr, Ruidoso; tel 505/257-2495. **Southwestern.** The simple, attractive decor features solid wood furnishings and white adobe walls displaying works by local artists. Basic Mexican dishes and some southwestern variations, plus charbroiled chicken, burgers, sandwiches, and salads. The most popular item is the fresh green chile chicken enchilada. **FYI:** Reservations accepted. Children's menu. **Open:** Daily 11am–10pm. Closed Dec 25. **Prices:** Main courses $4–$10. Maj CC. 🍴 🎗

Cattle Baron Steak and Seafood Restaurant, 657 Sudderth Dr, Ruidoso; tel 505/622-3311. **Seafood/Steak.** A handsome dining room, with low, adobe-style dividers and wood furnishings. The atmosphere is elegant and upscale, but still friendly. Specialties are steak, prime rib, and fresh seafood. In summer, diners in the waterfall room can watch a lovely, manmade waterfall cascading just outside a wall of windows. **FYI:** Reservations accepted. Children's menu. **Open:** HS Mem Day–Labor Day Sun–Thurs 11am–9:30pm, Fri–Sat 11am–10:30pm. Reduced hours off-season. Closed Dec 25. **Prices:** Main courses $6.95–$20.95. Maj CC. ♥ 🎗 ᕼ

Flying J Ranch, NM 48 N, Ruidoso; tel 505/336-4330. 10 mi N of Ruidoso. **Regional American.** A western-style "supper club," located in a large barn-like building with a high, rough wood ceiling and rough wood walls, and large windows. There's only one seating, at 6pm; a western music stage show follows. Diners share long picnic tables after going through the chuck wagon–style chow line. The choice of beef or chicken, simmered for several hours in barbecue sauce, comes with baked potato, ranch beans, biscuit, applesauce, and spice cake. **FYI:** Reservations recommended. Band. No liquor license. No smoking. **Open:** Mon–Sat 6–9:30pm. Closed Labor Day to Mem Day. **Prices:** PF dinner $12.50. Ltd CC. 😊 ⅃

The Hummingbird Tearoom, in Village Plaza, 2306 Sudderth Dr, Ruidoso; tel 505/257-5100. **American.** The dining room is small but airy and simply furnished. Classical music enhances the tearoom atmosphere. The menu features homemade soups, salads, and sandwiches; plus exotic desserts, which are served until 5pm during the summer in the adjoining dessert shop. Smoking is permitted only on the patio (open summer only). **FYI:** Reservations recommended. No liquor license. No smoking. **Open:** Mon–Sat 11am–2:30pm. Closed some hols; several weeks in Nov. **Prices:** Lunch main courses $3.25–$5.75. Ltd CC. ⚓ ⅃

La Lorraine, 2523 Sudderth Dr, Ruidoso; tel 505/257-2954. **French.** An elegant French restaurant with plush seating, attractive artwork, and a brick fireplace. Specialties include beef chateaubriand with béarnaise sauce for two; gourmet French rack of lamb; duck à l'orange; and chicken Provençal. **FYI:** Reservations recommended. Beer and wine only. **Open:** Lunch Mon–Sat 11:30am–2pm; dinner Mon–Sat 5:30–9pm. Closed Dec 1–7; 1 week in Apr. **Prices:** Main courses $13.95–$23.95. Maj CC. ♥ 🛥

Attraction 💼

Museum of the Horse, US 70 E; tel 505/378-4142. A collection of over 10,000 horse-related items, including saddles from all over the world, a Russian sleigh, a horse-drawn fire engine, and an 1860 stagecoach. The museum also has original works by American artists Frederic Remington, Charles M Russell, Frank Tenney Johnson, and Henry Alkins. **Open:** Daily 9am–5pm. Closed some hols. $$

RUIDOSO DOWNS

Map page M-3, D3

Motel 🏨

≣≣ **Inn at Pine Springs**, off US 70, PO Box 2100, Ruidoso Downs, NM 88346; tel 505/378-8100 or toll free 800/237-3607; fax 505/378-8215. Across from Ruidoso Downs Race Track. Just outside Ruidoso, this better-than-average standard motel is in a delightful mountain setting, surrounded by pine trees. **Rooms:** 100 rms and stes. CI 2:30pm/CO noon. Non-smoking rms avail. Rooms are uncluttered and spacious; many have great views of the surrounding hillsides. **Amenities:** 🛁 A/C, cable TV w/movies. Some units w/terraces. **Services:** 🛎 **Facilities:** 🛏 Whirlpool. Hiking, fishing, golfing, and horse racing are nearby, and downhill skiing is within 20 miles. **Rates (CP):** HS Mem Day weekend–Labor Day $60–$73 S; $70–$83 D; from $160 ste. Extra person $10. Children under 12 stay free. Min stay spec evnts. Lower rates off-season. Spec packages avail. Pking: Outdoor, free. Maj CC.

SALINAS PUEBLOS MISSIONS NATIONAL MONUMENT

Map page M-3, C2

The Spanish conquistadors' Salinas Jurisdiction, on the east side of the Manzano Mountains, was an important 17th-century trade center because of salt extracted by Native Americans from nearby salt lakes. Franciscan priests, utilizing local labor, constructed missions of adobe, sandstone, and limestone for the native converts. The ruins of some of the most durable—along with evidence of preexisting Anasazi and Mongollon cultures—are on display here.

The monument headquarters, on US 60 in Mountainair, serves as the information center, museum, and bookstore. The monument consists of 3 separate units: the ruins of Abo, Quarai, and Gran Quivira. **Abo,** located 9 miles west of Mountainair on US 60, boasts the 40-foot-high ruins of the Mission of San Gregorio de Abo, a rare example of medieval architecture in the United States. **Quarai,** 9 miles north of Mountainair on NM 55, preserves the largely intact remains of the Mission of La Purisima Concepcion de Cuarac (1630). **Gran Quivira,** 25 miles south of Mountainair on NM 55, maintains the ruins of 300 rooms, 6 kivas, and 2 churches (800–1300). The visitor center has a museum with artifacts from the site, an audiovisual presentation, and an art exhibit. For more information about the monument contact the headquarters at 505/847-2585.

SAN ANTONIO

Map page M-3, C2

Restaurant 🍴

Owl Bar and Cafe, NM 1 and US 380, San Antonio; tel 505/835-9946. 8 mi S of Socorro. 1 mi E of exit 139 off I-25. **Burgers/Steak.** This authentic western cafe has the original bar from a saloon and boarding house once owned by Augustus Hilton, the father of Conrad Hilton, who founded the successful hotel chain. Its green-chile cheeseburgers and onion rings are well regarded. Other burgers and sandwiches, plus a few dinners, are also offered. Attached to the cafe is a steakhouse, open only Friday and Saturday, 5 to 10pm, serving steaks and catfish. **FYI:** Reservations accepted. **Open:** Mon–Sat 8am–10pm. Closed some hols. **Prices:** Main courses $2.25–$10.95. Ltd CC.
♟

SAN JUAN PUEBLO

Map page M-3, B2   (N of Española)

The largest and northernmost of the Tewa-speaking pueblos, this is also the headquarters of the **Eight Northern Indian Pueblos Council,** which serves as a chamber of commerce and social-service agency. The pueblo is reached via NM 74, 1 mile off NM 68, 4 miles north of Española.

The **O'ke Oweenge Arts and Crafts Cooperative** focuses on the works of San Juan artists, who are known for their distinctive red pottery incised with traditional geometric symbols, silver jewelry, wood and stone carvings, embroidery, and paintings. Located on the main road through the pueblo is the **Tewa Indian Restaurant,** serving traditional pueblo food such as chiles, blue-corn, and posole. The **San Juan Tribal Lakes** are open to visitors for water sports and trout fishing. For more information call 505/852-4400.

SANTA FE

Map page M-3, B3

TOURIST INFORMATION

Santa Fe Convention and Visitors Bureau 201 W Marcy St, in Sweeney Center at corner of Grant St (tel 505/984-6760 or toll free 800/777-2489). Open Mon–Fri 8am–5pm.

Santa Fe County Chamber of Commerce 510 N Guadalupe St, Suite N (tel 505/983-7317). Open Mon–Fri 8am–5pm.

Hotels 🏨

≣≣≣ **Best Western High Mesa Inn**, 3347 Cerrillos Rd, Santa Fe, NM 87501; tel 505/473-2800 or toll free 800/777-3347; fax 505/473-5128. Exit 278 off I-25. A pleasant, basic hotel. **Rooms:** 211 rms and stes. CI 3pm/CO 11am. Express checkout avail. Nonsmoking rms avail. **Amenities:** 🛁 A/C, cable TV, refrig. Some units w/terraces. Coffeemakers in suites. **Services:** ✗ 🛏 🛎 🍴 Car-rental desk, masseur, babysitting. **Facilities:** 🏋 🏊 ⛳ 🅿 ♿ 2 rsts, 1 bar (w/entertainment), spa, whirlpool, washer/dryer. **Rates (CP):** HS May–Oct $99 S; $109 D; from $119 ste. Extra person $12. Children under 12 stay free. Lower rates off-season. Higher rates for spec evnts/hols. Pking: Outdoor, free. Maj CC.

≣≣≣ **Eldorado Hotel**, 309 W San Francisco St, Santa Fe, NM 87501; tel 505/988-4455 or toll free 800/955-4455; fax 505/982-0713. Exit 282 off I-25. Santa Fe's largest hotel is located a few blocks from the plaza. The lobby is quite large, with an impressive entrance and some compelling art. **Rooms:** 219 rms and stes; 8 ctges/villas. CI 4pm/CO 11am. Express checkout avail. Nonsmoking rms avail. Rooms are spacious with a well-coordinated Santa Fe decor. There are a variety of sizes, shapes, and options. The Presidential Suite is especially fine. **Amenities:** 🛁 🏋 🛎 A/C, cable TV w/movies, refrig, VCR, bathrobes. All units w/minibars, some w/terraces, some w/fireplaces, 1 w/Jacuzzi. **Services:** ✗ 🛏 VP 🛎 🍴 🐕 Twice-daily maid svce, masseur, babysitting. Butler service for rooms on the fifth floor and a few special rooms elsewhere. **Facilities:** 🏋 🏊 ⛳ 🅿 💻 ♿ 2 rsts, 2 bars (1 w/entertainment), spa, sauna, whirlpool, beauty salon. **Rates:** HS June 29–Sept 5 $239–$750 S; $239–$750 D; from $349 ste; from $269 ctge/villa. Children under 16 stay free. Min stay spec evnts. Lower rates off-season. Spec packages avail. Pking: Indoor, $5.95. Maj CC.

≣≣≣ **Hilton of Santa Fe**, 100 Sandoval St, PO Box 25104, Santa Fe, NM 87504; tel 505/988-2811 or toll free 800/336-3676; fax 505/986-6439. Exit 282 off I-25. Take St Francis Dr to Cerrillos Rd and go east on Cerrillos then west on Sandoval. The territorial architecture and southwestern decor makes the lobby very inviting and comfortable. Just 2 blocks from Santa Fe Plaza, the hotel is within easy walking distance of shops, galleries, restaurants, historical sites, cultural events, and museums. **Rooms:** 158 rms and stes. Exec-level rms avail. CI 4pm/CO noon. Nonsmoking rms avail. Rooms are done in southwestern style, very attractive and comfortable. **Amenities:** 🛁 🏋 🎬 A/C, cable TV w/movies, refrig, voice mail, in-rm safe, bathrobes. All units w/minibars, some w/terraces, some w/Jacuzzis. Executive rooms have coffee makers. **Services:** ✗ 🛏 🛎 🍴 Car-rental desk, babysitting. **Facilities:** 🏋 🏊 ⛳ 💻 ♿ 2 rsts, 1 bar, whirlpool. Guests have access to Club International for use of exercise and spa facilities. **Rates:** HS June–Oct $170–$230 S;

$190–$250 D; from $275 ste. Extra person $10–20. Children under 12 stay free. Min stay spec evnts. Lower rates off-season. Higher rates for spec evnts/hols. Spec packages avail. Pking: Outdoor, free. Maj CC.

≣≣≣ Hotel Plaza Real, 125 Washington Ave, Santa Fe, NM 87501; tel 505/988-4900 or toll free 800/297-7325; fax 505/988-4900. Exit 284 off I-25. In a convenient location within easy walking distance of Santa Fe Plaza. The territorial-style hotel contains both Indian and Spanish influences in the decor. **Rooms:** 56 rms and stes. CI 3pm/CO noon. Rooms are attractively decorated in southwestern style. **Amenities:** 📺 👁 🍴 A/C, cable TV. Some units w/terraces, some w/fireplaces, some w/Jacuzzis. VCRs are available. **Services:** ✗ 🔑 🆅🅿 📇 ↵ Masseur, babysitting. **Facilities:** 🛉 🔟 1 bar. **Rates (CP):** HS July–Oct $159 S or D; from $199 ste. Min stay spec evnts. Lower rates off-season. Higher rates for spec evnts/hols. Pking: Indoor, Maj CC.

≣≣≣ Hotel Santa Fe, 1501 Paseo de Peralta, Santa Fe, NM 87501; tel 505/982-1200 or toll free 800/825-9876; fax 505/984-2211. Exit 282 off I-25. Close to Santa Fe Plaza, with sculpture on the grounds, heavy-beamed ceilings, a kiva fireplace, and warm ambience. **Rooms:** 131 rms and stes. CI 4pm/CO noon. Nonsmoking rms avail. **Amenities:** 📺 👁 A/C, cable TV w/movies. All units w/minibars, some w/terraces. Suites have in-room safes, microwaves, and 2 telephones. **Services:** ✗ 🔑 📇 ↵ Masseur. **Facilities:** 🛗 🛉 🔢 👁 1 bar (w/entertainment), whirlpool, washer/dryer. There's a small sandwich and breakfast bar on premises. Guests have use of Club International's fitness center. **Rates:** HS May–Oct 15 $139 S or D; from $179 ste. Extra person $20. Children under 18 stay free. Lower rates off-season. Spec packages avail. Pking: Outdoor, free. Maj CC.

≣≣≣ Hotel St Francis, 210 Don Gaspar Ave, Santa Fe, NM 87501; tel 505/983-5700 or toll free 800/529-5700; fax 505/989-7690. Exit 284 off I-25. This historic hotel, close to the plaza, has a large old-fashioned lobby with a beautiful fireplace. It offers casual elegance and 1920s romance with a comfortable European ambience. **Rooms:** 83 rms and stes. CI 3pm/CO 11am. Nonsmoking rms avail. Rooms are quaint and charming, with old photographs on the walls, and furnished with a mixture of antiques and period reproductions. **Amenities:** 📺 A/C, cable TV, refrig, in-rm safe, shoe polisher. 1 unit w/terrace. **Services:** ✗ 🔑 📇 ↵ Babysitting. Afternoon tea is served daily in the lobby. Free local phone calls. **Facilities:** 🛉 🔟 👁 1 rst, 1 bar. **Rates:** HS May–Oct $105–$135 S; $135–$175 D; from $225 ste. Extra person $15. Children under 12 stay free. Min stay spec evnts. Lower rates off-season. Higher rates for spec evnts/hols. Spec packages avail. Pking: Outdoor, free. Maj CC.

≣≣≣ The Inn at Loretto, 211 Old Santa Fe Trail, Santa Fe, NM 87501; tel 505/988-5531 or toll free 800/727-5531; fax 505/984-7988. Exit 284 off I-25. Within easy walking distance of Santa Fe Plaza. The Loretto Chapel, with its famous "miraculous staircase," is here, and there are several shops and galleries located on the premises. **Rooms:** 137 rms and stes. CI 3pm/CO noon. Nonsmoking rms avail. Rooms are spacious, and handsomely decorated in Santa Fe style. **Amenities:** 📺 👁 A/C, cable TV, refrig. Some units w/terraces, 1 w/fireplace. **Services:** ✗ 🔑 📇 ↵ 🔔 Babysitting. **Facilities:** 🛗 🛉 🔢 🖥 👁 1 rst, 1 bar (w/entertainment), beauty salon, washer/dryer. Tennis and golf can be arranged by the hotel. **Rates:** HS July–Oct $160–$185 S; $175–$200 D; from $175 ste. Extra person $15. Children under 12 stay free. Lower rates off-season. Higher rates for spec evnts/hols. Spec packages avail. Pking: Outdoor, free. Maj CC.

≣≣≣≣ Inn of the Anasazi, 113 Washington Ave, Santa Fe, NM 87501; tel 505/988-3030 or toll free 800/688-8100; fax 505/988-3277. Exit 284 off I-25. An elegant hotel in the heart of downtown. **Rooms:** 59 rms and stes. CI 3pm/CO noon. Express checkout avail. Nonsmoking rms avail. Rooms are beautifully appointed, with great attention to detail. **Amenities:** 📺 👁 📲 🍴 A/C, cable TV w/movies, refrig, VCR, in-rm safe, shoe polisher, bathrobes. All units w/minibars, some w/terraces, all w/fireplaces. **Services:** ✗ 🔑 🆅🅿 📇 ↵ 🔔 Twice-daily maid svce, social director, masseur, babysitting. The service-oriented staff can fulfill practically any request. **Facilities:** 🛉 🔟 👁 1 rst (*see also "Restaurants" below*), 1 bar (w/entertainment), games rm. **Rates:** HS May–Oct $230–$260 S or D; from $390 ste. Extra person $20. Children under 12 stay free. Min stay spec evnts. Lower rates off-season. Spec packages avail. Pking: Indoor, $10. Maj CC.

≣≣≣ Inn of the Governors, 234 Don Gaspar Ave, Santa Fe, NM 87501; tel 505/982-4333 or toll free 800/234-4534; fax 505/989-9149. Exit 284 off I-25. A lovely property in downtown Santa Fe, with fresh flowers in the open and airy tiled-floor lobby. **Rooms:** 100 rms and stes. Exec-level rms avail. CI 4pm/CO noon. Nonsmoking rms avail. Attractive rooms are decorated in Santa Fe style. **Amenities:** 📺 👁 🍴 A/C, cable TV w/movies, refrig. Some units w/minibars, some w/terraces, some w/fireplaces. Stereos are available in some rooms. **Services:** ✗ 🔑 ↵ Babysitting. Complimentary coffee and newspaper daily; complimentary hors d'oeuvres on weekdays. **Facilities:** 🛗 🛉 🔢 👁 1 rst, 1 bar (w/entertainment). Pleasant al fresco dining in the courtyard. **Rates (CP):** HS July–Oct $125–$145 S; $135–$215 D; from $230 ste. Extra person $10. Children under 12 stay free. Lower rates off-season. Higher rates for spec evnts/hols. Spec packages avail. Pking: Outdoor, free. Maj CC.

≣≣≣≣ **Inn on the Alameda**, 303 E Alameda St, Santa Fe, NM 87501; tel 505/984-2121 or toll free 800/289-2122; fax 505/986-8325. Exit 282 off I-25. Has a cozy, attractively furnished lobby with library. **Rooms:** 66 rms and stes. CI 3pm/CO noon. Nonsmoking rms avail. Furnished in southwest decor with pizzazz. **Amenities:** 🛏 ⚱ A/C, cable TV, voice mail, bathrobes. Some units w/minibars, some w/terraces, some w/fireplaces. A third of the rooms have refrigerators. **Services:** ✕ ☎ 🛝 🛎 Masseur, babysitting. The complimentary breakfast can be delivered to the room. The hotel offers a Pet Program, with pet amenities and a walking map. **Facilities:** 🛝 🛶 ⊞ ♿ 1 bar, games rm, spa, whirlpool, washer/dryer. **Rates (CP):** HS May–Oct $140–$180 S; $155–$200 D; from $225 ste. Extra person $15. Children under 12 stay free. Lower rates off-season. Higher rates for spec evnts/hols. Spec packages avail. Pking: Outdoor, free. Maj CC.

≣≣≣ **La Fonda**, 100 E San Francisco St, PO Box 1209, Santa Fe, NM 87501; tel 505/982-5511 or toll free 800/523-5002; fax 505/988-2952. Exit 284 off I-25. This is the "Inn at the End of the Santa Fe Trail" in the oldest capital in the United States. When Santa Fe was founded in 1610, it already had a "fonda," or inn, and when the first successful trading expedition from Missouri arrived in 1821, the fonda welcomed the members. The name stuck, and this soon became the destination for trappers, traders, mountain men, merchants, soldiers, politicians, and all who followed. **Rooms:** 152 rms and stes. CI 3pm/CO noon. Nonsmoking rms avail. Each room uniquely decorated in New Mexico style. Flowers in the hallways. **Amenities:** 🛏 ⚱ A/C, cable TV w/movies, voice mail, in-rm safe. Some units w/terraces, some w/fireplaces. Refrigerators are available in some rooms. **Services:** ✕ ☎ 🛝 🛎 Masseur, children's program, babysitting. Santa Fe Detours Desk in the lobby can arrange excursions, from white water raft trips to city tours. **Facilities:** 🛝 🛝 ⊞ ♿ 2 rsts, 2 bars (1 w/entertainment), lifeguard, spa, whirlpool, beauty salon. The Bell Tower Bar, at the top of the hotel, is a great place to watch the sunsets. Several shops are located on the premises. **Rates:** $170 S; $165–$180 D; from $190 ste. Extra person $15. Children under 12 stay free. Min stay spec evnts. Spec packages avail. Pking: Indoor, $2. Maj CC.

≣≣≣ **La Posada de Santa Fe**, 330 E Palace Ave, Santa Fe, NM 87501 (Downtown/Plaza area); tel 505/986-0000 or toll free 800/727-5276; fax 505/982-6850. Exit 287 off I-25. A lovely old hotel on 6 acres, just 2 blocks from the Plaza. The grounds are a delight to stroll through. **Rooms:** 119 rms and stes. CI 3pm/CO noon. Express checkout avail. Nonsmoking rms avail. A wide variety of rooms are offered, each unique and individually decorated in Santa Fe style. **Amenities:** 🛏 A/C, cable TV w/movies, refrig. Some units w/minibars, some w/terraces, some w/fireplaces, 1 w/Jacuzzi. **Services:** ✕ ☎ 🛝 🛎 Masseur,

babysitting. **Facilities:** 🗟 🛝 ⊞ ♿ 1 rst, 1 bar, beauty salon. Guests have use of Santa Fe Spa and Ft Marcy Public Sports Complex. **Rates (AP):** HS May–Oct $128–$179 S or D; from $199 ste. Extra person $10. Children under 12 stay free. Lower rates off-season. Higher rates for spec evnts/hols. Spec packages avail. Pking: Outdoor, free. Maj CC.

≣≣≣ **Picacho Plaza Hotel**, 750 N St Francis Dr, Santa Fe, NM 87501; tel 505/982-5591 or toll free 800/441-5591; fax 505/988-2821. Exit 282 off I-25. An attractive hotel. Well-known flamenco dancer Maria Benitez performs here several nights a week in the summer. **Rooms:** 158 rms, stes, and effic. CI 4pm/CO noon. Express checkout avail. Nonsmoking rms avail. Condos are also available. **Amenities:** 🛏 ⚱ A/C, cable TV w/movies. Some units w/minibars, some w/terraces, some w/fireplaces, some w/Jacuzzis. Refrigerators and hair dryers are available on request. **Services:** ✕ 🛝 🛎 Babysitting. Complimentary shuttle service to downtown Santa Fe. **Facilities:** 🗟 🛝 ⊞ ♿ 1 rst, 1 bar (w/entertainment), whirlpool, washer/dryer. Guests have access to the Santa Fe Spa next door with its indoor pool, weights, exercise equipment, and racquetball courts. **Rates:** HS May 13–Oct 29 $108 S; $123 D; from $148 ste; from $145 effic. Extra person $15. Children under 12 stay free. Lower rates off-season. Higher rates for spec evnts/hols. Spec packages avail. Pking: Outdoor, free. Maj CC.

Motels

≣≣≣ **El Rey Inn**, 1862 Cerrillos Rd, PO Box 130, Santa Fe, NM 87504; tel 505/982-1931 or toll free 800/521-1349; fax 505/989-9249. Exit 278 off I-25. Take Cerrillos Rd exit into town; El Rey will be on the east side of street. One of the nicest choices on Cerrillos Rd, this motel has an old, classic, "Route 66" feel. **Rooms:** 85 rms and stes. CI 2pm/CO noon. Nonsmoking rms avail. Each room is unique, with a personal touch. There is a full range of choices from simple rooms to suites to efficiencies with kitchen, 2 bedrooms, and a fold-out bed in the living room. **Amenities:** 🛏 ⚱ 📺 A/C, cable TV, refrig, VCR. Some units w/terraces, some w/fireplaces. **Services:** 🛎 Babysitting. **Facilities:** 🗟 🛝 ⊞ ♿ Whirlpool, playground, washer/dryer. **Rates (CP):** $56–$99 S or D; from $95 ste. Children under 18 stay free. Pking: Outdoor, free. Maj CC.

≣≣≣ **Fort Marcy Compound**, 320 Artist Rd, Santa Fe, NM 87501; tel 505/982-6636 or toll free 800/795-9910; fax 505/984-8682. Exit 282 off I-25. Take St Francis Dr north through town. Drive east on Paseo de Peralta to Washington Ave and north on Washington to Artist Rd. A lovely complex just 4 blocks from Santa Fe Plaza and set on 9 acres of piñon tree–covered hills. **Rooms:** 145 effic. CI 4pm/CO 10am. Nonsmoking rms avail. All units are full condos and are individually owned and decorated. Pets are permitted in 11 units. **Amenities:** 📺 🛁 ☎ A/C, cable TV, refrig, VCR, stereo/tape player, voice mail. All units w/terraces, some w/fireplaces. **Services:** ✗ ↵ Babysitting. Although there's no daily maid service, there is a daily towel exchange. **Facilities:** 🏋 🛁 150 ⅙ Whirlpool, washer/dryer. Guests have use of the Fort Marcy Sports Complex, a public facility with a pool, racquetball courts, and weight and exercise equipment. **Rates (CP):** HS July 1–Sept 14 from $85 effic. Extra person $20. Children under 18 stay free. Min stay. Lower rates off-season. Higher rates for spec evnts/hols. Spec packages avail. Pking: Outdoor, free. Maj CC.

◼◼ Garrett's Desert Inn, 311 Old Santa Fe Trail, Santa Fe, NM 87501; tel 505/982-1851 or toll free 800/888-2145; fax 505/989-1647. Exit 284 off I-25. A pleasant, basic motel. **Rooms:** 82 rms and stes. CI 3pm/CO noon. Rooms are simple but attractively decorated in a southwestern style. **Amenities:** 📺 ☜ A/C, cable TV. Some units w/terraces. **Services:** ↵ Car-rental desk, babysitting. **Facilities:** 🏋 🛁 40 ⅙ 1 rst (*see also* "Restaurants" below), 1 bar, games rm. A new restaurant, Le Café on the Trail, recently opened in the hotel, serving excellent and French food and pastries. **Rates:** HS May–Oct $84–$99 S or D; from $100 ste. Children under 12 stay free. Lower rates off-season. Higher rates for spec evnts/hols. Spec packages avail. Pking: Outdoor, free. Maj CC.

◼◼ Howard Johnson, 4044 Cerrillos Rd, Santa Fe, NM 87501; tel 505/438-8950 or toll free 800/446-4656; fax 505/471-9129. Exit 278 off I-25. Modest motel at the south end of Cerrillos Rd. **Rooms:** 47 rms and stes. CI noon/CO noon. Nonsmoking rms avail. Simple, basic rooms. **Amenities:** 📺 A/C, cable TV w/movies. **Services:** ↵ Babysitting. **Facilities:** 🛁 ⅙ Spa. **Rates (CP):** HS Mem Day–Aug $69 S; $99 D; from $120 ste. Extra person $6. Children under 18 stay free. Lower rates off-season. Higher rates for spec evnts/hols. Spec packages avail. Pking: Outdoor, free. Maj CC.

◼◼ La Quinta Motor Inn, 4298 Cerrillos Rd, Santa Fe, NM 87501; tel 505/471-1149 or toll free 800/531-5900; fax 505/438-7219. Exit 278 off I-25. An attractive motel located close to an outlet mall and the city's largest shopping center. **Rooms:** 130 rms and stes. CI 2pm/CO noon. Nonsmoking rms avail. Rooms are standard but they are quite comfortable. **Amenities:** 📺 🛁 A/C, satel TV w/movies. **Services:** ↵ ↩ Babysitting. **Facilities:** 🏋 ⅙ Washer/dryer. A 24-hour restaurant is next door. **Rates (CP):** HS May–Oct $83 S; $91 D; from $97 ste. Extra person $8. Children under 18 stay free. Lower rates off-season. Pking: Outdoor, free. Maj CC.

◼ Park Inn Limited, 2900 Cerrillos Rd, Santa Fe, NM 87501; tel 505/473-4281 or toll free 800/279-0894; fax 505/471-5646. Exit 278 off I-25. A pleasant, basic motel. **Rooms:** 83 rms. CI 3pm/CO 11am. Nonsmoking rms avail. Rooms are simply but adequately furnished. **Amenities:** 📺 ☎ A/C, cable TV. **Services:** ↵ ↩ **Facilities:** 🏋 90 ⅙ Beauty salon, playground. **Rates:** HS June 1–Oct 9 $75–$85 S or D. Extra person $8. Children under 12 stay free. Lower rates off-season. Higher rates for spec evnts/hols. Spec packages avail. Pking: Outdoor, free. Maj CC.

◼◼ Santa Fe Budget Inn, 725 Cerrillos Rd, Santa Fe, NM 87501; tel 505/982-5952 or toll free 800/288-7600; fax 505/984-8879. Exit 282 off I-25. Take St Francis Dr to US 85 (Cerrillos Rd). Located close to Santa Fe Plaza. The small lobby has a rack of brochures for visitors. **Rooms:** 160 rms. CI 11am/CO 11am. Clean, basic motel rooms. **Amenities:** 📺 A/C, cable TV w/movies. **Services:** ↵ Babysitting. **Facilities:** 🏋 🛁 ⅙ There's a restaurant next door. **Rates:** HS July 4–Oct 25 $75 S; $75–$86 D. Extra person $9. Children under 12 stay free. Min stay spec evnts. Lower rates off-season. Higher rates for spec evnts/hols. Pking: Outdoor, free. Maj CC.

◼◼ Santa Fe Motel, 510 Cerrillos Rd, Santa Fe, NM 87501; tel 505/982-1039 or toll free 800/999-1039; fax 505/986-1275. Exit 282 off I-25. Take St Francis Dr to US 85 (Cerrillos Rd); go east on Cerrillos to motel. Clean and basic, close to Santa Fe Plaza. **Rooms:** 22 rms; 1 ctge/villa. CI 2pm/CO noon. There are standard motel rooms in the main motel; rooms in two 75-year-old adobe houses; and the Thomas House, a historic house that sleeps 6 and comes with a fully equipped kitchen, 1 bath, dining room, living room with fireplace, private garden, and breakfast patio. **Amenities:** 📺 A/C, cable TV. Some units w/terraces, some w/fireplaces. **Services:** ↵ Babysitting. **Rates:** HS May–Oct $75–$85 S; $80–$90 D; from $90 ctge/villa. Extra person $5. Children under 12 stay free. Lower rates off-season. Higher rates for spec evnts/hols. Pking: Outdoor, free. Maj CC.

◼ Santa Fe Plaza Travelodge, 646 Cerrillos Rd, Santa Fe, NM 87501; tel 505/982-3551 or toll free 800/255-3050; fax 505/983-8624. Exit 284 off I-25. A decent, basic motel. **Rooms:** 45 rms. CI 2pm/CO 11am. Nonsmoking rms avail. **Amenities:** 📺 🛁 ☎ A/C, cable TV. **Services:** ↵ **Facilities:** 🏋 🛁 ⅙ **Rates:** HS June 25–Aug 28 $71 S; $77 D. Extra person $6. Children under 12 stay free. Min stay spec evnts. Lower rates off-season. Higher rates for spec evnts/hols. Spec packages avail. Pking: Outdoor, free. Maj CC.

◼◼ Super 8 Motel, 3358 Cerrillos Rd, Santa Fe, NM 87501; tel 505/471-8811 or toll free 800/800-8000; fax 505/471-3239. Exit 278 off I-25. A pleasant, standard motel with a large lobby, located south of town. **Rooms:** 96 rms and stes. CI 4pm/CO 11am. Nonsmoking rms avail. Basic motel rooms with no frills.

Amenities: 📻 🕯 A/C, cable TV. **Facilities:** ♿ **Rates:** HS May–Sept $40 S; $46 D; from $57 ste. Extra person $2. Lower rates off-season. Pking: Outdoor, free. Maj CC.

Inns

▤▤▤ **El Paradero**, 220 W Manhattan Ave, Santa Fe, NM 87501; tel 505/988-1177. Exit 282 off I-25. An attractive bed-and-breakfast in an old Spanish farmhouse built between 1800 and 1820. Territorial details were added in the 1880s, and in 1912 the Victorian doors and windows appeared. The present owners have encouraged the eccentric look of the house in their renovations. Unsuitable for children under 4. **Rooms:** 14 rms and stes (4 w/shared bath); 2 ctges/villas. CI 2pm/CO 11am. No smoking. A wide variety of rooms, from simple to luxurious. Downstairs rooms front the courtyard, and the upstairs rooms have tile floors and baths. One room has a lovely view of the Sangre de Cristo Mountains. **Amenities:** 📻 🕯 No A/C or TV. Some units w/terraces, some w/fireplaces. Two of the casitas have small refrigerators, sinks, and stoves. **Services:** 🍴 🍷 Babysitting, afternoon tea served. Full breakfasts include different dishes rotating throughout the week, such as pancakes, eggs Benedict, huevos tostados, and huevos rancheros. Fruit is included. **Facilities:** 🛋 Guest lounge w/TV. **Rates (CP):** HS July–Oct $55–$70 S or D w/shared bath, $65–$130 S or D w/private bath; from $110 ste; from $130 ctge/villa. Extra person $15. Min stay wknds. Lower rates off-season. Pking: Outdoor, free. Ltd CC. There is a 3-day minimum stay required for suites. Closed: Christmas week.

▤▤▤ **Grant Corner Inn**, 122 Grant Ave, Santa Fe, NM 87501; tel 505/983-6678. Exit 282 off I-25. A charming, colonial manor bed-and-breakfast inn in downtown Santa Fe, decorated with antiques and historic photos. **Rooms:** 12 rms and stes (2 w/shared bath). CI 2pm/CO noon. No smoking. Rooms are charmingly decorated with antique quilts, brass and four-poster beds, armoires, and artwork. **Amenities:** 📻 🕯 A/C, cable TV, refrig, bathrobes. Some units w/terraces, 1 w/fireplace. **Services:** ✕ 🗝 🍷 Masseur, babysitting, afternoon tea and wine/sherry served. Breakfast is served by a crackling fire, or on the front veranda in the summer. **Facilities:** 🛋 🎱 ♿ 1 rst, games rm, guest lounge. **Rates (CP):** HS June–Oct $95 D w/shared bath, $85–$140 S or D w/private bath; from $130 ste. Extra person $20. Min stay spec evnts. Lower rates off-season. Pking: Outdoor, free. Ltd CC.

The Preston House, 106 Faithway St, Santa Fe, NM 87501; tel 505/982-3465. Exit 284 off I-25. A lovely bed-and-breakfast in a turn-of-the-century home close to the plaza, with a resident cat. Unsuitable for children under 10. Unrated. **Rooms:** 15 rms (2 w/shared bath). CI 3pm/CO 11am. No smoking. **Amenities:** 📻

🕯 A/C, TV, bathrobes. 1 unit w/terrace, some w/fireplaces. **Services:** 🗝 🍷 Babysitting, afternoon tea and wine/sherry served. The friendly and helpful staff can supply information on local attractions, and are happy to assist with tickets, dinner reservations, and other visitor needs. **Facilities:** 🛋 🎱 Guest lounge. **Rates (CP):** HS Mar–Oct $70–$80 S or D w/shared bath, $145–$145 S or D w/private bath. Extra person $15. Lower rates off-season. Pking: Outdoor, free. Ltd CC.

▤▤▤ **Pueblo Bonita**, 138 W Manhattan St, Santa Fe, NM 87501; tel 505/984-8001. Exit 284 off I-25. Adobe bed-and-breakfast is conveniently located close to Santa Fe's downtown attractions. The property has beautiful private courtyards, narrow brick paths, adobe archways, and shady gardens sheltered by huge trees. The second floor offers splendid views of downtown and the Sangre de Cristo Mountains. **Rooms:** 18 rms and stes. CI 2pm/CO noon. Each room is cozily furnished with Navajo rugs, baskets, and sand paintings; Pueblo and Mexican pottery; antiques; Spanish santos; and works by local artists. **Amenities:** 📻 🕯 Cable TV. No A/C. Some units w/terraces, all w/fireplaces. Suites have coffeemakers and refrigerators. Hair dryers are available on request. **Services:** 🗝 🍷 Afternoon tea and wine/sherry served. **Facilities:** 🛋 ♿ Washer/dryer, guest lounge. **Rates (CP):** HS May–Oct $80–$130 S or D; from $130 ste. Lower rates off-season. Pking: Outdoor, free. Ltd CC.

▤▤▤ **Territorial Inn**, 215 Washington Ave, Santa Fe, NM 87501; tel 505/989-7737; fax 505/986-1411. Exit 282 off I-25. Located just 2 blocks from the Plaza in an 1890s stone-and-adobe territorial-style house, this bed-and-breakfast has a cozy sitting room and a small patio area for pleasant summer relaxation. Unsuitable for children under 10. **Rooms:** 11 rms (3 w/shared bath). CI 3pm/CO 11am. No smoking. Rooms are individually decorated, light and airy. Many are decorated with early American antiques. **Amenities:** 📻 🕯 A/C, cable TV w/movies, bathrobes. 1 unit w/terrace, some w/fireplaces. **Services:** 🗝 📷 Babysitting, wine/sherry served. **Facilities:** 🛋 Washer/dryer, guest lounge. **Rates (CP):** $80–$90 S or D w/shared bath, $130–$150 S or D w/private bath. Extra person $15. Min stay wknds. Higher rates for spec evnts/hols. Pking: Outdoor, free. Ltd CC.

Resorts

▤▤▤▤ **The Bishop's Lodge**, Bishop's Lodge Rd, PO Box 2367, Santa Fe, NM 87504; tel 505/983-6377 or toll free 800/732-2240; fax 505/989-8739. Exit 282 off I-25. 3 mi N of the Plaza. 1,000 acres. Originally a retreat for the first bishop of Santa Fe, Bishop Jean Baptiste Lamy, and later a vacation home for the Pulitzer publishing family of St Louis, Bishop's Lodge is now a magnificent resort adjoining the national forest, just a few miles from downtown Santa Fe. The Bishop's chapel is still used for weddings. **Rooms:** 88 rms and stes. CI 3pm/CO noon. Rooms have an old New Mexican atmosphere and are beautifully furnished with art and old photos. **Amenities:** 🛏 🕭 A/C, satel TV, refrig, in-rm safe, bathrobes. Some units w/minibars, all w/terraces, some w/fireplaces. Hair dryers, VCRs, and computer/fax hookups are available. **Services:** ✕ 🍽 🚗 🖾 🕭 Twice-daily maid svce, social director, masseur, children's program, babysitting. **Facilities:** 🔄 🔖 🏌 🎿 🏂 🎣 🏐4 🏉 🏊150 🕭 1 rst, 2 bars (1 w/entertainment), lifeguard, lawn games, spa, sauna, whirlpool, playground. **Rates:** HS July–Sept 5 $195–$325 S or D; from $245 ste. Extra person $15. Children under 3 stay free. Lower rates off-season. MAP rates avail. Spec packages avail. Pking: Outdoor, free. Maj CC.

≣≣≣≣ **Rancho Encantado**, Route 4, PO Box 57C, Santa Fe, NM 87501; tel 505/982-3537 or toll free 800/722-9339; fax 505/983-8269. 6 mi N of Santa Fe, exit 282 off I-25. 160 acres. This fun resort 15 minutes north of downtown Santa Fe is especially popular for horseback riding and enjoying the wide open spaces of the West. **Rooms:** 26 rms and stes; 36 ctges/villas. CI 3pm/CO 11am. There is a wide range of accommodations, from individually owned villas in Pueblo Encantado, to simple rooms and spacious casitas. All are attractive and comfortable. **Amenities:** 🛏 🕭 🖾 A/C, satel TV w/movies, voice mail. Some units w/terraces, some w/fireplaces. Hair dryers, VCRs, and refrigerators are available. Villas have washers and dryers. **Services:** 🍽 🖾 🕭 Social director, masseur, babysitting. **Facilities:** 🔄 🔖 🏌 🏂 🎣 🏐2 🏊50 🕭 1 rst, 1 bar (w/entertainment), games rm, whirlpool. **Rates:** HS Apr–Oct $190 S; $210 D; from $260 ste; from $315 ctge/villa. Lower rates off-season. Spec packages avail. Pking: Outdoor, free. Maj CC.

Restaurants 🍴

Bobcat Bite, Old Las Vegas Highway, Santa Fe; tel 505/983-5319. 8 mi NE of Santa Fe. Take Old Las Vegas Hwy out of town past El Gancho. **Burgers.** Atmosphere reminiscent of a 1950s roadside hamburger joint. Locally popular for steaks and huge hamburgers, including a green chile cheeseburger. **FYI:** Reservations not accepted. No liquor license. **Open:** Wed–Sat 11:00am–7:50pm. Closed some hols. **Prices:** Main courses $3.50–$11.95. No CC. 👥

The Burrito Co, 111 Washington Ave, Santa Fe; tel 505/982-4453. ½ block NE of the Plaza. **Southwestern.** A popular place to stop for a quick bite, and a step above most fast food restaurants. Breakfasts include huevos rancheros and breakfast burritos, in addition to the usual bacon and eggs. Mexican fare includes blue corn chicken enchiladas smothered in red or green chiles and topped with cheese and beans, or posole topped with

sour cream. **FYI:** Reservations not accepted. Children's menu. No liquor license. No smoking. **Open:** Mon–Sat 7:30am–7pm, Sun 10am–5pm. Closed some hols. **Prices:** Main courses $2.99–$4.75. No CC. 🍴👥🕭

Cafe Escalera, 130 Lincoln Ave, Santa Fe; tel 505/989-8188. 1½ blocks N of the Plaza. **New American.** This second-floor cafe has an bright and airy atmosphere. The menu changes nightly, with an emphasis on fresh ingredients. Known for its homemade breads. **FYI:** Reservations recommended. **Open:** Mon–Wed 8:30am–9pm, Thurs–Sat 8:30am–10pm, Sun 5–9pm. Closed Dec 25. **Prices:** Main courses $4.50–$23.50. Ltd CC. ❤🕭

Cafe Pasqual's, 121 Don Gaspar Ave, Santa Fe; tel 505/983-9340. 1 block S of the Plaza. **International/Southwestern.** The menu features imaginative variations on both American and southwestern dishes. Specialties include chile-rubbed grilled salmon with corn pudding and grilled vegetables; roasted whole garlic with tomatillo salsa and warm brie; chicken mole enchiladas; and New Mexico lamb chops with fresh tomato mint salsa. There's a community table for single diners. **FYI:** Reservations recommended. Beer and wine only. No smoking. **Open:** HS May–Oct breakfast Mon–Sat 7am–3pm, Sun 8am–3pm; dinner daily 6–10:30pm. Reduced hours off-season. Closed some hols. **Prices:** Main courses $15.75–$23.75. Maj CC. ❤ 🍴

Carlos' Gosp'l Cafe, in Plaza II Executive Center, 125 Lincoln Ave, Santa Fe; tel 505/983-1841. 1 block N of the Plaza. **Deli.** A popular place for summer outdoor dining and for families seeking a filling, inexpensive lunch. Basic deli fare: sandwiches, soups, salads, and homemade desserts. **FYI:** Reservations not accepted. No liquor license. **Open:** Mon–Sat 11am–4pm. Closed some hols. **Prices:** Lunch main courses $2.95–$6.90. No CC. 🍴👥🕭

♣ **The Compound**, 653 Canyon Rd, Santa Fe; tel 505/982-4253. **Continental.** Located in an old adobe home, this elegant continental restaurant is noted for superb service. The specialty of the house is roast rack of prime lamb with mint sauce. Also on the menu are beef, veal, chicken, trout, and seafood. Entrees are served with saffron rice or braised potatoes, vegetables of the day, and fresh baked rolls. **FYI:** Reservations recommended. No smoking. **Open:** Tues–Sat 6pm–close. Closed Dec 25; Jan. **Prices:** Main courses $17.50–$28. Ltd CC. ❤🍴🕭

Cowgirl Hall of Fame, 319 S Guadalupe St, Santa Fe; tel 505/982-2565. Exit 282 off I-25. **Regional American/Barbecue.** Decked out in cowgirl memorabilia, this is a fun place and a smart choice for families with young children. A "kid's corral" has horseshoes, a play area, pin-the-tail-on-the-cow, and other activities to keep kids entertained. The menu includes sandwiches and a variety of chicken dishes—both American and New Mexican—as well as fish, beef, and vegetarian plates. Brisket and ribs and grilled salmon are house specialties. The specialty dessert is the "cowgirl's original ice cream baked potato," which is ice cream molded into a potato shape, rolled in spices, and topped with whipped cream and green pecans. The bar has a happy hour from 4–6pm and is open until 2am. **FYI:** Reservations recommended. Comedy/country music/singer. Children's menu. **Open:** Daily 11am–11pm. Closed some hols. **Prices:** Main courses $6.50–$12.95. Maj CC. ▮ ♨ 🖼 ♿

Coyote Cafe, 132 W Water St, Santa Fe; tel 505/983-1615. 1 block S and 1 block W of the Plaza. **Southwestern.** Decor is chic California/southwest, with painted tabletops and multicolored china. The menu changes seasonally, but includes a wide variety of southwestern appetizers and a variety of innovative fish, poultry, and meat entrees. The rooftop cantina is open daily 11am–10pm from April through September. **FYI:** Reservations recommended. No smoking. **Open:** HS May–Oct lunch daily 11am–1:45pm; dinner daily 5:30–9:45pm. Reduced hours off-season. **Prices:** PF dinner $39.50. Maj CC. ♿

El Farol, 808 Canyon Rd, Santa Fe; tel 505/988-9912. **Spanish.** Located in an historic building, this restaurant has old Santa Fe ambience throughout. The original bar is classic New Mexico, with entertainment each evening at 9:30. The specialty of the house is tapas (bar snacks or appetizers). There's a wide variety, both hot and cold, made with seafood, meats, chicken, and vegetables. Diners often make a meal of them. **FYI:** Reservations recommended. **Open:** Daily 11am–10pm. Closed some hols. **Prices:** Main courses $9.95–$22.95. Ltd CC. ▮ ♨

The Evergreen, Hyde Park Rd, Santa Fe; tel 505/984-8190. 8 mi E of Santa Fe. **Continental.** A rustic mountain lodge with handsome stone walls, viga-and-latilla ceiling, and a lovely outdoor patio. Specialties include rack of lamb and New York pepper steak. Also offered are chicken, trout, and pheasant. Transportation from downtown Santa Fe can be provided with an hour's notice. **FYI:** Reservations recommended. **Open:** HS May–Oct lunch Wed–Sun 11am–5pm; dinner daily 5–9pm; brunch–Sun 11:30am–3:30pm. Reduced hours off-season. **Prices:** Main courses $14.95–$23.50. Maj CC. ♥ ♨ 🔥 ⛰

Geronimo, 724 Canyon Rd, Santa Fe; tel 505/982-1500. Exit 282 off I-25. **Southwestern.** Housed in a lovely old Canyon Road adobe home, with attractively furnished, intimate dining rooms, and a front porch and side patio for outdoor dining. The innovative menu includes southwestern variations on a variety of classic dishes, such as ravioli stuffed with smoked chicken, mascarpone cheese, chile-dusted pecans, and green onion with a chipotle chile cream sauce. **FYI:** Reservations recommended.

Open: Lunch Tues–Sun 11:30am–2:30pm; dinner daily 6–10:30pm. **Prices:** Main courses $16.50–$21.50. Maj CC. ♥ ▮ ♨ 🔥

Green Onion, 1851 St Michael's Dr, Santa Fe; tel 505/983-5198. Exit 278 off I-25. **Burgers/Southwestern.** A locally popular sports bar, serving salads, burgers and hot dogs, a variety of sandwiches, and the usual Mexican plates. **FYI:** Reservations accepted. Children's menu. **Open:** Daily 11am–10pm. Closed Dec 25. **Prices:** Main courses $4.50–$9. Maj CC. ♿

$ **Guadalupe Cafe**, 313 Guadalupe St, Santa Fe; tel 505/982-9762. Exit 282 off I-25. **Southwestern.** A casual southwestern cafe in an attractive old building. New Mexico–style Mexican dishes, with a wide choice of enchiladas and burritos. **FYI:** Reservations accepted. Children's menu. Beer and wine only. No smoking. **Open:** Breakfast Tues–Fri 7–11am, Sat–Sun 8am–2pm; lunch Tues–Fri 11am–2pm; dinner Tues–Sun 5:30–9pm; brunch Sat–Sun 11am–2pm. Closed some hols. **Prices:** Main courses $5.75–$9.50. Ltd CC. 🖼 ♿

India Palace, 227 Don Gaspar Ave, Santa Fe; tel 505/986-5859. 2 blocks S of the Plaza. **Indian.** Quiet and serene atmosphere. Large choice of tandoori dishes; chicken, lamb, beef, seafood and vegetarian dishes; and Indian breads. **FYI:** Reservations recommended. Beer and wine only. **Open:** Lunch daily 11:30am–2:30pm; dinner daily 5–10pm. **Prices:** Main courses $6.95–$15.95. Maj CC.

Inn of the Anasazi Restaurant, in the Inn of the Anasazi, 113 Washington Ave, Santa Fe; tel 505/988-3236. 1 block N of the Plaza. **Southwestern.** Elegant southwestern-style restaurant features handpainted tables and walls and lovely custom-made china. The menu, which changes several times each year, features natural beef, lamb, and chicken as well as organically grown fruits and vegetables. **FYI:** Reservations recommended. Children's menu. No smoking. **Open:** Breakfast daily 7–10:30am; lunch daily 11:30am–2:30pm; dinner daily 5:30–10pm. **Prices:** Main courses $17.50–$29; PF dinner $35. Maj CC. ♥ VP ♿

Julian's, 221 Shelby St, Santa Fe; tel 505/988-2355. 2 blocks S of the Plaza. **Italian.** An elegantly simple restaurant with a central kiva fireplace, located in a historic building. The northern Italian fare features such specialties as saltimbocca alla Romana, veal sauteed with herbs, white wine, and marsala and topped with prosciutto, mozzarella, and Fontina cheese. Many other pasta, chicken, fish, and meat dishes. **FYI:** Reservations recommended. No smoking. **Open:** Daily 6–10pm. Closed Thanksgiving. **Prices:** Main courses $13–$26. Maj CC. ♥ ▮

La Casa Sena, in Sena Plaza, 125 E Palace Ave, Santa Fe; tel 505/988-9232. 1 block E of the Plaza. **Southwestern.** The main dining room, in an 1867 territorial-style adobe building, has landscape paintings on the walls and Taos-style handcrafted furniture. A lovely shaded courtyard is available for al fresco summer dining. Entrees include fish, seafood, chicken, and meats, plus a vegetarian dish. A specialty is baked Rocky Mountain trout stuffed with smoked salmon and herbs. A singing waitstaff serves customers in the more casual cantina, open daily 5pm to midnight. The cantina has a separate menu. **FYI:** Reservations recommended. Cabaret. **Open:** Lunch Mon–Sat 11:30am–3pm; dinner daily 5:30–10pm; brunch Sun 11am–3pm. **Prices:** Main courses $18–$24. Maj CC. ♥ ▐ ♠ &

Le Café on the Trail, in Garrett's Desert Inn, 311 Old Santa Fe Trail, Santa Fe; tel 505/982-7302. 3 blocks S of the Plaza. **French.** A relatively new French-style restaurant. The menu includes fresh pastas like linguini fisherman (scallops, shrimp, mussels, fish, garlic, tomato, and basil), angel-hair pasta with chicken (garlic, basil, parmesan, and cream sauce), and fettucine venitienne (julienne of mushrooms, chicken, and ham with velouté tomato). Hamburgers, poultry, fish, and veal dishes are also offered. **FYI:** Reservations recommended. Beer and wine only. **Open:** Daily 7am–9pm. Closed Dec 25. **Prices:** Main courses $7.50–$14.50. Ltd CC. ♥ ♠ ▣ &

Le Tertulia, 416 Agua Fria St, Santa Fe; tel 505/988-2769. Exit 282 off I-25. St Francis Dr N to Agua Fria St. **Southwestern/ Steak.** Located in a former convent, this elegant restaurant with a large dining room has a timeless feel. Classic New Mexico cuisine. House specialties include carne adovada and chiles rellenos. Also steaks and chops. **FYI:** Reservations recommended. Dress code. **Open:** Lunch Tues–Sun 11:30am–2pm; dinner Tues–Sun 5–9pm. Closed some hols; Dec 1–7. **Prices:** Main courses $7.25–$17.95. Maj CC. ♥ ▐ ♠ &

★ **Maria's**, 555 W Cordova Rd, Santa Fe; tel 505/983-7929. Exit 282 off I-25. **Southwestern.** A delightful restaurant with authentic Old New Mexico ambience. The floor is covered with Mexican tile, and there are old wooden tables and carved chairs. Fajitas—beef, chicken, shrimp, and vegetarian—are the specialty. Soups and salads are also served, and there is a daily lunch special. The margaritas, touted as the best in town, come in 41 varieties. **FYI:** Reservations recommended. Guitar. Children's menu. **Open:** Mon–Fri 11am–10pm, Sat–Sun noon–10pm. Closed some hols. **Prices:** Main courses $7.50–$15.95. Maj CC. ▐ ♠ ▣ &

The Natural Cafe, 1494 Cerrillos Rd, Santa Fe; tel 505/983-1411. Exit 278 off I-25. **International/Vegetarian.** A simple cafe with polished wood tables and an attractive flagstone patio for warm-weather dining. There are usually 4 or 5 specials and innovative international vegetarian dishes, fresh fish, and free-range chicken. Organically grown produce. Whole wheat french bread is baked daily. **FYI:** Reservations recommended. Children's menu. Beer and wine only. No smoking. **Open:** Lunch Tues–Fri 11:30am–2:30pm; dinner Tues–Sun 5–9:30pm. Closed some hols; Nov 15–30. **Prices:** Main courses $8.50–$16. Ltd CC. ♠

OJ Sarah's, 106 N Guadalupe St, Santa Fe; tel 505/984-1675. Exit 282 off I-25. **Regional American.** Simple, pleasant garden room. Breakfast is served all day: omelettes, papas fritas (home fries topped with red or green chiles and cheddar), breakfast burritos, pancakes, french toast, plus homemade breakfast breads and cereals. After 11am sandwiches, soup, salad, burgers, burritos, quesadillas, and enchiladas are available. **FYI:** Reservations not accepted. No liquor license. No smoking. **Open:** HS May–Oct daily 7am–2pm. Reduced hours off-season. Closed some hols. **Prices:** Lunch main courses $3.50–$6.75. No CC. ▦ &

★ **Old Mexico Grill**, in College Plaza South, 2434 Cerrillos Rd, Santa Fe; tel 505/473-0338. Exit 278 off I-25. **Mexican.** Classical Mexican decor to go along with classical Mexican cuisine. Mole, tacos, and fajitas, plus dishes with chicken, salmon, beef tenderloin, and baby-back ribs. **FYI:** Reservations not accepted. **Open:** HS June–Sept lunch Mon–Fri 11:30am–2:30pm; dinner Sun–Thurs 5:30–9:30pm, Fri–Sat 5:30–10pm. Reduced hours off-season. Closed some hols. **Prices:** Main courses $8.50–$17.50. Ltd CC. ▦ &

The Palace Restaurant and Saloon, 142 W Palace Ave, Santa Fe; tel 505/982-9891. 1 block W of the Plaza. **Continental/ Italian.** Located in a historic building close to the plaza, this restaurant is known for its Caesar salad and escargot portobello bruschetta appetizer. Also popular are baked shrimp and crab, pan-seared New Mexico lamb chops, and fettuccine pomodoro. All pastas, breads, and desserts are made on premises. The menu also includes chicken, sweetbreads, veal, salmon, and steak. **FYI:** Reservations recommended. Piano. **Open:** Lunch Mon–Sat 11:30am–4pm; dinner daily 5:45–10pm. **Prices:** Main courses $9.95–$19.95. Maj CC. ♥ ▐ ♠ &

Paul's, 72 W Marcy St, Santa Fe; tel 505/982-8738. 1 block N of the Plaza. **International.** An intimate restaurant where screens separating tables and low lighting help make for a romantic evening. The menu changes seasonally and depends on the availability of fresh ingredients. Paul's won the Taste of Santa Fe for best entree in 1992 and best dessert in 1994. **FYI:** Reservations recommended. Beer and wine only. No smoking. **Open:** Lunch Mon–Sat 11:30am–2pm; dinner Mon–Sun 5:30–9:30pm. Closed July 4. **Prices:** Main courses $12.95–$17.95. Ltd CC. ♥

The Pink Adobe, 406 Old Santa Fe Trail, Santa Fe; tel 505/ 983-7712. Exit 284 off I-25. **Continental/Southwestern.** Cozy, warm, intimate atmosphere, set in an old adobe home. Entrees include spaghetti, baked chicken, beef tournedos, lamb curry, pork Napoleon, lamb chops, grilled tuna, and fried shrimp Louisianne, plus several Mexican dishes. Especially popular is steak Dunigan—charred sirloin with fresh mushrooms and green chile, served with browned potatoes and Creole salad. **FYI:** Reservations recommended. Children's menu. No smoking. **Open:** Lunch Mon–Fri 11:30am–2:30pm; dinner daily 5:30– 10pm. Closed some hols. **Prices:** Main courses $10.25–$22.25. Maj CC. ❤ 🍴 🖼️ ♿

Pranzo Italia Grill, in Sanbusco Center, 540 Montezuma St, Santa Fe; tel 505/984-2645. Exit 282 off I-25. **Italian.** Sleek, attractive Italian bistro-style restaurant serving pastas, poultry, meat, and fish, plus pizza at lunch. There's a modified menu for late weekend nights. Smoking is permitted only in the lounge. **FYI:** Reservations recommended. No smoking. **Open:** Lunch daily 11:30am–3pm; dinner Sun–Thurs 5–10pm, Fri–Sat 5– 11pm. Closed some hols. **Prices:** Main courses $5.75–$17.50. Maj CC. 🍷 🖼️ ♿

Saigon Cafe, in Cordova Rd Shopping Center, 501 W Cordova Rd, Santa Fe; tel 505/988-4951. Exit 282 off I-25. **Chinese.** A simple Chinese restaurant with a luncheon buffet and popular dinners. **FYI:** Reservations not accepted. No liquor license. **Open:** Lunch Mon–Sat 11am–2:30pm; dinner Mon–Sat 5– 8:30pm. Closed some hols. **Prices:** Main courses $6.75–$9.95. Maj CC.

San Francisco Street Bar and Grill, in Plaza Mercado, 114 W San Francisco St, Santa Fe; tel 505/982-2044. 1½ blocks W of the Plaza. **New American.** A modern grill with tile floor, wood tables, rush-seated chairs, and photographs on the walls. Sand- wiches, hamburgers, steak, fresh fish, soups, salads, and home- made pasta. **FYI:** Reservations not accepted. Children's menu. No smoking. **Open:** Daily 11am–11pm. Closed some hols. **Prices:** Main courses $4.50–$10.95. Ltd CC. 🖼️ ♿

⭐ **Santacafé**, 231 Washington Ave, Santa Fe; tel 505/ 984-1788. 2 blocks N of the Plaza. **New American.** A cozy, intimate restaurant located in a historic house. The menu changes often but generally includes chicken, fish, lamb, steak, and 1 or 2 vegetarian dishes. **FYI:** Reservations recommended. Dress code. **Open:** Lunch Mon–Sat 11:30am–2pm; dinner daily 5:30–10pm. Closed some hols. **Prices:** Main courses $18.50– $24. Ltd CC. 🍴 🍷 🖼️ ♿

Sergio's Ristorante, in St Michael's Village West, 1620 St Michael's Dr, Santa Fe; tel 505/471-7107. Exit 278 off I-25. **Italian.** Bistro-style restaurant, with red-checked tablecloths at lunch, white at dinner. With homemade pasta and fresh pastries. There's a popular salad bar as well. **FYI:** Reservations accepted. Children's menu. Beer and wine only. No smoking. **Open:** Breakfast Tues–Sat 7–11am; lunch Mon–Sat 11am–2:30pm; dinner Mon–Sat 5–9pm. Closed some hols. **Prices:** Main cour- ses $5.95–$13.95. Maj CC. ♿

⭐ **The Shed**, in Sena Plaza, 113 ½ E Palace Ave, Santa Fe; tel 505/982-9030. ½ block E of the Plaza. **Southwestern.** Popular eatery that takes up several rooms of a rambling hacienda built in the late 1600s. Decorated with murals and lace curtains. New Mexican cuisine, with a few burgers and salads offered. Blue corn enchiladas and green chile soup are very popular. **FYI:** Reserva- tions not accepted. Beer and wine only. No smoking. **Open:** Mon–Sat 11am–2:30pm. Closed some hols. **Prices:** Lunch main courses $3.50–$6.75. No CC. 🍴 🍷 🖼️ ♿

Shohko-Cafe, 321 Johnson St, Santa Fe; tel 505/983-7288. 3 blocks W of the Plaza. **Chinese/Japanese.** A sushi bar that also offers some Chinese dishes and seafood specials. **FYI:** Reserva- tions recommended. Beer and wine only. **Open:** Lunch Mon–Fri 11:30am–2pm; dinner Mon–Sat 5:30–9:30pm. Closed some hols. **Prices:** Main courses $7.25–$15. Maj CC. ♿

Steaksmith at El Gancho, in El Gancho Club, Old Las Vegas Hwy, Santa Fe; tel 505/988-3333. 2½ mi E of Santa Fe; exit 284 off I-25. **Seafood/Steak.** Done in the style of an English pub, this restaurant serves steak and seafood, barbecue ribs, chicken, and New Mexican dishes. **FYI:** Reservations recommended. Children's menu. **Open:** Mon–Sat 5:30–10pm, Sun 5–9pm. Closed some hols. **Prices:** Main courses $8.95–$28.95. Maj CC. ❤ 🖼️ ♿

Szechwan Chinese Cuisine, 1965 Cerrillos Rd, Santa Fe; tel 505/983-1558. Exit 278 off I-25. **Chinese.** Basic Chinese, with a popular luncheon buffet. One specialty is tangerine delight: chunks of chicken, beef, and shrimp, with broccoli in a hot and spicy tangerine sauce. The menu lists over 80 items. **FYI:** Reservations accepted. Beer and wine only. **Open:** Daily 11am– 9:30pm. Closed Thanksgiving. **Prices:** Main courses $5.95– $12.95. Ltd CC. 🖼️ ♿

Tecolote Cafe, 1203 Cerrillos Rd, Santa Fe; tel 505/988-1362. Exit 278 off I-25. **American/Southwestern.** Breakfast is served all day in this New Mexican–style cafe. Items include carne adovada burrito, shirred eggs tecolote, corned beef hash, and sheepherder's breakfast. For lunch there's both standard New Mexican and American fare. **FYI:** Reservations not accepted. No liquor license. **Open:** Tues–Sun 7am–2pm. Closed some hols. **Prices:** Lunch main courses $2.95–$8.95. Maj CC. 🖼️

Tia Sophias, 210 W San Francisco St, Santa Fe; tel 505/ 983-9880. 2 blocks W of the Plaza. **Southwestern.** Casual restaurant, with both booths and tables. Standard New Mexico fare plus sandwiches and salads. **FYI:** Reservations not accepted. Children's menu. No liquor license. **Open:** Mon–Sat 7am–2pm. Closed some hols. **Prices:** Lunch main courses $2.95–$7.25. Ltd CC. 🎦

★ **Tiny's Restaurant & Lounge**, in Penn Rd Shopping Center, 1015 Penn Rd, Santa Fe; tel 505/983-9817. Exit 282 off I-25. **Seafood/Southwestern/Steak.** A favorite with locals since it opened in 1948. There are 2 dining rooms: one in an older part of the building with a bar-like atmosphere; the other newer and curved around an outdoor patio. Tiny's specialty is its award-winning fajitas. Also a variety of other New Mexican dishes, plus steak, seafood, burgers, and salads. **FYI:** Reservations recommended. Cabaret/guitar. Children's menu. **Open:** Lunch Mon–Fri 11:30am–2pm; dinner Mon–Sat 6–10pm. Closed some hols. **Prices:** Main courses $6.25–$14. Maj CC. 🍷 🖼

★ **Tomasitas Santa Fe Station**, 500 S Guadalupe St, Santa Fe; tel 505/988-5721. Exit 282 off I-25. **Southwestern.** Located in a former railway depot. Known for its chiles rellenos and enchiladas. Also served here are burritos, stuffed sopaipillas, chalupas, tacos, burgers, steak, and several vegetarian dishes. **FYI:** Reservations not accepted. Children's menu. **Open:** Mon–Sat 11am–10pm. Closed some hols. **Prices:** Main courses $4.75–$9.75. Ltd CC. 🍷 🖼 ⟨

Tortilla Flats, 3139 Cerrillos Rd, Santa Fe; tel 505/471-8685. Exit 278 off I-25. **Southwestern.** Southwestern-style restaurant with fast service. The usual New Mexican dishes are offered— enchiladas, chiles rellenos, tacos, quesadillas—plus Santa Fe trail steak (ribeye steak smothered with red or green chiles and topped with grilled onions) and green chile chops (2 pork chops smothered with green chile and topped with grilled tomatoes and onions). **FYI:** Reservations not accepted. Children's menu. **Open:** Daily 7am–10pm. Closed some hols. **Prices:** Main courses $4.75–$9.75. Ltd CC. 🖼

Toushie's, 4220 Airport Rd, Santa Fe; tel 505/473-4159. Exit 278 off I-25. **American/Mexican.** A simple restaurant and bar, with entertainment on weekends. Steak, seafood, and New Mexican dishes. **FYI:** Reservations accepted. Combo. Children's menu. **Open:** Mon–Fri 11am–9:30pm, Sat–Sun 4–11:30pm. Closed some hols. **Prices:** Main courses $4.95–$16.95. Maj CC. ⟨

$ **Zia Diner**, 326 S Guadalupe St, Santa Fe; tel 505/988-7008. Exit 282 off I-25. **American.** A popular, busy diner done in Santa Fe art deco style, with a nice outdoor patio for summer dining. Traditional all-American cuisine, including chicken-fried steak, meatloaf, mashed potatoes, and daily specials. The pies and cakes are well regarded. **FYI:** Reservations accepted. **Open:** Daily 11:30am–10pm. Closed some hols. **Prices:** Main courses $4.95–$9.25. Maj CC. 🍷 🖼 ⟨

Attractions 📷

HISTORIC BUILDINGS & MUSEUMS

Palace of the Governors, North Plaza; tel 505/827-6483. Built in 1610, the original capitol building has been in continuous public use longer than any other structure in the United States. Today it is a state history museum with a series of exhibits chronicling the 4 centuries of New Mexico's Hispanic and American history, from the 16th century Spanish explorations through the frontier era to modern times. Also in the collections are early Jesuit maps and rare Franciscan hide paintings, and an entire mid-19th century chapel. The bookstore has one of the finest selections of art, history, and anthropology books in the Southwest. There is also a print shop and bindery, in which limited edition works are produced on hand presses.

Outside the museum, beneath the long covered portal facing The Plaza, colorfully dressed Native American artisans sit shoulder-to-shoulder selling jewelry, pottery, beadwork, and paintings. **Open:** Mar–Dec, daily 10am–5pm. Closed some hols. $$

State Capitol, Paseo de Peralta and Old Santa Fe Trail; tel 505/ 986-4589. The only round capitol building in America, it derives its shape from a Native American *zia* emblem, which symbolizes the Circle of Life: 4 winds, 4 seasons, 4 directions, and 4 sacred obligations. Surrounding the capitol is a lush, 6½-acre garden containing dozens of varieties of plants—roses, plums, almonds, nectarines, and sequoias among them. **Open:** Mon–Fri 6am–7pm. Free.

Museum of Fine Arts, 107 W Palace Ave; tel 505/827-4455. The museum's permanent collection of more than 8,000 works emphasizes regional art, including numerous Georgia O'Keeffe paintings, landscapes and portraits by all the Taos masters, and more recent works by such contemporary greats as Luis Jimenez and Fritz Scholder. There is also a collection of Ansel Adams photography. **Open:** Daily 10am–5pm. Closed Mon, Jan–Feb, and some hols. $$

Center for Contemporary Arts, 291 E Barcelona Rd; tel 505/ 982-1338. Presents the work of internationally, nationally, and regionally known artists through gallery exhibitions, contemporary dance and new music concerts, poetry readings, performance-art events, theater, and video and film screenings. **Open:** Mon–Fri 9am–5pm, Sat noon–4pm. Closed some hols. Free.

Museum of International Folk Art, 706 Camino Lejo; tel 505/827-6350. Over 200,000 objects from more than 100 countries. Special collections include Spanish Colonial silver, traditional and contemporary New Mexican religious art, tribal costumes, Brazilian folk art, European glass, African sculptures, and East Indian textiles. In addition, the Hispanic Heritage Wing often presents art demonstrations, performances, and workshops. **Open:** Daily 10am–5pm; closed Mon, Jan–Feb. Closed some hols. $$

Museum of Indian Arts and Culture, 710 Camino Lejo; tel 505/827-6344. Interpretive displays detail tribal history and contemporary lifestyles of New Mexico's Pueblo, Navajo, and Apache cultures. More than 50,000 pieces of basketry, pottery, clothing, carpets, and jewelry is on continual rotating display. There are daily demonstrations of traditional skills, as well as regular performances of Native American music and dancing. **Open:** Daily 10am–5pm. Closed Mon, Jan–Feb, and some hols. $$

Wheelwright Museum of the American Indian, 704 Camino Lejo; tel 505/982-4636. Navajo medicine man Hastiin Klah took the designs of sand paintings used in healing ceremonies and adapted them into the textiles that are a major part of the museum's treasure. There are rotating single-subject shows of silverwork, jewelry, tapestry, pottery, basketry, and paintings. Outdoor sculpture garden. **Open:** Mon–Sat 10am–5pm, Sun 1–5pm. Closed some hols. $

Institute of American Indian Arts Museum, 108 Cathedral Place; tel 505/988-6281. Operated by the federal Bureau of Indian Affairs, the institute encourages Native American artists to create out of their own traditions and experiences. Representatives from 70 tribes display their current work in 4 to 5 major exhibitions a year. **Open:** Mon–Fri 8am–5pm, Sat–Sun 10am–5pm. $$

Indian Art Research Center, 660 Garcia St; tel 505/982-3584. One of the world's finest collections of southwestern tribal art. Admission is highly restricted; reservations must be made at least 2 weeks in advance. Entrance is free for Native Americans. $$$$

Santa Fe Children's Museum, 1050 Old Pecos Trail; tel 505/989-8359. Offers interactive exhibits in the arts, humanities, science, and technology. Special art and science activities and family performances are regularly scheduled. **Open:** Thurs–Sat 10am–5pm, Sun noon–5pm. $

Footsteps Across New Mexico, 211 Old Santa Fe Trail; tel 505/982-9297. This multimedia presentation provides an impressive introduction to the state. Slides, music, and a sculpted, 3-dimensional map combine to tell the New Mexico story, from pre-Hispanic Pueblo culture to the landing of the space shuttle at White Sands. **Open:** Mon–Sat 9:30am–5pm, Sun 9:30am–4pm. $$

El Rancho de las Golondrinas, 344 Los Pinos Rd; tel 505/471-2261. Otherwise known as Old Cienega Village Museum, this 400-acre ranch was once the last stopping place on the 1,000-mile El Camino Real from Mexico City to Santa Fe. Today, it is a living 17th- and 18th-century Spanish village comprising a hacienda, a village store, a schoolhouse, and several chapels and kitchens. There's also a working molasses mill, a wheelwright and blacksmith shop, shearing and weaving rooms, a threshing ground, winery and vineyards, and 4 water mills. **Open:** June–Sept, Wed–Sun 10am–4pm. $$

CHURCHES & SHRINES

St Francis Cathedral, Cathedral Place at San Francisco St; tel 505/982-5619. An architectural anomaly in Santa Fe, this Romanesque building was built between 1869 and 1886 by Archbishop Jean-Baptiste Lamy to resemble the great cathedrals of Europe. The small adobe Our Lady of the Rosary chapel on the northeast side of the cathedral is the only parcel remaining from Our Lady of Assumption Church, founded with Santa Fe in 1610. The new cathedral was built over and around the old church.

A wooden icon set in a niche in the wall of the north chapel, *La Conquistadora,* Our Lady of Conquering Love, is the oldest representation of the Madonna in the United States. Around the cathedral's exterior are doors featuring 16 bronze panels of historic note and a plaque memorializing the 38 Franciscan friars who were martyred in New Mexico's early years. There is also a large bronze statue of Bishop Lamy, and his grave lies under the main altar of the cathedral. **Open:** Daylight hours daily. Free.

Loretto Chapel, 211 Old Santa Fe Trail; tel 984-7971. Patterned after the famous Sainte-Chapelle church in Paris, it was constructed in 1873. The chapel is especially notable for its remarkable spiral staircase that makes 2 complete 360-turns with no central or other visible support. Entrance is through the Inn at Loretto. **Open:** Daily 9am–4:30pm. $

Santuario de Nuestra Señora de Guadalupe, 100 Guadalupe St; tel 505/988-2027. Built between 1795 and 1800 at the end of El Camino Real by Franciscan missionaries, this is believed to be the oldest shrine in the United States honoring the Virgin of Guadalupe, patroness of Mexico. Inside is the famous oil painting, *Our Lady of Guadalupe,* created in 1783 by renowned Mexican artist Jose de Alzibar. **Open:** Mon–Sat 9am–4pm, Sun noon–4pm. Free.

Cristo Rey Church, 1120 Canyon Rd; tel 505/983-8528. Huge adobe structure built in 1940 to commemorate the 400th anniversary of Coronado's exploration of the Southwest. **Open:** Daily 7am–7pm. Free.

Mission of San Miguel, 401 Old Santa Fe Trail; tel 505/983-3974. One of the oldest churches in America, it was built within a few years of the 1610 founding of Santa Fe. Severely damaged in the 1680 Pueblo revolt, the church was almost completely rebuilt in 1710. Among the highlights of the mission are San Jose Bell, reputedly cast in Spain in 1356, and a series of buffalo hides and deerskins decorated with Bible stories. **Open:** Mon–Sat 10am–4pm, Sun 1:30-4pm. Free.

PUEBLOS
Nambe Pueblo, Rt 1; tel 505/455-2036. The 700-year-old Tewa-speaking pueblo is located at the foot of the Sangre de Cristo range. A few of the original pueblo buildings still exist, including a large round kiva, used today in ceremonies. Pueblo artisans make woven belts, beadwork, and brown micaceous pottery.

    Nambe Falls make a 3-tier drop through a cleft in a rockface 4 miles beyond the pueblo, tumbling into Nambe Reservoir. A recreational site offers fishing, boating, hiking, camping, and picnicking. **Open:** Daily 8am–5pm. Free.

Pojoaque Pueblo, NM 11; tel 505/455-2278. The Poajaque Pueblo Tourist Information Center offers maps, brochures, and free tourist information, making this an important center for traveler services. Indigenous pottery, embroidery, silverwork, and beadwork are available for sale at the **Poeh Cultural Center and Museum.** There are also exhibits here that present the tribe's history and culture, as well as paintings by Tewa artists. Traditional dances are performed Saturday and Sunday at 11am and 1pm. **Open:** Daily sunrise–sunset. Free.

San Ildefonso Pueblo, NM 5; tel 505/455-3549. This pueblo is nationally famous for the matte-finish black-on-black pottery developed by resident Maria Martinez. At the **San Ildefonso Pueblo Museum** the pottery-making process is explained; it also maintains exhibits on pueblo history. Tours of the pueblo are offered from the visitor center. San Ildefonso Feast Day, January 22–23, is a good time to observe the social and religious traditions of the pueblo, when buffalo, deer, and Comanche dances are presented. **Open:** Summer, Mon–Fri 8am–5pm, Sat–Sun 9am–6pm; winter, Mon–Fri 8am–4:30pm. $

Tesuque Pueblo, US 84/285; tel 505/983-2667. Despite some concessions to the late 20th century, the 400 pueblo dwellers here are faithful to traditional religion, ritual, and ceremony.

Excavations confirm that there was a pueblo at the site in 1250. A mission church and adobe houses surround the plaza. **Open:** Daily 9am–5pm. Free.

ENTERTAINMENT VENUES
Santa Fe Opera, Old Taos Hwy; tel 505/982-3855. Located on a wooded hilltop 7 miles north of the city, the sweeping curves of this serene structure seem perfectly attuned to the contour of the surrounding terrain. At night, the lights of Los Alamos can be seen in the distance from the open-air amphitheater. The opera company is noted for its performances of great classics, little-known works by classical European composers, and American premieres of 20th-century works. **Open:** June–Aug. $$$$

Paolo Soleri Amphitheatre, 1501 Cerrillos St; tel 505/989-6310. This outdoor arena is the locale of many warm-weather events. More than two dozen concerts are presented here each summer, including the Santa Fe Summer Concert Series.

St Francis Auditorium, Lincoln and Palace Aves; tel 505/827-4455. This music hall, patterned after the interiors of traditional Hispanic mission churches, is noted for its acoustics. It hosts a wide variety of musical events, including the Santa Fe Chamber Music Festival in July and August. $$$$

Sweeney Convention Center, 20 W Marcy; tel 505/984-6760. Santa Fe's largest indoor arena hosts a wide variety of trade expositions and other events during the year. It's also the home of the Santa Fe Symphony Orchestra. $$$$

PARKS
Randall Davey Audubon Center, 1800 Upper Canyon Rd; tel 505/983-4609. This wildlife refuge occupies 35 acres at the mouth of Santa Fe Canyon. More than 100 species of birds and 120 types of plants live here, and a variety of mammals have been spotted, including black bears, mountain lions, and coyotes. **Open:** Daily 9am–5pm. Closed winter weekends. $

Old Fort Marcy Park, Artist Road. Marks the site of the first US military reservation in the Southwest. The Cross of the Martyrs, at the top of a winding brick walkway from Paseo de Peralta near Otero Street, is a popular spot for bird's-eye photographs. Free.

SANTA ROSA

Map page M-3, C3

Motels 🏨

▤▤ **Best Western Adobe Inn**, Business Loop 40 at I-40, PO Box 410, Santa Rosa, NM 88435; tel 505/472-3446 or toll free 800/528-1234; fax 505/472-3446 ext 100. Exit 275 off I-40. A pleasant, roadside motel. **Rooms:** 59 rms. CI 4pm/CO 11am. Nonsmoking rms avail. Rooms are clean and comfortable, with queen-size beds. **Amenities:** 🛏 A/C, cable TV w/movies. **Services:** � 🛎 🍽 Babysitting. **Facilities:** 🛗 ᵹ **Rates:** HS May 15–Aug $44 S; $48 D. Extra person $6. Children under 12 stay free. Lower rates off-season. Pking: Outdoor, free. Maj CC.

▤ **Motel 6**, 3400 Will Rogers Dr, Santa Rosa, NM 88435; tel 505/472-3045. Exit 277 off I-40. Basic lodging, perfectly adequate for an overnight stay. **Rooms:** 90 rms. CI 4pm/CO noon. Nonsmoking rms avail. Rooms are clean and functional. **Amenities:** 🛏 A/C, cable TV w/movies. **Services:** 🔺 🛎 🍽 Babysitting. **Facilities:** 🛗 ᵹ **Rates:** $32 S; $38 D. Extra person $3. Children under 18 stay free. Pking: Outdoor, free. Maj CC.

▤▤ **Super 8 Motel**, 1201 Will Rogers Dr, Santa Rosa, NM 88435; tel 505/472-5388 or toll free 800/800-8000; fax 505/472-5388. Exit 275 off I-40. A pleasant, basic motel, similar to others in the chain. **Rooms:** 88 rms. CI 4pm/CO 11am. Nonsmoking rms avail. **Amenities:** 🛏 🍴 A/C, cable TV. **Services:** 🚐 🛎 Babysitting. **Facilities:** 📦 ᵹ Washer/dryer. **Rates:** $34 S; $41 D. Extra person $6. Children under 12 stay free. Higher rates for spec evnts/hols. Spec packages avail. Pking: Outdoor, free. Maj CC.

Attractions 💼

Fort Sumner, US 84; tel 505/355-7705. Located on US 84, 44 miles southeast of Santa Rosa. In the early 1860s the US Army, under the command of Col Kit Carson, invaded the Mescalero Apache and Navajo homelands and forced the residents to march over 400 miles to Fort Sumner where they hoped to create a self-sustaining agricultural colony for captive Native Americans. The forced reservation experiment was a disaster, and in 1865 the entire group of Apache and Navajo escaped. Today, there is a museum that tells the story of the fort through artifacts, pictures, and documents; a Navajo shrine is maintained at the monument.

Behind the museum is the **Grave of Billy the Kid**, with a 6-foot tombstone engraved "William H Bonney, alias Billy the Kid, died July 16, 1881." Two previously slain comrades are buried with the outlaw. **Open:** Thurs–Mon 9am–5pm. $

Santa Rosa Lake State Park, 2nd St; tel 505/472-3110. Located on a dammed portion of the Pecos River, the park has camping, hiking, excellent fishing, and a visitor information center. **Open:** Daily 6am–9pm. $

SANTO DOMINGO

Map page M-3, B2 (SW of Santa Fe)

Attraction 💼

Santo Domingo Pueblo, NM 22; tel 505/465-2214. One of New Mexico's largest pueblos, this farming community on the east bank of the Rio Grande is also one of the state's most traditional. Dramatic Santo Domingo Pueblo feast day, held on August 4, hosts an incredibly lavish corn dance featuring over 500 dancers. Other ceremonies include Three Kings Day, January 6, with elk, eagle, buffalo, and deer dances; Candelaria Day, February 2, with the buffalo dance; the Easter spring corn dance and basket dance; the San Pedro's Day corn dance, June 29; and many traditional dances in the Christmas season. Photographs prohibited. **Open:** Daily sunrise to sunset. Free.

SAN YSIDRO

Map page M-3, B2

Attraction 💼

Zia Pueblo, 135 Capitol Square Dr; tel 505/867-3304. The pueblo is best known for its famous sun symbol, which is now the official symbol of the state of New Mexico. Zia has a reputation for excellence in pottery making; examples can be seen and purchased at the Zia Cultural Center. Photographs prohibited. **Open:** Daily sunrise–sunset. Free.

SILVER CITY

Map page M-3, D1

Hotel 🏨

▤▤ **Palace Hotel**, 106 W Broadway, PO Box 5093, Silver City, NM 88061; tel 505/388-1811. Built in 1890 and restored to its original elegance in 1990. Wonderful Victorian atmosphere. **Rooms:** 22 rms and stes. CI 2pm/CO 11am. All rooms are on the second floor and all are slightly different. Victorian furniture. Some rooms have transoms. **Amenities:** 🛏 ᵹ Cable TV, refrig. No A/C. Complimentary continental breakfast is served in the upstairs, sky-lit garden room, which can also be used by guests as a lounge. **Services:** Babysitting. **Facilities:** 🎱 Games rm. Access may be difficult for handicapped guests. **Rates (CP):** $30–$48 S or D; from $48 ste. Children under 18 stay free. Spec packages avail. Pking: Outdoor, free. Maj CC.

Motels

▤▤ **Copper Manor Motel**, 710 Silver Heights Blvd (US 180), PO Box 1405, Silver City, NM 88062; tel 505/538-5392 or toll free 800/853-2916. A clean, basic motel. **Rooms:** 67 rms. CI 1pm/CO 11am. Nonsmoking rms avail. **Amenities:** 🛋 A/C, cable TV. **Services:** ✗ 🛗 🕎 Security person makes the rounds all night. **Facilities:** 🏋 1 rst, 1 bar, whirlpool. **Rates:** $36–$43 S; $43–$48 D. Extra person $3. Pking: Outdoor, free. Maj CC.

▤▤ **Holiday Motor Hotel**, 3420 E US 180, Silver City, NM 88061; tel 505/538-3711 or toll free 800/828-8291. A quiet, pleasant motel, where guests can hear birds singing. Lobby recently renovated. **Rooms:** 80 rms. CI noon/CO noon. Express checkout avail. Nonsmoking rms avail. Rooms are attractive and restful, with an integrated decor. **Amenities:** 🛋 A/C, cable TV w/movies. **Services:** 🛗 🕎 🔊 Phone attachment for the hearing impaired available. A security guard patrols all night. **Facilities:** 🏋 🛗 2 rsts, playground, washer/dryer. **Rates:** HS May–Aug $44 S; $55 D. Extra person $4. Children under 12 stay free. Lower rates off-season. Higher rates for spec evnts/hols. Spec packages avail. Pking: Outdoor, free. Maj CC. Weekly rates available.

Inn

▤▤ **Bear Mountain Guest Ranch**, Bear Mountain Rd, PO Box 1163, Silver City, NM 88062; tel 505/538-2538 or toll free 800/880-2538. 4 mi NW of Silver City. 160 acres. Featuring a large, comfortable lobby with 2 stone fireplaces in a lovely, rustic setting. The area is a haven for bird watchers, with over 200 species in the vicinity. **Rooms:** 15 rms, stes, and effic; 3 ctges/villas. CI 2pm/CO noon. Rooms are individually decorated and have lots of windows. **Amenities:** No A/C, phone, or TV. Some units w/terraces. **Services:** 🔊 Bird-watching guide books and classes are available. Tours can also be arranged. **Facilities:** 🛗 Guest lounge. **Rates (AP):** $54–$95 S or D; from $105 ste; from $55 effic; from $105 ctge/villa. Spec packages avail. Pking: Outdoor, free. Ltd CC. Commercial and senior citizen rates available.

Attractions 🏛

Silver City Museum, 312 W Broadway; tel 505/538-5921. The museum is lodged in the 1881 H B Ailman House, a former city hall and fire station remarkable for its cupola and Victorian mansard roof. Collections include early ranching and mining displays, Native American pottery, and early photographs. Exhibits of pioneer life include 1 room about Silver City women, among them silent film actress Lillian Knight. **Open:** Tues–Fri 9am–4:30pm, Sat–Sun 10am–4pm. Closed some hols. Free.

Western New Mexico University Museum, 1000 W College Ave; tel 505/538-6386. Contains the largest exhibit of prehistoric Mimbres pottery in the United States. Also displayed are Casas Grandes Indian pottery, stone tools, ancient jewelry, historical photographs, and mining and military artifacts. **Open:** Mon–Fri 9am–4:30pm, Sat–Sun 10am–4pm. Closed some hols. Free.

Gila National Forest, 2610 N Silver St; tel 505/388-8201. Covers 3.3 million acres in 4 counties. The Gila, Aldo, Leopold, and Blue Range wildernesses make up nearly one fourth of the acreage. Within the forest are 1,490 miles of trails for hiking and horseback riding, and in winter, cross-country skiing and snowmobiling. **Open:** Daily sunrise–sunset. Free.

Gila Cliff Dwellings National Monument, NM 15; tel 505/536-9461. A 2-hour drive north from Silver City, the ruins can be found in 6 of the 7 natural caves in the southeast-facing cliff on the side of Cliff Dweller Canyon. In total there are about 42 rooms. The dwellings allow a rare glimpse inside the homes and lives of prehistoric Native Americans; about 75 percent of what is seen is original. A 1-mile loop trail, rising 175 feet from the canyon floor, provides access. Camping and picnicking are encouraged in the national monument; there are no accommodations closer than Silver City. **Open:** Visitor center, daily 8am–5pm. Closed some hols. Free.

SOCORRO

Map page M-3, C2

Motels 🛏

▤▤ **Econo Lodge**, 713 California St, PO Box 977, Socorro, NM 87801; tel 505/835-1500 or toll free 800/528-3118; fax 505/835-3261. Exit 150 off I-25. In a good location in the center of town, yet quiet. An easy walk to several restaurants. **Rooms:** 44 rms. CI 1pm/CO 11am. Nonsmoking rms avail. **Amenities:** 🛋 A/C, cable TV, refrig. Some units w/terraces. **Services:** 🕎 🔊 Continental breakfast is served in the lobby. **Facilities:** Whirlpool. **Rates (CP):** $39–$45 S; $45–$50 D. Extra person $3. Children under 18 stay free. Higher rates for spec evnts/hols. Pking: Outdoor, free. Maj CC.

≋Sands Motel, 205 California St NW, Socorro, NM 87801; tel 505/835-1130. Exit 150 off I-25. A modest, well-kept motel in the center of town. Within easy walking distance of restaurants. **Rooms:** 25 rms. CI 11am/CO 11am. Nonsmoking rms avail. Rooms are basic and cheerful. **Amenities:** 🛁 A/C, cable TV w/movies. **Services:** 🚐 🍴 🐾 **Rates:** $20 S; $26 D. Extra person $3. Children under 12 stay free. Pking: Outdoor, free. Maj CC.

≋≋ Super 8 Motel, 1121 Frontage Road NW, Socorro, NM 87801; tel 505/835-4626 or toll free 800/800-8000; fax 505/835-3988. Exit 150 off I-25. Standard motel. Helpful staff is bilingual. **Rooms:** 88 rms and stes. CI 1pm/CO 11am. Nonsmoking rms avail. **Amenities:** 🛁 A/C, cable TV w/movies. **Services:** 🚐 🍴 Continental breakfast served in the lobby. **Facilities:** 🎣 ⅋ Spa, whirlpool, washer/dryer. **Rates (CP):** $43 S; $47 D; from $66 ste. Extra person $4. Children under 12 stay free. Pking: Outdoor, free. Maj CC.

Restaurants 🍴

Don Juan's Cocina, 118 Manzanares Ave, Socorro; tel 505/835-9967. **Mexican.** Basic Mexican, with booths and tables and a patio. All the standards are available. **FYI:** Reservations accepted. No liquor license. **Open:** Lunch Mon–Fri 10am–2:30pm, Sat 10am–3pm; dinner Mon–Fri 4–9pm. Closed some hols. **Prices:** Main courses $4.25–$9.50. Maj CC. 🍴 ⅋

Frank and Lupe's El Sombrero, 210 Mesquite St NE, Socorro; tel 505/835-3945. Exit 150 off I-25. **Mexican.** Cheerful restaurant containing a charming atrium with water fountains as well as a fireplace. Homestyle Mexican cooking. Chile beer is served. The tortilla factory on the premises occasionally offers tours. **FYI:** Reservations recommended. Children's menu. Beer and wine only. **Open:** Daily 11am–9pm. Closed some hols. **Prices:** Main courses $1.75–$7.25. Ltd CC. 🍴 ⅋

Val Verde Steak House, 203 Manzanares Ave, Socorro; tel 505/835-3380. **Southwestern/Steak.** Located in the original dining room of the 1919 Val Verde Hotel, this beautifully restored restaurant displays paintings by local artists. The menu features a wide selection of steaks and seafood. House specialties include pepper steak, beef stroganoff, and the Val Verde enchilada. Weekday lunch specials, at $4.75, are a bargain. **FYI:** Reservations accepted. Children's menu. Beer and wine only. **Open:** Lunch Mon–Fri 11am–2pm; dinner Mon–Thurs 5–9pm, Fri–Sat 5–9:30pm, Sun noon–9pm. Closed some hols. **Prices:** Main courses $6.75–$32.50. Maj CC. 🖤

Attractions 💼

Bosque del Apache National Wildlife Refuge, NM 1; tel 505/835-1828. An estimated 300 permanent and migratory birds and more than 100 amphibians, reptiles, and mammals make their homes in the 57,000-acre reserve. Photographers and nature watchers can start the 15-mile driving tour, or 1¾-mile Bosque Trail walk, at the visitor center at the refuge entrance. **Open:** Daily sunrise–sunset. $

Old San Miguel Mission, 403 El Camino Real, NW; tel 505/835-1620. Completed in 1626 but abandoned during the Pueblo Revolt of 1680, this church was subsequently restored and a new wing was built in 1853. It boasts thick adobe walls, large carved vigas, and supporting corbel arches. Masses are held Saturday at 6:30pm, and Sunday at 10am and noon. **Open:** Daily 6am–6pm. Free.

Mineral Museum, Campus Rd; tel 505/835-5616. Located on the New Mexico Institute of Mining and Technology campus, this museum houses the largest geological collection in the state. Its more than 10,000 specimens include mineral samples from all over the world, fossils, mining artifacts, and photographs. **Open:** Mon–Fri 8am–5pm. Free.

TAOS

Map page M-3, A3

Hotels 🏨

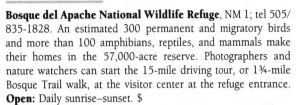

≋≋≋ Holiday Inn Don Fernando de Taos, 1005 Paseo del Pueblo Sur, PO Drawer V, Taos, NM 87571; tel 505/758-4444 or toll free 800/759-2736; fax 505/758-0055. 1½ mi S of Taos Plaza on NM 68. The decor sets this above the usual Holiday Inn. The lobby has white stucco adobe-like walls, a kiva-style fireplace, and a heavy-beamed, high ceiling. **Rooms:** 126 rms and stes. CI 2pm/CO 11am. Express checkout avail. Nonsmoking rms avail. Pleasant, spotless rooms are decorated with local art. **Amenities:** 🛁 ⅋ A/C, cable TV. Some units w/fireplaces. **Services:** ✕ 🚐 🖼 🍴 🐾 Twice-daily maid svce, car-rental desk, babysitting. **Facilities:** 🎣 🍸 🏊 ⅋ 1 rst, 1 bar (w/entertainment), whirlpool. The lobby bar has locally popular karaoke nights and a large-screen TV for sports events. **Rates:** HS Jan 19–Mar 31/May 28–Oct 16 $95 S; $105 D; from $125 ste. Extra person $10. Children under 19 stay free. Lower rates off-season. Higher rates for spec evnts/hols. Spec packages avail. Pking: Outdoor, free. Maj CC.

≋≋≋ Kachina Lodge de Taos, 413 Paseo del Pueblo Norte, PO Box NN, Taos, NM 87571; tel 505/758-2275 or toll free 800/

522-4462; fax 505/758-9207. ½ mi N of Taos Plaza traffic light. A pleasant, modern motel within walking distance of most Taos tourist attractions and several good restaurants. **Rooms:** 118 rms and stes. CI 2pm/CO 11am. Nonsmoking rms avail. Recently renovated rooms. **Amenities:** 🛅 A/C, cable TV. Some units w/terraces. **Services:** ✗ 🚗 🛎 ⊲⊳ A guest services desk in the lobby provides tourist and other information in the summer. **Facilities:** 🔓 🏃 400 ⅛ 2 rsts, 1 bar (w/entertainment), whirlpool, beauty salon, washer/dryer. A Taos Pueblo Indian family performs dances nightly, May through October. **Rates:** $100–$115 S or D; from $145 ste. Extra person $10. Children under 13 stay free. Higher rates for spec evnts/hols. Spec packages avail. Pking: Outdoor, free. Maj CC.

🏚🏚 **La Fonda de Taos**, South Plaza, PO Box 1447, Taos, NM 87571 (Taos Plaza); tel 505/758-2211 or toll free 800/883-2211. An historic, quaint hotel, with an old Taos feel. A trip back in time, with few modern amenities. The lobby is worth a visit in itself, with an outstanding collection of local art, crafts, and furniture. Hidden away in an office, but available to view for a fee, are the somewhat infamous paintings by the author D H Lawrence, a one-time Taos area resident. **Rooms:** 24 rms and stes. CI open/CO noon. Basic, comfortable rooms. **Amenities:** 🛅 No A/C or TV. 1 unit w/terrace. Few modern amenities are provided. **Services:** ⊲⊳ **Facilities:** Washer/dryer. **Rates:** HS Dec 18–Jan 3 $110 S or D; from $120 ste. Children under 18 stay free. Lower rates off-season. Pking: Outdoor, free. Maj CC.

🏚🏚 **Sagebrush Inn**, Paseo del Pueblo Sur, PO Box 557, Taos, NM 87571; tel 505/758-2254 or toll free 800/428-3626; fax 505/758-5077. 3 mi S of Taos. Historic adobe hotel with well-kept grounds. The original building is distinguished by arched doorways, heavy ceiling beams, and kiva fireplaces. **Rooms:** 80 rms and stes. CI 2pm/CO 11am. Nonsmoking rms avail. Many rooms have lovely views of the mountains and surrounding valley. **Amenities:** 🛅 A/C, satel TV. Some units w/terraces, some w/fireplaces. **Services:** 🛎 ⊲⊳ Babysitting. **Facilities:** 🔓 ♨2 300 2 rsts, 1 bar (w/entertainment), whirlpool. Guests have use of lawn chairs in a quiet, grassy courtyard. The lobby bar is a popular gathering spot for local residents, with frequent live country-and-western music. **Rates (BB):** $75 S; $90–$105 D; from $120 ste. Extra person $10. Children under 12 stay free. Higher rates for spec evnts/hols. Spec packages avail. Pking: Outdoor, free. Maj CC.

Motels

🏚🏚 **El Monte Lodge**, 317 Kit Carson Rd, PO Box 22, Taos, NM 87571; tel 505/758-3171 or toll free 800/808-8267; fax 505/758-1536. 2 blocks E of Taos Plaza. Within walking distance of Taos Plaza, this 1932 property is in a quiet,

residential area. All units face a lovely grassy picnic area with tall cottonwoods and a terrific view of Taos Mountain. **Rooms:** 13 rms. CI 2pm/CO 11am. Four units have kitchenettes ($10 additional charge). **Amenities:** 🛅 Cable TV, refrig. No A/C. Some units w/fireplaces. **Services:** 🛎 ⊲⊳ **Facilities:** 🏃 Washer/dryer. **Rates:** HS Thanksgiving–Easter $54–$59 S; $85–$95 D. Extra person $10. Lower rates off-season. Higher rates for spec evnts/hols. Pking: Outdoor, free. Maj CC. There's a $5 pet fee.

🏚🏚 **El Pueblo Lodge**, 412 Paseo del Pueblo Norte, PO Box 92, Taos, NM 87571; tel 505/758-8700 or toll free 800/433-9612; fax 505/758-7321. ½ mi N of Taos Plaza. A friendly place, good for families. Convenient to town attractions, yet quiet. **Rooms:** 49 rms, stes, and effic. CI 3pm/CO 11:30am. Rooms are in southwest style, with wood-beamed ceilings and American Indian motif decorations. **Amenities:** 🛅 ♨ 📺 A/C, cable TV, refrig. Some units w/minibars, some w/terraces, some w/fireplaces. **Services:** 🛎 ⊲⊳ **Facilities:** Whirlpool, washer/dryer. **Rates (CP):** HS June–Nov/Jan–Apr $63 S or D; from $73 ste; from $73 effic. Extra person $7. Lower rates off-season. Higher rates for spec evnts/hols. Spec packages avail. Pking: Outdoor, free. Maj CC.

🏚🏚🏚 **The Historic Taos Inn**, 125 Paseo del Pueblo Norte, PO Drawer N, Taos, NM 87571; tel 505/758-2233 or toll free 800/TAOS INN; fax 505/758-5776. A lovely combination of historic charm and modern convenience. The lobby/bar is popular with locals, with live entertainment, a central fountain under a skylight, and beautiful decor and ambience. **Rooms:** 39 rms. CI 4pm/CO 11am. Nonsmoking rms avail. Comfortable rooms exhibit a wonderful use of local art and designs and are furnished with standing armoires, built-in love seats, and kiva fireplaces. **Amenities:** 🛅 ♨ A/C, cable TV. Some units w/fireplaces. **Services:** 🛎 Twice-daily maid svce, babysitting. Refreshments served in courtyard near pool in summer. **Facilities:** 🔓 ⅛ 1 rst (see also "Restaurants" below), 1 bar (w/entertainment), whirlpool. Wheelchair access is from rear parking lot. **Rates:** HS July–Oct $85–$160 S or D. Children under 18 stay free. Lower rates off-season. Pking: Outdoor, free. Ltd CC.

🏚🏚 **Indian Hills Inn**, 233 Paseo del Pueblo Sur, PO Box 1229, Taos, NM 87571; tel 505/758-4293 or toll free 800/444-2346. 2 blocks S of Taos Plaza. This basic, comfortable motel is within walking distance of Taos Plaza and its shops and restaurants. **Rooms:** 50 rms. CI 2pm/CO 11am. The rooms have above-average artwork and framed antique maps on the walls, plus wall tiles and southwestern-motif bedspreads. The room quality is much nicer than expected for the rates. **Amenities:** 🛅 Cable TV w/movies. No A/C. **Services:** ⊲⊳ **Facilities:** 🔓 **Rates**

(CP): HS Nov–Feb/May–Sept $50 S; $60 D. Extra person $5. Children under 12 stay free. Lower rates off-season. Pking: Outdoor, free. Maj CC.

Quality Inn, 1023 Paseo del Pueblo Sur, PO Box 2319, Taos, NM 87571; tel 505/758-2200 or toll free 800/845-0648; fax 505/758-9009. 2 mi S of Taos Plaza. A clean, pleasant hotel, with a friendly and helpful staff. **Rooms:** 99 rms and stes. CI 2pm/CO 11am. Express checkout avail. Nonsmoking rms avail. Some rooms have nice local touches, such as copperwork-framed mirrors or RC Gorman prints on the walls. **Amenities:** A/C, cable TV, stereo/tape player, in-rm safe. Some units w/terraces. **Services:** X Breakfast included in the low season. **Facilities:** 1 rst, 1 bar, whirlpool. **Rates:** HS Dec 20–Jan 3/July–Aug $80–$85 S or D; from $150 ste. Extra person $7. Children under 18 stay free. Lower rates off-season. Spec packages avail. Pking: Outdoor, free. Maj CC.

Rancho Ramada, 615 Paseo del Pueblo Sur, Taos, NM 87571; tel 505/758-2900 or toll free 800/2-RAMADA; fax 505/758-1662. 1½ mi S of Taos Plaza. An attractive, modern motel. The lobby has several cozy sitting areas with local art and handcrafted furnishings. **Rooms:** 124 rms and stes. CI 3pm/CO noon. Express checkout avail. Nonsmoking rms avail. Clean, comfortable rooms. **Amenities:** A/C, cable TV. All units w/terraces, some w/fireplaces. **Services:** X Twice-daily maid svce. **Facilities:** 1 rst, 1 bar (w/entertainment), games rm, whirlpool. **Rates:** HS Mar 1–Mar 19/Nov 15–Feb 28 $95 S; $113 D; from $207 ste. Extra person $15. Children under 18 stay free. Lower rates off-season. Pking: Outdoor, free. Maj CC.

Resort

Quail Ridge Inn, NM 150, PO Box 707, Taos, NM 87571; tel 505/776-2211 or toll free 800/624-4448; fax 505/776-2949. 5 mi N of Taos. Turn right at blinking light. 7 acres. A pleasant family resort, with the best on-premise sports facilities in the area. It's out in the country yet convenient to town, skiing, and historic sites. **Rooms:** 110 rms, stes, and effic. CI 4pm/CO 11am. Rooms are spacious and modern, with southwestern touches. **Amenities:** Cable TV w/movies. No A/C. Some units w/terraces, all w/fireplaces. **Services:** Masseur, children's program, babysitting. **Facilities:** 1 rst, 1 bar, racquetball, squash, spa, sauna, steam rm, whirlpool, washer/dryer. **Rates:** HS July–Aug/Nov–Mar $85–$105 S or D; from $170 ste; from $110 effic. Extra person $10. Children under 12 stay free. Lower rates off-season. Spec packages avail. Pking: Outdoor, free. Ltd CC.

Restaurants

The Apple Tree, 123 Bent St, Taos; tel 505/758-1900. 1 block N of Taos Plaza. **Southwestern.** Located in an old adobe building that just oozes southwest charm. There are several small dining rooms, some with fireplaces, all decorated with attractive art. The menu has variations on southwestern cuisine, with beef, lamb, chicken, seafood, and vegetarian offerings. Specialties include velarde carnitas enchiladas—lean pork layered between blue corn tortillas with apple chutney, sour cream, and white cheddar cheese, and smothered in red or green chiles. All desserts and baked goods are made on premises. The chef will modify dishes to suit specific dietary needs whenever possible. **FYI:** Reservations recommended. Guitar/singer. Children's menu. Beer and wine only. No smoking. **Open:** Lunch Mon–Fri 11:30am–3pm; dinner daily 5:30–9pm; brunch Sat–Sun 10am–3pm. Closed Thanksgiving. **Prices:** Main courses $10.95–$18.95. Ltd CC.

Bent Street Deli and Cafe, 120 Bent St, Taos; tel 505/758-5787. **Eclectic.** Busy cafe atmosphere inside; pleasant patio outside, heated in winter. The menu consists of usual deli fare, with seafood and Italian specialties added for dinner. **FYI:** Reservations accepted. Guitar. Beer and wine only. No smoking. **Open:** Mon–Sat 8am–9pm. Closed some hols. **Prices:** Main courses $10–$13. Ltd CC.

Casa Cordova, NM 150, Taos; tel 505/776-2500. 8 mi N of Taos. **Continental.** This elegant restaurant in a charming old adobe building has a spacious courtyard with fountain, several dining rooms, and a cozy bar where patrons can relax and enjoy piano music along with their desserts or after-dinner drinks. The continental gourmet menu includes fish, seafood, chicken, quail, pork, lamb, veal, and steaks. There's also a wide selection of pastas. **FYI:** Reservations recommended. Piano. Children's menu. **Open:** Mon–Sat 4pm–close. **Prices:** Main courses $10.95–$20. Maj CC.

Doc Martin's, in The Historic Taos Inn, 125 Paseo del Pueblo Norte, Taos; tel 505/758-1977. **Continental/Southwestern.** Southwest decor in a historic adobe home, with comfortable chairs. The continental cuisine has a southwestern emphasis. A sample entree: roasted and grilled duck with red chile broth, posole, and mango relish. **FYI:** Reservations recommended. Guitar/singer. Children's menu. No smoking. **Open:** Breakfast Mon–Fri 8–11am, Sat–Sun 8–11:30am; lunch daily 11:30am–2:30pm; dinner daily 5:30–9:30pm. **Prices:** Main courses $14.50–$19.50. Ltd CC.

Dori's and Tony's Cafe, 402 Paseo del Pueblo Norte, Taos; tel 505/758-9222. **Italian/Southwestern.** Casual, friendly atmosphere, with seating inside or out. Posters and original art decorate the walls; art exhibits change regularly. Basic meals, fresh baked goods, and southwestern specialties are offered during the day. The dinner menu expands to include Italian dishes like lasagna and fettuccine alfredo, as well as a daily special. **FYI:** Reservations accepted. Guitar/singer. Children's menu. Beer and wine only. No smoking. **Open:** HS July–Sept daily 7am–9pm. Reduced hours off-season. Closed some hols. **Prices:** Main courses $7–$12. Ltd CC. 🍽 📷

★ **El Taoseño Restaurant**, 819 Paseo del Pueblo Sur, Taos; tel 505/758-4142. **American/Mexican.** A busy, local gathering place that's a favorite among many in the Taos community. The dining room is large and open, with paintings by local artists on display (and for sale). The breakfast burrito, served anytime, is locally famous. Mexican food, steaks, chicken, fish, burgers, and sandwiches can also be had. A separate lowfat menu is available. **FYI:** Reservations not accepted. **Open:** Mon–Sat 6am–10pm, Sun 6:30am–3pm. Closed some hols. **Prices:** Main courses $1.25–$11.95. Ltd CC.

The Garden Restaurant, in Taos Plaza, 127 N Plaza, Taos; tel 505/758-9483. **New American/Southwestern.** A casual, busy eatery on Taos Plaza. The menu includes a variety of beef, chicken, pasta, sandwiches, and burgers. Pollo de Taos is grilled chicken breast on warm sour cream and green chile sauce, topped with avocado slices; trout à la pecan is pan-fried trout with pecans, toasted in butter. **FYI:** Reservations accepted. Guitar. Children's menu. No liquor license. **Open:** Daily 7:30am–9pm. **Prices:** Main courses $7.95–$9.95. Maj CC. 📷

Lambert's of Taos, 309 Paseo del Pueblo Sur, Taos; tel 505/758-1009. 2½ blocks S of Taos Plaza. **New American.** Very attractive, combining southwestern decor and modern, casual elegance. Traditional American dishes are given a twist, like the pepper-crusted lamb with red wine demiglace and garlic pasta, and fresh Dungeness crab cakes with dipping sauce and pickled vegetables. All dinner entrees are offered in 2 sizes to suit different appetites. **FYI:** Reservations recommended. Children's menu. Beer and wine only. **Open:** Lunch Mon–Fri 11:30am–2:30pm; dinner daily 6–9pm. Closed July 4. **Prices:** Main courses $10.50–$18.50. Maj CC. 🍽 ♿

Mainstreet Bakery and Cafe, Guadalupe Plaza, Camino de la Placita, Taos; tel 505/758-9610. **New American.** A casual cafe popular with both locals and visitors. Several picnic-style tables are out front. The emphasis is on healthy sandwiches, fresh vegetables, and fresh baked goods. **FYI:** Reservations not accepted. Guitar. BYO. No smoking. **Open:** Wed–Sun 7:45am–10pm, Mon–Tues 7:45am–3pm. Closed Dec 25. **Prices:** Main courses $4.95–$12.95. No CC. 🍽 📷

★ **Michael's Kitchen**, 305 Paseo del Pueblo Norte, Taos; tel 505/758-4178. **Southwestern.** Cheerful and casual, with simple western decor and solid wood tables. The hearty fare is accented with southwestern and western flavors. The menu includes sandwiches and burgers, beef, chicken, fish, and Mexican items. Portions are ample, and breakfast is served all day. **FYI:** Reservations not accepted. Children's menu. No liquor license. **Open:** Daily 6am–8:30pm. Closed some hols; Apr and Nov. **Prices:** Main courses $6–$11.40. Maj CC. 📷

Stakeout Grill and Bar, Stakeout Dr, Taos; tel 505/758-2042. 8 mi S of Taos. Stakeout Dr exit off NM 68. **Seafood/Steak.** The Stakeout is located on a mountain slope south of Taos and offers incredible views of the Sangre de Cristo Mountains, Taos Valley, Rio Grande Gorge, and lovely sunsets. There are several dining rooms, and the outdoor patio is very popular in the summer months. Specialties include prime rib, grilled fillet of salmon, fresh rainbow trout baked with vegetables and herbs, veal, and roasted duck. **FYI:** Reservations recommended. Guitar/harp/jazz/piano. Children's menu. **Open:** Dinner daily 5–10pm; brunch Sun 10am–2pm. **Prices:** Main courses $13.95–$26.95. Maj CC. 🍽 📷 🏞 ♿

Villa Fontana, NM 522, Taos; tel 505/758-5800. 4½ mi N of Taos. **Italian.** Elegant, romantic atmosphere abounds in this adobe house decorated to feel like an Italian country home, with a few southwestern touches. Art by the owner/chef is displayed, and summertime outdoor dining offers terrific views of the mountains and surrounding valley. The northern Italian cuisine features such choices as pheasant breast with dried blueberries and demiglace, and grilled beef tenderloin with brandy, balsamic vinegar, and green peppercorns. **FYI:** Reservations recommended. Children's menu. Dress code. **Open:** Lunch Tues–Fri 11:30am–2pm. **Prices:** Main courses $19–$25. Maj CC. ♥ 🍽 📷 🏞 ♿

Attractions 💼

Taos Pueblo; tel 505/758-9593. The northernmost of New Mexico's 19 pueblos, located 2½ miles north of the Plaza, it has been the home of the Tiwa tribe for more than 900 years. Two massive, multistory adobe apartment buildings appear much the same today as when a regiment from Coronado's expedition first saw them in 1540. Houses are built one upon another to form porches, balconies, and roofs accessed by ancient ladders.

San Geronimo is the patron saint of the Taos pueblo, and his feast day on September 30 combines Catholic and pre-Hispanic traditions. Taos Pueblo Pow Wow, a dance competition and parade drawing tribes from throughout North America, is held in mid-July. Ask permission before taking photographs of individuals. **Open:** Daily, summer 8am–5pm, winter 9am–4pm. $

Millicent Rogers Museum, NM 522; tel 505/758-2462. Rogers was a wealthy Taos émigré who, in 1947, began to compile a magnificent array of beautiful Native American arts and crafts. Included in the collection are Navajo and Pueblo jewelry, Pueblo pottery, and paintings from the Rio Grande Pueblo people. The scope of the museum's permanent collection has been expanded to include Hispanic, religious, and secular arts and crafts, from Spanish and Mexican colonial times to the present. **Open:** Daily 9am–5pm. Closed some hols. $$

Martinez Hacienda, Lower Ranchitos Rd; tel 505/758-1000. This Spanish colonial–style, 21-room hacienda was built around 2 interior courtyards. It was the home of merchant and trader Don Antonio Martinez. Today many of the rooms are decorated with period furnishings; the rest of the hacienda has been turned into a "living museum" with weavers, blacksmiths, and wood carvers demonstrating their crafts. **Open:** Daily 9am–5pm. Closed some hols. $$

Kit Carson Home and Museum of the West, E Kit Carson Rd; tel 505/758-4741. A general museum of Taos history. The 12-room adobe home was built in 1825 and purchased in 1843 by Carson, the famous mountain man, Indian agent, and scout. A living room, bedroom, and kitchen are furnished as they might have been when occupied by the Carsons. An array of pioneer items are on display including antique firearms and trappers' implements. **Open:** Daily 9am–5pm. Closed some hols. $$

Ernest L Blumenschein Home and Museum, 222 Ledoux St; tel 505/758-0330. An adobe home with garden walls and a courtyard, parts of which date to the 1790s. It was the home and studio of Ernest Blumenschein and his family beginning in 1919. Period furnishing include European antiques and handmade Taos furniture in Spanish colonial style. Blumenschein was one of the founders of the Taos Society of Artists and an extensive collection of work by early 20th-century Taos masters is on display in several rooms of the home. **Open:** Daily 9am–5pm. Closed some hols. $$

The Fechin Institute, 227 Paseo del Pueblo Norte; tel 505/758-1710. Special exhibitions, concerts, and art workshops are offered in the former home of Russian artist Nicolai Fechin, who died in 1955. The adobe building is embellished with hand-carved doors, windows, gates, posts, fireplaces, and other features of a Russian country home. The house and adjacent studio are the location of Fechin Institute educational activities, as well as concerts and lectures. **Open:** June–Oct, Wed–Sun 1–5:30pm. $

Harwood Foundation Museum, 238 Ledoux St; tel 505/758-3063. This pueblo-style library-and-museum complex holds paintings, drawings, prints, sculpture, and photographs by the artists of the Taos area from 1800 to the present. Featured are paintings from the early days of the art colony by members of the Taos Society of Artists, including Oscar Berninghaus, Ernest Blumenschein, and Herbert Dunton. Also on display are 19th-century *retablos*, religious paintings of saints that have traditionally been used for decoration and inspiration in the homes and churches of New Mexico. **Open:** Mon–Fri 10am–5pm, Sat 10am–4pm. Closed some hols. Free.

Governor Bent House Museum, 117 Bent St; tel 505/758-2376. The residence of Charles Bent, the New Mexico Territory's first American governor. Bent was murdered in the 1847 Indian and Hispanic rebellion; his wife and children escaped by digging a hole through an adobe wall. The hole is still visible today. Period art and artifacts are displayed. **Open:** Daily 9am–5pm. $

Taos Volunteer Fire Department, 323 Placitas Rd; tel 505/758-3386. An excellent collection of the work of early Taos artists is on display here. The collection was started in the 1950s when volunteer Taos firemen asked their artist friends to decorate the station's recreation room. **Open:** Mon–Fri 8am–4:30pm. Free.

San Francisco de Asis Church, NM 68; tel 505/758-2754. This famous church with no doors or windows resembles a modernesque adobe sculpture. It has been photographed by Ansel Adams and painted by Georgia O'Keeffe. Displayed in an adjacent building is the painting *The Shadow of the Cross* (1896) by Henri Ault; in the dark, the painting mysteriously becomes luminescent, and the shadow of a cross forms over the left shoulder of Jesus's silhouette.

The church office and gift shop are across the driveway to the north of the church. A slide show is also presented here. **Open:** Mon–Sat 9am–4pm. Closed some hols. Free.

D H Lawrence Memorial, NM 522; tel 505/776-2245. This shrine to the controversial early 20th-century author is a pilgrimage site for literary devotees. The short uphill walk is littered with various mementos—photos, coins, messages from fortune cookies—placed by visitors. Lawrence lived in Taos off and on between 1922 and 1925. His ashes were returned here for burial. **Open:** Daily 8am–6pm. Free.

Kit Carson Park and Cemetery, Paseo del Pueblo Norte; tel 505/758-4160. Major community events are held in the park in summer. The cemetery, established in 1847, contains the graves of Carson and his wife; Charles Bent, the New Mexico Territory's first American governor; the Don Antonio Martinez family; and other noted historical figures and artists. **Open:** Daily sunrise–sunset. Free.

Rio Grande Gorge Bridge, US 64. This impressive bridge spanning the Southwest's greatest river rises 650 feet above the canyon floor. At different times of day the changing light plays tricks with the colors of the cliff walls.

TAOS SKI VALLEY

Map page M-3, A3

Hotels 🏨

≋≋≋ Amizette Inn, Taos Ski Valley Rd, PO Box 756, Taos Ski Valley, NM 87525; tel 505/776-2451 or toll free 800/446-TAOS. 18 mi N of Taos. A charming hotel, perfect for a romantic getaway or an enchanting escape for the skier. **Rooms:** 12 rms and stes. CI 2pm/CO 11am. Nonsmoking rms avail. Rooms are spacious, with separate sitting areas, lovely wood furniture, and panoramic views of the river and mountains. **Amenities:** 📺 👙 Satel TV. No A/C. Some units w/terraces. **Services:** 🍴 🛎️ 🕭 Twice-daily maid svce. **Facilities:** 🏊 👤 🦆 1 rst. **Rates (BB):** HS Dec–Apr $110–$143 S or D; from $132 ste. Extra person $20. Children under 5 stay free. Min stay HS. Lower rates off-season. AP and MAP rates avail. Spec packages avail. Pking: Outdoor, free. Maj CC.

≋≋ Austing Haus, Taos Ski Valley Rd, PO Box 8, Taos Ski Valley, NM 87525; or toll free 800/748-2932. 18 mi N of Taos. A clean, comfortable hotel, with interesting construction and beautiful woodwork. **Rooms:** 42 rms. CI 2pm/CO 11am. Nonsmoking rms avail. **Amenities:** 📺 Satel TV. No A/C. Some units w/terraces, some w/fireplaces. **Services:** 🛎️ 🕭 **Facilities:** 👤 🦆 👙 1 rst, washer/dryer. **Rates (BB):** HS Nov 24–Jan 2/Feb–Mar $100–$110 S or D. Extra person $25. Children under 5 stay free. Lower rates off-season. Spec packages avail. Pking: Outdoor, free. Ltd CC.

≋≋ The Inn at Snakedance, Hwy 150, PO Box 89, Taos Ski Valley, NM 87525; tel 505/776-2277 or toll free 800/322-9815; fax 505/776-1410. Combines old-world ambience and modern conveniences. **Rooms:** 62 rms. CI 4pm/CO 11am. Nonsmoking rms avail. Rooms furnished with locally built pine furniture and Taos art. **Amenities:** 📺 Cable TV, refrig. No A/C. All units w/terraces, some w/fireplaces. **Services:** 🆅🅿 Masseur. **Facilities:** 👤 🦆 🏋️ 👙 1 rst, 1 bar (w/entertainment), spa. The fitness center boasts state-of-the-art workout machines, separate massage room, and huge whirlpools. **Rates (BB):** HS Dec–Mar $175–$210 S; $195–$230 D. Extra person $20. Lower rates off-season. Spec packages avail. Pking: Outdoor, free. Ltd CC.

Attraction 🎒

Taos Ski Valley, NM 150; tel 505/776-2291. The preeminent ski resort in the southern Rocky Mountains. There are 73 trails and bowls, and between the 11,800-foot summit and the 9,200-foot base, 323 inches of light, dry powder fall annually. **Open:** Nov–Apr, daily 9am–4pm. $$$$

TESUQUE

Map page M-3, B3 (N of Santa Fe)

Restaurant 🍴

El Nido, NM 22, Tesuque; tel 505/988-4340. 5 mi N of Santa Fe. Tesuque exit off US 84/285 N. **Seafood/Southwestern/Steak.** Located in a delightful old building adorned with fascinating murals and possessing an Old Santa Fe ambience. Close to the Santa Fe Opera, it is a good spot for a pre-opera dinner. Salmon, prime rib, and sirloin are specialties, and beef, seafood, and chicken are also served. **FYI:** Reservations recommended. **Open:** Lunch Tues–Sat 11:30am–2pm; dinner Tues–Sun 5:30–10pm. Closed some hols. **Prices:** Main courses $9.95–$25.95. Ltd CC. 🍷 🖼️ 👙

TRUTH OR CONSEQUENCES

Map page M-3, D2

Motel 🏨

≋≋ Best Western Hot Springs Inn, 2270 N Date St, Truth or Consequences, NM 87901; tel 505/894-6665 or toll free 800/528-1234. Exit 79 off I-25. A basic motel in a pleasant setting. Personnel are friendly and helpful. **Rooms:** 40 rms. CI 1pm/CO noon. Nonsmoking rms avail. Simple, comfortable rooms. **Amenities:** 📺 A/C, satel TV. **Services:** 🚐 🛎️ 🕭 **Facilities:** 👙 1 rst (see also "Restaurants" below). **Rates:** $45–$50 S; $50–$57 D. Extra person $7. Children under 12 stay free. Pking: Outdoor, Maj CC.

Restaurants 🍴

K-Bob's Steakhouse, in Best Western Hot Springs Inn, 2260 N Date St, Truth or Consequences; tel 505/894-2127. Exit 79 off I-25. **Burgers/Steak.** A spacious, comfortable, and attractive restaurant, with artificial flowers in baskets. The menu features steaks, burgers, seafood, chicken, and Mexican dishes. Extensive salad bar. **FYI:** Reservations not accepted. Children's menu. Beer and wine only. **Open:** HS May–Sept Sun–Thurs 6am–9pm, Fri–Sat 6am–10pm. Reduced hours off-season. Closed Dec 25. **Prices:** Main courses $2.99–$12.99. Maj CC. 🎮 ⚬

La Cocina, 280 Date St, Truth or Consequences; tel 505/894-6499. Exit 79 off I-25. **Mexican.** Unusual Southwestern decor with local art and inlaid tile tables. Popular for Mexican combination plates and burritos, La Cocina also offers chicken, steaks, sandwiches, and enchiladas. The sopaipillas are huge. **FYI:** Reservations accepted. Children's menu. No liquor license. **Open:** Mon–Thurs 11am–9pm, Fri–Sun 11am–10pm. Closed some hols. **Prices:** Main courses $3.95–$14.50. No CC. 🎮

Los Arcos, 1400 N Date St Hwy 85, Truth or Consequences; tel 505/894-6200. Exit 79 off I-25. **Seafood/Steak.** An attractive, restful ambience, with subdued lighting, wrought iron tables, and several dining rooms. Mostly steak and seafood, with some chicken, shish kabob, ribs. Salad bar. **FYI:** Reservations not accepted. Children's menu. **Open:** Sun–Thurs 5–10:30pm, Fri–Sat 5–11pm. Closed some hols. **Prices:** Main courses $5.95–$25.95. Maj CC. ♥ 🖤 ⚬

Attraction 💼

Geronimo Springs Museum, 211 Main St; tel 505/894-6600. Exhibits of prehistoric Mimbres pottery, Spanish colonial artifacts, and historical murals. Outside is **Geronimo's Spring,** where the great Chiricahua Apache war chief is said to have taken his warriors to bathe their battle wounds. **Open:** Mon–Sat 9am–5pm. Closed some hols. $

TUCUMCARI

Map page M-3, B4

Motels 🛏

≡≡≡ **Best Western Discovery Motor Inn**, 200 E Estrella Ave, Tucumcari, NM 88401; tel 505/461-4884 or toll free 800/528-1234; fax 505/461-2463. Exit 332 off I-40. Stresses service. **Rooms:** 107 rms and stes. CI 4pm/CO 11am. Nonsmoking rms avail. Pleasant, modern, and comfortable furnishings. 1 king-size or 2 queen-size beds. **Amenities:** 🛁 ⚬ A/C, satel TV w/movies, refrig, VCR. Some units w/terraces, 1 w/Jacuzzi. **Services:** ✕ ⌔ ⚬ Babysitting. 24-hour front desk. **Facilities:** 🔥 ⬮ 🏊 ⚬ 1 rst, games rm, spa, sauna, whirlpool, washer/dryer. **Rates:** HS May 16–Sept 16 $42–$48 S; $48–$54 D; from $60 ste. Extra person $4. Children under 12 stay free. Lower rates off-season. Spec packages avail. Pking: Outdoor, free. Maj CC.

≡≡≡ **Best Western Pow Wow Inn**, 801 W Tucumcari Blvd, Tucumcari, NM 88401; tel 505/461-0500 or toll free 800/527-6996; fax 505/461-0135. Recently underwent complete renovation. **Rooms:** 93 rms and effic. CI 4pm/CO noon. Nonsmoking rms avail. All rooms and suites are at ground level. **Amenities:** 🛁 ⚬ A/C, cable TV w/movies, refrig. **Services:** ✕ ⬮ ⌔ ⚬ Babysitting. 24-hour desk. **Facilities:** 🔥 1 rst, 1 bar (w/entertainment), washer/dryer. **Rates:** HS Apr–June $40–$50 S; $45–$55 D; from $65 ste. Extra person $6. Children under 12 stay free. Lower rates off-season. Spec packages avail. Pking: Outdoor, free. Maj CC.

≡≡ **Comfort Inn**, 2800 E Tucumcari Blvd, Tucumcari, NM 88401; tel 505/461-4094 or toll free 800/221-2222; fax 505/461-4099. Exit 335 off I-40. A well-maintained motel, east of the main business district. **Rooms:** 59 rms. CI 4pm/CO 11am. Nonsmoking rms avail. Rooms are exceptionally light, clean, and airy. **Amenities:** 🛁 ⚬ A/C, cable TV w/movies. **Services:** ⌔ Babysitting. **Facilities:** 🔥 ⚬ **Rates:** HS June–Sept $52–$60 S; $58–$80 D. Extra person $6. Lower rates off-season. Higher rates for spec evnts/hols. Spec packages avail. Pking: Outdoor, free. Maj CC.

≡ **Friendship Inn**, 315 E Tucumcari Blvd, Tucumcari, NM 88401; tel 505/461-0330 or toll free 800/537-3893; fax 505/461-0330. Exit 332 off I-40. Completely acceptable lodging for the economy-minded. **Rooms:** 31 rms. CI 4pm/CO 11am. Nonsmoking rms avail. **Amenities:** 🛁 A/C, cable TV w/movies. **Services:** ⬮ ⌔ ⚬ Babysitting. **Facilities:** 🔥 ⚬ 1 rst. **Rates:** HS June–Sept $20–$25 S; $28–$35 D. Extra person $4. Children under 12 stay free. Lower rates off-season. Pking: Outdoor, free. Maj CC.

≡ **Safari Motel**, 722 E Tucumcari Blvd, Tucumcari, NM 88401; tel 505/461-3642. A small, well-maintained mom-and-pop motel. **Rooms:** 23 rms. CI 4pm/CO 11am. Nonsmoking rms avail. **Amenities:** 🛁 ⚬ A/C, cable TV. **Services:** ⌔ ⚬ Babysitting. **Facilities:** 🔥 Washer/dryer. **Rates:** $20–$26 S; $26–$30 D. Extra person $3. Children under 12 stay free. Pking: Outdoor, free. Maj CC.

Restaurants 🍴

Del's, 1202 E Tucumcari Blvd, Tucumcari; tel 505/461-1740. Exit 332 off I-40. **Mexican/Seafood/Steak.** Popular for reasonably priced steak and salad bar. Also seafood and Mexican dishes. **FYI:** Reservations not accepted. Children's menu. No liquor license. **Open:** Mon–Sat 11am–9pm. Closed some hols. **Prices:** Main courses $5.95–$15.95. Maj CC. 🎮

La Cita, 812 S 1st St, Tucumcari; tel 505/461-3930. **Mexican.** Variety of Mexican dishes. Specialties include fajitas and green chile chicken enchiladas. **FYI:** Reservations accepted. Children's menu. No liquor license. **Open:** Daily 11am–9pm. Closed Dec 25. **Prices:** Main courses $2.59–$5.99. Ltd CC. 🖳 ⅙

Attractions 💼

Tucumcari Historical Museum, 416 S Adams; tel 505/461-4201. On view are an early sheriff's office, an authentic western schoolroom, a hospital room of the early West, a real chuck wagon, a historic windmill, and a barbed-wire collection. **Open:** Mon–Sat 9am–5pm, Sun 1–5pm. Free.

Conchas Lake State Park, NM 104; tel 505/868-2270. The reservoir here is 25 miles long and has 2 modern marinas that provide facilities for boating, fishing, and waterskiing. The south side of the lake offers camping, picnic areas, and a 9-hole golf course. **Open:** Daily 6am–9pm. $

VADITO

Map page M-3, B3   (S of Taos)

Attraction 💼

Sipapu Ski Area, NM 518; tel 505/587-2240. The oldest ski area in the Taos region, located 25 miles southeast in Tres Rios canyon. Half of the 18 trails are classified as intermediate. **Open:** Dec–Mar, daily 9am–4pm. $$$$

WILLIAMSBURG

Map page M-3, D2   (S of Truth or Consequences)

Motel 🛏

📟 **Rio Grande Motel**, 720 Broadway, PO Box 67, Williamsburg, NM 87942; tel 505/894-9769. 4 mi S of Truth or Consequences, exit 75 off I-25. Attractive motel close to Elephant Butte and Caballo Lakes. **Rooms:** 50 rms and effic. CI noon/CO 11am. Nonsmoking rms avail. **Amenities:** 📺 A/C, cable TV. Kitchenette units have refrigerators, 2-burner hot plates, and dishes. Electric hookups to charge boat batteries are in every room. **Services:** 🛎 **Facilities:** 🛠 Playground, washer/dryer. Picnic ground and tennis and basketball courts are next door. **Rates:** $24 S; $32 D; from $285 effic. Higher rates for spec evnts/hols. Pking: Outdoor, free. Ltd CC.

ZUNI PUEBLO

Map page M-3, B1

Located 38 miles south of Gallup on NM 53. The largest and westernmost of New Mexico's 19 pueblos, Zuni is home to 8,084 members of the tribe. Zuni was built upon the ruins of the ancient site of Halona, an early pueblo destroyed by the conquistadors. Built in the early 1600s, the Zuni Mission was razed during the 1680 Pueblo revolt, rebuilt, and then destroyed yet again in 1849. Finally, in 1968, after 119 years, it was reconstructed as **Our Lady of Guadalupe Church**.

Thirteen miles southwest of Zuni are the ruins of **Hawikuh.** In all probability this is the famed "city of gold" spied in 1539 by the friar who incited the rush for the fabled **Seven Cities of Cíbola**. It was the largest Zuni pueblo of its day, until conquered by the Spanish. Though traditionally farmers, the Zuni are best known for their turquoise-and-silver inlay jewelry and other handcrafts, including stone animal fetishes. For camping, fishing, and hunting permits or for more information about the pueblo, call 505/782-4481.

INDEX

THE ROAD GUIDE FOR TODAY'S TRAVELER.

SAVE $4 OFF
GENERAL ADMISSION

Present coupon at Front Gate before bill is totalled. Not valid with any other discounts or special offers. Limit 6 guests per coupon. Photocopies not accepted. Operating hours and general admission prices subject to change without notice.

COUPON VALID THRU 12/31/95

PLU# 3175c/23176a An Anheuser-Busch Theme Park

BUSCH GARDENS.
TAMPA BAY, FLORIDA

SAVE $4 OFF
GENERAL ADMISSION

Present coupon at Front Gate before bill is totalled. Not valid with any other discounts or special offers. Limit 6 guests per coupon. Photocopies not accepted. Operating hours and general admission prices subject to change without notice.

COUPON VALID 3/31/95 THRU 10/29/95

PLU# 3175c/23176a An Anheuser-Busch Theme Park

ADVENTURE ISLAND
TAMPA'S WATER PARK

Limit six guests per certificate. Not valid with other discounts or on purchase of multi-park/multi-visit passes or tickets. Present certificate at Front Gate before bill is totaled. Redeemable only at time of ticket purchase. Photocopies not accepted. Certificate has no cash value. Operating hours and general admission price subject to change without notice. Valid through 3/31/95 only.

Sea World.
Orlando, Florida
Anheuser-Busch Theme Parks.

Make Contact With Another World®

©1994 Sea World of Florida, Inc.   PLU# 4556/4555

Discount valid for up to 6 people through 12/31/95.
Coupon has no cash value and is not valid with any other offers.
Offer subject to change without notice. Parking fee not included.
©1994 Universal Studios Florida. All Rights Reserved.

6101944075662

Name _____

Address _____

City _____ State _____ Zip _____

Phone (_____) _____

Name _____

Address _____

City _____ State _____ Zip _____

Phone (_____) _____

Name _____

Address _____

City _____ State _____ Zip _____

Phone (_____) _____

Name _____

Address _____

City _____ State _____ Zip _____

Phone (_____) _____

THE ROAD GUIDE
FOR TODAY'S
TRAVELER.

10% **10%**

STAY WITH US & SAVE!

Ramada Limiteds, Inns, Hotels, Resorts and Plaza Hotels offer you the value and accommodations you expect . . . And so much more!

- Over 750 convenient locations
- Children under 18 always stay free
- Non-smoking and handicap rooms available

10% **For reservations call 1-800-228-2828** **10%**

1-800-4-CHOICE
(1-800-424-6423)

Advance reservations through 1-800-4-CHOICE required. Based on availability at participating hotels and cannot be used in conjunction with any other discount.

TERMS AND CONDITIONS

Offer valid on an Intermediate (Group C) through a Full Size 4-Door (Group E) car for a 5-day minimum rental. Coupon must be surrendered at time of rental; one per rental. May not be used in conjunction with any other coupon, promotion or offer. Coupon valid at Avis corporate and participating licensee locations in the continental U.S. Offer not available during holiday and other blackout periods. Offer may not be available on all rates at all times. **An advance reservation is required.** Cars subject to availability. Taxes, local government surcharges and optional items, such as LDW, additional driver fee and refueling, are extra. Renter must meet Avis age, driver and credit requirements. Minimum age is 25 but may vary by location. Offer expires December 31, 1995.

Rental Sales Agent Instructions
At Checkout: • In CPN, enter **MUFA527.** • Complete this information:
    RA#_____ Rental Location_____
• Attach to COUPON tape.

© 1995 Wizard Co., Inc. 1/95 DTPS/

AVIS
We try harder.

DAYS INN
The Best Value Under The Sun.™

- **Available at participating properties.**
- **This coupon cannot be combined with any other special discount offer.**
- **Limit one coupon per room, per stay.**
- **Expires December 31, 1996.**

1-800-DAYS INN

Terms and Conditions

Advance reservations are required and blackout periods may apply. Present this certificate at time of rental or, for Gold rentals, at time of return, and receive $10 off Hertz Leisure Weekly rates at participating locations in the U.S. This certificate has no cash value, must be surrendered and may not be used with any other rate, discount or promotion. Standard rental qualifications, rental period and return restrictions must be met or offer is void. Weekly rentals require a minimum rental period of five days, including a Saturday night. Minimum rental age is 25. Taxes and optional items, such as refueling, are not included and are not subject to discount. All cars are subject to availability at time of rental. Certificate expires 12/31/95.

Hertz rents Fords and other fine cars.

HERE ARE SOME OF THE DETAILS YOU SHOULD KNOW:
Just mention promotion code TCB/MCBC087 when you reserve a compact through luxury size car and receive $20 off your weekly rental. Five-day minimum rental necessary to qualify for discount. This offer is valid at participating budget locations through 3/3/96 and is subject to vehicle availability. Car must be returned to renting location, except in some metro areas where inter-area drop-offs are permitted. Local rental and age requirements apply. Discount applies to time and mileage only and is not available in conjunction with any other discount, promotional offer, CorpRate™, government, or tour/wholesale rate. Refueling services, taxes and optional items are extra. Additional driver, underage driver and other surcharges are extra. Blackout dates may apply.

Terms and Conditions

- Offer includes 10% discount off all time and mileage charges on Cruise America or Cruise Canada vehicles only.
- Offer not available in conjunction with other discount offers or promotional rates.
- Excludes other rental charges, deposits, sales tax, and fuels.
- Normal rental conditions and customer qualification procedures apply.
- Members must reserve vehicles through Central Reservations only, at least one week in advance of pick up and mention **Frommer's America on Wheels** at time of reservation.

For reservations: 1-800-327-7799 - US and Canada

Rental Rates and Conditions

This offer is subject to availability and may not be used in conjunction with any other certificate or promotion. Offers apply only to economy through intermediate size car. Blackout periods may apply. This coupon has no cash value, and must be surrendered at time of rental. Coupon valid at all participating locations in the U.S. Taxes, fuel, LDW/CDW, under age and additional driver fees are extra. Some additional charges may apply.

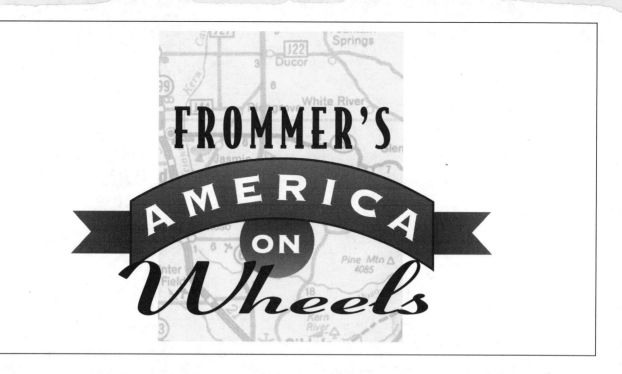

FROMMER'S AMERICA ON Wheels

THE ROAD GUIDE FOR TODAY'S AMERICA
FROM THE FIRST NAME IN TRAVEL

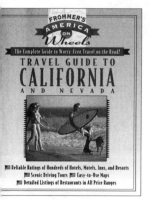

ISBN:0-02-860146-7

ISBN:0-02-860144-0

ISBN:0-02-860145-9

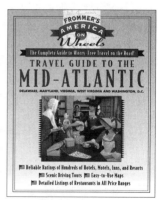

ISBN:0-02-860143-2

New titles coming in 1996

Northeast (includes Maine, Vermont, New Hampshire, Connecticut, Rhode Island, New York, and Massachusetts)

Northwest & North Central (includes Oregon, Washington, Idaho, Montana, Wyoming, North Dakota, South Dakota, Nebraska, Iowa)

Great Lakes (includes Michigan, Wisconsin, Illinois, Indiana, Ohio, Minnesota)

Southeast (includes South Carolina, North Carolina, Kentucky, Tennessee, Mississippi, Georgia, Alabama)

South Central (includes Louisiana, Arkansas, Oklahoma, Texas, Missouri)

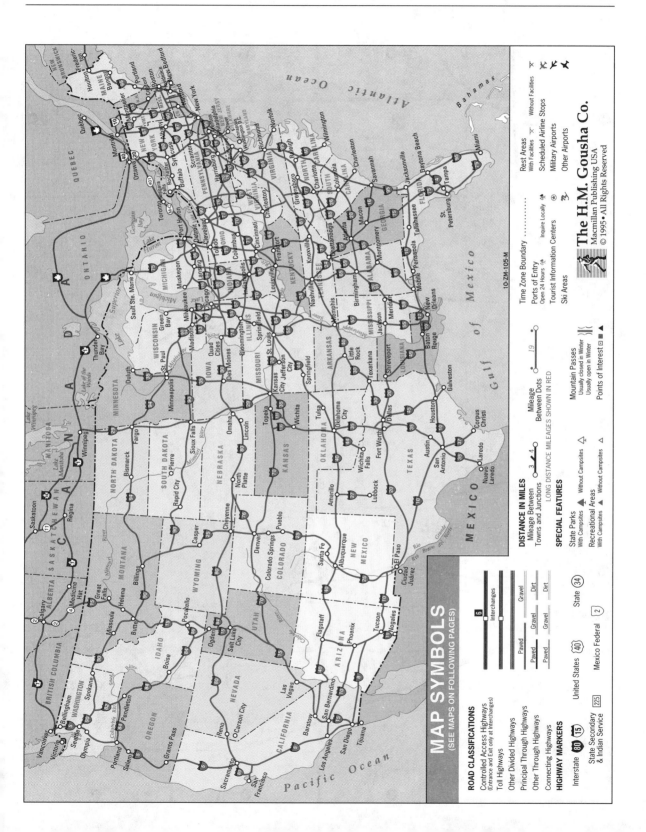

MAP SYMBOLS
(SEE MAPS ON FOLLOWING PAGES)

ROAD CLASSIFICATIONS

Controlled Access Highways
(Entrance and Exit only at interchanges)

Toll Highways

Other Divided Highways

Principal Through Highways

Other Through Highways

Connecting Highways

	Paved	Gravel	Dirt
	Paved	Gravel	Dirt
	Paved	Gravel	Dirt

6 Interchanges

HIGHWAY MARKERS

Interstate **90** **15**

State Secondary & Indian Service **225**

United States **40**

State **34**

Mexico Federal **2**

DISTANCE IN MILES

Mileage Between Towns and Junctions 3 ◦—◦ 4

Mileage Between Dots 19 ◦—◦

LONG DISTANCE MILEAGES SHOWN IN RED

SPECIAL FEATURES

State Parks
With Campsites ▲ Without Campsites △

Recreational Areas
With Campsites ▲ Without Campsites △

Mountain Passes
)(Usually closed in Winter
)(Usually open in Winter

Points of Interest ▣ ▲

Time Zone Boundary ·········

Ports of Entry
Open 24 Hours ✹ Inquire Locally ✹

Tourist Information Centers ⊛

Ski Areas ⤳

Rest Areas
With Facilities ⚡ Without Facilities ⚡

Scheduled Airline Stops ✈

Military Airports ✈

Other Airports ✈

The H.M. Gousha Co.
Macmillan Publishing USA
© 1995 • All Rights Reserved

10-ZM-105-M

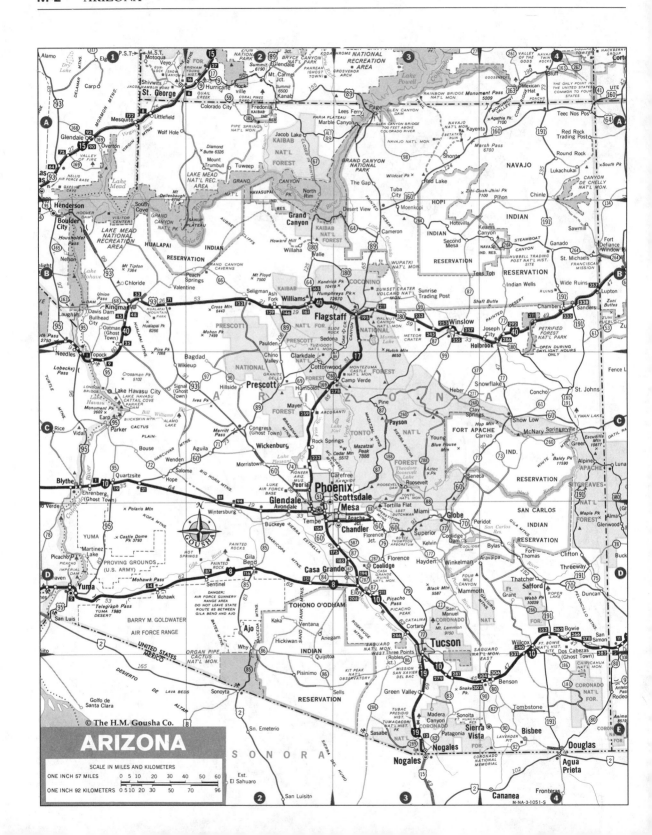

© The H.M. Gousha Co.

ARIZONA

SCALE IN MILES AND KILOMETERS

ONE INCH 57 MILES　　0 5 10　20　30　40　50　60

ONE INCH 92 KILOMETERS　0 5 10 20 30　50　70　96

M-NA-3-1051-S

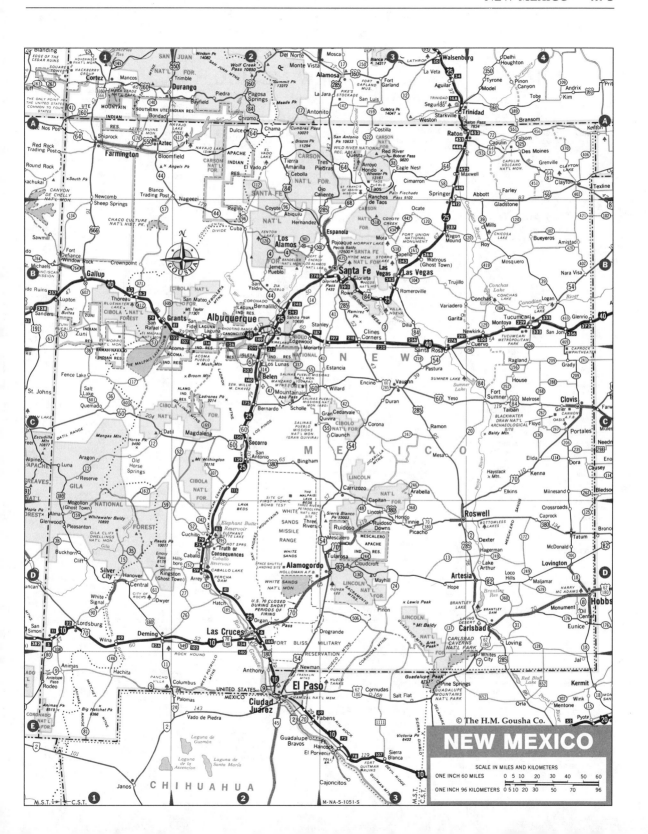

© The H.M. Gousha Co.

NEW MEXICO

SCALE IN MILES AND KILOMETERS

ONE INCH 60 MILES   0 5 10   20   30   40   50   60

ONE INCH 96 KILOMETERS   0 5 10 20 30   50   70   96

M-NA-5-1051-S

ARIZONA

Pop. (1990) 3,665,228
Area 113,575

COUNTIES

County	Co. Seat	County	Co. Seat
Apache	St. Johns	Mohave	Kingman
Cochise	Bisbee	Navajo	Holbrook
Coconino	Flagstaff	Pima	Tucson
Gila	Globe	Pinal	Florence
Graham	Safford	Santa Cruz	
Greenlee	Clifton		Nogales
La Paz	Parker	Yavapai	Prescott
Maricopa	Phoenix	Yuma	Yuma

CITIES AND TOWNS

1990 Census
• County Seat

Aguila C-2
Ajo D-2
Alpine C-4
Anegam D-2
Apache Junction
　18,100.............D-3
Aravaipa D-4
Ash Fork B-2
Avondale
　16,169.............D-2
Bagdad C-2
Benson 3,824 .....E-4
Bisbee • 6,288 ....E-4
Bouse C-1
Bowie.................D-4
Buckeye 5,038...D-2
Bullhead City
　21,951.............B-1
Bylas.................C-3
Cameron............B-3
Camp Verde
　6,243...............C-3
Carefree 1,666. ..C-2
Carrizo C-4
Casa Grande
　19,082.............D-3
Chambers B-4
Chandler
　90,533.............D-3
Chinle A-4
Chino Valley
　4,837...............C-2
Chloride B-1
Clarkdale 2,144.C-2
Clay Springs......C-4
Clifton • 2,840 ...D-4
Colorado City
　2,426...............A-2
Concho C-4
Congress
　(Ghost Town).C-2
Coolidge 6,927. .D-3
Coolidge Dam....D-4
Cortaro D-3
Cottonwood
　5,918...............C-2
Davis Dam B-1
Desert View B-3
Dos Cabezas
　(Ghost Town)..E-4
Douglas
　12,822.............E-4
Duncan 662.......D-4
Ehrenberg
　(Ghost Town)..C-1
Eloy 7,211 ....D-3
Flagstaff •
　45,857.............B-3
Florence •
　7,510...............D-3
Florence Jct. D-3
Fort Defiance B-4
Fort Grant..........D-4
Fort Thomas D-4
Fredonia 1,207. .A-2

Ganado B-4
Gila Bend
　1,747...............D-2
Glendale
　148,134...........D-2
Globe • 6,062....D-3
Grand Canyon ...B-2
Green Valley E-3
Greer C-4
Hayden 909 ......D-3
Heber.................C-3
Hickiwan D-2
Hillside C-2
Holbrook •
　4,686...............B-4
Hope..................C-1
Hotevilla............B-3
Humboldt...........C-2
Indian Wells B-4
Jacob Lake A-2
Joseph City B-4
Kaka..................D-2
Kayenta A-4
Keams
　Canyon B-4
Kelvin................D-3
Kingman •
　12,722.............B-1
Lake Havasu
　City 24,363 .....C-1
Lees Ferry A-3
Littlefield...........A-1
Lukachukai A-4
Lupton................B-4
Madera
　Canyon E-3
Mammoth
　1,845...............D-3
Marble
　Canyon A-3
Martinez Lake....D-1
Mayer C-2
McNary..............C-4
Mesa 288,091...D-3
Miami 2,018.......D-3
Moenkopi...........B-3
Mohawk D-1
Morristown.........D-2
Mount
　Trumbull..........A-2
Nogales •
　19,489.............E-3
North Rim A-2
Oatman (Ghost
　Town)..............B-1
Page 6,598 ....A-3
Parker • 2,897....C-1
Patagonia 888. .E-3
Paulden B-2
Payson 8,377 ....C-3
Peach Springs ...B-2
Peoria................D-3
Peridot D-3
Phoenix •
　983,403...........C-2

Pine C-3
Pisinimo E-2
Piñon B-4
Prescott •
　26,455.............C-2
Quartzsite
　1,876...............C-1
Quijotoba E-2
Red Lake A-3
Red Rock
　Trading Post ...A-4
Rock Springs.....C-2
Roosevelt C-3
Round Rock.......A-4
Safford • 7,359...D-4
St. Johns •
　3,294...............C-4
St. Michaels B-4
Salome C-1
Sanders B-4
San Manuel D-3
San Simon D-4
Sasabe E-3
Sawmill B-4
Scottsdale
　130,069...........D-2
Second Mesa.....B-3
Sedona 7,720 ...B-3
Seligman............B-2
Sells..................E-3
Seneca C-3
Sentinel D-2
Shonto A-3
Show Low
　5,019...............C-4
Sierra Vista
　32,983.............E-4
Signal (Ghost
　Town)..............C-1
Snowflake
　3,679...............C-4
Sonoita E-3
South Cove........B-1
Springerville
　1,802...............C-4
Sunrise Trading
　Post.................B-3
Superior 3,468...D-3
Tec Nos Pos A-4
Tempe
　141,865...........D-2
Tes Toh B-3
Thatcher
　3,763...............D-4
The Gap.............A-3
Three Points
　(Robles
　Junction) E-3
Threeway...........D-4
Tombstone
　1,220...............E-4
Topock...............C-1
Tortilla Flat........D-3
Tuba City A-3
Tucson •
　405,390...........D-3
Tuweep..............A-2
Valentine...........B-1
Valle..................B-2
Ventana.............D-2
Wenden..............C-1
Why...................D-2
Wickenburg
　4,515...............C-2
Wide Ruins B-4
Wikieup..............C-1
Willaha...............B-2
Willcox 3,122.....D-4
Williams 2,532 ...B-2
Window Rock B-4
Winkleman
　676..................D-3
Winslow 8,190 ...B-3
Wintersburg.......D-2
Wolf Hole A-1
Young C-3
Yuma • 54,923...D-1

NEW MEXICO

Pop. (1990) 1,515,069
Area 121,510

COUNTIES

County	Co. Seat	County	Co. Seat
Bernalillo		McKinley	Gallup
	Albuquerque	Mora	Mora
Catron	Reserve	Otero	Alamogordo
Chaves	Roswell	Quay	Tucumcari
Cibola	Grants	Rio Arriba	
Colfax	Raton		Tierra Amarilla
Curry	Clovis	Roosevelt	
De Baca			Portales
	Fort Sumner	San Juan	Aztec
Dona Ana		San Miguel	
	Las Cruces		Las Vegas
Eddy	Carlsbad	Sandoval	
Grant	Silver City		Bernalillo
Guadalupe		Santa Fe	Santa Fe
	Santa Rosa	Sierra	Truth or
Harding	Mosquero		Consequences
Hidalgo	Lordsburg	Socorro	Socorro
Lea	Lovington	Taos	Taos
Lincoln	Carrizozo	Torrance	Estancia
Los Alamos		Union	Clayton
	Los Alamos	Valencia	
Luna	Deming		Los Lunas

CITIES AND TOWNS

1990 Census
• County Seat

Abbott A-4
Abiquiu..............B-2
Acoma 2,590 .....C-2
Alamogordo •
　27,596.............D-3
Albuquerque •
　384,736...........B-2
Alma D-1
Amistad..............B-4
Animas...............E-1
Anthony E-2
Arabela C-3
Aragon C-1
Arrey D-2
Arroyo Hondo A-3
Artesia
　10,610.............D-4
Aztec • 5,479 .....A-1
Belen 6,547 ....C-2
Bernalillo •
　5,960...............B-2
Bernardo............C-2
Bingham.............C-2
Blanco Trading
　Post.................A-2
Bloomfield
　5,214...............A-1
Buckhorn D-1
Bueyeros B-4
Caballo D-2
Capitan 842 ....D-3
Caprock.............D-4
Capulin A-4
Garlsbad •
　24,952.............D-4
Carrizozo •
　1,075...............C-3
Causey 57 ....C-4
Cebolla A-2
Cedarvale C-3
Central 1,835.....D-1
Chama
　1,048...............A-2
Cimarron
　774..................A-3
Claunch..............C-3
Clayton •
　2,484...............A-4
Cliff D-1

Clines
　Corners...........B-3
Cloudcroft
　636..................D-3
Clovis • 30,954 ..C-4
Columbus
　641..................E-2
Conchas B-4
Corona 215........C-3
Costilla...............A-3
Coyote B-2
Crossroads D-4
Crownpoint.........B-1
Cuba 760 ....B-2
Cuchillo..............D-2
Cuervo B-4
Datil C-1
Deming •
　10,970.............D-1
Des Moines
　168..................A-4
Dexter 898 ....D-4
Dilia...................B-3
Dora 167............C-4
Dulce A-2
Duran.................C-3
Dwyer D-1
Eagle Nest
　189..................A-3
Edgewood...........B-2
Elida 201 ....C-4
Elkins C-4
El Vado A-2
Encino 131 ....C-3
Espanola
　8,389...............B-3
Estancia •
　792..................C-3
Eunice 2,676 .....D-4
Farley.................A-4
Farmington
　33,997.............A-1
Fence Lake.........C-1
Floyd 77.............C-4
Folsom 71..........A-4
Fort Sumner •
　1,269...............C-4
Gallup •
　19,154.............B-1

Garita B-3
Gladstone B-4
Glenrio B-4
Glenwood D-1
Glorieta B-3
Grady 110..........C-4
Gran Quivira C-3
Grants •
　8,626...............B-1
Grenville 24 ....A-4
Grier C-4
Hachita E-1
Hagerman
　961..................D-4
Hanover..............D-1
Hatch 1,136.......D-2
Hernandez..........B-3
Hillsboro D-2
Hobbs
　29,115.............D-4
Hondo................D-3
Hope 101............D-3
House 85............C-4
Jal 2,156............D-4
Jemez Pueblo
　1,750...............B-2
Kenna................C-4
Kingston
　(Ghost
　Town)..............D-1
Laguna...............B-2
Lake Arthur
　336..................D-4
Las Cruces •
　62,126.............D-2
Las Vegas •
　14,753.............B-3
Lincoln D-3
Loco Hills D-4
Logan 870..........B-4
Lordsburg •
　2,951...............D-1
Los Alamos •......B-2
Los Lunas •
　6,013...............C-2
Loving 1,243......D-4
Lovington •
　9,322...............D-4
Luna C-1
Magdalena
　861..................C-2
Maljamar............D-4
Maxwell 247.......A-3
Mayhill D-3
McDonald D-4
Melrose 662.......C-4
Mesa C-3
Mescalero D-3
Mills B-4
Milnesand..........C-4
Mogollon
　(Ghost
　Town)..............D-1
Montoya.............B-4
Monument D-4
Mora • B-3
Moriarty
　1,399...............B-3
Mosquero •
　164..................B-4
Mountainair
　926..................C-2
Nageezi B-2
Nara Visa...........B-4
Newcomb............A-1
Newkirk..............B-4
Newman E-2
Ocate B-3
Oil Center D-4
Ojo Caliente.......B-3
Old Horse
　Springs............C-1
Organ D-2
Orogrande..........D-2

Pastura C-3
Picacho..............D-3
Piñon D-3
Pleasanton D-1
Pojoaque B-3
Portales •
　10,690.............C-4
Quemado............C-1
Questa
　1,707...............A-3
Ragland C-4
Ramon................C-3
Ranchos de
　Taos.................A-3
Raton •
　7,372...............A-3
Red River
　387..................A-3
Regina B-2
Reserve •
　319..................C-1
Rodeo................E-1
Romeroville........B-3
Roswell •
　44,654.............D-3
Rowe B-3
Roy 362 ....B-4
Ruidoso 4,600 ...D-3
Ruidoso
　Downs 920.......D-3
Salt Lake C-1
San Antonio C-2
San Fidel B-2
San Jon 277 .....B-4
San Mateo B-2
San Rafael B-1
Santa
　Fe • 55,859 .....B-3
Santa
　Rosa • 2,263...C-3
San Ysidro
　233..................B-2
Sapello...............B-3
Scholle...............C-2
Sheep Springs ...B-1
Shiprock.............A-1
Silver City •
　10,683.............D-1
Socorro •
　8,159...............C-2
Springer
　1,262...............A-3
Stanley...............B-3
Taiban................C-4
Taos • 4,065 ......A-3
Tatum 768 ....D-4
Thoreau..............B-1
Three Rivers.......D-3
Tierra
　Amarilla • A-2
Tinnie................D-3
Tres Piedras.......A-3
Trujillo................B-3
Truth or
　Consequences •
　6,221...............D-2
Tucumcari •
　6,831...............B-4
Tularosa
　2,615...............D-3
Variadero............B-4
Vaughn 633 ....C-3
Wagon Mound
　319..................B-3
Watrous
　(Ghost
　Town)..............B-3
Whites City E-4
White Signal D-1
Willard 183 ....C-3
Wilna D-1
Yeso C-3
Zuni B-1

NA-1051-SX

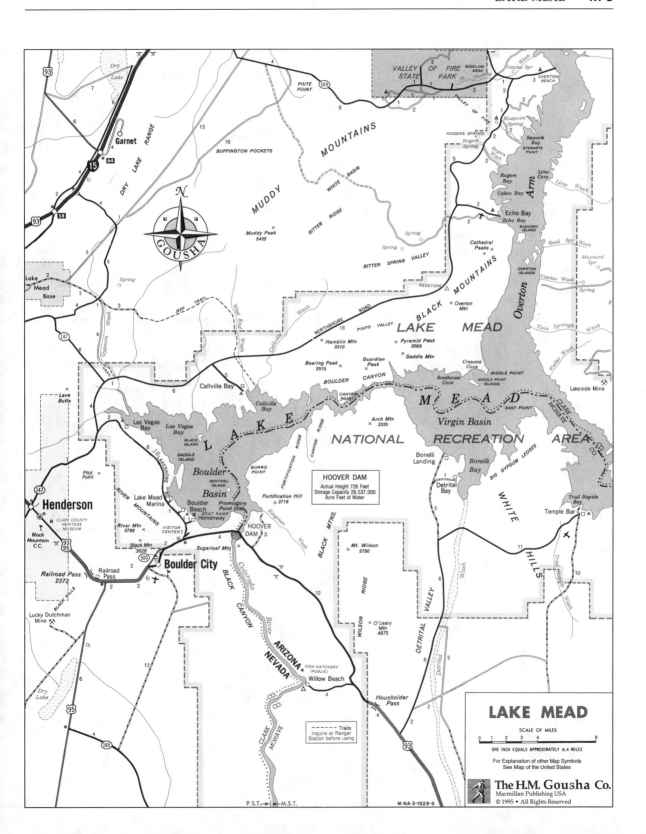

LAKE MEAD

SCALE OF MILES

0 1 2 3 4 6 8

ONE INCH EQUALS APPROXIMATELY 6.4 MILES

For Explanation of other Map Symbols
See Map of the United States

The H.M. Gousha Co.
Macmillan Publishing USA
© 1995 • All Rights Reserved

HOOVER DAM
Actual Height 726 Feet
Storage Capacity 28,537,000
Acre Feet of Water

Trails
Inquire at Ranger
Station before using

M-NA-3-1529-S

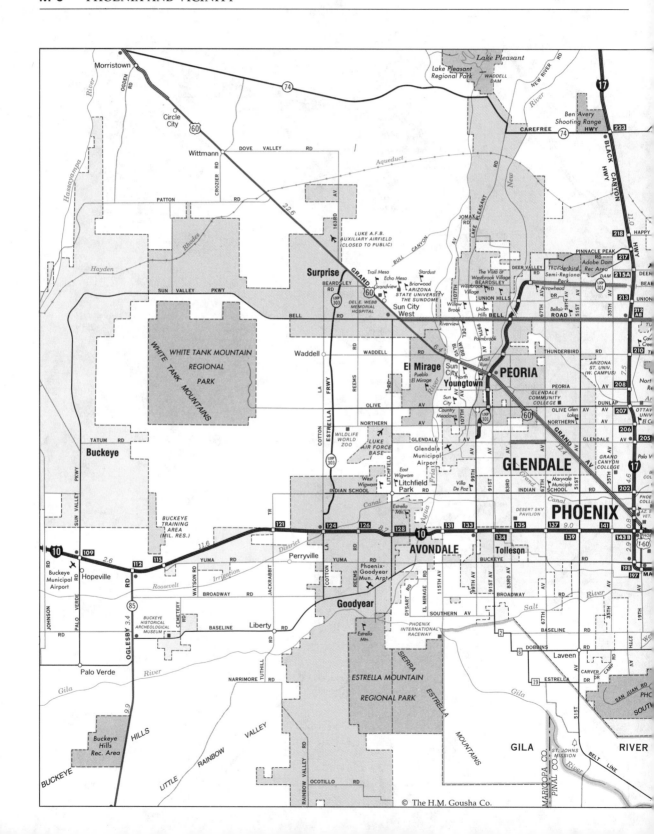

© The H.M. Gousha Co.

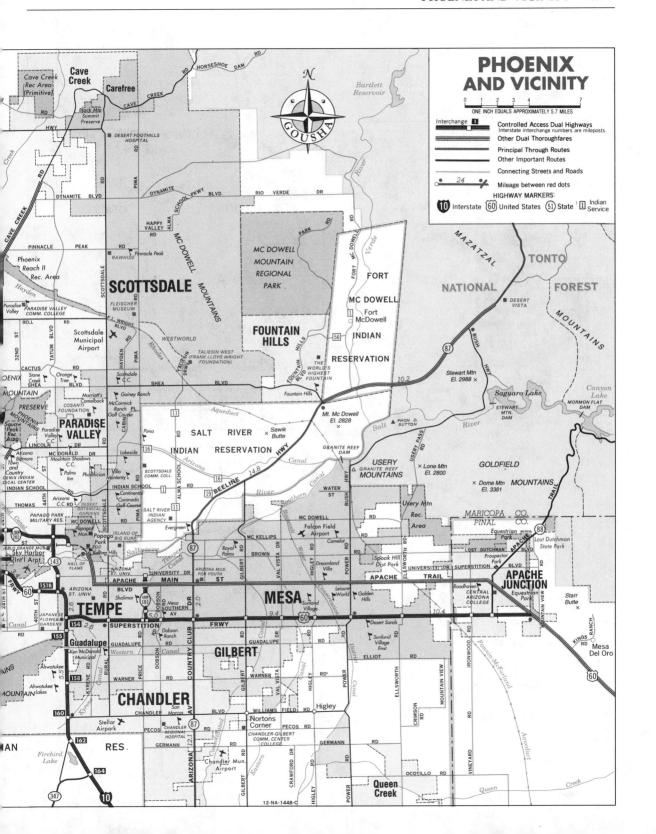

TUCSON
AND VICINITY

ONE INCH EQUALS APPROXIMATELY 4.5 MILES

Interchange

Controlled Access Dual Highways
(Entrance and exit only at Interchanges)
Other Dual Thoroughfares
Principal Through Routes
Other Important Routes
Connecting Streets and Roads
Mileage between red dots
Golf Courses   Recreation Areas
HIGHWAY MARKERS:
Interstate   United States   State

ZM-7-1777-S

© The H.M. Gousha Co.

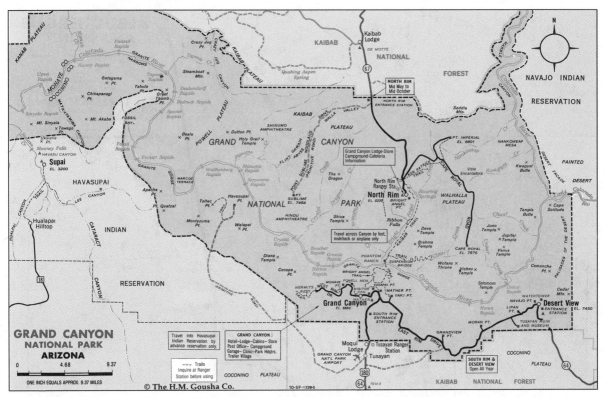

GRAND CANYON
NATIONAL PARK
ARIZONA

0   4.68   9.37
ONE INCH EQUALS APPROX. 9.37 MILES

Travel into Havasupai
Indian Reservation by
advance reservation only.

GRAND CANYON
Hotel—Lodge—Cabins—Store
Post Office— Campground
Garage— Clinic—Park Hdqtrs.
Trailer Village

--- Trails
Inquire at Ranger
Station before using

© The H.M. Gousha Co.

10-SF-1228-S

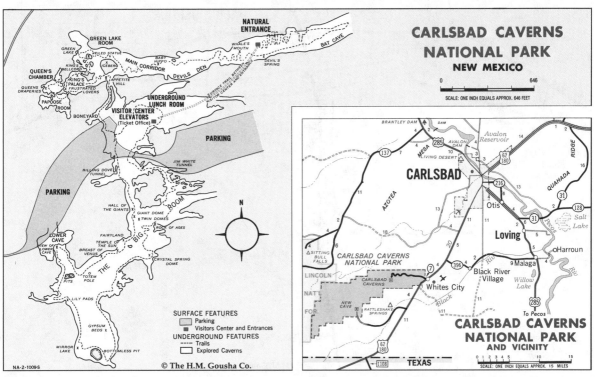

CARLSBAD CAVERNS
NATIONAL PARK
NEW MEXICO

0   646
SCALE: ONE INCH EQUALS APPROX. 646 FEET

SURFACE FEATURES
▨ Parking
■ Visitors Center and Entrances
UNDERGROUND FEATURES
--- Trails
☐ Explored Caverns

CARLSBAD CAVERNS
NATIONAL PARK
AND VICINITY

0 1 2.5 5   10   15
SCALE: ONE INCH EQUALS APPROX. 15 MILES

NA-2-1009-S

© The H.M. Gousha Co.

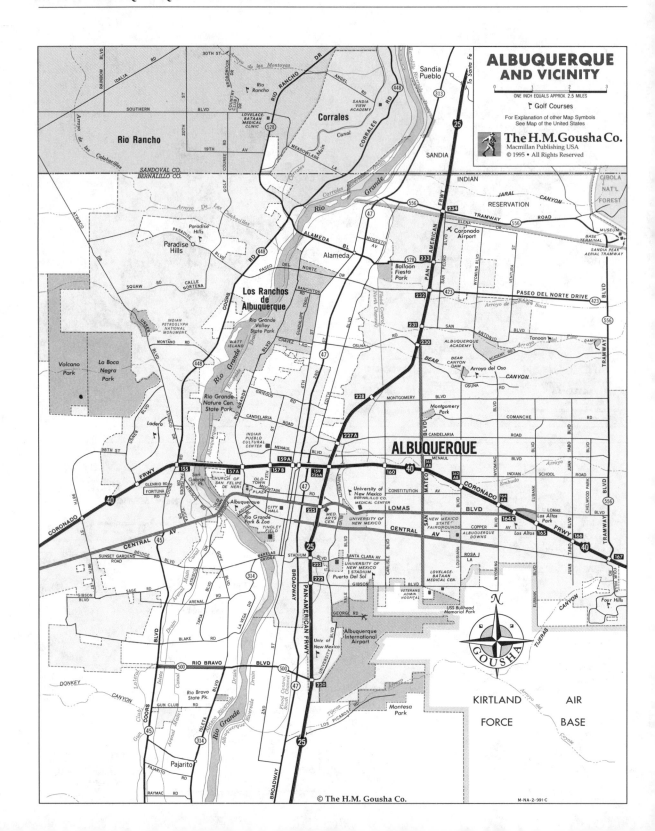

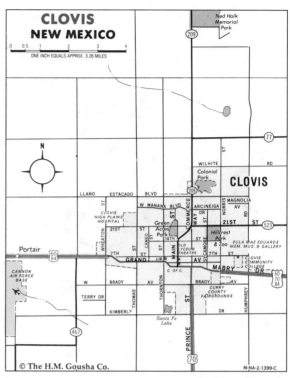

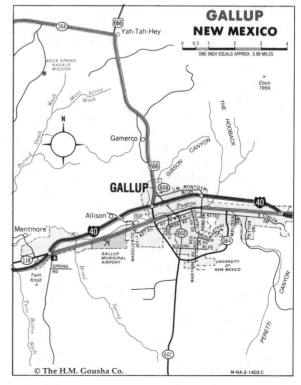

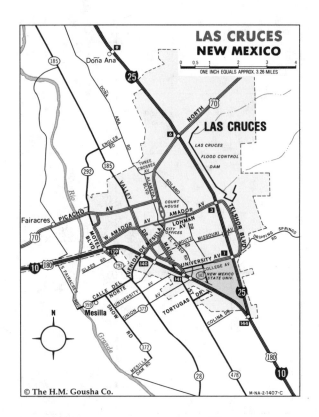

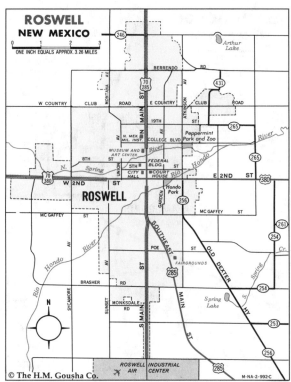

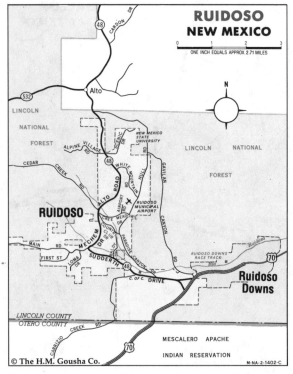

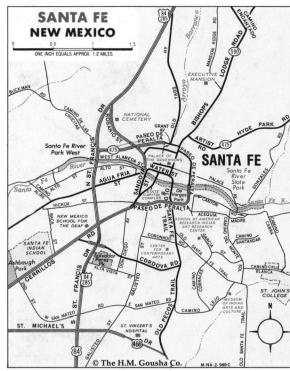

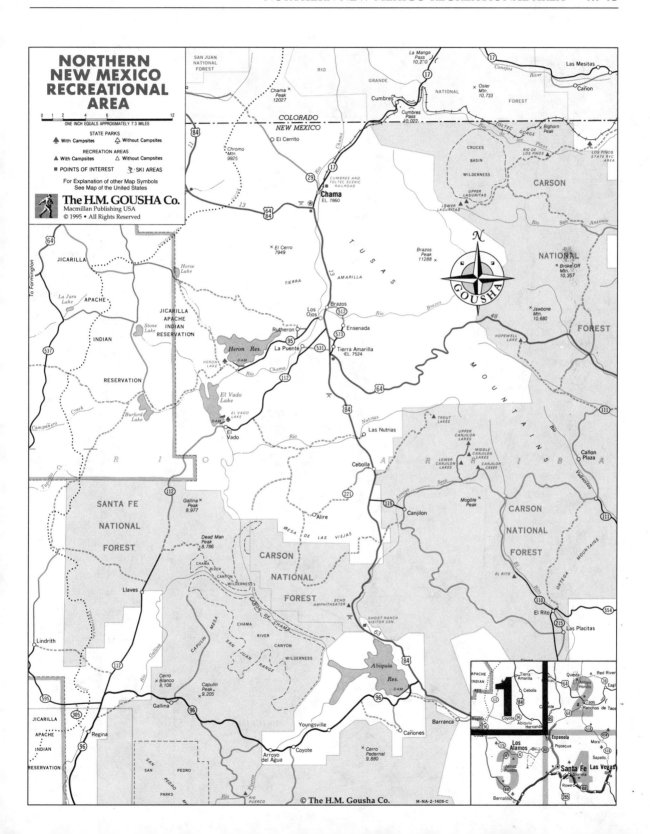

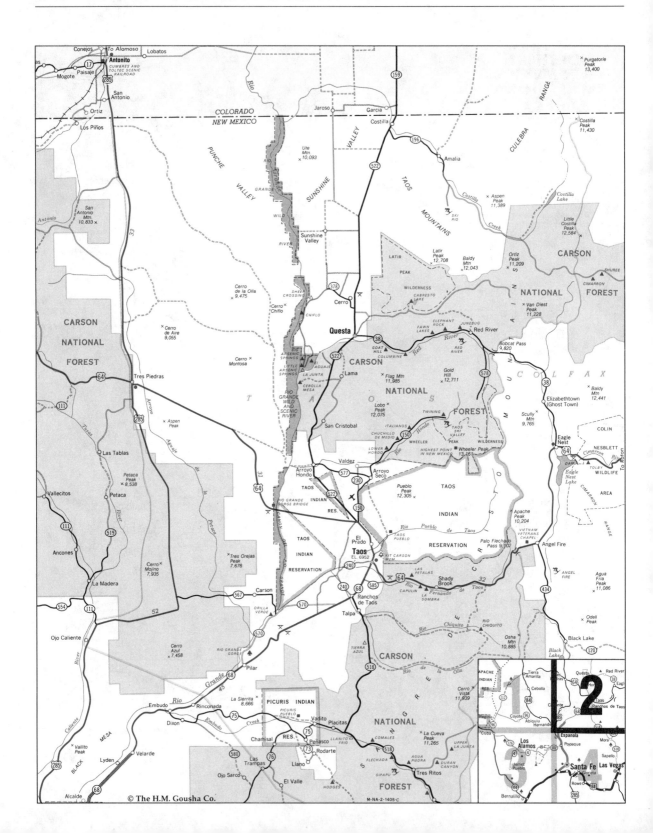

© The H.M. Gousha Co.

M-NA-2-1405-C

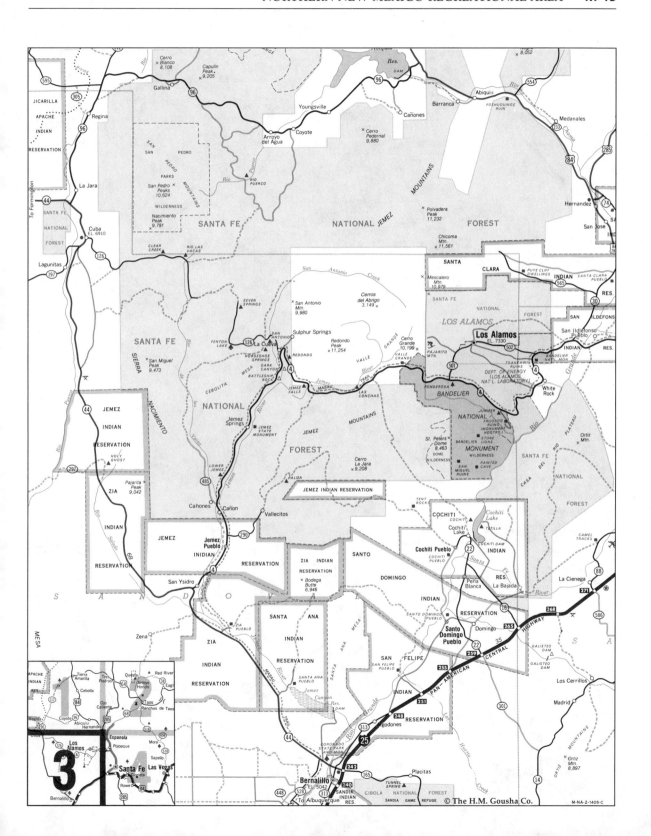

© The H.M. Gousha Co.

M-NA-2-1405-C

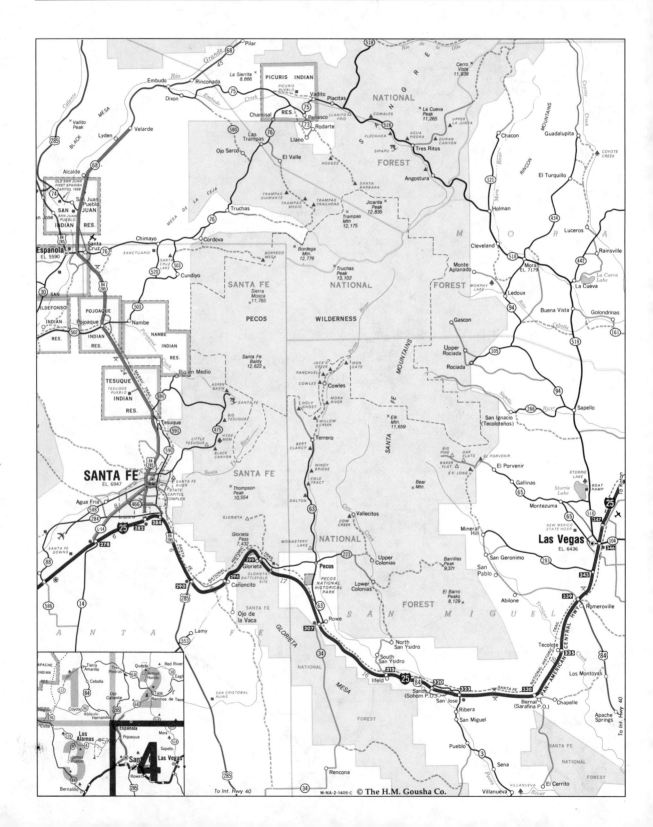